Northern France

And the Paris Region

Ludovic Piette: Jour de fête à Pontoise /Conseil Général du Val d'Oise

"... a village that affected him as a thing of whiteness, blueness and crookedness, set in coppery green, and that had the river flowing behind or before it - one couldn't say which ... Such a river sets one afloat almost before one can take up oars ... "

Henry James
The Ambassadors (1903)

Northern France bears the traces of English, Dutch, Flemish and Spanish influences; closer to Paris, in Île-de-France, visitors are reminded of the succession of sovereigns who made this their capital region, beginning with Clovis in 508. The northern shores are known as the Opal Coast, for the pearly light that bathes the fine sand, dunes and white cliffs. Set amid the nature reserves and wide beaches are charming and modern seaside resorts and active ports such as Boulogne, where the old town stands behind its ramparts, and Calais, where Rodin's powerful sculpture *Les Bourgeois de Calais* can now contemplate the Channel tunnel.

The Basilica of Saint Denis, witness to a millennium of royal funerals, marks the beginning of the Gothic style. Moving northward, the transitional gives way to the Flamboyant "stones of light"; the dazzling cathedral of Amiens is the largest religious edifice in France. Monarchs and their acolytes lived in the magnificence of the famed palaces of Île-de-France : Chantilly, Fontainebleau, Vaux-le-Vicomte and of course, Versailles, whose splendour staggers the imagination.

Near the Belgian border, the windmills and canals, the graceful Flemish architecture, the hearty enjoyment of mussels, chips and beer, lively carnivals with giant figures on parade, speak of yet another cultural heritage. From the modern metropolis of Lille, to the windy Somme valley, the legacy of the First World War, its memorial cemeteries and the *Flanders fields where poppies grow*, compels reflection on the strife which once afflicted this now peaceful land.

The river valleys of the Somme, the Seine, the Oise and the Marne have inspired artists by the beauty of their meanders, the lovely villages and the exceptionally intense northern light. Today's visitors will find many peaceful natural havens, for relaxation and sport, to refresh the spirit between visits to the wealth of museums and monuments; or perhaps a gently drifting row boat or a majestic shade tree will provide the perfect enticement for a day dream after an exploration of the region's culinary delights!

Contents

Key

	Sight	Seaside Resort	Winter Sports Resort	Spa
Worth a journey	★★★	≅≅≅	❋❋❋	⚘⚘⚘
Worth a detour	★★	≅≅	❋❋	⚘⚘
Interesting	★	≅	❋	⚘

Tourism

⊘	Admission Times and Charges listed at the end of the guide	►►	Visit if time permits
◉→	Sightseeing route with departure point indicated	**AZ B**	Map co-ordinates locating sights
♠♦♠♦	Ecclesiastical building	🛈	Tourist information
◨ ◩	Synagogue – Mosque	⊨ ∴	Historic house, castle – Ruins
▭	Building (with main entrance)	∪ ✿	Dam – Factory or power station
■	Statue, small building	☆ ∩	Fort – Cave
⊥	Wayside cross	⊓	Prehistoric site
◎	Fountain	▼ ᴠ	Viewing table – View
●■►	Fortified walls – Tower – Gate	▲	Miscellaneous sight

Recreation

🐎	Racecourse	🏃	Waymarked footpath
⛸	Skating rink	◆	Outdoor leisure park/centre
≋ ⊠	Outdoor, indoor swimming pool	🎿	Theme/Amusement park
⊿	Marina, moorings	♈	Wildlife/Safari park, zoo
⌂	Mountain refuge hut	❁	Gardens, park, arboretum
□■■■□	Overhead cable-car	◑	Aviary, bird sanctuary
🚂	Tourist or steam railway		

Additional symbols

══ ══	Motorway (unclassified)	⊠ ⊙	Post office – Telephone centre
❶ ❶	Junction: complete, limited	⊠	Covered market
⊞══	Pedestrian street	•✕•	Barracks
I═════I	Unsuitable for traffic, street subject to restrictions	△	Swing bridge
▥▥▥ ----	Steps – Footpath	∪ ✕	Quarry – Mine
🚆 🚌	Railway – Coach station	Ⓑ Ⓕ	Ferry (river and lake crossings)
□++++□	Funicular – Rack-railway	⛴	Ferry services: Passengers and cars
—— ●	Tram – Metro, Underground	⥥	Foot passengers only
Bert (R.)...	Main shopping street	③	Access route number common to MICHELIN maps and town plans

Abbreviations and special symbols

A	Agricultural office (Chambre d'agriculture)	**P**	Local authority offices (Préfecture, sous-préfecture)
C	Chamber of commerce (Chambre de commerce)	**POL.**	Police station (Police)
H	Town hall (Hôtel de ville)	🛡	Police station (Gendarmerie)
J	Law courts (Palais de justice)	**T**	Theatre (Théâtre)
M	Museum (Musée)	**U**	University (Université)
		●	Hotel

4

Using this guide

Your Michelin green guide is full of information of different kinds:

• **Thematic maps:** the main Sights, Touring programmes (must-sees for those on a tight schedule), Places to stay (choosing your day's destination point with regard to availability of hotels and the surroundings). The map on the bottom of this page shows which Michelin maps cover the area of this guide.

• **Introduction:** learn more about the region before you go, or as you tour; read about the landscape, history, customs, cuisine, art and contemporary development.

• **Towns and sights:** presented in alphabetical order for easy reference. Smaller villages are listed as excursions from the bigger places to visit.

Sections on major cities (Lille, Boulogne ...) include a selection of travelling tips, including suggestions for where to eat or have a drink and how to get the most out of your trip. Consult the **Michelin Red Guide France** for a complete selection of hotels and restaurants throughout the region.

• **Practical information:** useful addresses for planning your trip, looking for lodging, outdoor activities and more; opening hours and admission prices for monuments, museums and other tourist attractions (as indicated by blue clocks in the text); festival and carnival dates; suggestions for thematic tours on scenic railways, through nature reserves, etc.

• **Index:** lists attractions, famous people and events, and other subjects covered in the guide.

Let us hear from you. We are interested in your reaction to our guide, in any ideas you have to offer or good addresses you would like to share. Send your comments to Michelin Tyre PLC, Michelin Travel Publications, 38 Clarendon Road, Watford, Herts WD 1 1SX, U.K. or www.michelin-travel.com.

Bon voyage!

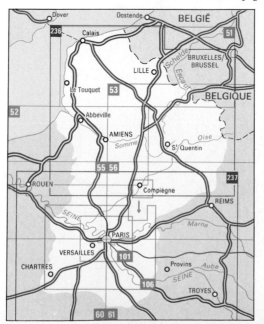

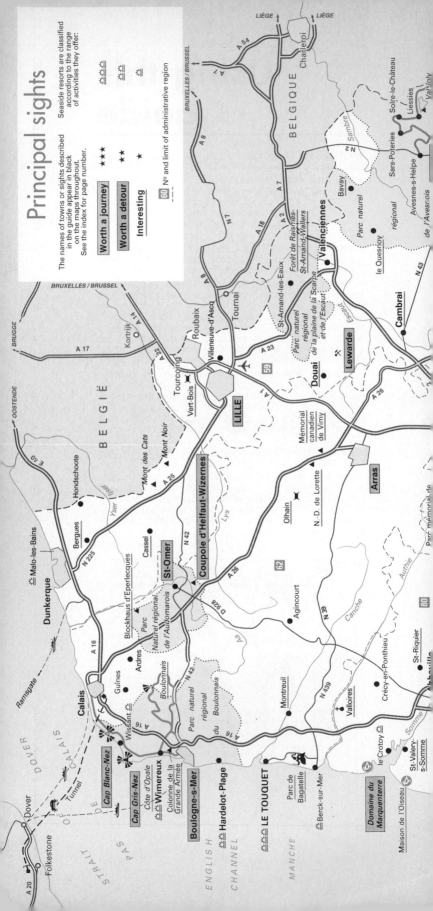

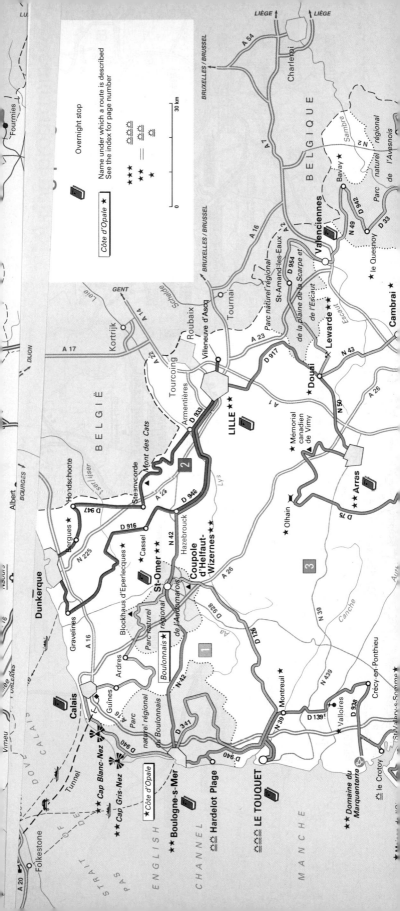

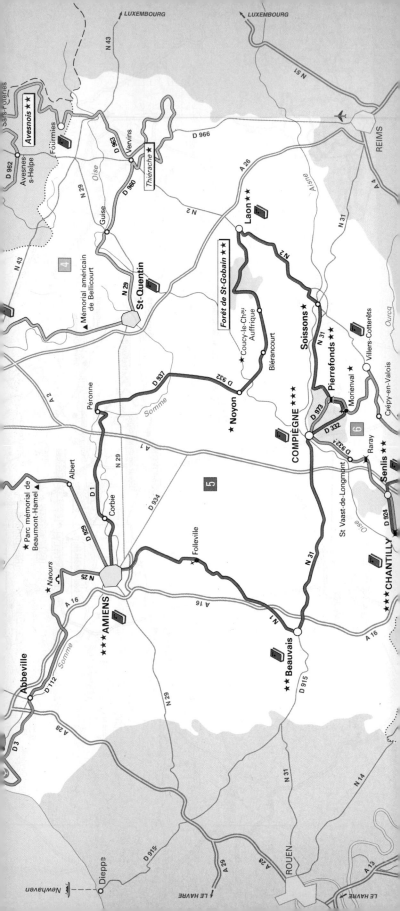

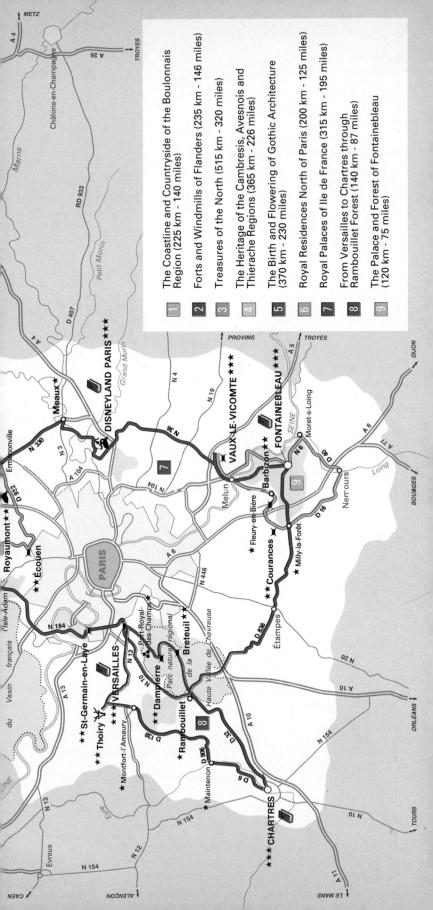

1 The Coastline and Countryside of the Boulonnais Region (225 km - 140 miles)

2 Forts and Windmills of Flanders (235 km - 146 miles)

3 Treasures of the North (515 km - 320 miles)

4 The Heritage of the Cambresis, Avesnois and Thierache Regions (365 km - 226 miles)

5 The Birth and Flowering of Gothic Architecture (370 km - 230 miles)

6 Royal Residences North of Paris (200 km - 125 miles)

7 Royal Palaces of Ile de France (315 km - 195 miles)

8 From Versailles to Chartres through Rambouillet Forest (140 km - 87 miles)

9 The Palace and Forest of Fontainebleau (120 km - 75 miles)

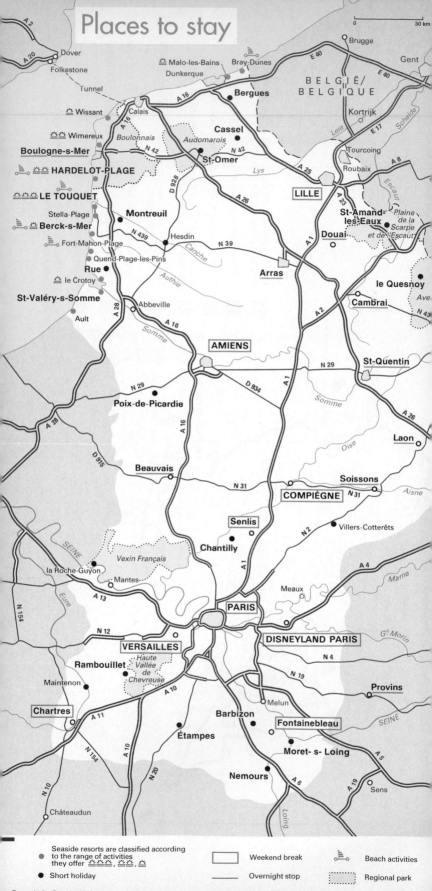

Places to stay

0   30 km

Dover
Folkestone
Tunnel
☆ Wissant
Malo-les-Bains
Dunkerque
Bray-Dunes
Bergues
BELGIË/
BELGIQUE
Gent
Brugge
E 40
Kortrijk
Cassel
Audomarois
St-Omer
Leie
Tourcoing
Roubaix
LILLE
St-Amand=
les-Eaux
Plaine
de la
Scarpe
et de l'Escaut
Douai
le Quesnoy
Cambrai
Arras
Wimereux
Boulogne-s-Mer
☆☆ HARDELOT-PLAGE
☆☆☆ LE TOUQUET
Stella-Plage
Berck-s-Mer
Fort-Mahon-Plage
Quend-Plage-les-Pins
Rue
le Crotoy
St-Valéry-s-Somme
Ault
Montreuil
Hesdin
Abbeville
AMIENS
St-Quentin
Poix-de-Picardie
Laon
Beauvais
Soissons
COMPIÈGNE
Senlis
Villers-Cotterêts
Chantilly
la Roche-Guyon
Mantes
Vexin Français
Meaux
Marne
PARIS
VERSAILLES
DISNEYLAND PARIS
Rambouillet
Haute
Vallée
de
Chevreuse
Provins
Maintenon
Melun
Chartres
Barbizon
Fontainebleau
Étampes
Moret-s-Loing
Nemours
Sens
Châteaudun

Seaside resorts are classified according
to the range of activities
they offer ☆☆☆, ☆☆, ☆

● Short holiday

☐ Weekend break

— Overnight stop

Beach activities

⬚ Regional park

Consult the Practical Information section at the back of the guide for further information on accommodation and where to s

Featured in this guide...

Descriptions of the sights listed below by theme may be found in the main section of this guide under the chapter headings appearing in CAPITAL LETTERS.

Famous people

The following list includes museums (musée), houses (maison) or studios (atelier) which perserve the memory of artists and prominent historical figures

Maison de **Van Gogh** (AUVERS-SUR-OISE)
Ancienne Auberge du Père Ganne (Historic inn frequented by the painters of the **Barbizon school**) (BARBIZON)
Atelier de **Rosa Bonheur** (FONTAINEBLEAU)
Musée de **Jeanne et Léon Blum**, Maison de **Victor Hugo** (JOUY-EN-JOSAS)
Maison natale du **Général de Gaulle** (LILLE)
Musée **Tourgueniev** (MARLY-LE-ROI), Musée **Alexandre-Dumas** (MARLY-LE-ROI and VILLERS-COTTERÊTS)
Musée **Rodin** (MEUDON and PARIS)
Musée **Maurice-Ravel**, Maison **Jean-Monnet** (MONTFORT-L'AMAURY)
Musée **Jean-Jacques-Rousseau** (MONTMORENCY)
Musée **Jean-Calvin** (NOYON)
Maison **Debussy**, atelier **Maurice Denis** (ST-GERMAIN-EN-LAYE)

War museums, memorials...

First World War

Parc Memorial de Beaumont-Hamel and other battlefields, South African and British memorials and cemeteries (ALBERT)
Caverne du Dragon (CHEMIN DES DAMES)
Clairière de l'Armistice (Armistice Clearing) (Forêt de COMPIÈGNE)
Mémorial australien (CORBIE)
Colline de NOTRE-DAME-DE-LORETTE (cemetery, museum)
Mémorial de Villeroy, Cimetière national de Chambry, Monument Notre-Dame-de-la-Marne (Vallée de l'OURCQ)
Historial de la Grande Guerre (PERONNE)
Mémorial américain de Bellicourt, (ST-QUENTIN)
Mémorial canadien de VIMY

Second World War

Musée de la Guerre (CALAIS)
Musée historique de la Seconde Guerre mondiale, Musée du Mur de l'Atlantique (La CÔTE D'OPALE)
Forteresse de Mimoyecques (GUÎNES)
Blockhaus d'Eperlecques (ST-OMER)

Modern art and architecture

Tour Perret (AMIENS)
Musée d'Art contemporain (sculpture garden) and Musée des Beaux-Arts (DUNKERQUE)
Palais des Beaux-Arts, Euralille (LILLE)
le Cyclope (MILLY-LA-FORÊT)
Musée National d'Art Moderne, Centre Georges-Pompidou, La Défense (PARIS)
Villa Savoye (POISSY)
Musée d'Art Moderne (VILLENEUVE D'ASCQ)

Most noteworthy châteaux

BRETEUIL	COURANCES	FERRIÈRES	PIERREFONDS
CHAMPS	DAMPIERRE	FONTAINEBLEAU	VAUX-LE-VICOMTE
CHANTILLY	ÉCOUEN	MAINTENON	VERSAILLES

Great Gothic cathedrals

AMIENS	CHARTRES	NOYON	ST-DENIS	SENLIS
BEAUVAIS	LAON	Notre-Dame (PARIS)	ST-OMER	SOISSONS

Lighthouses

Phare de Brighton (ST-VALERY-SUR-SOMME)   Le TOUQUET

Windmills

See Introduction: Rural housing in the North and Practical information: something different.

and specially for kids...

See also Practical information: Something different.

Parc ASTERIX	THOIRY (animal reserve)
Mer de Sable at Ermenonville	Aqualud, Parc d'attractions de Bagatelle
(Abbaye de CHAALIS)	(Le TOUQUET)
DISNEYLAND PARIS	Maison de l'Oiseau (ST-VALERY-SUR-SOMME)

St-Valery-sur-Somme

Introduction

Landscapes

Picardy, Artois, Île-de-France (the region around Paris) and Paris itself all lie within the vast geological area known as the Paris Basin which borders on Flanders and the great plain of Northern Europe beyond. The Paris Basin is linked by the Burgundy sill to the Rhône Basin (southeast) and by the Poitou sill to the Aquitaine Basin (west). The landscape of the Paris Basin comprises forests, lush alluvial valleys with slow-flowing rivers and limestone plateaux providing arable land, dotted with sandy patches. The climate tends towards stormy summers and temperate winters with damp springs and autumns. Under Clovis, Île-de-France was part of the Frankish kingdom, the first French territory with its two capitals Soissons and Compiègne. Clovis' descendants were deposed in 751 by Pépin the Short, whose son Charlemagne was consecrated King of the Franks by the Pope in Rome in 774. In 843 Charlemagne's kingdom was carved up and France was designated the land lying west of

16

the provinces bordering the Meuse, Saône and Rhône rivers. The former territory of the Franks was reduced to the Duchy of France and the two counties of Orléans and Étampes. It was only four centuries later that this duchy was called Île-de-France (the 'island of France' because of its position between the rivers Seine, Aisne, Oise and Marne). During the Norman invasion, the Duc de France valiantly defended Paris and one of the members of this House – Hugh Capet – was elected King of France at Senlis in 987. Hugh Capet's descendants governed France until 1848, except during the Revolution and the First Empire (1793 to 1814).

NORTHERN FRANCE

Picardy – This area northwest of Paris and Île-de-France is a land of plateaux and valleys but it also has a long coastline.

Plateaux – The wide and virtually flat plateaux of this former province are covered with a thick layer of silt which makes them very fertile and well suited to the cultivation of sugar-beet and cereals, fields of which stretch without interruption as far as the eye can see.

To the east, the **Santerre** (*Sana terra*: good earth) and **Vermandois** regions are characterised by large farms, often complemented by a sugar refinery or a distillery. St-Quentin, the administrative and industrial centre of the Aisne *département*, is the principal town.

To the east and south, the **Laonnois**, **Noyonnais** and **Soissonnais** regions mark the transition with Île-de-France, in particular the prestigious Valois region with its mantle of forests.

Western Picardy is sliced by wide valleys. Where the silt on the plateau was swept away the soil is poorer, as in the **Ponthieu** region where the villages have long, daubed walls devoid of windows. In the **Vimeu** region, where the chalk has decomposed into flinty clay, the cold, damp ground has created a mixed landscape of farmland criss-crossed by hedges and trees, cider-apple orchards and small, scattered villages. Near Beauvais the chalky, silt-covered plateau suddenly reveals a verdant hollow: the clayey **Pays de Bray**, a wooded area interspersed with meadows where stock-farming is the main activity.

Valleys – The verdant wide-mouthed valleys are bisected by the Somme, Authie and Canche rivers. These waters flow so slowly they have difficulty in making their way, losing themselves in ponds and marshes full of fish and waterfowl. The floors of the valleys are a mix of old peat bogs, rows of poplars, stock-farming fields and, on the outskirts of towns (Abbeville, Amiens, Péronne, Montdidier), vegetable gardens *(hortillonnages)* surrounded by canals.

Towns have developed along these valleys: Montreuil on the Canche, Doullens on the Authie, Péronne, Amiens, Abbeville on the Somme.

The capital of this region is Amiens, a great industrial centre with factories producing tyres, electronics, video games, domestic appliances car parts and chemical products.

Coast – To the south, near Ault, the Picardy plateau meets the sea, ending in a sharp cliff of white chalk banded with flint. North of the Somme Bay a maritime plain called the **Marquenterre** area has been created by debris torn from the Normandy coast and carried northward by the currents, gradually forming an offshore bar. Only the Somme, Authie and Canche rivers have carved a passage to the sea; there are therefore few large ports but several seaside resorts, the largest of them Le Touquet, beside the dunes.

Y Thierry

The Opal Coast at the Site des deux Caps

The coastal plain lies between the dunes and the old coastal bar, which is marked by a noticeable cliff. The drained and dried plain is now used for fields of wheat and oats, and for raising salt-pasture lambs on the grassy shores known as *mollières*.
In the past St-Valery-sur-Somme, Le Crotoy and Étaples were important ports; today they harbour only fishing boats and yachts.

Artois – The former province of Artois, which lies on an extension of the Picardy plateaux, is a rise of land running northwest to southeast. It ends in an escarpment of about a hundred metres (Vimy Ridge, Notre-Dame de Lorette Hill) which divides the Paris Basin from the Anglo-Belgian Basin. The great plain of Flanders begins at the foot of this escarpment. The Artois hills overlook the Boulonnais region to the northwest and the Lens plain and Arras' agricultural plain, fed by the Scarpe River, to the southwest. The well-watered hills of Artois are however bare to the southeast, in the **Ternois** region where there are outcrops of chalk; to the northwest, the chalky top layer of soil has decomposed into flinty clay resulting in lush, damp countryside which includes Hesdin Forest and mixed agricultural and meadow land.

Montreuil-sur-Mer – Rue du Clape-en-Bas

The **Boulonnais** region forms an enclave in the chalk layer, revealing outcrops of harder, older rocks; this "buttonhole" ends below the Channel.
The landscape of the Boulonnais is very different from neighbouring areas. In the north, where Artois rises again, the Upper Boulonnais forms a chalky plateau which in places reaches over 200m/650ft in altitude.
In the area where the land forms a hollow, the Lower Boulonnais, the wooded countryside is dotted with whitewashed farms. The clay creates meadows used for rearing the dappled-grey "Boulonnais draughthorses" and for other stock-breeding; the soil also supports Desvres and Boulogne forests, while Hardelot Forest grows in sandier soil.
Boulogne, France's foremost fishing port, stands at the mouth of the River Liane. To the north, the edge of the calcareous plateau forms the cliffs of the Opal Coast *(see La CÔTE D'OPALE)*.

Hainault and Cambrésis – Hainault (capital: Valenciennes) and Cambrésis (capital: Cambrai) are extensions of the chalky plateaux of Artois and Picardy, but are in addition covered with a thick layer of silt which is ideal for growing sugar beet and wheat; the per-acre harvests are excellent. The plateaux are divided by wide river valleys such as those of the Scarpe, Sambre, Selle and Escaut (Scheldt); meadows of fodder crops and pasture give them the look of farming country. The forests of St-Amand and Mormal appear where there is flinty clay, the result of decomposition of the chalk.

Thiérache and Avesnois – These two relatively hilly regions form the tail of the Ardennes uplands, covered at the western end by marl and chalk mixed with marl. The **Thiérache** is a damp region, part forest and part pasture. When carefully drained the cold, non-porous ground provides pasture for cows. The dairies produce butter, cheese and condensed milk. The **Avesnois** is crossed by the Helpe Majeure and the Helpe Mineure rivers, tributaries of the Sambre River. This region resembles the Thiérache but is marked by summits which rise to over 250m-820ft in places. It is also a region of pastures and is famous for its dairy cows and its cheeses, especially Maroilles.

Flanders – The Flemish plain, which continues into Belgium, is bounded to the south by the hills of Artois and to the east by the plateaux of Hainault and Cambrésis.

Coastal Flanders – The wet and windy *Blooteland* (bare land protected by dunes separating the area from the sea) has been gradually reclaimed from the sea since the Middle Ages. The engineers, including the famous **Coebergher**, came mostly from the Low Countries; they were able to drain the land gradually using great dams, canals and pumps, thus creating the marshes *(Moëres)*. It is today a low-lying region where the grey clay yields crops of sugar-beet, cereals, flax and chicory and the nearby pastures are grazed by sheep, pigs, horses and cattle. The flat countryside, scattered with great isolated farms built around square courtyards, is dominated by belfries, belltowers, windmills and, on the coast, the factory chimneys and harbour cranes of Dunkirk and Calais.

Inland Flanders – Known as *Houtland* (wooded land), in contrast with the bare maritime Flanders, the "Flemish lowlands" consist of lush countryside divided by rows of poplars, willows or elms. The *censes*, white-walled Flemish farms with red roofs, stand out against this green background.

A series of summits extends into Belgium; each standing independently from the others, they make up the chain of the **Monts des Flandres**. As well as providing beautiful meadows where cows, horses and pigs thrive, the rich soil is also used to grow various crops: cereals, fruit and vegetables in gardens among the St-Omer canals, plants for industrial processing (hops near Bailleul, flax in the Lys Valley, chicory, sugar beet).

Two small areas between Lille and Douai are different, however: they are the bare plateaux of the **Mélantois** and the **Pévèle** regions. The coal fields *(see Economy)* stretch from Béthune to Valenciennes and have given rise to a "black country" marked by slag-heaps, brick mining towns and mine-shaft frames.

Between the Lys Valley and the Escaut (Scheldt) River, there lies the industrial conurbation of Lille – Roubaix – Tourcoing – Armentières, traditionally largely devoted to textiles *(see LILLE)*.

ÎLE-DE-FRANCE

Pays de France – This arable plateau extending between St-Denis, Luzarches and the Dammartin-en-Goële ridge lay at the heart of royal territory. The layer of marl covering the subsoil has made the area extremely fertile and the huge fields are planted with wheat and beetroot.

Parisis – Parisis lies between the Oise and the Seine rivers and the Pays de France. This area was once occupied by the Gauls, who gave it its name and who christened the French capital. Parisis is an alluvial plain with few rivers which slopes towards the Seine; it is dominated by limestone hillocks covered in sand or grit.

Beyond the industrial suburbs of Paris, market gardens and orchards spread along the limestone slopes of the plain, while the sandy stretches bear forests.

Senlisis – This region has often been bracketed with Valois by geographers and historians but in fact it was part of the Crown territory, the central core of Ile-de-France. Senlisis, which is bordered by the Oise, the Dammartin-en-Goële ridge and the Valois itself, is one of the most picturesque regions near the capital. Arable land is found on the silty soils while the sandy areas have favoured the development of forestry.

Valois – Valois is surrounded by Senlisis and the rivers Oise, Automne and Ourcq; it acquired strategic importance as early as Roman times and has remained one of the most important regions in French history. First a county, then a duchy, Valois was twice given to one of the king's brothers. Twice the descendants of this royal line, known as the Princes de Valois, acceded to the throne.

Multien – Multien is an area of rolling landscapes and ploughed fields, bounded by the River Marne, the Valois and the Goële ridge. It was the scene of the fighting in September 1914.

French Vexin – Three rivers border this limestone platform: the Oise, the Epte and the Seine. West of the River Epte is the Normandy Vexin. The loess covering is an extremely fertile topsoil which favours cereal cultivation, especially wheat, and vegetable crops. Cattle rearing is concentrated in the valleys planted with poplar trees. The Buttes de Rosne, a series of outliers stretching from Monneville to Vallangoujard, are covered in woods. They include the strip of land running north of the Seine.

Mantois – Mantois is an enormous plateau situated between the rivers Eure and Oise; it consists of forests to the east and arable land to the west. The many brooks and streams which cut across it provide a pleasantly fresh, undulating appearance.

Hurepoix – It is bounded by Mantois, Beauce, Fontainebleau Forest and the Seine. Like other areas in Île-de-France, Hurepoix features a number of rises capped with limestone and sandstone which crop up between the valleys. Such geological diversity – sand, sandstone and limestone in the hills, marl in the vales – has produced a varied landscape and vegetation, which is one of the main attractions of the Hurepoix: market gardens spread along the valleys of the rivers Bièvre, Yvette and Essonne, the hillsides are covered in woodland and the plains below offer lush green pastures.

Gâtinais – The Gâtinais is defined by the River Seine, Hurepoix, Beauce and Champagne. The French Gâtinais, a clay plateau, lies east of the river Loing while the Orléanais Gâtinais (to the west) is an area of sand and sandstone. This second area is covered by Fontainebleau Forest, popular because of its splendid groves and sandstone boulders. The lush valley of the Loing is dotted with charming small towns.

French Brie – French Brie is located between the Seine and the Grand Morin rivers and has Champagne Brie as its northern border. These two regions differ for historical reasons: the former belonged to the King of France while the latter was the property of the Comte de Champagne. This area is watered by four meandering rivers: the Seine, Marne, Petit Morin and Grand Morin. A layer of non-porous marl which retains moisture is topped by a covering of millstone and siliceous limestone. This is the famous Brie limestone, which is itself covered with a fine blanket of fertile loess. The area has many large farms specialising in large-scale wheat, sugar-beet and vegetable cultivation. The less fertile pockets of land, around Sénart and Ferrières for instance, have been planted with forest.

FORESTS

Île-de-France has some magnificent forests, among them those of Rambouillet, Compiègne and Fontainebleau which feature among the finest in the country.
Woods and forests have a timeless appeal: lush greenery in springtime, shaded groves in summer, the deep russet tones of autumn or the crisp frosts of winter. Forests also provide a multitude of fauna and flora to study or flowers, fruit, nuts and mushrooms to harvest in season. Many also have charming picnic areas. Those who take time to understand the life cycle of a forest also understand its infinite variety.

State forests and private forests – Three types of forest exist in France: state, private and local authority forests. The most interesting for ramblers are state forests, run by the French Forestry Commission (ONF) since 1966: they have an extensive network of roads, paths and lanes, and their magnificent groves form a picturesque setting. The aim of the forest ranges is to preserve the natural habitat. The most beautiful French forests used to feature protected forest zones known as "artistic reserves" in which unusually striking trees were left untouched by the axe, even when they died. This practice was given up in favour of "biological reserves". Forests on private estates are not open to the public, apart from the roads that run through them.

Trees – Like all living things, trees breathe, reproduce and need nourishment. Mineral nutrients are drawn from the earth by the roots and distributed to all parts of the tree via the sap running through the trunk and leaves.
Every type of soil does not necessarily suit every species of tree. Chestnut trees, for instance, cannot survive on limestone sites, whereas oaks will flourish on a variety of soils.
Trees, like other plants, breathe through their leaves and reproduce through their flowers. Flowers will bear fruit providing they are fertilised by pollen of their own species. Very few trees have hermaphrodite flowers – presenting both male and female characteristics – like roses, acacias etc, and consequently the pollen is usually carried from the male flower to the female flower by insects, or sometimes by the wind. Trees may also reproduce by their shoots: if a youngish tree trunk is razed to the ground, a number of stool shoots will emerge from the stump. Conifers do not produce offshoots.
The trees of Île-de-France fall into two categories: deciduous and coniferous.

Deciduous – These trees shed their leaves every autumn and grow them again in the spring. Beeches, oaks, hornbeams, birches and chestnut trees belong to this category.

Coniferous – Coniferous species do not have leaves but needles instead, which they shed regularly throughout the year. The needles are renewed every four to five years. Their sap contains resin – they are also known as resinous trees – and the fruit is generally cone-shaped. Pines, cypresses, cedars and fir trees are all conifers, as is the larch, which loses its needles every year.

Trees of the Île-de-France forests – Most species of deciduous trees can be found around Paris; the most common are listed below.

Oak – One of the most esteemed forest trees, its hard but beautiful wood is used for both carpentry and ornamental woodwork. In former times oak bark was much sought after by local tanners. Some of the oaks tower 40m/132ft high with trunks over 1m/3ft in diameter. Trees can be felled up to the age of 250 years.

Beech – Although it resembles the oak in its habit, beech is slightly more elegant. The wood is mainly used for everyday furniture and railway sleepers but it is also popular as fuel. The trunk is cylindrical, the bark smooth and shiny; young shoots have a crooked, gnarled appearance. Beeches grow as tall as oaks but are no longer commercially viable beyond 120 years.

Hornbeam – A remarkably tough species, the hornbeam resembles beech; it also lives to the same age, but is shorter and its bark features numerous grooves.

Chestnut – This tree can grow to great heights and can live for several hundred years but is generally felled much younger as very old chestnut trees become hollow and prone to disease. Its wood was traditionally used by the cooperage industry for making staves, posts and stakes; nowadays it is used in the production of chip-board. Chestnut trees will grow only on siliceous soil.

Birch – Even when it reaches 25m/82ft in height the birch retains a graceful, slim trunk of white bark – which peels off in fine layers – and shimmering leaves. Damp, sandy soil is an excellent terrain for all varieties of birch. It makes excellent firewood but it is principally used for making wood pulp for use in the paper industry.

Oak   Beech

M. Viard /JACANA

Scots Pine – This species, the most commonly-found conifer in Île-de-France, is ideal for reafforestation, particularly in sandy terrain; since the mid-19C it has been planted in plots of land where there is meagre or non-existent vegetation. Scots pines have short needles (4 to 6cm/1.5 to 2.5in) which grow in pairs, smallish cones (3 to 5cm/1 to 2in) and reddish-ochre bark.
Foresters often plant Scots pines alongside exotic or Mediterranean (maritime pine) resinous species. A great favourite is the Corsican pine, a tall, handsome tree with a perfectly straight trunk; it can grow to 50m/165ft but old trees develop large grey patches on their bark.

The science of forestry – If a forest is not tended it will invariably deteriorate. In order to develop fully and reach their proper size, trees must be given breathing space and be placed in an environment which meets their specific requirements. The first step in a reafforestation campaign is to plant fir trees, which have few needs and which produce wood in a very short time. Their roots retain the earth, which the surface water otherwise washes away, and the needles build up thick layers on the ground. Next, hornbeams, birches and beeches are planted to increase the fertility of the soil, and finally oaks. Many of the beech groves are left as this species is considered to be commercially profitable.

Rotations – The prime concern of foresters is always to have trees ready for felling; consequently, when trees are felled foresters ensure they are immediately replaced with seedlings. For example, a forest may be divided into ten units and every five years the unit with the oldest trees is cleared and then replanted; this means that within 50 years the forest is entirely renewed while remaining commercially viable. This technique is known as rotation.
Forest managers try to avoid exposing a large sector of the forest as leafy plants such as hazel and mulberry trees can set in, which might choke the young shoots. Within each sector two, three or four groups are formed according to the trees' approximate age and a programme of successive felling is planned. This ensures that only limited areas are deforested at any one time.
Whatever the rotation for a given forest, its appearance is bound to change depending on the thickness of the vegetation and the forestry techniques which have been applied.
There are three types of plantation in Île-de-France:

Groves – After the land has been sown, natural selection sees that the weaker shoots are choked by the stronger ones. The trees – planted fairly close to one another – spread vertically. After some time the land is cleared around the finer species, to encourage them to develop, and eventually these are the only ones which remain. This grove, where the widely-spaced trees are all the same age, is called a *futaie pleine*; the rotation is rather long, 50 years or even 80 for very tall trees. *Futaie jardinée* is another type of grove, in which the trees are planted and cut at different times, so that the sector features a variety of "age groups"; older trees are always felled first.

A fully matured grove is a truly impressive sight, with its powerful trunks and its rich canopy of foliage producing subtle effects of light and shade.

Copses – The trees are younger. Rotation ranges from 5 to 30 years, depending on whether pit props, logs for heating or firewood is wanted. A copse is a sector of forest where a group of mature trees are razed to the ground once they have been cut. The shoots growing around the stump develop into a multitude of young bushy, leafy trees.

Copses with Standards – If, when cutting a copse, the finest trees are left standing, these will dominate the new shoots. If they survive a series of fellings, they will grow to be extremely strong. The utilisation of copses with standards produces both fuel wood (from the copses) and timber for industrial purposes (from the older species).

Fauna and flora – Forests contain not only trees but also countless varieties of plants and animals; hunts are still organised in certain forests.

Nature lovers always find forests fascinating as the rich, damp soil is remarkably fertile and can sustain moss, lichen, mushrooms, grasses, flowers, shrubs and ferns.

Flowers – April is the season of laburnum, hyacinths and daffodils. May brings hawthorn, lily-of-the-valley, columbine and the delightful catkins of the hazel tree. In June there is broom, heather, campanula, scabious and wild pinks. During the autumn russet and gold leaves are as attractive as the forest flowers.

Fruit – Wild strawberries and succulent raspberries ripen during July and August, while blackberries can be harvested in August and September together with the new crop of hazelnuts. October is the time for sloes and sweet chestnuts.

Mushrooms – Some varieties of mushrooms – the *Russula virescens, chanterelle comestible* and *mousseron* – are always edible. Other species are difficult to identify and may be dangerous. If in doubt, mushroom pickers should consult a professional mycologist or the local chemist *(pharmacien)*.

GARDENS IN ÎLE-DE-FRANCE

Three successive trends defined the official canons of ornamental gardening in Île-de-France, the home of many royal residences.

16C – During the 16C gardens were not considered an essential part of an estate, merely of the same category as outbuildings. They were generally of geometric shape and resembled a chessboard where each of the squares contained carefully-trimmed spindle and box forming arabesques and other elaborate patterns; these motifs were called *broderies*. Gardens were enclosed within a sort of cloister, made from stonework or greenery, from which visitors could enjoy a good view of the garden. The grounds themselves were cut across by paths featuring fragments of marble, pottery and brick. Though water did not play any significant part in the general appearance of the gardens, there were basins and fountains encircled by balustrades or tall plants; they were there to be observed in their own right and for people to admire their ornamental statues and water displays.

Most of them have now disappeared, at least in Île-de-France. There is, however, an outstanding example in Villandry in the Loire Valley *(see Michelin Green Guide, Châteaux of the Loire)*.

17C-early 18C: The Formal Garden – Although **André le Nôtre** cannot be credited with "inventing" the **formal French gardens**, he was undoubtedly the one person who raised this art form to absolute perfection. Its purpose was twofold: to enhance the beauty of the château it surrounded and to provide a superb view from within. The garden's main features were fountains, trees, statues, terraces and a sweeping perspective.

The château was fronted by a "Turkish carpet" of parterres with flowers and evergreen shrubs forming arabesques and intricate patterns. These were symmetrically flanked by basins with fountains, usually adorned with statues. Fountains were also placed on the terrace bearing the château and the upper lawns, which was the starting-point of the central perspective along a canal or a green carpet of lawn *(tapis vert)* lined with elegant groves of tall trees.

The groups of trees planted along the perspective were designed to be perfectly symmetrical. They were crossed by a network of paths: the clearings at the intersections offered splendid vistas extending into the far distance. Hedges lined the paths, concealing the massive tree trunks and providing a backdrop for marble statues; as hedges were fragile and expensive to maintain, however, most were later removed or greatly reduced in height from their original 6-8m/c20-26ft. Each grove of trees featured a "curiosity": a fountain with elaborate waterworks, perhaps, or a colonnade or a group of sculpted figures.

The enormous variety in designs and styles of the parterres and surrounding trees, bushes and hedges ensured that these formal gardens were never monotonous. They were conceived as an intellectual pursuit, giving pleasure through their stately proportions and perspectives, the skilful design and the sheer beauty of each detail.

Late 18C-19C: The Landscape Garden – In the 18C manipulating the landscape into rigid geometric patterns was deemed to be no longer fashionable: instead the tendency was to imitate nature. The landscape garden – also called the Anglo-Chinese garden – consisted of lush, rolling grounds dotted with great trees and rocks, pleasantly refreshed by streams and tiny cascades. A rustic bridge might cross a river flowing into a pond or lake covered with water-lilies and surrounded by willow trees, and a mill or dairy might add the final touch to this Arcadian scene. The 18C fascination for philosophy which characterised the Age of Enlightenment was also reflected in contemporary gardening which saw the introduction of symbolic or exotic monuments or **"fabriques"** (a technical term which originally referred to architectural works depicted in paintings). These follies were dotted throughout the grounds to enhance the landscape.

Antique temples and medieval ruins were particular favourites, and tombs and mausoleums became popular just before the Revolution; Chinese and Turkish sculptures were also fashionable. An unfinished temple, for instance, would remind visitors of the limits of science, while an oriental pagoda standing beside a crumbling tower symbolised the fragility of human achievements.

Sentimentality, romance and melodrama were popular features of many art forms and the trend also affected landscape gardens: a number of new sights made their appearance including the secret lovers' grotto, the bench of the tired mother, the grave of the rejected suitor etc.

Most of these estates were ravaged during the Revolution and few of their fragile monuments survived. Efforts are now being made to restore what was left. The most outstanding example of an 18C folly in the region is the Cassan Pagoda at L'Isle-Adam *(see illustration p 204)*.

Particularly fine gardens may still be found at Versailles, Vaux-le-Vicomte, Chantilly, Courances, St.-Cloud, Sceaux, Champs, Fontainebleau, Rambouillet and Ferrières.

Y. Arthus-Bertrand /EXPLORER

Aerial view of Vaux-le-Vicomte

Economy

NORD – PAS-DE-CALAIS

The landscapes, geographical location, temperate climate and agricultural resources of the Nord-Pas-de-Calais area have given it a high population density since the Middle Ages. It has always been a major trading sector. Very early on in their history, its towns acquired wealth from textiles and trade. They enjoyed a great deal of autonomy, symbolised by their belfries.

The region also has a coastal belt that includes Boulogne, France's leading fishing port. The Pas-de-Calais, the busiest maritime area in the world, constitutes the French side of the Straits of Dover, the narrowest stretch of water between the continent and Great Britain and the main trade route to northern Europe.

The industrial infrastructure in the Nord-Pas-de-Calais region is still the second largest in France. Although industrial employment is decreasing overall, the area's small and medium-size enterprises are implementing modernisation strategies aimed at expansion, especially in the export market. In doing so, they are taking full advantage of the proximity of vast European markets and the ease of access with the Nord-Europe high-speed train, the Channel Tunnel and the dense network of roads. This situation has attracted foreign investment (this is the leading region in France for inward investment with Coca-Cola, MacCain, IBM, Rank Xerox, 3M etc).

Metallurgy – The discovery and extraction of coal in the 19C attracted heavy industries (mining, iron and steelmaking) to the area. Mining ceased in 1990, leaving deep scars. Reconversion is currently underway.

The iron and steel industry has been through many crises over the past few decades. In days gone by, the main criteria leading to the opening of a works was proximity to raw materials. Since the 1960s, economies have acquired a global dimension and this, in addition to a reduction in transport costs, led to the importing of raw materials with higher mineral contents. The foundries and steelworks then moved towards ports and numerous traditional industrial sites closed down. Meanwhile, Dunkirk acquired one of the most efficient steelworks in Europe and Gravelines was selected as the site for an ultra-modern aluminium works (Pechiney).

French rail equipment (especially the VAL, the driverless subway first built in Lille in 1983 and now exported worldwide) is produced mainly in the Valenciennes and Douai areas. The automobile industry has works in Douai (Renault), Maubeuge (MCA, a Renault subsidiary), Douvrain (Française des Mécaniques) and Hourdain (Peugeot-Fiat).

The chemicals industry (9 000 jobs) has developed in the field of organic chemistry using tar and other coal by-products.

Textiles and Glassware – The textile and clothing industries, which had been traditional employers since the Middle Ages, have been seriously affected by international competition (especially from Third-World countries where wages are low). This has led to a need for huge increases in productivity in a market subject to the uncertainties of fashion. The enormous efforts made to achieve technical and commercial modernisation and train workers are unable to stem the constant flow of layoffs. Despite these difficulties, the Nord-Pas-de-Calais area still supplies all the national output of linen (Lys Valley), 95 % of worsteds, 22 % of woollen fabrics, 38 % of thread and 20 % of cottons, not forgetting the famous Calais and Caudry lace.

The glassware and crystal industries include the PPG works in Boussois, Sicover in Aniche and, best known of all, the Arques glass and crystal works which has enjoyed an outstanding increase in turnover and now exports to 160 countries.

Food-processing – The food-processing industry is now the region's leading sector. Regional produce supplies flour mills and biscuit factories in the Lille area, starch works, breweries etc. Chicory refineries enjoy a worldwide reputation. Beet has engendered a whole industrial sector with crushing mills, sugar and other refineries, and distilleries. All these buildings give the plain its own special landscape near Cambrai and Thumeries. Canning factories produce 30 % of the total national production of tinned vegetables and ready-prepared meals and 50 % of fish (Boulogne).

New Sectors – The region's geographical situation is ideal for the expansion of several different services (accounting for 62 % of total jobs): logistics, distribution, tourism, services for businesses etc. An important sector of employment is **mail order**. With a steadily increasing work force of 18 000, it provides regional companies with a wide range of business opportunities. Of the ten largest French companies in this sector, five operate from this area. The top two are La Redoute and Trois Suisses.

Coal Fields – Coal extraction in the coal fields of the Nord-Pas-de-Calais area dates from the 18C. The deposit in this region lies at the western end of a large coal depression which extends into Belgium (Borinage at Mons, Charleroi coal fields) and Germany (Ruhr coal fields).

After 270 years of extraction, all the mines have now closed.

The deposit – The coal fields extend eastwards from the hills of the Artois region for about 120km/75mi to the Belgian border; the deposit is from 4 to 12km/2.5 to 7.5mi wide and was mined to a depth of 1 200m/3 937ft. The irregularity of the seams, however, their small openings (sometimes less than 0.80m/3ft) and the presence of numerous geological flaws made extraction progressively harder and led to an increasing deficit.

Closure of the mines – A decline in the yield from these mines first appeared in the late 1950s. In 1959, when productivity still reached 29 million tonnes, a plan of progressive shutdown was implemented which led to the closure of the last pit on 21 December 1990.

Industrial Recycling – The pits employed up to 220 000 people in 1947 but since then they have gradually closed. A range of different industries developed around the working of the mines: production of oval coal briquettes, foundry and special coke; the manufacture of facing bricks; the sale of mine gas; the production of electricity in

Coal extraction

J. Dupont /EXPLORER

power stations which run largely on fuel products gathered from the slag heaps; the use of shale, also from slag heaps, for road foundations and as ballast for railway lines. Over 329 either flat or conical slag heaps remain today, of which about 70 are still commercially exploitable. With the prospect of imminent closure, the mining companies formed subsidiaries to take over from them; these make up the regional industrial group Filianor.

PICARDY

Despite being a rural area, Picardy nonetheless sustains lively industrial activities. Traditionally the region's industry was textiles but this has largely been replaced by metal-based industries (agricultural and car equipment, mopeds etc). Chemical products include glass (St-Gobain) and rubber (tyres in Amiens) in particular.

Linked to agriculture, the sugar refineries, food-manufacturing plants and especially the canning factories – based in the Santerre area at Estrée, Rosières and Péronne – all play an important part in the region.

ÎLE-DE-FRANCE

A high population density – Although Île-de-France covers only 2.2% of the surface area of France, over 18% of the French population resides in the province. This huge concentration of over 10 million inhabitants has gradually focused around the natural junctions of the Seine, Marne and Oise river basins. These large, slow rivers separate vast plateaux bearing rich countryside including the Brie and Beauce regions, and the large forests of Fontainebleau, Halatte, Rambouillet, Marly and St-Germain.

Today the development of the Paris region tends to respect these natural tracts and instead focuses urban and economic growth around the new towns: Cergy-Pontoise, Évry, St-Quentin-en-Yvelines, Marne-la-Vallée and Melun-Sénart.

The foremost industrial region in France – The Paris region employs over 15% of the national labour force. Alongside the various industries (metallurgy, mechanical engineering, electrical and electronics manufacturing, chemicals, clothing and fashion), highly specialised and ultra-modern businesses have also developed.

The Paris and Île-de-France region is the foremost business market in France.

The key on page 4 explains the abbreviations and symbols used in the text or on the maps.

Historical table and notes

Celts and Romans

BC	
Circa 300	The north of Gaul taken by a Celto-Germanic tribe, the Belgae.
57	Belgian Gaul brought into subjection by Caesar. Bavay, Boulogne and Amiens became important Roman centres.
AD 1C-3C	Roman peace. Northern France became part of the province of Second Belgium (capital Reims).
406	Frankish invasion.

Merovingians and Carolingians

486	Territory from the Somme to the Loire rivers occupied by Clovis following the defeat of the Roman army at Soissons: his kingdom was called Francia in Latin.
561	The kingdom of France divided into three parts: northern France incorporated into Neustria.
6C and 7C	Creation of bishoprics and founding of many abbeys.
768	Charlemagne crowned King of Neustria in Noyon.
800	Charlemagne proclaimed Emperor of the Western World.
9C and 10C	Norman and Hungarian invasions. Withdrawal of the abbeys into the towns.
911	The Duchy of Normandy created after the Treaty of St Clair-sur-Epte, ending Normans' ambitions in Île-de-France.
987	Hugh Capet, duke and suzerain of the land extending from the Somme to the Loire rivers, elected King of France in Senlis.

The Middle Ages

11C and 12C	Period of prosperity. Development of the clothmaking industry in Flanders, Artois and Picardy. Towns obtained charters and built belfries.
1180-1223	The Valois, Clermont, Meulan, Artois and Vermandois regions and the region around Amiens and Lille annexed to the royal kingdom by Philippe Auguste.
1214	Battle of Bouvines: victory for Philippe Auguste over the Count of Flanders and his allies King John of England, the Holy Roman Emperor Otto IV and the counts of Boulogne and Hainault.
1272	Ponthieu under the authority of the kings of England.
1314	Flanders annexed by Philip the Fair.
1337	Beginning of the Hundred Years War. The death of Philip the Fair and his three sons ("the accursed kings") resulted in a problem of succession: Philip the Fair's nephew, Philip de Valois, preferred by the French barons over his grandson, Edward III, King of England. The following century marked by battles between the French and the English who laid claim to the French Crown, as well as between the Armagnacs, supporters of the family of Orléans, and the Burgundians, supporters of the dukes of Burgundy.
1346	Battle of Crécy: victory for Edward III of England.
1347	Calais surrendered to the English with the famous episode of the Burghers of Calais.
1369	Marriage of Philip the Bold, Duke of Burgundy, with Marguerite, daughter of the Count of Flanders: Flanders under Burgundian authority.
1415	Battle of Agincourt: victory for Henry V of England.
1420	The Treaty of Troyes signed by Isabeau of Bavaria, wife of the mad king Charles VI, depriving the Dauphin of his rights of succession and designating her son-in-law, Henry V of England, heir to the French throne.
1422	Death of Charles VI. France divided between the English, the Burgundians and the Armagnacs. Charles VII, the legitimate heir, resident in Bourges.
1430	Joan of Arc taken prisoner at Compiègne.
1435	Picardy and the Boulonnais region yielded to the Duchy of Burgundy in the Treaty of Arras.
1441	English supremacy over Île-de-France ended with the liberation of Pontoise.

| 1477 | Invasion of Picardy, Artois, Boulonnais and Hainault by Louis XI following the death of Charles the Bold; only Picardy subsequently held. Marriage of Marie of Burgundy, daughter of Charles the Bold, to Maximilian of Austria: Flanders brought under Hapsburg control. |

From the Bourbons to the Revolution

16C	Through the House of Hapsburg, Flanders included in the empire of Charles V of Spain.
1520	Meeting between Henry VIII of England and François I at the Field of the Cloth of Gold, Guînes.
1529	Peace of Dames signed at Cambrai: claims to Artois and Flanders renounced by François I.
1557	St-Quentin taken by the Spanish.
1558	Calais taken from the English by the Duke of Guise.
1562	Beginning of the Wars of Religion.
1585	Philip II of Spain allied with the Catholic League (Treaty of Joinville).
1593	Henry of Navarre converted to Catholicism after capturing most of Île-de-France; crowned King Henri IV of France.
1598	Edict of Nantes.
1659	Following the Treaty of the Pyrenees, marriage agreed between Louis XIV and Maria-Theresa of Spain; Artois brought under French sovereignty.
1661	The construction of a huge palace at Versailles commissioned by Louis XIV.
1663	Marriage of Louis XIV with Maria-Theresa, who according to local custom was to inherit all of the Brabant region from her mother. When the inheritance passed to another heir, Louis XIV declared the war of "Devolution" on the Spanish Low Countries.
1668	Walloon Flanders given to Louis XIV under the Treaty of Aix-la-Chapelle.
1678	Louis XIV allowed to annexe the other northern towns under the Treaty of Nimegen.
1713	The frontiers of northern France definitively fixed (Treaty of Utrecht).
1789	French Revolution.

From the First to the Second Empire

1802	Treaty of Amiens.
1803	Napoleon's army mustered at the Boulogne Camp for a possible invasion of England.
1804	Napoleon crowned Emperor of the French.
1812	Russia invaded by Napoleon's troops.
1814	France invaded. Unconditional abdication by Napoleon at Fontainebleau as all Europe lined up against him. Louis XVIII returned from exile in England and enthroned in 1815.
1840	Attempted uprising against King Louis-Philippe organised by Louis-Napoleon in Boulogne.
1848	Louis-Napoleon elected President of the Republic; crowned Emperor (Napoleon III) in 1852.
1870-71	Franco-Prussian War. End of the Second Empire signalled by the defeat at Sedan: the Third Republic proclaimed. Paris besieged by Prussians: Alsace and part of Lorraine given up under the Treaty of Frankfurt.

20C

1914	Outbreak of the First World War. France attacked by German armies through neutral Belgium; four years of bloody trench warfare followed.
1915 to 1918	Battles throughout northern France and Flanders: in Artois (Neuville-St-Vaast, Vimy), in Picardy (Somme Valley, Chemin des Dames in the Aisne Valley, St Quentin) and in Île-de-France (Ourcq Valley, Battle of the Marne). 11 November: armistice signed in Compiègne forest.
1919	End of the War with the Treaty of Versailles.
1939	Outbreak of the Second World War. In June 1940 France overrun by the German army; occupation of much of the country. The "French State", established at Vichy, collaborated closely with the Germans. The north of France cut off from the rest of the country by a boundary. France's honour saved by General de Gaulle's Free French forces and by the courage of the men and women of the Resistance.

By 1942 all France occupied; the French fleet scuttled at Toulon. Allied landing in Normandy in June 1944, and in the south of France in August: Paris liberated. The "Dunkirk pocket" retaken by the Allies. The German surrender signed at Reims on 7 May 1945.

1976	Creation of the "Île-de-France" administrative region.
1987	Start of building works for the Channel Tunnel linking France and England.
1994	6 May: official opening of the Channel Tunnel.
1996	Inauguration of Evry cathedral.
1998	Inauguration of the Stade de France in Saint-Denis for the World Cup, won by the French team.

The chapter on art and architecture in this guide gives an outline of artistic creation in the region, providing the context of the buildings and works of art described in the Sights section.

Architecture and Art

ABC OF ARCHITECTURE

Religious architecture

MANTES-LA-JOLIE – Ground plan of Notre-Dame (12C-14C)

Basilical plan without transept: the sacristy was added in the 13C, the radiating chapels and the Chapelle de Navarre in the 14C.

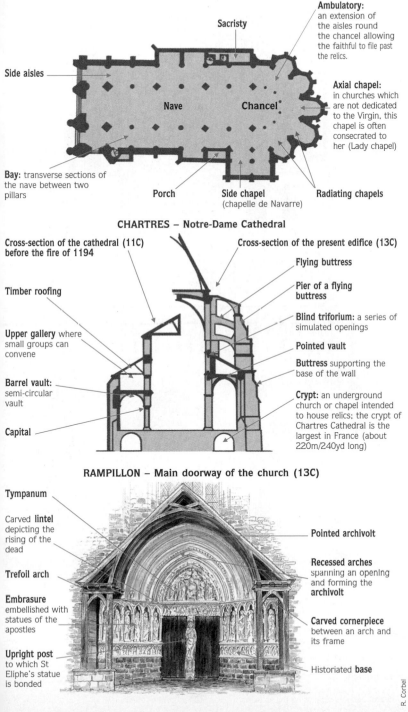

Ambulatory: an extension of the aisles round the chancel allowing the faithful to file past the relics.

Sacristy

Side aisles

Axial chapel: in churches which are not dedicated to the Virgin, this chapel is often consecrated to her (Lady chapel)

Nave

Chancel

Bay: transverse sections of the nave between two pillars

Porch

Side chapel (chapelle de Navarre)

Radiating chapels

CHARTRES – Notre-Dame Cathedral

Cross-section of the cathedral (11C) before the fire of 1194

Cross-section of the present edifice (13C)

Timber roofing

Flying buttress

Pier of a flying buttress

Blind triforium: a series of simulated openings

Upper gallery where small groups can convene

Pointed vault

Buttress supporting the base of the wall

Barrel vault: semi-circular vault

Capital

Crypt: an underground church or chapel intended to house relics; the crypt of Chartres Cathedral is the largest in France (about 220m/240yd long)

RAMPILLON – Main doorway of the church (13C)

Tympanum

Carved **lintel** depicting the rising of the dead

Pointed archivolt

Trefoil arch

Recessed arches spanning an opening and forming the **archivolt**

Embrasure embellished with statues of the apostles

Carved cornerpiece between an arch and its frame

Upright post to which St Eliphe's statue is bonded

Historiated **base**

R. Corbel

29

AMIENS – West front of the cathedral (13C)

The vast cathedral is the edifice which best reflects the blossoming of Rayonnant Gothic architecture.

Kings' gallery decorating the west front of many cathedrals: it includes 22 statues representing Christ's royal lineage

Finial: a flower-shaped ornament finishing off a pinnacle

Great rose-window

Gargoyle: a rainwater spout

Openwork **gallery** consisting of **trefoil arches** surmounted by quatrefoil openings

Tympanum made of four **historiated** bands

Gable: a steeply pitched ornamental pediment surmounting doorways and windows, here decorated with **crockets.**

Band: a carved ornamental strip

Canopy: a richly decorated baldaquin surmounting a statue

Recessed arches spanning an opening and forming the **archivolt**

Upright post to which a statue is generally bonded (here the "Beau Dieu")

Door leaf

Jambs: uprights supporting the archivolt

Embrasure embellished with statues carved in the **round**

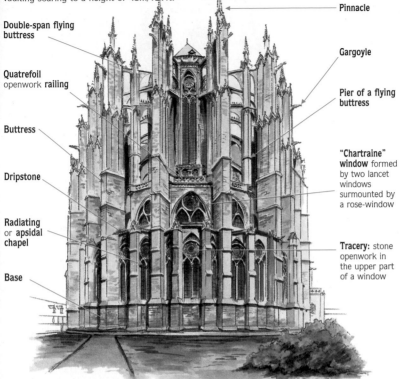

BEAUVAIS – East end of the cathedral (13C)

In spite of the missing spire (which collapsed in 1573) and nave (never built owing to lack of funds), the cathedral has a magnificent chancel representing the apogee of Gothic building techniques with vaulting soaring to a height of 48m/157ft.

Pinnacle

Double-span flying buttress

Gargoyle

Quatrefoil openwork **railing**

Pier of a flying buttress

Buttress

"Chartraine" window formed by two lancet windows surmounted by a rose-window

Dripstone

Radiating or **apsidal chapel**

Tracery: stone openwork in the upper part of a window

Base

SENLIS – Notre-Dame Cathedral (12C-13C)

Cell or **quarter:** a segment of vaulting defined by intersecting ribs

Intersecting ribs

Lunette: part of the ribbed vaulting which does not extend to the keystone

Pendant keystone

Transverse arch: a reinforcing arch under a vault

Tierceron: an intermediate rib

Tracery: delicate stone openwork in the upper part of a window

Clerestory window

Equilateral arch: a pointed arch whose radii are equal to its span

Gallery

Openwork railing

Composite pillar formed by several bonded columns

Pointed main arcade

R. Corbel

31

AIRE-SUR-LA-LYS – Organ of the collegiate church (1653)

This richly carved organ comes from the former Cistercian abbey of Clairmarais near Aire-sur-la-Lys.

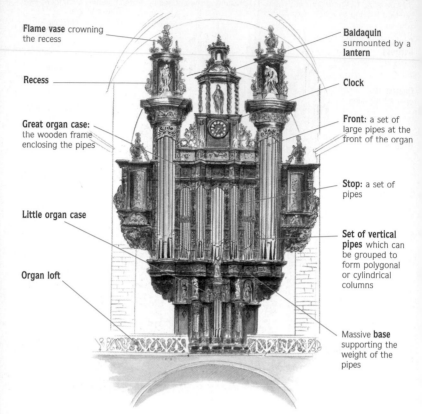

Flame vase crowning the recess

Baldaquin surmounted by a **lantern**

Recess

Clock

Great organ case: the wooden frame enclosing the pipes

Front: a set of large pipes at the front of the organ

Stop: a set of pipes

Little organ case

Set of vertical pipes which can be grouped to form polygonal or cylindrical columns

Organ loft

Massive **base** supporting the weight of the pipes

QUAËDYPRE – High altar and altarpiece of the church (late 17C)

In the 17C and 18C, altarpieces were architectural compositions towering above the altar and intended to channel the congregation's religious fervour.

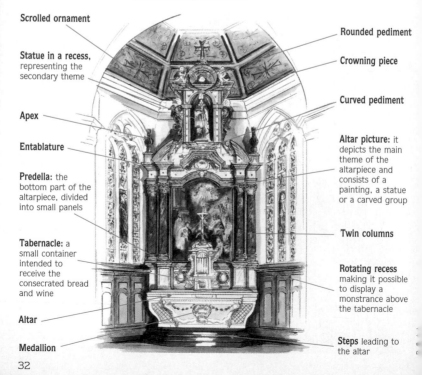

Scrolled ornament

Rounded pediment

Statue in a recess, representing the secondary theme

Crowning piece

Apex

Curved pediment

Entablature

Altar picture: it depicts the main theme of the altarpiece and consists of a painting, a statue or a carved group

Predella: the bottom part of the altarpiece, divided into small panels

Tabernacle: a small container intended to receive the consecrated bread and wine

Twin columns

Rotating recess making it possible to display a monstrance above the tabernacle

Altar

Steps leading to the altar

Medallion

Château de COURANCES (16C-17C)

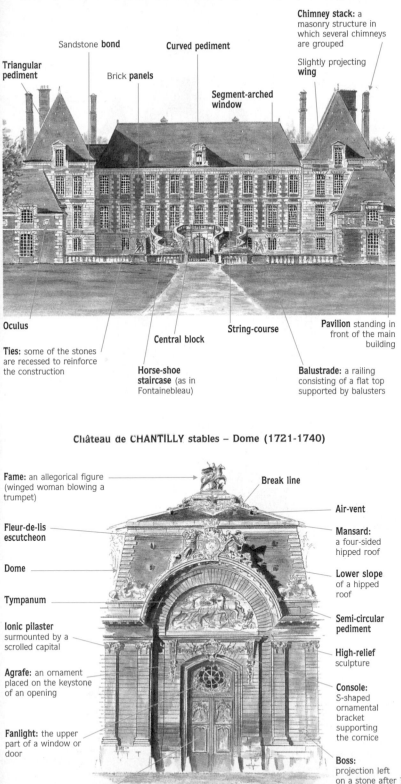

Triangular pediment

Sandstone **bond**

Brick **panels**

Curved pediment

Segment-arched window

Chimney stack: a masonry structure in which several chimneys are grouped

Slightly projecting **wing**

Oculus

Ties: some of the stones are recessed to reinforce the construction

Central block

Horse-shoe staircase (as in Fontainebleau)

String-course

Pavilion standing in front of the main building

Balustrade: a railing consisting of a flat top supported by balusters

Château de CHANTILLY stables – Dome (1721-1740)

Fame: an allegorical figure (winged woman blowing a trumpet)

Break line

Air-vent

Fleur-de-lis escutcheon

Mansard: a four-sided hipped roof

Dome

Lower slope of a hipped roof

Tympanum

Ionic pilaster surmounted by a scrolled capital

Semi-circular pediment

Agrafe: an ornament placed on the keystone of an opening

High-relief sculpture

Console: S-shaped ornamental bracket supporting the cornice

Fanlight: the upper part of a window or door

Boss: projection left on a stone after it has been cut

Door leaf

R. Corbel

33

RUE – Belfry (15C)

Symbolising the power of the city, the belfry was used as a watchtower as well as the aldermen's meeting place.

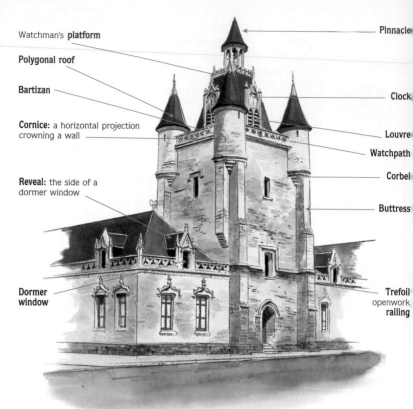

Watchman's **platform**

Polygonal roof

Bartizan

Cornice: a horizontal projection crowning a wall

Reveal: the side of a dormer window

Dormer window

Pinnacle

Clock

Louvre

Watchpath

Corbel

Buttress

Trefoil openwork **railing**

ARRAS – Façades overlooking the Grand'Place (15c-17C)

Left is the Hôtel des Trois Luppars (1467), the oldest house lining the square, right is a house dat 1684.

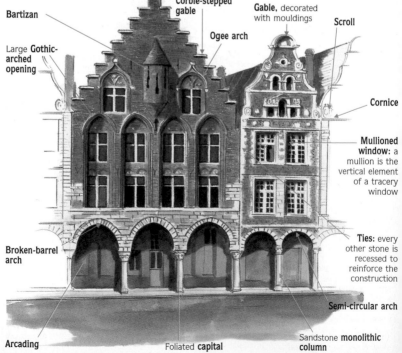

Bartizan

Large **Gothic-arched opening**

Corbie-stepped gable

Ogee arch

Gable, decorated with mouldings

Scroll

Cornice

Mullioned window: a mullion is the vertical element of a tracery window

Ties: every other stone is recessed to reinforce the construction

Broken-barrel arch

Semi-circular arch

Arcading

Foliated **capital**

Sandstone **monolithic column**

34

CHATOU – 19C pavilion

This type of pavilion, built of course-grained limestone, is characteristic of suburban domestic architecture.

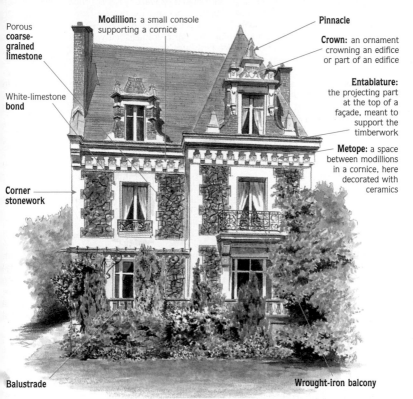

Modillion: a small console supporting a cornice

Pinnacle

Crown: an ornament crowning an edifice or part of an edifice

Entablature: the projecting part at the top of a façade, meant to support the timberwork

Metope: a space between modillions in a cornice, here decorated with ceramics

Porous **coarse-grained limestone**

White-limestone **bond**

Corner stonework

Balustrade

Wrought-iron balcony

Military architecture
LE QUESNOY – Fortifications (12C and 17C-19C)

These well-preserved fortifications, remodelled by Vauban from 1667 onwards, are set in green surroundings.

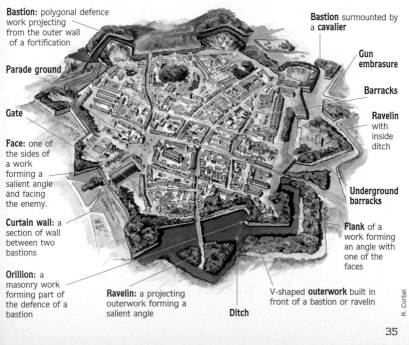

Bastion: polygonal defence work projecting from the outer wall of a fortification

Parade ground

Gate

Face: one of the sides of a work forming a salient angle and facing the enemy.

Curtain wall: a section of wall between two bastions

Orillion: a masonry work forming part of the defence of a bastion

Ravelin: a projecting outerwork forming a salient angle

Ditch

Bastion surmounted by a **cavalier**

Gun embrasure

Barracks

Ravelin with inside ditch

Underground barracks

Flank of a work forming an angle with one of the faces

V-shaped **outerwork** built in front of a bastion or ravelin

R. Corbel

35

LIVING LIKE KINGS

After the 15C, medieval castles were converted from fortresses into residential châteaux. Windows were enlarged, doors and openings were richly adorned. Towers, once strategic elements of the defensive structure, became decorative features, along with crenellated battlements and moats. By the second half of the 16C, such characteristics had become quite superfluous. Façades were embellished with statues and rows of superimposed columns. Roofs were high and presented a single slope.

The Château d'Écouen *(see p 175)* is a fine example of the French Renaissance style, as is the Richelieu Pavillon of the Louvre (1546-1654), in Paris. The style, which succeeded Gothic as the style dominant in Europe after the mid-16C, first developed in Italy. The name describes the "rebirth" of interest in Roman and Greek art and learning. By the early 17C, the Classical style of architecture had emerged, as expressed in the magnificence of royal palaces.

François I (reigned 1515-47)

The early phase of the French Renaissance culminated in the François I style *(see FONTAINEBLEAU, p 179)*. The decorative aspects mingle Gothic embellishments with elements inspired by Italian art, and the design features round arches and symmmetrical compostion. Many of the elegant buildings erected by the monarch bear his distinctive emblem: a crowned salamander.

Henri IV (r. 1589-1610) – Louis XIII (r. 1610-43)

Louis XIII was strongly influenced by the Henri IV style (Place des Vosges, Paris), which marked the beginnings of the Classical period of French architecture. The principal characteristics of this style, which prevailed during the first half of the 17C, are the exact symmetry of the main building and the use of brick panels set into white stonework. Carved ornamentation is limited and sober. Most often, the design is a central block flanked by two end pavilions *(see Château de COURANCES p 33)*. Louis XIII built the first palace in Versailles *(see p 335)* in this style, in brick, stone and slate.

Louis XIV (reigned 1643-1715)

Under the skilful hand of François Mansart, civil architecture gave up its straightforward character and acquired a less domestic, more noble appearance. The early period shows columns and pilasters which stand the height of a single floor of the château. Triangular and arched pediments top doorways and windows. Numerous chimneys sprout from the high roofs *(see Château de MAISONS-LAFITTE p 225)*.

Châteaux built during the second period are characterised by a high ground floor, a very high first floor and a relatively low second floor. The roof is concealed by a balustrade. The horizontal lines of the building are broken by rows of sturdy columns and tall windows. Ornamental sculpture is limited to the rooftop and the summit of the front pavilions, and inspired by classical models. Versailles *(see p 335)* represents the culmination of the high Classical period.

Louis XV (reigned 1715-74)

After 1700, the Louis XIV style and its harsh angles were mellowed by soft, rounded contours. Under Louis XV, oval spaces and curved surfaces were favoured. Windows and pediments display intricate ornamentation, while the rest of the façade remains austere, without columns; the roof is formed by two sloping planes *(see the stables at CHANTILLY p 33)*. Over time, Classical yielded more and more to Rococo (also known as Baroque classicism in France), which is distinguished by profuse, often semi-abstract ornamentation, and lightness of colour and weight.

Louis XVI (reigned 1774-92)

The influence of the elegant Louis XV style is still apparent in works of this period, but over-abundant curves are replaced by right angles. Columns make a conspicuous comeback, placed on unadorned façades. This phase is known as classicist, for many of the decorative motifs are inspired by Antiquity, a trend that introduced the so-called Pompeian and the Empire styles which followed *(see VERSAILLES: Petit Trianon p 360)*. The French Revolution brought an abrupt end to building in this style.

Fontainebleau – Galerie François I, fresco by Primaticcio

Renaissance: First Fontainebleau School – Ornate decoration in a free interpretation of the Italian masters. The frescoes framed by stuccowork are above the wainscoting. Coffered ceilings and rafters.

Gros-Bois – Dining room

Louis XIII style – The decorative features are more restrained. Above the wainscoting are huge tapestries or frescoes. The ceiling rafters are visible but in most instances the coffering has disappeared.

Versailles – Salon de Vénus

Louis XIV style – The decoration is luxurious in the materials used but understated in design. Marble panels decorate the walls. The ceiling is divided into painted compartments separated by gilded stuccowork.

37

Champs – Mme de Pompadour's bedchamber

Louis XV style – Right angles have been banished. Curves, scrolls and arabesques soften straight lines. Light-coloured wainscoting has replaced the marble panels. Mouldings with plant and floral motifs, volutes, cartouches and shells.

Versailles – Louis XVI's gaming room

Louis XVI style – The decoration is still elegant and light in colour but straigt lines have come back into fashion. The severity of the rectangular panels is relieved by reeds and ribbons or garlands.

Compiègne – Napoleon's bedchamber

Empire style – Antique green or crimson-red hangings have replaced the wainscoting. Straight lines and semicircular arches predominate. Heavy mouldings and motifs stand out against the dark woodwork.

RELIGIOUS ARCHITECTURE

Île-de-France and the regions north of Paris offer a rich variety of architectural styles: Gallo-Roman at Bavay and Romanesque at Morienval, Rhuis and Chartres; Gothic architecture throughout Île-de-France where it was born and the later Flamboyant Gothic mainly in Picardy; Renaissance influence may be found at Amiens and Cassel; Classical architecture flourished in and around Paris and the Baroque was embraced in Flanders.

Many of the earliest buildings of note were constructed for religious purposes and it is through these buildings that the development of architectural styles can best be followed. A church consisted basically of a chancel reserved for members of the clergy, where the high altar and the reliquaries were located, and of a nave which accommodated the congregation. This simple layout characterised the early churches which were built on a basilical plan. During the Romanesque period the plan of the church developed into the shape of a cross; the narthex at the entrance received those who had not been baptised; the nave was enlarged by aisles. In places of pilgrimage, an ambulatory and side aisles were added to the chancel to facilitate processions. Architects followed this layout as it was convenient for celebrating Mass and easy to build.

Romanesque (11C-12C)

Architects in Romanesque times knew how to build huge, lofty churches but, as the heavy stone vaulting often caused the walls to settle or cave in, they made the windows as small as possible and added aisles surmounted by galleries to support the sombre nave.

One of the main types of roofing in Romanesque churches is groined vaulting, in which two identical barrels meet at right angles. The barrel in line with the nave is supported by the transverse arch, while that set at a right angle is supported by the main arch or by a recess in the wall. Rhuis and Morienval churches and the Royal Doorway of Chartres Cathedral are splendid examples of Romanesque art.

Gothic (12C-15C)

The transition from Romanesque to Gothic architecture – which originated in Île-de-France – was a slow, natural process that developed in response to the demand for wider, higher and lighter churches. Typified by quadripartite vaulting and the use of pointed arches, Gothic art evolved from the sombre 12C Romanesque sanctuaries to the light 13C churches and the extravagantly ornate buildings of the 15C. It is rare, however, to find a church with entirely unified features reflecting a given period in history; building a church was a costly and lengthy operation subject to changes in public taste and building methods as the work progressed. Towards the late 13C famous personalities and guilds were granted the privilege of having a chapel built in their honour in one of the side aisles. In exchange they were expected to make a generous contribution towards the building or its maintenance.

Architects – The names of the architects of the great religious edifices are known to us only from the Gothic period onwards, through texts or through inscriptions carved around the "labyrinths" outlined on the floor of cathedrals; that is how Robert de Luzarches was revealed as responsible for the plans of Amiens Cathedral.

The most outstanding master builder in the north of France, however, was undoubtedly **Villard de Honnecourt**, born near Cambrai. The towers of Laon Cathedral, Vaucelles Abbey *(south of Cambrai)*, the chancels at St-Quentin and Cambrai *(no longer extant)* have all been attributed to him.

West Fronts – Most main façades were set facing west. Nave and aisles had their own doorway flanked by buttresses which were bare in the 12C and 13C, ornate in the 15C. The tympanum featured ornamentation and in the 14C its gable was elaborately carved, with crockets adorning the ramps. 13C rose windows were fairly small; in the 14C they were enlarged across the west front to provide light for the nave. As windows grew larger, façades became more delicate. A gallery was built at the base of the towers to break the rigid vertical perspective created by the buttresses and bell-towers; in the 15C this was reduced to a balustrade and the gables further embellished.

Ideally west fronts were to be richly decorated with stone carvings but in many cases they were the last part to be completed and architects were often obliged to forego ornamentation, and even towers, owing to insufficient funds; in others, however, even the transepts were given remarkable façades *(see Chartres)*.

Spires – After lightening the façades of Gothic churches architects turned to the spires; by the Flamboyant period the open-work masonry was markedly ornate. In the 19C numerous bell-towers in the region were given a spire by followers of Viollet-le-Duc.

Flying buttresses – In early Gothic churches the pillars in the nave were supported by masonry concealed in the galleries. During the 12C these walls were reduced to arches *(see below)* supported by sturdy piers. Soon afterwards the galleries themselves were replaced with a row of flying buttresses outside. A number of high openings could therefore be incorporated into the church interior, producing a far more luminous nave.

From then on, tall churches can be schematically described as stone frames consisting of columns supporting diagonal arches and resting on two or three levels of flying buttresses. The buttresses were in turn supported by a series of tall pillars bearing pinnacles.

Diagonal arches – Towards the end of the 11C groined vaulting was extremely common but, as it was difficult to build and liable to crack, a group of architects from England, Milan and Île-de-France decided to reinforce the groins.

They found that by building the diagonal arches first and by consolidating them with a small amount of rubble, vaulting that was both sturdy and light was achieved.

By supporting this vaulting on a series of arches, so that the weight of the masonry would have to be borne at the springing, the architects could dispense with the walls in between the arches and replace them with stained-glass windows; this in turn greatly enhanced the luminosity of the interiors.

This significant development heralded the age of quadripartite vaulting.

Vaulting – Quadripartite vaulting, in which the thrust is supported by four main arches, is easy to install in a square-shaped bay. In the 12C bays were enlarged and it was no longer possible to build them square: the pillars propping up the walls would have been too far apart. The problem was initially resolved by covering the bays two by two thus forming a square again: an extra transverse arch was then added and made to rest on slim pillars alternating with stout piers.

This type of vaulting – upheld by three diagonal arches – is known as sexpartite vaulting because of the number of its divisions.

When more sophisticated diagonal arches were able to support the vaulting above rectangular bays, the intermediary resting points were eventually discarded.

After the 15C, Flamboyant architects put in additional, decorative ribbing of complex design: it formed liernes and tiercerons, and subsequently stars and intricate networks. The main supporting arches were flanked by ornamental arches of no practical use. The keystones – usually pendant – grew thinner and longer.

Elevations – *(illustrations below)* Gothic elevations reflect the continual search for higher and lighter buildings.

Transitional Gothic (A) – The term Transitional Gothic covers the birth and early stages of Gothic architecture, from about 1125 to 1190. The first use of diagonal vaulting in France appeared over the ambulatory in the Romanesque abbey church at Morienval *(see p 244)*.

Though some Romanesque details, such as semicircular arches, can still be observed in early Gothic buildings, there were several significant changes. The new interiors presented four-storey elevations consisting of high clerestory windows at the top which lit the nave directly, a triforium (a narrow, arcaded passageway below the clerestory) and a gallery, which were instrumental in supporting the walls as high up as possible, and arcading at ground level. There were often openings behind the gallery but never behind the triforium.

The pillars of the main arches initially consisted of a thick column; this was later replaced by twinned columns supporting the arches and the colonnettes above. Laon Cathedral is a good example of early Gothic architecture. Semicircular transept endings like the famous south arm at Soissons Cathedral were also a feature.

| Transitional (12C) | Early Gothic (early 13C) | High Gothic (late 13C-early 14C) | Flamboyant (15C and 16C) |

Moret-sur-Loing – Maison de François I

Early Gothic (B) – This great period (c 1180 to 1250) when Gothic architecture was in its ascendancy produced some of France's finest masterpieces, among them Chartres Cathedral *(see illustration p 29).*

Characteristics include arches and windows pointed and shaped like a lancet; clerestory windows surmounted by a round opening; the gallery replaced by external flying buttresses. The numerous colonnettes originating from the vaulting rested on the shaft which bore the weight of all the main arches. This pier was generally a large round column flanked by four colonnettes.

High Gothic (C) – This was the golden age of the great cathedrals in France, lasting from about 1250 and the reign of St Louis to around 1375 when the Hundred Years War blocked the progress made by medieval architects.

At this time High Gothic, known as Rayonnant in French, reached its peak: the three-storey elevation (large arcades, triforium – the wall at the back now pierced with stained-glass – and tall clerestory windows) lightened the nave and formed one huge single stained-glass window in the chancels of churches with no ambulatory; the wall area was reduced to a minimum and the stringers supporting the vaulting were doubled by another series of arches. In many cases the colonnettes started from the ground, at the point where they surround the pillar of the main arches. Two slight mouldings – level with the main arches and the springers – were the only features to break the vertiginous ascent. Beauvais Cathedral is the most outstanding example of High Gothic *(see illustration p 31).*

Flamboyant Gothic (D) – This last stage in Gothic architecture, which could develop no further, succumbed to ornamental excess, aided by the fine, easily worked Picardy stone. The style owes its name to the flame shapes in the tracery of the bays and rose windows, and to the exuberant carved and sculpted decoration which tended to obscure the structural lines of the buildings: doorways were crowned with open-work gables, balustrades were surmounted by pinnacles, vaulting featured complex designs with purely decorative arches (called liernes and tiercerons) converging on ornately worked keystones. The triforium disappeared, replaced by larger clerestory windows. Arches came to rest on columns or were continued by ribbing level with the pillars. The latter were no longer flanked by colonnettes. In some churches, the ribs formed a spiral around the column.

Flemish civil architecture – From the late 13C the particular nature of Flemish Gothic architecture manifested itself in the civic buildings, belfries and town halls erected by the cities which had obtained charters.

Belfries – Symbol of the town's power, the belfry was either an isolated building (Bergues, Béthune) or part of the town hall (Douai, Arras, Calais). It was built like a keep with watchtowers and machicolations. The rooms above the foundations – which housed the prison – had diverse functions, such as guard-room. At the top, the bell-room enclosed the **chimes**. Originally these consisted of only four bells; today they often number at least 30 bells which play every hour, half-hour and quarter-hour. The bell-room is surrounded by watchtowers from which the sentry looked out for enemies and fires. At the very top is a weather vane symbolising the city: thus the lion of Flanders stands at Arras, Bergues and Douai.

Town halls – Town halls are often imposing with striking, richly embellished façades: niches, statues, gables and pinnacles might adorn the exterior.

Inside, the large council chamber or function room had walls decorated with frescoes illustrating the history of the town.

The most beautiful town halls (Douai, Arras, St-Quentin, Hondschoote, Compiègne) were built in the 15C and 16C. Many suffered damage and modification over the centuries and some were completely rebuilt in their original style, as at Arras.

41

Renaissance (16C)

Renaissance architecture, under the influence of Italian culture, favoured a return to classical themes: columns with capitals imitating the Ionic and Corinthian orders; façades decorated with niches, statues and roundels; pilasters flanking the windows. Quadripartite vaulting was replaced by coffered ceilings and barrel vaulting. Architects introduced basket-handled arches and semicircular or rectangular openings. Inverted brackets replaced flying buttresses. West fronts, and sometimes the north and south façades too, kept their heavy ornamentation. Spires were replaced by small domes and lantern towers. Isolated examples of Renaissance art – not widely adopted in the north of France – are the Maison du Sagittaire in Amiens and the Hôtel de la Noble Cour in Cassel.

Baroque and Classical (17C-18C)

Architecture – Through the 17C and 18C architecture presented two different faces, one Baroque – dominated by irregular contours, an abundance of exuberant shapes, generous carving and much ornamentation; the other Classical – a model of stateliness and restraint, adhering strictly to the rules of Antiquity: rows of Greek columns (Doric, Ionic and Corinthian), pedimented doorways, imposing domes and scrolled architraves. The Baroque style flourished in Flanders, Hainault and Artois which fell under Spanish influence, while the Classical style found favour in Picardy and Île-de-France.

The Baroque Chapelle du Grand Séminaire in Cambrai is one of many religious buildings erected in the 17C following the influence of the Counter Reformation and its main engineers, the Jesuits. Civil buildings include the House of Gilles de la Boé in Lille and the Mont-de-Piété in Bergues; the Mint in Lille, with its bosses and richly carved ornamentation, exemplifies **Flemish Baroque**.

The Petit Trianon at Versailles is a famous example of Classical architecture.

In Arras Baroque and Classical elements were combined for the town's splendid main squares framed by houses with arcades and volutes. Combined elements can also be seen at the abbeys in Valloires and Prémontré and at the Château de Long.

Sculpture – The finely grained and easily worked chalky stone found in Picardy was used for much decorative work and by the 13C the "picture carvers" in Amiens and Arras were already displaying the specific Picardy traits discernible throughout later centuries: lively, finely detailed figures going about their everyday life. The calendar at Amiens is a good example of this engaging art.

In the late 15C and early 16C the Picardy wood carvers *(huchiers)* became renowned through their work on the stalls in Amiens Cathedral; the door panels in St Wulfram's in Abbeville; the finely-worked frames of the "Puy-Notre-Dame" paintings.

Baroque art favoured abundant decorative sculpture: buildings were covered with a profusion of ornamental fruit, flowers, cornucopias, *putti*, niches, statues, vases etc.

Monasteries in Île-de-France

A considerable number of priory, convent and abbey ruins are to be found in Île-de-France, and numerous districts and street names recall the many religious communities which have not survived.

Abbeys in the history of Île-de-France – Abbeys would not exist if people did not feel a strong calling to take up ecclesiastical duties; on the other hand, abbeys would not exist if the clergy were not given land. After the 5C, when the victorious Franks divided up the Gallo-Roman territory, it would have been impossible for any religious community to survive without the help of donations. There were a great many aspiring monks in France up to the 18C and the different communities were almost entirely dependent on the generosity of benefactors. As the suzerain of Île-de-France was none other than the supreme ruler of France, the king, this region was graced with an abundance of local monasteries.

In the early days of Christianity, towards the late 4C, Île-de-France was covered with forests but the land was also fertile: the area attracted monks who wanted to live in peace and escape the terrible famine ravaging the country. Soon afterwards the Merovingian monarchs, who had been strongly backed by the clergy, encouraged the creation of religious foundations, to which they contributed quite considerably. The wealthy Carolingians continued to endow these abbeys and the practice was kept up by the Capetians and their vassals for over 800 years (Chaalis and Royaumont).

French kings favoured monasteries because the monks used to reclaim uncultivated land and because the monasteries were constantly praying for their patrons. Religious faith was strong from the 10C to the 17C, so a king might make a donation to an abbey for a variety of reasons: to thank God for a victory, to seek expiation for an offence committed against the Church, to express his own personal belief or to offer a dowry to dowager queens or royal princesses about to take the veil.

Religious Orders – The term abbey does not apply to just any Christian community whose members lead a frugal, secluded life; it in fact designates a group of men or women placed under the authority of an abbot or an abbess, who live according to a rule approved by the Pope. The monks' day is usually divided into chores related to community life, and spiritual and liturgical duties, which are the main purpose of the association.

Cloister, Abbaye de Royaumont

R. César /TOP

All abbeys have an abbot or abbess, who generally enjoys the same rank as a bishop. He or she is elected by fellow companions and incarnates the spiritual and temporal leader of the abbey. After the 16C, the Pope gave the king of France the right to appoint abbots and abbesses: these prelates were called commendatory abbots and usually lived in the king's entourage.

Sometimes, to administer new domains or to fulfil the wish of a patron who wanted to receive monks on his land, the abbots would build a priory. This small community was supervised by a prior who was answerable to the abbey. The Cistercians set up numerous granges, farming colonies run by lay brothers.

Monastic Rules – The Benedictine Order – created by St Benedict in the 6C – was undoubtedly the order which flourished the most in France: its members founded over one thousand abbeys throughout the country. The Benedictine rule was subsequently reformed and this led to the creation of two additional orders.

The first originated in the late 10C from Cluny in Burgundy but unfortunately all the Cluniac houses died out during the Revolution. The second – the Cistercian Order – was, and still is, extremely powerful. It was St Bernard of Cîteaux, also a native of Burgundy, who founded the order in the 11C. He was a firm believer in asceticism and introduced a number of new rules: he condemned elaborate ceremonial and the decoration of churches; monks could no longer be paid tithes, neither could they receive or acquire land; strict rules were laid down on diet, rest was limited to seven hours and monks had to sleep in their clothes in a common dormitory.

They shared their time between liturgical worship – 6 to 7 hours a day – manual labour, study and contemplation. In the 17C, Abbot de Rancé added further austerities to the Cistercian rule (silence, diet). This new rule was named after La Trappe, the monastery near Perseigne where it originated. It is presently enforced in abbeys of strict observance. The other two main orders which founded abbeys in France were the Augustinian friars and the Premonstratensian canons, both dating from the 12C.

Other communities include the Carmelite Order, the Order of St Francis (Franciscans and Capuchins), the Order of Preachers and the Society of Jesus (Jesuits). These however do not follow monastic rules and they do not found abbeys. Their activities (missionary work, caring for the sick) bring them into contact with the lay world. They live in convents or houses under the authority of the prior, the Mother Superior etc. A collegiate church is occupied by a community of canons accountable to their bishop.

Monastic buildings – The cloister is the centre of an abbey; its four galleries allow the nuns and monks to take their walks under cover. One of the cloister walls adjoins the abbey church, while another gives onto the chapter-house where monks meet to discuss community problems under the chairmanship of the abbot. The third gallery opens onto the refectory and the fourth onto the calefactory, the only room with heating where the monks study or do manual labour.

The dormitory is generally placed above the chapter-house. It communicates with the church by means of a direct staircase so that the monks may readily attend early morning and night Mass.

Lay brothers – believers who cannot or will not take holy orders – are granted a separate status. They spend most of their time in the fields and the workshops, and have their own dormitory and refectory. They may not enter the chapter-house or the chancel of the church. Since the Vatican II Council (1962-65) lay brothers have become more and more involved in the life of the community.

Visitors are not allowed to enter the "enclosure" and are lodged in the guest house. The poor are housed in the almshouse.

Monasteries also include an infirmary, a novitiate, sometimes a school, and the buildings needed to run the abbey: barns, cellars, winepress, stables and cowsheds.

RURAL HOUSING IN THE NORTH

The Coast, Inland Flanders and Artois – Whether in Picardy, Artois or Flanders, the same types of houses can be found along the coast: long and low to form a defence against the west winds which often bring rain. They are capped by high-pitched roofs covered with Flemish S-shaped tiles called *pannes*. Their whitewashed walls are cheered by brightly-coloured doors and shutters; the bases of the buildings are tarred against the damp.

Behind this apparent uniformity lie very different construction techniques.

In Picardy the walls consist of daubing on wood laths; in certain areas the surface is left plain, as in Ponthieu, but it is more usually whitewashed, giving a spruce look in summer to the flower-bedecked villages along the Canche and Authie rivers.

In Flanders the usual building material is more generally brick, sandy-coloured in maritime areas and ranging from red to purplish or brown further inland. The great Lille and Artois regional farms, known as **"censes"**, are built around a courtyard with access through a carriage gateway often surmounted by a dovecote.

Some large, partly stone-built farms in the Boulonnais hills are actually old seignorial homes and include a turret or fortifications, giving the impression of a manor house.

Hainaut, Avesnois, Thiérache and Soissonnais – In the Hainaut and Avesnois regions houses are massively built: they usually consist of one-storey brick buildings with facings and foundations in regional blue stone.

Their slate roofs are reminiscent of the nearby Ardennes region.

Construction in the Thiérache region, the land of clay and wood, consists of daubing and brick with slate roofs. There are many old dovecotes in the region, either over carriage gates or free-standing in courtyards. The fairly thickly scattered villages huddle around their fortified churches *(see La THIÉRACHE)*.

The houses in the Soissonnais region are similar to those of Île-de-France. Beautiful white freestone is used for walls and crow-stepped gables, contrasting with flat red roof tiles which take on a patina with the years.

Windmills – Up to the last century there were windmills throughout the windswept northern regions of France. In the early 19C there were nearly 3 000 windmills in northern France. Today no more than a few dozen still exist, registered, protected and restored by the Association Régionale des Amis des Moulins du Nord-Pas-de-Calais (ARAM).

Post mills, which are built of wood, are the most common in Flanders.The main body of the structure and the sails turn around a vertical post. On the exterior, on the side opposite the sails, a beam known as the "tail" is linked to a wheel which is turned to position the entire mill according to the wind direction. Some 14 of this type remain in northern France, including those at Boeschepe, Cassel, Hondschoote, Steenvoorde, Villeneuve d'Ascq and St-Maxent.

On a **tower mill** (or smock mill when made of wood) only the roof, to which the sails are attached, turns. This type of mill is more massive and is usually built of brick or stone; the Steenmeulen at Terdeghem near Steenvoorde is the only one still in working order, but there are other fine specimens at Templeuve and Watten (Nord) as well as Achicourt, Beuvry and Guemps (Pas-de-Calais) and Louvencourt (Somme).

Water mills – Water mills can also be seen throughout the region, particularly in the Avesnois, Ternois, Thiérache and Valenciennes areas. The shape and size of the wheel, which is the essential part of the mill, depends on the rate of flow of the river and on the specific features of the site. Some of these mills are open to the public: Felleries, Sars-Poteries, Marly (Nord), Esquerdes, Maintenay, Wimille and Wissant (Pas-de-Calais).

MILITARY ARCHITECTURE

Of the defensive systems in the north of France, relatively few date from the Middle Ages: the town walls of Boulogne and Laon, and the castles at Coucy, Rambures, Picquigny, Lucheux, Septmonts and Pierrefonds. In contrast, numerous 17C star fortifications along the northeastern border have been preserved, some in their entirety, as at Bergues and Le Quesnoy, others only partially: Avesnes, Maubeuge, Cambrai, Douai, St-Omer, Péronne.

Before Vauban – It was under the last of the Valois kings that the military engineers, who had studied Italian examples, adopted a system of curtain walls defended at the corners by bastions. Bastions in the shape of an ace of spades with projections to protect the men defending the curtain wall were introduced: this feature can be seen at Le Quesnoy. Bastions and curtain walls, usually with stone bonding, were crowned with platforms bearing cannon; raised towers allowed the moats or ditches and surrounding area to be watched. At the beginning of the 17C, Henri IV employed an engineer specialising in "castrametation" (fortification-building) as it was called: **Jean Errard** (1554-1610) from Bar-le-Duc, nicknamed the Father of French Fortification. In the north Errard fortified Ham and Montreuil and built the citadels at Calais, Laon, Doullens and Amiens which still stand today; in 1600 he published an authoritative *Treatise on Fortification* which served until Vauban's time.

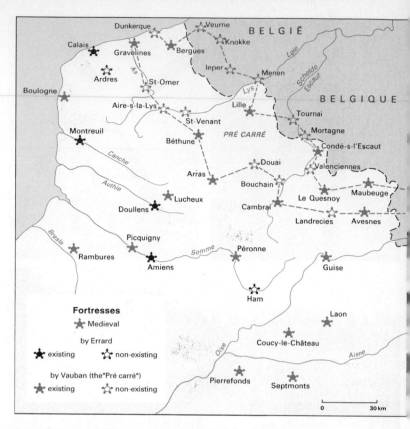

Fortresses

Medieval

by Errard
- existing
- non-existing

by Vauban (the "Pré carré")
- existing
- non-existing

0   30 km

The Age of Vauban – Inspired by his predecessors, **Sébastien le Prestre de Vauban** (1633-1707) established a system of his own characterised by bastions with half-moons surrounded by deep moats. Making the most of the natural obstacles and using local materials (brick in the north), he also tried to give an aesthetic quality to his works by giving them carved monumental stone gateways (Bergues, Lille, Maubeuge).

On the coast and along the border of Flanders and Hainaut, Vauban established a long line of double defences, known as the **"pré carré"**. These two close lines of fortresses and citadels were to prevent the enemy's passage and to ensure mutual back-up in case of attack.

The first line consists of 15 sites from Dunkirk and Bergues to Maubeuge, Philippeville and Dinant; the second runs a little way behind and includes 13 towns extending from Gravelines and St-Omer to Avesnes, Marienbourg, Rocroi and Mézières. Some of these strongpoints were Vauban's own creations such as the citadel at Lille, which he himself called the queen of citadels; others existed already and were remodelled.

For over a century this group of fortifications succeeded in defending the north of France, until the invasions of 1814 and 1815.

During the French campaign in 1940 Le Quesnoy, Lille, Bergues, Dunkirk, Gravelines and Calais all formed solid strongholds protecting the retreat of the Franco-British armies.

Atlantic Wall – The concrete bunkers of the Atlantic Wall which stretch along the coastline were erected by the **Todt Organisation** which from 1940 used prisoners of war for the task. In 1944 about 10 000 constructions were counted on the French coast: the Nord-Pas-de-Calais region was considered a war zone against England. In the deep forests of Eperlecques and Clairmarais enormous concrete installations were built for launching the V1 and V2 rockets on London. The Eperlecques Bunker *(see p 300)*, today designated a historic monument, is one of the most impressive examples of this type of monumental concrete architecture, along with the fort at Mimoyecques *(see p 197)*.

FAIENCE AND PORCELAIN IN ÎLE-DE-FRANCE

Faience – This is the term commonly applied to any ceramics made of porous clay and glazed with waterproof enamel. The enamel was initially transparent but, in the 9C, it became opaque thanks to the discovery in the Middle East of tin glaze. The Arabic influence throughout the Mediterranean Basin led to the development of faience in Moorish Spain and Italy from the 15C onwards. The Spanish island of Majorca gave its name to "majolicaware", the term describing Italian Renaissance ceramics. The name *faience* probably derives from Faenza, the Italian town renowned for its majolica.

Soft-paste porcelain figure (St-Cloud)

Porcelain water pitcher (Chantilly, 18C)

"Bachelier" vase (Sèvres, 18C)

Porcelain sauceboat (Vincennes, 18C)

Porcelain jardiniere (Mennecy, 18C)

Faience plate (Montereau, 19C)

Faience plate (Choisy-le-Roi, 19C)

R.M.N.

Faience developed in France in the 16C and 17C with leading potteries centres such as Nevers and Rouen; the latter influenced the early producers of faience in Île-de-France such as Pierre Chicaneau who settled in Saint-Cloud in 1674. In the 18C as porcelain became more popular, the number of potteries increased in the region and the first pieces of porcelain were produced. The famous ceramist Jacques Chapelle set up the works in **Sceaux** in 1748 and circumvented the Vincennes-Sèvres monopoly on faience by creating "Japanese-style faience". The Rococo style, vivid colours, and original decorations, many of them in relief, brought success to Sceaux until the end of the 18C. This period was marked by the discovery in England of "fine faience" or white lead-glazed earthenware. Its reasonable cost and elegance, along with the exceptionally liberal conditions laid down in the Treaty of Vergennes (1786), ensured its popularity and it was massively imported into France. This know-how was gradually taken over in Île-de-France by the works in **Montereau**, **Creil** and **Choisy-le-Roi**. The end of the 19C, however, confirmed the preference for porcelain and faience went into a decline.

Porcelain – Porcelain was discovered in China in the 12C. It is a thin, white ceramic ware that is slightly translucent. Body and glaze are fired together. In the 16C, the popularity of porcelain from the Far East led to numerous experiments in Europe to try and achieve a product that would rival it. The high level of imports by the French East India Company is indicative of European interest in this mysterious technique. Craftsmen did not know the exact nature of the paste used by the Chinese and they progressed by trial and error, using processes similar to the ones used for faience. A very fine marl used on its own was vitrified by the introduction of a sort of glass called "frit". The resulting ceramic was "soft-paste" porcelain; it could be scratched by steel. In the early 18C, the basic ingredient of porcelain, white china clay, was discovered in Saxony. The secrets of the production process were jealously kept in Meissen near Dresden. In France, it was not until 1769 that the output from a white china clay quarry near St-Yriex in the Limousin area enabled craftsmen to produce "hard-paste" porcelain. Sèvres produced porcelain exclusively from the beginning of the 19C onwards. This new product, in which body and glaze were fired together at very high temperature (1 400°C/2 500°F) was remarkably strong but more difficult to decorate. Only five colours are suitable for high-temperature firing – blue, green, yellow, purplish brown and reddish orange. The introduction of low-firing techniques revolutionised the production of faience and porcelain. The enamel was fired in succession at low temperatures, enabling the use of a wide range of fresh, vivid colours. The porcelain works in **St-Cloud** (1697-1766) were the first to master the techniques required to produce "soft-paste" porcelain. It was famous for its "white" ware and applied gilding which differed greatly from the technique used by Sèvres. Numerous porcelain works opened in quick succession in the 18C, with the backing of princes or the royal family. The works in **Chantilly** (1725-1800), for example, were set up by Cirquaire Cirou with the support of Louis-Henri de Bourbon, Prince de Condé. In **Mennecy**, it was the Duke de Villeroy who provided the necessary patronage in the face of ever-increasing privileges granted to some of the works. The one with the highest level of support was in **Vincennes**; Madame de Pompadour and Louis XV both took a keen interest in the company that set up works in **Sèvres** in 1756. The earliest designs were "natural" flowers and the works gradually specialised in the production of dinner services, statuettes and even veritable pictures in porcelain. Because of the processes used, the decoration and enamel combined perfectly, giving an incomparable blending. In its early days, the Sèvres porcelain works enjoyed exclusive rights to the use of gold on all its products. Even now, unless there is some technical reason against it, all its products must include some gold. "Biscuit-ware", another of the specialities of these works, is the term used to describe a production method in which the body of the paste is left unglazed so that the gracefulness of the statuettes is not altered.

STAINED GLASS

Since the early Middle Ages church windows have been adorned with coloured glass; unfortunately, none of these very early works have survived.

During the Gothic period, master glass-makers played an important role in the completion and the ornamentation of churches: thanks to them, both the clergy and the congregation could appreciate the shimmering light that came streaming through the roundels. Stained glass is not purely decorative, however: to the Church it is an invaluable teaching aid, permanently communicating catechism, sacred history and the lives of the saints.

The art of making stained glass – Stained-glass windows consist of juxtaposed pieces of coloured glass held together by strips of lead. The window is divided into panels to ensure perfect solidity. When the various coloured pieces have been selected and cut to shape, the glass-maker completes the shading and details of the figures with touches of *grisaille*: this is a brownish pigment containing silica which is painted on and which blends with the glass in the melt. The glass panels are then reassembled and fixed in place in the window. Patches of lichen may develop on stained-glass windows; it starts to attack the lead after 100 years and has been known to break through the glass after 300 to 400 years. It is man, however, rather than erosion who is to blame for the disappearance of numerous early stained-glass windows: in the 18C many were dismantled and replaced by plain glass, which afforded a better view of the aisles.

The development of stained glass – Technical developments in glass-making were prompted by artistic trends but also by the search for greater economy and the wish to produce lighter tones.

12C – Stained-glass windows were small, with fairly heavy borders. The ornamentation around the main figures was extremely limited.

13C – To ensure perfect cohesion between the panels and the leading, the iron armatures were fastened to the walls.

The clerestory windows presented tall, isolated figures whereas lower windows, which could be observed more closely, had medallions depicting scenes from legends, eg the lives of the saints: this genre is known as *historiated stained glass*. Panels included architectural features and embellishments. Borders were heavy and the scenes show a marked attempt at realism. Historiated roundels were set in a *grisaille* framework enhanced by brightly painted rose-windows. The daily lives of craftsmen were evoked in lively anecdotal scenes. The lower windows were generally divided into panels composing geometric motifs (stars, diamonds, cloverleaves).

Notre-Dame-de-la-Belle-Verrière
Detail of 12C-13C stained glass, Chartres Cathedral

P. Tetrel /EXPLORER

14C – The loss of wealth led to a considerable increase in window space. For reasons of economy, more and more *grisaille* was produced, its starkness softened by delicate shading and graceful foliage motifs. Angels and rosy cherubs adorned the barer parts of the windows. Borders became smaller and lettering made an appearance. In the second half of the 14C glass-makers discovered that silver staining could be used to accentuate a variety of bright colours: yellow on a white background, light green on blue, amber on red etc.

15C – The leading was no longer produced using a plane, but instead stretched on a wire-drawing bench: the lead strips were thinner, therefore more flexible and able to hold together larger and thinner panes of glass than previously. Glass-makers worked with a lighter type of glass and the colours used in the decoration were less vivid. In some churches two thirds of the window was taken up by *grisaille*: these panels featured Gothic canopies with high gables and openwork pinnacles. The craftsmanship was of a remarkable quality: master glass-makers began to sign their own work and to introduce original themes.

16C – Stained glass drew inspiration from the works of the great painters and from contemporary engravings. Glass-makers had become masters at cutting glass from large sheets – using a diamond and no longer a red-hot iron – and they also excelled at painting with enamels. Stained-glass windows developed into large, transparent paintings in which minute attention was given to detail, perspective and design. In some buildings religious themes were replaced by classical scenes taken from Antiquity.

17C and 18C – The use of coloured glass decreased. Stained glass was painted and decorated with enamels.

LANDSCAPE PAINTING

Although many painters were employed in the internal decoration of châteaux and abbeys around Paris, it was not until the 19C that painters began to show an interest in the surrounding landscapes.

Until the 18C, French masters had used landscapes merely as a background to their work, either as a decorative element or to enhance the atmosphere through composition and colour. It was so poorly regarded that often a major artist painting a portrait or other subject would leave the background landscape to be painted by a studio assistant. The two most celebrated French landscape painters were the 17C classicists Nicolas Poussin and Claude Lorrain: Poussin gave his views the heroic qualities of his subject and Lorrain painted scenes of a lost, idyllic Antiquity.

Camille Corot (1796-1875) – Corot was the pioneer of contemporary landscape painting in France. He lived in Barbizon from 1830-35 and worked outdoors in Fontainebleau Forest and all over Île-de-France, studying the contrasts and soft hues of light in the undergrowth, along shaded paths and on the edge of the plain. He later took up painting lakes in a search for more delicate variations; the ponds at Ville-d'Avray (south of St-Cloud), with their subtle reflections, were his favourites.

Moret bridge

Painters of the Oise – The group was founded in 1845 by two of Corot's followers, Charles-François Daubigny and Jules Dupré. Daubigny (1817-78) liked to paint the rippling waters of the River Oise and the greenery and blossoms of the orchards and groves. He led a peaceful life: his work paid well and received universal acclaim. He could often be found working on the Île de Vaux near Auvers, or in a small rowing boat he had converted into a studio. Jules Dupré (1811-89), a close friend of Théodore Rousseau, used darker colours and belonged to the Barbizon School. He seldom left his house in L'Isle-Adam.

In 1865 the lithographer and satirical cartoonist Honoré Daumier (1808-79) moved from the capital to Valmondois in Île-de-France, when he met with serious financial difficulties.

In 1866 **Camille Pissarro** (1830-1903) settled in Pontoise for two-years at first. Uninterested in the nearby streams and rivers, he concentrated on meadows, grassy slopes, country villages and street scenes featuring peasant women, which he portrayed in a deliberately poetic manner. His gift for expressing light, his qualities as a teacher and his kindliness made him the father figure of the Impressionist movement.

The Barbizon School – Its representatives drew inspiration from the landscapes of Fontainebleau forest and the nearby Bière plain. The founder of the movement was **Théodore Rousseau** (1812-67) who settled in a modest country cottage in 1847 and stayed there until his death. Diaz and Charles Jacque were among his close friends. They remained cheerful and humorous despite the lack of success of their paintings and their consequent penury; it was only towards the end of the Second Empire that their talent was acknowledged. Troyon (1810-65) specialised in rural scenes representing cattle. Barye, the highly respected animal sculptor, also took up landscape painting because of his love of nature. The charms and hardships of country life were particularly evoked in the work of **Jean-François Millet** (1814-75), who lived in Barbizon from 1849 until his death.

The artists of this school generally favoured the dark colours of tree bark and undergrowth and their preferred subjects included dusk, soft lighting and stormy skies; these sombre tones were criticised by their detractors who claimed they painted with "prune juice".

Around 1865 a new group of artists fell under the spell of these magical woodlands: Pierre-Auguste Renoir, Alfred Sisley and Claude Monet settled in Chailly. Though they did not associate themselves with the Barbizon community, they did however accept advice from their elders: Diaz encouraged the young Renoir to work with lighter tones. Here too the seeds of Impressionism were being sown.

Impressionism – The second-generation artists wanted their work to capture the essence of light itself and to reflect the vibrant quality of colour; the term "Impressionist" was actually coined by a sarcastic journalist in 1874, but was adopted by the group as they felt it conveyed the double revolution they had brought about in the field of painting.

The Impressionist Revolution – The Impressionist movement revolutionised artistic conventions on two counts: it paid little attention to form and it invented a new technique. Until then, the representation of reality was fundamentally important and no artist would have dared to neglect the lines and shapes of his subject, whether a portrait, still-life painting or landscape. Painters showed little concern for light and its effects, considered a minor component: priority was given to subject matter. For the Impressionists, light and the analysis of its effects became the principal subject: all the rest – contours, scenes, people – was simply an excuse to paint light.

Religious and historical works as well as family portraits and everyday scenes were no longer interesting in themselves. The Impressionists' favourite subjects were those which played with light: water, snow, fabrics, flesh, flowers, leaves, or fruit.

They wished to capture the infinite depths of the skies, the shimmering of light on water, a dress or a human face. When depicting the undergrowth, they wanted to show how the russet tones glitter in sunlight, how bright colours sparkle...

Such fleeting and indefinite concepts were no longer attainable using traditional techniques. As priority was given to the vibration of light around the edges of objects, the process that applied paint along contours was banished. Traditionally, the layers of paint were applied slowly and acquired their definite colour after the oil had solidified; they were then coated with varnish to produce a transparent effect and to give depth to the colours. Naturally this technique was far too lengthy to capture the ephemeral quality of light and as a consequence the Impressionists developed a technique more suited to their purpose, one which involved very little oil and which dispensed with varnish: their art consisted in applying quick, small dabs of colour. The exact shade was conveyed by the juxtaposition of touches of pure colour, the final effect being assessed by the eye of the viewer.

The Impressionists were harshly criticised, even insulted at times, and it was only after a twenty-year struggle that their work was fully acknowledged. Île-de-France with its rivers, lakes, gardens, orchards, showers of rain, mists, elegant ladies and regattas gave them countless sources of inspiration.

Gare St-Lazare by Claude Monet (Musée d'Orsay)

The Painters – The Impressionist School was founded in Honfleur where **Claude Monet** (1840-1926), a painter from Le Havre, was encouraged by the seascape specialist Eugène Boudin to paint landscapes. **Boudin** (1824-98), a friend of Corot's, was also a precursor of Impressionism: his paintings are full of air and light. Following his example, Monet and later the Dutch artist Jongkind worked on the luminosity of the landscapes around the Seine estuary. They were joined by Bazille and **Sisley**, whom they had befriended in Gleyre's studio, and began to paint around Fontainebleau forest too, though they remained separate from the Barbizon School. Pissarro, Cézanne and Guillaumin, who met at the Swiss Academy, were called "The Famous Three" *(Le Groupe des Trois)*.

The painters were strongly supported by **Édouard Manet** (1832-83), one of their elders who was upsetting artistic conventions and scandalising the public with his bold colours and compositions. It was Manet who encouraged the Impressionists to pursue their efforts at painting light. In 1863, following clashes between the artists and the official salons which refused to show these new works, a now-famous independent exhibition of the rejected works (Salon des Refusés) was set up on the orders of Napoleon III; it gave birth to and led to the naming of the Impressionist movement.

In 1871 small groups of amateur painters, pupils and friends, including **Paul Cézanne**, joined Pissarro at Pontoise and Docteur Gachet in Auvers. Another group based in Argenteuil and Louveciennes included **Renoir**, Monet, Sisley and Edgar Degas, who had originally studied under Ingres. Monet's innovative technique put him at the head of the movement and inspired both Manet and later Berthe Morisot.

In the 1880s, Renoir moved to Chatou just west of Paris, where he frequented the Maison Tomaise, a restaurant first opened in 1815 and now restored. After 1880 the group broke up but its members remained faithful to painting with light colours. Sisley moved to Moret, drawn to the River Loing, while Monet settled in Giverny on the banks of the Epte *(see Michelin Green Guide Normandy)*. For practical reasons, Pissarro left the Oise valley to live in Eragny, near Gisors.

Georges Seurat (1859-91) remained in Paris but concentrated on the landscapes around the capital and along the Channel coast. His technique amounted to breaking down the subject matter into small dabs of colour, each consisting of a series of dots *(points)*. Maximilien Luce (1858-1941) also experimented with this method – known as Pointillism or Divisionism – in the vicinity of Mantes.

Cézanne later returned to Aix-en-Provence where through the use of colour, tone and accentuated outlines he developed stylised masses which laid the foundations for the Cubist movement.

Renoir travelled to Algeria and Venice which inspired him to paint some of his finest works. Degas and Toulouse-Lautrec (1846-1901) lived in Paris; they were fascinated by circuses and theatres where the swirling dancers and performers were showered with complex illuminations created by artificial lighting.

The Dawn of the Twentieth Century – The followers of the **Nabis** and **Fauve** movements, which preceded Cubism and the new art forms born in the wake of the First World War, also set up their easel or sometimes even their studio in the picturesque outskirts of Paris. On his return from a stay in Pont-Aven where Paul Gauguin had shown him the magic of composing in flat, bold colours, Paul Sérusier converted his friends from the Académie Julian to the same style and formed the Nabis movement (a Hebrew word meaning prophet). **Maurice Denis** (1870-1943) became the leader of the group, which included Bonnard, Roussel, Vuillard, Maillol, Vallotton and others.

The early Fauves (meaning "wild beasts") included extremely diverse artists – Matisse, Dufy, Braque, Derain, Vlaminck, Rouault, Marquet. Their paintings of bright, even violent colour created an uproar when they were first shown. The painters, never a coherent group, were influenced by the paintings of **Van Gogh** who had died in 1890 leaving a collection of brilliant canvases composed of strong, vigorous brushstrokes of pure colour.

The coasts and countryside of the north of France and the region around Paris continue to attract many artists.

Folklore and traditions
of the North

For dates of festivals and other events see the Calendar of Events at the end of the guide.

The people of Picardy and the north of France belong to the "Picardy nation" which used to spread from Beauvais to Lille and from Calais to Laon, extending as far as Tournai and Mons. The common language of this "nation" formed a bond between its inhabitants, who are known for being hard workers with a taste for good food and lively merry-making. Even now, the slightest excuse can be found to organise a feast or a get-together in an *estaminet* (the Walloon word for a café) for a beer or two. Natives of Flanders, Artois, Lille and Picardy all have this same fondness for gatherings which is reflected in their many group activities: carnivals, celebrations, patron saint days, village fairs and associations (each village has its own band).

The Ducasse or Kermesse – The words *ducasse* (from *dédicace*, meaning a Catholic holiday) and *kermesse* ("church fair" in Flemish) now both designate a town or village patron saint's day. This holiday has preserved aspects of its religious origins (Mass and procession) but today also includes stalls, competitions, traditional games, jumble sales, etc.

Carnivals – Carnival-time is an occasion to dress up in costume and watch parades of floats and giant figures; it traditionally takes place on Shrove Tuesday *(Mardi Gras)* – as in Dunkirk, where it lasts for three days – but in reality, however, carnival parades take place throughout the year in the North.

Famous Giants – Giants originate from various myths, legends and stories and include:
– legendary founders, such as Lydéric and Phinaert in Lille.
– famous warriors like the Reuzes from Dunkirk and Cassel, said to originate from Scandinavia.
– historic figures, such as Jeanne Maillotte in Lille, the inn-keeper who fought off the "Howlers"; the beautiful Roze in Ardres, who saved the town from dragonnades; the Elector of Bergues, portraying Lamartine; Roland in Hazebrouck, one of Baudouin of Flanders' Crusaders, who distinguished himself at the taking of Constantinople.
– famous couples, like Martin and Martine, the two jack o' the clocks of Cambrai; Colas and Jacqueline, the gardeners of Arras; Arlequin and Colombine in Bruay; Manon and Des Grieux in Hesdin.
– popular figures, like Gédéon, the bell-ringer of Bourbourg, who saved the belfry chimes from being stolen; the pedlar Tisje Tasje of Hazebrouck, symbol of the Flemish spirit, with his wife Toria and his daughter Babe Tisje; Pierrot Bimberlot in Le Quesnoy; and Ko Pierre, a drum major, in Aniche.
– legendary heroes: Gargantua in Bailleul; Gambrinus, the king of beer, in Armentières; Yan den Houtkapper, the woodcutter who made a pair of wooden boots for Charlemagne, in Steenvoorde; Gayant of Douai, said to have delivered the town from brigands.
– representatives of trades, like the vegetable gardener Baptistin in St-Omer; the miner Cafougnette in Denain; and the fisherman Batisse in Boulogne.
– or simply a child, like the famous Binbin in Valenciennes.
Giants are often accompanied by their families – as they do marry and are given large families – and are surrounded by skirted horses, devils, bodyguards and wheels of fortune. Sometimes they have their own hymn, such as the Reuzelieds in Dunkirk and Cassel.

Materials – Traditionally the giants' bodies are made from a willow frame on which a painted *papier mâché* head is placed. Once dressed in their costumes, the giants are then carried by one or more people who make them dance in the procession.
The tallest is Gayant in Douai, who is 8.40m/almost 28ft tall.
As giants are often now made of heavier materials (steel tubing, cane, plastic), they are frequently pulled along in carts or on wheels rather than carried.

Town Chimes – Chimes in town belfries, which regularly sound out their melodic tunes, lend a rhythm to life in northern French towns. Since the Middle Ages, when four bells were tapped by hand with a hammer, there have been many additions: a mechanism, a manual keyboard, pedals, all of which have made it possible to increase the number of bells (62 in Douai) and to increase the variety of their sounds.
Carillon concerts are held in Douai, St-Amand-les-Eaux and Maubeuge (east of Valenciennes).

Traditional Games and Sports – Traditional entertainments remain popular: marionettes, ball games, real tennis, ninepins, darts, lacrosse (an ancestor of golf), archery (which is also a traditional sport of the Valois area), cock-fighting, pigeon-breeding etc.

Northern Giants

Yan
den Houtkapper
Steenvoorde

Martin
and Martine
Cambrai

Gayant and
his wife
Douai

The Sailor's
wife
*Grand-Fort
Philippe*

Mother Reuze *Cassel*

Archery – In the Middle Ages archers were already the pride of the Counts of Flanders, who would have the archers accompany them on all their expeditions. As soon as individual towns were founded the archers formed associations or guilds. They appeared at all public ceremonies, dressed in brightly-coloured costumes, brandishing the great standard of their association.

Today archery is practised in several ways. A method particular to the North is vertical or "perch" shooting, which consists in firing arrows upward to hit dummy birds attached to gratings suspended from a pole. At the top of this pole, about 30m/98ft off the ground, is the hardest target of all, the "**poppinjay**" *(papegai)*. Archers must hit this bird with a long, ball-tipped arrow and the winner is proclaimed "King of the perch".

In winter the sport is practised indoors: arrows are shot horizontally at a slightly tilted grating.

Still grouped in brotherhoods, the archers gather every year to honour their patron, St Sebastian.

Crossbow – The art of the crossbow, which also dates from the Middle Ages, has its own circle of enthusiasts organised in brotherhoods. Their gatherings, colourful events featuring these curious weapons from another time, are often given evocative names such as the King's Crossbow Shoot.

Javelin – This feathered arrow measuring 50-60cm/20-24in is thrown into a tightly tied bundle of straw which serves as a target. It is the same principle as for the game of darts, which is played in many cafés.

The Game of "Billons" – A *billon* is a tapering wooden club about 1m/3ft long, weighing about 2-3kg/4-7lb. Two teams throw their *billons* in turn towards a post 9m/30ft away; the aim is to land the narrower end of the club nearest to the post and this may be achieved by dislodging the *billons* of the opposing team.

Bouchon – Teams face each other in cafés, and knock down the cork and wood "targets" with their metal paddles. The best players participate in competitions at local festivals.

Cock-Fighting – Cock-breeders and anxious gamblers watch bloody and vicious fights to the death between roosters.

Pigeon-Breeding – Pigeon fanciers *(coulonneux)* raise their birds to fly back to the nest as quickly as possible: for pigeon-racing competitions, which are very popular, the birds are carried in special baskets to a distance of up to 500km/310mi and must then return to their dovecote at record speed. A pigeon can fly over 100km/60mi per hour on average.

Singing Finch Competitions – Finches have also become part of the folklore in the north of France, where they participate in trilling contests. Some can trill as many as 800 times an hour.

Ratting Dogs – Cruel ratting competitions have always had a certain popularity in this region. Three rats are put in a cage, then a dog; spectators time how long it takes the dog to kill its adversaries; the fastest dog is the victor.

To choose a hotel or a restaurant,
to find an auto mechanic,
*consult the current edition of the **Michelin Red Guide**.*

Food and drink

The Cuisine of Picardy – Soups are the great local specialities, in particular thos made from tripe *(tripe)*, pumpkin *(potiron)* or frogs *(grenouille)*, as well as the famou vegetable soup *(soupe des hortillons)*. The people of Picardy and Artois love thei vegetables: beans from Soissons, Laon artichokes, St Valery carrots, peas from th Vermandois and leeks which are used in a delicious pie, the *tarte aux porions*.
Starters include duck pâté in a pastry case *(pâté de canard en croûte)* (prepared i Amiens since the 17C), snipe pâté *(pâté de bécassines)* from Abbeville and Montreui eel pâté *(pâté d'anguilles)* from Péronne. The *ficelle picarde* is a ham pancake in creamy mushroom sauce.
Duck, snipe and plover, eel, carp and pike from the River Somme are often on th menu. Seafood (shrimps known as *sauterelles*, cockles called *hemons*) is common, a well as sole, turbot, fresh herring and cod, often cooked with cream.

Flemish Cuisine – Flemish cooking, washed down with beer and often followed by glass of gin or a *bistouille* (coffee with a dash of alcohol), contains several typica dishes:
– rabbit with prunes or raisins and pigeon with cherries.
– home-made potted meat made from veal, lard, rabbit and sometimes chicken *(potje vleesch)*.
– mixed stew of veal, mutton, pork offals, lard and vegetables *(hochepot)*.
– braised beef in a beer sauce flavoured with onions and spices *(carbonade)*.
– eel sautéed in butter and stewed in a wine sauce with herbs *(anguille au vert)*.
– small smoked herrings, a speciality of Dunkirk *(craquelots)*.
Among the other specialities of the north of France are chitterling sausage *(andouillettes)* from Arras and Cambrai, trout from the Rivers Canche and Course, an cauliflowers from St-Omer.

Cheeses of the North – Local cheeses, except for that from **Mont des Cats**, are strong most come from the Thiérache and Avesnois regions, areas rich in pasture. The bes is **Maroilles**, created in the 10C by monks from Maroilles abbey: it has a soft centr with a crust washed in beer, similar to cheese from Munster. The other cheeses i the region are derived from it: **Vieux Lille**, also called Maroilles gris (grey Maroilles) **Dauphin** (Maroilles with herbs and spices); **Cœur d'Avesnes** or Rollot; and the deliciou **Boulette d'Avesnes** (Maroilles with spices, rolled in paprika). **Flamiche au Maroilles**, a creamy highly-flavoured quiche, is one of the most famous dishes from the northern regio of France.

Brie – The Brie region in Île-de-France is famous for its soft cow's milk cheeses wit surface mould. There are two types – Brie and double or triple-cream cheeses (**Lucullus Grand Vatel, Gratte-Paille** etc) often made from the fat left over from the production c Brie, a mythical cheese that already enjoyed a reputation for excellence in the 13C Brie was as popular with the commoners of Paris as with royalty and it was th outright winner of a competition organised during the Congress of Vienna in 181 bringing together all the best cheeses from throughout Europe. There are certai characteristics common to all Brie cheeses. They are made from partially-skimmed raw cow's milk, the rind is white with reddish marks, the cheese is soft in texture and pale yellow in colour, the fat content is approximately 45%, and the maturing period does not exceed seven weeks. Setting these features aside, several varieties of Brie have developed and they differ depending on the area of production. The best-known are Brie de Meaux and Brie de Melun.

Cakes – The local pancakes *(crêpes)*, waffles and sweet breads *(tartines* and *brioches)* can make entire meals in themselves; the brioches with bulging middles are called *coquilles*.

Tarts, such as the delicious *tartes au sucre* sprinkled with brown sugar, are often served for dessert. Sweets are accompanied by the light, chicory coffee which people from the region drink at any time of the day.

Brown Sugar Tart Recipe – Mix 375g/13oz flour, 90g/3oz sugar, 20g/0.7oz yeast blended with warm water, with 1 egg yolk and 60g/2oz butter. Knead and leave the dough to rise until it has doubled in size. Put into a greased sponge tin and leave the dough to rise again for 30min. Add 100g/3.5oz brown sugar and dot with knobs of butter. Bake for 30min in a hot oven (220°C – Thermostat 7).

Beer – Gambrinus, the king of beer, is greatly revered in the north of France as is St Arnould, the patron saint of brewers. Beer *(la bière)* was already known in Antiquity; in Gaul, later, it was called *cervoise*. During the Middle Ages brewing beer was a privilege of the monasteries; it spread enormously in Flanders under John the Fearless, Duke of Burgundy and Count of Flanders, who developed the use of hops.

The Brewing Process – Beer is obtained by the mashing and fermentation of a mixture of water and malt, flavoured with hops. Barley grains are soaked in water (malting) until they germinate. The malted barley, dried and roasted in a kiln, becomes **malt**. This is powdered and then mixed with pure water and hops and cooked, according to each manufacturer's secret procedure. This operation, called brewing, transforms the starch in the malt into sugar and makes it possible to obtain the **wort**. With the addition of a raising agent, the wort begins to ferment.

Beer brewing was formerly undertaken simply by a brewer, with his boy hand-

Brewers in Lille

ling a sort of pointed shovel *(fourquet)*, but is now a large and sophisticated industry. Much of French beer and lager (paler, "aged" beer containing more bubbles and often less alcohol) is produced in the Pas-de-Calais region, which is rich in water, barley and hops; the hops grown in Flanders have a particularly strong flavour. The largest breweries are in the areas around Lille-Roubaix and Armentières, and the Scarpe and Escaut (Scheldt) river valleys. On the eve of the First World War, the region had 2600 breweries; today, there are only 17 left. Many small breweries are, however, now operating locally.

Different beers have their own characteristics: the traditional, slightly-bitter lager *(bière blonde)* of the north; the relatively sweet and fruity regional dark beer *(bière brune)* or the richly-flavoured, amber-red beer *(bière rousse)*.

Consumption has decreased over the past dozen years or so and is now at the level of 39.3 l/86 pints per person a year.

Gin – Gin is made from wheat, oats, malted barley and rye turned into meal. After cooking, the action of the yeast causes them to ferment.

The resultant "cereal wine" is distilled with juniper berries and the drink begins to produce its characteristic aroma.

Gin is still produced in the Nord-Pas-de-Calais region, in Houlle, Wambrechies and Loos. Another drink produced in Loos is an aperitif called le *chuche-mourette*, consisting of *crème de cassis* and gin.

57

The Hall of Mirrors, Château de Versailles

ABBEVILLE

Population 23787
Michelin map 52 folds 6, 7 or 236 fold 22

Abbeville (pronounced Abb'ville) is the capital of the Ponthieu region and stands on the edge of the River Somme, about 20km/12mi from the sea. In the 19C artists flocked to its medieval streets overlooked by the towers of the Collégiale St-Vulfran; since the Second World War it has taken on a more modern aspect.

HISTORICAL NOTES

The town derives its name from the Latin *Abbatis Villa* meaning abbot's villa, and originally developed around the country house of the abbot of St-Riquier. From the 13C to the 15C Abbeville became the property of the English, the Burgundians and the French, depending on the outcome of the struggles for possession of the Somme Valley. Abbeville finally became French under Louis XI in the 15C.

In 1514 the young and attractive Mary of England (Henry VIII's sister) was married here to King Louis XII – then aged 52 – who died of consumption the following year.

Enlightened Capitalists: the Van Robais – This Dutch family settled in Abbeville as a result of Colbert's wish to free the national economy from its dependence on foreign imports by manufacturing products in France.

Josse Van Robais arrived in Abbeville in 1665 to establish a factory making fine cloth, aided by various privileges, not least of which was a guaranteed monopoly. Van Robais brought with him his family, his Protestant chaplain, about 50 workers and his weaving looms, which he installed in Faubourg Hocquet.

Thus the Royal Tenter Works (Manufacture Royale des Rames) was founded, one of the first "integrated" businesses, dealing not only with all aspects of spinning and weaving but also with the finishing (dressing, fulling, dyeing etc).

The firm's success was consolidated by Josse's grandson, Abraham Van Robais (1698-1779): during the 18C about 2500 people were employed, 250 of whom were weavers. All that remains of the factory built between 1709 and 1713 at 264 chaussée d'Hocquet are the main entrance and a dovecot (1712).

The Father of Prehistory: Boucher de Perthes (1788-1868) – Jacques Boucher de Perthes was a handsome and intelligent man, the multi-talented author of a minor masterpiece called "Portraits" written in the style of La Bruyère. In 1825 after a wild and worldly youth he succeeded his father as Head of Customs in Abbeville, which at the time was a busy seaport.

He became passionately interested in prehistory, scanning the alluvial layers of the Somme – exposed by dredgers widening the canal – in search of the sharpened flints which, he believed, should accompany the bones of prehistoric peoples. From 1830 he was assisted by the doctor, **Casimir Picard**. Following Picard's death in 1841, Boucher de Perthes struggled on, continuing to explore the woodland peat of La Portelette – close to what is now Abbeville station – and the quarries of St-Acheul, near Amiens. From the study of his finds he gathered material for a work on "Celtic and Antediluvian Antiquities" in which he asserted his belief in the existence of Paleolithic man, contemporary to the large extinct pachyderms.

His discoveries were met with scepticism. Boucher de Perthes would pay 10 centimes for an oddly-shaped rock or stone, and one of his cousins recalled how, on meeting a peasant breaking rocks, she asked what he was doing: "Making prehistoric axes for M Boucher de Perthes" was the reply.

The tragic days of May-June 1940 – After the German breakthrough at Sedan and the Panzer drive to the sea, Abbeville became a nerve centre for the French Resistance. From 20 May intense bombing by Stukas struck the town centre, almost all of which burned, destroying 2000 houses and leaving hundreds of people dead or wounded. At night, the Germans entered the town and established a large bridgehead on the south bank of the Somme, extending as far as Huppy and Bray-lès-Mareuil, with the well-fortified Caubert Heights (Monts de Caubert) as a strong point. A fierce counter-attack by the French 4th Armoured Division under **Colonel de Gaulle** and by the Scots reduced the German pocket but did not succeed in breaching the Caubert Heights' defences.

SIGHTS 2hr

Collégiale St-Vulfran – St Wulfram's Collegiate Church, which resembles a cathedral, was begun in 1488; the west front was built first, but construction of the nave was interrupted in 1539 owing to lack of money, and it was not until the 17C that the chancel was finished in neo-Gothic style. During the bombing of 1940 the nave and chancel vaults collapsed. The building was very badly damaged and is currently undergoing restoration.

The west front is best viewed from the west side of the square. It was in this square that, in 1766, a young man of 19, Chevalier de la Barre, was beheaded and burnt at the stake after being condemned for damaging one of the crucifixes on one of the bridges in Abbeville. Voltaire tried in vain to obtain a pardon for him.

★West Front – The Flamboyant west front shows how late-15C architecture had become merely a vehicle for sculpture. Flanked by small watch-turrets, the towers rise to 55m/180ft; between them the open gable supports a statue of the Virgin accompanied by St Wulfram and St Nicholas. In the corner of the Gothic gable above the central doorway stands a group representing the Trinity.

Central Doorway – The piers are decorated with statues of bishops: St Nicholas *(left)* and St Firmin of Amiens *(right)* standing on a sculpted base and holding an open book. The carvings depict his martyrdom, and the emblem of the coopers of whom he was patron.

The door has preserved its Renaissance panels, masterpieces by the Picardy wood-carvers *(huchiers)*. In the centre the figures of the Evangelists are framed by St Peter *(left)* and St Paul *(right)*. Scenes from the life of the Virgin can be seen above a frieze of horsemen.

The panels were given by Jehan Mourette, the head of a brotherhood of poets (Confrérie du Puy Notre-Dame d'Abbeville), who is commemorated in an inscription dated 1550.

Left Doorway – This doorway tells the legend of St Eustace: on the tympanum, his foot on the shield of the draper-hosiers, St Eustace sees his children being eaten, one by a lion, the other by a wolf; to the left, a relief shows him being thrown into the sea by a sailor, in front of his wife, from a ship on which he had tried to stow away.

Right Doorway – This doorway was the gift of the guild of haberdashers; their shield of a purse and scales can be seen under the three famous statues carved by Pierre Lheureux in 1501-02. These statues represent: the Assumption of the Virgin Mary *(on the tympanum)* and the Virgin Mary's sisters *(on the piers)*; bare-breasted Mary the mother of Cleophas, one of the two pilgrims on the road to Emmaus, on the left; on the right, Mary Salome and her two children, John the Evangelist and James the Great.

Buttresses – The second buttress on the left features figures of St Peter and St Andrew, the latter carrying the cross of his martyrdom, with the bull's head emblem of the butchers at his feet.

Interior – The height of the nave (only 31.70m/103ft compared to a width of 37m/120ft) is further accentuated by the slenderness of the pillars devoid of capitals. Note the keystones painted in their original colours and decorated with coats of arms. From the nave, notice the abstract stained-glass windows in the chancel which were designed by William Epstein.

★Musée Boucher de Perthes ⊙ – Facing the square, which is graced by the statue of the local sailor Courbet (1827-1885), stand the museum buildings: a 13C belfry, a small 15C edifice (formerly the Mint) and a new building to the rear.

The main room on the ground floor displays paintings: 16C works from the Confrérie du Puy Notre-Dame (portrait of Jehan Mourette and his wife), a 17C Deposition by the Flemish artist Van Mol, and from the 18C four mythological canvases by François le Moine, portraits by Largillière, a self-portrait by Lépicié and genre scenes by the local artist Choquet.

The Mint and the grand staircase exhibit medieval sculpture (corbels and friezes from local houses, 15C altarpiece from the Charterhouse at Thuison), local ceramics (faience from Vron, glazed earthenware from Sorrus) and tapestries (fragment from the Artemis series).

The vaulted rooms of the old belfry provide an ideal setting for the medieval statues and ivories, in particular the superb silver Virgin and Child (1568).

The second floor houses the Boucher de Perthes prehistoric collections and the archeological discoveries made in the Somme valley and St-Acheul.

Église du St-Sépulcre – Only the bell-tower, the piers and archivolts of the nave, the two side aisles and the Chapel of the Holy Sepulchre remain from the original 15C building, which was altered substantially in the late 19C into Flamboyant Gothic style. The vaulting and pavement were renovated following severe damage during the Second World War. The contemporary **stained-glass windows★★** by Alfred Manessier represent the Passion and the Resurrection of Christ.

Old House – *29 rue des Capucins, on the corner of rue des Teinturiers*.
This corbelled house is an example of 15C-16C domestic architecture.

★Château de Bagatelle ⊙ – *Southeast of the town, at 133 route de Paris*.
Abraham Van Robais had Bagatelle built c 1740 as his villa in the country, where he could relax and receive his business clients. It originally consisted of only the ground floor to which was added, 15 years later, an attic storey with bull's-eye windows to provide living accommodation; the mansard roof dates from about 1790. In spite of subsequent additions this is a charming residence, characterised by a harmony and unity of style. Sedaine, the dramatist, said in 1770, "This retreat would please even the gods. Modern art is so beautiful here that it seems to have been created by Nature itself."

On the ground floor, the Rococo decoration of the rooms – furnished with period pieces – has a light and elegant touch. The hall leads into the summer salon, a room with no fireplace. The picture panels above the door cases are painted with cherubs representing Morning, Noon and Night; the panelling is carved with arabesques in the Pompeiian style.

In the winter salon, the decoration of the sculpted panels and chimneypiece is highlighted in blue. The fine chandelier with porcelain flowers from the Royal Vincennes factory, the wall lights, the panelling and the consoles in the dining room all belonged to the Van Robais; the rest of the furniture is also 18C. A graceful double staircase with a wrought-iron balustrade was ingeniously adapted to fit the hall, to give access to the low-ceilinged first-floor rooms with their delicate Louis XV woodwork, and Louis XVI garland and ribbon motifs.

The formal French garden contains parterres and statues, and "Mme Roland's hillock" (butte de Mme Roland) where the wife of the future minister – at that time Inspector of Factories in Picardy – used to take her lunch.

The botanical park contains a large and varied collection of plants, some rare.

Château de Bagatelle

EXCURSIONS

Monts de Caubert – *5km/3mi. Leave Abbeville by* ④ *on the town plan.*
At the first sharp bend before a road junction, turn left onto the narrow road running along the crest of the rise. 1.5km/1mi further on is a wayside cross from which there is a good view over the Somme valley, Abbeville and the plains of Ponthieu beyond.

The Vimeu Region – *Round trip of 35km/22mi – about 1hr.*
The Vimeu region of Picardy, between the Rivers Somme and Bresle gets its name from a tributary of the latter. It seems like an isolated plateau, grooved by green valleys with hedged meadows full of apple trees. This farming country also contains many châteaux and villages hidden among the trees. Locksmithing and wrought-iron making have been the traditional occupations of the area since the 17C. Nowadays, the region produces mainly locks and bathroom or kitchen taps.

Friville-Escarbotin – *15km/9mi west of St-Valery-sur-Somme.*
The **Musée des Industries du Vimeu** ⊙ traces the history of small-scale metalwork: locksmithery, taps and fittings, ironmongery, shipchandlery etc. The ground floor displays 19C machines (pedal-worked drill) and reconstructed workshops: locksmith's shop, keymaker's workshop, local foundry. Among the collections of locks, bars and bolts, note the display of 135 padlocks, the smallest of which is made from a gold coin. The first floor displays modern objects (audiovisual presentation).

St-Maxent Windmill – *13km/8mi south of Abbeville.*
This timber windmill, which was in use until 1941, retains its post, its counterbalancing "tail", its roof of chestnut shingles, its three storeys for sifting, and its mechanism and millstones.
Continue north on N 28 for 3km/2mi.

Huppy – *10km/6mi south of Abbeville.*
Home of the 17C sculptor JB Poultier, this village also boasts a 15C and 16C **church** ⊙ (Renaissance stained glass) and a 17C **château** *(private)*, where Colonel de Gaulle established his headquarters on 29 May 1940 *(plaque)*; he was promoted to General on 1 June.
Return to Abbeville by N 28.

ALBERT

Population 10010
Michelin map 52 fold 9 or 236 fold 25

The town, which was originally called Ancre, from the river which flows through it, was the seat of a marquess; the title was acquired in 1610 by Marie de Medici's favourite, Concino Concini. Following his tragic death in 1617, which heralded the queen mother's disgrace, Louis XIII offered Ancre to Charles d'Albert, Duc de Luynes, who gave it his name.

Albert was almost totally destroyed during the Battle of the Somme in 1916 and the Battle of Picardy in 1918 *(see Introduction: Historical Notes)* and is today a well-planned, modern town. Méaulte, a large suburb to the south, is the home of aircraft factories founded by Potez but now run by the Aérospatiale.

Basilique Notre-Dame-de-Brébières – The basilica is a popular place of pilgrimage *(see Calendar of Events)*. The tower (70m/230ft high) is surmounted by a poignant statue of the Virgin and Child by Albert Roze. Inside, the 11C Miraculous Virgin is venerated.

BATTLEFIELDS *Round trip of 34km/21mi – 45 min.*

A circuit east and north of Albert commemorates the British and South African soldiers under Douglas Haig who fell during the Allied attack in summer 1916 (Battle of the Somme).

Take D 929 northeast towards Bapaume.

On the right lies a British cemetery.

La Boisselle – Traces of explosions still suggest some of the violence of the fighting which occurred in this village.

Take D 20 on the right.

Cross Bazentin and Longueval, around which lie several British cemeteries, then turn left.

Mémorial sud-africain et musée commémoratif du bois de Delville ⊙ – The Battle of Delville Wood in July 1916 saw, over five days and nights, some of the fiercest fighting and worst devastation which resulted in the deaths of over 1 000 South African men, who were attached to the 9th Scottish Division. The original dense wood was blasted out of existence, apart from a single hornbeam which is now carefully tended.

A memorial and a museum were built to commemorate the many South African soldiers who lost their lives during both World Wars.Inside the museum housed in a replica in miniature of Capetown Castle there are paintings, bronze panels, and display cases containing uniforms and relics of the men who came from so far away to fight on the battlefields of France.

Return to D 20 and turn right onto D 107; turn left onto D 929.

Pozières – This British cemetery is encircled by columns which give it a majestic air. The names of 14690 men who went missing in action are engraved on the memorial.

Turn right into D 73.

Mémorial britannique de Thiepval – The brick-built triumphal arch overlooks the Ancre valley and is visible from afar. The memorial, surrounded by a lawn, bears the names of 73367 British soldiers who went missing in action in the Thiepval area.

Continue on D 73.

The **Tour d'Ulster** *(right)*, a replica of a tower near Belfast, was erected in memory of the dead of the 36th Irish Division.The road then runs through the Ancre Valley.

★**Parc-mémorial de Beaumont-Hamel** – This wind-swept plateau was the site of a battle fought by the Newfoundland Division in 1916 on the opening day of the Battle of the Somme. Some 700 Newfoundlanders were killed or wounded that first day. The area has been preserved and developed, and now displays trenches, outposts, firing parapets, twisted iron rods suggesting bullet-blasted bushes etc. The monument, topped by a Newfoundland Caribou, includes a viewing platform: view of the battlefield.

At the base of the monument – a huge, bronze New-World Caribou (the emblem of the Regiment) – tablets bear the names of 820 men with no known grave. A platform provides good **views** over the battlefield. It stands in the largest of the memorial parks, and was opened by Earl Haig in 1925.

Return to the Ancre valley and turn right onto D 50 to Albert.

AMIENS★★★

Conurbation 156 120
Michelin map 52 fold 8 or 236 fold 24

Amiens, the capital of Picardy, is an important communications centre and the setting for a beautiful cathedral. Devastated during the two world wars, it is now essentially a modern town, sheltering the precious remains of its past in picturesque areas. The ramparts were replaced in the 18C by circular boulevards; a lively shopping street runs from Gare du Nord to the Maison de la Culture.

The town has always been an economic, artistic and intellectual centre, and a university was founded there in 1964.

The delicious gastronomic specialities include chocolate wafers, macaroons, pancakes filled with ham and mushrooms with a white sauce *(ficelles Picardes)* and the famous duck patés encased in pastry *(pâtés de canard en croûte)*.

HISTORICAL NOTES

St Martin's Cloak – In Gallo-Roman times Amiens was the capital of a Belgian tribe, the Ambiani; in the 4C the town was converted to Christianity by Firmin and his companions. At that time **St Martin**, a horseman in the Roman legion stationed here, met a beggar shivering in the north wind; he sliced his cloak in two with his sword and gave half to the poor man. This episode is recalled in a low-relief by J Samson (1830) on the north wall of the law courts (Palais de Justice), Place d'Aguesseau.

Birth of an Industry: Textiles – Affiliated to the Hanse of London (a merchants' guild), Amiens was very prosperous in the Middle Ages. The cloth business and wine trade, the port, and the influx of pilgrims who came to worship the relic said to be the head of John the Baptist, all contributed to the bustling atmosphere. **Woad**, a precious tinctural plant found locally and in the Santerre area, was treated here where it was known as *waide*; when milled the plant produces a beautiful blue, which was exported to England. The late 15C saw the production of a woollen serge mixed with silk, *sayette*, which gave the products of Amiens *(Articles d'Amiens)* a far-reaching reputation. The famous **"Amiens Velvets"** were introduced during Louis XIV's reign.

Steely Assaults – The valleys of the Somme and the Aisne rivers are major obstacles to invaders from the north, and being the bridgehead, Amiens has suffered many attacks. In 1918, during the Battle of Picardy, the town was attacked by Ludendorff and bombarded with 12 000 shells. It was set ablaze in 1940 during the Battle of the Somme. In 1944 its prison was the target of a dangerous aerial attack aimed at helping the imprisoned Resistance members to escape.

Where to stay and eat

Hôtel Carlton – 42 Rue Noyon; modern hotel near the station.

Hôtel Holiday Inn Express – 10 Boulevard Alsace-Lorraine; modern hotel facing the Tour Perret.

Restaurant Couronne – 64 Rue St-Leu; attractive meals, moderate prices.

Restaurant Vivier – 593 Route de Rouen; seafood.

Main entertainment venues

Maison de la Culture – Place Léon-Gontier.

La Comédie de Picardie – 62 Rue des Jacobins.

Maison du Théâtre – 18 Rue des Majots.

Cirque municipal – Place de Longueville.

Night Life

Rue Cauvin – A pedestrian precinct lined with cafés such as Chez Marius (excellent choice of beers, student atmosphere).

Place Gambetta – Le Forum, Le Cambridge, set out around an open-air theatre.

Rue du Don – Vents et Marées (café with comic strip exhibition) on the water's edge.

Place du Don – Numerous cafés including Couleur Café (rum cocktails), and Riverside.

Quartier Saint-Leu – A district with a cabaret atmosphere. Includes La Lune des Pirates (bar, rock concerts and pavement café), the Nelson Pub (blues and French songs), and Au XVIe siècle, a great favourite with students.

Post-War Changes – As sixty per cent of Amiens was destroyed it had to undergo considerable reconstruction, the most prominent of which is around Place Alphonse-Fiquet (the station and Perret Tower), in the area around the Maison de la Culture, the Pierre de Coubertin Sports Centre and the Faidherbe district (**BY**). The town's edges are being redefined by other new buildings.

Traditional industries still hold sway in the city – knitting wools and the famous velvets – though the Longpré industrial zone is home to substantial metallurgical and chemical plants, major alternatives to the textile business. Factories producing tyres, car parts and electronic equipment have also been established.

Local Heroes – Amiens was the birthplace of several writers including **Choderlos de Laclos** (1741-1803), famous for *Les Liaisons Dangereuses*, Paul Bourget (1852-1925) and **Roland Dorgelès** (1885-1973), author of *Les Croix de Bois*, as well as the physician **Édouard Branly** (1844-1940) who invented the coherer, a device for detecting radio waves.

In Place René-Goblet a monument commemorates another local hero: Marshal Leclerc de Hauteclocque who distinguished himself during the Second World War.

★★★CATHÉDRALE NOTRE-DAME (CY) *1hr 30min*

Amiens cathedral is the largest Gothic building in France (145m/475ft long with vaults 42.5m/139ft high).

In 1218 the Romanesque church on the site was destroyed by fire. Bishop Evrard de Fouilloy and the people of Amiens immediately decided to build a replacement, something exceptional worthy of sheltering the "head of John the Baptist", the precious relic brought back in 1206 from the fourth crusade by Wallon de Sarton, Canon of Picquigny. The plans of the church were entrusted to **Robert de Luzarches** who was succeeded by Thomas de Cormont and then his son Renaud. The cathedral was begun in 1220 and the speed with which it was built explains the remarkable unity of style, though the towers remained uncrowned until the beginning of the 15C. The cathedral was later restored by Viollet-le-Duc; it miraculously escaped damage in 1940.

Exterior

The west front *(see illustration in Architecture and Art)* of Amiens cathedral has a horizontal emphasis, consisting of several bands: the three doorways; the two galleries including the Kings' Gallery *(galerie des rois)* with its enormous figures; the great Flamboyant rose-window (renewed in the 16C) framed by twinned open bays; and the small bell-ringers' gallery *(galerie des sonneurs)* topped by light arcading between the towers. Elegant sculptures – some damaged by pollution – further enhance the ensemble. The **central doorway** is framed by the Wise and Foolish Virgins who, together with the Apostles and the Prophets on the piers, escort from a respectable distance the famous **Beau Dieu**, a noble and serene Christ standing on lavender and basil. He is the focal point of this enormous carved Bible. The tympanum portrays the Last Judgment presided over by a more archaic and severe God with a procession of virgins, martyrs, angels and damned souls in the arching above. The lower sections have quatrefoil low reliefs framing the Virtues (women with shields) and Vices.

The **left doorway** is dedicated to **St Firmin** the evangelist of Amiens and to the Picardy region.

The quatrefoils on the base enclose lively representations of a **Calendar** symbolised by the signs of the Zodiac and the corresponding Labours of the Months.

Above, St Ulphe, a virgin hermit, stands ranged with various local bishops and martyrs including the decapitated St Acheul and St Ache, holding their heads in their hands.

The **right doorway** is dedicated to the **Mother of God**. On the central pier, the crowned Virgin presides over scenes from Genesis. In the embrasures, the large statues portray the Annunciation, the Visitation, and the Presentation in the Temple *(right)*,

---

High-tech

A new method has been developed to clean stone. The technique, using a pulse laser, was first tested in Amiens. The laser functions by very short impulses, emitting a low-intensity light which fritters away the surface layer without any mechanical action. This technique is used to remove the layer of grime without damaging any traces of paintwork. Medieval cathedrals used to be brilliantly coloured and up to 13 layers of paint have been found in some places. There is currently some debate as to whether the multicoloured decor should be restored.

It takes about three days to clean a bracket and ten days for a statue. The restoration of the west front has been scheduled until the year 2000.

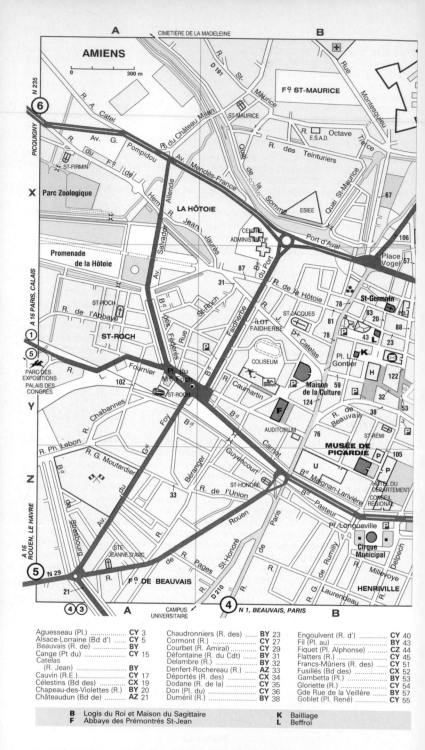

AMIENS

Aguesseau (Pl.)	**CY** 3	Chaudronniers (R. des)	**BY** 23	Engoulvent (R. d')	**CY** 40
Alsace-Lorraine (Bd d')	**CY** 5	Cormont (R.)	**CY** 27	Fil (Pl. au)	**BY** 43
Beauvais (R. de)	**BY**	Courbet (R. Amiral)	**CY** 29	Fiquet (Pl. Alphonse)	**CZ** 44
Cange (Pt du)	**CY** 15	Défontaine (R. du Cdt)	**BY** 31	Flatters (R.)	**CY** 45
Catelas		Delambre (R.)	**BY** 32	Francs-Mûriers (R. des)	**CY** 51
(R. Jean)	**BY**	Denfert-Rochereau (R.)	**AZ** 33	Fusillés (Bd des)	**CY** 52
Cauvin (R.E.)	**CY** 17	Déportés (R. des)	**CX** 34	Gambetta (Pl.)	**BY** 53
Célestins (Bd des)	**CX** 19	Dodane (R. de la)	**CY** 35	Gloriette (R.)	**CY** 54
Chapeau-des-Violettes (R.)	**BY** 20	Don (Pl. du)	**CY** 36	Gde Rue de la Veillère	**BY** 57
Châteaudun (Bd de)	**AZ** 21	Duméril (R.)	**BY** 38	Goblet (Pl. René)	**CY** 55

B	Logis du Roi et Maison du Sagittaire	**K**	Bailliage
F	Abbaye des Prémontrés St-Jean	**L**	Beffroi

the Magi visiting Herod, Solomon and the Queen of Sheba *(left)*. The quatrefoils show the life of the Virgin and of Christ; the tympanum celebrates the Assumption.

Walk along impasse Coron.

On the north side, note the statue of Charles V (**4**) on the 14th buttress supporting the tower

Go round the cathedral to the right, passing a giant St Christopher (**1**), an Annunciation (**2**), and, between the 3rd and 4th chapels, a pair of woad merchants with their sack (**3**).

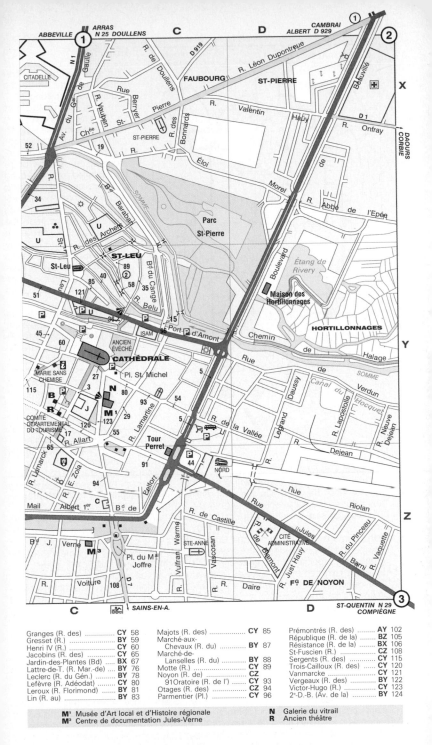

M¹	Musée d'Art local et d'Histoire régionale	**N**	Galerie du vitrail
M³	Centre de documentation Jules-Verne	**R**	Ancien théâtre

Follow Rue Cormont to Place St-Michel.

From here there is a fine view of the east end with its pierced flying buttresses, and the soaring lead-covered chestnut **spire** (112.70m/370ft high).

Retrace your steps and enter the cathedral through the south doorway.

The **south doorway**, known as the Golden Virgin Doorway because of the statue which used to adorn the pier, is dedicated to St Honoré who was bishop of Amiens. Visitors can mount the 307 steps of the towers, for a close up view of the spires and statuary atop the cathedral, and a wide-angle view of the city below.

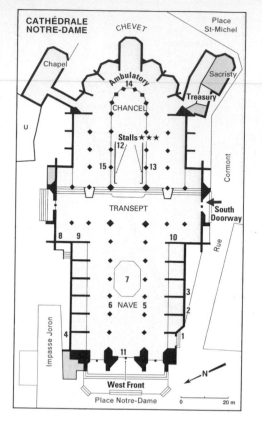

CATHÉDRALE NOTRE-DAME

CHEVET

Place St-Michel

Chapel

Ambulatory 14

Sacristy

CHANCEL

Treasury

Stalls ★★★

12

15 ◆ ◆ 13

Cormont

TRANSEPT

South Doorway

8 9

10

Rue

3

7

2

6 NAVE 5

1

Impasse Joron

4

11

—N→

West Front

Place Notre-Dame

0   20 m

Interior

The sheer size and the amount of light inside the cathedral are striking.

The **nave** is the highest in France, reaching 42.50m/139ft. Its elevation consists of large and exceptionally high arcades surmounted by a band of finely detailed foliage, a blind triforium and a clerestory; 13C recumbent bronze effigies of the cathedral's founding bishops lie in the third bay: Evrard de Fouilloy (**5**) and Geoffroy d'Eu (**6**); the latter faces towards the St-Saulve chapel which contains a figure of Christ in a long gold robe.

On the flagging, renewed in the 19C, the meandering lines of the labyrinth (**7**) have been restored. In the past the faithful would follow the lines on their knees, as a Way of the Cross. At the centre, the names of those responsible for the cathedral are inscribed: Robert de Luzarches, Thomas and Renaud de Cormont (the original stone is in the Picardy Museum).

The **north transept** is adorned with a 14C rose-window with star-shaped central tracery. The font (**8**), to the left of the door, dates from 1180 and was originally used to wash the dead. On the west wall a painted sculpture in four parts represents Christ and the money-lenders in the Temple (**9**) (1520).

The **south transept**, which is illuminated through a Flamboyant rose-window, bears on its west wall four scenes in relief (**10**) portraying the conversion of the magician Hermogene by St James the Great (1511).

The perspective back down the nave reveals its elegance and the boldness of the organ loft supporting the **great organ** (**11**) (1442) with its delicate golden arabesques, crowned by the majestic rose-window at the west end.

The **chancel** is enclosed within a beautiful 18C choir screen, wrought by Jean Veyren. The 110 Flamboyant oak stalls★★★ ☉ were created between 1508 and 1519 by the master cabinet-makers Arnould Boulin, Antoine Avernier and Alexandre Huet. They are arranged in two rows and surmounted by wooden tracery, and are presided over by two master-stalls destined for the king and the dean of the chapter. Over 4000 figures on the misericords, stall ends, canopies, pendentives and brackets realistically and spiritedly evoke Genesis and Exodus, the life of the Virgin Mary, scenes of 16C life in Amiens such as craftsmen at work, and comical episodes culled from medieval fables. One worker carved himself holding his mallet (**12**) and inscribed his name: Jehan Turpin.

In the **ambulatory** on the right, on the choir screen above two recumbent effigies, eight remarkable carved and coloured stone groups (1488) under delicate Gothic canopies evoke the **life of St Firmin** (**13**), his martyrdom and his exhumation by St Saul three centuries later. The highly expressive figures are wearing 15C dress: the nobles in sumptuous attire, the humble poorly dressed and the executioner in curious breeches.

Behind the main altar, facing the central chapel containing a 19C gilded statue of the Virgin Mary, are the tomb of Cardinal de la Grange (1402) and the much larger tomb of Canon Guislan Lucas, famous for its **Weeping Angel** (**14**) carved by Nicolas Blasset (1628). In the apsidal chapels vestiges of the 13C stained-glass windows remain.

The choir screen north of the chancel bears scenes from the **life of St John** (**15**) (1531) - read from right to left. Executed with less verve than the scenes of the life of St Firmin, they nevertheless reveal a striking wealth of detail and imagination; the desert is strangely represented as a forest. A quatrefoil shows the arrival of John the Baptist's head (visible in the treasury) in Amiens in 1206.

Trésor ⊘ – The collection was put together in the 19C and 20C; it is housed in the cloisters and a room next to the sacristy. The old treasure disappeared during the Revolution apart from the "face of John the Baptist", displayed on a silver gilt platter.

Among the other treasures, note the three pieces from the abbaye du Paraclet near Amiens: the cross decorated with filigree work and engraved stones (13C), the votive crown and the reliquary vase (14C), as well as St Firmin's reliquary, beautiful 13C Mosan work.

★★MUSÉE DE PICARDIE (BZ)

The building housing the Picardy Museum was constructed between 1855 and 1867 for the Picardy Society of Antiquaries and is an imposing example of Napoleon III architecture.

Basement: archeology

In addition to the Egyptian antiquities (serpentine statuette of Imenhotep) and Ancient Greek exhibits (head of Kuros), the collection includes items uncovered during digs in the region.

St-Acheul, one of the suburbs of Amiens, has given its name to a Paleolithic period, the **Acheulian**. Numerous biface tools were discovered on this site.

Among the objects from the Neolithic period, note the earthenware vase from Belloy-sur-Somme which was used for grinding grain, and a superb double-bladed axe from Renancourt.

During the Bronze Age, metal working developed mainly along the Somme Valley, as is obvious from the excavations carried out in Le Plainseau, a district of Amiens (weapons, axes, jewellery). The Iron Age that followed is illustrated by the reconstruction of the sanctuary in Ribemont-sur-Ancre (ossuaries, weapons).

Remains of the ancient town of **Samarobriva**, which had a population of 20 000 in the 2C, include sections of its baths, forum, amphitheatre and miscellaneous utilitarian objects such as glassware and ceramics.

Albert Roze (1861-1952)

During his 30 years as principal of the Beaux-Arts School in Amiens and his 26 years as director of the Musée de Picardie, Albert Roze remained faithful to his native province. In spite of the fact that his most successful work was Jules Verne's funeral monument, he became famous through two very different effigies, which both represent Picardy: the Golden Virgin of the belfry of Notre-Dame de Brébières in Albert and Marie without a shirt, a half-naked little nymph symbolising spring, which created a scandal when it was inaugurated. It used to be the crowning piece of a clock situated on place Gambetta in Amiens and, after the Second World War, it was placed rue Duvesel by public demand.

Ground floor

Among the many objects representing **medieval art**, note the ivory bookbinding depicting scenes from the life of St Rémi (9C), a whalebone statuette of a horseman (12C) and a large collection of gold and silver plate. The sculptures formerly adorned the cathedral or various churches and abbeys in the region that have been destroyed over the years. There is a grotesque figure *(marmouset)*, a representation of Mary Magdalene from a lost rood screen, the central stone from the labyrinth in Amiens cathedral, the Adam and Eve capital from the former abbey in Corbie, the font from the abbey in Sélincourt, the recumbent figure of Robert de Bouberch from the Franciscan friary in Abbeville, and the Passion altarpiece decorated with rough, unpolished characters from the church in Méharicourt.

In the rotunda, the American artist Sol LeWitt created a mural using Indian ink wash.

In addition to the works by local sculptors Albert Roze *(Head of an Old Woman from Picardy)* and Nicolas Blasset *(Ecce Homo)*, sculpture is represented by 19C Romantic and Realist works including animal bronzes by Barye and Monard, busts by

---

Confrérie du Puy Notre-Dame

This literary and religious society devoted to the glorification of the Virgin Mary was founded in Amiens in 1389. The master of the brotherhood was elected on an annual basis and used to recite his "royal hymn" from a podium or *puy*. The refrain or *palinode* was unusual in that it was a play on words based on the name of the donor who from 1450 onwards, was required to offer to the cathedral a votive painting referring to the theme of the *palinode*.

Elshoecht *(Marguerite)*, Falguière *(Gambetta)*, Dalou *(Reading)* and Rodin *(Puvis de Chavannes)*, and statues by Nanteuil *(Eurydice)* and Dumont *(Love)*.

The Grand Salon contains huge historical paintings (18C-19C) by Van Loo and Vernet.

First floor – Enormous murals by Puvis de Chavannes adorn the main stairway and first-floor rooms. The Notre-Dame du Puy gallery and part of the following room house the works of art of the Confrérie du Puy Notre-Dame d'Amiens.

Some of these paintings on wood have retained their sumptuous frames, fashioned by those who carved the cathedral stalls. François I is recognisable in the panel with a Renaissance canopy (1518) entitled *Au juste pois, véritable balance* ("True scales, just weight"); Henri IV appears under the Gothic canopy bearing the poem entitled *Terre d'où prit la vérité naissance* ('Land where Truth was born") (1601). The remarkable *Virgin with Palm Tree* (1520) in its high openwork wood frame shows the Virgin Mary surrounded by saints and the donors and their family, with Amiens Cathedral in the background.

The Nieuwerkerke gallery presents 17C paintings from the Spanish School (Ribera: *Miracle of St Donatus of Arezzo* and El Greco: *Portrait of a Man*), the Dutch School (Frans Hals: *Portrait of Langelius the Pastor*) and the French School (Simon Vouet: *Repentant Magdalene*).

Subsequent rooms exhibit 18C French painting including works by Oudry, Chardin, Fragonard and Quentin de La Tour, as well as the nine *Chasses en pays étrangers* ("Hunts in Foreign Lands") by Parrocel, Pater, Boucher, Lancret, Van Loo and De Troy for Louis XV's small apartments at Versailles. Italian masters (Guardi, Tiepolo) express the charm of Venetian painting.

The Charles-Dufour gallery is dedicated to 19C French landscape painters and in particular to the Barbizon School (Millet, Isabey, Corot, Rousseau).

Modern art is represented by Balthus, Masson, Fautrier, Dubuffet, Picabia.

ADDITIONAL SIGHTS

Musée d'Art local et d'Histoire régionale (CY M¹) – The **Hôtel de Berny★** was built in 1634 to accommodate the meetings of the treasurers of France, and is a good example of the Louis XIII style with its pink brick bonding and stone trimmings. It derives its name from the last owner, Gérard de Berny (1880-1957), who dedicated himself to creating the refined interior on view today and then bequeathed the building to Amiens as a museum of local art.

The furniture and woodwork come from other residences in the region. The dining room features an immense fireplace attributed to Jean Goujon and elegant 18C panelling which used to adorn the entrance hall of the Château de Grange-Bléneau owned by the Marquis de La Fayette. On the first floor, note the Louis XVI gilded room which came from a local mansion, with furniture from an Abbeville residence, and the panelling from the library of the old abbey at Corbie.

Paintings show Amiens as it used to be, while several portraits present local celebrities: M and Mme Choderlos de Laclos, Jules Verne, Branly and Parmentier, the "inventor" of the potato in France.

Quartier St-Leu

Puppets

Famous for its string puppets dating back to about 1785, Amiens now boasts its own puppet theatre. Known in the Picardy dialect as a **cabotans**, puppets are about 50cm/19in in height, carved out of wood and operated from above. The king of St-Leu (the district existed in medieval times) is **Lafleur**. He is the leader of the cabotans and is undoubtedly the most expressive embodiment of the spirit and character of the Picardy people.

Since the 19C, but arguably from an earlier date, this mythical, truculent, bold, irreverent, and brave character with a fiery temper has expressed plain common sense and described the nobility and pride of the province in the language of his ancestors. Wherever he is, wherever he comes from, and however far away he is, he is always recognisable for his impressive height, his characteristic gait, and most of all, his 18C valet's livery of beautiful red Amiens velvet. He is often accompanied by his wife Sandrine and his friend Tchot Blaise. His motto is "Drink, eat and do nothing".

Lafleur et Sandrine

In the 19C each of the 20 quarters in the city had its own puppet theatre. With the arrival of the cinema and sporting events at the turn of the century, however, the theatres gradually closed down.

After many ups-and-downs, the professional puppeteers of Picardy who manage the theatre known as **Chés Cabontans d'Amiens** have moved into the St-Leu district's old velvet works in Rue Edouard-David. The theatre was founded in 1933 by Maurice Domon and has been directed since 1969 by Françoise Rose. Its aim is to maintain the old traditions.

A puppet workshop *(67 rue du Don, St-Leu district)* enables the public to see a woodcarver at work.

★Hortillonnages (**DY**) – These small vegetable gardens known as **aires** have been worked since the Middle Ages by market gardeners or *hortillons* (from the Latin hortus = garden) who supplied the local population with fruit and vegetables. The gardens stretch over an area of 300ha/740 acres amid a network of canals or **rieux** fed by the many arms of the Somme and Arve rivers. When the canals are dredged, the alluvium fertilises the land which is in danger of reverting to marshland.

At present, fruit trees and flowers are tending to replace vegetables and the gardeners' huts are becoming weekend holiday homes.

The long black punts have a sloping bow called a *cornet* that enables them to berth. They used to transport the produce to the "market-on-the-water". Nowadays, they take visitors through the "floating gardens" amid typical marshland plants (water lilies, reeds, foxtails and arrowhead) and birds (moorhens, coots, crested grebe) and give them a chance to appreciate the tranquillity of their surroundings.

The **"market-on-the-water"** to which the market gardeners come to sell their produce is held every year on the third Sunday in June. In September, the town holds a riverside festival.

The towpath is also a pleasant place for a walk.

Tour Perret (Perret Tower) (CZ) – The reinforced concrete "lookout tower" (26 floors, 104m/340ft high) stands on Place Alphonse-Fiquet. Its architect, **Auguste Perret** (1874-1954), the man who rebuilt Le Havre, was also responsible for the railway station.

Centre de documentation Jules-Verne (CZ M³) – **Jules Verne** (1828-1905) was born in Nantes but he spent much of his life in Amiens where he wrote *Voyages extraordinaires*. He played an active part in local life and was a town councillor. One of his short stories is even entitled *Une ville idéale, Amiens en l'an 2000* ("An Ideal Town, Amiens in the year 2000"). He is buried in the cemetery at La Madeleine, beneath overhanging branches and amid mausoleums. His home, the so-called "house with a tower" provides a vast amount of information (more than 18000 documents) about the writer and his works. It also contains a reconstruction of his study, a number of personal effects, a model of the *Nautilus*, and his portrait in the form of a hologram.

A few of the titles in the Voyages extraordinaires series:

1873	*Around the World in Eighty Days*
1874	*The Mysterious Island*
1876	*Michel Strogoff*
1877	*Les Indes noires*
1879	*Les Tribulations d'un Chinois en Chine*
1886	*Robur le Conquérant*
1892	*Le Château des Carpathes*
1895	*L'Île à hélice*

Cirque municipal (BZ) – The circus was inaugurated in June 1889 by Jules Verne, then a town councillor. It was built to plans by the architect Emile Ricquier and can seat an audience of 3000.

Logis du Roi et Maison du Sagittaire (CY B) – The King's Lodging (1565), featuring a pointed-arch door decorated with a Virgin with a Rose, is the seat of the **Rosati** of Picardy, a society with the motto "Tradition, Art and Literature". The adjacent building is the **Sagittarius House** (1539) with its Renaissance front, which owes its name to the sign of the Zodiac embellishing its two arches.

Old Theatre (CY R) – The Louis XVI façade was the work of Rousseau in 1780; the building now houses a bank. Three large windows are framed by elegant low reliefs depicting garlands, medallions, muses and lyres.

Galerie du Vitrail (CY N) – A master glassmaker, who may be watched working, displays his collection of stained glass including 13C pieces.

Maison de la Culture (BY) – This construction by Sonrel and Dutilleul, supported by a blind tower, presents large glazed façades mounted on piles. It houses large and small theatres (1050 and 300 seats), a 200-seater cinema, two contemporary art galleries, an information centre, a restaurant, and studios belonging to the Centre de Musiques vivantes.

Abbaye des Prémontrés St-Jean (BY F) – The beautiful 17C and 18C classical buildings of the old Premonstratensian abbey dedicated to St John have been restored and now house the University of Amiens. The main courtyard is flanked by two wings at right angles, built of brick and stone. The façade is decorated with a wrought-iron balcony and sculptures.

Bailliage (BY K) – The restored front is all that remains of the bailiff's residence built under François I in 1541, presenting mullioned windows, Flamboyant gables and Renaissance medallions. On the right, note the "fool" wearing a hood with bells.

Bell-tower (BY L) – The enormous bell-tower in Place au Fil consists of a square 15C base and an 18C belfry surmounted by a dome.

Église St-Germain (BY) – The church dedicated to St Germanus was built in Flamboyant Gothic style in the 15C; its tower leans slightly.

*Quartier St-Leu (CY) – Several arms of the Somme flow through this district, which has undergone widescale renovation in an effort to preserve its special charm. Craft and antique shops, cafés and restaurants now occupy the spaces where tanners, millers, weavers and dyers once worked.

From the bridge known as Pont de la Dodane, there is a fine **view** of the cathedral.

A stroll through the streets (rue Bélu, rue des Majots, rue Motte, rue d'Engoulvent) lined with small colourful half-timbered houses gives a feel of the area's discreet charm.

Église St-Leu, a 15C hall-church with three aisles, has a 16C Flamboyant Gothic bell-tower.

Pont du Cange (CY 15), a bridge built during the reign of Louis-Philippe, leads to **place Parmentier** where a "riverside market" is held on Saturday mornings.

Take the Baraban footbridge to the new **Parc St-Pierre** and its landscaped gardens.

Parc zoologique (Zoo) (AX) – The zoo is pleasantly located by the **Promenade de la Hôtoie**, laid out in the 18C, and its lake. The lawns are encircled by branches of the River Selle where swans, pelicans, cranes and pink flamingoes flutter. The zoo proper features giraffes, lions, panthers, elephants...

EXCURSIONS

Sains-en-Amiénois – *9km/5.6mi south along D 7.* The **church** contains a 13C **tomb** and recumbent effigies of St Fuscien and his companions, Victoric and Gentien, who were martyred in the 4C; below, a bas-relief portrays their decapitation.

Boves – *11km/6.8mi by ③ on the town plan.* The **ruins** of the 12C castle overlook this small town, which from 1630 was the seat of a marquess. Road D 167 leads to the grassy courtyard, and from there to the motte bearing two imposing sections of wall from the keep.

From the top there is an extensive **view:** south over the lakes of Fouencamps, north to Amiens.

Conty – *22km/14mi south by D 210 then right onto D 920.* **Église St-Antoine** is a 15C and 16C church in a unified Flamboyant style; its right side offers a curious row of projecting gargoyles. The tower is crowned with a pyramid-shaped roof, like the collegiate church in Picquigny, and bears traces of cannonballs dating from the 1589 siege of Conty by the Catholic League; in the corner, a statue of St Anthony the hermit. On the left of the west front, steps lead down to St Anthony's fountain.

ARRAS★★

Conurbation 79 607
Michelin map 53 fold 2 or 236 fold 15

Arras, the capital of the Artois region, hides its little-known artistic beauties behind a serious, reserved appearance. The city, a religious, military and administrative centre, is surrounded by boulevards that replaced the old Vauban-like fortifications. Chitterling sausages *(andouillettes)* and chocolate hearts are the local gastronomic specialities.

HISTORICAL NOTES

Influence in the Middle Ages – The Roman town of Nemetacum, capital of the Atrebates, was founded on the slopes of Baudimont hill, which is still known as La Cité today. In the Middle Ages the town developed around the Benedictine abbey of St Vaast, forming the district known as La Ville. From that time on, Arras grew from being a grain market and the centre of woollen cloth manufacture to being a cradle of art, patronised by bankers and rich Arras burghers.

In terms of literature, the town is famous for its troubadours *(trouvères)* such as Gautier d'Arras, **Jean Bodel**, author of *Le Jeu de saint Nicolas*, and above all the 13C **Adam de la Halle** who brought dramatic art to Arras with his play *Le Jeu de la Feuillée*. From 1384 the manufacture of high-warp tapestries, under the patronage of the dukes of Burgundy, brought Arras widespread fame – and the word *arras* passed into English to indicate a tapestry wall-hanging.

It was at this time that the workshops in Arras, competing with those in Tournai, made delightfully realistic hangings, such as the *Life of St Piat and St Éleuthère* (1402) which today hangs in Tournai Cathedral.

Youth of "The Incorruptible" – **Maximilien de Robespierre**, whose father was an Artois Council barrister, was born in Arras in 1758. Orphaned at an early age, the young man went to school in Arras from 1765 to 1769; as the *protégé* of the bishop, he

Grand'Place

received a scholarship to attend the Louis-le-Grand School in Paris. Robespierre became a barrister on his return to Arras, pleading most notably for a citizen of St Omer accused of having put a lightning rod on the roof of his house.

Not only accepted by the Arras Academy but also affiliated with the **Rosati** (an anagram of "Artois") poetic society, Robespierre met Carnot, who was garrisoned in Arras at the time, and Fouché, a schoolteacher. During this period the pale young man, later the spirited leader of the Revolution, courted young ladies for whom he wrote verse. In Arras Robespierre knew **Joseph Lebon** (1765-1795), a member of the Oratorian order who was mayor of the town during the Reign of Terror. During this time the former priest presided over the destruction of many churches and regulary sent aristocrats and rich farmers to the guillotine set up in Place du Théâtre. Lebon himself was later to perish under the blade in Amiens.

Arras and the Battles of Artois – During the First World War, the front was until 1917 constantly near Arras which suffered heavy shelling as a result. The most violent conflicts took place in the strategically-important hills north of the town. After the Battle of the Marne the retreating Germans fought to hold on to them, their backs to the rich coal basin, clinging to Vimy Ridge and the slopes of Notre-Dame-de-Lorette Hill. In the autumn of 1914 they emerged to attack Arras, but were stopped after battles at Ablain-St-Nazaire, Carency and La Targette.

In May and June 1915 General Foch, in command of the French forces in the north, attempted to pierce the German ranks; his troops took Neuville St-Vaast and Notre-Dame-de-Lorette. The attack failed at Vimy, however, which was won only in 1917, by the Canadians.

★★★ MAIN SQUARES *1hr*

The two main squares in Arras, the theatrical-looking Grand'Place and place des Héros, which are joined by the short rue de la Taillerie, are extremely impressive. They existed as early as the 11C but have undergone many transformations through the centuries. Today's magnificent façades are remarkable examples of 17C and 18C Flemish architecture. The local council of the period was careful to control the town's development, permitting citizens to construct only "in stone or brick, with no projecting architectural elements". The houses in these squares, though of different heights and widths, décor and details, form a rhythmical whole: this is largely due to the consistent use of walls laid in brick and stone; pilasters and ties; scrolled gables and curvilinear pediments. The façades, formerly embellished with carved shop-signs, a few of which remain, rest on monolith-columned arcades which protected market stallholders and customers alike from inclement weather.

Today the squares hold their colourful market on Saturdays. As evening comes they take on a different charm when the gables, discreetly floodlit, stand out against the night sky. Although badly damaged during the First World War, the squares have undergone extensive restoration with impressive results.

The **Grand'Place** covers an area of 2ha/5 acre. The moderate height of the surrounding houses emphasises the vastness of this open space, empty except on market days.

The oldest house, dating from the 15C *(no 49, north side)*, has three Gothic arches surmounted by a great corbie-stepped gable *(see illustration in ABC of architecture)*.

The smaller and livelier of the two squares, **place des Héros**, is surrounded by shops and overlooked by the belfry. Note the shop signs at no 9, The Three Cockerels; no 11, The Mermaid; no 15, The Admiral; no 17, The Salamander; no 23, The Unicorn; and no 62, The Whale.

*Hôtel de ville and belfry ⊘ **(BY H)** – The town hall was destroyed in 1914 and rebuilt in the Flamboyant style. The beautiful front, with its uneven arches, stands on the western side of place des Héros and the graceful 75m/246ft belfry rises over the more severe-looking Renaissance wings.

On the ground floor, the Gothic-vaulted lower room called the **Guard-room** displays the giant town mascots, Colas and Jacqueline, together with chilling photographs of Arras in ruins in 1918.

Upstairs, the **Banqueting Hall** offers a view of the square through eight Flamboyant bays. A fresco by **Hoffbauer** which recalls Breughel's style runs above the carved wainscot; it describes daily life in 16C Arras (notice the 12C cathedral from which a procession issues; the building was destroyed in 1799).

From the top of the belfry *(take the lift in the basement then walk up 43 steps)*, the view embraces the squares, the town and the surroundings. The cathedral's 40 bells are also visible.

Downstairs, an audio-visual presentation on the history of Arras is an excellent introduction to the town. The tour of the underground passages starts here.

Circuit des souterrains ⊘ – *In the basement of the town hall.*
As early as the 10C galleries were cut into the limestone bank on which the town stands. Since then a complex network has been created, consisting of vast rooms supported by sandstone pillars, recessed staircases leading from one level to another (up to 13m/42ft difference), corridors etc. This "underground city" has served as a refuge in times of trouble, a shelter during wars (during the First World War the British set up a field hospital here) and above all as an enormous wine cellar, as the famous **caves** *(boves)* are at the ideal temperature for storing wine.

★★ANCIENNE ABBAYE ST-VAAST (BY) *1hr*

The old abbey was founded in the 7C by St Aubert on the hill overlooking a tributary of the Scarpe River, and was entrusted with the relics of the first bishop of Arras. **Cardinal de Rohan**, commendatory abbot, began reconstructing the abbey buildings in 1746 in a style combining balance and elegance to produce an austere sense of beauty; they were deconsecrated during the Revolution, then restored after 1918. They stand to the right of the cathedral. The gardens offer

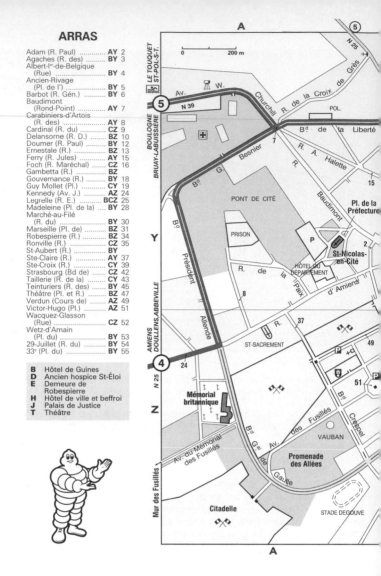

a view across to the austere west front. The porch of the main entrance (in place de la Madeleine), surmounted by the abbey's arms, opens into the elegant main courtyard. The central part of the abbey, straight ahead, contains the museum; wings to the side house the library, multimedia library and offices.

★ **Musée des Beaux-Arts** ⊘ – The **Italian Room** (**1**) decorated with the original lions from the belfry (1554) in Arras is used as a reception area. The tour begins in a series of small rooms on the left (**2** and **3**) containing the Gallo-Roman archaeology collection bronze bust of Bacchus, porphyry statue of Attis from a 2-3C sanctuary in honour of Attis and Cybele (bearing witness to the influence of Near Eastern religions carried abroad by the army and merchants), cinerary urns from the burial grounds in Baralle, remains of paintings, and coinage from Beaurains. There are models of the *fanum* (a rural sanctuary built to a central layout) in Duisans, a Germanic sanctuary, and a Theodosian barracks. The galleries around the small cloister, known as the Cour du Puits, contain some fine medieval sculptures and paintings including

14C funerary mask – Musée des Beaux-Arts

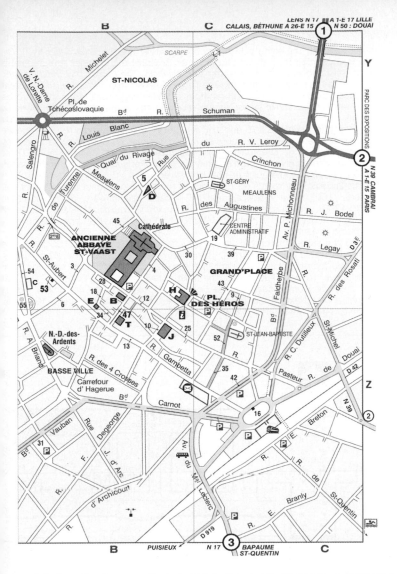

capitals from the former cathedral, Bishop Frumauld's Romanesque tombstone (12C) and the delightful 13C **angels of Saudémont***, whose twinkling almond-shaped eyes and slight smiles indicate that they were the work of a master craftsman. The 14C is represented by a delicately carved female **funerary mask**, a *Virgin and Child* by Pépin de Huy, and the remarkable gravestone of the Sacquespée family. A tapestry made in Arras, depicting a scene from the legend of St Vaast (St Vaast and the Bear), wooden statues of St George and St Sebastian and a recumbent figure of Guillaume Lefranchois in the form of a skeleton (1446) all date from the 15C while the 16C is illustrated by triptychs by Bellegambe *(Christ with his Torturers, Adoration of the Christ Child)* and an *Entombment* by Vermeyen.

Note the harmonious proportions of the **refectory** at the east end. A tapestry bearing the arms of Cardinal de Rohan hangs above the great marble fireplace.

The spacious main cloister, which used to lead through a peristyle into the minster, contains capitals carved with garlands and rosettes.

The staircase is decorated with a fine series of paintings by Giovanni Baglioni (1571-1644) entitled *Apollo and seven Muses*. It used to hang in the gallery of the Palais du Luxembourg in Paris until Rubens took charge.

The **first floor** is given over to paintings from the 16C to 18C. The small rooms on the front of the building contain works by the 17C and 18C French school such as the *Martyrdom of St Matthew* (1617) by Claude Vignon, the first work painted by the artist in Rome and indicative of Caravaggio's influence, the *Portrait of P de Montesquiou* by Nicolas de Largillière, *Dogs Fighting over Their Prey* (1632) and *The Death of the Children of Bethel* (1653) by Laurent de La Hyre.

The other rooms contain 18C works by Boullongne, Vien, a fine neo-classical *Aspasie* by Marie Geneviève Bouliar and works by the local artist Dominique Doncre.

In the **gallery** on the south side of the small cloister are the *Fruit Seller* by P Van
Boucle, a painting from the studio of Pieter Brueghel the Younger (the original is
in Brussels) showing *The Numbering at Bethlehem*, *The Parrot*, *Jay*, *Bullfinch* and
Chaffinch by Adriaen Van Utrecht, *The Three Angels at Abraham's House* by Barent
Fabritius, who studied with Rembrandt, as is evident in the use of the same bronze
tones and *St Francis of Assisi* shown receiving the stigmata, an early work by
Rubens.

The east gallery contains 17C and 18C sculptures. It leads into the recently opened
Salle des Mays de Notre-Dame, a room so-named because it contains huge works by
La Hyre, Philippe de Champaigne *(The Birth of the Virgin)* and Jouvenet. These
works used to be given to Notre-Dame Church in Paris every springtime between
1603 and 1707 by the guild of gold and silversmiths .

On the **2nd floor**, the rooms on the front of the building contain the ceramics collections: 16C Italian majolica, mid-17C glazed earthenware, Arras porcelain
(1770-1790) and more especially porcelain made in Tournai (18-19C) decorated
with light, delicate motifs (note the "Buffon bird dinner service" commissioned by
the Duc d'Orléans in 1787).

Around the small cloister are works by various schools of early 19C landscape
artists: Barbizon, Lyon and Arras. The paintings are by Corot *(The Woodcutters
Wives, Mortefontaine)* and Constant Dutilleux *(Woodland Path)*. One spacious room
is given over to large 19C works, the most noteworthy being Delacroix' *Disciples
and the Holy Women Carrying the Body of St Stephen* and Chassériau's *Young
Shepherd Boy*. Next to this room is the Salle Louise-Weiss containing 19C small
paintings by Monticelli, Ribot and Ravier.

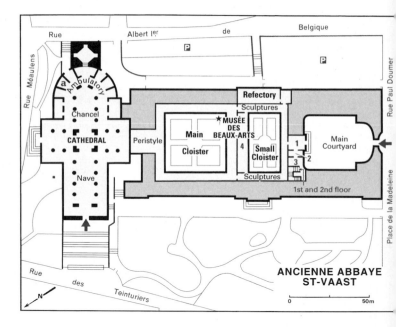

Cathédrale ⊘ (**BY**) – The old abbey church of St Vaast was built according to
plans prepared by Contant d'Ivry in the 18C. It was finished in 1833 and elevated
to a cathedral, to replace Notre-Dame-de-la-Cité.

The Classical façade is graced by a monumental flight of steps; the luminous interior
presents an Antique splendour. A line of lofty columns bearing Corinthian capitals
flanks the nave, transept and chancel. Enormous 19C statues of saints, from the
Pantheon in Paris, adorn the side aisles.

In the ambulatory's second chapel stands the beautiful 17C **Christ Bound** (**a**); the fourth
chapel contains the kneeling figures of Philippe de Torcy (1652) and his wife. The
right transept is decorated with large frescoes, in which St Vaast may be seen taming
a bear. To each side of the altar is a *Nativity* and a *Resurrection* by Desvallières.

ADDITIONAL SIGHTS

Place du Théâtre (**BZ 47**) – It was in this lively square that the guillotine stood
during the darkest hours of the Revolution. The **theatre** (**BZ T**) dates from 1784
(though its façade is restored), and was built where the fish market once stood;
it faces the **Ostel des Poissonniers** (1710), a narrow Baroque house carved with sea
gods and mermaids.

In rue des Jongleurs, note the majestic 18C **Hôtel de Guines** (**BY B**); at no 9 rue Robespierre (**BY E**) the former residence of the famous revolutionary may be seen.

Palais de Justice (**BZ J**) – The Law Courts, the former seat of the Artois government (1701), is embellished with Corinthian pilasters, while its side entrance (1724) is decorated with Regency shells.

Place du Wetz-d'Amain (**BY 53**) – The square is graced by a pretty Renaissance house, to which a Classical stone porch was added later. It served as refuge to the monks of Mont St-Éloi.

Place de l'Ancien-Rivage (**BY 5**) – The square-turreted house (**D**) was the former St-Éloi hospice, founded in 1635 by one of the town's goldsmiths.

Basse-ville (**BZ**) – This district lies between the town and the citadel. It is arranged regularly around the lovely, octagonal **place Victor-Hugo** (**AZ 51**), built in 1756.

Église Notre-Dame-des-Ardents safeguards fragments of the Holy Taper. This miraculous candle was entrusted by the Virgin Mary to two minstrels, to cure ergotic poisoning in the 12C. The silver reliquary is to the left of the high altar, in a latticed recess *(lighting below, to the right)*.

A **stele** has been erected along **Promenade des Allées** (**AZ**), under a peristyle decked with roses. It honours the Rosati and depicts a marquess and a 20C man watching a procession of muses.

Citadel ⊘ (**AZ**) – This pentagonal-shaped citadel, built to plans by **Vauban** between 1668 and 1672, is encircled by a grassy moat. It was built less to protect the town from Spanish troops than to keep a watch on the inhabitants, and its nickname was "The Great Useless". Today it is occupied by an Army regiment.

The tour takes in a model of the citadel, the old arsenal and the Baroque Chapelle St Louis.

Mur des Fusillés – *Access by the road between the memorial and the citadel.* Plaques line one of the bastions southwest of the fort, in memory of the Resistance members martyred here.

Mémorial britannique (**AZ**) – *Access by boulevard Charles-de-Gaulle.* The British memorial was erected in memory of the many British soldiers lost in the Battles of Artois (1914-18).

Place de la Préfecture (**AY**) – This square was the heart of medieval Arras. Today the *préfecture* (county council) occupies the former bishop's palace, finished in 1780. The 19C **Église St-Nicolas-en-Cité** ⊘ rises on the site of Notre-Dame-de-la-Cité cathedral, which was destroyed by angry mobs after the Revolution. It houses a triptych depicting *The Climb to Calvary*, painted in 1577 by P Claessens of Bruges.

Parc ASTÉRIX★★

Michelin map 106 fold 9

Access from Paris: – *By car: A 1 motorway, exit "Parc Astérix". By train: RER line B to Roissy-Charles-de-Gaulle, then by shuttle bus to the park.*

Asterix the Gaul, hero of the famous cartoon strip by Goscinny and Uderzo known throughout the world and translated into several languages, provides the theme for this 50ha/123 acre fun park; it is a fantasy world for all ages which offers a journey into the past

TOUR ⊘ *allow a day*

The park presents carefully reconstructed "historical" sections, various attractions, shows and audio-visual displays and offers a choice of snacks and meals (**Halte des Chevaliers, Fastes de Rome**...).

Via Antiqua – Situated at the entrance to the park, this "street" is lined with houses symbolising, through their architecture, Asterix' various journeys across Europe (Germany, Helvetica, Hispania etc.). It leads to a huge rock from which the popular hero greets visitors.

Gaule Antique – The very heart of this area is the Village d'Astérix, a veritable Gallic village consisting of huts, where visitors can meet such well-known figures as Obelix with his menhirs, Panoramix, Assurancetourix the bard in his hut perched in the tree-tops. Here and there are fights, festivities or hunting scenes. The **Balade d'Astérix** reveals a few strange scenes and a tour of the **Forêt des Druides** attracts young and not so young visitors alike. Nearby, the atmosphere is much damper at the **Grand Splatch**.

But the most popular site is a Stone Age village built on piles, which gets its wealth from the production of menhirs. An ingenious delivery system called **Menhir Express**★★ takes anybody who dares on a trip through a network of canals bristling with surprises!

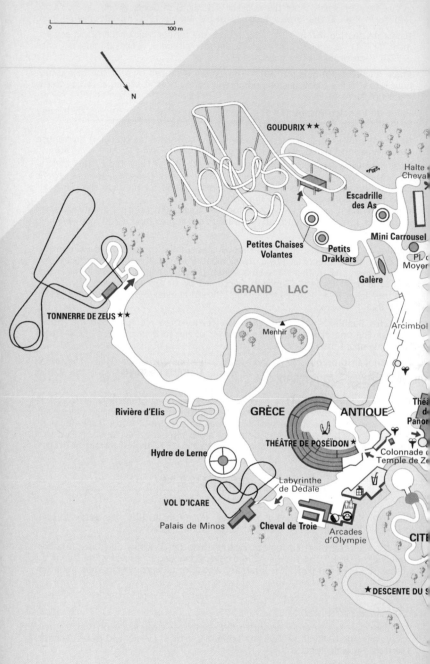

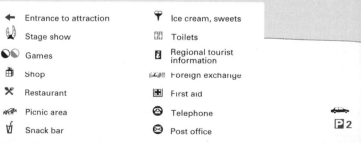

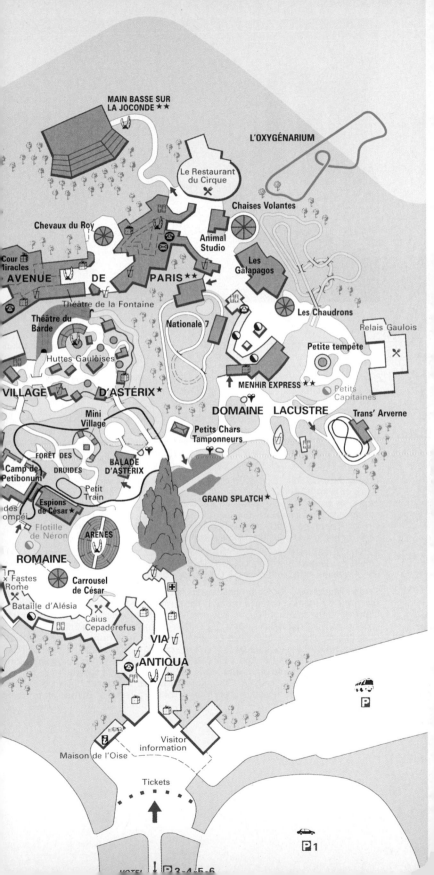

Descente du Styx

Grèce Antique – The entrance to this part of the park is marked by the colonnade from the Temple of Zeus. The **Vol d'Icare** (Icarus' flight) takes visitors out of Daedalus' labyrinth but only after defeating the terrible **Hydre de Lerne** or incurring the wrath of the gods by taking a ride on the impressive **Tonnerre de Zeus★★** (top speed 80kph/50mph) can you enjoy a well-earned rest along the **Rivière d'Elis** or with the dolphins in the **Théâtre de Poséidon★**.

Empire Romain – In the arena are terrible fights between gladiators and some amazing circus acts performed by the **Stars de l'Empire**. If you wish to know what is afoot in the Gallic village, join the **Espions de César★** (Caesar's spies) who have devised a very efficient surveillance system (5m/16ft above ground level).
And why not brave Hell itself by trying the **Descente du Styx★**?

Moyen Âge – A long journey in time takes place along **Avenue de Paris★★**. Ten centuries of history are illustrated here, each period represented by people in costume, typical shops and its own special atmosphere. The Middle Ages relive through street entertainers, glassmakers and potters living and working in dark, mysterious streets. There are interesting demonstrations of ancient crafts and a strange carnival regularly livens up the medieval square.

17C – To illustrate this colourful period, the king's **musketeers** confront the Cardinal's musketeers in a seemingly endless series of pitiless duels. Artistic and literary life is remembered, too, through **La Fontaine's fables**.

Temps Modernes – Going on holiday has not always been plain sailing as you can see from the numerous adventures to be encountered along the **Nationale 7** main highway to the south of France. However, it may not be necessary to leave for the country as the **Oxygénarium** (a new 1999 attraction) has been specially designed to offer city-dwellers the combined benefits of water and fresh mountain air: guaranteed thrills! More excitement is round the corner with **Goudurix★**, a gigantic roller coaster taking visitors through a succession of vertiginous drops, swooping round corners, and going into spins and loops, all at breathtaking speed.
This trip through time ends in 1930, in **Main basse sur la Joconde★**, a splendid enactment of a historical detective story during which a gang of thieves attempts to steal the Mona Lisa.

Michelin Maps are updated constantly.
Always travel with the latest edition.

AUVERS-SUR-OISE★

Population 6 129
Michelin map 106 fold 6

This village stretches over 7km/4.5mi from the River Oise to the escarpment edging the Vexin plateau. The old path, now a series of narrow streets winding their way from Valhermeil to Cordeville, still carries the memory of the artists who brought it fame. Here and there, panels indicate the scenes portrayed by Impressionist painters. It is the district around the church, however, which constitutes the favourite "place of pilgrimage" for art lovers.

Doctor **Paul Gachet** (1828-1909) moved to Auvers in 1872, although he retained his surgery in Paris. An enthusiastic painter and engraver, with an unquenchable thirst for novelty and an extremely wide and varied medical experience — in epidemics, war wounds and mental disorders — he was the centre of attraction for a new generation of painters, known as the "Impressionists" *(see p 52)* who came to stay and paint locally.

The 1870s were therefore an exciting period for a great many artists who were stimulated by Pissarro's presence at Pontoise. Cézanne's talent blossomed during his three visits to Auvers and Pontoise (1873, 1877 and 1881), when he painted about a hundred canvases, working both outdoors and in the doctor's studio. In May 1890 **Van Gogh** was invited here by Paul Gachet. The doctor-cum-artist managed to calm his guest for a while by encouraging him to throw himself into work but this state of well-being was only a brief interlude: overcome by another bout of madness and guilt over his financial dependence on his brother Theo, Van Gogh shot himself in an open field and died in his room at the Ravoux inn on 29 July 1890.

SIGHTS

Church – The best view of the church is from the back of the terrace, near the east end. The well-proportioned chancel and 12C bell-tower were depicted by Van Gogh in one of his expressive paintings, now in the Orsay Museum in Paris.
A bust portraying the painter Charles-François Daubigny stands at the foot of the church.

Monument de Van Gogh – In the Van Gogh Park located in rue du Général-de-Gaulle. Van Gogh's statue is the work of the sculptor Ossip Zadkine.

Van Gogh's grave – The famous Dutch painter is buried in the cemetery that lies on the plateau *(follow the road behind the church)*. His tomb stands against the left hand wall. His brother Theo, who gave

Church at Auvers by Van Gogh (Musée d'Orsay, Paris)

Musée d'Orsay, Paris /EDIMEDIA

him moral support all his life and who died soon after him, rests by his side. **View** of Auvers' bell-tower.

★**Maison de Van Gogh** ⊘ – This is actually the **Auberge Ravoux**, an inn made famous by the celebrated artist who stayed there several months before his tragic death. It has been carefully restored and has retained its interior decoration and its sector of activity *(local cuisine and wines)*. Outside are panels describing the artist's eventful life. The small garret he occupied has remained unchanged and, despite the absence of furniture, gives some insight into the aescetic conditions under which he lived *(tours restricted to five visitors at a time because of the lack of space)*. The tour ends with a moving audio-visual presentation illustrating Van Gogh's stay in Auvers.

Musée de l'Absinthe ⊘ – The famous green liqueur reached the peak of its popularity in the cafés of the 19C. It was often described as the **"green muse"** and was closely linked to the life of the artists of the day who spent a great deal of time in cafés. The documents, posters and objects displayed in the museum bring back to life the history of a drink which had a profound social influence until it was banned in 1915.

Stopover

OUR SELECTION

Auberge Ravoux – Opposite the town hall. ☎ 01 30 36 60 60. Closed Sunday evenings and Monday lunchtime. Van Gogh once lived here and the restaurant has retained its artist-café tradition. It is advisable to book well in advance as the number of places is limited. Fixed menu: 180 F.

Maison-Atelier de Daubigny – **Charles-François Daubigny** (1817-1878), the landscape painter, settled in Auvers on the advice of his friend Camille Corot. He had studio-house built in 1860 and asked his family and friends to take part in the interior decoration. Charles, his son Karl and his daughter Cécile as well as Corot and Daumier left a mark of their artistic inspiration on the walls or the doors. Charles Daubigny decorated his daughter's childhood bedroom with panels depicting some of Perrault's tales (Tom Thumb and Little Red Riding Hood), which express his deep love for her.

Daubigny loved to paint on the River Oise, aboard a small boat specially designed. Later on, Monet followed his example (note the boat in the garden). In 1890, Van Gogh painted Daubigny's garden and, in his last letter to his borther Theo, he gives details about the colours he chose for the painting and asks his advice.

Château d'Auvers – This 17C château, which has been restored and laid out with extensive use of audio-visual presentations, offers visitors a chance to enjoy a **"Journey Back to the Days of the Impressionists"★** ⊘ and gain some insight into the wonderful adventure that was Art in the 19C. Using reconstructions of interiors and the projection of some 500 works, it brings to life the Paris of the time, a city undergoing immense change thanks to the work of Baron Haussmann, and a city where the wealthy middle classes led a bustling, frivolous life with little appreciation of the new style of painting.

Although some of the artists fed on the capital's atmosphere for their works (Degas, Toulouse-Lautrec), most of them preferred to travel on the brand-new railway from Paris to the seaside in search of new sources of inspiration. They found it in the open-air bars (guinguettes) in Asnières and Chatou, along the banks of the Seine and the Oise (Argenteuil, Vétheuil, Auvers-sur-Oise etc.), in the lush countryside of the Paris basin (haystacks by Monet and Thornley), in the sea, the harbours (Le Havre), the cliffs (Étretat) and the beaches.

The Impressionists have left many other reminders of their stay in Auvers. Spend a day here to take a peak at the home of Dr Gachet and the Maison du Pendu immortalised by Cézanne. The surrounding area is full of scenic beauty, thanks to the vast fields of corn that so inspired the artists.

Use the map in the "brochure-pass" issued at the Maison Van Gogh to locate the various sites with ease.

L'AVESNOIS★★

Michelin map 53 folds 6, 7 or 236 fold 29

The Avesnois region, which lies south of Maubeuge and extends along the Belgian border, is known for its undulating countryside of orchards, woodlands and pastures dotted with black-and-white heras of Friesians and its pretty villages of brick, slate and stone.

The **Helpe Majeure River** (58km/36mi long) drains the area, making its way through the Ardennes shale, outcrops of which can be seen downstream from Eppe-Sauvage.

The vast forests and the cluster of lakes around Liessies and Trélon are traces of a period when the great abbeys – Maroilles, Liessies and St-Michel – dominated the region, constructing mills and forges on every river. Some of the local churches contain works of art from these abbeys.

Many small industries developed in the 18C and 19C: glassmaking at Sars-Poteries, Trélon and Anor, wood turning at Felleries, spinning at Fourmies, marble quarrying at Cousoire etc.

Today the museums at Sars-Poteries, Felleries, Trélon and Fourmies recall the time when the region was highly populated and active.

The Avesnois area forms part of the Parc naturel régional du Nord-Pas-de-Calais.

AVESNES TO FOURMIES 70km/43mi – about 4hr

It is advisable to follow this itinerary in the afternoon, when the museums are open.

Avesnes-sur-Helpe – The quiet town which gave the region its name stands on the south bank of the river; it has preserved some of its Vauban-like fortifications. From March to September 1918 the German army's Chief of Staff, **Hindenburg**, with his deputy Ludendorff, set up his headquarters here. **Place du Général-Leclerc** is the town's main square, surrounded by old houses with high slate roofs. It was here that in June 1918 Kaiser Wilhelm II reviewed his troops, which included Jenny, the famous elephant mobilised by the Germans to move logs for trench shelters. A graceful onion dome tops the 60m/197ft belfry-porch of **Église St-Nicolas** (1534). Inside the hall-church there are two monumental Louis XV altarpieces with paintings by Louis Watteau. A double staircase with wrought-iron balustrades fronts the 18C Classical **town hall** in blue Tournai stone. **Square de la Madeleine** (*behind the church*) provides a bird's-eye view of the Helpe Valley.

Leave Avesnes by D 133 (east) towards Liessies.

Just outside Avesnes there is a good view (*right*) of the town's beautiful surroundings and its ramparts.

At Sémeries turn right onto D 123 towards Etrœung, then left onto D 951.

Sains-du-Nord – The **Maison du Bocage** ⊙, a branch of the Fourmies-Trélon Folk museum, has been established in a farm. Exhibitions present life and work in the woodlands and pastures of the Avesnois (stock farming, cheese-making etc).

Take D 80 to Ramousies.

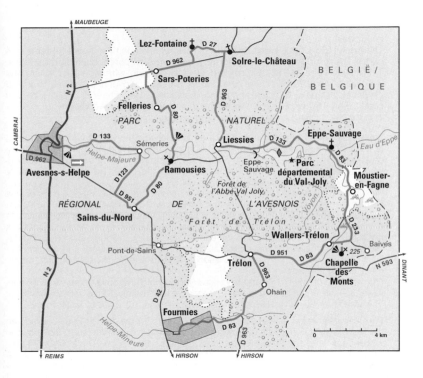

Ramousies – The 16C **church** ⊙ contains two beautiful Renaissance altarpieces, from Antwerp workshops, which once belonged to Liessies Abbey. One depicts the life of St Sulpice; the other represents the Passion.
The 13C crucifix was from the oldest calvary in northern France.

Continue along D 80 to Felleries.

On leaving the village there is a lovely **view** of the region.

Felleries – Since the 17C the town's inhabitants have specialised in *bois-joli*: turned wood and cooperage. These workshops developed at the same time as the textile industry, the former making bobbins and spindles for the latter.

Musée des Bois-Jolis ⊙ – This museum, housed in a 16C water mill, brings together a wide variety of treen (wooden) items made in Felleries: butter moulds, salt boxes, spindles, tops etc.

Sars-Poteries – Since the 15C the earth around Sars has been used by potters, and many small pottery workshops exist locally although larger factories specialising in pipes, ducts etc. have all closed. In the 19C, two glassworks were set up specialising in dinner services and bottles. In 1900, they employed a work force of 800 but by 1938 the economic slump forced them to close.

★ Musée-Atelier du Verre ⊘ – Housed in the former home of the glassworks manager, this museum boasts an unusual collection of popular glassware made by the workers for their own use. The pieces were nicknamed *bousillés* (meaning "made after working hours") and they enabled the workers to make full use of their talent, artistry and imagination.

There are highly ornate engraved lamps, large dishes, "revenge inkwells" (so named because the glass workers did not know how to write but they had the most beautiful inkwells), strange "Passion bottles" containing representations of the instruments of Christ's Passion (these bottles were taken on pilgrimages to Notre-Dame de Liesse) and a range of miscellaneous objects. As a result of local digs, the museum has built up a collection of grey-sandstone objects with glazed cobalt-blue decoration (17C and 18C).

In association with the glass workshop, the museum welcomes international artists and, by doing so, extends its contemporary glass collection.

The **watermill** ⊘ north of the village was built in 1780 and still contains its great wheel and workings.

Take D 962 east, then turn left.

Lez-Fontaine – In the 15C church the wooden vaults are decorated with paintings dating from 1531.

Solre-le-Château – The seigneurial château no longer exists but there are still many 17C and 18C houses. The sober Renaissance **town hall** (late 16C) has an austere bell-tower.

The lovely 16C Gothic **church** is made of local blue stone. The powerful **belfry** was part of the fortifications; its base forms a most unusual porch, open on three sides. The mauve spire (1612) is crowned by a large bulb with openings where the watchman stood. Inside there is a double transept, wooden barrel-vaulting with carved tie-beams in the nave and diagonal vaulting in the chancel. The church also contains an 18C organ, 16C stained glass and Renaissance woodwork.

From Solre-le-Château, take D 963 south towards Liessies.

Liessies – The village originated with an 8C Benedictine abbey which had exclusive use of the surrounding woods. The monks drained the boggy marshlands by creating ponds for breeding fish. The abbey prospered and by the 17C the abbots were powerful lords, but the Revolution led to the break up of the 13C abbey church and the monastic buildings.

The abbey park, situated near the church, is open to the public. Several trails enable visitors to discover the local fauna and flora as well as former monastic buildings. Summer exhibitions are organised in the church and in the Bûcher aux Moines (inside the park). The 16C parish **church** stands near the site of the old abbey. It contains beautiful 15C to 18C statues and remnants of the abbey, including a precious Romanesque cross of gilded copper decorated with chased enamelwork and gemstones. Just outside the village, the 18C **Château de la Motte** was formerly a monks' retirement home; it is now a hotel.

From Liessies follow D 133 and the Helpe Valley, which becomes more winding, narrower and wilder, while its undulating slopes are increasingly dotted with thick woods. The waters of the River Helpe (originally Eppe) used to operate small forges.

★ Parc départemental du Val-Joly – The construction of the dam at Eppe-Sauvage on the Helpe Majeure created a magnificent 180ha/445-acre reservoir surrounded by the wooded banks of the River Helpe and its tributary, the Voyon. The 200ha/494-acre park has many leisure facilities including swimming, tennis, sailing, fishing, riding, footpaths and cycle tracks, archery, and boat or pedalo hire. There is also an arboretum, an aquarium, and a pike-breeding centre. The park includes a campsite and catering facilities. An old farm has been converted to hold exhibitions on the region.

Eppe-Sauvage – This village, close to the Belgian border, nestles in a pretty location in the hollow of a basin formed where the Helpe and the Eau d'Eppe rivers meet. In **Église St-Ursmar**, with its 16C chancel and transept, there are two remarkable 16C painted wood triptychs. One is dedicated to the Virgin Mary, the other to St Ursmar of Lobbes, patron saint of the Hainaut region.

After Eppe-Sauvage, the valley opens out and becomes less wooded; marshes, called *fagnes*, are frequent along its floor. A beautiful manor farm may be seen.

Moustier-en-Fagne – This small village derives its name from a 16C priory, or *moustier*, which was a daughter-house of Lobbes Abbey. Olivetan Benedictines, who devote themselves to painting icons, live in the monks' quarters. They are near the **church** dedicated to St Dodon, the hermit invoked for back ailments, who was originally from this village. A handsome **manor house** is visible *(left)* on entering Moustier-en-Fagne. Known as the Spanish House *(Maison Espagnole)*, it was built of brick and stone in 1560 in a Gothic style: its features include a crow-stepped gable and an ogee arch over its door, ornamented by two angels bearing a crown.

Continue south and, 2km/1mi beyond Moustier, fork left onto D 283, then turn right.

The top of a knoll (225m/738ft high) affords a clear **view** of **Trélon Forest** (about 4 000ha/10 000 acres) and the Helpe Valley.

Chapelle des Monts – *15min on foot over wild heath.*
This 18C chapel is surrounded by a grassy terrace and age-old lime trees. The quarries and lime kiln date from the 19C.

Wallers-Trélon – Built entirely in blue stone, this beautiful village owes its unique appearance to the numerous quarries nearby.

Nature trails allow visitors to discover the unusual flora of the **Monts de Baives**, which flourishes owing to the chalky soil.

Blue-stone oratories

Blue-stone oratories have been built in the Avesnois and Thiérache regions since 1550; they are located in various places, mostly on the roadside, but also in fields, along ancient footpaths and even in woods or set in walls. These characteristic constructions consist of a narrow shaft surmounted by a fine recess, closed off by wire mesh as in Le Favril or Dimont, and a larger crowning piece. Each recess was intended to hold one or several polychrome statues carved by the clog-makers of Mormal Forest. The oratories were erected for various reasons: in thanksgiving for a cure (as in Bérelles), to ask for a favour, one of the most common reasons (in Bas-Lieu, for instance, St Leonard was asked to help children who were late in starting to walk, in Wignehies, on the other hand, favours were asked of St John), to protect a village from an epidemic (the cholera epidemic in Maresches in 1849), to assert a certain social status (the oratory in Hestrud was payed for in 1758 by François Patou), to abide by a family tradition (as did the Mary family in Cartignies). The Avesnois region is said to possess more than 700 blue-stone oratories including some 40 of them in the village of Cartignies alone.

Take D 83 south; turn right onto D 951 to Trélon.

Trélon – Formerly known for its glass industry, Trélon is today the location of the **Atelier-musée du verre**⊘, a branch of the Fourmies-Trélon folk museum. In the heart of the old hall of the 19C glassworks, which still contains two kilns from 1850 and 1920 together with their equipment, glassworkers demonstrate the blowing and shaping of glass. Through objects and photographs, the exhibitions present the history of the industry locally, as well as today's techniques for flat and hollow glass.
South beyond Ôlhain the route follows the Helpe Mineure Valley, and is bordered by a sprinkling of ponds.

Fourmies – *See Fourmies.*

AZINCOURT

Population 250
Michelin map 51 fold 13 or 236 fold 13 – 6km/4mi south of Fruges

Situated in the middle of the hills of Artois, this flower-decked village recalls one of the most famous battles in the Hundred Years War.
The **Battle of Agincourt**, which was fought on 25 October 1415, was one of the bloodiest defeats ever suffered by the French aristocracy which lost 10 000 men and saw 1 500 men taken prisoner, including the poet Charles d'Orléans. The site chosen as the battlefield left little space for the knights to manoeuvre and the land was waterlogged; the horses were quickly bogged down. Moreover, the knights were hindered by the medieval concept of warfare and were obliged to fight on foot in their heavy armour. Despite superiority of numbers, they were massacred by the English archers concealed behind a fence and by the English footsoldiers armed with axes and leaded clubs. The victory gave greater weight to Henry V's claims to the throne of France.
Up to 1734 this fateful spot was known locally as Carrion (La Carogne).
A calvary erected in 1963 recalls this historic episode, as does, at the junction of D 104 and the road to Maisoncelle, an inscription at the foot of the pine-encircled menhir.

Musée de Traditions populaires et d'Histoire locale ⊘ – Documents, photographs, copies of arms and armour, and small models depict the weaponry of the time. The events of the battle are evoked in a video presentation. A model shows the battlefield. Some of the 14C paving found on the site of the old castle are also on show in a display case.
A round trip *(map provided)* leaving from the museum leads to the battlefield where a viewing table and various maps are displayed.

BARBIZON★★

Population 1 407
Michelin map 106 fold 45
10km/6mi northwest of Fontainebleau – Local map Forêt de FONTAINEBLEAU

The village of Barbizon, which was part of Chailly until 1903, was a popular spot with landscape painters *(see Introduction: Landscape Painting)* and still carries memories of the artists who made it famous. The Bas-Bréau coppices nearby are reminders of a time when, according to the Goncourt brothers, "every tree was like an artist's model surrounded by a circle of paint-boxes".

The Barbizon Group – Breaking the rules of studio work and official art, the Barbizon artists were landscape painters who perfected the technique of working directly from nature after two great masters: Théodore Rousseau (1812-67) and Jean-François Millet (1814-75). The local people were happy to welcome these nature-loving artists who rose at dawn and whose genius and mischievous nature enlivened local weddings and banquets. Next came the writers, seduced by the beauty of the forest and the congenial atmosphere of this small, international community: George Sand, Henri Murger, the Goncourt brothers, Taine etc. Thereafter, Barbizon remained a fashionable spot.

Millet, a patriarch with nine children, died after a life of hard work, his eyes forever riveted on the landscapes of the Bière plain. Like Rousseau, he was buried at **Chailly Cemetery** *(plan of graveyard at entrance)*.

LA GRANDE RUE *1hr – From the junction of D 64 to the forest.*

Barbizon is a long high street (Grande Rue) lined with hotels, restaurants and villas. Many of these buildings bear commemorative plaques of the artists who stayed there.

★**Auberge du Père Ganne** ⊙ – This was a popular meeting-place for artists, many of whom had rooms here. The inn has now become the **Musée de l'École de Barbizon.** A lively educational audio-visual display describes "Ganne's painters" who revolutionised art and brought life and laughter to the inn by their tricks. The "Officers'" dining room on the ground floor is representative of their habit of decorating all the wood panelling in the inn as a means of paying for their keep. They decorated cupboards, doors, the sideboard, the fireplace, in fact any flat surface, all of them ideal as supports for the talents of the artists. On the first floor the museum has numerous paintings indicating the influence of Barbizon on Impressionists through the "Back to Nature" theme. Some of the artists such as Charles Jacque or Constant Troyon favour animal paintings; others such as Millet prefer to illustrate the relationship between Man and Nature, the "cry of the earth..... a drama swathed in splendour". *Haystacks in the plain* or *Haystacks at Sunrise* by Chaigneau are precursors of the famous haystacks painted by Monet. Painting "on the motif" changes the brushstrokes, thickening them as on the *Landscape with Elm Trees* by A Knyff. The lack of popular enthusiasm for this School was probably due to the dark colours which were soon to be replaced by the brilliant hues of the Impressionists.

The Gleaners by Millet (Musée d'Orsay, Paris)

Our selection

Hostellerie de la Clé d'Or – 73 Grande-Rue, ☎ 01 60 66 40 96, fax 01 60 66 42 71. Close to the famous Fontainebleau Forest, this former posting-house overlooking a pleasant garden calls for relaxation. Double room from 370F, fixed menu: 160F.

L'Angélus – 31 Grande-Rue, ☎ 01 60 66 40 30. Housed in a picturesque old building, this restaurant is nicely decorated. Fixed menu: 175F.

Bizon's Club – 1 Grande-Rue. Main discotheque in the Fontainebleau Forest. Young crowds can enjoy techno music in a large hall while their seniors dance in the basement to music of the 1980s.

Maison-atelier de Théodore Rousseau – Behind the war memorial is the small house that is now an annex of the Barbizon School museum. It is used for temporary exhibitions and contains a collection of old photographs of Fontainebleau Forest during the days of the "Colourists".

Monument de Millet et de Rousseau – A bronze medal embedded in the rock is the work of Henri Chapu. Behind this monument, a plaque set into another rock commemorates the centenary of the setting up of the first artistic reserve in 1853 at the instigation of Rousseau.

BAVAY★

Population 3 751
Michelin map 53 fold 5 or 236 folds 18, 19

Bavay was originally the capital of the old Belgian tribe the Nervii; today it is a small town with low houses, known for its confectionery called "chiques de Bavay".

Bagacum during the Roman Peace – At the time of Caesar Augustus, Bagacum was an important town in Roman Belgium. The town, a judicial and administrative centre, seat of a curia, military post and supply centre, was at the junction of seven roads that led to Utrecht, Boulogne, Cambrai, Soissons, Rheims, Trier and Cologne, this last being the busiest. The routes, still recognisable in the present road network, were furrowed by the pedestrians and carts which dug these ruts, traces of which can be found in the forum.
Ravaged at the end of the 3C, Bagacum never regained its former splendour.

SIGHTS

Remains of the Roman City – In 1942 Canon Biévelet began searching on a site cleared in the bombing of 17 May 1940, during which Bavay had been badly damaged. Excavations revealed the remains of a large group of monumental buildings: a civil basilica, a forum, a portico above a horseshoe-shaped underground gallery *(cryptoporticus)* and a room over a deep cellar stand along an east-west axis. A few houses have also been found south of the walls built after the invasions of the second half of the 3C.

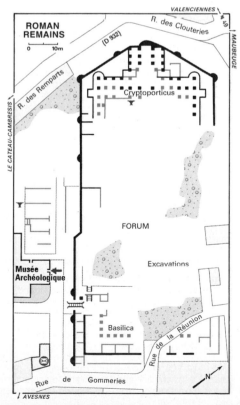

Archives du musée de Bavay

Musée archéologique
de Bavay – Jupiter

Musée archéologique ⊘ – Housed in a large modern building, the archeological museum exhibits various objects found during excavations. An audio-visual show presents daily life, trade, religious life and craft activities at the time of Bagacum. The numerous pots, dishes and vases with busts of divinities on them are a reminder that Bavay was an important pottery production centre. Delightful bronze figurines are among the treasures from a bronze-founder's hoard.

Grande Place – The brickwork of the 17C belfry contrasts with the 18C town hall, built of granite, next to it. A fluted column in the square supports a statue of Brunhilda, Queen of Austrasia, who took a great interest in road networks.

EXCURSION

Bellignies – *3km/2mi north of Bavay on D 24.*
In the 19C Bellignies-les-Rocs, in the middle of the Hogneau Valley, developed a marble industry. Over 1 000 people worked there: the men cut, the women polished. It was an important business right up to the Second World War.

Musée du Marbre et de la Pierre bleue ⊘ – The tools traditionally used to cut and polish marble are displayed in the museum, together with typical examples of the workshops' output: clocks, bases etc.

BEAUVAIS★★

Conurbation 57 704
Michelin map 55 folds, 9, 10 or 236 fold 33

Beauvais was ravaged by the bombing of June 1940 but despite this retained its striking cathedral, an architectural masterpiece almost defying the laws of gravity.

Bishops and Burghers – Beauvais, the Gallic capital of the Belgian tribe the Bellovaci, was destroyed by the Romans to create a fortified camp. The city was rebuilt and enclosed within walls during the Middle Ages; today boulevards straddle the moat. From the 11C the city had as its lord a bishop, who was often in conflict with the town's wealthy merchants and jealous of their franchises. One of the bishops, Pierre Cauchon, has a dubious claim to fame: while the town wanted to surrender to Charles VII, Cauchon rallied to the English. Chased out of Beauvais in 1429 by the burghers, he took refuge in Rouen where, on 30 May 1431, he sent Joan of Arc to the stake.

Jeanne Hachette – On 27 June 1472 Beauvais was besieged by Charles the Bold, Duke of Burgundy, who was marching on Paris with 80 000 men. The town had no troops so men and women ran to the ramparts and watched in horror as ladders were laid against the fortifications. Jeanne Laîné, the daughter of a humble craftsman, saw an assailant appear at the top of the wall, a standard in hand. She threw herself on him, tore away his banner and struck him with a hatchet, sending him flying into the moat below. This example fired the courage of the others; the resistance gained momentum, giving time for reinforcements to arrive. Charles lifted the siege on 22 July.
Each year, at the end of June, Beauvais honours Jeanne "Hachette".

Tapestries, stained glass and ceramics – In 1664 Colbert founded the Manufacture nationale de Tapisserie. The artisans worked on horizontal looms producing low-warp tapestries in wool and silk which are noted for being extremely fine; they were usually used as upholstery. The great days of Beauvais tapestries date from when the painter Oudry was directing the works, from 1734 to 1753. The workshops, which were evacuated to Aubusson in 1939, were unable to return to Beauvais after the buildings were destroyed in 1940. The looms were relocated to the Gobelins Works in Paris and remained there until they could go back to Beauvais in 1989.
Beauvais' 16C stained glass is also famous, particularly that by the Leprince family. Glazed earthenware and stoneware, manufactured locally since the 15C, have made the Beauvais region one of the great ceramic centres of France.

★★CATHÉDRALE ST-PIERRE *1hr*

The history of the cathedral has been tumultuous. Its unique appearance is due to the great technical drama of its construction and the desperate efforts of the bishops and chapters to raise the necessary funds: an exhausting struggle which was prolonged over four centuries but finally abandoned before the enormous project was completed. During the Carolingian period a small cathedral, Notre-Dame, was erected; known as the **Basse-Œuvre**, now only three of the nave's bays remain complete, adjoining the newer building.

In 949 another cathedral was begun, but it was destroyed by two fires.

Subsequently, in 1225, the bishop and chapter decided to erect the biggest church of its day, a New Work **(Nouvel-Œuvre)** dedicated to St Peter.

While building a grandiose cathedral might seem a reasonable ambition in the Gothic period, in this case aspiration overcame sense. When the construction of the chancel was started in 1238, the clergy and the master builders wanted to better both past and future architects: the height to the vault's keystone was to be slightly above 48m/158ft, making the roof (68m/223ft high) about the height of the towers of Notre-Dame in Paris.

It took twenty-five years to archieve this feat but for once the medieval architects had overestimated their ability. The pillars were too widely spaced and the buttresses on the piers too weak. In 1284 the chancel collapsed: forty more years of work and an enormous amount of money went into saving it. The three large arches of the chancel's right bays were reinforced by the addition of intermediary piers, the flying buttresses multiplied, the abutments strengthened.

No sooner had this task been finished than the Hundred Years War prevented any continuation. The cathedral still only consisted of a chancel and its dependent parts. In 1500 the bishop decided to resume work and entrusted the construction of the transept to Martin Chambiges, assisted by Jean Vast; the first and most important thing, however, was to obtain funds.

The sale of exemptions from Lenten fasting, donations from the clergy, collections and François I's gift of part of the revenue from the royal monopoly of the sale of salt were not enough to cover the mounting costs. The citizens of Beauvais appealed to Pope Leo X, patron of Michelangelo and Raphael, who understood only too well, having financial problems of his own, and a solution was found: the sale of indulgences. This scandalised the German monk Luther and partly triggered the Reformation. Leo X authorised the bishop of Beauvais to sell indulgences and the work continued. In 1550 the transept was finally completed.

Unfortunately, instead of building the nave next, it was decided to erect an open-work tower over the transept crossing, surmounted by a spire. The cross at the top of the spire was positioned in 1569, at a height of 153m/502ft (Strasbourg's is 142m/466ft). As there was however no nave to counterbalance the thrusts, the piers gave way, on Ascension Day in 1573, just as the procession had left the church.

Beauvais – The Cathedral

After that, despite tremendous efforts and sacrifices, the clergy and people o Beauvais were able to restore only the chancel and the transept: the unfinishec cathedral would never again have a spire, and would never have a nave.

★ **Chevet** – *See illustration in the Introduction: ABC of architecture.* The chancel dates from the 13C. Like the Flamboyant transept arms, it is shored up by flying but tresses with high piers which rise up to the roof. The transept arms were to have been very long and framed by towers.

South transept façade – The façade is richly decorated and bears two high turret: flanking the **Portail de St-Pierre** (St Peter's Doorway), the embrasures, tympanum anc arching of which are adorned with niches beneath openwork canopies. It is toppec with a high gable crossing a gallery. A large rose-window with delicate tracery sur mounts them, and is crowned by a gable with colonnettes.

The **door leaves★** are good examples of early, Italian-influenced Renaissance sculp ture. They are the work of Jean le Pot: on the left, St Peter healing a lame mar at the door of the Temple; on the right, the Conversion of St Paul (in the back ground, the walls of Damascus and St Paul escaping, lowered in a basket).

★★★ **Interior** – The dizzying height of the vaults (almost 48m/157ft high) is immedia tely apparent: they are nearly as tall as the Arc de Triomphe in Paris. It is here that the possibilities opened up by Gothic art become clear. The generous transep is almost 59m/193ft long, and the chancel is extremely elegant. There is an open triforium. The clerestory (18m/59ft high) is as tall as the vaults of the Church o St-Germain-des-Prés in Paris. Seven chapels open off the ambulatory. Near the par close, note the layout of the great arches in the bays on the south side of the church. Additional arches were built in the 14C after the catastrophe of 1284 Traces of the original pointed arches can still be seen.

★★ **Stained-glass windows** – The transept features most of the 16C compositions. The south rose-window, the work of Nicolas Leprince (1551), is dedicated to the Crea tion, with the Eternal Father occupying the central medallion; note the wonderfull clear green tones. Underneath, ten Prophets and ten Apostles or Doctors stand in two rows. Opposite, in the north transept, there are ten Sibyls counterbalancing the Prophets (1537). The rose window and the lower gallery (parable of the Wis and Foolish Virgins) are by Max Ingrand (1954). In the chapel of the Sacred Hear (chapelle du Sacré-Cœur) (**1**) the "Roncherolles" window (1552) offers a close-u view of Renaissance stained-glass making.

The **radiating chapels** which were devastated in 1940 and are currently undergoing restoration have had their windows replaced by contemporary glass masters.

The **apsidal chapel** still retains three 13C windows: the life of an unidentified sain *(left)*; the Tree of Jesse and the Childhood of Christ *(centre)*; scenes from the reli gious drama by Rutebeuf, the *Miracle of Theophilus (right)*.

A 16C altarpiece (**3**) from the Église de Marissel *(see below)* can be seen in a sid chapel. A Crucifixion scene is portrayed above the Death of the Virgin.

★ **Astronomic Clock** ⊙ – This monumental clock was made by the engineer Louis-August Vérité from 1865 to 1868. It comprises 90 000 parts and has been reassemblec several times. The lower part resembles a fortress with numerous windows at which appear an assortment of figures, among them Vérité, the prefect, the bishop etc In the glazed openings 52 dials show the length of the days and nights, the sea sons, the time of the Paris meridian etc.

The Last Judgmen unfolds in the uppe part of the clock which represents th Celestial City: a coc flaps its wings an crows, and Christ seat ed in His glory signal the angels to blow their trumpets. The the Judgment take place, and Virtue is le to heaven while Vice dragged to hell by th Devil.

To the right of the as tronomical clock is a old 14C clock (**2**) wit chimes that pla psalms correspondin to the different pe riods of the year.

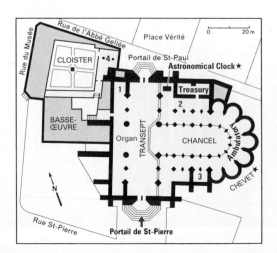

Cloister – Two early-15C galleries have wooden ceilings; one of them extends into a sort of vaulted shelter which dates from the 16C and supports the Chapter-house (**4**) above.

Return to the cathedral and leave by the north door, known as the Portail de St-Paul.

North transept façade – This side is less ornate than the south façade, with unadorned buttresses. The doorway's tympanum features a tree bearing thirteen coats of arms: they were probably intended to represent the genealogy of François I, the cathedral's great benefactor.

The door panels were again sculpted by Jean le Pot, but in the Gothic style: the four Evangelists *(right)*, and the four great Doctors of the Church *(left)*.

Return to the south doorway by going westwards around the cathedral.

Basse-Œuvre – Traces remain of the old 10C cathedral built from salvaged Gallo-Roman quarry stones known as *pastoureaux*. It served as the parish church until the Revolution.

ADDITIONAL SIGHTS

★Église St-Étienne – The nave and the transept of the church dedicated to St Stephen are Romanesque. Their restraint, softened by the "Beauvais-style" bracketed cornices, contrasts with the architectural richness of the chancel, rebuilt a little after 1500 in a refined Flamboyant style. The chancel, which is higher than the nave, is encircled by chapels. The tower flanking the west front, built from 1583 to 1674, served as the town belfry.

The left aisle gives on to a Romanesque doorway with a finely carved tympanum and arching; the wall, with three hollowed-out arcades above, features unusual brick and stone masonry. From this side a good view is offered of the north transept's lovely Wheel of Fortune, symbolising the frailty of earthly things: a rose-window, showing ascending figures *(right)* who, on reaching the height of their climb, are brought down by Destiny *(left)*.

The Romanesque nave possesses rib-vaulting and blocked galleries. The transept crossing offers a good view over the aisles and their archaic Gothic vaulting: note that the arc of the transverse arches is slightly too generous; when seen from an angle, the rounded or faceted ribs of the pointed arches appear to rise crookedly.

★★Stained-glass windows – The chancel's stained-glass windows, by Engrand Leprince, are among the most beautiful preserved from the Renaissance period; among them is the extraordinary Tree of Jesse★★★ with its stunning design, colours and translucency.

On the left at the beginning of the ambulatory, a very low, late-15C former funerary chapel with finely interwoven ribs serves as the baptistery.

A 16C wooden statue of St Wilgefortis hangs in the right aisle; the crucified young Portuguese girl is shown with the beard which grew after she had implored the Virgin to save her from a heathen marriage as she had made a vow of chastity.

Ancien palais épiscopal – The fortified doorway of the former bishop's palace is flanked by two large towers with pepperpot roofs. It was built by Bishop Simon de Clermont de Nesle with 8 000 *livres* of fines that the town had to pay after the riot of 1306 during which the bishopric was pillaged. At the far end of the courtyard stands the main body of the palace; set ablaze in 1472 by the Burgundians, it was rebuilt by Louis Villiers de L'Isle Adam around 1500 and retains an elegant Renaissance façade which was restored in the 19C.

Beauvais, Église St-Étienne –
Detail from the Tree of Jesse

Urbano /GEMOB

★ Musée départemental de l'Oise ○ – The vaulted rooms of the entrance to the museum contain the sculpture collections. The left tower houses woodcarvings from churches and abbeys (a 16C St Barbara by Jean Le Pot) and sculpted fragments from some of Beauvais' timber-framed houses, numerous in the town until 1940 (sign from a spice and mustard shop). In the right tower, with its frescoes of mermaids playing musical instruments, there are stone carvings from the Middle Ages (tympanum from St Giles' church, a king's head, St James).

On the upper floor the museum periodically displays the tapestries bequeathed to the cathedral by Nicolas d'Argillères, *The Legend of the Gauls* (16C).

Cross the garden.

The basement, halls and attics of the palace are devoted to archeology, fine arts, decorative arts and regional ceramics. The 12C and 16C cellars house the archeological collections from recent excavations at local sites: Chevincourt, Verberie, Tartigny, Bulles. Note the Gallic warrior from St-Maur, the 1C AD metal statuette and the stele carved with a bearded Mercury (3C).

Remarkable local ceramics (16C to 18C) are exhibited on the first floor: large pieces of glazed earthenware including a piece known as "The Passion Dish" *(plat "de la Passion")* and a decorative finial (the hurdy-gurdy player). The art galleries present the 16C French School, in particular *The Resurrection of Christ* by Antoine Caron (1521-99), and the 17C and 18C Italian and French Schools. The French landscape artists of the 19C include Corot *(The Fountain from the French Academy in Rome* and *The Old St-Michel Bridge, Paris)*.

The old assizes in the law courts house the enormous unfinished painting by Thomas Couture (1815-79), *The Enlisting of the Volunteers of 1792,* surrounded by preparatory sketches.

The second floor recreates France at the turn of the century and during the Roaring Twenties through a collection of paintings (decorative panel by Édouard Vuillard and spectacular stairway decor by Maurice Denis, *The Golden Age)*, and through exceptional sets of furniture: two Art Nouveau dining rooms, the Parrot Salon *(salon Les Perroquets)* with Beauvais tapestry-work.

Works by the local master potter Auguste Delaherche (1857-1940) also reflect this turbulent period.

Some 600 everyday ceramic items from the Pays de Bray (19C and early 20C) are displayed under the imposing 16C roof: dishes, jugs and pitchers, salt cellars, decorative tiles, sweet-dishes, fountains, funerary monuments etc.

Reconstruction of a Pays de Bray potter's workshop.

Galerie nationale de la Tapisserie ○ – Housed in a low-roofed building beyond the cathedral's east end, the gallery stages exhibitions giving an overview of French tapestry from the 15C to the present day. Building work revealed the walls of the old Gallo-Roman fortified town *(castrum)*; the important remains have been left exposed within the gallery.

Manufacture nationale de la tapisserie ○ – After over 40 years' exile, the national tapestry works returned to the town in 1989 thanks to the redevelopment of the old slaughter-houses by the local architect Desgroux. Today the factory contains about a dozen looms. The weavers work under natural light and follow the artist's cartoon, weaving on the reverse side and monitoring their work with a mirror. The entire production is reserved for the State.

Église de Marissel ○ – *1.5km/1mi east along rue de Clermont and rue de Marissel which branches off to the sight.*

The village is now almost a suburb of Beauvais and its restored church rises on a terrace from where the cathedral's huge mass is visible, 2km/1.25mi away. A painting by Corot from 1866, now in the Louvre, made the church famous.

The building is the result of sporadic construction from the 11C to the 16C; the spire dates from only the last century.

The 16C west front with its Flamboyant doorway was inspired by the cathedral. The east end, the oldest and most surprising part, has a Romanesque chapel wedged between the Gothic transept and flat-ended chancel. To get an impression of the earlier sanctuary, imagine greater height on the tiny Romanesque belltower, ignoring the high roof of the nave against which it now abuts.

EXCURSIONS

Château de Troissereux – *8km/5mi northwest of Beauvais.*

The stone and brick castle, standing near the River Thérain; was built in the Renaissance style, in the late 16C or early 17C. The interior decoration and the furniture date from the 18C.

A pavilion overlooking the main courtyard contains a very old clockwork, probably older than that of Beauvais cathedral's 14C clock.

The English-style park, adorned with ornamental ponds and a "grand canal", shelters a great variety of birds including rare species.

★**Gerberoy** – *21km/13mi northwest of Beauvais by D 901. After Lachapelle-sous-Gerberoy, turn left.*

This fortified town perched on a knoll was forgotten from the 17C until the painter Le Sidaner (1862-1939) fell under its charm and settled here. Since then numerous figures from the worlds of the arts and letters have come to live in the old, timber-framed houses (restored) which line the cobbled streets.

The gateway which gave access to the castle leads to the modest 15C collegiate church. A shaded walk now follows the line of the old ditches.

BERGUES★

Population 4 163
Michelin map 51 fold 4 or 236 fold 4

Bergues is now a wealthy little Flemish town leading a peaceful life within ramparts which overlook a region famous for its pastures, butter and cheese. It grew rich on the wool trade and rivalled Dunkirk (Dunkerque).

The warm tones of the buildings' yellow-ochre bricks are reflected in the waters of the moat which partly surrounds the town. Despite having been badly damaged in 1940, Bergues has retained its old character through the austere but harmonious rebuilding of the bombed districts. The winding streets, the large squares and the silent quays along the edge of the River Colme are reminiscent of Bruges.

SIGHTS *1hr 30min*

Town Walls – The walls, pierced by four gateways and surrounded by a deep moat, date partly from the Middle Ages (Bierne Gate, Beckerstor, curtain wall east of Cassel Gate) and partly from the 17C, when the defences were developed by Vauban after the Treaty of Aix-la-Chapelle (1668), which gave Bergues to France (eastern hornwork, Cassel Gate, Hondschoote Crown). These fortifications were used by the French troops during the 1940 defence of Dunkirk, and the Germans had to use Stukas and flame-throwers to breach the walls.

★**Couronne d'Hondschoote** – On the north side of the walls, Vauban used the branches of the River Colme to build an extensive system of bastions and ravelins completely surrounded by large moats filled with carp, pike-perch and tench; viewed from above, this defensive system forms a sort of crown, hence its name.

Porte de Cassel – This gateway was built in the 17C; its triangular pediment features a carved sun, Louis XIV's emblem. From the outside, there is a view to the right over the medieval curtain wall towards the towers of St Winnoc.

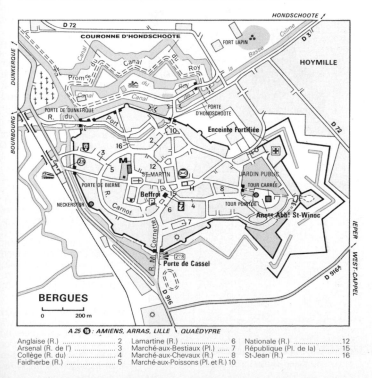

BERGUES

0   200 m

Ancienne abbaye de St-Winoc – Only ruins remain of this famous Benedictine establishment founded by St Winnoc on the Groenberg, a rise surrounded by marshes. Most of the buildings were destroyed during the Revolution; all that survives is the 18C front door, the Tour Pointue (rebuilt in 1815) which marks the site of the abbey's façade and the 12C-13C square tower of the transept crossing, supported by reinforced buttresses.

Belfry ☉ – Built in the second half of the 16C, set ablaze in 1940 and dynamited by the Germans in 1944, the belfry was rebuilt by Paul Gélis who sought to preserve the main structure of the former edifice while simplifying the exterior decoration. As a result, Bergues' belfry again stands out against the pale Flemish sky. The belfry (54m/177ft high) is made of yellow bricks known as "sand bricks" and is surmounted by the lion of Flanders; the **carillon** ☉ comprises 50 bells. From the top there is a good view over the Flemish plain.

On the façade of the town hall (**H**) nearby, a bust of **Lamartine** recalls that the writer, brother-in-law to M de Coppens d'Hondschoote, was elected M.P. of Bergues in 1833, after a first, unsuccessful attempt two years earlier.

Mont-de-piété (**M**) – Sensitively restored after the War, like the nearby church dedicated to St Martin, this building is the work of **Wenceslas Coebergher** (1561-1634), an extraordinary character who was painter, architect, economist and engineer; in the Flanders region he occupied himself with the draining of the Moëres, the marshes near Hondschoote, and introduced the first pawnshops *(monts-de-piété)*. This pawnshop was inaugurated in 1633 and continued in business until 1848. The elegant building with a Baroque gable is constructed of brick and white stone, and includes an ingenious combination of decorative elements: pilasters, niches, cartouches, pediments.

A museum is housed inside.

Musée municipal ☉ – The most outstanding of all the paintings in the municipal museum is undoubtedly the *Hurdy-Gurdy Player*, a vast canvas by Georges de la Tour (1593-1652) exhibited on the first floor. There are also works by several 16-17C Flemish artists including a sketch by Rubens, portraits by Van Dyck, Cossiers and Simon de Vox, a painting entitled *Chaste Suzanne* by Jan Metsys, still lifes by Gysbrecht and Van Son etc.

The natural history section on the 2nd floor includes a particularly extensive collection of birds and butterflies. The collection of 16C and 17C drawings is displayed on a rotating basis.

EXCURSIONS

Quaëdypre – *5km/3mi southeast along D 916 and D 37*. This village, located on a small hill, has a **hall-church** ☉ with three equal aisles and an interior decorated with

E. Revault /PIX

Le Mont-de-Piété in Bergues

17C carved woodwork: high altar *(see Introduction: ABC of architecture)* with a painting by Goubau, an artist from Aubverp who was Largillière's tutor; communion table, pulpit and confessional from the Dominican church in Bergues; organ loft and stalls formerly in St Winnoc's Abbey, Bergues.

West-Cappel – *10km/6mi southeast along D 110 then D 4*. This is a peaceful village on a rise. Église St-Sylvestre,☉ rebuilt in the 16C in "sand bricks", boasts a mighty porch-belfry, three aisles and a taller chancel. The interior features stained-glass windows, some dating from the 16C; a 17C communion table; an interesting pulpit; the reclining effigy of Ludwine Van Cappel (15C) *(back of the north aisle)*.

Den Leeuw Windmill ☉ – *8km/5mi south via D 916 then turn right onto D 110*. On the outskirts of **Pitgam** stands a wooden post mill dating from 1776.

BLÉRANCOURT

Population 1 268
Michelin map 56 fold 3 or 236 folds 36, 37

Only a few sections survive from the former château of the dukes of Gesvres, built in the 17C by Salomon de Brosse and abandoned during the Revolution. In 1917 a group of American women led by a Miss Ann Morgan moved into the remaining parts. They came to give help to areas devastated by the war.

Musée national de la coopération franco-américaine (National Museum of Franco American Cooperation) ⊙ – Two monumental entrances lead into the main courtyard surrounded by a moat. Pavilions frame the second doorway: the right one contains the library, documents and archives, the left one is filled with memorabilia concerning Miss Morgan. The two wings of the museum itself partly recreate the château's ground floor. The left wing *(temporarily closed)* is dedicated to the American Revolution. The right wing (Florence Gould pavilion) displays paintings and sculptures executed between 1800 and 1945 by French artists in the United States and by American artists in France. Finish the tour with a stroll through the garden planted with American trees and the arboretum.

Musées nationaux

18C engraving depicting the "Independance" coiffure

BOULOGNE-SUR-MER★★

Conurbation 95 930
Michelin map 51 fold 1 or 236 fold 1

Boulogne, once a Roman city, is situated where the Liane Valley opens up after running between steep hills. The town has a commercial port, ferry terminal and fishing harbour and has a rough but appealing look and busy streets. Literary historian St Beuve was born here in 1804; another local figure was the engineer **Frédéric Sauvage** (1786-1857), the inventor of the propeller used in steam navigation (statue on Marguet bridge opposite the tourist office).
The town itself is divided into an upper town, which is the administrative and religious centre enclosed within ramparts and overlooked by its basilica, and the lower town, the commercial and maritime area which was rebuilt after the war.

The Miracle of Our Lady – In 636 during Dagobert's reign a boat with neither crew nor sails came aground on the shore at Boulogne, carrying a statue of the Virgin Mary. At the same time, the congregation praying in the chapel (which stood on the site of the present basilica) were notified of the event by an apparition of the Virgin. This miracle led to the establishment of a famous **pilgrimage** which was undertaken by fourteen kings of France and five kings of England.
The prestige of the statue of Notre-Dame de Boulogne was sometimes used for political ends. Louis XI, for example, appropriated the county that belonged to the Dukes of Burgundy by declaring that the Madonna which was held in such great esteem in Boulogne was the real "Lady" of the town, that as king he was her vassal on Earth and that he was therefore taking charge of the town's interests.

"Imperial" Boulogne – Boulogne is linked to Bonaparte because from 1803 to 1805 he kept his troops mustered at the **Boulogne Camp** *(camp de Boulogne)* for a possible invasion of England. On 26 August 1805 Napoleon I, crowned a year earlier, finally abandoned his project in order to set his Grande Armée against the Austrians.
In August 1840 the future Napoleon III tried to raise the town against Louis-Philippe, but the attempt floundered and he was imprisoned in Ham Fort.
Every year in July the town holds a Napoleonic festival with the re-enactment of a Napoleonic battle fought in period costume.

THE PORT

Boulogne-sur-Mer – The fishing port

The foremost **fresh fish port** on mainland Europe, Boulogne is also the European centre of the fish trade and the home of an international industrial fish-processing complex (freezing, canning, smoking and salting). About fifteen industrial trawlers, 90 small-scale fishing boats and 40 coastal boats, together with foreign ships, supply the port. There are also imports from northwest Europe. The **fish auction** (la criée) is interesting on Wednesdays. It is held in the building beside the Loubet basin in the Capélure district at 5am and lasts about 1hr.

Boulogne ranks 9th as a **commercial port** in France with imports of manganese ore, paper and paper pulp, timber and chipboard, frozen foods, and exports of iron alloys, cement and flour.

Boulogne is a **ferry port** specialising in links with Great Britain. The Boulogne-Folkestone route is covered by Hoverspeed which runs a catamaran service for vehicles and passengers.

Completely destroyed during the war, the harbour installations have since been reconstructed and enlarged, and now extend beyond Boulogne to Le Portel where the commercial port is located. The **outer harbour** is protected by two jetties, one of which, the digue Carnot is 3250m/over 2mi long. The main part of the harbour is the Sarraz Bournet deep-water dock with a western pier for large cargo ships, and an eastern pier for the ore ships supplying the Paris-Outreau metallurgical complex. The **inner harbour** consists of a tidal dock reserved for ferries, small trawlers and yachts and the Napoleon and Loubet docks for the big fishing boats. The ferry terminal (**Y**) has four quays and three gangways. At night the sorting of the trawled fish takes place in the refrigerated markets alongside Loubet dock. **Quai Gambetta** (**YZ**), overlooked by tall buildings, is busiest when the trawlers unload their catch, some of which is sold on the spot.

Beach (**Y**) – Already quite well known in the 18C, this beach of fine, white sand became very fashionable from the mid 19C onwards. An equestrian statue of San Martin stands on the promenade. The general spent the last few months of his life in Boulogne.

★★★ NAUSICAA ⏱ (Y) 3hr 30min

Nausicaa, the **Centre National de la Mer**, is a recent development on the site of the old casino, opposite the ferry terminal on the edge of the beach. It was designed by architect Jacques Rougerie who specialises in buildings with a maritime theme, and Christian Le Conte, a specialist in museography.

This complex, which is the largest sea life centre in Europe, aims to provide information about fauna in warm and cold ocean environments, the rational management of marine resources and the trades linked to them. It strives to increase public awareness of problems of pollution and excessive exploitation of the sea's resources, two problems which are threatening this vast communal reserve.

Visitors are invited to undertake a voyage to the centre of the sea, in a building dappled with bluish light and filled with aquatic music. There are huge aquariums providing a variety of information. Nausicaa is also a scientific research centre with a 40m/130ft long test basin designed by the Institut français pour la recherche et l'exploitation de la mer (IFREMER). It is used to simulate the working of hydro-dynamic fishing boats.

Journey through the World's Seas – Visitors step into the world of plankton. The circular aquarium contains jellyfish.

After being informed about the reproduction cycle of species from tropical seas and the Mediterranean, visitors are able to discover some magnificent specimens and observe their habits: mimicry, grouping together in shoals, occupation and defence of a hunting ground Video terminals provide information about the senses of fish in general followed by a rapid look into a reconstructed marine environment at depths below 3000m/9843ft, which gives

> ### Plankton
> This generic name refers to organisms that cannot withstand maritime currents.
> They vary in size from the microscopic phytoplankton (plant plankton), to zooplankton no bigger than the head of a pin, and to several tens of metres for certain jellyfish extended by their filaments. Plankton is of vital importance. It forms the basis of all marine life, producing organic matter from mineral salts and the energy afforded by sources of light. It generates much of the planet's oxygen.

an idea of the kind of fauna living at such depths, near sources of warm water.

Next comes the Espace "diamant des thons", a strange aquarium shaped like a reverse pyramid and containing a shoal of sérioles (of the tuna family); an optical illusion gives visitors the impression that they, like the fish, are moving beneath the surface of the sea. On their way to the flat-fish aquarium, visitors discover in turn the fish and invertebrates of the local coastline in connection with tidal movements, wrecks which are the favourite haunt of moray and ecosystems of the Mediterranean and the North Sea which have fewer species but a more plentiful supply and are ideal fishing grounds.

After this tour of the World's seas, a footbridge and a long corridor lead visitors to an area where the relationship between man and the sea over thousands of years is explained.

Total immersion in spectacular settings – A celestial dome (25m/82ft in diameter), beneath which the "Blue Planet" is suspended, forms the setting of the area devoted to resources from the sea; visitors are shown how, nowadays, towns and ports occupy most of the available coastline and are given information about the various means of maritime transport and codes.

Visitors then arrive on the beach of a paradisiacal island surrounded by the greenish-blue waters of a lagoon. From the pontoon, they can observe the lagoon full of colourful fish on one side, and the open sea with characteristic shoals of fish on the other. Steps lead beneath the surface to a vast panoramic window which reveals a stunning landscape with tropical fish darting among coral formations. An audio-visual show (use special glasses to get the 3-D effect) is devoted to the various uses of marine resources. Visitors then aim for the underwater observatory to be confronted with Californian sea-lions diving and swimming through the waves. The aerial observatory shows the same sea-lions stretched out on the rocks in a typical Californian setting of cliffs and log cabins.

An escalator leads to the hands-on basin, full of cod, pollack and turbot, where children can stroke the friendly thorn-back rays.

The tour takes visitors to a reduced-scale fish farm where the new fish-farming techniques are described. The adjacent area is devoted to various fishing techniques and a film shows night work aboard a trawler in the North Sea.

The visit ends with the spectacular Anneau des sélaciens, a panoramic circular tank filled with sharks.

Off the foyer are a cinema, a multimedia library, souvenir shops, a restaurant, bar and cafeteria.

★★LA VILLE HAUTE *3hr*

The upper town, enclosed by ramparts, stands on the site of the old Roman *castrum* or fortified town. It is overlooked by the enormous dome of Notre-Dame basilica and is popular with tourists in summer, offering pleasant strolls along the ramparts or through the streets and past the historic buildings of the walled town.

Ramparts

The fortifications were built in the early 13C by Philippe le Hurepel, Count of Boulogne and son of Philippe-Auguste, on the foundations of the Gallo-Roman walls and were strengthened in the 16C–17C. The ramparts form a rectangle (325m/1 066ft by 410m/1 345ft) reinforced by the **castle** to the east, and are pierced by four gates – Gayole, Dunes, Calais and **Degrés (X)** which is pedestrian only – flanked by two towers. The parapet walkway is accessible from each gateway and offers lovely **views★** of the town and the port.

At the western corner the **Tour Gayette (X B)**, a former jail, was the site of the take-off for the balloon flight in 1785 by **Pilâtre de Rozier** and Romain who were attempting to cross the Channel; they crashed near Wimille, just north of Boulogne.

A pyramid-shaped monument **(V K)** surmounted by a statue stands in the garden between Boulevard Auguste-Mariette and the ramparts; it is dedicated to another local figure, **Mariette** the Egyptologist, whom the statue shows in Egyptian costume.

Stroll through the Upper Town (VX) – Enter the ramparts through the western porte des Dunes into Place de la Résistance, around which stand:

– The **library** in the old Annonciades Convent. The 17C buildings and the cloisters house study and exhibition rooms, while the main reading room occupies the 18C chapel with its superb coffered ceiling, visible through the windows from the square.

– The **law courts (J)** dating from 1852, with a neo-Classical façade, statues of Charlemagne and Napoleon in two niches.

– The 13C Gothic **belfry** ⊘ *(access from the Hôtel de Ville)*, with a 12C base (the former keep from the castle of the counts of Boulogne) and an 18C octagonal section at the top. It houses Gallo-Roman statues and regional antique furniture as well as a beautiful stained-glass window portraying Godefroy de Bouillon.

The top of the belfry *(183 steps)* offers an extensive **view★** of Boulogne and its surroundings.

Place de la Résistance leads into **place Godefroy-de-Bouillon** located at the junction of the four main streets. The square owes its name to the leader of the first crusade, who was a member of the House of Boulogne.

The 18C façade of the **Hôtel de Ville (H)** of red brick with stone dressings, contrasts sharply with the primitive Gothic belfry.

Opposite the town hall stands the Louis XVI **Hôtel Desandrouin (F)**; Napoleon stayed here several times from 1803 to 1811.

Follow rue de Puits-d'Amour alongside Hôtel Desandrouin and turn right.

Rue Guyale (X 24) – The merchants' guildhall used to stand on this street, which has been restored and reveals the back of the Annonciades Convent and the rough-stone façades of the old houses, one of which is occupied by the Tourism Development Office.

At no 58 **(V E)** is the oldest house in Boulogne (12C).

From place Godefroy-de-Bouillon take rue de Lille.

Basilique Notre-Dame (V) – *Access via the south transept in rue de Lille.* The basilica was built from 1827 to 1866 on the site of the old cathedral (destroyed after the Revolution) and has preserved the Romanesque crypt. It is a popular place of

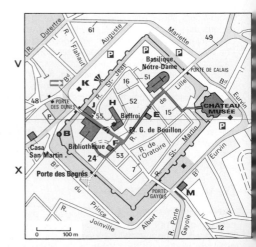

BOULOGNE-SUR-MER
VILLE HAUTE

B	Tour Gayette
E	Maison ancienne
F	Hôtel Desandrouins
H	Hôtel de ville
J	Palais de Justice
K	Monument à Mariette
M	Musée d'Histoire naturelle

Boulogne-sur-Mer – Château-musée

pilgrimage. Inside, a powerful Corinthian colonnade supports the building. The superb, soaring **dome★** with its circle of large statues rises behind the chancel; beyond it, in the central chapel, stands the wooden statuette of Our Lady of Boulogne (Notre-Dame de Boulogne), crowned with precious stones. Every year the statuette is carried in a procession during which the traditional sun-shaped headdresses, bonnets and Indian shawls of the region are worn.

★ Crypt and Treasury ⊘ – Under the basilica, a labyrinth of underground passages links 14 chambers. One of them houses the Treasury which contains religious statues and objects (chalices, reliquaries) from various churches in the region, and the relic of the Holy Blood offered by Philip the Fair to Our Lady of Boulogne.

Continue through several rooms, among them St Luke's Hall adorned with 19C *grisaille* and another containing traces of a 3C Roman temple, to the **crypt of the painted pillars** dating from the 11C, discovered during the construction of the new basilica.

Take rue du Château opposite.

★ Château-musée ⊘ (**V**) – Formerly the residence of the counts of Boulogne, this powerful-looking polygonal building was the first in western Europe to abandon the traditional keep. Flanked by round towers, it protected the most vulnerable part of the ramparts facing the plateau; in the 16C a horseshoe bastion was added on one side. The castle is separated from the ramparts by a moat, which was spanned by a drawbridge.

The varied collections are displayed in rooms throughout the four floors of the castle, including the count's hall, the towers, the chapel, the guard-room etc.

The archeology of the Mediterranean is represented by an Egyptian section – sarcophagi and numerous funerary objects, the gift of Mariette the Egyptologist – and also by a beautiful group of **Greek vases★★**, among them a black-figure jug portraying the suicide of Ajax.

Beyond this are rooms containing ceramics and earthenware from the main French and foreign manufacturers (Rouen, Nevers, Delft) and remarkable pieces of porcelain (St-Cloud, Sèvres, Vincennes). The Boulogne Camp and Napoleon (bust by Canova, twin-cocked hat) are evoked on the stairway and landing of the 3rd level. In the next room, works by painters of the Opal coast reveal the artistic talent that flourished around Boulogne in the 19C.

Among the ethnographic collections, the **Eskimo and Aleutian masks★★** brought back from a voyage to North America by the anthropologist Pinart, and the objects from the South Sea Islands including a Maori battle canoe from New Zealand, are particularly interesting. Three rooms are devoted to 17C, 18C and especially 19C painting: Corot, Boudin and Fantin-Latour, together with sculptures by Rodin, Pompon and Carpeaux.

The enormous guardroom displays collections from the Middle Ages and the Renaissance: copper and brassware, wood and stone sculptures, Gothic furniture and woodwork, an exceptional glazed earthenware finial, paintings, and coins. The archeological collections are exhibited in the underground rooms, which rest largely on the 2C and 3C Gallo-Roman walls, and in La Barbière, a superb Gothic room.

ADDITIONAL SIGHTS

Église St-Nicolas (Z) – The church, standing in place Dalton where the market i
held *(Wednesdays and Saturdays)*, is the oldest in Boulogne despite its Classica
façade. It was built from 1220 to 1250, and underwent many alterations at th
beginning of the 16C (apse, transept, chancel vaults, chapels) and in the 18C whe
the nave was rebuilt. The 17C high altar features spiral columns and a fine paint
ing of *The Flagellation* by Lehmann, a pupil of Ingres.

Musée d'Histoire naturelle ⊘ **(Z M)** – The museum has a collection devoted t
the study of paleontolgy, including life-size models of dinosaurs in their natura
environment, as well as various species of reptiles and fish from the Jurassic era
Four rooms are devoted to comparative anatomy and zoology, with two diorama
illustrating the ecology of the forests and the coastal cliffs. Many mineral sample
and sea shells are on exhibit.

Casa San Martin ⊘ **(Y)** – From 1848 to 1850 this house was inhabited by th
Argentinian general San Martin who, in 1816, freed his country from Spanish rul
and then also liberated Chile (1817) and Peru (1821). He died in a room on th
second floor, in 1850: mementoes of the illustrious soldier.

Calvaire des marins (Y) – *From Nausicaa, access by rue de la Baraque-de-l'Empe
reur and rue de la Tour-d'Odre.*
The calvary stands on the plateau where once stoodthe tour Odre, a Roman light
house collapsed in the 17C, owing to the crumbling of the cliff. The calvary an
the sailors'chapel also collapsed recently; fortunately, the calvary was saved an
now stands near a new chapel (1996) shaped like a ship. From the calvary's sur
roundings and the platform of the neighbouring wartime bunker there is a plungin
view★ over the beach, Nausicaa, the channel entrance, the harbour area and th
English coast when the weather is clear. Not far from here, following the cliff,
marker indicates the site of the hut from which the Emperor stood watching th
coast of England as well as the Napoleonic powder magazine.

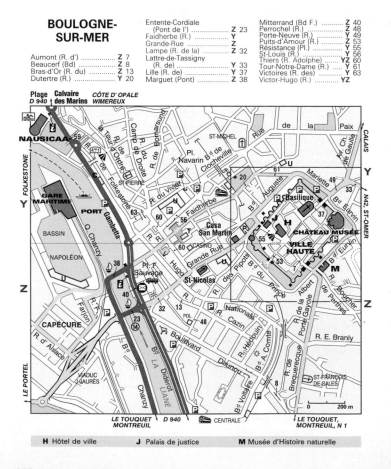

H Hôtel de ville	**J** Palais de justice	**M** Musée d'Histoire naturelle

EXCURSIONS

★**Colonne de la Grande Armée** ⊙ – *3km/2mi north by N 1 and turn left on a small road.*
Designed by the architect **Eloi Labarre** (1764–1833) to commemorate the Boulogne Camp, the column was started in 1804 but only finished under Louis-Philippe. The column is of marble from nearby Marquise, rises 54m/177ft high and is 4m/13ft in diameter. On its base, a bronze lowrelief portrays Field Marshal Soult offering the plans of the column to the Emperor. A staircase *(263 steps)* leads to the square platform (190m/623ft above sea level) from where the **panorama**★★ extends over the lush countryside of the Boulogne region and, on a clear day, across the Channel as far as the white cliffs of Dover. Other sights include Cap Gris-Nez *(north)*, the jetties of Boulogne's port, the rocks of Le Portel, Alprech Point lighthouse, the Upper Town *(west and south)* and the triumphal avenue which leads to the column *(east)*.

Monument de la Légion d'honneur – *2km/1.25mi north by D 940 and a path to the right.*
This obelisk marks the site of the throne on which Napoleon I sat on 16 August 1804, for the second distribution of the Legion of Honour decorations (the first took place on 14 July 1804 at the Invalides in Paris). The troops were deployed in a huge semicircle on the slopes of Terlincthun Valley; 2000 men received their crosses, arranged for this ceremony in the shields and helmets of the ancient military heroes Du Guesclin and Bayard.

Château de Pont de Briques – *5km/3mi south on N 1.*
This modest 18C château *(private)* became famous because Napoleon stayed there when he came to visit the troops at the Boulogne Camp; his apartments were in the right wing. The emperor dictated his plan of campaign against Austria – which ended with his victory at Austerlitz in December 1805 – in the salon here.

Viewpoint of St-Étienne-au-Mont – *5km/3mi along D 52 then right up a steep hill (13%).*
From the cemetery adjacent to the isolated hilltop church (alt 124m/407ft), there is a fine **view**★ of the Liane Valley; Boulogne, over which towers the dome of Notre-Dame basilica, can be seen downstream whereas, the inland scenery is dominated by the dark Boulogne Forest.

Le Portel – *5km/3mi southwest.*
The town has a sandy **beach** dotted with rocks and bordered by a raised promenade, facing the small isle on which stands **Fort de l'Heurt**, built by Napoleon in 1804. A statue of Our Lady of Boulogne watches over the Epi jetty.
Alprech Point lighthouse perches on the cliff, to the south.

Hardelot-Plage – *15km/9mi south by D 940 (Z) and D 113ᴱ.*
This elegant seaside and sporting resort features a magnificent, gently-sloping beach of fine sand. Leisure facilities include paths for walking, riding and cycling; golf; sailing; a country club with tennis courts and a swimming pool.
The **château** north of the village, by the Lac des Miroirs, retains some of its 13C fortifications. In the 19C it was bought by an Englishman who had the château rebuilt in the style of Windsor Castle with crenellations and turrets.

Forêt de Boulogne – *10km/6mi east by N 42 and D 341.*
The road climbs the slopes of **Mont Lambert** (189m/620ft); a television aerial rises from the top.
The forest covers 2000ha/4940 acres and contains forest roads, bridle paths, parking facilities and picnic areas. The lush Liane Valley borders the forest to the south and east; the village of **Questrecques** nestles in delightful surroundings.

Le BOULONNAIS★

Michelin map 51 fold 1, 2 or 236 fold 1, 2

The Boulonnais is a region of lush countryside around Boulogne. Its complex relief is due to the juxtaposition of differing geological formations: marble in Marquise, sandstone in Outreau and chalk in Desvres and Neufchâtel, where it lies under a layer of clay. In some places, outcrops rise over 200m/656ft in altitude.
The plateau between Guînes and the River Aa is intermittently bare or dotted with copses and affords an unrestricted view in all directions; here and there great farms surrounded by thickets and pastures grow cereals and sugar beet.
The Wimereux, Liane, Hem and Slack Valleys are deep and narrow, providing fertile ground for orchards (cider apples) and meadows. A local breed of cow grazes peacefully here, in addition to the Northern Blue and the Flemish Red cows; sheep are put out to pasture with Boulonnais draughthorses, which are powerful grey animals capable of pulling as much as a ton in weight.

The modest villages with their low, white-washed stone houses are devoted to stoc
farming; they are scattered around the manor houses, which were Royalist dens durin
the Revolution.
The Boulonnais forms part of the nature park known as the Parc naturel région
Nord–Pas-de-Calais.

Typical landscape of the Boulonnais region

ROUND TRIP STARTING FROM BOULOGNE

75km/46mi – about 3hr

★★**Boulogne** – *See Boulogne-sur-mer.*

Take N 42 east; 3km/2mi on, beyond the roundabout, turn onto D 232.

This picturesque road, edged with beeches and old elms, descends sharply into th
freshness of the **Wimereux Valley** which is carpeted with meadows and scattered wit
copses.

Souverain-Moulin – The château and its outbuildings look very attractive in the
leafy setting.

*Take D 233 (east) to Belle, then turn left onto D 238 and right onto D 251. Tur
right again onto D 127.*

Le Wast – Many local people take walks which end at this charming village. Th
church ⊘ features a Romanesque portal with Eastern-looking festoons, and rounde
arches supported by capitals decorated with acanthus leaves which curve to forr
scrolls. St Ide, the mother of Godefroy de Bouillon and the founder of the priory
was buried here in the 12C.
The **Maison du Parc national régional du Nord-Pas-de-Calais, zone du Boulonnais** is situated i
the **Manoir du Huisbois** ⊘ a beautiful 17C house of local grey stone. The informatio
centre provides documentation, a library, a video centre and exhibitions all relat
ing to the Boulonnais. A trail starting here leads through typical countryside
farmland crisscrossed by hedges and trees.

Château de Colembert – *(Private)*. This vast 18C building stands out from its lus
surroundings at the foot of Mont Dauphin (201m/659ft high).

Join N 42 to Saint-Omer and take D 224 left to Licques.

Licques – All that remain of the Premonstratensian abbey founded in the 12C an
rebuilt in the 18C, are the abbey church's tall nave (late-18C) and a few building
from the same period, now occupied by the presbytery, the town hall and th
school. 2km/1.25mi along D 224 north towards Ardres, the road offers a goo
view over Licques and the Hem River basin.

*Licques is famous for its turkeys introduced in the area in the 17C by the monk
of the local abbey and celebrated today on the third Sunday in December.*

From Licques, follow D 191 west through Sanghem and Hermelingen.

Beyond Le Ventu the road begins to climb, overlooking the entire region. Ther
are beautiful **views**★ over the verdant, undulating Boulonnais countryside.

At Hardinghen, take D 127 southwest and D 127ᴱ to Réty.

Rety – The small Flamboyant **church** ⊘ (late 15C; 12C tower) has decorative stone-work which creates a chequered effect. Inside, note the chancel's carved keystone in the centre of a stone crown. The cemetery has been turned into an attractive garden.

Turn left beyond Rety onto D 232. After crossing D 127ᴱ, turn right to Hydre-quent.

Hydrequent – The **Maison du marbre et de la géologie** ⊘ is a centre concentrating on the formation of marble and coal in the Boulonnais. The marble, which is actually limestone formed during the Carbaniferous Era or the later, Jurassic period, is rich in fossils as can be seen on the various display panels. 26 different types of marble exist. During the Primary Era this region was covered by a lush forest (model showing the animals and giant plants whose decomposition eventually formed coal). The Marquise quarry yields a type of "marble" which has been used for many buildings, among them Canterbury Cathedral in England; granules of the rock were used more recently for the vaults of the Channel Tunnel. The plaster cast of a dino-saur skeleton found locally (during the building of the motorway in 1991) and an audio-visual presentation of the quarryman's trade may also be viewed.

Return to D 232.

Almost immediately, a pretty mill beside the River Slack comes into view *(left)*.

In Wierre-Effroy take D 234 to Conteville-lès-Boulogne, then take D 233 along the banks of the Wimereux River.

Wimille – The graves of the aeronauts Pilâtre de Rozier and Romain are in the old cemetery.

Return to Boulogne.

Musée de l'Air et de l'Espace du BOURGET★★

LE BOURGET AIR AND SPACE MUSEUM
Michelin map 101 folds 7 and 17 – Michelin plan 20

ccess: *Leave Paris by motorway A 1 then follow signs.*

e Bourget airfield was created in 1914 and rapidly became an important airport and ilitary air base. It was from here that Nungesser and Coli set off in their *White Bird* n 8 May 1927 in a doomed attempt to reach the American coast. Thirteen days later, the early hours of 22 May, Lindbergh successfully landed his *Spirit of St Louis* in aris, after achieving the first nonstop solo flight across the Atlantic in the history of viation. Costes and Bellonte were the first to accomplish this feat in the opposite rection when *Question Mark* landed on 1 September 1930.

nce the Charles-de-Gaulle airport at Roissy became operational, Le Bourget has been sed mainly for private aircraft and business flights.

very two years, Le Bourget hosts the International Air and Space Show *(see Calendar f Events)*.

Visit of the museum ⊘ – The museum has been laid out in the former terminal building at Le Bourget and it boasts some extraordinary collections retelling the history of the conquest of the skies. The adventure began with **hot air balloons**★ after the experiment carried out by Rozier and Arlandes in 1783 and a 1.6:3 model of their balloon can be seen in the museum, to recall the event. This first success resulted in the rapid expansion of flying. The decisive step came with the crossing of the English Channel. It cost the lives of Rozier and Romain in their balloon in 1785 but was a triumph for JP Blanchard the same year. A veritable fashion for hot air balloons then took over the interior design sector. The museum has more than 400 objects reflecting this enthusiasm including knickknacks, wall fabrics, engravings, ceramics, and furniture (note the copy of G Tissandier's desk). Later, balloons were to prove very useful in military operations or as a means of transport (postal services, means of escape for statesman Gambetta) during the Franco-Prus-sian war of 1870. The system was perfected and the balloons could then be steered. They provided inspiration for a great painter and photographer, Nadar. Meanwhile, Jules Verne was forecasting the days of machines "heavier than air" in his novel *Robur le Conquérant*.

The **Grande Galerie**★★ traces the early years of aviation and has the largest collec-tion in the world dealing with this period. The first prototypes were gliders, like the one flown by Massa-Biot (1879). Some of the aircraft were inspired by bionics, among them the Clément Ader's strange *Éole*, which was designed after observa-tion of a bat. The pioneers had boundless imagination and the lightness of the aircraft structures is decidedly perplexing. Among the earliest aircraft, note Farman's *Voisin* (first round 1km/0.6mi trip, in Issy-les-Moulineaux, 1907), the

Musée de l'Air et de l'Espace – Concorde

elegant and popular *Levasseur Antoinette* (1908), the *Blériot-XI* which succeede
in flying across the Channel etc. With the outbreak of the First World War, avi
tion underwent rapid progress. Aircraft structures and power were increased ar
the skies became the setting for the first aerial battles. This period is well repr
sented with Guynemer's *Spad-VII* and the *Spad-XIII* painted in the colours of flyir
ace René Fonck (75 victories). Note the basket of an enormous Zeppelin and th
"squadron's bar" reconstructed in an Adrian-type prefab where the drabness
lightened by the songs of Maurice Chevalier.

After the war, aeronautics continued to develop and records were made or broke
Hall A contains the famous *Potez-53* (it achieved average speeds
322kph/200mph over a distance of 2 000km/1 243mi in 1933), the very powerf
Caudron 714R (900 hp), the *Breguet XIX* "Nungesser-Coli" in which Costes ar
Le Brix made the first successful crossing of the South Atlantic in 1927. The Secor
World War is represented in **Hall B** by some fearsome fighters such as the *Spitfi
MK-16* used by the Free French Airforce, the *YAK-3* painted in the colours of th
Normandie-Niemen squadron, or the enormous *P-47 Thunderbolt* (a 2 000t
fighter bomber). The first jet-engined planes appeared at the end of the war. **Hall**
has an exhibition of amazing prototypes with thermopropulsion such as the *Ledu
010* and the *Nord-1500 Griffon*. The **other three halls** cover the French Air For
since 1945 *(Mystère-IV, Super Sabre)*, aerial sports *(Stampe et Vertongen* bi-plai
from Belgium and the first autogiros), and the conquest of space *(Diamant* lau
cher, reproduction of the famous *Sputnik* space capsule). Outside are examples
French technology at its best with a gigantic model of *Ariane-V*, 45m/146ft hig
and a Concorde in its new shed.

Château de BRETEUIL★★

Michelin Map 101 fold 31

Access from Paris: *Pont de Sèvres and N 118 towards the motorway to Chartres (A 1(
Take the Saclay exit and follow the signs to Chevreuse (N 306 then D 906). Fro
Chevreuse, the château is signposted.*

Tour ⊘ – This château, which was known for many years as Brévilliers, is built
the Louis XIII style in brick and stone. It consists of a main building flanked
two low wings. The tour begins with an introduction to the most famous membe
of the family, including Gabrielle-Émilie de Breteuil, a brilliant scientist who w
known for her long love affair with Voltaire, and Louis-Auguste de Breteuil, amba
sador and government minister during the reign of Louis XVI.

On the first floor, the family memorabilia takes on quite another dimension thanks
the waxwork figures which bring back to life a few historical events. Louis XVI
shown with Louis-Auguste de Breteuil and Marie-Antoinette, signing the arre
warrant for the Cardinal de Rohan who was implicated in the mysterious affair of t
Queen's necklace. Note the Dauphine's spinning wheel and the portrait of the Dauph
(the future Louis XVII) by Koucharsky. Further on is Louis XVIII, sitting in the act
wheelchair used by him and thought to have been made by Jacob. He is talking bu
ness with Duc Decazes and Charles de Breteuil. The lacquer bedchamber whi
accommodated so many illustrious guests provides the setting for a tableau w
Proust while in the smoking room the figures represent Henri de Breteuil, Gambe
and the future Edward VII laying down the bases of the Entente Cordiale (1904)
The château's most outstanding exhibit remains the **Teschen table★★**, a table inl
with stones, gems and petrified wood. The play of light across its surface sho
it off to its full advantage. This superb piece of craftsmanship was given to Lou
Auguste de Breteuil (1730-1807) by Empress Maria Teresa of Austria. He h
been the successful mediator during discussions leading to the Treaty of Tesch
(1779) which put an end to a serious regional conflict between the Empire a
Prussia. The Breteuil family's international importance is also illustrated by its lir

with the British royal family, an example of which was Edward VII's visit to the château on 3 May 1905. The sumptuous meal served to him is remembered in the dining room where the table has been laid and in the kitchens reconstructed as they were at that time.

★★The park – Lying on the edge of a plateau overlooking the upper Chevreuse Valley, the 75ha/185 acre park provides some beautiful views and diverse landscapes. Near the château are the **formal French gardens** created by the Duchênes in accordance with Lenôtre's principles. They include a lake, 16C dovecote, statues and topiaried yews and boxwood. The **Princes' Garden** is vividly and variously coloured with flowering cherries, roses and some outstanding peonies. The harmonious setting is completed by waxwork tableaux in the outbuildings representing several of **Perrault's Fairy Tales**. Play areas have also been laid out for younger visitors. At the bottom of the slope are two lakes in romantic, untamed surroundings, an ideal place for a stroll.

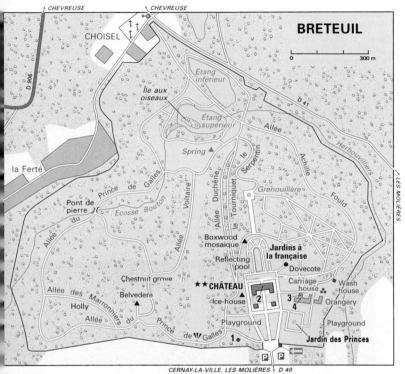

Perrault's Fairy Tales
1 - Little Red Riding Hood, **2** - Sleeping Beauty, **3** - Puss in Boots, **4** - Tom Thumb, **5** - Wild Ass's Skin

CALAIS

Conurbation 101768
Michelin map 51 fold 2 or 236 fold 2

Calais is divided into two distinct districts: the administrative and industrial centre, Calais-Sud, and the maritime centre, Calais-Nord, which was rebuilt after the last war. The town gave its name to the Pas-de-Calais, the strait known on the north side of the Channel as the Straits of Dover. The history of the town has been enormously influenced by its proximity to the English coast, only 38km/23.5mi away, and on a clear day the white cliffs of Dover are visible from the promenade and the vast sandy beach west of Calais harbour's entrance.

The Burghers of Calais – After his success at Crécy **Edward III** of England needed to create a powerful base in France. He began the siege of Calais on 3 September 1346 but eight months later had still not been able to breach the valiant defence led by the town governor, Jean de Vienne; in fact, it was famine that forced the inhabitants to capitulate in the end.

Six burghers, led by **Eustache de Saint-Pierre**, prepared to sacrifice themselves in order that the other citizens of Calais would be spared the sword. In thin robes, "barefoot, bareheaded, halters about their necks and the keys to the town in their hands", they presented themselves before the king to be delivered to the executioner. They were saved by the intercession of Queen Philippa of Hainault who pleaded for mercy for them.

Calais was in the hands of the English for over two centuries and was liberated onl
in 1558, by the Duke of Guise. This was a mortal blow to **Mary Tudor**, Queen of England
who said: "If my heart were laid open, the word "Calais" would be engraved on it."

Port Activity – Calais is the leading passenger port in France and the second in th
world. It has always had a close association with England.

Harbour traffic was not reduced as a result of the opening of the Channel Tunnel. I
1996 over 18 million passengers passed through the port together with 3.2 millio
private vehicles and 765 000 lorries. To cope with this level of activity, Calais is equippe
with efficient cross-Channel installations. The ferry port is directly linked to the Euro
pean motorway network (A 26 and A 16) and the loading and unloading of vehicle
has been simplified by special equipment. P & O-Stena Line and Seafrance, two hug
car-ferry companies, provide 60 daily crossings between Calais and Dover lasting 75min
In addition, Hoverspeed runs hovercraft (35min), catamarans and fast ferries on th
Calais-Douvre route.

Traditionally, Calais has always been a leading commercial port, importing and export
ing minerals, aggregates, sugar and various other products totalling 25 million tonnes
which ranks Calais in fourth place among French ports.

Lace – Together with Caudry-en-Cambrésis, Calais is the main centre of machine-mad
lace, employing about 2 000 workers using over 350 looms. Englishmen from Not
tingham introduced the industry at the beginning of the 19C; quality was improve
around 1830 when the first Jacquard looms were introduced.

75 % of Calais' lace is exported, to 140 different countries; 80 % of it is used for lin
gerie, 20 % for dresses (wedding gowns, cocktail and evening dresses, off-the-pe
and designer clothing). Traditional lace made with the Leavers machine is entitled t
a quality label created in 1991, representing a peacock.

The town has also diversified into textiles, wood, paper pulp, chemicals and foods.

SIGHTS *3hr*

★★ Monument des Bourgeois de Calais (Monument to the Burghers of Calais) (**DY**) – Thi
famous work by Rodin is located in between the hôtel de ville and Parc St-Pierre
It dates from 1895 and exemplifies the sculptor's brilliance: the bronze group is si
multaneously full of vitality and pathos. Each of the six lifesize figures should b
admired separately: their veins and muscles exaggerated, their forms tense an
haughty, they express the heroic nobility of the men obliged to humiliate them
selves before the king of England.

The Burghers of Calais by Rodin

CALIS

B Tour du guet
H Hôtel de ville
M¹ Musée des Beaux-Arts et de la Dentelle
M² Musée de la Guerre

Hôtel de ville (DY H) – The beautiful and graceful town hall is built of brick and stone in the 15C Flemish style yet dates only from the turn of the century. The belfry (75m/246ft) can be seen for miles in all directions; the sound of its bell is very appealing. Inside, a **stained-glass window** which recalls the departure of the English diffuses the sunlight over the grand staircase.

Harbour – Walk around the old Bassin du Paradis, where the Louis XVIII Column recalls the king's landing in 1814; follow the quays (Monument des Sauveteurs) to the end of the harbour entrance.
The Courgain district *(right)*, which was rebuilt after the war, is where many sailors live. The lighthouse is located behind this area.

Le phare (**CX**) – The lighthouse (53m/174ft tall; *271 steps*) was built in 1848 to replace the watchtower beacon. From the top there is a surprisingly wide and splendid panoramic **view★★** over Calais, the harbour, the basins, the town's stadium, Place d'Armes and the unexpectedly large Church of Our Lady.

Place d'Armes (**CX**) – Before the devastation of the war, this was the heart of medieval Calais. Only the 13C **watchtower** (**B**) has survived. The belfry and the town hall beside it are popular subjects for artists.

★**Musée des Beaux-Arts et de la Dentelle** ⊘ (**CX M¹**) – The fine arts and lace museum gives an insight into changes in sculpture over the 19C and 20C and styles of painting between the 16C and 20C.

Musée des Beaux-Arts et de la Dentelle, Calais

Calais lace depicting the Blériot-XI crossing the Channel

Ground floor – One of the rooms illustrates 19C **sculpture** centred on the works of Rodin and the studies he made for *The Burghers of Calais*. The concept of modern sculpture is made quite clear through the works of Rodin's predecessors, including Carrière-Belleuse, Carpeaux, Barye, and of some of his students, Bourdelle and Maillol.

A large section (a lace and fashion museum is scheduled to be opened at a later date in a former tulle-making factory) deals with machine-made **Calais lace** and with hand-made lace. The history of lace is illustrated by production techniques, haute-couture dresses, pieces of lace and lingerie from the 17C to the present day (the museum owns more than 400 000 examples of machine-made lace). All the exhibits are set within the economic and social context of the time.

First floor – This floor houses extensive collections of **paintings** from the 17C to the 19C by the Flemish and North-European schools.

There are also works by modern and contemporary artists such as Jean Dubuffet *(Landscape around Calais)*, Félix Del Marle *(Construction-Colour)*, Picasso *(The Old Man)*, Fautrier *(Nude with Raised Arms)*, Lipchitz, Arp....

Musée de la Guerre ⊘ (**CY M²**) – Opposite the town hall, in the middle of Parc St Pierre, there is a large bunker that was used as a telephone exchange by the Germans during the Second World War. Posters, tracts, memorabilia and letters in some of the rooms evoke the Resistance, the occupation of Calais and the Battle of Britain. The documents and the museum's simplicity make this a moving visit.

Église Notre-Dame (**CDX**) – Construction of the church started at the end of the 13C, when the nave was built. The building was finished during the English occupation at the end of the 14C, which explains the surprising look of the tower, chancel and transept: despite being in France, they recall the English perpendicular Gothic style. In 1691 Vauban had a large cistern built on the north side. The wedding of Captain Charles de Gaulle with a young Calais woman was celebrated here in 1921.

The star ratings are allocated for various categories:- regions of scenic beauty with dramatic natural features- cities with a cultural heritage- elegant resorts and charming villages-ancient monuments and fine architecture, museum and picture galleries.

CAMBRAI★

Population 33 092

Michelin map 53 fold 3, 4 or 236 fold 27

Cambrai stands in the centre of a rich cereal and sugar beet region, on the east bank of the River Escaut (or Scheldt). Traditionally cambric linen was made here, bleached in the sunny meadows then used to make up handkerchiefs and fine lingerie. In gourmet terms, Cambrai is known for its small chitterling sausages (andouillettes), its tripe and its mint-flavoured sweets (bêtises de Cambrai).

The town is built of white limestone and is overlooked by the three towers of the belfry, the cathedral and St Gery's Church. Once military and archiepiscopal, Cambrai today looks peaceful, a ring of boulevards having replaced the ramparts.

The yachting marina at Cantimpré can cater for up to 50 leisure craft.

The "Swan of Cambrai" – In 1695 François de Salignac de La Mothe-Fénelon (1651-1715), a great lord, man of the Church and famous writer, was made archbishop of Cambrai. **Fénelon** was venerated by his flock for his gentleness and charity, and learned while in Cambrai that Rome had condemned his Maximes des Saints; this work defended quietism, a doctrine made fashionable by Mme Guyon, which exalted the "Pure Love of God". In response the former tutor of the Duke of Burgundy first climbed into the pulpit to preach obedience to the Church's decisions and then wrote a pastoral letter to the same effect, thus showing an admirable humility.

The charity of the "Swan of Cambrai" was often called upon during the Spanish War of Succession: starving peasants from the surrounding Cambrai region poured into the archdiocese, where Fénelon welcomed them. On one occasion a cow was lost on the way to the archbishop, who immediately set out on foot with a servant to find the animal; he found the cow and was able to return it to its poor owner. Fénelon died at Cambrai after a carriage accident.

Raoul de Cambrai – This 12C chanson de geste describes a historical event, the struggle between Raoul de Cambrai, who was unjustly deprived of his father's estate, and the descendants of Herbert de Vermandois in the 10C. The epic tale also paints a picture of feudal morals and ethics.

OLD TOWN 1hr 30min

Porte de Paris (AZ) – This town gate, a vestige of the medieval fortifications, is flanked by two round towers dating from 1390.

Follow avenue de la Victoire towards the town hall, visible at the end of the street. Place du St-Sépulcre appears shortly on the left.

Cathédrale Notre-Dame (AZ) – Originally dedicated to the Holy Sepulchre, the abbey church was elevated to the rank of cathedral after the Revolution. It was built in the 18C and has been altered several times since; the tower dates from 1876. An 18C convent building stands to the right.

The rounded chapels terminating the transept arms are decorated with large trompe-l'œil grisailles, painted in 1760 by the Antwerp artist Martin Geeraerts. They represent the Virgin Mary (south) and Christ (north). Fénelon's tomb, sculpted by David d'Angers in 1826, is in the apsidal chapel. The prelate raises himself, looking heavenward in a Romantic burst of emotion; his hands are particularly fine.

A statue of Fénelon by Auricoste stands on the left of the cathedral.

Chapelle du Grand Séminaire (AZ B) – The chapel is set back from the square. It was completed in 1692 and formerly belonged to the Jesuit school; its lively and theatrical Baroque façade nevertheless retains a symmetry through the regular arrangement of windows, pilasters, scrolls and firepots.

Among the richly carved decor, note the high-relief sculpture of the Assumption, which was added in the 19C during restoration.

Église St-Géry – The Entombment by Rubens

Maison espagnole (AZ E) – *Tourist office*. This wooden house, its gables sheathed in slate, dates from the late 16C. It is possible to see the medieval cellars and, on the first floor, the oak carvings which once adorned the façade.

Note the 17C and 18C private residences along rue du Grand-Séminaire, rue de l'Epée and rue de Vaucelette. One of them houses the fine arts museum.

Place Fénelon (AY 16) – The square is located on the site of the old cathedral, a splendid Gothic structure demolished after the Revolution. The 17C entrance porch still remains from Fénelon's **archiepiscopal palace**.

Église St-Géry ⊙ **(AY)** – Overlooked by a tower (76m/249ft tall), the old church of St Aubert's Abbey rises on the site once occupied by a temple believed to have been dedicated to Jupiter Capitolinus. Construction of this austere Classical building lasted from 1698 to 1745. The ambitious plans called for a chancel with an ambulatory and radiating chapels, preceded by a monumental canopy resting on four colossal Baroque columns.

The beautiful **rood screen** (1632), which formerly closed off the chancel entrance, was moved to the west end of the nave. It is a good example of the Baroque style with its contrasting red and black marble and its carved decoration by Gaspard Marsy, creating an impression of movement or even agitation: *putti* on the wing, alabaster statues and high-relief carvings relating the miracles of Christ. The monumental pulpit, installed in 1850, was the work of Cambrai craftsmen. The chancel contains 18C furniture: an altar and, in particular, the wood panels with medallions depicting the lives of St Augustine and St Aubert.

The north transept houses Rubens' enormous dramatic painting, **The Entombment★★**. The 14C **statue** in the south transept was discovered in 1982 during excavations in the crypt and represents a bishop.

Cross Place du 9 Octobre to reach Place Aristide-Briand.

Place Aristide-Briand (AYZ 6) – The square was entirely rebuilt after the First World War and is dominated by the cold and majestic lines of the **hôtel de ville (H)** which was rebuilt at the end of the 19C but was set ablaze during the First World War. Its reconstruction in the 1920s, together with that of the square itself, respected the old façade and its Louis XVI peristyle; this was largely due to the commitment of the Parisian architect, Antoine. The hall is surmounted by a columned bell-tower, flanked by the town's two jacks o' the clock, Martin and Martine. According to legend these two individuals, who appear in parades as giants, were 14C blacksmiths who dealt with the lord ravaging the region by felling him with hammer blows. The bronze figures (2m/6.5ft tall), dressed as turbanned Moors, date from 1512; they strike the town bell with their hammers to sound the hour.

The southwest corner of the square marks the beginning of a long avenue, Mail St-Martin, which offers a good view of the 15C-18C **belfry (AZ K)** (70m/230ft tall), which is all that remains of St Martin's Church.

Cambrai – Musée des Beaux-Arts:
Fragment of a 14C Annunciation

ADDITIONAL SIGHTS

Musée des Beaux-Arts ⊙ **(AZ M)** – The town museum is housed in a mansion built for the Comte de Francqueville c 1720. It has been restored and substantially extended, with the addition of two new buildings.

The **archeology** department occupies the vaulted 18C cellars. Three themes recall the Gallo-Roman period: ceramics (model of a kiln), housing and funerals (burial urn). Exhibits from the Merovingian period include funerary artefacts from sites near Cambrai, Les Rues-des-Vignes (pairs of gilded silver fibulae) and Busigny, all of which were explored in 1986. The section devoted to osteo-archeology gives a clearer insight into man during the Dark Ages (age of the deceased, traces of disease or illness etc).

An audio-visual presentation based on a relief map of the town serves as an introduction to a tour of the department devoted to **Cambrai and its heritage**.

CAMBRAI

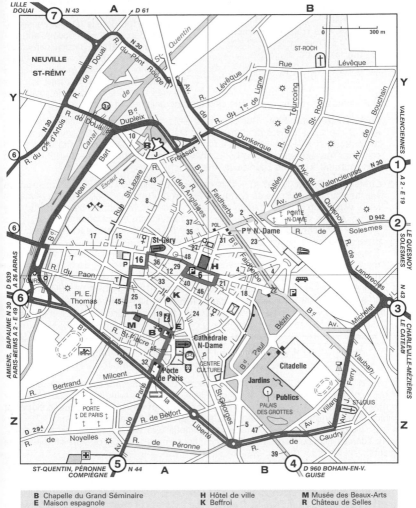

B Chapelle du Grand Séminaire   **H** Hôtel de ville   **M** Musée des Beaux-Arts
E Maison espagnole   **K** Beffroi   **R** Château de Selles

The many sculptures come from religious buildings that have been demolished. The set from the Abbaye St-Géry in Les Monts-des-Boeufs (12C) consists of three statue-columns representing the seasons, a capital and small tympana, one of which illustrates the legend of Pyramus and Thisbe. The blue stone **choir screen★** from the chapel in the Hôpital St-Julien dates from 1541. Alabaster statues, including a late 16C statue of St Sebastian come from the former cathedral church. The last room contains the impressive painted **processional carriage of the canonesses of Ste-Aldegonde de Maubeuge★** (18C), carved out of wood. A painting by Van der Meulen is a graphic description of the capture of Cambrai by Louis XIV in 1677.

The **Fine Arts** section gives a panoramic overview of Dutch painting in the late 16C and 17C. The collection includes still-life paintings by Nicolas Van Veerendael, *Portrait of a Man* by Mirevelt, *Entombment* by Hendrick de Clerck (1690), *The Interior of Antwerp Cathedral* by Hendrick Van Steenwick (1613), *Dido and Aeneas Hunting* by Jan Miel, and *The Card Players* by Rombouts.

The 18C French school is represented by Berthelemy *(Esther Fainting)*, Jacques de Lajoue *(Astronomy)*, and PA Wille *(The Dying Moments of a Beloved Wife)*. In the 19C and 20C, portraits, religious subjects and landscapes predominate with Carolus Durand, Boudin, Utrillo, Marquet, Othon Friesz etc.

> **Beguine convents**
>
> Beguine convents consisted of small terraced houses forming an enclosure for single women or widows wishing to lead a life of devotion and charity. There were eleven of them in Cambrai. The Béguinage St-Vaast, which dates from 1354, was transferred to rue des Anglaises in 1545. This is the last such enclosure still existing in France.

The museum also has a sculpture collection, with works by Rodin, Camille Claudel, Bourdelle, Zadkine and the contemporary artist Georges Jeanclos (he carved the doorway for St-Ayoul's Church in Provins).

Jardin public (**BZ**) – The park was laid out in the late 19C when the ramparts were destroyed, on old military grounds; it includes the Batiste garden consisting of lawns decorated with flowers and statues, the Monstrelet garden named after the 15C chronicler, with its bandstand, and the Caves garden situated alongside the 16C-17C **citadel** built by Charles V of Spain. Only the royal gate and a barracks remain, while the countermine galleries lie underground.

Porte Notre-Dame (**BY**) – This piece of the old fortifications was built at the beginning of the 17C; it owes its name to the statue of the Virgin Mary which adorns the outer face. The gate is unusual for its diamond-shaped stones and its grooved columns. The sun representing Louis XIV was added to the pediment after the town was captured from the Spanish by the French.

Château de Selles ⊘ (**AY R**) – This castle dates back to the 13C; its construction was attributed to Nicolas de Fontaine, bishop of Cambrai. It allowed the owner to keep watch on the craftsmen's quarter and the windmills belonging to the bishop. It also stood guard over the main trading route to Flanders.

The five projecting corners were reinforced by round towers; each originally had three storeys with ogival vaulting.

The castle is unusual in having a corridor *(gaine)* running all the way around inside the walls and connecting the towers. This corridor, which was used as a prison in the 16C, is covered with period graffiti. From 1520 onwards, the moat was filled in and the castle was integrated into the town's fortifications. The 18C stone and brick barracks have just been restored; they now house the law courts.

CASSEL★

Population 2 177
Michelin map 51 fold 4 or 236 fold 4

Cassel is a small town that is Flemish in both its customs and appearance: an enormous cobbled main square (Grand' Place), narrow, winding streets and low whitewashed houses. It stands on a **site**★ at the top of Cassel Hill, the green slopes of which, formerly dotted with windmills, overlook the flat Flanders region.

Local traditions are still celebrated: the religious fête with its mass, parades, traditional games and competitions; archery; the carnival; the procession of the Reuze giants.

Two regional specialities may be sampled here: Cassel butter and cheese from Mont des Cats.

Two World Wars – From October 1914 to June 1915 **General Foch** had his headquarters at Cassel. From here he followed the progress of the battle of Flanders which was raging on the banks of the Yser. He stayed at the Hôtel de Schoebecque at no 32 of what is now rue du Maréchal Foch.

In May 1940 members of the British expeditionary corps retreating towards Yser and Dunkirk fought a fierce rearguard action at Cassel, which resulted in 2 000 dead and 1 000 prisoners on the battlefield.

"Cassel Hill" – The highest point of the region (176m/577ft high) and a link in the Flemish hill-range, the hill looks surprisingly large rising in the middle of the Flemish plain; although about 30km/18mi from the coast, it is used as a landmark by sailors. Its peak is made up of a very hard ferruginous layer.

To the east, **Mont des Récollets** (159m/521ft high) owes its name to a convent of Recollect nuns which existed there from 1615 to 1870.

SIGHTS *1hr*

Public Gardens – The gardens at the top of the hill occupy the site of a medieval castle which once incorporated a collegiate church, the crypt of which remains. An equestrian statue of General Foch stands in the garden's centre, together with an 18C wooden **windmill** ⊘ from Arneke which was re-erected here to replace the castle's original windmill.

A tour of the terrace offers an excellent **panorama**★★ *(viewing platforms)* over the picturesque jumble of Cassel's old rooftops, and beyond to the hills of Flanders and the plain, as far as the North Sea and the belfry of Bruges; a local saying maintains that "from Cassel you can see five kingdoms: France, Belgium, Holland, England and, above the clouds, the Kingdom of Heaven".

Grand' Place – The main square, irregularly shaped and cobbled, extends along the hillside near the church. It still has an attractive group of 16C, 17C and 18C houses on its south side, among them the Hôtel de la Noble Cour.

Hôtel de la Noble Cour – Under the Ancien Régime this 16C-17C house was the seat of the court in which the local lord dispensed justice. A high roof dotted with blind dormer windows crowns the façade, which is entirely of stone – unusual in the North – pierced by large windows with alternately triangular and curvilinear pediments; the elegant Renaissance doorway, flanked by grey marble columns, is decorated with Fames in the spandrels and with Sirens and foliate scrolls on the frieze.
The **museum** ⊘ includes the Archive Room with its Louis XV woodwork, the Grande Salle (Flemish furniture and 17C and 18C objects), the Court Room (collection of faiences and northern French porcelain), the Salon de la Châtellenie (Louis XV woodwork, Louis XVI furniture), and Foch's office, preserved as it was in 1915. The ground floor houses reconstructions of a Flemish interior and a bar.

Collégiale Notre-Dame ⊘ – This is a Gothic Flemish church with three gables, three aisles, three apses and a square tower over the transept crossing. Foch often came here to pray and meditate.

Ancienne chapelle des Jésuites – Pleasant 17C brick and stone façade.

EXCURSIONS

Steenvoorde – *8km/5mi by D 948*. This typical small Flemish town with painted houses under red tiled roofs was once famous for its sheets; today it is the home of one of the largest dairies in the area.
The town celebrates the legend of its giant, Yan den Houtkapper: he was a woodcutter who made a pair of everlasting boots for Charlemagne; in return he was given a suit of armour, which he still wears for the processions in which he is the hero.

Windmills ⊘ – Three well-preserved windmills can be seen near the town. The first, the **Steenmeulen** at Terdeghem *(on D 947 south)*, is a truncated brick mill; the other two, the **Drievemeulen** *(on D 948 west)* and the **Noordmeulen** *(on D 18 northwest)*, are wooden postmills.

Situated 12km/7.5mi north of Steenwoorde and 5km/3mi east of Wormhout, the Café des Orgues, 2 Rue des Orgues in Herzeele, is the favourite haunt, every Sunday (except in January) from 4pm to midnight, of lovers of waltzes, tangos and polkas, who dance to the sound of three hurdy-gurdies made by Mortier between 1912 and 1939.

Wormhout – *10km/6mi north via D 218 and D 916*.

Moulin Deschodt ⊘ – This wooden post mill is the last of 11 windmills which stood in the town in 1780.

Musée Jeanne-Devos ⊘ – This charming Flemish house, flanked by a dovecote and set within lovely gardens at the end of a cul-de-sac, is the old Wormhout presbytery (18C). It was inhabited by Jeanne Devos who collected, until her death in 1989, a multitude of objects from daily life. A photographer by profession, she left thousands of photographs portraying the ordinary and extraordinary lives of the villagers nearby.

Abbaye de CHAALIS★
Michelin map 106 fold 9

The estate lies on the edge of Ermenonville Forest opposite the Mer de Sable theme park *(see Excursions)* and, during the 19C, it evoked the gentle, romantic charm suggested by religious contemplation. Later, and up to 1912, Chaalis inspired its last owners to collect works of art and to entertain some of the most notable personalities of their time.

A prosperous abbey – Chaalis was a Cistercian abbey *(see Introduction: Monasteries in Île-de-France)*, built on the site of a former priory in 1136 by Louis the Fat. The monks led a pious and modest country life, husbanding the land, cultivating vines, keeping bees and fishing in the lakes.
St Louis paid frequent visits to the abbey: he took part in the monks' prayers and duties, even waited on them, cared for the sick and watched over the dying.

Decline – During the 16C the abbey was held *in commendam* and the abbots were appointed by the king. The first was Cardinal Ippolito d'Este, son of Alfonso d'Este and Lucrezia Borgia, a distant cousin of François I (the Cardinal's brother, Ercole II d'Este, married Renée of France, the second daughter of Louis XII). Better known as Cardinal of Ferrara, this enthusiastic art lover had his private chapel decorated with murals and commissioned fine gardens but he nevertheless preferred his Tivoli residence, the Villa d'Este, where he died in 1572.

In the 18C the ninth abbot, one of the Great Condé's grandsons, attempted a costly operation to restore the abbey to plans by Jean Aubert, the architect who designed the Great Stables at Chantilly. It was a disaster; after only one side of the building had been completed (1739, currently the Château-Museum) work stopped owing to lack of funds. This financial crisis prompted Louis XVI to close down the abbey in 1785. During the upheaval of the French Revolution, Chaalis was badly pillaged and the greater part of the building destroyed.

Restoration – The estate frequently changed hands. Romantic painters and poets appreciated the melancholy charm of the old walls and their lush, verdant setting. In 1850 the highly distinguished Mme de Vatry bought the abbey ruins; she converted the 18C building into a château, had the park refurbished and entertained lavishly.

These efforts were continued by Mme de Vatry's heirs and by the last owner, Nélie Jacquemart-André, the widow of banker Edouard André who founded the Paris museum which bears her name. She died in 1912 and bequeathed the estate to the Institute of France. Its first curator was the art critic Louis Gillet (1876-1943); his successor, the art historian Émile Mâle, died here in 1954.

Abbaye de Chaalis

★FORMER ABBEY *1hr*

★**Church Ruins** – Ready for consecration in 1219, Chaalis Abbey was the first Cistercian church built in the Gothic style. Of the original buildings there remain a staircase turret, the northern transept arm surrounded by radiating chapels – an unusual feature – and a section of wall from the north aisle with blind arcades reminiscent of the old cloister.

Chapelle de l'abbé – Built around 1250, the chapel is a fine example of Gothic splendour from the time of the Sainte-Chapelle in Paris. On the right, a bronze bust portraying Mme Jacquemart-André marks the site of her grave. Beyond the chapel a strange 16C crenellated wall with asymmetrical merlons sets the boundaries of the rose garden. Above the heavy archway, the coat of arms of Cardinal Louis d'Este, nephew of Cardinal of Ferrara, is displayed.

From north of the château there is a fine perspective of the park with its flower beds and dazzling lake, restored in the 19C.

★**Château-Musée** ⊘ – The personality and taste of Mme André are revealed as soon as one enters the **Salle des Moines** which houses Italian 15C Gothic furniture, small paintings, two panels from an altarpiece painted by Jean de Bellegambe, many religious statues (14C-16C French) and a few objects from the abbey.

This mixture of styles is apparent in the ground-floor gallery, containing various busts, chests and glass-cabinets and leading successively to the **dining room** (hunting scenes by Oudry and Desportes), the **library**, the **Medici hall** (Renaissance tapestries and furniture bearing the arms of the Medici family), the **billiard room** *(The Capture of Namur* and *The Capture of Valenciennes by Martin des Batailles)*, the strange **Indian drawing room** (chests, altars, arms...) and the **large drawing room** (portraits by Nicolas de Largillière and Van Loo).

The main staircase gives access to the **private apartments of Mme André**: a long corridor with silvered-leather double doors leading to the Eagles' Room decorated in Empire style, then to the bedroom in two parts separated by a pair of imposing columns (hue gilt-wood tester bed dating from the Louis XV period); next come the water-green and gold bathroom and the boudoir with its tapestry, *The Country Ball*, after a design by Boucher.

The first-floor gallery, decorated with Renaissance paintings and furniture, ends with the famous **panels painted by Giotto★★**, depicting St John the Evangelist and St Lawrence. The former cells have been turned into guest rooms fitted with bathrooms. The last rooms are devoted to the Henri Amic bequest (wooden objects from St Lucia, Japanese intos and netsuke) and to the **Galerie Jean-Jacques Rousseau** (collection donated to the Institut de France by the last Marquis de Girardin in 1923).

EXCURSIONS

Ermenonville *– 3km/1mi south on N 330.* In May 1778 **Jean-Jacques Rousseau** was invited to stay at the Château d'Ermenonville *(private)* by the Marquis de Girardin, who had acquired the estate in 1763, and it is here that Rousseau rekindled his passion for nature: he walked, daydreamed in the park and taught music to his host's children, until his sudden death on 2 July from a stroke.

The **Parc Jean-Jacques Rousseau★** ⊙, which the marquess had transformed from sandy, swampy land into a superb landscaped garden in the French style with shaded paths, graceful vistas, elegant rockeries and charming brooks, still contains some strategically sited monuments.

Living like lords

Château d'Ermenonville – ☎ 03 44 54 00 26, fax 03 44 54 01 00. Separated from its park by the road which runs through the village, the castle has retained its elegant outline and offers a blend of modern luxury and refined 18C decoration. Double room from 890F, fixed price menus from 195F.

Mer de Sable ⊙ *– 0.5km/0.25mi south on N 330.* The sand deposits date from the Tertiary Era and at the end of the Ice Age this region was probably one vast sandy moor covered with wild heather.

The landscape has been developed into themed areas evoking China, the Wild West or Morocco through characteristic scenery. Various scenes – of Indians attacking trains, fights beside a ranch, or displays of horsemanship – animate the different areas. The small train tour of the desert and the shows are complemented by various thrilling attractions (white-water rides, head-first slides etc) and more peaceful games. A glass-blower demonstrates his skill and sells his production on the site.

Forêt d'Ermenonville – After 1840 the clearings in the vast heather-covered moor were planted with maritime and Scots pines, and country lanes have now been marked out as suitable for walks. Cars are not allowed on the forest roads except along the "Longue Route" leading to the crossroads and on the section linking Baraque de Chaalis to the commemorative monument marking the crash of the Turkish Airlines DC 10 on 3 March 1974, in which 346 people died.

The southwest of the forest, which enchanted Corot, is not accessible though the road from Mortefontaine to Thiers offers views of the lake and the wilder landscape.

The length of time given in this guide
- for touring allows time to enjoy the views and the scenery;
- for sightseeing is the average time required for a visit.

Château de CHAMPS★★

Michelin map 101 fold 19 – Michelin plan 19

Access from Paris: *RER line A 4.*

Champs, built with the funds of two unfortunate financiers at the end of Louis XIV's reign, is characteristic of 18C architecture and decoration.

TOUR *about 1hr 30min*

★**Château** ⊘ – When the construction of Champs was completed by JB Bullet in 1708, his contemporaries were struck by the many changes made in the name of comfort. The rooms no longer communicated, the corridors were improved, each bedroom had its own closet and boudoir and a proper dining room was designed (until then the tables were laid in an antechamber). Mezzanines connecting with the ground floor by means of hidden staircases were built at the end of each wing: they provided accommodation for the guests' domestics.

On the ground floor, visitors are shown round the great salon, the dining room and the smoking room, with its portrait of Louis XV by a representative of the Van Loo School. The **Salon chinois**★★ is decorated with ornamental chinoiserie panels painted by Huet. The armchairs are upholstered with Beauvais tapestry depicting scenes from the *Fables* of La Fontaine: one of the collections executed after the cartoons of Oudry, director of the National Tapestry Works at Beauvais.

The boudoir is decorated with attractive Chinese pastoral scenes.

On the first floor, the Music Room offers a superb view of the park. Mme de Pompadour's bedroom may be visited – the marquess rented the château in 1757 – and the corner drawing room, embellished by superb rococo **wainscoting**★ and a portrait by Drouais of Mme de Pompadour dressed for gardening.

★★**Park** ⊘ – The park is a masterpiece of French gardening. Originally created by Claude Desgots, one of Le Nôtre's nephews, it was redesigned by Duchêne in the early 20C and features a sweeping perspective with elaborate boxwood patterns, fountains and groves.

The CHANNEL TUNNEL

Michelin map 51 folds 1, 2 or 236 fold 2

The "Chunnel" is the realisation of more than two centuries of dreams and unfinished projects.

History – Over the past 250 years there have been 27 proposals, the oldest of which was made in 1750 by a M Desmarets, who wanted to rejoin Britain to the mainland by a bridge, a tunnel or a causeway. From 1834 onwards, Aimé Thomé de Gamond, who is known as the "Father of the Tunnel", put forward several different propositions, all of them technically viable. In 1880, 1 840m/over 1mi of galleries were dug out on the site called the "Puits des Anciens". 2 000m/1.25mi were tunnelled out on the English side before the work was stopped. During a Franco-British summit conference in September 1981, the idea of building a fixed link was again mooted by British Prime Minister Margaret Thatcher and French President François Mitterrand. In October 1985, after an international competition, four projects were shortlisted and it was the Eurotunnel project which was finally selected, on 20 January 1986. A Franco-British treaty was signed on 12 February 1986 in Canterbury Cathedral with a view to the construction of the tunnel.

Facts and figures – The Channel tunnel was dug from access points near the French and English coasts. There was a 10m/32.5ft shaft near Folkestone and a gigantic earthwork 65m/211ft deep with a diameter of 50m/162.5ft in Sangatte. Most of the tunnel lies at a depth of 40m/130ft below the seabed, in a layer of blue chalk. Enormous tunnel-digging machines bored their way through the rock at a rate of 800 to 1 000m/867 to 1 083yd a month.

The **trans-Channel link** consists, in fact, of two railway tunnels 7.60m/25ft in diameter connected every 375m/406yd to a central service gallery 4.80m/16ft in diameter built for the purposes of ventilation, security, and system maintenance. The tunnels contain a single track and the trains run in one direction only, taking passengers and freight. The tunnels have a total length of 50km/31mi of which 24mi are beneath the Channel, 3km/2mi are beneath French soil and 9km/5.5mi are under English soil. They link two terminals, near Calais and Folkestone, accessible from special slip roads.

THE TERMINAL

The terminal is located at **Coquelles**, 3km/2mi from the coast. It covers 700ha/1 729 acres.

Cité Europe – This site includes a vast two-storey shopping centre designed by architect Paul Andreu. It has a hypermarket, more than 100 shops, 12 cinemas and the **cité gourmande** where there are more than thirty bars and restaurants, each frontage representing a different European country.

Coquelles – Tunnel-digging machine

RAILWAY SERVICES

Le Shuttle – *Folkestone to Calais.* The green and blue shuttle is 775m/0.5mi long. Passenger shuttles have one two-storey train for cars and one single-storey train for coaches and caravans. There are special shuttles for TGV's. A *rame* consists of 147 coaches, including one for embarkation and another for disembarkation. The Shuttle operates round the clock throughout the year. Departures vary depending on the volume of traffic (2 to 4 services every hour during the day, 1 per hour at night). The crossing lasts 35 minutes, including 28 minutes in the tunnel.

Eurostar – High-speed trains run by the French, Belgian and British railway companies run a daily service between Paris, Brussels and London. It takes approximately 3 hours to travel from Paris-Gare du Nord to London-Waterloo. There are also several trains a day between Lille and London.

Michelin green tourist guides
Landscapes
Monuments
Scenic routes, touring programmes
Geography
History, Art
Places to stay
Town and site plans
Practical information
A collection of guides for travelling in France and around the world.

119

Château de CHANTILLY★★★

Access from Paris: *SNCF Rail link from Gare du Nord.*

The name Chantilly brings to mind a château, a forest, a racecourse and the world of horse racing in general. Because of its remarkable setting, its park and the treasures in its museum, the Château de Chantilly is considered one of the major sights in France. Chantilly is also rapidly becoming an important cultural centre thanks to the activities of the Centre des Fontaines with its library boasting 600 000 titles (philosophy, art, religion etc).

HISTORICAL NOTES

From Cantilius to the Montmorency – Over the past 2 000 years, five castles have occupied this part of the Nonette Valley. Above the ponds and marshes of the area rose a rocky island where **Cantilius**, a native of Roman Gaul, built the first fortified dwelling. His name and achievement gave birth to Chantilly. In the Middle Ages the building became a fortress belonging to the Bouteiller, named after the hereditary duties he carried out at the court of the Capetians; originally in charge of the royal cellars, the Bouteiller de France was one of the king's close advisers.
In 1386 the land was bought by the chancellor, M. d'Orgemont, who had the castle rebuilt. The feudal foundations bore the three subsequent constructions. In 1450 the last descendant of the Orgemont married one of the Barons of Montmorency and Chantilly became the property of this illustrious family. It remained in their possession for 200 years.

Constable Anne, Duc de Montmorency – Anne de Montmorency was a devoted servant to a succession of six French kings from Louis XII to Charles IX. This formidable character gained a reputation as warrior, statesman, diplomat and patron of the arts. For forty years, apart from a few brief periods, he remained the leading noble of the land, second to the king. Childhood friend and companion-in-arms to François I, close adviser to Henri II, he even had some influence over Catherine de' Medici, who looked favourably upon the man who had advised her on cures for her infertility.
Constable Anne owned 600 fiefs, over 130 castles and estates, four mansions in Paris and numerous posts and offices. He was immensely wealthy. When he went to court he was escorted by 300 guards on horseback. Through his five sons and the husbands of his seven daughters he controlled most of the country's highest positions and had connections with Henri II, as well as with all the other most distinguished French families.
In 1528 the feudal castle of the Orgemont was demolished and the architect Pierre Chambiges replaced it with a palace built in the French Renaissance style. On a nearby island Jean Bullant erected the charming château which still stands today: the Petit

Château de Chantilly

Château. It was separated from the Grand Château by a moat − now filled in − which was spanned by two superimposed bridges. An aviary was set up in the tiny garden on the island. Constable Anne ordered great loads of earth and built the terrace which bears his statue.

Plans were made for new gardens and the best artists in town were hired to decorate the two palaces. Chantilly had become one of the most celebrated estates in France and even Charles V expressed his admiration when he was shown round it.

In 1567 Montmorency, aged 75, engaged in hostilities against the Protestants and perished in the Battle of St-Denis. It was no easy task to kill this energetic soldier: five strokes of the sword cut his face to ribbons, two blows of the bludgeon smashed his head and an arquebus caused his spine to snap. Before collapsing, Constable Anne broke his opponent's jaw with the pommel of his sword.

The last love of Henri IV − Henri IV often stayed at Chantilly, with his companion-in-arms Henri I de Montmorency, the son of Constable Anne. At the age of 54 the king fell in love with his host's ravishing daughter Charlotte, aged only 15. He arranged for her to marry Henri II de Bourbon-Condé, a shy and gauche young man, whom the king hoped would prove an accommodating husband. The day after the wedding, however, Condé left the capital with his wife. Henri IV ordered them to return to Paris.

The young couple fled to Brussels, where they stayed under the protection of the king of Spain. Henri IV raged, implored, threatened and even went as far as to ask the Pope to intervene, but he was murdered by Ravaillac. Only then did the two fugitives return to France.

Sylvie and her poets − Henri II de Montmorency, the godson of Henri IV and the most brilliant and extravagant knight at court, married Marie-Félicie Orsini, god-daughter to Marie de Medici. A charming, generous and highly educated young woman, she was a close friend of the poets Mairet and Théophile de Viau. The latter − to whom she extended her protection when he was taken to court by the Parlement de Paris − addressed her as Sylvie. The name remained associated with the pavilion built for Henri IV in 1604, a retreat where Marie-Félicie spent many enjoyable hours. Encouraged by Louis XIII's brother, the scheming Gaston d'Orléans, Henri de Montmorency plotted against Richelieu. He was defeated at Castelnaudary near Toulouse and made a prisoner after receiving eighteen wounds, including five by bullets. The last of the Montmorency was beheaded in Toulouse in 1632. By way of an apology, Henri II de Montmorency bequeathed to Cardinal Richelieu the two *Slave* statues by Michelangelo, now in the Louvre; those at Chantilly and Écouen are replicas. Beside herself with grief, Marie-Félicie withdrew to the Visitation convent in Moulins and remained there until her death.

The Great Condé – Charlotte de Montmorency and her husband the Prince of Condé – the couple persecuted by Henri IV – inherited Chantilly in 1643 and the Château remained family property until 1830. Descendants of Charles de Bourbon, like Henri IV, the Princes of Condé were of royal blood and the heir apparent to the title was called the Duke of Enghien.

The Great Condé was the son of Charlotte and Henri II. He applied himself to renovating the Château de Chantilly with the same energy and efficiency he had shown in military operations. In 1662 he commissioned Le Nôtre to redesign the park and the forest. The fountains at Chantilly were considered the most elegant in France and Louis XIV made a point of outclassing them in Versailles. The work lasted twenty years and the result was a splendid achievement, part of which still stands today.

All the great writers of the 17C stayed at Chantilly including Bossuet, Fénelon, Bourdaloue, Boileau, Racine, La Fontaine, Mme de la Fayette, Mme de Sévigné, La Bruyère (who was tutor to the prince's grandson) and Molière, to whom Condé granted permission to perform *Tartuffe*.

The last of the Condé – The Prince of Condé died in Fontainebleau in 1686, to the king's great dismay. During the religious ceremony preceding the burial, Bossuet delivered a funeral oration which became famous.

The great-grandson of the Great Condé, Louis-Henri de Bourbon, alias "Monsieur le Duc", was an artist with a taste for splendour, who gave Chantilly a new lease of life. He asked Jean Aubert to build the Grandes Écuries, a masterpiece of the 18C, and set up a porcelain factory which closed down in 1870.

The Château d'Enghien was built on the estate by Louis-Joseph de Condé in 1769. His grandson the Duke of Enghien, who had just been born, was its first occupant. The father of the newly born baby was 16, his grandfather 36. The young prince died tragically in 1804; he was seized by the French police in the margravate of Baden and shot outside the fortress of Vincennes on the orders of Bonaparte.

During the French Revolution the main building was razed to the ground though the smaller château was spared. Louis-Joseph was 78 when he returned from exile. His son accompanied him back to Chantilly and the two of them were dismayed: their beloved château was in ruins and the park was in a shambles. They decided to renovate the estate. They bought back the plots of their former land, restored the Petit Château, redesigned and refurbished the grounds. The prince died in 1818 but the duke continued the work. He was an enthusiastic hunter and at the age of 70 he hunted daily. Thanks to his efforts, Chantilly became the lively, fashionable place it had been in the years preceding the Revolution. As in former times, the receptions and hunting parties attracted crowds of elegant visitors. The renovation and restoration work was a source of income for the local population.

The duke was worried by the Revolution of 1830, which raised his cousin Louis-Philippe to the throne, and considered returning to England. A few days later, he was found hanging from a window at his castle in St-Leu. He was the last descendant of the Condé.

The Duke of Aumale – The Duke of Bourbon had left Chantilly to his great-nephew and godson the Duke of Aumale, the fourth son of Louis-Philippe. This prince gained recognition in Africa when he captured Abd el-Kader and his numerous relations. The Revolution of 1848 forced him to go into exile and he returned only in 1870; in 1873 he presided over the court martial which sentenced Marshal Bazaine.

From 1875 to 1881 the duke commissioned Daumet to build the Grand Château in the Renaissance style. This castle, the fifth, still stands today. Back in exile between 1883 and 1889, he died in 1897 and the Institute of France inherited his estate at Chantilly, together with the superb collections that constitute the Condé Museum.

The first races – The first official race meeting was held in Chantilly on 15 May 1834 at the instigation of the members of the Société d'encouragement, an association founded in 1833. The patronage of both the Duke of Orléans and the Duke of Nemours, and the fashionable trends introduced by the Jockey Club dandies, appreciative of the soft grassy track, combined to make these races a major social event (*Prix du Jockey-Club* in 1836, *Prix de Diane* in 1843); before the opening of Longchamp in 1857, Parisian races used to be run on the hard ground of the Champ-de-Mars. The hunting parties, concerts, firework displays and aquatic entertainments at Chantilly delighted racegoers and socialites.

By the end of the 19C the races had attracted huge crowds of visitors and the Northern France Railways set up a transport system whose efficiency has never been matched. In 1908 it became necessary to introduce 40 to 50 special trains composed of 16 carriages. A group of trains taking passengers back to Paris (leaving every three minutes) were even permitted to run on the wrong side of the track between Chantilly and St-Denis, a rare breach of regulations indeed.

The riding capital – With a total of over 3000 horses trained on the tracks in and around Chantilly, the Condés' town may be considered the capital of French thoroughbreds.

Jobs for 1000 stable-lads and a number of related occupations employ 10% of the farming population of the Oise *département*. Each stable-lad rides three horses every morning.

WHERE TO STAY AND EAT

BUDGET

La Calèche – 3 Avenue du Maréchal-Joffre, ☎ 03 44 57 02 55. Nice simple hotel with restaurant, situated near the racecourse. Double room from 240F.

OUR SELECTION

Tour d'Apremont – In Apremont, 7km/4mi north of Chantilly along D 606 and a small road, ☎ 03 44 25 61 11. Closed Monday, evenings except Friday and Saturday, and from 11 to 21 February. Golf course with two kinds of restaurant: a bistro (closed evenings and Monday) serving specialities from Picardy from 90F upwards; and a restaurant proposing regional and Japanese specialities (fixed menus starting from 150F).

LUXURY

Château de la Tour – Situated in Gouvieux, 3.5km/2.2mi east of Chantilly, ☎ 03 44 62 38 38, fax 03 44 57 31 97. This luxury hotel has all the charm of an Anglo-Norman manor house; the vast wooded park includes a heated summer swimming pool. Double room from 690F.

The racecourses – *Private.* 100 trainers attend to their respective charges from sunrise to noon, either on the sandy or grassy tracks of the four courses, or along the sand-covered paths of the forest (in particular the "Route du Connétable" also known as the "Piste des Lions").
Numerous race meetings take place during the racing season in June *(see Calendar of Events).*

THE CHÂTEAU

Several roads lead to the château. From Chapelle-en-Serval, crossing Chantilly Forest, the château suddenly rises into view from the carrefour des Lions; it appears to be floating on the water in a superb setting of rocks, ponds, lawns and stately trees.
From Paris, take N 16; do not drive through the town but turn right after the lower road and into the shady Route de l'Aigle which skirts the racecourse.
The road from Senlis through Vineuil offers a good view of the château and its park; leaving Vineuil, turn left at each junction.
Try to picture the Château de Chantilly at the time of the Condé when the two main buildings were still divided by an arm of water: the 16C Petit Château (or barbican) and the Grand Château, for which Daumet used the foundations of the former stronghold.
Cross the constable's terrace, which bears the equestrian statue of Anne de Montmorency, and enter the main courtyard through the main gateway (Grille d'Honneur), flanked by the two copies of Michelangelo's *Slaves.*

★★MUSEUM ⊘

The museum contains a superb collection which according to Raoul de Broglie, former curator, would be impossible to put together today, even with unlimited purchasing power. In the days when the Duke of Aumale was building up his collection, an enlightened amateur could still take advantage of unexpected lucky breaks. One of the best works by Largillière cost 450 francs.
The layout of the museum may surprise visitors. Unlike contemporary collections, the works of art are not classified according to their period or their artist. Italian and Flemish Primitive paintings are found next to 19C works, and illuminated manuscripts side by side with oil paintings.
The Duke of Aumale did not intend to establish a gallery for didactical purposes; he merely wanted to build up a fine art collection. He therefore hung them in chronological order of purchase though favourite works were sometimes placed in a separate room. The curators have respected his layout.
According to the terms of the duke's legacy, the Institute must agree "to make no changes to the interior and exterior architecture of the château". Moreover, it is not allowed to lend any of the exhibits.
The reception hall is the starting point for guided tours of the chapel and the various apartments – if a group has already formed, it is best to join it – as well as for unaccompanied tours of the collections. It is advisable to interrupt a visit to the collections if the custodians announce a guided tour of the apartments.

★ **Appartements des Princes** ⊘ – Situated in the Petit Château, this suite, occupied by the Great Condé and his descendants, was embellished with Regency and rococo **wainscoting**★★, especially in the 18C thanks to the Duke of Bourbon. It was not occupied by the Duke of Aumale who had taken up residence on the ground floor. The antechamber and part of the library, the work of the Duke of Aumale, are located on the site of the old moat.

Chantilly – Cabinet des Livres

★**Cabinet des Livres (Library)** (**1**) – It contains a splendid collection of manuscripts, including **The Rich Hours of the Duke of Berry** *(Les Très Riches Heures du duc de Berry)* with 15C illuminations by the Limbourg brothers. This extremely fragile document is not permanently exhibited but visitors may see a facsimile by Faksimile Verlag of Luzern.

Another interesting reproduction is the psalter of Queen Ingeburge of Denmark.
Among the ornamental motifs feature the monogram of the Duke of Aumale (H O for Henri d'Orléans) and the Condé coat of arms (France's "broken" coat of arms with a diagonal line symbolising the younger branch of the family).

Chambre de Monsieur le Prince (**2**) – This title referred to the Condé Prince who was on the throne, in this case the Duke of Bourbon (1692-1740), who had a wainscot installed at the far end of the room, into which were embedded panels painted by C Huet in 1735. The famous Louis XVI commode was designed by Riesener and made by Hervieu.

Salon des Singes (**3**) – A collection of monkey scenes *(singeries)* dating from the early 18C is a masterpiece by an anonymous draughtsman; note the fire screen depicting the monkeys' reading lesson.

Galerie de Monsieur le Prince (**4**) – The Great Condé had ordered his own battle gallery, which he never saw completed (1692). The sequence was interrupted from 1652 to 1659 during his years of rebellion. A painting conceived by the hero's son portrays him stopping a Fame from publishing a list of his treacherous deeds and asking another Fame to issue a formal apology.

Chapelle – An **altar**★ attributed to Jean Goujon and 16C wainscot and stained-glass windows from the Chapel at Écouen were brought here by the Duke of Aumale. The apse contains the **mausoleum** of Henri II de Condé *(see above)* (bronze statues by J Sarrazin taken from the Jesuit Church of St-Paul-St-Louis in Paris) and the stone urn which received the hearts of the Condé princes. Up to the Revolution, the Condé necropolis was at Vallery in Burgundy, where another sepulchral monument celebrating Henri II still stands.

★★**The collections (Grand Château)** – Cross the **Galerie des Cerfs** (**A**) with its hunting theme; note the 17C Gobelins tapestries.

Galerie de Peinture (**B**) – The variety of paintings here reflects the eclectic tastes of the Duke of Aumale. Military events are illustrated on huge canvases *(Battle on the Railway Line* by Neuville, Meissonnier's *The Cuirassiers of 1805)*. Orientalism is well represented with Gros' work, *The Plague Victims of Jaffa*, H Vernet's *Arab Sheikhs holding Council*, and *The Falcon Hunt* by Fromentin. Note, too, the famous portrait of *Gabrielle d'Estrées in her Bath* (16C French school), the portraits of Cardinals Richelieu and Mazarin by Philippe de Champaigne, and *The Massacre of the Holy Innocents* by Poussin.

Rotonde (C) – The *Loreto Madonna* by **Raphael**, **Piero di Cosimo's** portrait of the ravishing Simonetta Vespucci, who is believed to have been Botticelli's model for his *Birth of Venus*, and Chapu's kneeling statue of Joan of Arc listening to voices are exhibited here.

Salle de la Smalah et Rotonde de la Minerve (D) – Family portraits of the Orléans (17C, 18C and 19C) and of Louis-Philippe's relations in particular: Bonnat's picture of the Duke of Aumale at the age of 68.

Cabinet de Giotto (E) – A room devoted to Italian Primitives: *Angels Dancing in the Sun* (Italian school, 15C).

Salle Isabelle (F) – Numerous 19C paintings including *Moroccan Guards* by Delacroix, *Horse ILeaving the Stables* by Géricault, and *Françoise de Rimini* by Ingres.

Salle d'Orléans (G) – The glass cabinets contain **soft-paste Chantilly porcelain** manufactured in the workshops founded in 1725 by the Duke de Bourbon (armorial service bearing the Condé coat of arms or the Duke of Orléans' monogram).

Salle Caroline (H) – 18C painting has pride of place here, with portraits by Largillière and Greuze, *Young Woman Playing with Children* by Van Loo, *The Worried Lover* and *The Serenade Player* by Watteau, or *Snowstorm* by Everdingen.

Cabinet des Clouet (K) – A precious collection of small and extremely rare **paintings★★** executed by the **Clouets**, Corneille de Lyon etc, portraying François I, Marguerite de Navarre (stroking a little dog), Henri II as a child etc.

Galerie de Psyché (L) – The 44 **stained-glass windows** (16C) that tell the story of the loves of Psyche and Cupid came from Constable Anne's other family home, Château d'Écouen.

★★★ Santuario (N) – It houses the museum's most precious exhibits: Raphael's *Orléans Madonna*, named after the noble family, *The Three Ages of Womanhood*, also known as *The Three Graces*, by the same artist; *Esther and Ahasuerus*, the panel of a wedding chest painted by Filippino Lippi and forty miniature works by Jean Fouquet, cut out of Estienne Chevalier's book of hours, a splendid example of French 15C art.

Cabinet des Gemmes (P) – It contains jewels of stunning beauty. The Pink Diamond, alias the Great Condé (a copy of which is permanently on show), was stolen in 1926 and subsequently found in an apple where the thieves had hidden it. The room also boasts an outstanding collection of enamels and miniatures.

Tribune (R) – Above the cornice of this polygonal room are painted panels representing episodes from the life of the Duke of Aumale and the house of Orléans.

The paintings include *Autumn* by **Botticelli**, *Love Disarmed* and *Pastoral Pleasures* by **Watteau**, a portrait of Molière by **Mignard**, and on the "Ecouen Wall", three superb works by **Ingres**: a self-portrait, *Madame Devaucay* and *Venus*.

★Petits Appartements ⊘ – *Access by the stairway off the reception hall.* The Duke of Aumale had these private appartments designed and decorated by painter Eugène Lami specially for his marriage in 1844.

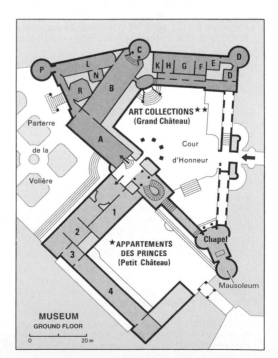

MUSEUM
GROUND FLOOR

0   20 m

Château de CHANTILLY

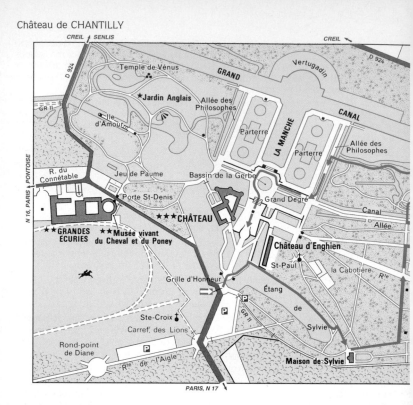

Château d'Enghien – *Return to the terrace outside the main château.* The 18C château is set back to the right; access to it is limited to the curators whom the Institute chooses from among its own members (one member of the French Academy, one member of the Académie des Beaux-Arts, and one member from one of the other Academies).

★★PARK ⏱ *about 1hr*

Follow the route indicated on the plan and walk past the pond (Étang de Sylvie).

Maison de Sylvie – *(Private)* This is a small garden pavilion where Marie-Félicie enjoyed meeting her close friends. The Duke of Aumale added on a rotunda and decorated it with Louis XV panelling of hunting scenes which he had brought back from his retreat in Dreux Forest, which also belonged to the Orléans family.

Chapelle St-Jean – The chapel was erected on the estate by Constable Anne in 1538, with six other chapels, in memory of the seven churches of Rome he had visited in order to gain the indulgences granted to those who undertook this pilgrimage. He obtained from the Pope the same privileges for the chapels at Chantilly. Two other chapels still stand on the estate: St Paul's, located behind the Château d'Enghien, and Ste-Croix, on the lawns of the racecourse.
Take Allée Blanche along the banks of the Canal des Morfondus.

La Chute – These tiered waterfalls mark the start of the Grand Canal.
Return along Allée Blanche; cross the Canal des Morfondus at the footbridge.

Le Hameau – Dating from 1775, it was built before the more famous Trianon at Versailles *(see p 361)*. Under the influence of Jean-Jacques Rousseau, French princes used to seek new horizons by creating miniature villages.
The mill and a few half-timbered buildings may be seen. These used to accommodate a kitchen, a dining room and a billiard room. The barn provided a drawing room that was restored by the Duke of Aumale. All the big parties included supper in this charming spot in the park.
Skirt the brook by the small village.

★**L'Aérophile** ⏱ – A thrilling trip on board the world's largest **aerostat**. A huge balloon 32m/104ft high takes 30 visitors at a time up to 150m/488ft above this enchanting spot. This type of attraction was very popular by late 19C high society, in the Tuileries Gardens in Paris for example. Technical progress has made it much more accessible to the general public today, with lower prices and greater attention to safety. The flight is majestic and silent, and there is an unforgettable **panoramic view★★** of the Chantilly estate and surrounding area. On clear days, Senlis Cathedral is visible in the distance and occasionally the Eiffel Tower in Paris.

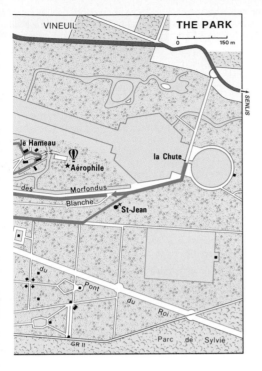

Les Hydrophiles – Electric boats glide along the Grand Canal, offering unusual vistas of the castle and the park.

Parterres – The parterres are framed by two avenues of young lime trees, called "The Philosophers' Path" because the great writers who visited Chantilly used to pace up and down the shaded avenue, exchanging their views and ideas. Le Nôtre diverted the course of the River Nonette to make the Grand Canal and La Manche. The circular Vertugadin lawns lie along the line of La Manche, flanked by delightful stretches of water. Between La Manche and the round basin (Bassin de la Gerbe) stands Coysevox's statue of the Great Condé, framed by the effigies of La Bruyère and Bossuet (statues of Molière and Le Nôtre, seated, may be seen in the near distance). A monumental stairway (Grand Degré) leads from the parterres up to the terrace; on either side of these imposing steps are grottoes, their carved decoration representing rivers.

★★GRANDES ÉCURIES (STABLES)

Jean Aubert's masterpiece constitutes the most stunning piece of 18C architecture in Chantilly. The St-Denis Gateway – built astride the road leading to town – marks the site of an uncompleted pavilion. The most attractive façade of the stables overlooks the racecourse.
At the time of the Condé, this architectural complex housed a total of 240 horses, 500 dogs and around 100 employees (grooms, drivers, whips etc.).

★★ **Musée Vivant du Cheval et du Poney** ⊘ – This museum is brought to life by the 28 saddle and draught animals – 18 horses and 10 ponies – bred in France or in the Iberian peninsula which occupy the stalls and boxes built in the days of the Duke of Aumale.
In the central rotunda, 28m/92ft high, admire the water playing in the **fountain**, the basin of which was once used as a trough.
The exhibition in the east gallery focuses, through paintings and models, on the harness, the rider's costume and the general atmosphere of the competition in 30 equestrian events throughout the world.
Thirty-one rooms set up in the former sheds present the art of horse riding and a number of related professions: the blacksmith's trade, a veterinary's operating theatre etc. The last room illustrates France's betting system, the "PMU".
The tour ends with a demonstration of **dressage**★ *(about 30min)*. The excellent acoustics, the rider's smart costume and the comments on the various exercises make it a delightful experience. Equestrian entertainments on the theme "Riding and the Arts" take place in the kennels' quarry at night.

★JARDIN ANGLAIS

The landscaped English-style garden was laid out on the surviving relics of Le Nôtre's park in 1820. Its charm derives from the pleasant groves (plane trees, swamp cypresses, weeping willows) rather than from the symbolic monuments: remains of a Temple of Venus and of Love (l'île d'Amour).

FORÊT DE CHANTILLY

The vast wooded area covers about 6300ha/15500 acres and has been reshaped by hunting enthusiasts over 500 years. Tree species which are sparse in some places because of the poor soil and abundance of game include oaks, hornbeams, lime trees and Scots pines in copses and groves, with additions of oak and beech seedlings since 1973.

The network of paths through the forest is suitable for country walks, and the light soil favours riding activities; training sessions take place at Carrefour du Petit Couvert every morning. The forests of Coye, Orry and Pontarmé are reserved for walkers.

Étangs de Commelles – They were used as fishponds by the monks from Chaalis Abbey. The road provides access to the car parks and to the causeways that criss-cross the water, which makes it possible to explore the area around the ponds on foot.

Château de la Reine Blanche – In 1825 this old mill was restored in the troubadour style by the last of the Condés, the Duke of Bourbon, who used it as a hunting pavilion.

It stands on the site of a legendary château believed to have been built by Queen Blanche of Navarre, wife of Philippe VI of Valois, after her husband's death around 1350. Part of the lodge is now occupied by a pancake house.

An avenue of age-old beeches completes this delightful site★.

CHARTRES★★★

Population 39 595
Michelin map 106 folds 37, 38

Access from Paris: *SNCF Rail link from Paris gare Montparnasse.*

Chartres is the capital of Beauce, France's famous corn belt, but for tourists the town is known mainly for the Cathedral of Our Lady, a magnificent edifice now on UNESCO's World Heritage list, which reigns supreme over a picturesque setting of monuments and old streets.

HISTORICAL NOTES

A town with a destiny – Since ancient times Chartres has always had a strong influence over religious matters. It is believed that a Gallo-Roman well, located on the Chartres plateau, was the object of a pagan cult and that in the 4C this was transformed into a Christian cult by the first evangelists. Adventius, the first known bishop of Chartres, lived during the middle of the 4C. A document from the 7C mentions a bishop Béthaire kneeling in front of Notre-Dame, which points to the existence of a Marian cult.

In 876 the chemise said to belong to the Virgin Mary was given to the cathedral by Charles the Bald, confirming that Chartres was already a place of pilgrimage. Up to the 14C the town of Chartres continued to flourish. Three representations of the Virgin are the subject of a special cult which has survived through the ages: Notre-Dame-de-Sous-Terre, Notre-Dame-du-Pilier and Notre-Dame-de-la-Belle-Verrière, but the cathedral features altogether 175 different illustrations portraying Mary.

Note that neither the cathedral nor the crypt contains any tombs; Chartres is a temple devoted exclusively to the Virgin, who remains protected from corruption.

The Pilgrimage – Chartres Cathedral was consecrated to the Assumption of the Virgin Mary in 1260; in the Middle Ages it attracted huge crowds of pilgrims. The sick were housed in the northern gallery of the crypt. When the cathedral was thronged with visitors, the nave served as a shelter and provided night-time accommodation. A second statue – Notre-Dame du Pilier – was placed in the upper church for the adoration of the faithful.

In 1912 and 1913 the writer and poet **Charles Péguy** made the pilgrimage to Chartres. The strong influence it had on his work inspired a small group of enthusiasts after the First World War to follow suit and led later, in 1935, to the establishment of the "Students' Pilgrimage" *(see Calendar of Events)*. Now extended to include other young people, the pilgrimages end with a mass in the cathedral.

An exceptional man – In the **Église St-Jean-Baptiste** in the Rechèvres district to the north of the town lies the body of the abbot **Franz Stock**, whose tomb is still a place of pilgrimage.

This German priest, chaplain to the prisons of Paris from 1940 to 1944, refused to retreat with the Wehrmacht and was taken prisoner. At the Morancez prison camp near Chartres he founded a seminary for the prisoners of war and was the Superior there for two years. He died in February 1948 at the age of 43.

A bird's-eye view – For a view of the cathedral rising up above the Eure Valley, stand behind the Monument aux Aviateurs Militaires, a memorial to the French Air Force high above the east bank of the river. The **view**★ is impressive. A few typical gable ends are visible in the old town and the roofs of two churches, St-Aignan and St-Pierre, can also be seen.

View of the cathedral from the garden of Église St-André, Chartres

G. Guttot /DIAF

★★★CATHEDRAL *1hr 30min*

The 4000 carved figures and the 5000 characters portrayed by the stained-glass windows demanded a lifelong commitment from the specialists who studied them. The most famous expert is probably Étienne Houvet, a custodian who died in 1949; he photographed the building in minute detail and built up a supremely interesting collection.

A neat, swift construction – The building rests upon the Romanesque cathedral erected by Bishop Fulbert in the 11C and 12C: there remain the crypt, the towers and the foundations of the west front, including the Royal Doorway, and fragments of the Notre-Dame-de-la-Belle-Verrière stained-glass window. The remaining sections of the cathedral were built in the wake of the Great Fire of 1194; princes and dignitaries contributed generously to the work, while the poor offered their labour.

These efforts made it possible to complete the cathedral in 25 years, and to add on the north and south porches 20 years later, with the result that the architecture and decoration of Notre-Dame form a harmonious composition almost unparalleled in the history of Gothic art. By some miracle, the Wars of Religion, the French Revolution and the two World Wars spared the famous basilica, which Rodin referred to as "the Acropolis of France" on account of its aesthetic and spiritual value. Only the cathedral's "forest" – the superb roof timbers – were destroyed by flames in 1836, and subsequently replaced by a metal framework.

Exterior

Beneath the cathedral close, where it is planned to build an international medieval centre, archeological excavations covering an area of some 1200m²/12912sq ft are currently in progress. The remains of two 13C houses have been uncovered.

West front – The two tall spires and the Royal Doorway form one of the most perfect compositions encountered in French religious art. The New Bell-Tower on the left was in fact built first; the lower part dates back to 1134. Its present name dates from the 16C, when Jehan de Beauce erected a stone spire (115m/377ft high) to replace the wooden steeple which had burned down in 1506. The Old Bell-Tower (c 1145 to 1164) (106m/384ft) is a masterpiece of Romanesque art, foming a stark contrast to the ornate Gothic construction. The Royal Doorway and the three large windows above date from the 12C. Everything above this ensemble was built at a later date: the rose-window (13C), the 14C gable and the king's gallery featuring the Kings of Judah, the ancestors of the Virgin Mary. On the gable, the Virgin Mary is depicted presenting her son to the Beauce area.

The **Royal Doorway★★★** (Portail Royal), a splendid example of late Romanesque architecture (1145-1170), represents the life and triumph of the Saviour. The Christ in Majesty on the central tympanum and the statue-columns are famous throughout the world. The elongated features of the biblical kings and queens, prophets, priests and patriarchs study the visitors from the embrasures. While the faces are animated, the bodies remain rigid, in deliberate contrast to the figures adorning the arches and the capitals. The statues were primarily designed to be columns, not human beings

Chartres – The Royal Doorway

North porch and doorway – Leave the west front on your left and walk round the Cathedral, stepping back to get a clear view of its lines. The nave is extremely high and unusually wide. The problem of how to support it was brilliantly resolved with the construction of three-tiered flying buttresses; the lower two arcs were joined together by colonnettes. The elegant Pavillon de l'Horloge near the New Bell-Tower is the work of Jehan de Beauce (1520).

The ornamentation of the north porch is similar to that of the doorway, executed at an earlier date. The characters – treated more freely than those on the Royal Doorway – are elegant and extremely lively, illustrating a new, more realistic approach to religious art. The statue of St Modesta, a local martyr who is pictured gazing up at the New Bell-Tower, is extremely graceful.

Once again, the decoration of the three doors refers to the Old Testament. The right door pays tribute to the biblical heroes who exercised the virtues recommended in the teachings of Christ. The central panel shows the Virgin Mary and the Prophets who foretold the coming of the Messiah. The door on the left presents the Annunciation, Visitation and Nativity, together with the Vices and Virtues. In the bishopric's garden, the raised terrace commands a view of the town below lying on the banks of the Lower Eure River. Before reaching the garden gate, look left and note the archway straddling a narrow street. It used to open in the walls of the Notre-Dame cloister.

East end – The complexity of the double-course flying buttresses – reinforced here with an intermediate pier as they cross over the chapels – and the succession of radiating chapels, chancel and arms of the transept are stunning. The 14C St Piat Chapel, originally separate, was joined to Notre-Dame by a stately staircase.

South porch and doorway – Here, the upper stonework is concealed by a constellation of colonnettes. The perspective of these planes, stretching from the arches of the porch to the gables, confers to this arm of the transept a sense of unity that is lacking in the north transept.

The theme is the Church of Christ and the Last Judgment. In the Middle Ages, these scenes would usually be reserved for the west portal but in this case the Royal Doorway already featured ornamentation. Consequently, the scenes portraying the Coming of a New World, prepared by the martyrs, were destined for the left-door embrasures, while those of the Confessors (witnesses of Christ who have not yet been made martyrs) adorn the right door.

Christ reigns supreme on the central tympanum. He is also present on the pier, framed by the double row of the 12 Apostles with their lean, ascetic faces, draped in long, gently folded robes.

Among the martyrs, note the statues standing in the foreground: St George and St Theodore, both admirable 13C representations of knights in armour. These figures are quite separate from the columns – the feet are flat and no longer slanted – and are there for purely decorative purposes.

The most delightful feature of the sculpted porch is the display of medallions, grouped in sets of six and placed on the recessed arches of the three doorways: the lives of the martyrs, the Vices and Virtues etc.

Returning to the west front, note the Old Bell-Tower and its ironical statue of a donkey playing the fiddle, symbolising man's desire to share in celestial music. At the corner of the building, stop to admire the tall figure of the sundial Angel.

★**Access to New Bell-Tower** ⊘ – The tour *(195 steps)* leads round the north side and up to the lower platform of the New Bell-Tower. Seen from a height of 70m/230ft, the buttresses, flying buttresses, statues, gargoyles and Old Bell-Tower are most impressive. It is still possible to recognise the former Notre-Dame Cloister thanks to the old pointed roof. Enclosed by a wall right up to the 19C, this area was frequented by clerics – especially canons.

Interior

Enter the cathedral by the Royal Doorway. The nave (16m/52ft) is wider than any other in France (Notre-Dame in Paris 40ft, Notre-Dame in Amiens 46ft), though it has single aisles. The vaulting reaches a height of 37m/121ft and the interior is 130m/427ft long. This nave is 13C, built in the style known as early or lancet Gothic. there is no gallery; instead, there is a blind triforium *(illustration, see Introduction: Religious Architecture)*.

As Notre-Dame was a noted place of pilgrimage, the chancel and the transept had to accommodate large-scale ceremonies; they were therefore wider than the nave. In Chartres, the chancel, its double ambulatory and the transept form an ensemble 64m/210ft wide between the north and south doorways.

Note the gentle slope of the floor, rising slightly towards the chancel; this made it easier to wash down the church when the pilgrims had stayed overnight.

The striking state of semi-darkness in the nave creates an element of mystery which was not intentional: it is due to the gradual dimming of the stained glass over the centuries.

★★★**Stained-glass windows** – The 12C and 13C stained-glass windows of Notre-Dame constitute, together with those of Bourges, the largest collection in France. The Virgin and Child and the Annunciation and Visitation scenes in the clerestory at the far end of the chancel produce a striking impression.

West front – These three 12C windows used to throw light on Fulbert's Romanesque cathedral and the dark, low nave that stood behind, which explains why they are so long.

The scenes *(bottom to top)* illustrate the fulfilment of the prophecies: *(right)* the Tree of Jesse, *(centre)* the childhood and life of Our Lord (Incarnation cycle) and *(left)* Passion and Resurrection (Redemption cycle).

Visitors may feast their eyes on the famous 12C "Chartres blue", with its clear, deep tones which are enhanced by reddish tinges, especially radiant in the rays of the setting

H. Champollion/MICHELIN

Chartres Cathedral –
Central Window of the west front:
Detail of the Redemption cycle

sun. For many years, people believed that this particular shade of blue was a long-lost trade secret. Modern laboratories have now established that the sodium compounds and silica in the glass made it more resistant to dirt and corrosion than the panes made with other materials and in other times. The large 13C rose window on the west front depicts the Last Judgement.

Transept – This ensemble consists of two 13C rose-windows, to which were added a number of lancet windows featuring tall figures. The themes are the same as those on the corresponding carved doorway: Old Testament (north), the End of the World (south).

The north rose (rose de France) was a present from Blanche of Castille, mother of St Louis and Regent of France, and portrays a Virgin and Child. It is characterised by the fleur-de-lis motif on the shield under the central lancet and by the alternating Castile towers and fleurs-de-lis pictured on the small corner lancets. The larger lancets depict St Anne holding the infant Virgin Mary, framed by four kings or high priests: Melchizedek and David stand on the left, Solomon and Aaron on the right.

The centre roundel of the south rose shows the risen Christ, surrounded by the Old Men of the Apocalypse, forming two rings of 12 medallions. The yellow and blue chequered quatrefoils represent the coat of arms of the benefactors, the Comte de Dreux Pierre Mauclerc and his wife, who are also featured at the bottom of the lancets.

The lancets on either side of the Virgin and Child depict four striking figures – the Great Prophets Isaiah, Jeremiah, Ezekiel and Daniel – with the four Evangelists seated on their shoulders.

The morality of the scene is simple: although they are weak and lacking dignity, the Evangelists can see further than the giants of the Old Testament thanks to the Holy Spirit.

★**Notre-Dame-de-la-Belle-Verrière** (**1**) – *(illustration, see Introduction: Stained Glass)* This is a very famous stained-glass window. The Virgin and Child, a fragment of the window spared by the fire of 1194, has been mounted in 13C stained glass. Admire the superb range of blues.

Other stained-glass windows – The aisles of the nave and the chapels around the ambulatory are lit by a number of celebrated stained-glass windows from the 13C verging on the sombre side. On the east side, the arms of the transept have received two works of recent making, in perfect harmony with the early fenestration: St Fulbert's window (south crossing **2**), donated by the American Association of Architects (from the François Lorin workshop – 1954), and the window of Peace (north crossing **3**), a present from a group of German admirers (1971).

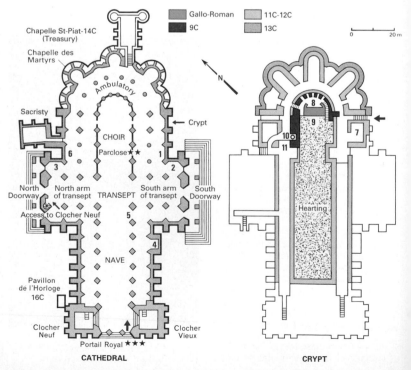

CATHEDRAL   CRYPT

The Vendôme Chapel (**4**) features a particularly radiant 15C stained-glass window. It illustrates the development of this art, which eventually led to the lighter panes of the 17C and 18C.

★★Parclose – The screen was started by Jehan de Beauce in 1514 and finished in the 18C. This fine work consists of 41 sculpted compositions depicting the lives of Christ and the Virgin Mary. These Renaissance medallions, evoking Biblical history, local history and mythology, contrast sharply with the Gothic statues of the doorways.

Chancel – The marble facing, the Assumption group above the high altar and the low-relief carvings separating the columns were added in the 18C.

Organ (**5**) – The case dates from the 16C.

Vierge du Pilier (**6**) – This wooden statue (c 1510) stood against the roodscreen, now sadly disappeared. The richly clothed Virgin is the object of a procession celebrated annually *(see Calendar of Events at the end of the guide)*.

Treasury ⊘ – Chapelle St-Piat has been built to house the cathedral treasury. It is linked to the east end of the cathedral by a Renaissance staircase. Inside are some superb items of church plate.

Chapelle des Martyrs – This chapel has been refurbished and now contains the **Virgin Mary's Veil**, laid out in a beautiful glass-fronted reliquary. Pilgrims used to pray to this veil, calling it a tunic or "Holy Chemise".

★Crypt ⊘ – *Entrance outside the cathedral, on the south side (see plan above)*. This is France's longest crypt (220m/722ft long). It dates largely from the 11C and

Where to stay

BUDGET

Ibis Centre – 14 Place Drouaise, ☎ 02 37 36 06 36, fax 02 37 36 17 20. Modern and functional hotel situated in the town centre. Double room from 330F.

LUXURY

Grand Monarque – 22 Place des Épars, ☎ 02 37 21 00 72, fax 02 37 36 34 18. Luxury hotel situated on one of the town's main squares. Double room from 585F, fixed menu from 227F.

Eating out

BUDGET

Dix de Pythagore – 2 Rue Porte Cendreuse, ☎ 02 37 39 02 38. Closed Sunday evening, Monday and from 15 to 31 July. Small convivial restaurant in the old town. Fixed menu from 92F.

OUR SELECTION

Buisson Ardent – 10 Rue au Lait, ☎ 02 37 34 04 66. Situated in one of the streets leading down to the cathedral, this restaurant offers a warm atmosphere on the first floor of an old house. Fixed menu from 128F.

FOR GOURMETS

La Truie qui file – Place de la Poissonnerie, ☎ 02 37 21 53 90. Closed Sunday evening and Monday. High-class restaurant housed in a splendid 15C timber-framed building. Choice of fixed menu from 180F. Less expensive alternative for lunch and dinner in **Les Caves de la Maison**, at the same address (fixed menu: 100F).

On the town

Information – The tourist office, Place de la Cathédrale, provides information about public transport, special events and guided tours of the town.

Arts and Crafts – The town is famous for its stained glass and there are a large number of craftsmen perpetuating the tradition, in restoration work and in the creation of new pieces.
Galerie du Cloître, 8 Cloître Notre-Dame; Galerie du Vitrail, 17 Cloître Notre-Dame; Galerie d'Art Serpente, 6-8 Rue Serpente.

Theatre – Boulevard Chasles.

Having a drink – L'Académie de la Bière, 8 Rue du Cheval-Blanc; The Dickens Pub, 13 Place du Châtelet; Le Saxophone, 20 Place des Halles.

features Romanesque groined vaulting. It is a curious shape; the two long galleries joined by the ambulatory pass under the chancel and the aisles and open onto seven chapels. The central area, which has been filled in, remains unexplored. Of the seven radiating chapels, only three are Romanesque. The other four were added by the master architect of the Gothic cathedral to serve as foundations for the chancel and the apse of the future building.

St Martin's Chapel (**7**), by the south gallery, houses the originals of the statues on the Royal Doorway: the sundial Angel etc.

A staircase, starting from the ambulatory, leads down to a lower crypt.

Crypte St-Lubin (**8**) – This crypt served as the foundations of the 9C church. A thick, circular column with a visible base backs onto a Gallo-Roman wall (**9**), its bond easily recognisable by the alternating bricks and mortar. The crypt was a safe place that protected the cathedral treasures in times of social unrest or natural disaster. Thus, the Chemise of the Virgin survived the Great Fire of 1194.

Puits des Saints-Forts (**10**) – The lower part of this 33m/108ft deep shaft has a square section characteristic of Gallo-Roman wells. The coping is contemporary. The name dates back to 858; it is believed that several Christian martyrs from Chartres were murdered during a Norman attack, and their bodies thrown down the well.

Chapelle Notre-Dame-de-Sous-Terre (**11**) – A sacred retreat where pilgrims indulge in fervent praying. Since the 17C the chapel, together with the north gallery of the crypt, has played the part of a miniature church. It originally consisted of a small alcove where the faithful came to venerate the Virgin. The interior of the chapel and its decoration were refurbished in 1976. On this occasion, the 19C statue of the Virgin was replaced by a more hieratic figure, based on the Romanesque model, enhanced by a Gobelins tapestry.

ADDITIONAL SIGHTS

★**Old Town** (**Quartier St-André and banks of the Eure**) – *Follow the route indicated on plan below*. This pleasant walk leads past the picturesque hilly site, the banks of the Eure River, an ancient district recently restored and the cathedral which is visible from every street corner. In the summer season, a small **tourist train** ⊘ tours the old town.

Église St-André – This Romanesque church *(deconsecrated)* was the place of worship of one of the most active and densely-populated districts in town. Most of the trades were closely related to the river: millers, dyers, curriers, cobblers, tanners, drapers, fullers, tawers, serge makers etc. The church was enlarged in the 13C, and in the 16C and 17C it received a chancel and an axial chapel resting on arches that straddled the Eure River and rue du Massacre. Unfortunately, both these structures disappeared in 1827 leaving a much less picturesque church.

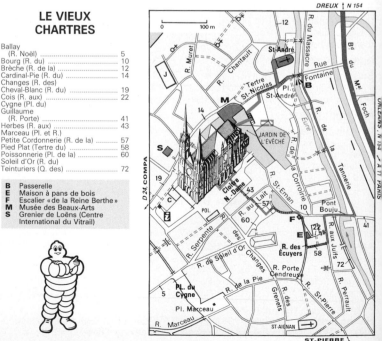

LE VIEUX CHARTRES

B Passerelle
E Maison à pans de bois
F Escalier «de la Reine Berthe»
M Musée des Beaux-Arts
S Grenier de Loëns (Centre International du Vitrail)

Cross the Eure by a metal footbridge (**B**); there is a good **view**★ of the old hump-back bridges. At the foot of the shortened nave of St Andrew's lie the remains of the arch that once supported the chancel. Wander upstream; the wash-houses and races of former mills have been prettily restored. Rue aux Juifs leads through an ancient district which has recently been renovated, featuring cobbled streets bordered by gable-ended houses and old-fashioned street lamps.

Rue des Écuyers – This is one of the most successful restoration schemes of the old town. At nos 17 and 19 the houses have 17C doorways with rusticated surrounds, surmounted by a bull's-eye window. Stroll along the street to rue aux Cois. The corner building is a delightful half-timbered villa (**E**), with an overhang in the shape of a prow. Opposite stands Queen Bertha's stairturret (**F**), a 16C structure, also half-timbered.

Grenier et cellier de Loëns (**S**) – From the 12C onwards, this half-timbered barn with treble gables in the courtyard of the old chapter house was used to store the wine and cereals offered to the clergy as a tithe. Renovated to house the **Centre international du Vitrail** ⊘ which organises stained-glass exhibitions, the building now features a large hall with beautifully restored roof timbering and a magnificent 12C cellar with three aisles.

Musée des Beaux-Arts ⊘ (**M**) – The museum is housed in the old bishop's palace and occupies the first terrace of the bishopric's gardens. The large, handsome edifice which was built over four centuries consists of a 15C section arranged around an interior courtyard, a 17C and 18C façade, and an early-18C wing overlooking the garden.

On the ground floor, note the foyer with its horseshoe-shaped staircase and the chapel used for temporary exhibitions. The drawing rooms contain the 18C collections with paintings by Boucher, Fragonard, Watteau, Chardin etc. as well as faience, pewter and a fine collection of old musical instruments.

The upper floor contains collections of works from Primitive painting to the 19C: *Fire in Chartres Cathedral in 1836* by FA Pernot, *Horses at Rest* by Corot and *Crucifixion* by Q Massys. Two of the rooms contain wooden statues, many of them painted, dating from the 16C to 19C.

The old sacristy, close to the chapel, houses 12 unusually large **enamels**★ representing the Apostles, by Léonard Limousin. They were commissioned by François I in 1545 and offered by Henri II to Diana of Poitiers, for her residence at Anet. In the basement are sculptures, medieval religious artefacts (enamels, superb processional Cross) and archeological exhibits discovered locally (cruciform fibulae).

The museum's new rooms house the permanent modern art collections as well as temporary exhibitions. There are several works by Vlaminck (*The House in Auvers, Red Bouquet with Anemones*) and J Guérin (*Flower Woman with the Poplar*). Also South Sea Island collection and works by master glass painter Navarre.

Rue du Cygne – The street has been widened into a little square planted with trees and shrubs *(flower market on Tuesdays, Thursdays and Saturdays)* and is at present an oasis of calm in this lively shopping district in the town centre.

At the end of rue du Cygne, on place Marceau, a monument celebrates the memory of the young local general who died at Altenkirchen (1796) at the age of 27. His ashes have been shared among Chartres (funeral urn under the statue on place des Épars), the Panthéon and the Dome Church of the Invalides in Paris.

★**Église St-Pierre** – This 12C and 13C Gothic church used to belong to the Benedictine abbey of St-Père-en-Vallée. The belfry-porch dates from pre-Romanesque times. The Gothic **stained-glass windows**★ can be traced back to a period that is not represented in Chartres Cathedral: the late 13C and early 14C, before the widespread introduction of yellow staining.

The oldest stained glass is that in the south bays of the chancel, portraying tall, hieratic figures from the Old Testament.

The windows in the semicircle of the chancel, with the most vivid tones, were mounted around 1300. Here the characters have been treated more freely.

The last windows to be installed were those in the nave (c 1305-15). They feature an alternation of medallions and religious figures Apostles, bishops, abbots).

Monument de Jean Moulin – **Jean Moulin** was *préfet* (chief administrator) of Chartres during the German invasion; on 17 June 1940, despite having been tortured, he resisted the enemy and refused to sign a document claiming that the French troops had committed a series of atrocities. As he was afraid of being unable to withstand further torture, he attempted to commit suicide.

Moulin was dismissed by the Vichy government in November 1940 and, from then on, he planned and coordinated underground resistance, working in close collaboration with General de Gaulle.

Arrested in Lyons on 21 June 1943, he did not survive the harsh treatment he received from the Gestapo. In December 1964 he was honoured in the Panthéon.

★ **Le COMPA: Conservatoire du Machinisme et des Pratiques Agricoles** ⊙ – *West of the town by D 24* . The museum is located in a strikingly converted, semicircular former railway shed. The spacious, modern-looking building, encircled by neat lawns offering a good view of Chartres and the cathedral, contains splendid, gleaming old machines and tools of copper, wrought iron or wood.

An **audio-visual display** depicts changes in farming practices in a voyage through time and space.

Tools and machines – At the museum's core stands an assortment of machines grouped according to function: seeders, binder-harvesters, combine-harvesters... Note the American MOLINE tractor, from 1910.

Land, men and methods – A comparison of two farming concerns in different regions of France, in 1860 and today, provides a better understanding of rural life. Ploughs from around the world illustrate the diversity in methods used by workers on the land.

Galerie des inventeurs et des inventions – The 80m/262ft long gallery introduces the figures responsible for major agricultural developments over the centuries.

The ideas and innovations of Pliny the Elder, Olivier de Serres, Henri de Vilmorin and, more recently, Ferguson and the national agricultural research centre (INRA) are explained through information panels and fascinating interactive displays.

Varions types of cereals are also displayed. Visitors can even consult and print off a regional recipe.

Salle des tracteurs – The tour ends with an exhibition of tractors, the oldest dating from 1816, the most recent from 1954.

Musée de l'École ⊙ – A classroom belonging to the old teachers' training college houses teaching aids and furniture evoking the schools of yesteryear: abacuses, magic lanterns using paraffin, books advocating humanist ethics, a collective money-bank with a separate compartment for each pupil etc.

Maison Picassiette ⊙ – *East of the town, 22 Rue du Repas* Built and decorated by Raymond Isidore (1900-64), this house offers an amazing medley of naive art. A number of monuments and numerous religious scenes are suggested by mosaic compositions made with extremely diverse materials: pieces of crockery, fragments of tinted glass, dollops of cement etc. Visitors are given a complete tour of the house, including the "chapel", the Black Courtyard ("tomb" crowned by a replica of Chartres Cathedral), the summer house (frescoes); the garden is dotted with statues and features a large-scale mosaic depicting Jerusalem.

Le CHEMIN DES DAMES

Michelin map 56 folds 4, 5 or 236 folds 37, 38, 39

Chemin des Dames, which means Ladies' Way, follows a ridge separating the Aisne Valley from the Ailette Valley. It derives its name from the daughters of Louis XV, known as *"Mesdames"*, who followed this route to get to the Château de la Bove, home of their friend the Duchess of Narbonne.

Nivelle Offensive – In 1914, after the Battle of the Marne, the retreating Germans stopped here, having realised that the location was an excellent defensive spot which they fortified by making use of the quarries *(boves or creuttes)*, hollowed out of the ridge.

General Nivelle, commander of the French armies from December 1916, searched for a way of penetrating their defence along Chemin des Dames. In spite of the difficult terrain, riddled with machine gun nests, on 16 April 1917 he sent an army under Mangin to attack the German positions. The French troops occupied the ridges following the first assault but the Germans clung onto the slopes of the Ailette Valley: the terrible French losses that ensued, together with the failure of the venture, caused a crisis of morale which provoked mutinies in parts of the French army.

FROM SOISSONS TO CORBENY
52km/32mi – about 3hr 30min

★ **Soissons** – *See Soissons.*

Drive northeast out of Soissons and take N 2 towards Laon.

Carrefour du Moulin de Laffaux – On this hill (169m/549ft), which marks the western extremity of the Chemin des Dames, stands the Monument aux Morts des Crapouillots, a memorial to those killed by trench mortar shells *(behind the restaurant)*. Laffaux windmill used to stand here.

A few miles further on, turn right onto D 18 (Chemin des Dames).

Signs along the route indicate the eight historic sites (equipped with parking and rest areas) where informative panels explain the stakes at play:

1 Fort de la Malmaison: fortifications date from the early 20C
2 Royère viewpoint: colonial troops

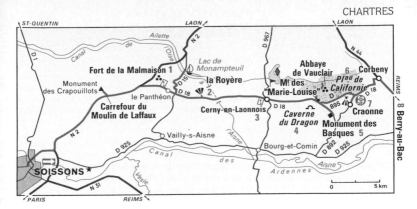

3 Cerny-en-Laonnois: necropolis and memorial
4 Caverne du Dragon: museum
5 Monument des Basques: Fighting France
6 Plateau de Californie: daily life in the trenches
7 Craonne Arboretum and village: mutineers
8 National assault vehicle monument, Berry-au-Bac: armoured vehicles

Fort de la Malmaison – This fort was taken by the colonial troops of the 38th Regiment from the Prussian guard in 1917. Malmaison Cemetery: German graves (1939-45).

Cerny-en-Laonnois – Near to the cross-roads with D 967 stand the Chemin des Dames memorial, chapel, and a French military cemetery (5 500 graves) which is neighbour to a cemetery for the German soldiers who died here too.

Caverne du Dragon ⊙ – The galleries dug out in the Middle Ages for the extraction of stone used to build Vauclair Abbey were baptised "Dragon's Cave" by the Germans. In 1915, they used it as a barracks (command post, dormitory, chapel, cemetery). Now a museum of remembrance, it serves to illustrate the daily life of soldiers through displays and videos. The sculptures, graffiti and carvings made by soldiers are moving reminders of their lives. A film and an animated model, "Theatre of Operations", demonstrate significant episodes of the conflict and explain the strategic importance of the site. From the entrance building *(shop, cafeteria)*, there is a view over the Aisne valley.

D 18 follows the top of the ridge known as Hurtebise's Isthmus, which extends to the northeast on the Craonne plateau formed by the Vauclair and Californie plateaux.

Monument des Marie-Louise ⊙ – In March 1814 the Hurtebise farm was fought over in the **Battle of Craonne** in which Napoleon, newly-arrived from Corbeny, was victorious over Blücher. A hundred years later in September 1914 the same farm was the object of fierce fighting in which the Basques of the 36th Division excelled themselves. Memorial to both battles.

Turn left onto D 886 which descends into the Ailette Valley.

Abbaye de Vauclair ⊙ – The ruins of this Cistercian monastery, founded in 1134 by St Bernard, were uncovered in 1966. The best-preserved parts of the abbey are the undercroft, the refectory, the chapter-house and the calefactory. The foundations of the abbey church and the guest house are also visible. A herb garden with medicinal plants has existed since 1976 and an exhibition gallery stands nearby.
All around, the ancient monastic forest of Vauclair covers 1 000ha/2 471 acres.

Return to Chemin des Dames and follow D 18 for another 2km/1mi.

Monument des Basques – The Hurtebise farm was again the centre of conflict in 1914, during which Basque soliders from the 36th Division distinguished themselves. A monument commemorates their heroism.

Turn back and take D 895 to the right.

To the right, stands the observation point from which Napoleon directed the Battle of Craonne in 1814 (now his statue stands there).

Plateau de Californie – First an observatory *(right)* comes into view, from where Napoleon directed the **Battle of Craonne** in 1814 (statue of the Emperor). Further away, opposite a large car park, a viewing table explains the 1917 offensive.

Arboretum – Where the path leads back to D 18, an arboretum has been erected on the site of the old village of Craonne. A new village has been built farther down the hill.

Corbeny – Kings came to Corbeny Abbey the day after their coronation, in order to pray to the relics of St Marcou who had the power to cure the king's evil (scrofula).

COMPIÈGNE★★★

Conurbation 67 057
Michelin maps 56 fold 2 and 106 fold 10 inset or 236 fold 35
Local map see Forêt de COMPIÈGNE

Compiègne, which was a royal residence long before it hosted the brilliant parties and receptions of the Second Empire, is bordered by one of the most beautiful forests in France. The town has become one of the busiest in Picardy, owing largely to its industry and its university (Benjamin Franklin University of Technology, Royallieu Research Centre).

HISTORICAL NOTES

Origins – Charles the Bald had a palace built to resemble the one in Aix-la-Chapelle (Aachen) built for Charlemagne and ceded to Charles' brother, Louis, in 843 when the Treaty of Verdun divided up the Carolingian Empire. He also founded an abbey which from the 10C preserved the relics of St Cornelius. The town developed around this royal abbey of St Cornelius (today only the 14C cloister remains), which preceded St Denis as the royal necropolis and centre of culture. Ramparts were built around Compiègne in the 13C; Charles V reinforced them and in 1374 added a castle that was the foundation for the palace.

Joan of Arc Imprisoned – In May 1430 the Burgundians and the English were camping beneath Compiègne's town walls, on the north side of the River Oise. **Joan of Arc** came to examine the enemy position and returned on the 23rd after a few days' absence, entering the town from the south. That same evening she attempted an assault, crossing the river and chasing the Burgundian vanguard from their Margny encampment. However, reinforcements came to the aid of the Burgundians from Clairoix and Coudun, while the English came from Venette, stealing along the Oise to attack from the rear; the French had no choice but to give ground. The Maid of Orléans covered the retreat with a handful of men. She reached the moat just as the commanding officer in Compiègne gave the order to raise the drawbridge, fearing the enemy would slip inside with the last of the French soldiers. A short skirmish ensued. A Picardy archer toppled Joan of Arc from her horse and she was immediately taken prisoner. The place of capture is located near place du 54ème-Régiment-d'Infanterie, where Frémiet's equestrian statue of the Maid of Orléans stands.

The Palace of Louis XV – All the kings of France enjoyed staying in Compiègne which they often visited. Yet, with four main buildings haphazardly arranged around a central courtyard, the château was not an obvious royal residence. Louis XIV said, "At Versailles, I am lodged like a king; at Fontainebleau, like a prince; and at Compiègne, like a peasant." He had new apartments built facing the forest. His 75 visits here were marked by sumptuous feasts and, in particular, great military camps. The largest of these was in 1698, the last time the King stayed at Compiègne.

When Louis XV ordered the complete reconstruction of the palace in 1738 he was less interested in outdoing his predecessor, who had built so much, than in having a place where he could reside with his court and ministers. The architect Jacques Gabriel and his successor **Jacques-Ange Gabriel** were limited by the town and its ramparts, which obliged them to rebuild on the old foundations. As a further inconvenience, they could not destroy an old building until a new one had been completed, as the King refused to cease his visits to Compiègne during the rebuilding work.

Louis XV's master plan of 1751 was brought to a halt by the Seven Years War. Louis XVI continued the project and achieved a great deal but left it unfinished. In fact, it was not until 1785 that he was finally able to occupy the royal apartments, which would later accommodate Napoleon I. The south wing was finished that same year. Marie-Antoinette had personally overseen its arrangement, decor and furnishing but never actually stayed here herself. A great terrace was built in front of the palace's façade, which looked out onto a park. This terrace was connected to the gardens by a monumental central flight of steps, replacing the moat that had formerly been part of Charles V's fortifications.

From 1789 to 1791 the work continued, though at a slower pace, as the King hoped to withdraw to Compiègne. In 1795, in the aftermath of the Revolution, the furnishings were completely dispersed through auctions which lasted five months.

After the Revolution the palace served first as a military school, then as an engineering college. In 1806 it became an Imperial residence and Napoleon I had the palace entirely restored by the architect Berthaut, the painter Girodet and the decorators Redouté and the Dubois brothers.

Wedding Palace – It was in Compiègne Forest that, on 14 May 1770, the future Louis XVI was introduced to Marie-Antoinette of Austria for the first time; the young Dauphin was paralysed with shyness.

On 27 March 1810 the great-niece of Marie-Antoinette, Marie-Louise of Austria, was to arrive in Compiègne. She had married Napoleon I by proxy and this time the groom was impatient. Despite torrential rain, the Emperor ran to meet the princess and threw himself soaking wet into her carriage, smothering the terrified Marie-Louise with demonstrations of affection. The dinner planned in Soissons was cancelled and instead

Where to stay

BUDGET

Hôtel de Flandre – 16 Quai République, ☎ 03 44 83 24 40, fax 03 44 90 02 75. Closed 24 December to 4 January. Functional soundproof hotel situated on the banks of the River Oise. Double room from 270F.

OUR SELECTION

Hôtel les Beaux-Arts – 33 Cours Guynemer, ☎ 03 44 92 26 26, fax 03 44 92 26 00. Closed 1 to 15 August. Comfortable hotel, close to the town centre; original modern decoration. Double room: 450F.

LUXURY

Château de Bellinglise – Located in Élincourt-Ste-Marguerite, 16km/10mi north of Compiègne along D 142, ☎ 03 44 96 00 33, fax 03 44 96 03 00. Lovely 16C stone and brick residence in the Matz Valley; elegant period furniture. Double room from 965F.

Eating out

BUDGET

Le Bistrot des Arts – 35 Cours Guynemer, ☎ 03 44 20 10 10. Closed Saturdy lunchtime and Sunday, from 10 to 24 August and from 21 December to 4 January. The highly polished furniture and the prints create the bistro atmosphere of this popular restaurant. Fixed menu: 110F.

OUR SELECTION

Auberge du Buissonnet – In Choisy-au-Bac, 5km/3mi east of Compiègne, ☎ 03 44 40 17 41. Closed Sunday evening and Monday, and from 10 to 21 October. This restaurant, situated on the edge of the forest has a pleasant terrace overlooking the garden and the pond. Fixed menu: 139F.

On the town

Au Relais du Château – 24 Rue d'Ulm, ☎ 03 44 40 03 45. Close to the palace, this shop sells local produce and provides regional dishes. Cycle hire.

Les Jardins d'Eugénie – 17 Rue Legendre, ☎ 03 44 40 00 88. Have a drink, tea or even a meal in pleasant surroundings; large Art deco window.

L'Espace Café – 8 Rue Napoléon, ☎ 03 44 40 10 64. Pleasantly situated in the shopping area of the town centre, this pavement café is very lively as soon as the weather is fine.

City-Hall – 1 Rue Legendre, ☎ 03 44 40 80 40. Located on the right of the town hall, this discotheque benefits from its central position.

the Emperor and his bride had supper at Compiègne. Some days later the wedding ceremonies were celebrated at St-Cloud, serving only as the consecration of a union imposed at Vienna and willingly accepted at Compiègne.

In 1832 Louis-Philippe, who transformed the real tennis court into a theatre, married his daughter Louise-Marie to the first king of Belgium, Leopold of Saxe-Coburg.

The Second Empire "Series" – Compiègne was the favourite residence of Napoleon III and Empress Eugénie. They came every autumn for four to six weeks to enjoy the hunting season, receiving the kings and princes of Europe. They also received the celebrities of the time, arranged in five "series" of about 80 people, grouped by "affinities". Lodging the guests often posed great difficulties and many distinguished individuals had to content themselves with rooms under the eaves.

The hunts, theatrical evenings, charades and balls left the guests with little free time. Romantic and political intrigue mixed freely. One rainy afternoon, to amuse the Imperial couple and their guests, the writer Mérimée composed his famous dictation, comprising the words with the greatest spelling difficulties in the French language. The Empress made the highest number of mistakes, 62; Pauline Sandoz, Metternich's daughter-in-law, had the least with three. The luxuries and endless frivolities intoxicated the courtiers, who delighted in waltzes and long forest outings. The events of 1870 interrupted this joyous life and the work on the new theatre. During the emperor's long periods of residence at Compiègne most of the First Empire furniture was replaced.

The World Wars – From 1917 to 1918 the palace was the general headquarters of generals Nivelle and then Pétain. In 1919 a fire damaged most of the royal apartments. The armistices of 11 November 1918 and 22 June 1940 *(see Clairière de l'Armistice under Forêt de COMPIÈGNE)* were signed in the forest. Compiègne suffered heavy bombing during the Second World War. **Royallieu**, a district south of the town, served from 1941 to 1944 as a centre from which prisoners were sent to various Nazi concentration camps (a memorial stands at the entrance to the military camp as well as in Compiègne railway station).

★★★ PALACE *2hr*

Viewed from the square the palace is paradoxically "a Louis XV château built almost entirely from 1751 to 1789".

This austerely Classical château covers a vast triangular area (3ha/7.5 acres); indeed, the regularity of its arrangement is even rather monotonous. The decoration inside and the collection of 18C and First Empire tapestries and furnishings is, however, exceptional. Among the many details unifying the various apartments are fine *trompe-l'œil* paintings by Sauvage (1744-1818) over the doors.

The Second Empire Museum and the Transport Museum are also in the palace.

The new theatre, on which work began in 1867 during the reign of Napoleon III, was never completed because of the Franco-Prussian War in 1870. An association was set up in 1987 to rehabilitate it and organise productions there. As a result, the **Théâtre Impérial**, in which the interior layout is reminiscent of the opera house in Versailles, has become popular as a venue for concerts and operettas.

★★Historic Apartments (Appartements Historiques) ⓥ

HISTORIC APARTMENTS

The Historic Apartments of the palace begin with rooms devoted to its history; beyond them rises the Queen's Grand Staircase, or Apollo Staircase, which led directly to the queen's apartments; further still is the entrance hall or Gallery of Columns which precedes the Grand Staircase (**1**). Climb the staircase with its beautiful 18C wrought-iron balustrade to the landing where a great Gallo-Roman sarcophagus lies; it served as the font in the vanished abbey church of St Cornelius and is a relic of very early Compiègne. The first-floor Guard-Room (1785) (**2**) leads into the antechamber or Ushers' Salon (**3**), which gave access to both the King's apartment *(left)* and the Queen's *(right)*.

The main courtyard and the principal body of the château are on different levels: the sovereigns' apartments were built on the old ramparts and are therefore on the ground floor on the garden side (on the same level as the terrace), but on the first floor on the side facing the courtyard.

Appartement du Roi et des Empereurs (King's and Emperors' Apartment)

This apartment houses exceptional groups of objects, works and memorabilia.

Salle à manger de l'Empereur (4) – The decor and furnishings in the dining room are First Empire (early 19C). Pilasters and doors, surmounted by *grisaille* paintings by Sauvage, stand out against the fake rose-pink onyx. One of Sauvage's paintings is an extraordinary *trompe-l'œil* representing Anacreon. It was here that on 1 May 1814 Louis XVIII entertained Czar Alexander, who was still hesitating about returning the Bourbons to the throne of France. Under the Second Empire a private theatre was established here, with those close to the empress taking part in charades and revues.

Salon des cartes (5) – First designated as the Nobles' Antechamber under Louis XVI, then as the Senior Officers' Salon under Napoleon I, this room ended up as the *Aide-de-Camp* Salon or the Card Salon under Napoleon III. The furnishings comprise elements from the First Empire (chairs covered in Beauvais tapestry) and from the Second Empire. Note the games: quoits and a pin table.

Salon de famille (6) – This room was once Louis XVI's bedchamber (large mirrors hide the alcove). The **view★** onto the park extends the length of the avenue to the Beaux Monts.

The furnishings recall Empress Eugénie's taste for mixing styles: Louis XV armchairs, unusual little seats for two (called *confidents*) or for three *(indiscrets)* etc.

Salle du Conseil (7) – Unfortunately only the original table has been returned; the rest of the furniture from the council chamber has been lost. Together with Versailles and Fontainebleau, Compiègne was one of the three châteaux where the king held counsel. Representatives of the Republics of Genoa and of the Kingdom of France signed two successive treaties here (1756 and 1764) which accorded France the right to garrison troops in the maritime citadels of Corsica. An immense tapestry illustrates *The Crossing of the Rhine by Louis XIV*.

Chambre de l'Empereur (8) – The Emperor's bedchamber has been restored to its appearance during the First Empire, with Jacob-Desmalter furnishings and friezes representing eagles.

Bibliothèque de l'Empereur (9) – Formerly the King's Great Cabinet, this room was used as a library during the First Empire. The bookcase and the furnishings are by Jacob-Desmalter; the painted ceiling is the work of Girodet.

Palace – Salon Bleu

Appartement de l'Impératrice (Empress' Apartment)

These rooms comprised the queen's principal apartments, the only ones in which Marie-Antoinette ever stayed; later, they were particularly favoured by Empresses Marie-Louise and Eugénie.

Salon du Déjeuner (10) – The delightful breakfast room, with pale blue and yellow silk hangings, was prepared for Marie-Louise in 1809.

Salon de musique (11) – This was one of Empress Eugénie's favourite rooms; she furnished it herself. The Louis XVI pieces, from the apartment of Marie-Antoinette at St-Cloud, recall that the last sovereign consort of France was keeping the memory of the unfortunate queen alive.

Chambre de l'Impératrice (12) – The majestic tester bed is enclosed by white silk curtains and gold-embroidered muslin. Paintings by Girodet represent the seasons and the Morning Star appears in the centre of the ceiling. The round boudoir leading to the bedchamber, also built for Marie-Louise, served as a dressing-room and for taking baths. The last three of these interconnecting rooms form a decorative First Empire ensemble. Seats are arranged formally around a couch in the **Grand Salon (13)**; the **Salon des Fleurs (14)** owes its name to the eight panels painted with lily-like flowers, after Redoute; the **Salon Bleu (15)** strikingly contrasts blue walls and seats with a red marble fireplace and console tables. These rooms belonged to the imperial prince at the end of the Second Empire.

Salle à manger de l'Impératrice (16) – The walls of this modestly sized room are lined with stucco-marble, of a caramel colour more elegantly known as "antique yellow". It was here that the Archduchess Marie-Louise dined with the Emperor for the first time.

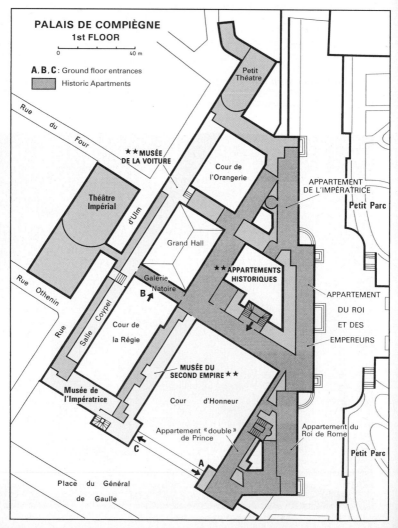

PALAIS DE COMPIÈGNE
1st FLOOR

0   40 m

A, B, C: Ground floor entrances

Historic Apartments

Rue du Four

★★MUSÉE DE LA VOITURE

Théâtre Impérial

Rue Othenin

Rue

d'Ulm

Salle Coypel

Galerie Natoire

B

Cour de la Régie

Grand Hall

★★APPARTEMENTS HISTORIQUES

Cour de l'Orangerie

Petit Théatre

APPARTEMENT DE L'IMPÉRATRICE

Petit Parc

APPARTEMENT DU ROI ET DES EMPEREURS

MUSÉE DU SECOND EMPIRE ★★

Musée de l'Impératrice

Cour d'Honneur

Appartement «double» de Prince

C

A

Place du Général de Gaulle

Appartement du Roi de Rome

Petit Parc

Galerie des chasses de Louis XV — The room is hung with Gobelins tapestries, which were woven as early as 1735 in accordance with sketches by Oudry. One represents a hunt along the River Oise and includes the silhouettes of Compiègne and the old Royallieu abbey. The series continues in the **Galerie des Cerfs** (**17**), formerly the Queen's Guards' Room, then the Empress' Guards' Room.

Galerie du Bal — The room (39m by 13m/128ft by 43ft) was constructed within a few months for Marie-Louise's arrival, by gutting two floors of small apartments. The ceiling paintings glorify the Emperor's victories; the mythological scenes at the end of the room are by Girodet. Throughout the Second Empire the gallery served as a dining room at the time of the "series", the sovereigns presiding from the centre of an immense table set up for the occasion.

Galerie Natoire — The room was built by Napoleon III to lead to the **Grand Théâtre** (built on the other side of rue d'Ulm but never finished). The gallery is decorated with *The Story of Don Quixote*, a series of **paintings★** by Natoire (1700-77) in the heroic style. These were copied at Beauvais to create the tapestries hanging today in the Aix-en-Provence Tapestry Museum.

Salle Coypel — In this room a second series of episodes, by Coypel, continue the Don Quixote story (1714-34) in a more light-hearted style. These paintings were also recreated by the Gobelins tapestry weavers.

Chapel — The First Empire chapel is surprisingly small for such a vast château, as the great chapel planned by Gabriel was never built. It was here on 9 August 1832 that the marriage took place between Princess Louise-Marie, eldest daughter of Louis-Philippe, and Leopold I, King of Belgium. Princess Marie of Orléans, the French king's second daughter, designed the stained-glass window.

Appartement double du Prince, appartement du roi de Rome

Appartement double du Prince — Napoleon I had this apartment arranged to receive a foreign sovereign and his or her consort. This excellent group of Empire rooms comprises a dining room, four salons and a great bedchamber (original wallpaper, silk hangings, furniture).

Appartement du roi de Rome — The apartment has been restored to its appearance in 1811, when Napoleon I's son (five months old at the time) stayed in it for one month. All the original furnishings adorn the salon-boudoir, bathroom, boudoir, bedchamber and main drawing room. In the middle of the apartment a room (**18**) has been restored to appear as it did at the end of the 18C (Queen Marie-Antoinette's games room).

★★Musée du Second Empire ⊙

The museum is located in a series of small, quiet drawing rooms and presents life at Court and in the outside world, and the arts, during the Second Empire.

Beyond the first room, displaying Daumier's humorous drawings, a space is devoted to the "beauties" of the period. Princess Mathilde (1820-1904), one of the reign's great figures, has pride of place here. She was for a brief time the fiancée of Louis-Napoleon, her close cousin. After her Spanish marriage she devoted herself entirely to her salon in rue de Courcelles, which was much frequented by the important writers and artists of the day, and to her château in St-Gratien.

The museum owns the famous Winterhalter painting, *The Empress with her Ladies-in-Waiting* (1855).

Among the many sculptures by Carpeaux in the last rooms, note the bust of Napoleon, aged by the fall of the Empire, and the statue of the Imperial Prince with his dog.

Musée de l'Impératrice — This collection was bequeathed by M and Mme F Ferrand and includes memorabilia of official life and life in exile, as well as the more popular objects associated with Empress Eugénie. Among the more moving items are those evoking the Empress and her son, the Imperial Prince, who was massacred by the Zulus.

★★Musée de la voiture ⊙

The museum was created in 1927 on the initiative of the Touring Club of France. None of the authentic royal carriages has been preserved in France. The collection of antique carriages features berlin coaches for travelling or ceremonial use in particular; these carriages were mounted on a base with two shafts, safer than a single shaft, to which the horses were harnessed.

Grand Hall — About fifty carriages are on display in what was formerly the kitchen courtyard, now covered over: the oldest, a travelling berlin coach which belonged to the kings of Spain, dating from c 1740; the berlin coach used by the pope in Bologna, and the one in which Bonaparte made his entrance to the town in 1796; 18C and 19C travelling carriages, including one used by Napoleon in Russia; the travelling brougham used by the Duke of Angoulême for the Trocadero campaign, and that of Field Marshal Maison.

A mail-coach, a charabanc, a Madeleine-Bastille omnibus and Orsay broughams are also on show, as well as the ceremonial berlins used by Napoleon III and the president of the Republic.

The collection includes the 1878 Mancelle de Bollée vehicle and a strange steam stage-coach by the same builder, which it is hard to imagine running without horses; a tracked vehicle, a 1924 Citroën from the Croisière Noire (the first trans-African car expedition), and the salon-coach (Compagnie du Nord) used by Napoleon III to travel between Paris and Compiègne.

Kitchens and Outbuildings – The evolution of the two-wheeler, starting with the heavy ancestors of the bicycle, hobbies which the rider set in motion by pushing off, can be seen in the former pantries. Pedals appeared with the 1863 Michaux velocipede. The penny-farthing, built out of iron tubing, had an unusually large front wheel to increase its speed. Developments such as the invention of the chain belt, which first appeared on the English tricycle, rendered wheels of disproportionate size unnecessary. The true bicycle became possible in about 1890. The army took advantage of the idea by developing a folding velocipede just before the First World War.

The exhibition in the large former kitchens of the palace follows the development of the **automobile**, from De Dion and Trépardoux's steam car to Guynemer's 1914 Sigma-Ballot open touring-car, the form of which already shows the technical efforts made to increase speed. Between these two extremes in the evolution of the car there is the Panhard No 2, the first car equipped with a four-stroke Daimler engine; the 1895 vis-à-vis by Bollée & Son which was one of the entrants in the race from Paris to Marseille-en-Beauvaisis (north of Beauvais); the De Dion-Bouton series; the large 1897 wagonette belonging to the Duchess of Uzès, the first woman driver; the 1899 "Never-satisfied" on Michelin tyres, which was the first car to attain speeds of 100kph/62mph; and the little 1900 4-CV Renault, the first saloon car. Steam, combustion and electric motors are also exhibited, showing the various ideas of the researchers and creators of the automobile industry.

First Floor – These rooms are devoted to foreign vehicles and their accessories: Dutch and Italian cabriolets, a Sicilian cart, palanquin, sleighs, coachmen's clothes etc.

PARK

From a crossroads, three avenues lead into the forest. The gardens are known as the Petit Parc; the main entrance gate is to the left, when facing away from the town. The Grand Parc surrounds it and is part of the forest.

Petit Parc – Cross the trench which, at the time of Napoleon's investiture, was the only trace of the formal French gardens planned by Gabriel, together with the terraces planted with lime-trees alongside it.

The Emperor's guiding idea was "to link the château as soon as possible to the forest, which is the true garden and the real beauty of this residence". The enclosing wall which blocked the view of the woods was taken down and replaced by iron railings. Beyond, the openness of avenue des Beaux-Monts creates a magnificent linear perspective (4km/6mi long), which was originally to have been closed with a monumental gateway to remind the Emperor's young bride of Schönbrunn. Impatient to reach the forest without having to go through the town, Napoleon had a central ramp built for carriages between the terrace and the park; this was unfortunately at the expense of the glorious flight of steps by Gabriel. From then on the Petit Parc was replanted as a formal English garden and lost its importance. The present layout dates from the Second Empire.

ADDITIONAL SIGHTS

★**Hôtel de ville** – This remarkable building was constructed under Louis XII in the late-Gothic style. It was restored during the last century and the façade statues date from this period. They represent, from left to right around the central equestrian statue of Louis XII: St Denis, St Louis, Charles the Bald, Joan of Arc, Cardinal Pierre d'Ailly who was born in Compiègne, and Charlemagne.

The belfry consists of two floors and a slate-covered spire, flanked by four pinnacled turrets. At the base of the spire, three figures, called *picantins* and dressed as Swiss foot-soldiers from the period of François I, ring the hours and the quarter-hours.

Two wings were added to the old building during its restoration.

★**Musée de la Figurine historique** ⊘ – In *Hôtel de la Cloche, to the right of the Hôtel de ville*.

The museum houses over 100 000 model figures in tin, lead, wood, plastic, paper and cardboard; they are sculpted wholly or partly in the round, or are flat. A visit here offers an interesting retrospective of the development of dress, along with an evocation of historical events throughout the ages. The presentation, in rooms lit only by the display, allows leisurely contemplation of the various scenes. Note in particular *The Review of French Troops at Betheny* in 1901 in front of the Czar of Russia and President Loubet (12 000 figures made by A Silhol, who participated in the parade himself); *The Battle of Waterloo* created by Charles Laurent from 1905 to 1923, which is completed by an audio-visual presentation; and *The Return of the Emperor's Ashes* with the veterans of the Napoleonic wars.

Église St-Jacques – The church features a 15C tower, the highest in the town, at one of the corners of its west front. This was the parish church of the king and the court, hence funds provided for the chancel to be reworked in marble in the 18C and for the addition of

Compiègne – Hôtel de ville

carved-wood panels at the base of the nave's pillars. The harmony of the Gothic style at the time of St Louis is particularly evident in the chancel with its narrow, clerestory-lit triforium and the 13C transept. An ambulatory was added in the 16C. The 13C stone Virgin and Child in the north transept, known as "Our Lady of the Silver Feet" *(Notre-Dame aux pieds d'argent)*, is the subject of much veneration. A chapel in the north aisle houses three 15C painted wooden statues. They came from the calvary which surmounted the old rood beam.

Tour de Beauregard – This former royal keep or "Governor's Tower", now in ruins, is located on the site of Charles the Bald's palace. The tower is all that remains from the time when Joan of Arc *(see above)* made her last, fatal military assault, which she began by leaving the town via the old St Louis bridge on 23 May 1430.

Musée Vivenel ⊘ – Compiègne's municipal museum is located in the Hôtel de Songeons; it is a pleasant building dating from the early 19C, the garden of which is now a public park.

The ground floor is devoted to Antiquity: Greek and Roman marbles and bronzes; Antique ceramics including a remarkable group of **Greek vases**★★ discovered in Etruria and Southern Italy *(Magna Graecia)*; Egyptian sculptures and funerary objects (mummified sacred animals) dating largely from the New Empire (1580 to 1085 BC) and the Saitic Period (663 to 525 BC).

France's successive civilisations, from prehistory to the end of the Gallo-Roman period, are evoked through the tools, weapons and various objects found at excavation sites; archeological activities have been conducted in the region from the time of Napoleon III's campaigns. Note the three bronze helmets dating from *c* 600 BC. In the room devoted to the Gallic sanctuary at Gournay-sur-Aronde, two great showcases display weapons and iron objects, and bones from animals which were ritually sacrificed.

The first-floor rooms have preserved their Directoire wainscoting. The painting collections are displayed here (large altarpiece representing the Passion by Wolgemut, Dürer's teacher), together with ceramics (pitchers in "Flemish stoneware", Italian majolicas), ivories, Limousin enamels etc.

Discover the suggested Touring Programmes at the beginning of the guide
Plan a trip with the help of the Map of Principal Sights.

Forêt de COMPIÈGNE★★

COMPIÈGNE FOREST

Michelin map 106 fold 10 (inset) or 237 folds 7,8

The State forest of Compiègne (14 500ha/35 800 acres) is a remnant of the immense Cuise Forest which extended from the edge of Île-de-France to the Ardennes. It embraces delightful beech groves, magnificent avenues, valleys, ponds and villages. The forest occupies a sort of hollow with the Oise and Aisne river valleys on two sides. A series of hills and promontories sketches a sharply defined crescent to the north, east and south. These peaks rise on average 80m/262ft above the sandy base of the hollow, which is grooved with numerous rivulets. The largest of these, the ru de Berne, links a series of ponds.

The forest is crisscrossed by 1 500km/930mi of roads and footpaths. François I first cut great rides through the trees, with Louis XIV and Louis XV later contributing to extend this network in order to create an ideal place for hunting.

The grounds, once the lands of Frankish kings, are today used by three different hunts.

Types of trees – The most common species in the forest are beech (40%), oak (30%) and yoke-elms (15%). Beech in particular occupies the south plateau and its slopes, and the area immediately surrounding Compiègne itself. Oak, which was planted long ago, thrives in the better-drained clay soil, as well as on the Beaux Monts. Since 1830 Norway pine and other conifers have grown in the poor, sandy soil where oaks would find it difficult to thrive.

A paved cycle path runs between Compiègne (east from Carrefour Royal along Route Tournante) and Pierrefonds.

Fishing regulations – A board in front of the forest warden's house at Étangs de St-Pierre lists the clubs and organisations which issue permits and licences.

★★LES BEAUX MONTS

① Tour starting from Compiègne

18km/11mi – about 1hr

★★★**Compiègne** – *See COMPIÈGNE*

Leave Compiègne by Avenue Royale. At Carrefour Royal, turn left onto Route Tournante; the road crosses the long perspective of Avenue des Beaux-Monts in two bends. At Carrefour du Renard turn right onto Route Eugénie and cross Carrefour des Vineux. The road rises to offer a good view of Avenue des Beaux-Monts from about halfway up the hillside. Continue as far as Carrefour d'Eugénie.

Carrefour d'Eugénie – Some of the forest's oldest **oak trees★★** stand around this junction. The most ancient ones date from the time of François I.

Take the winding road on the left which climbs to Les Beaux Monts.

★★**Les Beaux Monts** – Stop at the summit, near the Beaux Monts viewpoint *(point de vue)*; from here the **view★** stretches along the straight line of the avenue through the forest all the way to the palace, barely visible 4km².5mi away.

Continue to the junction and the Point de vue du Précipice.

Point de vue du Précipice (Precipice Viewpoint) – Here the extensive **view★** overlooks the woody stretches of the Berne River Valley and Mont St-Marc.

Return to the junction and take the road on the right down from Les Beaux Monts.

The road runs through a magnificent grove of oaks and beeches and reaches a straight road. *Turn right; Cross Route Eugénie and take the first road on the right.*

Chapelle St-Corneille-aux-Bois – The secluded chapel was founded in 1164; it later passed to the Abbey of St-Corneille in Compiègne. François I added a hunting lodge but its appearance today dates only from the time of Viollet-le-Duc (19C); the Gothic construction of the 13C chapel, however, has remained intact. The wardens of Compiègne Forest came here before the days of the French Revolution to hear Sunday mass.

Continue to D 14; turn right to return to Compiègne (Vieux-Moulin-Compiègne).

★★CLAIRIÈRE DE L'ARMISTICE

② Direct road to the historic site

6km/3.5mi northeast of Compiègne 1hr visit

Leave Compiègne by N 31. Go straight across Carrefour d'Aumont and continue to Carrefour du Francport where you will see the Monument to the liberators of Alsace and Lorraine and the car park.

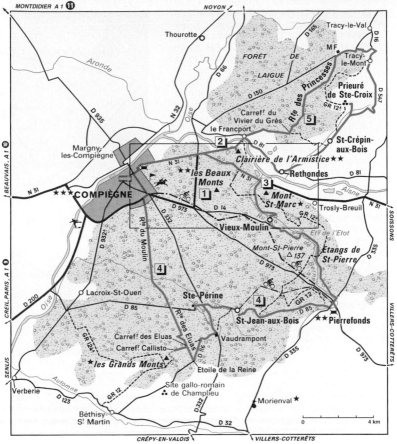

A site where a network of tracks existed for heavy artillery installations was cleared to make room for the private train of the allied forces' commander-in-chief, Field-Marshal Foch, and for that of the German plenipotentiaries. The tracks were linked to the Compiègne-Soissons line at Rethondes Station.

Today, rails and flagstones, marking the site of the railway carriages, surround a memorial commemorating the date.

On 7 November 1918 Maréchal Foch's private train arrived.

On 8 November, during the first few hours of daylight, the train arrived from Tergnier with the German negotiators. At 9am, they entered Foch's carriage-office. The Germans sat down at the conference table; General Weygand went to fetch the Maréchal who greeted the Germans in the following terms:

"Whom do I have the honour of addressing?"

"The plenipotentiaries sent by the German government," replied Erzberger, the group's leader. He handed the Commander-in-Chief the delegation's letters of credit and Foch withdrew to study them. When he had done so, he came back and, without sitting down, asked,

"What is the purpose of your visit?"

"We have come to hear the proposals of the Allied forces with a view to achieving an armistice on land, sea and in the air," replied Erzberger.

"I have no such proposals," answered Foch.

Oberndorff, the diplomat, broke in,

"If you prefer, Sir, we could say that we have come to ask under what conditions the Allies would agree to an armistice."

"I have no conditions!" Erzberger then read out the note from President Wilson stating that Maréchal Foch was authorised to indicate the armistice conditions.

"Are you asking for an armistice?" asked the Maréchal. "If you are, I can tell you the conditions under which it could be achieved."

Oberndorff and Erzberger declared that they were indeed seeking an armistice.

Weygand then read out the conditions and it took him one hour to do so (the document had to be translated). Everybody listened in silence. Three days were then granted to the Germans to study the proposals.

General von Winterfeldt, the only army officer in the German delegation, asked for a suspension of hostilities during the period allowed for consideration of the draft armistice. Foch refused. On the evening of 10 November, a radio message from

147

Germany authorised the plenipotentiaries to sign the armistice. At about 2am, the Germans returned to the Maréchal's carriage and, at 5.15am, the agreement was signed. It came into effect on the same day, at 11am. During the morning, Maréchal Foch travelled in person to Paris to announce the good news to Raymond Poincaré, the President of the Republic, and to Clémenceau, the French Prime Minister.

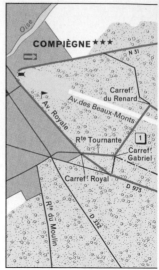

On 14 June 1940, 22 years later, during the Second World War, the German Army entered Paris; on 21 June, at 3.30pm the French armistice delegation was received by Hitler and governement dignitaries in the same car of the same private train, then located in its 1918 position. The leaders withdrew together and the representatives of the German high command gave their interlocutors the detailed document listing the victors' terms for an armistice.

It was signed on the evening of 22 June.

The clearing and its historic monuments were then ransacked by the occupation forces. Only the statue of Foch was spared.

Wagon du maréchal Foch ⊙ – The original, historic dining-car which was converted into an office for Field Marshal Foch was exhibited in the courtyard of the Invalides in Paris from 1921 to 1927 then returned to the forest clearing and placed in a shelter built for the purpose. Transported to Berlin as a trophy in 1940, it was destroyed in the Thuringia Forest in April 1945. In 1950 it was replaced by another carriage from a similar series. The places occupied by the delegates are indicated and the actual objects they used in 1918, put aside safely at the time, are now back inside the carriage.

The shelter also houses a large room devoted to the two armistices (11 November 1918 and 22 June 1940); the display includes contemporary newspapers, original documents, photographs, dummies in military uniform and remains of the original carriage.

★LE MONT ST-MARC AND THE PONDS

③ From Compiègne to Pierrefonds

26km/16mi – about 1hr 30min

Leave Compiègne by N 31.

Pont de Berne – It was here that the Dauphin, the future Louis XVI, met Marie-Antoinette for the first time; the future queen had just arrived from Vienna.

Turn right towards Pierrefonds. At Vivier-Frère-Robert turn left onto Route du Geai.

★**Mont St-Marc** – The slopes of this long rise are covered with beeches. On reaching the plateau, turn left into the forest road which follows the edge; there are good views of the Berne and Aisne River valleys, Rethondes and Laigue Forest. The road follows the northern promontory of the hill. 2.5km/1.5mi further along, **Carrefour Lambin** offers a particularly fine **view** of the Aisne Valley.

Return by the same road and fork left onto the first road suitable for vehicles; Drive down Route du Geai and continue towards Pierrefonds.

Turn right and continue along the main street in Vieux-Moulin.

Vieux-Moulin – This former woodcutters' village later became a wealthy community of holiday homes. The little church, with a belfry resembling a Chinese hat, was rebuilt in 1860 at Napoleon III's expense.

Turn left at the junction with the war memorial and take Route Eugénie (on the south bank) to Étang de l'Étot.

Étangs de St-Pierre – These ponds were created to stock fish; they were dug by members of the Celestine community from the priory of Mont-St-Pierre, to the west.

Empress Eugénie's former chalet is now a forest warden's house with exhibitions on the forest.

1km/0.5mi beyond the last pond, at a fork near the edge of the forest, take the small road left that climbs up to the hilltop districts of Pierrefonds.

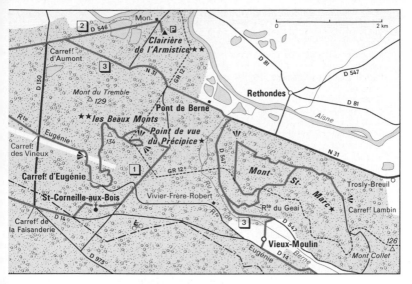

★LES GRANDS MONTS

④ From Pierrefonds to Compiègne

27km/17mi – about 1hr 30min

★★**Château de Pierrefonds** – *See PIERREFONDS.*

Leave Pierrefonds by D 85, heading west.

The road first rises to a wooded plateau, where the beautiful beech groves were largely destroyed during storms in 1984; it then descends into St-Jean-aux-Bois.

St-Jean-aux-Bois – This charming village was appropriately renamed "Solitude" in 1794. The 12C monastic buildings which were at the heart of the village can be seen along one side of it, marked by a moat filled with water. The Benedictine nuns left their abbey for Royallieu (on the outskirts of Compiègne) in 1634 as the forest was no longer safe; for a while Augustine canons took their place but in 1761 St-Jean was abandoned by its religious inhabitants.

The old fortified gate leads to the esplanade and the last vestiges of the abbey: the church, the chapter house and the doorway to the "Small Courtyard" (formerly farm buildings). The architectural purity of the 13C **church**★ is remarkable. Inside, the sober harmony of the transept and chancel create an impression of grandeur. The slenderness of the columns separating each transept arm into two bays emphasises the church's height. The arrangement here – which was common later, in the 16C – is the only example in the region from that period. The *grisailles* recall the luminous atmosphere of the nave in the 13C.

The **chapter-house** *(salle capitulaire)* is located on the south side of the church; dating from c 1150, it is the oldest part of the structure. It serves today as a chapel annex and is generally open only for worship.

Ste-Périne – The pond surrounded by plane trees and poplars, and the woodland house in an old priory form an attractive sight.

The nuns of Ste-Périne (a linguistic contraction of Pétronille) occupied this hermitage from 1285 to 1626. Fear for their safety forced them to move first to Compiègne, then to Paris, then la Villette, Chaillot and finally Auteuil, where a retirement home still bears their name.

Turn round; turn right onto the main road to Crépy-en-Valois and at Vaudrampont turn right onto D 116.

At Etoile de la Reine roundabout turn sharp right onto Route des Éluas and first left onto an unpaved road; park at Carrefour Callisto.

★**Les Grands Monts** – This southern part of the forest is divided into the plateau and the swamps. The short trip described below *(30min on foot there and back)*, along an overhanging path shaded by beech groves, introduces some of the area's characteristics. Walk down Route des Princesses; immediately after the barrier turn left into the well-maintained path marked with yellow indicators which goes around the promontory. Turn back when the path becomes less well cleared and reaches the bottom of the gully.

Turn round; continue along Route des Éluas which runs downhill and round a hairpin bend.

Return to Compiègne by following the long Route du Moulin.

A further intinerary ⑤ might take in the village of **Rethondes**, the church at **St-Crépin-aux-Bois**, and the 16C ruins of the beautiful priory church of the old **Prieuré Ste-Croix-d'Offémont**; Route des Princesses is a popular starting point for rambles.

CORBIE

Population 6 152
Michelin map 52 fold 9 or 236 fold 24

Corbie is a small town between the Somme and the Ancre rivers; it developed around the Benedictine abbey, where the powerful abbots held the title of Count and were allowed to mint coinage.

A Cradle for Saints – The monastery was founded in 657 by St Bathild, wife of the Frankish king Clovis II, and in Carolingian times became a centre of Christian civilisation under the direction of St Adalard, Charlemagne's cousin. More than 300 monks took part day and night in the constant worship of the Lordt; St Paschase Radbert wrote the first theological treatise on the Eucharist; apostolic activity developed. The abbey spread to Corvey in Westphalia, which was to become the main centre of evangelism in northern Europe under the impetus of St Anschaire (or Oscar), who was born in Corbie in 801.
In the 11C St Gerard, a monk from Corbie, retreated to the area between the Garonne and the Dordogne, founding the Monastery known as La Sauve Majeure. **St Colette** (1381-1447), the daughter of a local carpenter, lived as a recluse and was favoured with several visions. She came out of seclusion to establish several convents of Poor Clares.

SIGHTS

Museum ⊘ – It is essentially devoted to the history of the abbey and contains Carolingian pottery, 16C coins, copies of manuscripts from the former library and a relief map of the siege of Corbie in 1636.

From the vast Place de la République go through the 18C **monumental gateway** to the abbey; the cloister and convent buildings were razed during the Revolution.

Église St-Pierre ⊘ – The construction of the former abbey church lasted from the 16C to the 18C but in 1815 the transept and chancel were knocked down, since they were by then in a state of collapse.
The stylistic unity of the remaining buildings is due to the architects' continued use of the Gothic style throughout the Renaissance and Classical periods: this accounts for the ribbed vaults in the three aisles, the rose-window, the twin towers pierced by twin bays, and the west front featuring three doorways with broken arches, all following the style of Gothic cathedrals. Part of the decoration borrows from the Classical repertory, notably the cartouches on the porch coving.
The **interior** is now only about 36m/118ft long, as opposed to 117m/384ft originally (see the model of the church before the Revolution). The Treasury at one time contained 113 reliquaries which were often venerated by the French kings and some of which have been preserved. The works of art include:
– the 15C statue of Our Lady of the Door *(south aisle, last pillar)*;
– St Bathild, an example of majestic 14C statuary *(end of south aisle, right of altar)*;
– a head of St Peter (13C) *(a pillar of north aisle)*;
– the 15C tomb of Abbot Raoul de Roye, the tutor of St Colette *(north aisle)*.

Chapelle Ste-Colette – The chapel was built in 1959 on the site of the house in which St Colette was born and contains a 16C statue of the saint kneeling.

EXCURSIONS

La Neuville – *2km/1mi northwest, on right bank of the River Ancre.*
Above the doorway of the early-16C church is a large, interesting **bas-relief** showing Christ's entry into Jerusalem on Palm Sunday. The relief is remarkable for its clarity and wealth of detail: spectators perched in the trees, in the background a miller wearing a cotton bonnet at the window of his mill. etc.

Australian Memorial – *3km/2mi south. Leave Corbie by D 1 (towards Amiens) and in Fouilloy turn left onto D 23 towards Villers-Bretonneux.*
In spring 1918 the hills around **Villers-Bretonneux** were fiercely fought over by the Germans and the Australians, following the German offensive on Picardy; more than 10 000 Australian men lost their lives. A memorial and a cemetery recall their sacrifice. Extended **view** towards the River Somme and Amiens.

La CÔTE D'OPALE★

The OPAL COAST

Michelin map 51 folds 1,2 or 236 folds 1,2

The **Côte d'Opale** extends from Baie de Somme all the way round to the Belgian border; its name is derived from the creamy colour of the waves washing against the coast. The name was first used in 1911 by a local painter, Édouard Lévêque.
The most spectacular part of the coastline is between Boulogne and Calais, where the cliffs skirt the Boulonnais hills. Between the sea and the sky there is only the Opal Coast bluff, characterized by promontories separating the small, dry valleys (**crans**), which are similar to the *valleuses* of the region around Dieppe, Le Havre and Rouen. A strong north-south current wears away the base of the cliffs, sometimes causing large parts to collapse. Research has shown that the cliff is eroded by about 25m/27yd every hundred years.
This part of the coast has been declared a major national site and named **Site des deux Caps** ⊘; it offers enjoyable rambles and nature trails.

Seaside restaurants

Enjoy seafood, mussels and chips or just a glass of local beer while gazing at the sea and the sand in one of the establishments listed below:

Zuydcoote – La Grande Marée, a *brasserie* with a large dining room and an overhanging terrace.

Malot-les-Bains – Le Bistrot de la plage (the bistro on the beach).

Calais – L'Aquar'aile with its blue and white decoration and panoramic view through its large windows.

Cap Blanc Nez – Le Thomé de Gamond, next to the museum, on top of Mont d'Hubert.

Cap Gris Nez – Le Bar du Cap offers a view of the cliffs and the sea against a background of fields.
From La Sirène (speciality: lobster), there is a view of Wissant bay and Cap Blanc Nez.

Wimereux – La Légioise (speciality: seafood) overlooks the sea wall.

Boulogne – Restaurant de Nausicaa provides a panoramic view of the beach and the port whereas La Matelote faces the sea.

Hardelot – L'Océan is situated on the seafront.

Le Touquet – Panoramic restaurant of the Novotel hotel, facing the sea, with bar and terrace on the water front.

Berck – Le Grand Bleu, panoramic restaurant situated on the 5th floor of the Inter Hotel Neptune.

Fort-Mahon – La Terrasse, a restaurant with large windows directly overlooking the sea wall.

Le Crotoy – Les Tourelles, a strange red-brick building dating from the end of the 19C, situated on the Butte du Moulin.

Cayeux – Le Parc aux Huîtres, facing the bay, a peacefully convivial establishment.

Mers-les-Bains – Le Bellevue, a restaurant situated by the beach, which lives up to its name of "fine view".

FROM BOULOGNE TO CALAIS *49km/30mi – about 2hr 30min*

★ **Boulogne** – *See BOULOGNE.*
Leave Boulogne by D 940.

D 940 is a winding coastal road offering glimpses of the sea, the ports and the beaches, leading across hill crests which are intermittently bare or covered with closely cropped meadows.
To the north the road comes to the Escalles *cran*, looking like a mountain pass at an altitude of less than 100m/328ft. Car parks flank the road, allowing access to the sea or to walks among the dunes.

Wimereux – The opening to the Wimereux Valley *(see Le BOULONNAIS)* is the site of a large and popular seaside resort for families. A walk on the promenade built along the sand and pebble beach affords views of the Straits of Dover, the Grande

Armée Column and Boulogne. The promenade narrows to a path leading to **Pointe aux Oies**, where on 6 August 1840 the future Napoleon III landed prior to his attempt to win over the garrison stationed at Boulogne.

Between Wimereux and Ambleteuse the road runs beside tall dunes.

On a beach with lifeguards in attendance, pay attention to the colour of the flag flying near the lifeguard station:

Green: Lifeguards in attendance. Swimming authorised and not considered dangerous.

Orange: Lifeguards in attendance. Swimming considered dangerous.

Red: Swimming prohibited.

Ambleteuse – This picturesque village stands on a hillside above the mouth of the River Slack, where boats can to beached. Ambleteuse was formerly a naval base protected by **Fort d'Ambleteuse** ⊘, built by Vauban between 1685 and 1690. Napoleon based part of his flotilla here at the time of the Boulogne Camp *(see BOULOGNE-SUR-MER)*. Today it is a beach among the coastal dunes, from which Boulogne's harbour entrance and, in clear weather, the white cliffs of the English coast, are visible.

The **Musée historique de la Seconde Guerre mondiale** ⊘ on the outskirts of Ambleteuse retraces the full story of this conflict, from the conquest of Poland in 1939 to the Liberation. About a hundred different uniforms are exhibited, together with equipment worn or used by the armies involved in the war.

3km/2mi after Audresselles, turn left onto D 191.

★★**Cap Gris-Nez** – This "grey-nose cape" looks out to the English coast less than 30km/19mi away. The gently sloping cliffs rise to 45m/148ft. The lightouse (28m/92ft tall) with beams visible 45km/28mi away, was rebuilt after the war. It stands at the tip of a bare, windswept peninsula dotted with the remains of ruined German pillboxes. The Gris-Nez branch of CROSS (Centre Régional d'Opération de Secours et de Sauvetage) is located underground; the organisation is responsible for watching over these waters, where maritime traffic is the heaviest in the world, and provides aid of any kind when needed. The crumbling debris from the cliffs mingles with the rocky reef known as "the Whales" *(Les Épaulards)* because, seen from a distance, it looks hump-backed and throws up spray.

Straight ahead, the **view★** extends to the English cliffs which appear white next to the blue of the sky, while on the French side the folds of the coastline, including the characteristic dry valleys between the cliffs, are visible. Cap Blanc-Nez *(right)* and Boulogne *(left)* may also be seen.

A memorial recalls that on 25 May 1940 the naval officer Ducuing and his sailors died here, defending the signal station against Guderian's armoured tanks.

The **Musée du Mur de l'Atlantique** ⊘ is in the Todt battery, a Second World War pillbox which served as a German missile launching base; missiles 2m/6ft long were fired on England from here. There are collections of arms and uniforms inside the museum.

Cap Gris-Nez

⚓ **Wissant** – This splendid beach of fine, firm sand is well sheltered from the eastern winds and currents. It forms a vast curve between Cap Gris-Nez and Cap Blanc-Nez. Villas stand among the dunes overlooking the shore.

The **Musée du Moulin** ⊙ is housed in a flour mill driven by hydraulic power. It is well preserved and features pinewood parts, cast-iron waterwheels and a conveyor belt to lift the goods.

★★**Cap Blanc-Nez** – The "white-nose cape" is a vertical mass of chalk cliffs rising 134m/440ft above the waves, offering extensive **views**★ over the English cliffs

---

"Flobarts" from Wissant

These fishing boats, whose origin goes back to the 17C, were used all along the Opal Coast for fishing herring, mackerel, cod and sole. Built of wood in the shape of half a walnut shell, they measured 5m/16ft in length and 2m/6.5ft in width and could land on a beach or any other place where there was no harbour. In addition, owing to their flat bottom and reduced draught, they hardly felt the impact of the waves. In the 1950s, engines replaced the traditional sails and the boats were launched with the help of tractors. Most of them have now been replaced by more efficient vessels; however, a few flobarts are still used as pleasure sailing boats.

A flobart festival takes place every year during the last weekend in August.

---

and the French coast from Calais to Cap Gris-Nez.

The **Musée National du Transmanche** ⊙, located on Mont d'Hubert, faces Cap Blanc-Nez; it retraces the turbulent history of the strait, which scientists and scholars have always used to promote their ideas. The story began in 1751 with Nicolas Desmarets, who was the first to think of linking France to England. Later, Aimé Thomé de Gamond suggested a variety of options: a tunnel constructed of metal tubes, a concrete undersea vault, a pontoon, an artificial isthmus, a mobile bridge and a viaduct-bridge. He even dived to the bottom of the strait several times to collect numerous geological samples. Channel crossings were eventually achieved by balloon (Blanchard), plane (Blériot), steamboat (the first regular line was established in 1816), raft, on skis etc. Lower down, near D 940, stands the monument to **Latham** (1883-1912), the pilot who attempted, unsuccessfully, to cross the Channel at the same time as Blériot. Between **Sangatte** and Blériot-Plage, the chalets are built directly on the seawashed dunes. It is here that the Channel Tunnel emerges.

Blériot-Plage – The beautiful beach extends along to Cap Blanc-Nez. At Baraques (500m/550yd west of the resort), near D 940, a monument commemorates the first aerial crossing of the Channel, by **Louis Blériot** (1872-1936). On 25 July 1909 he landed his airplane in a valley in the Dover cliffs, after a flight of approximately half an hour.

Calais – See CALAIS.

COUCY-LE-CHÂTEAU-AUFFRIQUE★

Population 1 058
Michelin map 56 fold 4 or 236 fold 37

Coucy extends along a promontory overlooking the Ailette valley on an impressive defensive **site**★, further sheltered by its medieval walls which used to incorporate 28 towers. Unfortunately, during the First World War the proud town suffered greatly from being in the front line of battle and in 1917 the Germans blew up the castle's keep.

The Lord of Coucy – "I am not a king, nor a prince, a duke or a count either. I am the Lord (Sire) of Coucy" was the proud boast of the castle's owner, Enguerrand III (1192-1242) who, after fighting loyally and valiantly at Bouvines, sought to take possession of the French throne during Blanche of Castille's regency.

SIGHTS

Château ⊙   A bailey is entered before the castle proper. To the right of the bailey's entrance the Guard-Room (Salle des Gardes) contains a model and documents relating to Coucy. The foundations of a Romanesque chapel are visible on the approach to the castle, which stands as an irregular quadrilateral at the end of the promontory. The great round towers which used to surround it were over 30m/98ft high and were even stronger than the royal keeps. They were built with hoardings.

The round **keep** measured 31m/101ft in diameter and 54m/177ft high; its walls, which had admirable limestone bonding, were 7m/23ft thick; the whole was protected by an additional external defence, the "shirt". The interior contained three levels covered by Gothic vaults; a well, 65m/213ft deep, provided water for the inhabitants.

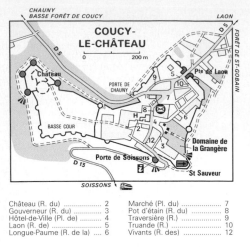

Château (R. du)	2	Marché (Pl. du)	7	
Gouverneur (R. du)	3	Pot d'étain (R. du)	8	
Hôtel-de-Ville (Pl. de)	4	Traversière (R.)	9	
Laon (R. de)	5	Truande (R.)	10	
Longue-Paume (R. de la)	6	Vivants (R. des)	12	

The dwellings had been rebuilt by Enguerrand VII at the end of the 14C, then finished at the end of the 15C by Louis of Orléans, Charles VI's brother, who had bought Coucy from Enguerrand VII's daughter. Remains of two large chambers (Salle des Preuses and Salle des Preux) exist, with a cellar underneath. From the west tower there is a good view over the Ailette and Oise river valleys.

Porte de Soissons – This gate, which was built in the 13C, is reinforced by the Coucy tower and now houses the history museum.

Musée historique ⊙ – A model of the town and the castle are among the exhibits, together with engravings and old photographs, and figures dressed in period costumes. From the platform there is a good view over the Ailette Valley.

Église St-Sauveur ⊙ – This church nestles at the edge of the ramparts. Apart from the Romanesque west front (12C) and the 14C Gothic aisles, the building was almost totally rebuilt after the First World War.

Domaine de la Grangère – This garden belonged to the Governor's House where in 1594 César, Duke of Vendôme, was born, the bastard son of Henri IV and Gabrielle d'Estrées, Duchesse de Beaufort. The lip of the well is made from a keystone from the castle keep.

Porte de Laon – This entrance dates from the 13C and played a major defensive role at the promontory's base; it is the only entrance with easy access and is therefore guarded by two huge round towers, with walls 8m/26ft thick at their base.

BASSE FORÊT DE COUCY

Leave Coucy by Porte de Chauny; at the junction at the foot of the promontory, take D 934 towards Noyon, through Montoir.

Bois de Montoir – A 380mm motar was concealed in this stretch of woodland. On several occasions in 1915, it fired on Compiègne which is 40km/25mi away, forming enormous shell holes.

Folembray – The kennels of the Rallye-Nomade Hunt are located here; the hounds are used for deer hunting. François I enjoyed staying in the château with his favourite Françoise de Châteaubriand.

Château de COURANCES★★

Michelin map 106 fold 44 5km/3mi north of Milly.

The luxuriant vegetation and limpid waters surrounding the château de Courances make this setting one of the most attractive sights in Île-de-France.
Built around 1550 by Gilles le Breton for Cosme Clausse, Secretary of Finance to Henri II, the château acquired its present appearance in the 17C. It is a good example of the Louis XIII style: a brick building with sandstone bonding, pointed roofs and a sparsely-decorated exterior. In the 19C the front was embellished with a replica of the horse-shoe staircase at Fontainebleau *(See illustration in Introduction: ABC of architecture)*. The château is still surrounded by a moat and a splendid avenue on the opposite side of the road completes this sweeping perspective.

★★**Park** – The approach to the château is very grand. Walk through the gate and cross the "forecourt", a vast stretch of lawn divided by a central path and flanked by two canals reflecting the plane trees.
The park, designed by Le Nôtre, extends behind the château and the rear façade overlooks a lush, green lawn. A path leads to the Grand Canal, which receives the waters of the École. Another path, set at right angles, skirts the small cascades and leads to the flower beds, offering a lovely view of the château mirrored in the crystal-clear water.

Château de Courances, garden façade

Before returning to the gate, turn right *(when level with the château)* towards the ruins of an old fuller's mill and its gushing stream. From the embankment on the left, admire the Japanese garden and, further back, the falls of an old mill.

Château ⊙ – From the south terrace, there is a view of the park. The tour includes a number of living-rooms, low-ceilinged chambers and annexes. Note the corner dining room, tastefully decorated with walnut wainscot and ornamental plates, and the Monkeys' Gallery, named after three 16C tapestries with scenes of monkeys mimicking man.

EXCURSION

Château de Fleury-en-Bière – *4km/2.5mi northeast on N 372 and right into D 11.* The château *(private)* dates from the 16C and was designed for Cosme Clausse *(see above).* The stately proportions of the courtyard, sealed off from the street by a stout wall, can be glimpsed from the entrance. At the far end, surrounded by a moat, stands the brick and stone château, flanked on its right side by a large stone tower. Several huge outbuildings stand on either side of the building. The gracious Romanesque chapel *(set back to the right)* serves as a parish church.

CRÉCY-EN-PONTHIEU

Population 1 491
Michelin map 52 fold 7 or 236 fold 122

The name of Crécy conjures up pictures of the defeat of King Philippe VI of France at the hands of Edward III of England on 26 August 1346, at the beginning of the Hundred years war.
Crécy is today a peaceful little town on the edge of a farmed basin at the source of the River Maye, facing the plateau on which Crécy Forest stands.

Church – The interior houses four large canvases from the Poussin School presenting the story of Moses. The paintings came from the now-ruined Dommartin Abbey *(near Tortefontaine on D 119, north of Crécy).*

Moulin Edouard III – *1km/0.5mi north on D 111.*
Beside the road *(right)* stands a hillock on the site of the windmill from where the King of England directed the battle. From the top there is a good **view** over the undulating plain *(viewing table).*
A memorial just off the battlefield marks the spot where the Prince of Wales took a bunch of ostrich feathers from the body of the Duc de Luxembourg; the feathers became the personal crest of the monarch's son and are still used to this day.

Edward III had landed in Normandy with 4 000 men-at-arms and 10 000 long-bowmen; they rampaged through Normandy as far as Poissy. When Philip VI advanced with 12 000 men-at-arms and thousands of other troops, Edward took up a defensive position at Crécy. An attack was then launched by the French cavalry, in a spirited but ill-planned move. The assault disintegrated under the hail from the English archers, backed up for the first time in European history by bombardments; in the resulting carnage, 20 000 Frenchmen fell on the battlefield. Philip's ally John the Blind, the old king of Bohemia, was killed while being carried to his badly-wounded son at the heart of the battle; the spot where he fell is marked with the Bohemia Cross (Croix de Bohême) *(on D 56 southeast of Crécy)*. Edward went on to besiege Calais.

FORÊT DE CRÉCY *29km/18mi round trip - about 1hr*

The forest, which covers an area of 4 300ha/10 625 acres, has been laid out for tourism with lay-bys and picnic areas, signposted footpaths and bridlepaths, and the "Circuit des vieux chênes" or "Old Oak Trail" which can be followed by car or bike. The forest lies on the plateau to the south of the Maye River and is the natural habitat of deer, wild boar and pheasants. It is carpeted with lily-of-the-valley in springtime. Viewing tables have been set out on the edge of the forest in Forest-Montiers and Forest-l'Abbaye.

From Crécy, take the Forest-l'Abbaye road (D 111) to the crossroads at Le Monument then turn right onto the Forest-Montier road through the woodland.

The Forest-Montier road runs past some superb beech and oak copses.

Continue to Le Poteau de Nouvion then turn right onto the forest road called Le Chevreuil, to the crossroads at Les Grands-Hêtres hunting hide.

Hutte des Grands-Hêtres – This part of the forest, crossed by a footpath called Sentier des deux Huttes, is absolutely outstanding.

Return to Poteau de Nouvion and turn right towards N 1 and Forest-Montiers.

Forest-Montiers – It was here that St Riquier founded a hermitage, later to become a monastery (*moutier* in French). It was also here that François I's son, Charles, died of plague at the age of 23.

Take N 1 in a northerly direction.

Bernay-en-Ponthieu – See Bernay-en-Ponthieu.

The River Maye forms a myriad of lakes and ponds in the area around Bernay-en-Ponthieu.

Turn right onto D 938 and return to Crécy-en-Ponthieu.

The road overlooks the wide **Maye Valley** with its alternating fields of crops, meadows and thickets. The southern slopes are topped by the Crécy Forest.

CRÉPY-EN-VALOIS

Population 13 222
Michelin map 56 folds 12,13

Crépy is in the heavily forested Valois, one of the oldest regions in France. The upper part of the town is strategically placed on a plateau between two streams.

The Valois dynasty – For over two and a half centuries, from 1328 to 1589, the French throne was occupied by the descendants of Charles I, comte de Valois and brother of Philip IV the Fair. The last representatives of this dynasty, Charles VIII, François I, Henri II and III, contributed to the development of Italian – therefore Renaissance – art in France, while giving kingship a new, authoritarian stamp.

Capital of the Valois – The Counts and subsequently the Dukes of Valois made Crépy their new capital. A 10C castle, as well as several monasteries and churches, testify to the importance Crépy had acquired between the 11C and the 14C. It was only after Henri II's reign that the princes showed a preference for Villers-Cotterêts. In 1790 the reorganisation of the French *départements* split the old Valois territory between Oise and Aisne. Crépy's golden age was over.

★OLD TOWN *1hr 30min*

Place Gambetta – This square has retained its quaint medieval charm. Among the 18C buildings, the **Maison des Quatre Saisons** (no 15) features four Rococo grotesque masks representing the four seasons. There are a number of fine house fronts dating from the 13C, 16C and 17C.

Follow rue des Ursulines, then turn right onto rue du Lion.

At no 5, note the 14C mansion **Hôtel du Lion** with its crow-stepped gables.

Église St-Denis – The majestic 16C transept consists of two bays. The nave was built in the 12C, the aisles in the 15C. The south aisle presents several small stone slabs celebrating the memory of the Ursuline nuns *(see below)*.

Abbaye St-Arnoul ⊙ – The ruins of this abbey – the necropolis of the counts of Valois – are at their most impressive when seen from the edge of the walls they dominate. On the opposite side stand the remains of a Gothic church. Excavations have uncovered a series of 11C colonnettes with their capitals, belonging to a former crypt.

Take the opposite direction to St-Denis and return to the town centre along a cobbled street; after a bend it leads to the **Maison de l'Intendant des Ursulines**, a superb 18C building and further along, to the entrance of the Ursuline convent. This was a teaching order present in Crépy from 1623 to 1791.

Return to place Gambetta and turn right onto rue Gustave-Chopinet.

Vieux Château – This building houses some charming collections from the musée de l'Archerie et du Valois.

Musée de l'Archerie et du Valois ⊘ – Archery is a traditional sport in the Valois area. Groups originated from part-civilian, part-military associations set up in the Middle Ages to train the militia in peacetime.

Wary of the strong religious and loyalist views of the archers, the members of the 1789 Constituent Assembly incorporated them into the National Guard. Archers' associations reappeared in the 19C, for social and sporting purposes.

The exhibitions in the museum's low-ceilinged chambers illustrate the history and folklore behind this sport in a particularly lively manner: archery, the internal hierarchy of the companies of archers, and the ceremony of the "provincial bouquet" during which a solemn procession was held around a bouquet of honour arranged in a commemorative vase. The display cases also show the history of the bow and crossbow, from "primitive" weapons to present-day competition bows made of tropical timber, metal, glass fibre etc.

J.M. Guinot /Musée de l'Archerie

18C statuette of
Saint Sebastian,
patron saint of archers

The room dealing with representations of St Sebastian, patron saint of archers, forms a happy transition between the museum and the upper chapel and large quardroom where, beneath magnificent 16C rafters, there is an exhibition of **sacred art**★ consisting mainly of statues from local rural churches including a Madonna and Child from Le Luat (early 16C), a Virgin Mary suckling from Nanteuil-le-Haudouin (15C), several statues of St Martin and St Sebastian, a Madonna from Rully (15C), St John the Baptist (13C), etc.

ADDITIONAL SIGHT

Église St-Thomas – *Entrance in Rue St-Lazare.* These distinguished ruins are the remains of a Gothic church built outside the ramparts in 1182 in memory of Thomas Becket, Archbishop of Canterbury, twelve years after he was murdered in his own cathedral. The ruins include the west front, the first bay of the nave, the truncated tower and its 15C spire. The rest of the grounds are now a garden.

Le CROTOY ⌓

Population 2 440
Michelin map 52 fold 6 or 236 fold 21

Le Crotoy is reached by a scenic route (D 940) which runs alongside grass-covered sandbanks *(mollières)*. The town was once a fortress, with a castle in which Joan of Arc was imprisoned in 1430 before being taken to St Valery and then to Rouen. Today it is an attractive and popular seaside resort overlooking the Somme Bay.

The Port – The port is not far from place Jeanne d'Arc, the resort's lively centre, and is used by small coastal fishing trawlers (which catch shrimps, flatfish and herrings); casting on the Somme's bed brings in plaice and eel.

Butte du Moulin – The hill is reached from the church by rue de la Mer and offers an extensive **view**★ from the terrace over the Somme Bay, St Valery, Le Hourdel and the open sea.

Chemin de fer de la baie de Somme ⊘ – A train comprising old carriages with viewing platforms pulled by steam or diesel engines runs between Le Crotoy, Noyelles, St Valery and Cayeux-sur-Mer providing a journey (16km/10mi) of discovery through this lush area bordered by the River Somme's grassy sandbanks.

Château de DAMPIERRE★★

Michelin map 101 fold 31

Dampierre, situated in the narrow upper part of the Chevreuse Valley, is closely associated with two distinguished families, the Luynes and the Chevreuse. The château still belongs to the latter.

From 1675 to 1683 Jules Hardouin-Mansart rebuilt the Château de Dampierre for Colbert's son-in-law the Duke of Chevreuse, a former student at Port-Royal and the mentor of the Duke of Burgundy.

TOUR ⊘

The main body of the château, surrounded by a moat, opens onto a courtyard flanked by stables and outbuildings. In front of it are two buildings with arcades. The pinkish tones of the brick harmonise with the sober stone string courses and columns, contrasting sharply with the darker hues of the park.

On the ground floor, visitors may admire Cavelier's statue of Penelope in the hall leading to the drawing rooms embellished with Louis XV wainscot, the suite occupied by Marie Leszczynska, and an imposing dining room decorated with Louis XIV panelling.

The first floor houses the Royal Suite, which accommodated Louis XIV, Louis XV and Louis XVI. The splendid 17C and 18C furnishings are beautifully preserved and reminiscent of the King's suite at Versailles. Note the furniture, portraits, wainscot, medallions and overdoor panels by old masters.

The most amazing achievement stands at the top of the great staircase. The Salle de la Minerve is a formal reception room by Duban from the Restauration period. Ingres was commissioned to paint a fresco representing the Golden Age; it was never completed. The duc Honoré de Luynes, who conceived the whole project, ordered a colourful 3m/10ft statue of Minerva, a miniature replica of the legendary gold and ivory Minerva of the Parthenon executed by Phidias in the 5C BC.

★**Park** ⊘ – A walk round the castle starting from the right will lead you to a large ornamental pond, the favourite spot of many anglers. Water is omnipresent in this vast romantic park: canals, fountains and waterfalls embellish this green open space at the heart of the forest, in the centre of the picturesque Vallée de Chevreuse. The park and the castle form one of the rare protected estates near the capital

EXCURSIONS

Vaux de Cernay – *4km/2.5mi south by D 91, 30min to 2hr walk.* The road *(D 91)* weaves up the wooded narrow valley, past a restaurant and across a brook by a mill, Moulin des Roches.

Park near the Chalet des Cascades.

The slopes surrounding the oaks and beeches are dotted with sandstone boulders, little falls and whirlpools.

Château de Dampierre

Étang de Cernay — The pond was created by the monks of the local abbey to stock fish. A memorial to the 19C landscape painter Léon-Germain Pelouse stands at the top of the embankment, near a stately oak tree.

The walk may be continued for another 30min or 1hr by following the wide path which veers right and leads straight up to the wooded plateau. From the edge of the plateau turn back, bear right and return along the cliff path that skirts the promontory.

★ **Abbaye des Vaux-de-Cernay** ⊙ — The abbey was founded in the early 12C. It came under Cistercian rule but was abandoned in 1791 by its last twelve monks and sold. The Rothschild family who bought the abbey in 1873 restored and preserved it until the Second World War. It has now been converted into a hotel.

In the **grounds**, the ruins of the abbey church may be seen (late-12C façade with rose-window), and the monk's building, now a concert hall.

Stopover

OUR SELECTION

Auberge du Château "Table des Blot" — 1 Grande rue in Dampierre, ☎ 01 30 47 56 56, fax 01 30 47 51 75. This 17C inn facing the castle has retained its old-world charm. Double room from 400F, fixed menu: 170F.

LUXURY

Abbaye des Vaux-de-Cernay — In Cernay-la-Ville, ☎ 01 34 85 23 00, fax 01 34 85 11 60. Luxury, peace and quiet, nature and the prestigious setting of the former Cistercian abbey. Double room from 890F, fixed menu: 255F. The abbey also serves afternoon tea. The **Hôtel des Haras**, also on the estate, ☎ 01 34 85 34 30, is less expensive: double room from 390F.

DISNEYLAND PARIS★★★

Michelin map 106 fold 22

Standing on the Brie plain about 30km/18mi east of Paris is a unique development in Europe: Disneyland Paris.

The enormous site, which was designed as a complete holiday resort and will continue to develop until the year 2017, already consists of the **Disneyland Paris theme park** and a resort complex offering accommodation and other recreational facilities.

Not far from the hotels, the main entertainment centre, **Disney Village**, recreates the American way of life with shops, restaurants and a variety of entertainment. At a slight distance from the complex lies **Golf Disneyland Paris** with its 27 hole course.

A magician called Walt Disney — Walt Disney's name is linked to innumerable cartoon strips and animated cartoons which have entertained children throughout the world, and the heroes of his creations — Mickey Mouse, Minnie, Donald, Pluto, Pinocchio, Snow White etc — no one can forget.

He was born Walter Elias Disney in Chicago in 1901, the fourth child of Flora and Elias Disney. Walt soon showed great ability in drawing. After the First World War, in which he served as an ambulance driver in France, he returned to the United States where, in Kansas City, he met a young Dutchman called Ub Iwerks, who was also passionate about drawing. In 1923 the pair produced in Hollywood a series of short films called *Alice Comedies*. In 1928 Mickey Mouse, the future international star, was created. There next followed the era of the Oscar-winning, full-length animated cartoon films: *The Three Little Pigs* (1933), *Snow White and the Seven Dwarfs* (1937), *Dumbo* (1941). Disney productions also developed to include films starring real people, such as *Treasure Island* (1950) and *20000 Leagues Under the Sea* (1954), and some mixing the two, for instance *Mary Poppins* (1964) which won six Oscars. On 15 December 1966 the man who had spent his life trying to bring dreams to life died; the Walt Disney Studios continued to make films, however, remaining faithful to Walt's ideas: *The Aristocats*, *Who Killed Roger Rabbit?* (which won four Oscars), *The Little Mermaid* (two Oscars), *Beauty and the Beast* (1991), *Aladdin* (1992), *The Lion King* (1994), *Pocahontas*, *The Hunchback of Notre-Dame*, *Hercules* (1997) and *Mulan, a Chinese legend* (1998).

Access

RER – Line 4 A. Station: Marne-la-Vallée – Chessy (35min from centre of Paris).

TGV – From the new station, there is a direct high-speed train link to Lille (1hr), Lyon (1hr 55min), Avignon (4hr 10min), and Marseille (under 5hr).

Shuttles from Orly and Roissy-Charles de Gaulle airports.

Car – Motorway A 4. Follow signs to Metz and Nancy. Leave the motorway at exit 14.

General information

Information / Bookings: From the UK: ☎ 09 90 030 303; from the US: ☎ W-DISNEY; from France: ☎ 01 60 30 60 30.

Minitel: 3615 DISNEYLAND.

Internet: www.disneylandparis.com

Accommodation

Most of the hotels, situated around Lake Disney or along the Rio Grande, illustrate various regions of the USA through typical architecture, folk traditions or culinary specialities. They are linked to the rest of the complex by a shuttle service (yellow buses). Rooms are designed to accommodate four persons. Hotel residents can often go into the theme park before the general public. Below is a selection of establishments; prices are quoted as a guideline only as they can vary according to the season and special offers.

Newport Bay Club – ☎ 01 60 45 55 00, fax 01 60 45 55 33. This establishment's attractive architectural style suggests a New England seaside resort around the turn of the century. Facilities: swimming pool, fitness centre, sauna, jacuzzi, massage, games room... Room from 850F. Two restaurants: **Cape Cod**, fixed menu: 145F and **Yacht Club**, fixed menu: 150F.

Sequoia Lodge – ☎ 01 60 45 51 00, fax 01 60 45 51 33. The sturdy stone and wood façades are modelled on those of buildings in the American national parks. Facilities: swimming pool, fitness club, jacuzzi, sauna, games room... Room from 715F. Two restaurants: **Hunter's Grill**, fixed menu (evening meal only): 150F; **Beaver Creek Tavern**, fixed menu: 150F.

Hôtel Cheyenne – ☎ 01 60 45 62 00, fax 01 60 45 62 33. A typical town of the American West has been recreated here with its saloon and wooden houses. You may meet some cowboys round a street corner. Facilities: children's playground, pony rides, games room... Room from 545F. Restaurant: **Chuck Wagon Café**, *à la carte* meal around 150F.

Hôtel Santa Fe – ☎ 01 60 45 78 00, fax 01 60 45 78 33. The ochre-coloured, cube-shaped buildings are reminiscent of a small New-Mexico town. Inside the atmosphere is enlivened by the rhythm of the music. Facilities: children's playground, games room... Room from 445F. Restaurant: **La Cantina**, *à la carte* meal around 130F.

Davy Crockett Ranch – ☎ 01 60 45 69 00. This secluded bungalow village situated in the Citry wood, suggests the land of trappers. There is a variety of entertainment (not necessarily free) and a fine tropical swimming pool which delight young children and adults alike. No shuttle service to and from the theme park. Bungalows from 425F. Restaurant: **Crockett's Tavern**.

Where to eat

In addition to the **hand carts selling snacks**, Disneyland Paris also has a number of self-service or traditional **restaurants** offering a wide choice of cuisine from several different countries. Only the traditional restaurants have a licence to sell alcohol. The most popular are:

Walt's – an American Restaurant – Mainstreet USA inside the theme park. Refined atmosphere and mementoes of the Walt Disney family. Fixed menu: 155F.

The Lucky Nugget Saloon – Frontierland. Music-hall shows in a very lively saloon. Fixed menu (Tex Mex): 85F.

Blue Lagoon Restaurant – Adventureland. Seafood served on terraces adjacent to the attraction "Pirates of the Carribean". Fixed menu: 175F.

The Steakhouse – Disney Village. A Chicago red-brick warehouse turned into an elegant restaurant for amateurs of meat and good wine. Fixed menu: 210F.

Ice cream, snacks and soft drinks are on sale in all the lands and there are also fast food outlets.

Picnics – Drinks and food may not be taken into the park. A picnic area is therefore provided outside the park between the car park and the esplanade.

Services

Information/Bookings – The **City Hall** information office in Town Square supplies the programme of shows.

Day passes/Re-admission – See the chapter entitled *Admission times and charges* at the end of the guide.

Tip – Some attractions have long queues; it is therefore advisable to try them during the parade at the end of the day.

Currency – There is an exchange bureau at the main entrance. Cash dispensers are to be found in **Liberty Arcade** and **Discovery Arcade**.

Handicapped visitors – A Guide to Special Services can be obtained from **City Hall**.

Left-luggage and lockers – Near the main entrance and under Main Street Station.

Photo, push-chair, wheelchair hire – Cameras and camcorders can be hired from **Town Square Photography**. Push-chairs and wheelchairs are available from **Town Square Terrace**.

Pets – Pets are not admitted to the park, with the exception of guide dogs for the blind. There is a Pets' Creche near the visitors' car park.

Baby changing rooms, Lost Children Rendez-vous Point, First Aid – Near the **Plaza Gardens Restaurant**.

✲✲DISNEYLAND PARIS THEME PARK ⏲

This theme park, like those in the United States (Disneyland in California opened in 1955 and Magic Kingdom in Florida opened in 1971) and Japan (Tokyo Disneyland, 1983), is a realisation of Walt Disney's dream of creating "a small, enchanted park where children and adults can enjoy themselves together".

The large Disneyland Paris site (over 55ha/135 acres) comprises five territories or "lands", each with a different theme. As well as the spectacular shows featuring amazing automatons in particularly detailed settings, each region has shops, ice cream vendors, restaurants and self-service restaurants.

Every day, the **Disney Parade★★**, a procession of floats carrying all the favourite Disney cartoon characters, takes place. On some evenings and throughout the summer the **Main Street Electrical Parade★★** adds extra illuminations to the fairytale setting. The fireworks display spectacularly rounds off an eventful day.

Listed below are descriptions of the main attractions only; for more detailed information and plans refer to the Michelin Green Guide Disneyland Paris.

The Newport Bay Club

Main Street USA

The main street of an American town at the turn of the 20C, lined with shops and restaurants with Victorian-style fronts, is brought to life as though by magic. Horse-drawn street cars, limousines, fire engines and Black Marias transport visitors from Town Square to Central Plaza (the hub of the park) while colourful musicians play favourite ragtime, jazz and Dixieland tunes. On each side of the road are **Discovery Arcade** and **Liberty Arcade** (exhibition and diorama on the famous Statue of Liberty at the entrance to New York harbour).

From Main Street station a small steam train, the **Disneyland Railroad★**, travels across the park and through the **Grand Canyon Diorama**, stopping at the station in each land.

Frontierland

The conquest of the West, the gold rush and the wild West with its legends and folklore are brought together in Thunder Mesa, a typical western town, and Big Thunder Mountain a strange, arid wall of rock like the mountains of Mounment Valley (Arizona, Utah). It rises on an island washed by the Rivers of the Far West. The waters here are plied by two handsome **steamboats★**, the *Mark Twain* and the *Molly Brown*.

★★★**Big Thunder Mountain** – In the mountain, there's an old gold mine... On the banks of the lake, in the buildings belonging to a mining company, are crowds of travellers patiently waiting to board the **Mine Train**. The trip in the hurtling carriages racing down the track at top speed includes explosions and risks of rock falls. A thrilling ride for those who enjoy heart-pounding excitement.

★★★**Phantom Manor** – A dilapidated manor house stands high above the Rivers of the Far West. It used to be the home of people who had struck it lucky during the gold rush. Inside, strange things happen. The walls stretch and shrink. The tour through the rooms and basement continues in small black cars that take you to the ghost town of Thunder Mesa. When you leave, take a stroll to the **Boot Hill** cemetery and have a look at the strange tombstones.

★**The Lucky Nugget Saloon** – This horseshoe-shaped saloon – every western town had its saloon – is richly decorated. Dinner show: **Lilly's Follies** starring bright, sparkling dancers.

Adventureland

From Central Plaza, go through Adventureland Bazaar, a sort of desert fortress containing several exotically foreign shops. Adventureland conjures up pictures of exotic adventures, travel to far-distant lands, treasure island, and pirates.

★★★**Pirates of the Caribbean** – This fortress is easy to spot – the skull and crossbones fly at the top of its walls. Cross the underground passages which reserve a few surprises then go on board a small boat and watch the attack and ransacking of a Spanish harbour town by pirates. There are several different scenes, all with superb decors and lots of action.

★★★**Indiana Jones et le Temple du Péril** – In the jungle lies a ruined temple; courageous archeologists in wagons enter it and defy the laws of gravity. This is not for the faint-hearted.

★★**La Cabane des Robinson** – The Swiss Family Robinson survived a shipwreck and were able to salvage a few objects and building materials that enabled them to build a tree house in a giant banyan tree (an Indian fig). A staircase leads up to the various rooms with their wonderful furniture.

Fantasyland

The land of legends and fairytales is indicated by Sleeping Beauty's castle. It is a village in which the houses symbolise various European countries. Strolling around it are such well-known figures as Mickey Mouse, Donald Duck, Pinocchio, Captain Hook, Chip 'n Dale, to name but a few. They will all be delighted to pose for a photograph.

★★**Le Château de la Belle au Bois Dormant (Sleeping Beauty's Castle)** – On the upper floor, stained-glass windows and Aubusson tapestries recount episodes from this famous fairy story. Below, in the depths of the castle, a huge scaly dragon appears to be sleeping...
From the ramparts, there is a magnificent view of Fantasyland.

★★**It's a Small World** – A "cruise" that takes visitors past dolls dressed in national costume, singing and dancing in sets that represent their home countries. A hymn in praise of the gentleness and liveliness of children all over the world.

★**Alice's Curious Labyrinth** – An episode from *Alice in Wonderland* in which the path to the Queen of Heart's castle is full of surprises.

★**Peter Pan's Flight** – Like Peter Pan, the boy who never grew up, the trip takes visitors over the rooftops of London and the Never-Never Land, and past episodes from the story of Peter Pan... all in small boats.

Space Mountain

Les voyages de Pinocchio – The misadventures of Pinocchio drawn from the story by Carlo Collodi. Meet Gepetto, Jiminy Cricket, Stromboli, and Monstro the Whale.

Blanche-Neige et les Sept Nains (Snow White and the Seven Dwarfs) – In the mysterious forest crossed by small waggons is the wicked witch who cast a spell on Snow White.

Le Carrousel de Lancelot – This is an enchanting merry-go-round of brightly-painted horses.

Discoveryland

This is the world of past discoveries and dreams of the future with the great visionaries such as Leonardo da Vinci, Jules Verne and HG Wells and their wonderful inventions.

Space Mountain – This superb attraction, which is unique to Disney, was inspired by Jules Verne's novel *From the Earth to the Moon.* A huge copper and bronze mountain encompasses a gigantic cannon pointing skywards awaits the most audacious visitors. After being catapulted towards the cosmos, they experience a mind-bending, and highly acrobatic, intergalactic trip.

Star Tours – A breathtaking trip on a spaceship. Based on George Lucas' famous film, *Star Wars.*
A stopover at the **Astroport Services Interstellaires** is highly recommended. Use the **Photomorph** to change your looks (peals of laughter guaranteed) and have your photo taken.

"Chérie, j'ai rétréci le public" (Darling I have shrunk the audience) – An extraodinary experience awaits you in the hall of the Imagination Institute: the famous professor Wayne Szalinski is giving a public demonstration of his shrinking machine. Are you volunteering? If so, hang on... the settings may not be spot on!

Le Visionarium – Ever dreamt of travelling back in time? This is your chance, in an amazing machine which offers a "voyage through time". Using the surround-vision process, the audience travels right across Europe and meets a number of famous people.

*DISNEY VILLAGE

Next to the theme park and Lake Disney, Disney Village can be seen from afar, with its tall steel columns reaching for the sky. At night the whole area is flooded with light.
The main street of this American town offers continuous entertainment and a convivial atmosphere. On summer evenings, it is particularly lively once the theme park is closed for the night. Shops, restaurants and bars are crowded out. In the street, games of skill take place while tightrope walkers, acrobats on stilts, jugglers and musicians arouse the crowd's enthusiasm. Night-owls can then go on to the discotheque. The quality of the shows, the increasing number of cinemas in the **Multiplexe Gaumont**, the reputation of establishments such as **Planet Hollywood**, have insured the success of this "village" which attracts a growing number of visitors from the Île-de-France region.

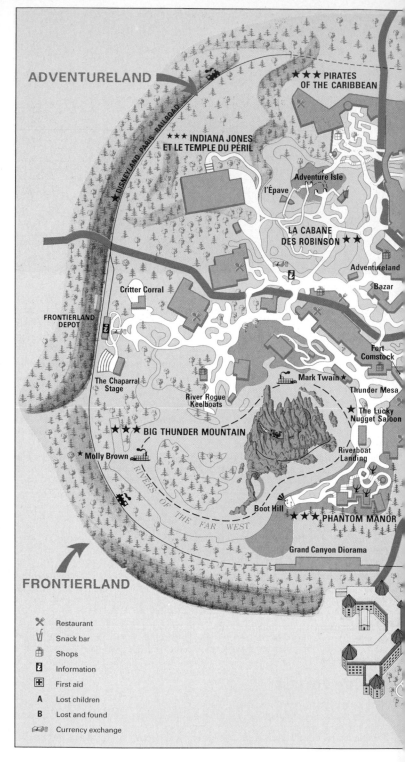

ADVENTURELAND

★★★ **PIRATES OF THE CARIBBEAN**

★★★ **INDIANA JONES ET LE TEMPLE DU PÉRIL**

Adventure Isle

l'Épave

LA CABANE DES ROBINSON ★★

Adventureland Bazar

Critter Corral

FRONTIERLAND DEPOT

Fort Comstock

The Chaparral Stage

Mark Twain ★

Thunder Mesa

River Rogue Keelboats

★ The Lucky Nugget Saloon

★★★ **BIG THUNDER MOUNTAIN**

★ Molly Brown

Riverboat Landing

Boot Hill

★★★ **PHANTOM MANOR**

FRONTIERLAND

Grand Canyon Diorama

RIVERS OF THE FAR WEST

✕	Restaurant
ⱱ	Snack bar
⌨	Shops
🅙	Information
✚	First aid
A	Lost children
B	Lost and found
▱▱	Currency exchange

★★ **Buffalo Bill's Wild West Show** – The famous adventures of pioneer William Frederick Cody (1846-1917), alias Buffalo Bill, inspired this dinner-show which, complete with horses, bison, cowboys and Indians, evokes the epic days of the Wild West. The Texas-style meal, is served on tin plates. There is non-stop action with unexpected turns, special effects and plenty of laughs.

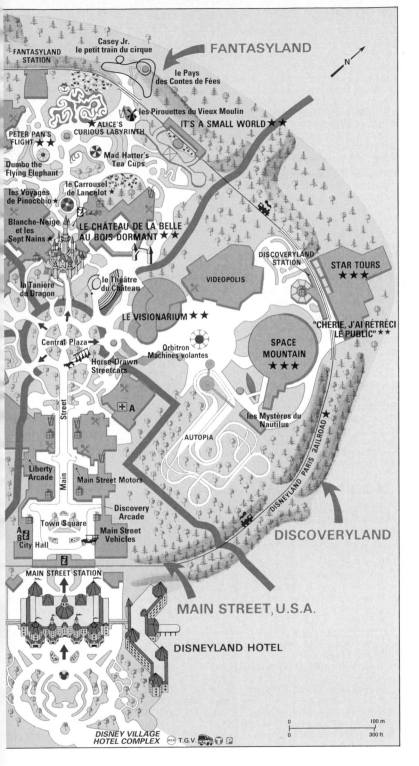

FANTASYLAND STATION

Casey Jr.
le petit train du cirque

FANTASYLAND

N

le Pays
des Contes de Fées

les Pirouettes du Vieux Moulin

★ ALICE'S
CURIOUS LABYRINTH

IT'S A SMALL WORLD ★★

PETER PAN'S
FLIGHT ★★

Mad Hatter's
Tea Cups

Dumbo the
Flying Elephant

le Carrousel
de Lancelot ★

les Voyages
de Pinocchio ★

DISCOVERYLAND
STATION

STAR TOURS
★★★

Blanche-Neige
et les
Sept Nains ★

LE CHÂTEAU DE LA BELLE
AU BOIS DORMANT ★★

VIDEOPOLIS

la Tanière
du Dragon

le Théâtre
du Château

"CHÉRIE, J'AI RÉTRÉCI
LE PUBLIC" ★★

LE VISIONARIUM ★★

Central Plaza ▶

Orbitron
Machines volantes

SPACE
MOUNTAIN
★★★

Horse-Drawn
Streetcars

les Mystères du
Nautilus ★

A

AUTOPIA

Liberty
Arcade

Main Street Motors

Discovery
Arcade

DISNEYLAND PARIS RAILROAD

Town Square

Main Street
Vehicles

DISCOVERYLAND

A B
City Hall

MAIN STREET STATION

MAIN STREET, U.S.A.

DISNEYLAND HOTEL

0   100 m
0   300 ft

DISNEY VILLAGE
HOTEL COMPLEX   RER T.G.V.

Billy Bob's Country Western saloon – For those who wish to prolong their journey back to the days of daring cowboys, this saloon is the ideal place to go after the show, for it is their favourite haunt, with beer flowing freely and country music creating a convivial atmosphere.

DOUAI★

Conurbation 199 562
Michelin map 51 fold 16 or 236 fold 16

Douai stands on either side of the River Scarpe, which flows through its centre; despite the bomb damage of 1940, the town has preserved the 18C layout and buildings that gave it the aristocratic look Balzac evoked in his *Recherche de l'Absolu*.

Despite the number of large industrial firms – comprising metallurgy (Arbel, Renault), chemicals and food, a national printing works and France's fourth-ranking river freight trade – Douai appears as more of a legal centre, with a Court of Appeal, a relic of the Flanders Parliament which sat here from 1713 to the Revolution.

The town also enjoys a distinguished reputation for intellectual activity, which began with the elegiac poetess **Marceline Desbordes-Valmore** (1786-1859) who was born here, and is maintained by the many educational institutions which have taken the place of the university, founded in the 16C but transferred to Lille in 1887.

Parade of the Gayants – On the Sunday after 5 July, five giant figures of the Gayant family are paraded through the town in medieval costume, accompanied by folklore groups singing songs associated with this family: Gayant, the father (7.50m/25ft tall, weighing 370kg/816lb), his wife Marie Cagenon (6.50m/21ft tall) and their children Jacquot, Fillion and Binbin. They are escorted by a wheel of fortune and the artillerymen's fool, a skirted horse. The giants appear in the town during the two days that follow, then return on Tuesday night to their house. Gayant, the oldest giant in the north (1530), is also the most popular. The week before his appearance is enlivened with concerts, ballets, folklore evenings, organ recitals and bell-ringing.

After the giants retire, a torch light procession takes place, preceding the regattas, parade and fireworks display of 14 July. These popular rejoicings bring together the citizens of Douai, who refer to themselves in jest as "Gayant's children".

Jean Bellegambe, painter of Douai and its region – The artist Jean Bellegambe (1470-1534), who seems to have spent his entire life in Douai, appears to have been a likeable character with wide-ranging artistic talent.

He mastered the transition from the Gothic tradition (religious subjects treated with realistic detail and harmonious colours) to the Italian influence of the Renaissance (works decorated with columns, pilasters, shells and garlands) which he linked with the objective, intimate realism of the Flemish school and the intellectualism of the French school. The latter is marked by a choice of subjects which are sometimes difficult to understand.

Bellegambe worked a great deal for the abbeys of the Scarpe Valley, and Douai's landscape and buildings can often be recognised in his works: the belfry and town gates, the towers of the abbey church of Anchin, Flines woods and the watery landscapes of the Scarpe and Sensée rivers. These representations testify to the painter's deep love for his region.

BELFRY AND SURROUNDING AREA *1hr*

Start from Place d'Armes, a part-pedestrian zone with pavement cafés and fountains. L'**Hôtel du Dauphin** is the only remaining 18C house here; its façade is adorned with trophies. It now houses the tourist office.

Walk along rue de la Mairie.

★ **Belfry** ⊘ (**D**) – Douai's belfry is one of the best known in northern France and has been made famous not only by the description given by Victor Hugo who stopped briefly in the town in 1837 but also by Corot's fine painting, now in the Louvre. It is an imposing square Gothic tower, sombre and grim, and was built from 1390 to 1410; it stands 64m/210ft tall (40m/131ft from the ground to the platform).

The top of the belfry bristles with turrets, dormer windows, pinnacles and weathervanes, and is crowned with a Flemish lion "that turns with a flag in its paws" (Victor Hugo).

The current peal of 62 bells is on the fourth floor. The bells replaced the famous ones which were destroyed by the Germans in 1917. They play the tune of the Scottish Puritans on the hour; on the half-hour, a boating song; at quarter past and quarter to the hour, a few notes of Gayant's tune.

From the top of the tower *(192 steps)*, Douai and its industrial suburb may be seen through the louvre-boarding.

Inside the **town hall** *(hôtel de ville)* (**H**) the Gothic Council Chamber (15C), the old chapel (now the main hall), the White Salon with 18C wood panelling and the state room are open to visitors.

Follow the vaulted passageway and cross the courtyard of the town hall to rue de l'Université.

This street passes beside the old 17C **pawnshop** *(mont-de-piété)* (**E**), now a food and agriculture research laboratory; it then leads to the 18C **theatre** (**T**) with its Louis XVI façade.

In Rue de la Comédie to the right stands the Hôtel d'Aoust (**L**), a beautiful example of Louis XV architecture. Note the rococo door and the allegorical statues representing the four seasons decorating the façade overlooking the courtyard. It is today the headquarters of the Northern Collieries Board (Direction des Houillères du Nord); indeed, Douai was formerly the heart of the French coal mining basin *(see Introduction: Economy)*.

Continue along rue de la Comédie and turn right onto rue des Foulons.

Along the left-hand side of rue des Foulons, literally "Fullers' Street", a reminder of the linen-drapers of the Middle Ages, are a few 18C houses. At no 132, note the **Hôtel de la Tramerie (K)** built in the Louis XIII style.

Follow rue de la Mairie on the right to return to the town hall.

Douai is proud of its two peals of bells, one in the belfry and the other a peripatetic peal of 50 bells which travels the length and breadth of France. A French bell-ringing school was founded in Douai by Jacques Lannoy, who still runs it today.

The belfry at Douai

Demolin /CAMPAGNE CAMPAGNE

★MUSÉE DE LA CHARTREUSE ⊘ *1hr*

The museum is installed in an interesting group of 16C, 17C and 18C buildings, which were once the old charterhouse. On the left is the Hôtel d'Abancourt; on the right, beneath a huge square tower, is the building in the Flemish Renaissance style constructed for the Montmorency family. This is where the first Carthusian monks settled in the 17C. They built the small cloister, the refectory, the chapterhouse and the church, which was completed in 1722. The great cloister and the monks' cells were destroyed in the 19C.

The museum is in two parts: the Fine Arts Section, and Archeology and Naturel History Section.

Fine Arts Section – The collections consist principally of fine early paintings.

Room 1 – Early Flemish, Dutch (the Master of Manne, the Master of Flemalle) and Italian paintings.

Passage – Plan of the Charterhouse.

Room 2 – Large 16C altarpieces from other abbeys are on display here, in the old refectory. Especially noteworthy are **Anchin Polyptych★** by Bellegambe portraying the Adoration of the Cross or the Adoration of the Holy Trinity, depending on whether the leaves are open or closed, and the Marchiennes Polyptych by Van Scorel (Utrecht School, 16C), dedicated to St James and St Stephen.

Room 3 – The room includes two masterpieces of the Italian Renaissance: Veronese's *Portrait of a Venetian Woman* and Carracci's *Scourging of Christ* in which the *chiaroscuro* effect was used to create a work of rare intensity. The bronze *Venus of Castello* recalls the work of the famous sculptor and architect Giambologna. Although he conducted most of his career in Italy, in Rome and particularly Florence, he was born in Douai in 1529 and trained in Flanders.

Room 4 – Relief map of Douai in1709.

Rooms 4-5-6 – 16C Flemish and Dutch Mannerism is exhibited: works by Rolandt Savery *(Village Brawl)*; the Antwerp artists Jean Matsys, son of Quentin *(The Healing of Tobias)*, and Frans Floris *(The Holy Family)*; the Dutchmen Van Hemessen *(The Scour-*

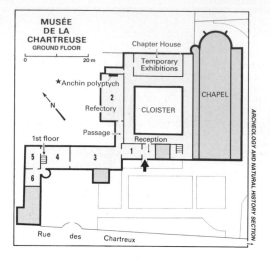

ging of Christ), Van Reymerswaele *(St Jerome),* Goltzius *(The Young Man and the Old Woman)* and Cornelis Van Haarlem *(Baptism of Christ).*

Take the staircase in Room 4 to the first floor.

Rooms 7-8 – Works by Rubens and Jordaens; landscapes by Momper and Govaerts; a witchcraft scene by David Teniers.

Rooms 9-10 – These rooms feature an interesting series of lesser 17C Dutch masters: still-life paintings by Van der Ast and Abraham Mignon; *The Child* by Cuyp; a view of Haarlem by Berckheyde; a landscape by Ruisdaël; *The Young Musician* by Duyster.

Rooms 11-12 – The French school (17C-19C) is well represented here by portrait painters: Le Brun *(Louis XIV on Horseback),* Vivien, Largillière, Nattier, François de Troy *(The Franqueville Family),* Boilly, Chardin *(Still Life),* David *(Mme Tallien).* Works by Impressionist painters are also on show: Renoir, Sisley and Pissaro and Post-Impressionists including Cross, Bonnard and Maurice Denis.

Return to the ground floor.

Cloister – The cloister vaults are pointed despite having been built in 1663, in the middle of the Classical period. The red brickwork contrasts pleasantly with the white stone of the ribs and the framing, carved with Baroque designs.

Chapter house – The chapter house was built in the same year as the cloister (1663) and in the same style; it now holds temporary exhibitions.

Archeology and Natural History Section – *Turn left on leaving the Charterhouse and left again into rue St-Albin.*
The evolution of man is traced from the Paleolithic Age to AD 400 through the findings of excavations in the north of France (first floor). The collection includes a cast of Biache Man's skull, discovered at Biache-St-Vaast, about 13km/8mi from Douai; the man is thought to have lived c 250000 BC.
The Gallo-Roman period is illustrated through material found at Bavay (statuettes) and at Lewarde (busts). There are some interesting models of the Merovingian village of Brebières and the necropolis at Hordain.
On the ground floor, an **aquarium** includes freshwater and saltwater fish from around the world (from African lakes and tropical oceans etc). There are also collections of exotic butterflies and stuffed birds found locally, some of them nesting birds, others migratory.

ADDITIONAL SIGHTS

Église St-Pierre ⊘ – The main features of this former collegiate church are the 16C-17C stone belltower, the 18C brick nave and chancel faced with stone, and the 18C apsidal chapel surmounted by a graceful bulb. Stand to left of the church for the best view.
Inside, the chancel is as long as the nave; it was reserved for canons and members of Parliament. Note the 18C organ case originally from Anchin Abbey, and the three 18C paintings in the right transept arm. They were the work of Deshayes (*The Marriage of the Virgin Mary,* centre) and Ménageot.
The Modern Style boutique in rue Bellegambe *(opposite the church)* features a shop front decorated with sunflowers. Slightly further on *(no 5)* is the birthplace of painter Henri-Edmond Cross (1856-1910).

Palais de Justice ⊘ **(J)** – The courts date from the early 16C but were almost entirely rebuilt in the 18C; they were once the refuge of Marchiennes Abbey and then became the seat of the Flanders Parliament. The main front, rebuilt under Louis XVI by the architect Lillois Lequeux, has a severe-looking central porch.
Turn left immediately beyond the porch. Enter by the glass door then climb the staircase and continue to the end of the corridor.

The first-floor courtroom, called the **grande salle du parlement** (1762), is furnished with a vast marble fireplace, carved Louis XV woodwork, a portrait of Louis XIV and allegorical paintings by Nicolas Brenet (1769).

In 1972 buildings were constructed on the site of the old tribunal; they contain two courtrooms.

The brick façade overlooking the River Scarpe bears traces of the original Gothic arching.

The old prison, from which a famous 18C French adventurer escaped, has been turned into an **exhibition centre** *(enter from the riverside)*. The items on show illustrate the history of the town and the law courts.

Quai de la Scarpe – The quaysides along the Scarpe River, no longer frequented by barges, provide a pleasant walk. Old houses can be seen.

From the landing-stage by the law courts, **boat trips** ⊘ are organised on the river during the tourist season.

Porte de Valenciennes – This monumental gateway today stands alone, 15C Gothic on one side and late-17C Classical on the other.

Église Notre-Dame ⊘ – The church, formerly abutting the ramparts, has always been part of Douai's history. The sandstone and brick nave was built in the early 13C. The 14C Gothic chancel has five bays; the ribs of the pointed vaults are stone, the cells brick. The five-sided apse is pierced by tall lancet windows. The church has been restored since the damage of 1944.

Parc Charles Bertin – The landscaped park (5ha/12 acres) laid out in 1904 lies on the site of an old bastion on the other side of the boulevard.

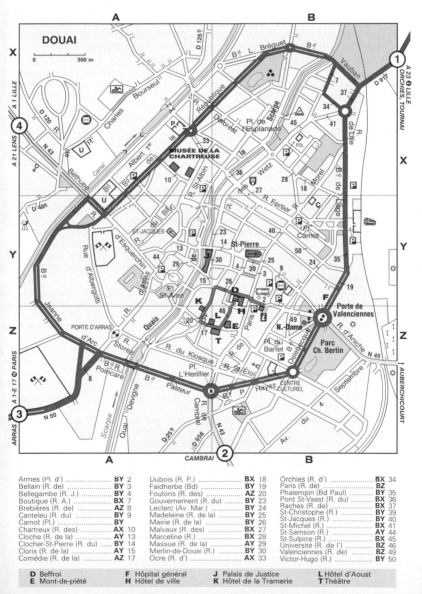

Armes (Pl. d')	**BY** 2	Dubois (R. P.)	**BX** 18	Orchies (R. d')	**BX** 34
Bellain (R. de)	**BY** 3	Faidherbe (Bd)	**BY** 19	Paris (R. de)	**BZ**
Bellegambe (R. J.)	**BY** 4	Foulons (R. des)	**AZ** 20	Phalempin (Bd Paul)	**BY** 35
Boutique (R. A.)	**BX** 7	Gouvernement (R. du)	**BY** 23	Pont St-Vaast (R. du)	**BX** 36
Brebières (R. de)	**AZ** 8	Leclerc (Av. Mar.)	**BY** 24	Raches (R. de)	**BX** 37
Canteleu (R. du)	**BY** 9	Madeleine (R. de la)	**BY** 25	St-Christophe (R.)	**BY** 39
Carnot (Pl.)	**BY**	Mairie (R. de la)	**BY** 26	St-Jacques (R.)	**BY** 40
Chartreux (R. des)	**AX** 10	Malvaux (R. des)	**BX** 27	St-Michel (R.)	**BX** 41
Cloche (R. de la)	**AY** 13	Marceline (R.)	**BX** 28	St-Samson (R.)	**AY** 44
Clocher-St-Pierre (R. du)	**BY** 14	Massue (R. de la)	**AY** 29	St-Sulpice (R.)	**BX** 45
Cloris (R. de la)	**AY** 15	Merlin-de-Douai (R.)	**BY** 30	Université (R. de l')	**BZ** 46
Comédie (R. de la)	**AZ** 17	Ocre (R. d')	**AX** 33	Valenciennes (R. de)	**BZ** 49
				Victor-Hugo (R.)	**BY** 50

D Beffroi	**F** Hôpital général	**J** Palais de Justice	**L** Hôtel d'Aoust
E Mont-de-piété	**H** Hôtel de ville	**K** Hôtel de la Tramerie	**T** Théâtre

EXCURSIONS

Flines-les-Raches – *11km/7mi north by exit ①, on D 917 and D 938.*
The village has a curious **church**, which is entered through a very old brick and sandstone belfry-porch (some say dating back to AD 800). The narrow nave opens onto chapels from various periods. In the first two chapels on the right, the roof beams are decorated with historiated corbels; they bear the arms of Philippine Torck, Abbess of Flines from 1561 to 1571.

★★Centre historique minier de Lewarde – *See Centre historique minier de LEWARDE.*

DUNKERQUE

DUNKIRK – Conurbation 192 852
Michelin map 51 folds 3, 4 or 236 fold 4

The "heroic town" of Dunkirk (Dunkerque) was 80% destroyed during the Second World War. Since its rebuilding it has expanded rapidly, both commercially and industrially, owing to the enormous growth of its port.

Church of the Dunes – Until the 7C the site on which Dunkirk stands was covered by sea. Its name, which means "church of the dunes", did not appear until 1067. Until the end of the 17C, possession of this poorly defended fishermen's town was fought over by Spanish, French, English and Dutch alike. In 1658 it was taken by Turenne after the Battle of the Dunes and fortified shortly after by Vauban.

Evacuation of Dunkirk (May-June 1940) – From 25 May to 4 June, Dunkirk was the scene of a bloody battle at the time of the evacuation of Allied forces who were cut off from their bases after the German breakthrough at Sedan and the subsequent push towards the coast. The boats in Dunkirk's port and on the beaches from Malo to Bray-Dunes made the journey back and forth between the French coast and England. Despite the limpet mines, torpedoes, bombs and the pounding of heavy German shells, almost 350 000 men were rescued, about two-thirds of them British.

★★THE PORT

Dunkirk is classed as France's third largest port, having had over 35 million tonnes of traffic in 1996. Imports (28 million tonnes) including minerals, chemical and petroleum products, coal, sand and gravel, metallurgical products, oil-bearing seeds, timber, oils and textiles are higher than exports (a quarter of the total traffic) which encompass petroleum and metallurgical products, early vegetables and fruit, cement, sugar, fertilizer, cereals, heavy goods and tunkey factories.
Since 1987 the eastern and western ports have been linked by a **deep-water canal** to the Nord-Pas-de-Calais region of France (3 600 t), Belgium (1 300 t) and the Paris Basin (600 t). The port installations cover 7 600ha/18 800 acres and extend along 15km/9mi of coastline.

Port-Est – The eastern port has a **harbour basin** 6km/4mi long, and 385ha/950 acres of wet docks, divided into six open basins and specialised industrial basins, in addition to storage installations. It is serviced by an outer harbour (80ha/198 acres) and three locks, the largest of which, the Charles-de-Gaulle Lock (365m by 50m/400yd by 55yd) can receive 125 000-tonne vessels. Well equipped for ship repairs, the port has four dry docks and one floating dock. The quays extend north to the entrance of the deep-water canal and handle heavy-cargo ships as well as the local steel production and cereal traffic (three silos).

Port-Ouest – The western port, in use since 1975, has the advantage of a very deep (20.50m/67ft) and very large (560ha/1 380 acres) outer harbour with a wharf which can receive 300 000-tonne oil tankers.
It contains a rapid-transit port to which ships gain access without having to pass through any locks and 2km/1.5mi of quays. In order to receive the largest container vessels, this rapid-transit port has a series of quays equipped with storehouses, powerful hoisting equipment (three cranes) and 80ha/198 acres of marshalling yards. Metallurgical industries are established on the west side of the harbour basin, near the crude oil reserves and the power station at Gravelines. The coal and minerals terminal is accessible to 180 000-tonne ships.

The Industrial Complex – Dunkirk's port activity is largely linked to the size of the industrial complex established here.
The **iron and steel industry** is represented by Sollac, Dunkirk's "factory on the water", which produces a large percentage of France's steel. On the other hand, French **fine-grade iron and steel** is well known owing to the Ascométal firm's Dunes works (between Malo-les-Bains and Bray-Dunes). The plant specialises in making bars, wheels, rail axles and oil drilling pipes. Péchiney opened a plant here in 1990, producing **aluminum**.

The **petroleum industry** is represented by the presence of the BP, Elf and Total installations; the **petro-chemical** industry is especially important, with the Copenor plant producing ethylene and polyethylene here, among other products; the Stocknard port terminal is equipped to handle deliveries of liquid chemical products.

The 840km/522mi long Franco-Norwegian gas pipeline NorFra, which is linked to the Draupner oil rig in the North Sea, supplies a third of the total French needs in natural gas.

Other companies include GTS Industries (large pipes), Air Liquide, Lafarge (cement works) and, at Coudekerque-Branche, the Lesieur factory (cooking oil). Dupont de Nemours specialises in analytical chemistry for the agriculture industry and Ajinomoto is a food-processing company. Both of them are recent arrivals in Dunkirk.

Tour of the Eastern Port

⬚ **Tour on foot** – *About 1hr.*

Start from Place du Minck (**CY 53**) (fish market) between the Bassin du Commerce and the *cale aux pêcheurs* and cross the old citadel district, where the customs forwarding agents are established today. The channel and the marina are on the right. Cross Trystam Lock and turn right towards the **lighthouse**. The tower, built between 1838 and 1843, is 59m/194ft tall and its 6000 watts produce beams which can be seen 48km/30mi away. From the top the **view** extends to the impressive harbour installations, the beach at Malo-les-Bains and the surrounding area. Beyond the floating docks is Watier Lock. The eastern port's control tower stands at its entrance, to the right on the bunker; there is a good **view** of the port and harbour entrance from the terrace. The view also includes the long jetty where the French troops embarked in 1940.

Jean Bart, the "king's official privateer"

During the wars fought by Louis XIV, the privateers of Dunkirk destroyed and captured 3000 ships, took 30000 prisoners and wiped out Dutch trade. The most intrepid of all the privateers was **Jean Bart** (1650-1702). He was as famous as the privateers from Saint-Malo, Duguay-Trouin and Surcouf, and was a virtuoso of the North Sea trade routes. Unlike pirates, who were outlaws attacking any and every passing ship and, in many cases, murdering the crews, privateers were granted "letters patent" from the sovereign entitling them to hound warships and merchant vessels. In 1694, Jean Bart saved the kingdom from famine by capturing 130 ships loaded with wheat. His success owed much to the existence of an ultra-modern arsenal and the constant presence of a royal fleet. He was a simple, plain-spoken man but his exploits were many and varied. As a result, he was raised to the nobility in 1694 then, three years later, was given the rank of Commodore. It is said that Louis XIV announced the appointment personally. "Jean Bart, I have appointed you to the rank of Commodore". The brave seafarer is said to have replied, "Sire, you were right to do so." The following year he avoided a combat with nine large ships while taking the Prince de Conti to Poland. Once the

Jean Bart

B.N. Paris /HARLINGUE-VIOLLET

danger was past, the prince said to him, "Had we been attacked, we should have been captured." "Never," replied Jean Bart. "We should all have been blown sky high for my son was in the munitions hold and he had orders to set light to a powder keg as soon as I gave the command."

★ **Musée portuaire** (**CZ M³**) – Laid out in a former tobacco warehouse dating from the 19C, this attractive museum gives an insight into the history and operating of the port of Dunkirk, Northern France's huge maritime gateway. Dunkirk used to specialise in fishing and trade but, from the 1960's onwards, it also became a major industrial port. The work of the pilots, access to the harbour, ship repairs, product handling, coastal fishing and Icelandic fishing are all described through dioramas, model ships, maps, paintings, engravings and the tools once used by dockers. The Ateliers et Chantiers de France, which closed down in 1987, built more than 300 ships.

In the 17C, Dunkirk became the main privateering harbour, with Jean Bart to defend it. *The Battle of Texel* (a copy of a painting by Isabey kept in the Musée de la Marine in Paris), engravings, and models of privateers' boats illustrate his exploits.

DUNKERQUE

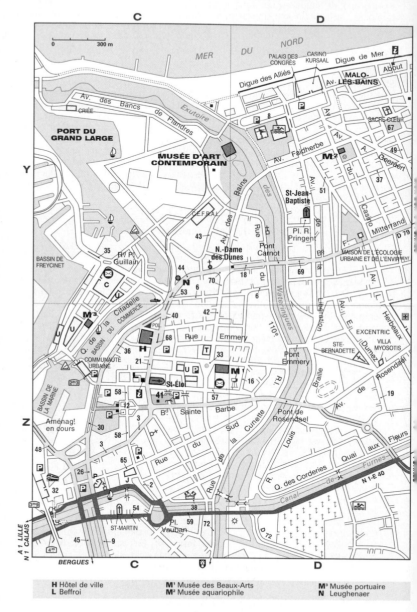

H Hôtel de ville
L Beffroi

M¹ Musée des Beaux-Arts
M² Musée aquariophile

M³ Musée portuaire
N Leughenaer

In a gallery on the second floor are some thirty models of sea-going craft, showing the diversity in types of ships and giving an indication of technological progress. They include a fully-armed brig, a frigate, a paddle steamer, a 20C petroleum carrier etc.

Every year exhibitions are organised around a specific topic linked to the sea or the harbour.

In the basin opposite the museum is a three-master, the *Duchesse Anne*, once a sailing school ship (1902). There are also two light vessels, the *Dyck* (1911) and the *Sandettie* (1949), and an old barge.

2 **Boat trips** ⊙ – Boats leave from the Bassin du Commerce, the largest of the three old basins, and cruise the entire length of the port. The trip takes visitors past the tug basin, the workshops (dry docks), the various locks, the wet docks and storage areas, the sugar terminal (Trans Terminal Sucrier), the BP refinery and the petroleum wharves, the EDF power station, the Sollac iron and steel plant, the mineral basin and the dike known as Le Break.

ADDITIONAL SIGHTS

★**Musée d'Art contemporain** ⊙ (**CDY**) – The Museum of Contemporary Art stands in the middle of a **sculpture park**★ designed by landscape gardener Gilbert Samel. The paths climb outcrops and run down slopes, leading past great stone pieces by the sculptor Dodeigne, metal structures by Féraud and compositions by Viseux, Arman and Zvenjjorovsky, all against the backdrop of the North Sea.

Architect Jean Willerval bore in mind the existing garden when he built his modern concrete building sheathed in white ceramic. This rather sober structure is preceded by a superb portico by Philippe Scrive; it is made of azobe, an African wood. In 1994, the museum changed its original purpose and, as a result, its collection of paintings and sculpture was transferred to the Museum of Fine Arts. It is now devoted to contemporary earthenware and glassware. Inside the forum, ramps lead up to the first floor and its eight rooms containing displays of modern ceramics. The permanent collection, exhibited on the upper floor, consists of works by Camille Virot, Thiébaut, Chagué, Gérard Quinchez, Gilles Suffren, Philippe Goodridge. Working under the heading of **"Dialogues in ceramics"**, the museum aims to increase public awareness of this art form through temporary exhibitions, beginners workshops, and books on the artists.

Belfry ⊙ (**CZ L**) – Built in the 13C and heightened in 1440, it served as the bell-tower to **Église St-Éloi** which burnt down in 1558. This high tower (58m/190ft) contains a peal of 48 bells which play "Jean Bart's tune" on the hours and other popular tunes on the quarter hours. The tourist office is housed on the ground floor. A war memorial has been erected under the arch opposite Église St-Éloi.

Église St-Éloi ⊙ (**CZ**) – The church was built in the 16C and remodelled in the 18C and 19C. It has a neo-Gothic west front and a pyramid roofline along the side aisles and apse. The proportions appear odd since the suppression of the transept; the church is 68m/221ft long and 53m/172ft wide.

Note the size of the five aisles with quadripartite vaulting supported by elegant piers, and its apse with radiating chapels. The restored pointed windows feature stained glass by the master glassworker Gaudin. On the north side of the chancel, a white marble slab marks the tomb of **Jean Bart** *(see box above)*.

Place Jean-Bart – On this square at the centre of the town stands a statue of the famous corsair, Jean Bart, by David d'Angers (1848).

★ **Musée des Beaux-Arts (Fine Arts Museum)** ⊙ (**CZ M'**) – This museum (rebuilt 1973) houses beautiful collections of 16C to 20C paintings and documents tracing Dunkirk's history. In the entrance hall, a panel of 540 Delft tiles portrays the bombardment of the port in 1695.

On the ground floor there is a local history section mainly concerning the privateer Jean Bart. Note the strange 17C money box in the shape of a chained captive from the Église St-Eloi. The money placed in it was used to buy back slaves.

In the modern art gallery (1950-1970) are works by César, Arman, Hartung, Mathieu, E Pignon, Kijno, Vasarely, Soulages, Karel Appel (17 painted sculptures making up the "circus") formerly displayed in the Museum of Contemporary Art.

On the first floor the 16C and 17C **Flemish school** is well represented: F Pourbus the Younger *(Head of a Child)*, Snyders *(Fruit Vendor)*, Jean de Reyn (several portraits), Francken *(The Feast of Herod)*, Robert van der Hoecke *(Snow Effects)*, Teniers the Younger *(Village Fête)*, Van Dyck *(Head of a Bearded Man)*.

The **Dutch school** offers interesting portraits of women by Morelse, Aert de Gelder and Bylert, still lifes by Van der Poel and Claez. Among the 18C Italian painters, note the work of Magnasco *(Adoration of the Magi)*.

The **French school** from the 17C to the 20C contains canvases by Largillière, Vignon, Riguaud, Lesueur, Hubert Robert, Vernet, Corot, Boudin, and Carrier-Belleuse.

The natural history section in the basement includes reconstructions of the region's natural habitats (marshes, beaches etc.).

Hôtel de ville (**CZ H**) – Built in 1900 by Louis Cordonnier, who designed the Peace Palace in the Hague, it includes a 75m/246ft central belfry. Inside, a stained-glass window by Félix Gaudin commemorates Jean Bart's return following his victory at Texel (off the Netherlands) in 1694.

Leughenaer (**CY N**) – The liar's tower (Leughenaer is Flemish for a liar) is the only vestige of the Burgundian walls and 28 towers which encircled the city in the 14C. It owes its name to a watchman's mistake.

Dunkerque – Musée d'Art contemporain

Chapelle Notre-Dame-des-Dunes (CY) – The chapel was rebuilt in the 19C; it contains a wooden statue of the Madonna which has been worshipped by sailors since 1405. Votive offerings.

Église St-Jean-Baptiste – This modern, brick-built church (1962), shaped like the prow of a ship, stands separately from its wooden belfry which rises like a mast. Inside there is a lovely Christ surrounded by four angels.

⌂MALO-LES-BAINS (DY)

Founded before 1870 by a local shipowner named Malo, this seaside resort has become the residential district of Dunkirk. The large, gently sloping beach of fine sand extends east of the port; it is flanked by a promenade beside which stands the casino.

Musée aquariophile ⊘ (**M²**) – The aquarium's 21 tanks hold 150 species of fish of various origins, some of them from the Dunkirk region.

EXCURSIONS

Gravelines – *13km/8mi west.*
The town is enclosed within classic, Vauban-style ramparts with brick bastions and stone courses; it was an important part of Dunkirk's defence in 1940. The 1742 powder magazine, now set within pleasant gardens, houses the **Musée du Dessin et de l'Estampe originale** ⊘ specialising in prints and engravings and temporary exhibitions.
The town also boasts a large sports centre *(Sportica)*, a harbour full of yachts and sailings boats, and a Flamboyant church with a Renaissance front portal.
To the northeast rise the towers of the Nuclear Power Station.

La Côte des Dunes (From Malo-les-Bains to Bray-Dunes) – *13km/8mi northeast by D 79 and D 60.*
The road bypasses Dunes Fort which gave its name to the Battle of the Dunes (1658), then continues past the Ascométal company's Dunes plant.

Zuydcoote – The town found literary fame with the novel *Weekend in Zuydcoote* by Robert Merle, on which a film was based evoking the tragic episodes of the 1940 evacuation. The great sanatorium, transformed into a hospital, was at that time the setting of dramatic scenes, with an influx of wounded whose number reached 7 000.

Bray-Dunes – A promenade runs along the beach which stretches all the way to la Panne in Belgium; it is a popular spot for sand yachts. On the promenade, a stele commemorates the soldiers who fought until 4 June 1940.

Château d'ÉCOUEN**

Access is through the forest, on foot; cars must be parked at the entrance to the forest.

The château, nestling in a park (17ha/42 acre), overlooking the plain was originally intended for Constable Anne de Montmorency *(see p 122)* and his wife Madeleine of Savoy, who lived here from 1538 to 1555.

When Constable Anne's grandson Henri II de Montmorency was beheaded in 1632, the château reverted to the Condé family but was later confiscated during the Revolution. Napoleon I salvaged the estate in 1806 by founding the first school for the daughters of members of the Légion d'Honneur there. In 1962 the château and its grounds were handed over to the Ministry of Culture, who undertook to turn it into a state museum devoted to Renaissance art.

TOUR *1hr*

Exterior – The Château d'Écouen reflects the transition of French art from the Early Renaissance period (Château of the Loire) to the High Renaissance during Henri II's reign.

Courtyard – The buildings feature pavilions at each corner and are surmounted by elaborate dormer windows with carved pediments. The beautiful east range was destroyed in the 18C and replaced by a low entrance wing.

Porticoes with Classical-style columns decorate the buildings. The most outstanding one is to the left, on the south wing (Anne de Montmorency's residence) built by Jean Bullant to house Michelangelo's famous *Slaves* in the niches on the ground floor. The statues (the originals are in the Louvre) were a gift to Anne de Montmorency from King Henri II.

North Terrace – Sweeping **view** of the surrounding cereal-growing countryside.

★★ Musée national de la Renaissance ⊘ – Some of the exhibits on display belonged to the Renaissance collections of the Cluny Museum in Paris. Écouen Museum presents a wide range of works dating from the 16C and early 17C, which introduce visitors to the various branches of the decorative arts: furniture, wainscots, tapestries and embroideries, ceramics, enamels etc.

Painted fireplace in the Château d'Écouen

R. Mazin /DIAF

175

Most of the exhibits were made in France, Italy or the Netherlands. They represent a small selection but the ambience they create is in keeping with the life of wealthy nobility during the Renaissance.

The original interior decoration consists mainly of grotesques, painted on the friezes below the ceiling and the embrasures of the windows. But it is for its **painted fireplaces** that Écouen is famed. Created during the reign of Henri II, these chimneypieces are representative of the first Fontainebleau School: the central biblical scene is painted on an oval or rectangular medallion, surrounded by grotesques, garlands of fruit and motifs in leather; the hazy landscapes depicting antique ruins, fortresses and humble cottages are in imitation of Niccolo dell'Abbate.

Ground Floor – The monograms A and M (Anne de Montmorency and Madeleine of Savoy) have been included in the decoration of the chapel, built in 1544 and covered with painted vaulting resting on diagonal arches. This heraldic motif reappears in different places (musicians' gallery, panelling in the oratory, the vaulting in the sacristy). The Passion Altarpiece is adorned with enamelling and a copy of Leonardo da Vinci's *Last Supper*.

Several rooms are devoted to a particular trade or technique and illustrate various aspects of Renaissance life; note a clock of German origin in the shape of a ship known as Charles V's clock, now shown incorporated into a 16C collector's cabinet and, in the reconstruction of a 16C goldsmith's workshop, a goldsmith's work bench set in an inlaid chest. It comes from the Kunstkammer of Augustus I in Dresden. The northwest pavilion was formerly occupied by Catherine de' Medici.

First Floor – In the south wing, visitors are shown round the constable's bedroom and Madeleine of Savoy's suite, both interesting on account of the period furniture. The west wing is almost exclusively taken up by the **Tapestry of David and Bathsheba★★★** (1510-1520) which runs from the Abigail pavilion to the king's bedchamber, along the Psyche Gallery. The 75m/246ft hanging divided into ten sections tells of the romance between King David and Bathsheba. The outstanding quality of the tapestry – woven with wool and silk threads, as well as silver braid – is equalled only by that of *The Hunts of Maximilian* in the Louvre, without doubt the two most precious examples of 16C Brussels tapestry work existing in France.

The hanging ends in the King's Apartment, situated in the northwest pavilion. *(For explanations of the monograms read the paragraph entitled "Henri II's Château" in the chapter on Fontainebleau).*

The king's suite occupied the northern wing. One of the rooms contains the floor tiles made specially for the château in 1542 by the Rouen potter Masseot Abaquesne. The winged victory on the central panel of the monumental fireplace was taken from a similar design in the François I Gallery at Fontainebleau.

The two tapestries are part of the famous *Fructus Belli* made in Brussels to cartoons by Jules Romains.

Second Floor – In the northeast pavilion, many pieces of Isnik pottery (mid-16C to early 17C) are exhibited in glass cabinets, illustrating the exotic tastes of 16C collectors. The first room in the north wing presents religious stained glass painted in *grisaille*; admire the *Virgin and Child*, dated 1544.

The second hall deals entirely with French ceramics (Bernard Palissy, Saint-Parchaira, and Masséat Abaquesne's work, *The Flood*) and there is a reconstruction of another floor designed specially for the château, showing the arms of the Constable, those of his wife, of Henri II and Catherine de' Medici.

The fifteen marriage chests *(cassoni)* on show in the northwest pavilion form a remarkable ensemble; these painted panels are taken from wooden chests that were presented to newlyweds in sets of two.

The cabinets in the west gallery contain enamels (pieces by Léonard Limosin including portraits of Claude of Lorraine and Antoinette of Bourbon), tin-glazed pottery or majolica from Deruta in Italy and glasses (goblets belonging to Anne de Bretagne and Catherine de' Medici).

The southwest pavilion concentrates on silverware (cutlery, jewellery), mainly of German origin. There is an extraordinary Daphne by the great Nuremberg goldsmith, Wenzel Jammitzer (1508-1585). Above the chapel is the former library of Constable Anne which still has some of the original gilded wainscoting. It is representative of the world of books during the Renaissance period.

ADDITIONAL SIGHT

Église St-Acceul – The chancel by Jean Bullant is the most interesting part of the building. The complex rib patterns of the vaulting *(temporarily concealed by supporting timber)* date it to the 16C.

St Acceul features several Renaissance **stained-glass windows★**; those in the north aisle are dated 1544: *Dormition and Assumption of the Virgin, Annunciation and Visitation, Nativity and Adoration of the Magi.*

Château de FERRIÈRES★

Michelin map 101 fold 30

The shooting parties on Ferrières estate, the luxurious furnishings of the château and the precious collections gathered by the members of the Rothschild dynasty were the talk of the town for over 100 years.

The landscape park – created at the same time as the Bois de Boulogne – is extremely attractive, especially in the vicinity of the lake.

A Challenge to Tradition – In 1829 James de Rothschild, founder of the French line of the family, acquired 7 500 acres of hunting grounds formerly belonging to Fouché, with a view to building a villa which would accommodate his invaluable collections and satisfy his taste for splendour. The baron did not choose a professional architect: he broke with tradition and hired **Joseph Paxton**, the English glasshouse and garden designer with a penchant for modern materials such as iron and glass. Already famed for the Crystal Palace in London (destroyed in 1936), Paxton erected a rectangular building flanked by square towers, with a central hall equipped with zenithal lighting. Construction work was completed in 1859. The decoration, left in the hands of the baroness, was entrusted to the French specialist Eugène Lami.

On 16 December 1862 Napoleon III paid an official visit to the Rothschilds in their new residence. Delighted by the splendid apartments and the 800 head of game for his day's shoot, the Emperor planted a sequoia tree as a commemorative gesture.

Less than 10 years later, Jules Favre – in charge of Foreign Affairs in the new National Defence government – turned up at the gates of the château on 19 September 1870. In his capacity as Minister, Favre came to see Chancellor Bismarck, who was staying at Ferrières with Kaiser Wilhelm I of Prussia, to ask him to agree to an armistice. The chancellor however made this conditional on the surrender of Strasbourg, Toul and Bitche, and further implied that the cession of Alsace and part of Lorraine was inevitable. Jules Favre left the premises the following morning but it was not until 28 January 1871 that Paris fell to the hands of the enemy.

In 1977 Baron Guy de Rothschild and his wife Marie-Hélène donated their château and part of the estate to the Confederation of Paris Universities.

TOUR ⏱ *2hr*

Exterior – Its architecture reflects the various styles of the Renaissance period, including the odd eccentricity that was acceptable in the 19C. Although balusters, galleries and colonnades reigned supreme, the façades were each different. The most striking and the most typically English is the main front overlooking the lake, with its centrepiece flanked by turrets and its display of superimposed galleries. Step back to take in the tall decorative stone chimneys, reminiscent of the Château de Chambord.

Interior – A pavilion sporting a large clock is fronted by the main entrance porch which bears the baron's monogram (JR) and the family coat of arms (the five Rothschild arrows).

The main staircase leads to the central hall – 40m/130ft wide and 12m/40ft high under the glass ceiling – now stripped of its paintings and tapestries. Above the main door, a row of telamones and caryatids in bronze and black marble support a musicians' gallery. The use of such statues was a popular decorative feature in the mid 19C. The Salon bleu, overlooking the park, has busts of the Empress Eugénie and Bettina de Rothschild, the first proprietress of the château. The Louis XVI salon is the most typical example of Eugène Lami's work: it features off-white wainscoting with pinkish hues, a painted ceiling inspired by Boucher and reproduction Louis XVI furniture. Opposite is the Salon rouge, in which the 1870 negotiations took place. It now presents an exhibition on the history of the estate.

Musée de l'Imaginaire ⏱ – This small museum housed on the second floor showcases a changing collection of paintings and sculptures by an international group of contemporary artists who express their extravagant visions in the style known as Fantastic Realism. The works are shown here before being offered for public sale.

★**Park** ⏱ – The park designed by Paxton boasts a number of superb compositions, mainly consisting of ornamental coniferous trees: cedars of Lebanon, numerous Atlas cedars – including the highly decorative blue form – and sequoias, introduced into France around 1850.

Several individual trees also deserve a mention: a Lebanese cedar with unusually long, spread-eagled branches, swamp cypresses, with twigs which turn deep russet and drop off in winter, copper beeches, groves of plane trees and, on the far side of the lake, feathery weeping species, adding an autumnal touch to the tableau. Outside the park, the Allée des Lions presents an imposing driveway of stately sequoias.

FOLLEVILLE

Population 63
Michelin map 52 fold 18 or 236 fold 34

This modest village located on a hill at the end of the Noye Valley was once the seat of an important fief. The ruins of a castle (13C-16C), once owned by the illustrious Lannoy and Gondi families, stand as testimony to the town's former importance.

A Valiant Knight – **Raoul de Lannoy**, the son of a Flemish family, was Chamberlain and Counsellor to Louis XI, Charles VIII and Louis XII. He achieved great glory in 1477 at the siege of Le Quesnoy, and Louis XI presented him with a gold chain saying: "Because, my friend, you are too furious in combat you must be chained to contain your ardour, as I do not want to lose you." This chain is exhibited in Folleville church. During the Italian campaign Lannoy was named Governor of Genoa by Louis XII, and died there in 1513.

Monsieur Vincent's First "Mission" – In January 1617 a humble, wise old priest – **Vincent de Paul** – travelled through the lands of Françoise de Gondi, heiress of the fief of Folleville through her mother Marie de Lannoy. The region was in an advanced state of secularisation. Horrified, the priest entered the pulpit and preached such an eloquent sermon that a general confession ensued. Following this experience, in 1625 Vincent founded the Congregation of the Priests of the Mission, later known as Lazarists.

CHURCH ⏱ *1hr 30min*

The exterior of this early-16C church is decorated with remarkable carvings: 16C statue of St James on the corner of the west front and a Virgin and Child in the niche of a buttress.

Nave – A Renaissance font stands near the entrance; the white Carrara marble basin is carved with the symbolic chain and the coat of arms of the Lannoy family. In the south aisle the pulpit from which Vincent de Paul preached still stands.

★**Chancel** – The chancel is constructed in a largely Flamboyant architectural style but also features numerous Renaissance decorative elements. Note the finely carved ribbed vault.

The first **tomb**★★ on the left is that of Raoul de Lannoy and his wife Jeanne de Poix. The white marble sarcophagus was made in Genoa in 1507, when Raoul de Lannoy was still alive, by the Milanese sculptor Antonio Della Porta and his nephew Pace Gaggini; the recumbent effigy of Lannoy is portrayed wearing the gold chain he was given by Louis XI. The base is adorned with graceful weeping children, the family coat of arms and an epitaph. The recess in which the tomb lies is a masterpiece of French art with its delicate sculptures and carvings. The background is garlanded with sweet peas *(fleurs de pois)*, a reference to de Lannoy's wife. It is crowned by a double ogee framing a graceful Virgin and Child emerging from a fleur-de-lis and surmounted by a tent-shaped canopy; a trellised enclosure, a daisy chain, cherubs and the symbols of the Evangelists complete the composition.

The second **tomb**★ shows the progress of funerary art, moving in 50 years from recumbent effigies to kneeling stone figures. Among those kneeling are François de Lannoy, Raoul's son who died in 1548, and his wife Marie de Hangest. The base of the white marble surround is decorated with figures of the Cardinal Virtues (Prudence, Temperance, Fortitude and Justice).

The tomb of Raoul de Lannoy
and Jeanne de Poix, Folleville

Recess and piscina – A pointed arch beyond the altar opens on to a large festooned recess revealing a sculpted Christ appearing to Mary Magdalene; on either side angels carry the instruments of the Passion. On the right of the altar, a pretty piscina is decorated with statuettes of St Francis and John the Baptist, the patron saints of François de Lannoy and Jeanne de Poix.

FONTAINEBLEAU★★★

Population 15 714
Michelin map 106 folds 45, 46 or 61 folds 2, 12

Access from Paris: *SNCF Rail link from Gare de Lyon*

It was not until the 19C that Fontainebleau – which long remained a hamlet named Avon – started to develop, owing to the growing popularity of country residences and the general appreciation of its unspoilt forest. This residential area has also acquired a large number of tertiary sector companies including various workshops and laboratories, a research centre for one of France's top engineering colleges, the European Institute of Business Management and a contemporary archive library, a branch of the National Archives. However, Fontainebleau essentially owes its fame to the castle and the park named on UNESCO's World Heritage list.

Military and equestrian traditions – Throughout French history, whether under monarchic or republican rule, independent units have been posted to Fontainebleau. Tradition, it seems, favoured the cavalry, present in the 17C with the king's bodyguard. A number of racecourses and riding schools were created under Napoleon III; the Centre national des sports équestres perpetuates this tradition *(see Calendar of Events)*, while the forest caters for riding enthusiasts.

The history of the town has been marked by several military organisations, notably the École spéciale militaire (1803 to 1808, before St-Cyr), the polygon-shaped École d'application d'artillerie et du génie (1871 to 1914) and the SHAPE (Supreme Headquarters, Allied Powers, Europe) headquarters of NATO, which gave the town a cosmopolitan touch from 1947 to 1967.

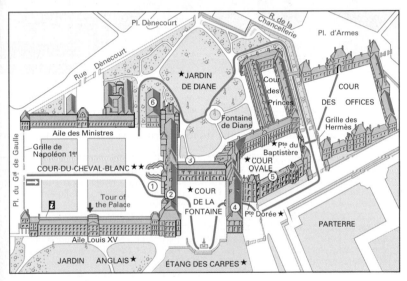

1) Horseshoe Staircase
2) Aile des Reines Mères
3) Galerie François Ier
4) Aile de la Belle Cheminée
5) Ballroom
6) Real Tennis Court

★★★PALACE ⊙

The Palais de Fontainebleau owes its origins to royalty's passion for hunting; it owes its development and decoration to the kings' delight in amassing works of art and displaying them in their "family home". This palace has an extremely distinguished past; from the last of the Capetians up to Napoleon III, it was designed for and occupied by French rulers.

A hunting lodge – A spring – called Bliaud or Blaut fountain in the middle of a forest abounding in game – prompted the kings of France to build a mansion here. The exact date is not known but it was probably before 1137 as a charter exists issued under Louis VII from Fontainebleau, dating from that year. Philip Augustus celebrated the return of the Third Crusade here during the Christmas festivities of 1191 and St Louis founded a Trinitarian convent, whose members were called Mathurins; Philip the Fair was born here in 1268; unfortunately he also died here following a serious riding accident.

The Renaissance – Under François I almost all the medieval buildings were pulled down and replaced by two main edifices, erected under the supervision of Gilles Le Breton. The oval-shaped east pavilion – built on the former foundations – was linked to the west block by a long gallery. To decorate the palace, François I hired many artists; he dreamed of creating a "New Rome" furnished with replicas of Classical statues.

Fontainebleau, main façade

The actual building consisted of rubble-work as the sandstone taken from the forest was too difficult to work into regular freestones. The harled façades are enlivened by string-courses of brick or massive sandstone blocks.

The Fontainebleau School – 16C – The teams of painters and stucco workers were supervised by Rosso, one of Michelangelo's pupils and a native of Florence, and by Primaticcio, a follower of Giulio Romano who came from Bologna. They developed a decorative technique strongly inspired by enigmatic allegories. Attention to detail, which typified late Gothic architecture, was no longer in vogue beyond the Loire Valley as it had been during the Early Renaissance. The Fontainebleau artists were more intent on depicting a dreamy form of elegance, characterised by the representation of human bodies arched into arabesques.

These painters formed the First Fontainebleau School, which blossomed during the reign of François I. The school created a style of decoration incorporating both stucco and paintings – exemplified by the François I Gallery – in semi-miniature works referred to as "French style" by the Italians.

Rosso died in 1540. Primaticcio was sent to Rome to make moulds of famous Antique statues – the *Laocoon*, the *Belvedere Apollo* – which were brought back to Fontainebleau and cast in bronze.

In his private suite *(Appartement des Bains)*, the king could feast his eyes on masterpieces by Raphael and Leonardo da Vinci *(The Mona Lisa)*, while the Pavillon des Armes housed the gold and silver plate, jewellery and miscellaneous curios that delighted contemporary royalty.

Henri II's château – Henri II pursued the efforts undertaken by his father. He gave orders to complete and decorate the ballroom, which remains one of the splendours of Fontainebleau Palace. The monograms – consisting of the royal H and the two intertwined Cs of Catherine de' Medici – were legion. In a form of ambiguity that was generally accepted in its day, the two C's placed immediately beside the H form a double D, the monogram of the King's mistress Diane de Poitiers.

When Henri II was killed in a tournament, his widow Catherine de' Medici sent her rival to Chaumont-sur-Loire *(see the Michelin Green Guide Châteaux of the Loire)* and dismissed the architect in charge of the building work Philibert Delorme, who was Diane's protégé. He was replaced by the Italian Primaticcio; those working under him, including Niccolo dell'Abbate, favoured light, cheerful colours.

Henri IV's palace – 17C – Henri IV, who adored Fontainebleau, had the palace enlarged quite significantly. The irregular contours of the Oval Court were corrected and he gave orders to build the kitchen Court and the Real Tennis Court *(Jeu de Paume)*. These he had decorated by a new group of artists of largely Flemish, and not Italian, inspiration: frescoes were replaced by oil paintings on plaster or canvas.

M. Beaugeois/PIX

In the same way, the plain wood panelling highlighted with gilding gave way to painted wainscot. This was the Second Fontainebleau School, whose representatives moved in Parisian circles.

The House of Eternity – Louis XIV, XV and XVI undertook numerous renovations aimed at embellishing their apartments. The Revolution spared the château but emptied it of its precious furniture. Napoleon, who became consul, then emperor, thoroughly enjoyed staying at the palace. He preferred Fontainebleau to Versailles, where he felt haunted by a phantom rival. He called the palace "The House of Eternity" and left his mark by commissioning further refurbishments. The last rulers of France also took up residence in this historic palace. It was eventually turned into a museum under the Republic.

Exterior *1hr*

★★ **Cour du Cheval Blanc** or **des Adieux** – This former bailey was used only by domestics but its generous size soon earmarked it for official parades and tournaments. It was sometimes called the White Horse Court after the day Charles IX set up a plaster cast of the equestrian statue of Marcus Aurelius in Rome; a small slab in the central alley marks its former location.

The golden eagles seemingly hovering above the pillars of the main gate remind visitors that the Emperor had this made into his main courtyard. He gave orders to raze the Renaissance buildings that lay to the west of the court but kept the end pavilions. It is clear, walking between the two long wings, that only the one on the left with its brick courses has retained the elegance that characterised the work of Gilles Le Breton, François I's favourite architect. The right wing – which boasted the Ulysses Gallery decorated under the supervision of Primaticcio – was dismantled by Louis XV and rebuilt by Jacques-Ange Gabriel.

At the far end of the court the main block, fronted by a balustrade marking the site of the former moat, was completed in several stages from the reign of François I to that of Louis XV. Nonetheless the façades show a certain unity of style. The large horizontal planes of the blue slating are broken by the white façades, the trapezoidal roofs and the tall chimneys of the five pavilions. The celebrated horseshoe staircase executed by Jean Du Cerceau during the reign of Louis XIII is a harmoniously-curved, extravagant composition showing clearly royalty's taste for splendour. The staircase served as a majestic backdrop on many occasions. Saint-Simon described the arrival of the 11-year-old Princess Marie Adélaïde of Savoy at Fontainebleau on 5 November 1696 for her betrothal to the Duke of Burgundy. "The entire Court was assembled waiting to receive them on the horseshoe staircase, with the crowd standing below, a magnificent sight. The King led in the princess, so small that she seemed to be emerging from his pocket, walked very slowly along the terrace and then to the Queen Mother's apartments which were to become hers...".

The Farewell – On 20 April 1814 the Emperor Napoleon appeared at the top of the horseshoe staircase; it was 1pm. The foreign army commissioners in charge of escorting him away were waiting in their carriages at the foot of the steps. Napoleon started to walk down the staircase with great dignity, his hand resting on the stone balustrade, his face white with contained emotion. He stopped for a moment while contemplating his guards standing to attention, then moved forward to the group of officers surrounding the Eagle, led by General Petit. His farewell speech, deeply moving, was both an appeal to the spirit of patriotism and a parting tribute to those who had followed him throughout his career. After embracing the general, Bonaparte kissed the flag, threw himself into one of the carriages and was whisked away amid the tearful shouts of his soldiers.

★ **Cour de la Fontaine** – The fountain at the edge of the pond *(Étang des Carpes)* used to yield remarkably clear water. This was kept exclusively for the king's use and to that end the spring was guarded by two sentinels night and day.

The present fountain dates back to 1812 and is crowned by a statue of Ulysses. The surrounding buildings feature stone masonry and the whole ensemble forms a pleasant courtyard. At the far end, the Galerie François Ier is fronted by a terrace; it rests on a row of arches which once opened onto the king's bathroom suite.

The **Aile de la Belle cheminée** on the right was built by Primaticcio around 1565. The name originated from the fireplace that adorned the vast first-floor hall until the 18C. At that point in history Louis XV – who had turned the room into a theatre and rechristened it Aile de l'Ancienne Comédie – dismantled the fireplace, and the low-relief carvings were scattered. The monumental external steps consist of a dog-legged staircase with two straight flights in the Italian style.

On the left the Queen Mothers' and Pope's wing ends in the Grand Pavillion built by Gabriel.

★**Étang des Carpes (Carp Pond)** – In the centre of the pond – alive with carp – stands a small pavilion built under Henri IV, renovated under Louis XIV and restored by Napoleon. It was used for refreshments and light meals.

The pavillon of the Étang des Carpes

★**Porte Dorée** – Dated 1528, this gatehouse is part of an imposing pavilion. It was the official entrance to the palace until Henri IV built the Ponte du Baptistère. The paintings by Primaticcio have all been restored and the tympanum sports a stylised salamander, François I's emblem. On the two upper levels are Italian-style loggias. The first floor – its loggia sealed off by large bay windows – used to house Mme de Maintenon's suite.

The ballroom is flanked by an avenue of lime trees. The view from the bay windows is splendid and it is regrettable that the initial plans to build an open-air loggia were changed on account of the climate. The east end of the two-storeyed chapel dedicated to St Saturnin can be seen in the distance.

★**Porte du Baptistère** – The gateway opens onto the Oval Court. The base of the gateway is the rustic entrance with decorative sandstone that once held the drawbridge across the old moat. It opened onto the Cour du Cheval-Blanc and was designed by Primaticcio. It is crowned by a wide arch surmounted by a dome. The door is named after the christening of Louis XIII and his two sisters, Élisabeth and Chrétienne, celebrated with great pomp on a dais on 14 September 1606.

★**Cour Ovale** ⊘ – This is by far the most ancient and the most interesting courtyard of Fontainebleau Palace. The site was the bailey of the original stronghold; of the latter there remains only the keep, named after St Louis, although it was probably built prior to his reign. François Ier incorporated it into the structure he had erected on the foundations of the old castle, shaped like an oval or rather a polygon with rounded corners. Under Henri IV, the courtyard lost its shape, although not its name; the east side was enlarged, the wings were aligned and squared by two new pavilions framing the new Porte du Baptistère. The general layout of the palace was preserved.

Cour des Offices – Its entrance faces the Porte du Baptistère and is guarded by two arresting sandstone heads depicting Hermes, sculpted by Gilles Guérin in 1640. The Cour des Offices was built by Henri IV in 1609; it is a huge oblong, sealed off on three sides by austere buildings alternating with low pavilions. With its imposing porch executed in the style of city gates, it bears a strong resemblance to a square. Walk through the gate and admire its architecture from Place d'Armes; the sandstone front presents rusticated work and has a large niche as its centrepiece.

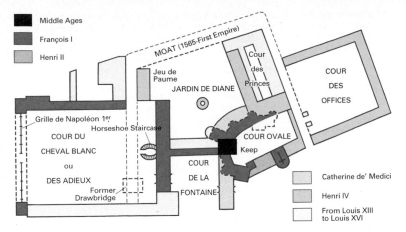

- Middle Ages
- François I
- Henri II

MOAT (1565-First Empire)

Jeu de Paume
JARDIN DE DIANE

Cour des Princes

COUR DES OFFICES

Grille de Napoléon 1er
Horseshoe Staircase
COUR DU
CHEVAL BLANC
ou
DES ADIEUX
Former Drawbridge

COUR DE LA FONTAINE

COUR OVALE
Keep

- Catherine de' Medici
- Henri IV
- From Louis XIII to Louis XVI

Continue the tour of the palace exterior. The east and north wings of the Cour des Princes are two functional buildings designed or redesigned under Louis XV to provide further accommodation for members of the court.

★**Jardin de Diane** – The queen's formal garden created by Catherine de' Medici was designed by Henri IV and bordered by an orangery on its northern side. In the 19C the orangery was torn down and the park turned into a landscape garden. Diana's fountain, an elegant display of stonework dated 1603, has survived in the middle of the grounds. It has now resumed its original appearance; the four bronze dogs formerly exhibited in the Louvre Museum sit obediently at the feet of their mistress, the hunting goddess.

★★★Grands Appartements ⊙

The main apartments are reached by the stucco staircase (**a**), the Galerie des Fastes (**b**) and the Galerie des Assiettes (**c**) which features 128 beautifully decorated pieces of Sèvres porcelain.

★**Chapelle de la Trinité** – The chapel takes its name from the Trinitarian church set up on the premises by St Louis. Henri IV had the sanctuary reinforced by vaulting and then decorated. Martin Fréminet (1567-1619), one of the lesser-known followers of Michelangelo, painted the arches with strong, vigorous scenes characterised by perspective and a daring use of foreshortening. The scenes represent the mystery of the Redemption and a number of figures from the Old Testament. It was in this chapel that Louis XV was wedded to Marie Leszczynska in 1725 and that Louis Napoleon, later to be Napoleon III, was christened in 1810.

★★★**Galerie de François Ier** – This gallery was built from 1528-30 and was originally open on both sides, resembling a covered passageway. When Louis XVI enlarged it in 1786, he filled in the windows giving onto Diana's garden. A set of false French windows was fitted for reasons of symmetry. The greater part of the decoration – closely combining fresco and stucco work – was supervised by Rosso, while the wood panelling was entrusted to an Italian master carpenter. François I's monogram and his emblem the salamander were widely represented.

The scenes are difficult to interpret and there are no enlightening documents, though they seem to split into two groups, one on either side of the central bay which is adorned with an oval painting depicting two figures: Danaë by Primaticcio and the Nymph of Fontainebleau (1860) after Rosso.

The east side, near a bust of François Ier, features mostly violent scenes, perhaps referring to the recent misfortunes of the French king (the defeat of Pavia, the king's captivity in Madrid), the inescapable nature of war and death (the battle between the Centaurs and the Lapiths, Youth and Old Age, the Destruction of the Greek fleet). Beneath the vignette depicting Venus and Love at the edge of a pond, note the miniature picture set in a tablet, representing the château around 1540 with both the gallery and the Porte Dorée clearly visible.

On the west side, near the entrance, the decor exemplifies the sacred qualities of the royal function – Sacrifice, the Unity of the State – and the concept of filial piety in the old-fashioned sense of the word (the twins Cleobis and Biton): the king, his mother Louise of Savoy and his sister Marguerite d'Angoulême were devoted to one another.

The most striking scene is the portrait of an elephant whose caparison bears the royal monogram; the pachyderm no doubt symbolises the perennity of the monarchy.

★★ Escalier du Roi – The staircase was built in 1749, under Louis XV, in what was once the bedchamber of the Duchess of Étampes, François I's favourite. The murals – the history of Alexander the Great – were by Primaticcio (note Alexander taming Bucephalus above the door) and dell'Abbate (Alexander placing Homer's books in a chest, on the far wall). Primaticcio's stucco work is highly original; the upper frieze is punctuated by caryatids with elongated bodies.

★★★ Salle de Bal (Ballroom) – This room (30m/100ft long and 10m/33ft wide) was traditionally reserved for banquets and formal receptions. It was begun under François Ier and completed by Philibert Delorme under Henri II. A thorough restoration programme has revived the dazzling frescoes and paintings by Primaticcio and his pupil dell'Abbate. The marquetry of the parquet floor, completed under Louis-Philippe, echoes the splendid coffered ceiling, richly highlighted with silver and gold. The monumental fireplace features two telamones, cast after Antique statues in the Capitol Museum in Rome.

Appartements de Mme de Maintenon – Note the delicate wainscoting in the Grand Salon, most of which was executed in the 17C.

★★ Appartements royaux – At the time of François Ier, Fontainebleau featured a single suite of apartments laid out around the Oval Court. Towards 1565, the regent Catherine de' Medici gave orders to double the curved building between the Oval Court and Diana's Garden. Subsequently, the royal bedrooms, closets and private salons overlooked Diana's Garden. The original suite now houses antechambers, guard-rooms and reception rooms where the king used to entertain his guests.

Salle des Gardes (1) – Late-16C ceiling and frieze.

Salon du Donjon – A wide arch leads from the Salle du Buffet (**2**) to a chamber in the oldest tower of the castle. Until the reign of Henri IV this sombre room was occupied by French kings, who used it as a bedroom (**3**) hence its other name, the St Louis Bedroom. The equestrian low-relief sculpture (c 1600) portraying Henri IV on the fireplace came from the Belle Cheminée *(see above)*. It was carved by Mathieu Jacquet.

Salon Louis XIII (4) – It was here that Louis XIII was born on 27 September 1601. His birth is evoked by the coffered ceiling which depicts Cupid riding a dolphin (the word *dauphin* means both dolphin and heir to the throne). The panel with painted wainscoting is crowned by a set of 11 pictures by Ambroise Dubois; the Romance between Theagenes and Chariclea, works dating from c 1610.

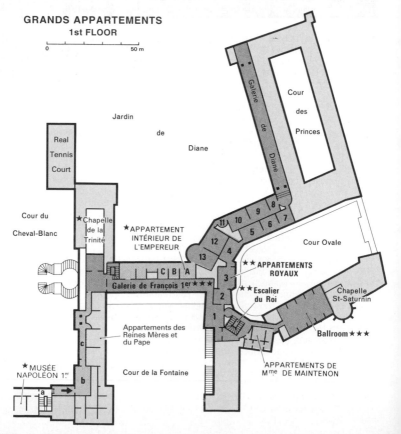

GRANDS APPARTEMENTS
1st FLOOR

La Chambre de l'Impératrice

Salon François Ier (5) – Of Primaticcio's work there remains only the fireplace.

Salon des Tapisseries (6) – This room, having been the queen's chamber, the guard-room and the queen's first antechamber, became the empress's principal drawing room in 1804, the guard-room once more in 1814 and finally the Tapestry Salon in 1837.

The fireplace dates from 1731 and the Renaissance ceiling in pine wood is the work of Poncet (1835). The furniture was made during the Second Empire (mid 19C). The tapestries telling the story of Psyche were manufactured in Paris in the first half of the 17C.

Antichambre de l'Impératrice (7) – Formerly the queen's guard-room, this chamber was built on the site of the old royal staircase; the ceiling and panelling are both dated 1835. The Gobelins tapestries, executed after cartoons by Le Brun, illustrate the four seasons. The Second Empire furniture features a console, a carved-oak writing desk (Fourdinois, 1865) and a set of armchairs of English inspiration. Note the two Indian-style enamel vases produced by the Sèvres factory.

Galerie de Diane – This long gilt passageway (80m/263ft) was decorated during the Restoration and turned into a library under the Second Empire.

Salon blanc or **petit salon de la Reine (8)** – In 1835 the room was decorated with furnishings from an earlier period: Louis XV wainscoting, Louis XVI fireplace inlaid with bronze etc. The furniture is Empire: chairs in gilt wood by Jacob Frères, settee, armchairs and chairs from St-Cloud, mahogany console and heads of fantastic animals in bronzed, gilt wood (Jacob Desmalter).

Grand Salon de l'Impératrice (9) – This drawing room, formerly the queen's gaming room, features a ceiling painted by Berthélemy; the scene is Minerva crowning the Muses.

The furniture dates from the reign of Louis XVI (chests by Stöckel and Beneman, seats upholstered with painted satin, a carpet made by the Savonnerie works) or from the First Empire (seats and chests by Jacob-Desmalters, the so-called

"Seasons Table" made of Sèvres porcelain and painted by Georget in 1806-1807, and a carpet rewoven to an old design) The two sets of furniture are displayed in turn.

Chambre de l'Impératrice (10) – This used to be the queen's bedroom. The greater part of the ceiling was designed for Anne of Austria in 1644; the wood panelling, the fireplace and the top of the alcove were created for Marie Leszczynska in 1747 and the doors with arabesque motifs were installed for Marie-Antoinette in 1787. The brocaded silk was rewoven according to the original pattern in Lyon at the end of Louis XVI's reign. Among the furniture note Marie-Antoinette's bed, designed in 1787 by Hauré, Séné and Laurent, a set of armchairs attributed to Jacob Frères and several commodes by Stöckel and Beneman (1786). The vases are Sèvres porcelain.

Boudoir de la Reine (11) – This delightful room was designed by Marie-Antoinette. The wainscoting was painted by Bourgois and Touzé after sketches by the architect Rousseau. The ceiling – representing sunrise – is the work of Berthélemy. The roll-top writing desk and the work table were made by Riesener in 1786.

Salle du Trône (12) – This was the king's bedroom from Henri IV to Louis XVI; Napoleon converted it into the throne room. The ornate mural paintings, dating from several periods, were harmonised in the 18C. Above the fireplace is a full-length portrait of Louis XIII, painted in Philippe de Champaigne's studio.

Salle du Conseil (13) – This room was given a semicircular extension in 1773. The ceiling and panelling are splendid examples of Louis XV decoration.
Five pictures by Boucher adorn the ceiling, representing the four seasons and Apollo, conqueror of Night. The wainscoting presents an alternation of allegorical figures painted in blue or pink monochrome by Van Loo and Jean-Baptiste Pierre.

★**Appartement Intérieur de l'Empereur** ⊘ – Napoleon had his suite installed in the wing built by Louis XVI, on the garden side running parallel with the François Ier Gallery.

Chambre de Napoléon (A) – Most of the decoration – dating from the Louis XVI period – has survived. The furniture is typically Empire.

Petite chambre à coucher (B) – A little private study which Bonaparte furnished with a day bed in gilded iron.

Salon de l'Abdication (C) – According to tradition, this is the room in which the famous abdication document was signed on 6 April 1814. The Empire furniture in this red drawing room dates back to that momentous time.
The François Ier Gallery leads to the Vestibule du Fer-à-cheval, at the top of the curved steps of the same name. This was the official entrance to the palace from the late 17C onwards. Both the gallery of the chapel and the Appartements des Reines-Mères give onto this hall.

★**Musée chinois** ⊘ – This small museum, commissioned by Empress Eugénie on the ground floor of the Gros Pavillon, comes as a surprise because of the contrast between the comfortable, heavy furniture and the slender elegance of the objects on show. The collection was originally the booty captured during the Franco-British conflict with China in 1860, especially as a result of the ransacking of the imperial palace. The following year, a delegation of Siamese ambassadors completed the collection with a number of opulent presents, an event which was faithfully recorded in a painting by Gérôme.
The tour begins in the **antechamber** decorated with two luxurious Siamese palanquins. The **"nouveaux salons"** beyond are decorated with crimson wall hangings, padded armchairs, ebony furniture and objects from China and Siam. Most of the collection, however, is to be seen in the **cabinet de laque** decorated with 15 panels from an 18C Chinese fan. Note the four large tapestries on the ceiling and the huge glass-fronted cabinet filled to the brim with objects, including a copy of the Siamese royal crown.

★Musée Napoléon Ier

The **museum** ⊘ is dedicated to the Emperor and his family; it occupies 15 rooms on the ground level and first floor of the Louis XV wing. Exhibits include portraits (paintings and sculptures), silverware, arms, medals, ceramics (Imperial service), clothing (coronation robes, uniforms) and personal memorabilia. Thanks to the numerous works of art and furniture adorning their interior, these apartments have kept their princely character.
The rooms on the first floor evoke the Coronation (paintings by François Gérard), the Emperor's various military campaigns, his daily life (remarkable folding desk by Jacob Desmalter), the Empress Marie-Louise in formal attire or painting the Emperor's portrait (picture by Alexandre Menjaud) and the birth of Napoleon's son, the future King of Rome (cradles).
The ground floor presents the Emperor's close relations. Each of the seven rooms is devoted to a member of the family: Napoleon's mother, his brothers Joseph, Louis, Jérôme and sisters Elisa, Pauline and Caroline.

Petits Appartements et galerie des Cerfs ⊙

These rooms are located on the ground floor below the François Ier Gallery and the Royal Suite overlooking the Jardin de Diane.

Petits Appartements de Napoléon Ier – This suite comprises François I's former bathroom suite (located beneath the gallery and converted into private rooms under Louis XV for the king, Mme de Pompadour and Mme du Barry), and the ground floor of the new Louis XVI wing, situated under the Imperial Suite. The rooms opening onto the garden have been decorated with Louis XV wainscoting and Empire furniture.

★**Appartements de l'Impératrice Joséphine** – This suite of rooms adorned with Louis XV panelling was designed for Joséphine in 1808. It lies beneath the grand royal suite.

The study, with its large rotunda, is located beneath the Council Chamber (1st floor). The Empire furniture here has a feminine touch: Marie-Louise's tambour frame, her easel etc. The Salon Jaune constitutes one of the palace's most perfect examples of Empire decoration. The gold-coloured wall hangings provide an elegant setting for Jacob-Desmalter's choice furniture set off by a large Aubusson carpet with a white background.

★**Galerie des Cerfs** – The gallery is decorated with numerous deer heads (only the antlers are genuine). The mural paintings were renovated under Napoleon III; they show palatial residences at the time of Henri IV, seen in perspective. It was in this gallery that Queen Christina of Sweden had her favourite, Monaldeschi, assassinated in 1657. The original casts used to make Primaticcio's 1540 replicas of Antique statues are on display in the gallery.

★GARDENS

These consist of the Jardin de Diane *(see above)*, the Landscape Garden, the parterre and the park.

Follow the route indicated on the map below.

★**Grotte du Jardin des Pins** – This rare ornamental composition carved in sandstone reveals the popular taste, copied from the Italians, for ponds, man-made features and bucolic landscapes in vogue towards the end of François I's reign. The rusticated arches are supported by giant telamones. The frescoes have disappeared.

★**Jardin Anglais** – The garden was created in 1812 on the site of former gardens – featuring a pine grove – redesigned under Louis XIV and abandoned during the Revolution. The Bliaud or Blaut fountain – which gave its name to the palace – plays in a small octagonal basin in the middle of the garden.

Parterre – This formal garden was laid out under François Ier, reviewed under Henri IV and eventually redesigned by Le Nôtre. The Tiber and Romulus Basins take their name from a Classical-style sculpture which adorned them in the 16C

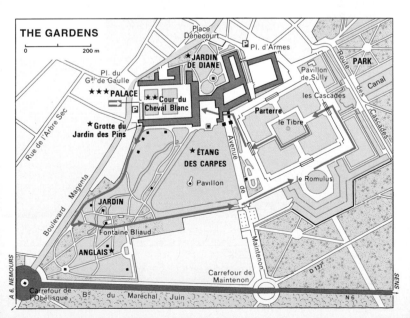

THE GARDENS

and then the 17C. The Tiber – melted down during the Revolution – was cast after the original (in the Louvre) a second time and is now back in the place Louis XIV had assigned it. Skirt the Canal du Bréau to get a broad view of the palace.

Until the 18C, a series of cascades marked the end of this first group of tiered fountains. At present there remains only a basin of the same name, its ornate niches adorned with marble statues.

Park – The park was created by Henri IV, who filled the canal in 1609 and had the grounds planted with elms, pines and fruit trees. Sixty years before the installation of the Grand Canal at Versailles, this dazzling sight was a great novelty for the *Ancien Régime*, as were the aquatic displays.

ADDITIONAL SIGHT

Musée Napoléonien d'Art et d'Histoire Militaires ⊘ (**AY M**) – The museum contains around one hundred figures, complete with full equipment and weaponry: swordsmen and veterans from the Imperial Grand Army, soldiers who fought for the conquest of Algeria and the Second Empire.

The first floor houses a **collection** of statutory **swords and sabres**★ dating from the 19C.

EXCURSIONS

Croix du Calvaire – *5km/3mi from the Palace. Leave by boulevard Maréchal-Leclerc (direction ② on the map above). Just before the swimming pool, take the second turning on the left and proceed along Route de la Reine Amélie.*

Almost a mile after the road starts to rise, turn left to reach the esplanade and calvary; admire the fine **view** of the town nestling amidst woodlands.

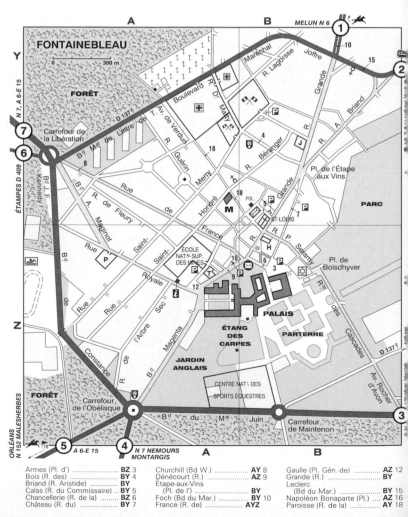

Stopover

BUDGET

Croquembouche – 43 Rue de France, ☎ 01 64 22 01 57. Small convivial restaurant, cosy and refined atmosphere. Fixed menu: 125F.

OUR SELECTION

Legris et Parc – 36 Rue Paul Seramy, ☎ 01 64 22 24 24, fax 01 64 22 22 05. This hotel and restaurant with its pleasant terrace was the Marquis de Cavoye's former mansion. Double room from 460F, fixed menu: 120F.

LUXURY

L'Aigle Noir – 27 Place Napoléon, ☎ 01 60 74 60 00, fax 01 60 74 60 01. Situated near the palace, this luxury establishment is fitted with the most modern equipment and pleasantly decorated. Double room from 1050F. Fixed menu: 180F in the restaurant.

On the town

Le Montijo – 27 Place Napoléon. Piano bar of the Aigle Noir Hotel (see above): jazz-band, piano or guitar concerts in convivial atmosphere on Thursday and sometimes Friday evenings.

Le Diam's – 7 Rue Denecourt. Bar serving cocktails in huge glasses inside coconut shells filled with foaming dry ice... for those who like a change of scenery (parrot on the edge of the glass and monkey up a palm tree). Karaoke every night.

Billard Adacémie – 14 Rue des Pins. Billiard club open to the public from 2pm to 1am.

Auberge de l'Île – Chez Fernand – 21 Quai de la République in Samois-sur-Seine. Famous bar where guitarist Django Reinhardt would often have a drink with actors Bourvil and Fernandel or poet Jacques Prévert. Numerous mementoes of jazz musicians; the River Seine flows past the terrace. Concerts sometimes given on Saturday nights until dawn.

Avon; By-Thomery – *Leave Fontainebleau by Boulevard du Maréchal-Juin and at the junction, Carrefour de Maintenon, fork left to D 137ᴱ.*

Église St-Pierre – Built in the 11C, this church features a Romanesque nave surmounted by diagonal arches. The belltower was erected in the 13C, the Renaissance door dates from the 15C. The Gothic chancel, the work of architect Jean du Montceau, was completed in 1555. Note, among the tombstones, that of the Marquess of Monaldeschi, the favourite of Queen Christina of Sweden who had him assassinated at Fontainebleau in 1657. The recently-restored porch was erected in the 18C.

Leave Avon and proceed along D 137 then turn right on entering By-Thomery.

Atelier de Rosa Bonheur ⊘ – Rosa Bonheur (1822-99), an animal painter widely acclaimed by her contemporaries, bought the château de By in 1859 to satisfy her need for space (she had numerous pets) and quiet. Empress Eugénie paid her a visit when she was awarded the French order of merit, the Légion d'Honneur. Another famous visitor, Buffalo Bill, gave her one of his outfits, which is still exhibited in the corridor.
The tour includes the study (portrait of the artist by Achille Fould, banker and government minister to Napoleon III), the studio (stuffed animals, deer antlers, her last, uncompleted picture) and a closet furnished with her bed, her wardrobe and a glass cabinet of memorabilia.

Musée départemental Stéphane-Mallarmé in Vulaines-sur-Seine ⊘ – *Leave Fontainebleau on the Avon road then take the first turning on the left after the Valvins bridge.* Housed in **Stéphane Mallarmé**'s former home on the banks of the Seine, this little museum gives an insight into the life of the poet who was so fond of this picturesque spot. "The water, light and greenery all play music..." On the upper floor, the apartments have been restored and reflect his lifestyle quite accurately. They contain personal memorabilia and the original furniture. Visitors can also see his small garden, which has been carefully restored.

Château de Bourron ⊘ – *7km/4.5mi south. Michelin map 237 fold 37. Leave Fontainebleau by ④ the N 7 and turn left at Bourron-Marlotte.*
Built on the remains of a medieval stronghold in the late 16C, the château consists of an austere central block flanked by two perpendicular pavilions; these are fronted by two low wings (stables). The stone and brick patterns of the façades and the horse-shoe staircase are reminiscent of the Cour du Cheval-Blanc at Fontainebleau. On the northern side, a swivel bridge spanning the moat leads to another horse-shoe staircase. The parterre to the south affords a good view of the stately and harmonious proportions of the château. Note the delightful Ste-Sévère spring, which flows into the Grand Canal to the north of the park. Louis XV came to the château de Bourron to meet his father-in-law Stanislas Leszczynski, the dethroned King of Poland, who was staying on the estate.

Forêt de FONTAINEBLEAU★★★
FONTAINEBLEAU FOREST
Michelin map 106 folds 44, 45, 46

This lovely (25 000ha/62 000 acres) forest is largely State-owned and has always provided magnificent hunting grounds. It is immensely popular with ramblers and climbing enthusiasts.

GENERAL APPEARANCE OF THE FOREST

Geological formation – The relief of the forested area comprises a series of parallel sandstone ridges running in an east-west direction. These ridges are thought to be the result of a tropical spell during the Tertiary Era, when strong winds gradually accumulated sand deposits in this part of the Paris Basin. The sand dunes subsequently solidified into a hard sandstone matrix and were then buried beneath deposits of

A PRACTICAL GUIDE TO THE FOREST

Forests have a fragile ecosystem and should be protected as much as possible. In particular, it is forbidden to light fires, leave rubbish, pull up plants or rip branches from the trees, or walk elsewhere than along the footpaths.
Please comply with the safety instructions indicated near army training grounds.

Hiking – Over the past few years, many more footpaths have come into being and there is now a wide choice. The paths are marked with one or more identifying signs to guide you:

Grande randonnée (GR) – White and red.

Petite randonnée (PR) – Yellow.

Tour du massif de Fontainebleau (TMF) – Green and white (superimposed lines).

The marks referring to the Denecourt and Colinet paths (blue), which are older than the others, have been retained on certain maintained footpaths.
For full details of all these marks and signs, consult the *Guide des Sentiers de Promenade dans le Massif Forestier de Fontainebleau* published by the Association des Amis de la Forêt de Fontainebleau (on sale at the tourist office and in bookshops).

Cycling — Paved forest roads are popular with cyclists.

Mountain bikes are permitted in certain reserved areas. Mountain bike rides and cycle hire are available from Top Loisirs, 73 bis Avenue de Fontainebleau, Veneux-les-Sablons; ☎ 01 60 70 10 88.

Equitation – Several stables hire horses for rides in the forest:

Centre équestre de Recloses, Chemin du Clos-de-la-Bonne à Recloses; ☎ 01 64 24 21 10.

Centre hippique de Marlotte, 23 Rue Allongée, Bourron-Marlotte; ☎ 01 64 45 94 04

Climbing – Numerous sites have been officially approved and are maintained for rock climbers. For information, contact the Club Alpin Français, 24 Rue Laumière, Paris; ☎ 01 53 72 88 00.

Orienteering – Beginners' courses and equipment hire from Top Loisirs (for address and phone number, see above).

Trim course – Situated at La Faisanderie near the Carrefour du Coq.

The Fontainebleau forest

Beauce limestone, which resulted in the preservation of the area's rolling landscape. Where the upper layer of Beauce limestone was spared by erosion, the valley sides culminate in small **hillocks**. They reach a maximum height of 144m/475ft and bear some of the forest's most charming groves.

Where the limestone has eroded revealing the sandstone, the resultant rocky areas are known locally as **platières**.

These **moorlands** covered with heather and other shrubs are often cracked and dotted with ponds. When the sandstone layer has many crevices and holes, water seeps through and starts to wash away the underlying sands. The upper sandstone strata is no longer supported and crumbles as a result, producing picturesque rocky clusters, the famous Fontainebleau **rochers**. **Vales** or **plains** averaging 40-80m/130-260ft in height are found where the sandstone layer has been eroded away, exposing the sand or the Brie marl and limestone beneath. The planting of conifers fertilises the soil, making it possible to grow beeches. These produce humus and are eventually replaced by oaks, the ideal tree species for a forest.

Forest layout – The forest is divided into 747 plots maintained in such a way as to provide the finest possible trees.

Most of the forest (9/10ths) consists of copses and thickets; the remainder is moorland and rock. Sessile oaks cover 8 000ha/19 768 acres, Norway pines 7 500ha/18 532 acres, and beeches 1 500ha/3 706 acres. The other species (hornbeam, birches, maritime and Corsican pines, larches, chestnuts, acacias, and service trees) are reminders of older attempts at acclimatisation or the remains of lightly-wooded moorland. 416ha/1 028 acres constitute a biological reserve.

Denecourt-Colinet footpaths – Footpaths laid out by the "two Sylvains" (Denecourt and Colinet) take tourists to the most famous spots in the forest. Sylvain Denecourt served with Napoleon's Grande Armée. He removed rocks and boulders from caves, cleared the finest beauty spots, and laid out 150km/93mi of waymarked footpaths. On carefully selected trees or rocks, discreet blue lines topped by numbers (1 to 16) indicate the main paths. Blue letters (also explained in the guide edited by the Amis de la Forêt) and stars are also used as markings on specific sights. Colinet, once a civil servant with the Ponts et Chaussées (Ministry of Public Buildings and Works) continued where his predecessor had left off. The markings were completed, after 1975, by the inclusion of white enamelled signposts bordered in green at all the main junctions.

"Bleau" and "Bleausards" – By 1910, a few climbing enthusiasts from the Club Alpin Français had already begun to train at Le Cuvier-Châtillon, la Dame-Jeanne, l'Éléphant etc, camping overnight near their favourite rock if necessary.

In the inter-war years, the idea of a rock climbing school became commonplace among climbers in France. Fontainebleau was the ideal spot for climbers living in Paris, especially for the members of the Groupe de Haute Montagne.

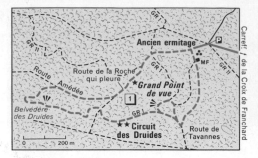

Described by one of the great mountain guides of Chamonix as "rocks ideal for scouring pots and pans", the compact sandstone in the forest provide a challenge and a few valuable examples of potential difficulties: overhanging ledges, and slabs of rocks which, if there are many in succession, are a good preparation for climbs in the Alps, Himalayas or Andes. Many a well-known climber has come here to train.

Since then, the "Bleausards" have continued to practise their sport in the forest. There are more than one hundred climbs marked out with arrows on the rocks.

Each of them is a succession of climbs, descents and, in some cases, jumps; there are never any walks along paths.

★★GORGES DE FRANCHARD

⬚1 Round tour starting from La Croix de Franchard

30min to 2hr on foot there and back.

From the Croix de Franchard crossroads, drive to the spacious shady esplanade at the Ermitage de Franchard, a very popular spot at weekends.

Ancien ermitage de Franchard – A hermitage developed here in the 12C, and in the 13C a community moved in to look after the pilgrims. By the 19C, the pilgrimage had become a country fête held on the Tuesday after Whitsun. Today only the chapel walls remain, incorporated into the forest warden's house.

★**Grand Point de vue** – *30min on foot there and back.* Beyond the warden's garden skirt the sandy track on the left and climb towards the rocks without changing direction. This leads to a very sandy road (route de Tavannes); after 300m/330yd a mushroom-shaped rock will appear ahead. At the plateau turn right and on reaching the rock bear left to a bench overlooking the ravine. The view of the gorge is breathtaking.

To return to the hermitage, walk down three steps and bear left. This path returns to the route de Tavannes.

★★**Circuit des Druides** – *2hr* – Beyond the Grand Point de vue shown on the map, go down three steps and turn right. Follow the blue markings indicating Denecourt-Colinet path 7 which wends its way through a labyrinth of half-splintered boulders, some of them forming overhangs. At the bottom of the "gorge", cross a sandy road beside an isolated oak tree and climb back up among the rocks (follow the "⬚" signs) to the "second belvedere" marked by a star. Remain on the edge of the plateau. There is a wonderful view of the gorge and across the **Belvédère des Druides** (marked "P"). Go down to the easterly footpath and, at the bottom of the gorge, join the "route Amédée". Turn right. At the first crossroads, turn left onto the Route de la Roche-qui-Pleure which climbs back up the hill and through a gap in the side of the plateau to the hermitage. *(Do not follow the path with the blue signs; it zigzags its way up through the rocks on the left.)*

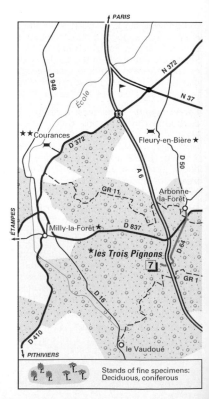

Stands of fine specimens:
Deciduous, coniferous

★GORGES D'APREMONT

② Round tour starting from Barbizon

10km/6mi – about 3hr 30min on foot

Leave Barbizon by allée aux Vaches, the continuation of Grande Rue, a magnificent tree-lined avenue that was so well-known to artists. This road leads to the **Carrefour du Bas-Bréau**, an intersection near a cluster of trees now protected by a preservation order spearheaded by a group of artists.

★**Chaos d'Apremont** – *45min on foot there and back from the crossroads.*
Follow the path marked in blue left of the refreshment chalet *(buvette)* and continue up amid the rocks; at the top bear right and follow the edge of the plateau. Views are over the wooded slopes of the gorge and the Bière plain. The path veers left: a clump of acacia and pine trees marks the entrance to the **Caverne des Brigands** *(take a torch)*.
Return to the car.
Take the Sully road up through the woods to the bare plateau high above the distant ravines.

★**Grand Belvédère d'Apremont** – *15min on foot.* 1 700m/just over a mile from the crossroads called Le Bas-Bréau, park at the junction with the "road" to Le Cul-de-Chaudron. Progress along the plateau and turn left onto the path with blue markings. At a crossroads with a Denecourt-Colinet sign, turn right.
The path runs downhill past boulders and rocks. Bear left, remaining above the rocks. Below is the "gorge", its slopes strewn with blocks of stone. To the west is the Plaine de Bière.
Return to the car and to Carrefour du Bas-Bréau.

★★**Circuit du Désert** – *3hr 30min on foot.* This part of the forest is famous for its barren and desert-like appearance that was so well known to artists and, later, to film directors.
Take the old road from Barbizon to Fontainebleau; after a mile turn south into the road to le Clair Bois. Take the first lane on the right, Route de la Chouette, over a pass and down to the Désert d'Apremont, a valley dotted with oddly-shaped boulders. Bear left into path no 6 marked in blue. On reaching the rock resembling an animal with two snouts (reference N), bear right. At the Carrefour du Désert take the blue-marked path which lies between Route du Clair-Bois and Route de

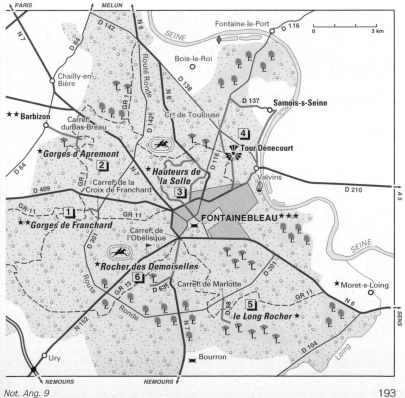

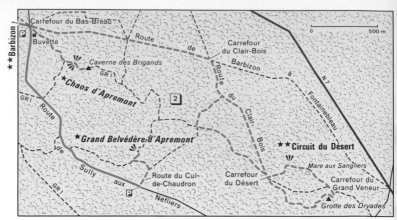

Milan; it leads to a ravine framed by boulders, then along a rocky ledge.
Immediately after the Grotte des Dryades, marked with a star, bear left and walk down path "6-6" and up the far side of the valley to the raised platform; the pond called Mare aux Sangliers lies to the left. The prominent part of the plateau offers a good **view** of the Désert d'Apremont and the Bière plain.

Return to the car via carrefour du Désert and route du Clair-Bois.

LE LONG ROCHER

⑤ Round tour starting from Carrefour de Marlotte

1.5km/1mi – then 2hr on foot there and back

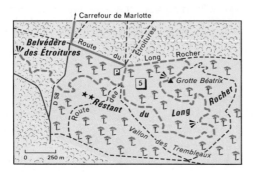

From Route Ronde branch off towards Marlotte.

After 0.5mi, before reaching a steep slope, turn left into Route du Long Rocher, a sandy forest lane (ONF board: "Zone de Silence de la Malmontagne").

Park at the next crossroads (barrier).

Take Route des Etroitures (first turning on the right).

After 100yd, turn right onto path no 11, marked in blue.

Belvédère des Étroitures – *Trail marker U.* Admire the view of Marlotte and the Loing Valley.

Turn round and follow the blue-marked path which soon begins to wend its way between the boulders in the shade of the pine trees. It then winds here and there along a seemingly aimless route until it reaches the top of the plateau, the "Restant du Long-Rocher".

★★ **Restant du Long Rocher** – The edge of the plateau, strewn with boulders, offers several good views of the southern and northern areas of the forest through the pine trees. Return to blue path and continue in an easterly direction. Leave the plateau via the steep slope which includes Grotte Béatrix. Walk past a series of boulders used for exercise by mountaineering schools *(red arrows)*.

Further along, the path rises slightly; branch off left and take the steep, clearly marked track down. This leads back to Route du Long Rocher; bear left to return to the starting point.

LES TROIS PIGNONS

⑦ Round tour starting from Arbonne

2.5km/1.5mi – then 3hr on foot there and back

Leave from the southern end of Arbonne (junction of the Fontainebleau-Milly road.

Take the Milly road but immediately turn left into the Achères-la-Forêt road (D 64). After 1mi the road veers towards the motorway; turn right under it. Park the car. Les Trois Pignons massif is an unusual extension of Fontainebleau Forest: it is a stony, barren site, unique in Île-de-France, with dry valleys, eroded peaks and other peculiarities which are common to sandstone landscapes.

From the car park go straight ahead and follow the road past two houses on the right. At the corner of the fencing, bear right and walk to the edge of a sandy depression, to the starting point of Dene-court-Colinet path no 16.

On the other side of the depression, directly opposite the plaque, is the first blue mark. The path crosses a flat stretch of land dotted with boulders and leads past the platform of the old Noisy telegraph transmitter to the plateau. An hour's walk will bring you to a chestnut grove. The path follows the recesses of the impressive Gorge aux Chats and continues southeast and then south, crossing a sandy, rocky area cleared of trees.

★★ **Point de vue de la Vallée Close** – The edge of the plateau offers a good **view**★★ of the uplands. In the foreground, a monument crowned by a cross of Lorraine honours the local Resistance network.

The blue path then turns north and descends eastwards, avoiding the wide sandy track previously explored to lead through oak coppices and heathers back to the starting point.

Suggestions for additional tours:

– north of Fontainebleau ③ **Hauteurs de la Solle★** along **Route Louis-Philippe★** and **Route du Gros-Fouteau★** through ancient groves and then to the **Rochers du Mont Ussy★** where a pleasant path leads through pine trees;

– a round trip northeast of the town ④ taking in **Tour Dénecourt**, a 19C tower offering **panoramic views★**, and **Samois-sur-Seine,** an attractive and once-important town on the banks of the river;

– to the southwest ⑥, pleasant rambles through the Cirque des Demoiselles and to the **Rocher des Demoiselles★**.

FOURMIES

Population 14 505
Michelin map 53 fold 16 or 236 fold 29. Local map see L'AVESNOIS

Fourmies is a busy town which developed an important textile industry in the 19C; it is surrounded by huge forests and a series of lakes. The lakes were created by monks from Liessies and it is from them that the best-known of these, the **Étangs des Moines** with fishing, boating and swimming facilities, derive their name.

Écomusée de la région Fourmies-Trélon – The museum's aim is to preserve and promote the different economic and cultural aspects of life, past and present, in the region. Established with the help of the local population, the museum has branches specialising in different areas: industrial activity is featured at the Textile Museum *(see below)* and at the Glass Workshop-Museum, Trélon; rural activities at the Maison du Bocage in Sains du Nord

The environmental heritage can be seen in the natural setting of the Baives Hills (Monts de Baives) at Wallers-Trélon *(see L'AVESNOIS)* and along the **Observation trails** in **Wignehies** *(Sentiers d'Observation sur la Commune de Wignehies)* ⊙. An audio-visual presentation *(15min)* in the textile museum presents an overall view of the region and the museum satellites.

★ **Musée du Textile et de la Vie sociale** ⊙ – The museum, which is housed in an old spinning mill, displays a collection of textile machines from the late 19C to the present day, all in working order.

Photographic records, reconstructions – of a textile laboratory, a hosiery work-shop, and a street with a bar and shops – evoke the life of the locals over a century and retraces the events which marked their history (the strike of 1 May 1891 during which soldiers opened fire killing nine people in the crowd).

EUROPE on a single sheet:
Michelin Map 70, *at a scale of 1:3,000,000.*
Tourism, roads, relief, index of names.

FRANCE MINIATURE★

Michelin map 106 folds 28, 29

Access from Paris: *A 13 then A 12 to St-Quentin. Rejoin N 10 and head for Rambouillet. In Trappes, take D 23 to Élancourt.*

This theme park, laid out in Élancourt on a 5ha/12-acre site, is shaped like a gigantic relief map of France, bordered by lakes forming the coastline. In it are almost 2 000 models of the main sights and historic buildings in France, built to a scale of 1:30.

TOUR ⊙

Like Gulliver setting foot in Lilliput, visitors begin by climbing to the top of the Alps (altitude 9m/29ft!) for a panoramic view of France Miniature. In the middle of the mountains, plains and rivers is a network of footpaths that take visitors through all the French provinces and show them the most outstanding architectural sights and the most representative industrial developments. The Roman arena in Arles, the Pont du Gard, the Château de Chambord, the railway bridge at Gabarit (16m/52ft long), the Futuroscope in Poitiers, the Hospice de Beaune and the 10m/32ft high Eiffel Tower are as enthralling and interesting as Versailles, the dam at Bort-les-Orgues or the already famous Stade de France in St-Denis. Miniature trains, boats, planes and cars create a sense of movement amid the landscapes.

GUÎNES

Population 5 105
Michelin map 51 fold 2 or 236 fold 2

Guînes, now a busy cereal market town, was the seat of a powerful count, a vassal of the English crown for more than 200 years, from 1352 to 1558.

The Field of the Cloth of Gold – The famous encounter between **François I** of France and **Henry VIII** of England took place near Guînes, on the road to Ardres, in 1520. The 17-day meeting from 7 June now known as the Field of the Cloth of Gold *(Camp du Drap d'or)* was convened to discuss a possible Anglo-French alliance; however, it developed into a competition of one-upmanship.
François was staying in Ardres, Henry stayed with the count at Guînes castle; each was accompanied by his queen and a substantial court: the gentlemen of the Knight King were so sumptuously dressed that the contemporary writer Martin du Bellay was moved to note that "they carried their mills, their forests and their fields on their backs."

The Field of the Cloth of Gold by Bouterwek, Guînes

The camp was arranged around jousting rails. On one side the English king occupied a "crystal palace" which sparkled in the sun, on the other François I sheltered under a tent of gold brocade; the surroundings had been arranged by the painter Jean Bourdichon. This luxurious display proved fruitless however; Henry was irritated by the French King's extravagance, the crystal palace was damaged by the wind and he was toppled by his royal adversary during a contest.

Humiliated and angry, Henry returned to Gravelines and two weeks later made an alliance with the Emperor Charles V of Spain, undertaking not to enter into any fresh partnership with François for two years.

Musée municipal E.-Villez ⊘ – Numerous archeological remains, documents, objects, maps (Mercator atlas of 1609), engravings and paintings evoke the history of the town from its origins to the 20C.

FORÊT DE GUÎNES

The road from Guînes enters this hilly area which is densely covered with varied species (oaks, beech, hornbeam, birch) and extends (785ha/1940 acres) to the northern edge of the Boulonnais region.

The road ends at the **Clairière du Ballon.** To the left and slightly set back, the **Colonne Blanchard** in marble marks the spot where, on 7 January 1785, the balloon flown by Jean-Pierre Blanchard (1753-1809) and the American physician John Jeffries landed, having achieved the first aerial crossing of the Channel.

EXCURSIONS

Forteresse de Mimoyecques (MimoyecquesFort) ⊘ – *10km/6mi southwest by D 231 and D 249 from Landrethun-le-Nord.*

Because of its position 8km/5mi from the coast and 150km/93mi from London, Mimoyecques was chosen as the launch site for the formidable V3 howitzer, invented after the V1 and V2, to bombard London. To fire these shells the Germans had developed enormous, 130m/426ft long cannons. Work began in September 1943 when thousands of prisoners were forced to dig the 600m/1968ft rail tunnel under 30m/98ft of chalk, and the trenches where the cannon's were to be installed. The Allied forces bombed Mimoyecques from November 1943, and in July 1944 a Tallboy bomb pierced the concrete roof; this resulted in flooding which put an end to the works.

The huge scale of the project can still be seen, including the impressive tunnel where over 40 trains daily brought materials from Germany.

Ardres – *9km/5.5mi east on D 231.*

This pleasant and peaceful market town, where François I stayed during the Field of the Cloth of Gold, was prosperous in Gallo-Roman times and later became a frontier town coveted by the English and the Spanish. The town lake *(swimming, fishing, sailboarding facilities)* was formed over the old peat bogs, out of which turfs were cut for fuel from Antiquity until the 19C.

The triangular, paved main square is bordered by picturesque old houses with pointed roofs. The old 17C Carmelite chapel stands opposite the east end of the 14C-15C church.

GUISE

Population 5976
Michelin map 53 fold 15 or 236 fold 28

Guise (pronounced Gu-eez) lies in a pleasant setting at the bottom of the Oise Valley; despite its modern appearance the town has preserved an old district, near the church at the foot of the hill.

Elevated to a duchy by François I, Guise gave its name to an illustrious family – a junior branch of the House of Lorraine – whose most famous members were: **François de Guise** (1519-63) who defended Metz against Charles V of Spain, retook Calais from the English and who was assassinated; and **Henri de Guise** (1550-88), head of the Catholic League during the Wars of Religion, who was assassinated in the castle in Blois on the orders of Henri III.

Guise was the birthplace of **Camille Desmoulins** (1760-94), the son of a lieutenant in the bailiff's court. The most famous French journalist at the time of the Revolution, Desmoulins publicly denounced the violence and injustices being committed in its name and was guillotined as a traitor for saying so.

In 1914 General de Lanzerac's army held back German troops attempting so cross the Orse, thereby allowing the French troops time to regroup for the Battle of the Marne.

SIGHTS

★Château Fort des Ducs de Guise ⊙ – *Access from the town, beyond Église St-Pierre.*

The castle was built in medieval times (11C) from Ardennes sandstone. Later, in the 16C, it was one of the first fortresses in France to have bastions added to it, at the instigation of the first Dukes of Guise, Claude and François. Situated in the path of invaders of the Oise Valley, the castle was further reinforced by Vauban the following century. The buildings cover an area of 17ha/42 acres. After being subjected to artillery bombardments during the First World War, it was subsequently used as a quarry for materials and later as a rubbish tip.

In 1952 Maurice Duton, a local man, decided to save the castle with the help of young volunteers who were brought together under an organisation which they named the Club du Vieux Manoir.

Enter the castle through the restored 16C Porte Ducale which faces the town. From the Bastion de la Haute Ville cross the medieval passageway - which leads to the vaulted carriage entrance - to reach the prison and the large storeroom in which 3 000 men were garrisoned during sieges; continue along the vaulted passageway to the remains of the Palais du Gouverneur and the medieval keep. The foundations of the Collegiate Church, Eglise St-Gervais-St-Protais, are also visible. The guard-rooms in la Charbonnière and l'Allouette bastions have been turned into a museum exhibiting finds from excavations, including the coat of arms of François de Guise, the second Duke, and of his wife the Duchess of Este and Ferrara. Follow a series of underground passages to return to the Bastion de la Haute Ville and the Galerie des Lépreux.

Familistère Godin ⊙ – The creation of a workers' co-operative was the brainchild of Jean-Baptiste André Godin (1817-88), the founder of factories producing heating and cooking appliances. Godin was a daring businessman who wished to put his ideas about the welfare of mankind into practice by building a "Social Palace" (1859-1883), which included 500 modern homes, schools, swimming-pool, theatre, wash-house, garden and general store. In 1880, Godin created a co-operative for capital and labour and ownership of the factory was gradually transferred to the workers.

The dwellings, built around courtyards with glazing supported on wooden or metal frameworks, can still be seen today. On each floor, walkways allow public access. The east wing houses JB Godin's flat (no 265 on the first floor) as well as a show-flat reconstructed as it was in 1880. The theatre is the venue of various events. On the other side of the River Oise are the Godin factories which still operate.

EXCURSION

Vadencourt – *Round trip of 17km/10mi - About 30min. Leave Guise by D 946 to Étreux and after 3km/2mi turn left onto D 693.*

The road offers a good **view** *(left)* over the Oise Valley. Follow D 693 into the valley of the Sambre canal (Canal de la Sambre à l'Oise) - which joins the Sambre to the Oise and the Noirieux, a tributary of the Oise - crossing it at Tupigny; D 66 follows the northwest side of the valley.

Popular with anglers, Vadencourt sits in a pleasant spot at the confluence of the Oise and the Noirieux rivers.

The 12C **church** has beautiful capitals.

From D 66 turn left beside the church; D 960 returns to Guise.

L'HAŸ-LES-ROSES

Population 29 591
Michelin map 101 fold 25 – Michelin plan 22

This town, located in the suburbs just south of Paris, is famed for its spectacular rose garden, occupying a corner of a pleasant **park**.

★★Roseraie (Rose Garden) ⊘ – The garden was created in 1892 and subsequently embellished by Jules Gravereaux, a man passionately fond of roses who was also one of the founders of the famous Parisian department store Le Bon Marché.

The flower beds are planted with thousands of wild and grafted roses from all over the world. The gardens also feature a display of arches, trellises and colonnades for the climbing varieties which will delight visitors. The selection of roses is extended every year.

This impressive collection of roses, regrouped typologically, allows the visitor to trace the evolution of this noble flower from the prickly rose *(Rosa acicularis)* to the most recent award-winning hybrids.

The rose garden at L'Haÿ-Les-Roses

Coupole d'HELFAUT-WIZERNES★★

Michelin map 51 fold 3 or 236 fold 4

This gigantic rocket-launching pad, built in 1943, is one of the most imposing relics of the Second World War. It has now been turned into a **Centre d'histoire de la guerre et des fusées** (Centre devoted to the history of war and rockets). Following the destruction in 1943 of the Éperlecques Bunker *(see p 302)*, Hitler decided to build a new one. The Todt organisation built a protective dome 72m/236ft in diameter and 5m/16ft thick, railway tunnels to convey the rockets, and miles of underground galleries to stock them. Adjusted in a top secret centre headed by Wernher von Braun in Peenemünde, on an island in the Baltic Sea, V2 rockets were built by the prisoners of the DoraNordhausen concentration camp who were made to work day and night. They were the first rockets to reach the stratosphere and they marked the beginning of man's venture into space.

In spite of the heavy bombing which lasted from March to September 1944 and involved 5t Tallboy bombs, the dome was hardly damaged but the thrust forward of Allied forces in July 1944 forced the Germans to abandon the site before the launching pad was completed. V2 rockets were launched subsequently towards London and Antwerp from mobile bases, causing heavy casualties.

At the end of the war, von Braun joined the Americans and became one of the initiators of the Apollo space programme.

TOUR

The tour starts in a tunnel through which travelled all trains arriving from Germany and continues along underground galleries intended for the storage of rockets. Visitors then proceed with the audio-guided tour by taking a lift up a 40m/131ft shaft which brings them beneath the huge dome weighing 55 000t. Two exhibitions, relying heavily on audio-visual techniques (documentaries lasting 7 to 20min including rare archive

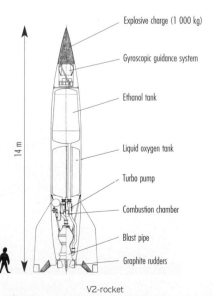

V2-rocket

pictures, laser show) present German secret weapons (V1 flying bombs and V2 rockets) and the life of the local population in northern France from 1940 to 1944. One of the most moving sequences of the tour is focused on the last letter of a young member of the Resistance which shows up on a reconstruction of the Mur des fusillés (execution wall) of the Lille citadel. An area is devoted to rockets and the conquest of space from 1945 to 1969 with models of Titan, Soyouz, Saturn, Ariane and a 20min film entitled *From the Earth to the Moon*.

A working model shows the firing site as it should have been; next to it, visitors can see a V1 flying bomb and an authentic V2 rocket, 14m/46ft high weighing 12t. On the way back, the itinerary takes in the large octagonal hall, which remained unfinished, where rockets were prepared for launching (they were loaded with liquid oxygen and explosives) before being conveyed upright through two tunnels leading to two outside launching pads.

The centre, situated on a site symbolising Nazi madness, is both a memorial and an instructive place.

Other bunkers of the Second World War have also been turned into museums: the Éperlecques Bunker, the Mimoyecques Fortress, the Todt Battery near Cap Gris-Nez, the former headquarters of the 15th Army in Tourcoing, the bunker situated in Calais town centre.

HONDSCHOOTE

Population 3 654
Michelin map 51 fold 4 or 236 folds 4,5

This Flemish-speaking town, which is bedecked with flowers in summer, centres on its main square (Grand-Place). Until the 17C the town produced a lightweight serge cloth *(sayes)* in 3 000 workshops, a prodigious number for a town with a population of only 28 000.

Hôtel de ville ⊙ – The building, which is dated 1558, was built on the main square in a Gothic-Renaissance style. The stone front is articulated by high mullioned windows linked by fine mouldings of curves and counter-curves. The rear façade is brick and stone, with a pointed tower crowned with an onion dome.

On the ground floor, a display of inscriptions by the writer Lamartine shows his affection for the local Coppens family, and a large painting portrays the 1793 Battle of Hondschoote in which the French triumphed over the English and the Austrians. On the first floor, an exhibition room displays ten 17C paintings showing nine noblewomen and Joan of Arc, together with works by Dutch painters. The inn beside the town hall dates from 1617.

Hondschoote – The Noord-Meulen

Église – This hall-church type of building, with a tower at the west front and parallel aisles of equal height, is common in the maritime region of Flanders. The 16C tower (82m/269ft high) dominates the town; it was the only thing to survive the fire of Hondschoote in 1582. The aisles were rebuilt in the early 17C. Inside, the lyre-shaped organ case and the pulpit are 18C Flemish Baroque.

The savings bank *(Caisse d'Épargne)* opposite is installed in the former manor house of the Coppens family, the lords of Hondschoote.

Moulin Spinnewyn ⊘ – The wind mill bears the name of its former owner. It was rebuilt in 1993 for the bicentennial commemoration of the Battle of Hondschoote (8 September, 1793).

Noord-Meulen ⊘ – *500m/550yd north of Hondschoote, near D 3.*
This windmill is thought to be the oldest windmill in Europe – its foundation dates back to 1127 – and was in use until 1959. The wooden cabin rests on a timber pivot and brick base.

To commemorate the bicentenary of the Battle of Hondschoote a new post mill was built in 1993.

LES MOËRES

The marshes – which extend as far as Furnes in Belgium – are below sea-level and were flooded over from 1645 to 1746 and again in 1940. Reclaimed from the sea in the 17C using 20 windmills and protected by dykes, the marshes now provide fertile polders which are dotted with large farms and crisscrossed by canals full of tench, bream and pike. On the horizon stand the belfry, factories and cranes of Dunkirk.

Leave Hondschoote by D 947 and turn left onto D 3 towards Bergues, along the Canal de la Basse Calme; turn right onto D 79, then take the small road leading to the village of Les Moëres. Return to Hondschoote by D 947.

L'ISLE-ADAM
Population 9 979
Michelin map 106 fold 6 or 55 fold 20

In 1014 a castle built on one of the islands in the River Oise was ceded to Adam de Villiers by Robert II the Pious, Hugh Capet's son. The former erected a priory on the estate. In 1364 the fief was purchased by Pierre de Villiers, whose descendants gained widespread recognition: Jean (1384-1437), Maréchal de Bourgogne, served two Dukes of Burgundy, John the Fearless and Philip the Good, before becoming one of the king's followers; Philippe (1464-1534), Commander of the Order of St John of Jerusalem, and subsequently Grand Master of the Order of Malta, heroically defended Rhodes against Suleiman the Magnificent for five months, and succeeded in obtaining Malta as headquarters for the order.

In the 16C the land came into the hands of Constable Anne de Montmorency. Louis XIII later offered the estate to Henri II of Bourbon, Prince de Condé. In 1646 Armand de Bourbon, Prince de Conti, moved in with his lavish court.

Honoré de Balzac was a regular visitor to L'Isle-Adam and several of his novels are set in the area. In the 19C Villiers de L'Isle-Adam, the author of *Cruel Tales*, was to become one of the great names of French literature. L'Isle-Adam was also home to Henri Prosper Breuil (1877-1961), the renowned archeologist.

The site – The château belonging to the Conti was razed during the Revolution. The old bridges – in particular Cabouillet Bridge, a 16C stone construction with three arches – command a pleasant view of the Oise, which is still frequented by traditional rowing boats *(boat hire office on the beach)*.

L'Isle-Adam has one of France's largest inland beaches, now a popular water sports centre: it features numerous facilities for yachting, sailing, rowing, canoeing etc.

Église St-Martin ⊘ – Like the church in Montmorency *(see MONTMORENCY)*, this church is typical of 16C architecture and presents highly intricate vaulting. It was consecrated on 1 October 1567, in the presence of Constable Anne. The tower erected in 1869 is a replica of the one adorning Église de la Trinité in Paris.

The interior offers a vast collection of well-preserved furnishings. The 1560 **pulpit★** – of German origin – features inlaid panels and portrays numerous statues, grouped in sets of four: Great Prophets, Evangelists, Doctors of the Church, Cardinal Virtues (also the three Theological Virtues).

On the northern side stands the funeral chapel of Louis-François de Bourbon (1717-76), the penultimate descendant of the Conti dynasty, Grand Prior of France of the Order of Malta. The remains of the original monument (1777), including the prince's medallion, have been reassembled.

Musée Louis-Senlecq – *46 Grande-Rue (between the post-office and the church).*
Housed in a former 17C school, this art and history museum displays the town's collections gathered since 1939. The painting gallery is particularly interesting; it

L'Isle-Adam – The pagoda at Cassan

J.-P. Nacivet /EXPLORER

contains the works of important groups of artists (Émile Boggio, Jules-Romain Joyant and Jules Dupré. Note the fine painting by Vlaminck entitled *Houses under snow.*

Centre d'Art Jacques-Henri-Lartigue – *31 Grande-Rue.*
Jacques-Henri Lartigue (1894-1986) was a famous photographer and a prolific painter: his foundation owns no fewer than 300 of his paintings exhibited in rotation. His style changed with time but his vigorous brushstrokes and his very bright colours are easily recognisable. The centre also organises temporary exhibitions featuring contemporary artists.

Pavillon chinois de Cassan – *To the northeast, along rue de Beaumont. Enter through the main gateway of the former park.*
This quaint pavilion overlooking a lake was built to adorn the landscape park of Cassan. The estate used to belong to the financier Bergeret (1715-85), an enthusiastic art lover and patron of Fragonard; the rest of the estate has been turned into a residential area.
The pagoda, brightly decorated in red, green and saffron tones, stands on a stone base resting upon arches that house the spillway for the waters of the park (ponds and canals).

The pagoda-shaped roof is supported by a peristyle of eight wooden pillars. It conceals the elaborate network of imbricated domes which act as a lantern and crown the room, decorated with paintings. The mast at the top of the pavilion features several tiers of rings adorned with small bronze bells.

Stopover

Le Gai Rivage *(Our selection)* – 11 Rue Conti. ☎ 01 34 69 01 09. Situated on the way into town, near the bridge, this restaurant (with terrace) offers fine views on the banks of the River Oise. Fixed-price menu: 220F.

Forêt de L'Isle-Adam – This State-owned forest, which covers an area of 1 500 ha/3800 acres, is separated from the Forêt de Carnelle by the Presles Valley. Oak trees make up two-thirds of the thickets and copses; the remainder of the forest is beech, chestnut, hornbeam, birch and lime.
The forest was very carefully enclosed and maintained for hunting by the Princes de Conti until 1783 (the words *portes* and *grilles*, both meaning "gate", are frequently found in local place names). Nowadays, several major roads cut through it including D 64 to Paris and N 184, newly-routed to avoid the banks of the Oise river.
The forest varies in altitude from 27m/88ft to 193m/627ft. The forest is in fact a series of copses. The area adjacent to L'Isle-Adam is fairly flat. The area near Maffliers is higher and more hilly. It is crossed by a network of roads fanning out from the remarkable star-shaped crossroads known as **Le Poteau La Tour.**

Abbaye de JOUARRE★

Michelin map 106 fold 24 or 56 fold 13

Jouarre stands on a hilltop high above the last loop of the Petit Morin River before it flows into the Marne.

The town already had two abbeys in the 7C. The monastery was short-lived but the convent adopted the Benedictine rule and survived. It soon acquired a prestigious reputation and the great ladies of France, among them Madeleine d'Orléans, François I's half-sister, were flattered to receive the title of Abbess.

Badly damaged during the Hundred Years War, the abbey was rebuilt several times, particularly in the 18C. When the abbey was seized during the Revolution, it was the residence of a fervent, united religious community, close observers of monastic rules and widely praised by Jacques Bossuet. The monastery resumed its activity c 1837. The **principal offices** are celebrated according to Benedictine liturgy.

ABBEY AND CRYPT *1hr*

Tower – Only the tower remains from the old medieval sanctuary; it once served as bell-tower and porch to the 12C Romanesque church. The interior has been carefully restored: three vaulted rooms, furnished by Madeleine d'Orléans in the 16C, house abbey memorabilia (note the armorial bosses) and temporary exhibitions.

★**Crypt** ⊘ – It lies behind the parish church, at the end of place St-Paul. This square presents an imposing 13C cross resting on a stone base with the Virgin and Child in the centre of a four-lobed medallion. The crypt consists of two formerly underground chapels which were linked in the 17C.

Crypte St-Paul, the mausoleum of the founding family, is considered to be one of the oldest religious monuments in France.

The crypt is divided into three aisles by two rows of three columns dating from Gallo-Roman times, made of marble, porphyry or limestone. It is believed that the capitals were made of white marble from the Pyrenees. The famous Merovingian wall near the entrance presents a primitive stone mosaic with geometric motifs (oblongs, squares, diamonds etc).

The most striking sarcophagus is the Tomb of St Agilbert, Bishop of Dorchester and later of Paris, the brother of Theodechilde; Christ sits enthroned, surrounded by the Chosen Few with upraised arms. One of the galleries affords a good view of the bas-relief at the head: Christ circled by the four Evangelists' symbols (man, lion, bull, eagle). The tomb of St Osanne - an Irish princess who allegedly died in Jouarre - presents a 13C recumbent figure. The most elaborate decoration is that of the sarcophagus of Theodechilde, the first abbess of Jouarre. A display of large cockleshells adorns a Latin inscription in honour of the wise Virgins.

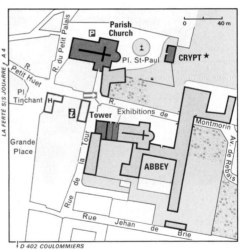

The **crypte St Ébrégésile** is a small Romanesque church beyond the first crypt. An archeological dig carried out in 1989 revealed that it had been built between Merovingian walls. The capitals in the crypt are Merovingian, as is Bishop Ebrégésile's sarcophagus which was discovered in 1985 to the left of the altar.

Recent excavations have revealed the nave of the modest St-Ébrégesile Church, along with several Merovingian sarcophagi.

Above these two crypts, a former chapel (17C) houses the **Musée Briard** ⊘, presenting exhibits relating to regional folklore and history: costumes, tools, paintings etc.

ADDITIONAL SIGHT

Église Paroissiale – *Enter by the south transept (see plan) at the end of the cul-de-sac.*

It was rebuilt after the Hundred Years War and completed in the early 16C.

The north arm of the transept features a 16C Entombment (studio of Michel Colombe), a 15C *Pietà* and two reliquaries (12C and 13C) covered in silver-gilt with enamels, cabochon and filigree work. The south aisle contains a 16C statue of Our Lady of Jouarre. The windows in the chancel and side aisles comprise many pieces of 16C stained glass.

JOUY-EN-JOSAS

Population 7 687
Michelin map 101 fold 23 - 6km/3.5mi southeast of Versailles
Michelin plan 22

This town has retained a noble aspect owing to the neat, tidy houses and the substantial estates, partly preserved after being ceded to various research and academic centres. The village was once a secluded spot favoured by memorable visits from Victor Hugo. The former French President Léon Blum and the bacteriologist Professor Albert Calmette are buried in Jouy cemetery.

A textile centre - In 1760, at the age of 22, **Christophe-Philippe Oberkampf** founded his first textile workshop, specialising in a type of printed calico known as *toile de Jouy*. In 1783 the factory became the Royal Works; business thrived. Oberkampf recruited his first skilled workers in Switzerland, and they in turn trained new apprentices. He showed a great interest in scientific advancement and modern machinery, and during the Continental Blockade he obtained permission from Napoleon to despatch several envoys to Switzerland, Alsace and even England. This gifted manufacturer employed up to 1 300 workers, a remarkably high number for the time.

The commercial losses sustained during the Napoleonic Wars, the foreign invasion (in which Oberkampf perished) and the advent of competition (over 300 firms in 1815) dealt a deathblow to the Royal Works. In 1843 the company was forced to file a petition for bankruptcy.

SIGHTS

Musée de la toile de Jouy ⊘ – *54, Rue Charles-de-Gaulle.*
The museum is housed in the 19C Château de l'Eglantine, once the home of Maréchal de Canrobert who won fame during the Crimean War. The rooms on the

Toile de Jouy

ground floor contain displays explaining the techniques used and the history of this famous product. Copper plates and cylinders or blocks of wood are used to print the pattern on the fabric. The Salon d'Oberkampf has been reconstructed with waxwork figures, some superb pieces of furniture stamped with the name of the cabinetmaker (Jacob) Jouy hangings and family portraits.

On the first floor are some fine show cases containing examples of the various motifs used in Jouy during the 18C and 19C. Note the various sets of bedclothes. Other French manufacturers (in Nantes, Rouen, Bordeaux, Alsace etc) are also represented.

Église – *Place de la Division-Leclerc.*
The 13C base of the bell-tower is the oldest part of the building. Inside, at the far end of the single aisle, note the **Diège★**, a restored 12C painted wooden Virgin.

Musée de Jeanne et Léon Blum ⊘ – *4 Rue Léon-Blum.*
The estate which the former French president acquired in 1945 and on which he lived until his death in 1950 provides an interesting insight into his life and political career. Several of the rooms contain documents relating to his early days, his literary works (essays, reviews) and his role in both the Socialist movement and French current affairs. The main room houses his writing desk and most of his private collection of books.

Maison de Victor Hugo – *Rue Victor-Hugo. Private.*
A plaque indicates the small house rented by the poet for his mistress Juliette Drouet in 1835. His stay here inspired the writing of *Olympio*.

EXCURSION

Bièvres – The **Musée Français de la Photographie★** ⊘, at no 78 rue de Paris, in the direction of Le Petit Clamart, presents a history of photography from technical and artistic viewpoints. The displays are being completely rearranged and the new museum is due to open in 2002. The many interesting exhibits range from Da Vinci's studies to the very latest apparatus, relying on sophisticated technology.

The crucial discoveries of Nicéphore Niepce, who took the first photograph on 5 May 1816, are explained, as are Daguerre and his photographic process, the advent of amateur photography in 1888 (George Eastman-registered trademark "Kodak"), the invention of the miniature camera (Leica) in 1925 etc.

The museum highlights the continuous, sometimes naïve quest for technical advancement, together with the craftsmanship involved; the large-format cameras are masterpieces of cabinet-making and leatherwork. The first-floor collections are devoted to the bygone industry of amateur photography: plate cameras from the golden years (1910-1945).

15 000 apparatuses, including 300 Kodak cameras, and about a million photographs are on show.

LAON★★

Population 26 490
Michelin map 56 fold 5 or 236 fold 38

Laon occupies a splendid **site★★**, perched (over 100m/328ft high) like an acropolis on a rock, crowning a tall outcrop of land which overlooks the plain. The Carolingian town is a celebrated tourist destination on the borders of Picardy, the Paris Basin and Champagne incorporating a famous cathedral, interesting sights and houses in medieval streets overlooking a wide horizon.

There are two districts in the Ville Haute: the **Cité**, Laon's original heart around the cathedral; and the **Bourg**. An automatic cable railway, the **Poma**, links the old town to the railway station in the modern town at the base of the mount. The **Le Nain brothers** (17C), born here, evoked the life and people of Laon in their paintings.

HISTORICAL NOTES

Tertiary Age "Island" – At the northeastern edge of the Parisian Basin, following a line linking the towns of Monterau, Épernay, Reims, Corbeny and Bruyères, there is a sheer-sided chalky promontory; this is known by geologists as the "Île-de-France cliff". The rise on which Laon stands is a kind of island, set slightly apart from the other Tertiary Age formations and now strangely eroded. Once covered with grapevines, the land is still pitted with natural caves *(creuttes)*.

Carolingian Capital – Ancient Laudunum was the capital of France for a time during the Carolingian period (9C-10C). Berthe au grand pied, Charlemagne's mother, was born in Samoussy (northeast of Laon) and Charles the Bald, Charles the Simple, Louis IV d'Outremer, Lothar and Louis V all lived on "Mount Laon" in a palace near the Ardon Gate. The reign of the Carolingians finally came to an end with the arrival of Hugh Capet, who took Laon by treachery; Charlemagne's descendants were driven out and Capet established himself in Paris.

Cathedral City – St Remigius, who was born in Laon, founded the first bishopric in the 5C; under Hugh Capet the bishops became dukes and peers with the privilege of assisting the king during coronation ceremonies at Reims.

From the Carolingian period on, Laon became a renowned religious and intellectual centre, thanks to Jean Scot Erigène and Martin Scot in the 9C; to Anselm and Raoul of Laon in the 11C, under whose auspices the "Laon School", flourished; and to Bishop Gautier de Mortagne in the 12C, who had the cathedral built. In the 13C the town was surrounded with new ramparts and from the 16C Laon was a powerful military stronghold which was besieged on several occasions, once by Henri IV in 1594. In 1870 the munitions magazine exploded; over 500 people were killed or injured.

★★CATHEDRAL DISTRICT 2hr 30min

★★Cathédrale Notre-Dame (BY) – Laon boasts one of the oldest Gothic cathedrals in France; it was begun in the 12C and completed in about 1230. The cathedral's main feature is the traces of Romanesque architecture evident in its structure, in common with Noyon and Soissons cathedrals. These traces may be seen in the lantern tower and galleries, in the shape of some of the rounded arches and in the style of manys capitals. There were originally seven towers: two on the west front, one over the transept crossing and four on the transept arms, two of which lost their spire during the Revolution.

The west front is one of the loveliest and most unusual in existence. The beautifully balanced appearance is due to the three deep porches decorated with majestic statuary (reworked in the 19C) and in particular to the famous towers (56m/184ft tall). The man thought to have designed them, **Villard de Honnécourt** said: "I have been in many lands but nowhere have I seen more beautiful towers than those of Laon." These towers, imposing yet light in appearance, are pierced by large bays and framed by slender turrets. They bear great oxen on their corners, recalling the

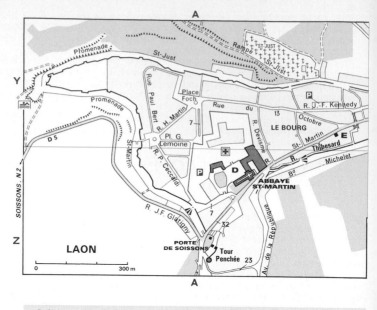

B Cloître **D** Bâtiments abbatiaux **E** Hôtel du Petit St-Vincent **J** Palais épiscopal

legend of the ox which appeared miraculously to help a struggling team of yoked oxen working on repairs to the cathedral. The two towers of the transept arms are built in the same way (60m/196ft and 75m/246ft).

Interior – The interior is 110m/360ft in length, 30m/98ft in width and 24m/78ft in height (Notre-Dame de Paris: 130m/426ft, 45m/147ft, 35m/114ft). The **nave★★★**, roofed with sexpartite vaulting, rises to a magnificent height through four levels: great arches, galleries, a blind triforium and a clerestory. Beyond the nave, the wide chancel terminates in a flat east end, as in Cistercian churches. The chapter numbered 80 canons assisted by 50 chaplains.

The transept crossing offers a good view of the nave, chancel, transept arms and the Norman-style lantern tower (40m/131ft high). Beautiful 13C stained-glass windows grace the apse's lancet bays and rose-window, dedicated to the Glorification of the Church; the rose-window in the north transept also contains 13C stained glass representing the Liberal Arts.

The chancel railings and the organ date from the 17C. The south transept leads to the 13C **chapter-house** *(salle capitulaire)*; the bays look out onto a pretty cloister (**BY B**) from the same period.

Leave the cathedral by the south transept and follow the outer wall of the cloister, which is decorated with a frieze of sculpted foliage; on the corner is an Angel with sundial.

Hôtel-Dieu (BY) – In the past the bays and wide tierce-point arches of the 12C two-storey former hospital opened onto the street; today they are bricked up. The building has retained its great Gothic ward with three aisles which now houses the tourist office, and the room on the ground floor called the Passers-by Room.

Palais épiscopal (BY J) – The palace, today used by the law courts, is preceded by a courtyard offering a view of the east end of the cathedral. The 13C building on the left rests on a gallery of pointed arches, its capitals decorated with plant motifs. Upstairs, the Grande Salle du Duché (over 30m/98ft long) today serves as the Assize Court.

The building at the far end was built in the 17C; it contained the bishop's apartments which lead directly to the two-storey 12C chapel. The lower chapel was reserved for servants and was used mainly for the Eucharist; the upper chapel *(visible through the glass door)*, in the form of a Greek cross, served for religious ceremonies in the bishop's presence.

The **Maison des Arts** ⊙ (**BY T**), opposite the palace, opened in 1971. It stands on the site of the third hospital founded in the 13C. The cultural centre comprises an exhibition hall, reading room, theatre, meeting rooms and a function or conference room.

In rue Sérurier (**BY**) no 53 has a 15C entrance and no 33 bis incorporates the 18C door of the old town hall. The 16C-17C Dauphin Inn, at no 7-11 rue au Change (**BY**), still has its beautiful wooden gallery.

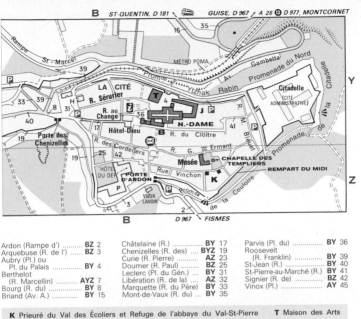

ADDITIONAL SIGHTS

★**Rempart du Midi et porte d'Ardon** (**BZ**) – The 13C Porte d'Ardon or Porte Rayée,
stands at the end of the South Ramparts, flanked by watchtowers with pepperpot
roofs; the gate overlooks a picturesque old public wash-house and drinking-trough.
The ramparts offer good **views**★ over St Vincent's plateau crowned by the Arsenal
(right), once St Vincent's Abbey, and the hills separating the Laon plain from the
Ailette Valley *(ahead)*.
The South Ramparts end in a **citadel** built for Henri IV by Jean Errard *(see Introduction: Military architecture)*; walk round it along Promenade de la Citadelle which
offers views of the plain dotted with other, small Tertiary Age hillocks.

★**Museum** ⊙ (**BZ**) – The archeological collection is remarkable: Greek figure vases,
baked clay figurines, 3C BC Greek head of Alexander the Great. There is also a
prehistory section. Local finds are displayed on the mezzanine: bronzes and ceramics, Merovingian and Gallo-Roman jewellery.
The first-floor rooms are devoted to painting: a 15C diptych fragment by the
Master of the Rohan Hours; the Le Nain brothers; 17C still-life paintings by
Desportes, 18C works by the Laon painter, Berthélemy.

★**Chapelle des Templiers** ⊙ (**BZ**) – The building recalls the Temple commandery
founded here in the 12C which, after the order was suppressed, passed to the
Knights of St John of Jerusalem. A peaceful flower garden has replaced the Knights
Templar's cemetery but the Romanesque chapel has been preserved; it is octagonal with a gabled bell-tower and a small chancel with an semicircular apse. The
porch and the gallery were added in the 13C and 14C. The interior houses two
statue-columns of prophets from the west front of the cathedral and the 14C
recumbent effigy of Guillaume de Harcigny, Charles VI's doctor.
On leaving, turn right into rue G Ermant and round into rue Vinchon, which is
lined with old houses (**BZ K**): no 44 was the 13C Val des Écoliers Priory (15C
chapel and 18C portal) and no 40 the Val-St-Pierre Abbey refuge (15C-16C).

★**Église St-Martin** ⊙ (**AZ**) – This 12C-13C former Premonstratensian abbey church,
restored after the fire in 1944, is a beautiful example of the early Gothic style. The
square offers a good general view; note the long, Romanesque-looking nave, the
height (35m/114ft) and arrangement of the two towers at the corner of the nave
and the transept (Rhenish influence) the tall south transept with its rose-window
and arcades.
The west front soars up, pierced by a great bay; its gable is decorated with a high-
relief carving of St Martin sharing his cloak with a pauper. The tympana over the
side doors depict the Decapitation of John the Baptist *(right)* and the Martyrdom
of St Lawrence, who was roasted alive *(left)*.

Interior – The chancel and the transept chapels have flat east ends, following Cistercian custom. Recumbent figures lie near the entrance: Raoul de Coucy, a Laon
Knight (late 12C) and Jeanne de Flandre, his sister-in-law, abbess of Sauvoir-sous-

Laon – Notre-Dame Cathedral

Laon (14C). The wooden panels in the nave are in the Louis XV style and those in the chancel Louis XIII. A 16C Christ of Compassion stands to the right of the Chapelle St-Eloi, separated from the church by a Renaissance stone screen.

Abbey Buildings (AZ D) – The restored 18C section, visible from the cloister, houses the **library** (bibliothèque). A fine elliptical stone staircase leads to the first floor.

★**Porte de Soissons (AZ)** – The gate was built in the 13C from quarried stone and reinforced with round towers. It stands in a park containing a monument to Marquette (1637-75), a Jesuit from Laon who discovered the Mississippi River. A curtain wall links the gate to the great **Tour Penchée** or leaning tower, so-named following subsidence.

Rue Thibesard (AYZ) and Porte des Chenizelles (BY) – Rue Thibesard follows the sentry path along the ramparts, offering unusual **views**★ of the cathedral; its towers rise above the old slate roofs with their red brick chimneys.
Continue along rue des Chenizelles, an old, cobbled street, to the 13C **Porte de Chenizelles.** The two towers create a narrow passageway through to rue du Bourg.

Hôtel du Petit St-Vincent (AY E) – The building was constructed in the first half of the 16C as the town refuge for St Vincent's Abbey, which was outside the ramparts. The main body of the Gothic building by the road is surrounded by turrets and flanked with an entrance vault surmounted by a chapel. A later wing set at right angles and overlooking the courtyard has an enclosed stairway framed by pilasters and surmounted by the figure of a drunk. The mansion now contains the offices of the tourist board.

On Michelin road maps at a scale of 1:200,000, places with a hotel or restaurant listed in the Red Guide are underlined in red.

Centre historique minier de LEWARDE★★

LEWARD MINING HERITAGE CENTRE

Michelin map 53 fold 3 or 236 fold 16 (8km/5mi southeast of Douai)

The **Centre Historique Minier de Lewarde** ⊙ is housed in the converted buildings of the Delloye Colliery which operated from 1930 to 1971. The museum's design has adapted the original structure to provide exhibition rooms, a restaurant, a conference, a film theatre etc.

Tour

An exhibition describes life in and around the mine from the economic, technical, social and human point of view including the discovery of coal and the mining of the seams over a period of three hundred years (animated model of mine working centre no 10 in Oignies), mining techniques (shafts, cutting) and their development, the everyday life of the miners with its disasters and illnesses (fire-damp explosions, silicosis, strikes).

Lewarde — Tour of the mine

After touring the offices of the manager and accountant and the surveyors' room at their own speed, visitors are taken on a guided tour of the surface installations by an ex-miner (cloakroom, showers also known as the "hangman's room" because of the hooks on which the miners used to hang up their clothes, helmets and boots), lamp room, infirmary etc. A small train then takes visitors to shaft no 2 where they descend to the galleries by lift. A 450m/487yd walk through the galleries (audio-visual presentation and reconstruction of men working the coal face) gives a clear insight into changes in miners' lives from 1930 to the present day.

A tour of the processing building (extraction machines, coal-screening room) and the pit stables completes the visit. A vast collection of fossils is also on display, shown in the context of the formation of the mining basin 300 million years ago.

LILLE★★

Population 174 034 – Conurbation 950 265

Michelin map 51 fold 16 or 236 fold 16

Lille, the lively capital of French Flanders, today enjoys a role as a regional and European metropolis owing to its location on major north-south and east-west routes. The city's handsome appearance is due to successful efforts over several years to preserve and restore the lovely 17C and 18C buildings and monuments of the old district; at the same time, much modernisation has taken place: the rebuilding of the district known as St-Sauveur; the construction of the **Forum** (**FZ**); the creation of Villeneuve-d'Ascq, a new town 8km/5mi east and the building of the Euralille centre.

LIFE IN LILLE

The typical Lille citizen is reliable and hardworking but also a *bon vivant* who likes his food and appreciates a beer or two in one of the city's many brasseries. Place du Général-de-Gaulle, the pedestrianised place Rihour and nearby streets, particularly rue de Béthune with its numerous cinemas, are always lively.

Cultural Activity – Lille is now a major cultural centre following the establishment of a philharmonic orchestra, the opening of Opéra du Nord in Lille, the lyric workshop in Tourcoing, the Northern France ballet company and the institution of several theatre companies (including La Métaphore, the national company). Several cultural festivals take place here every year; the autumn festival includes concerts, fine arts, and theatre and dance performances.

Folklore – Folklore still plays an active part in the city, as it does in much of northern France; every district of Lille has its own feast day *(ducasse)*.

La Grande Braderie – *First weekend in September.* From Sunday evening (8pm) to Monday afternoon (1pm) the whole of Lille – it is a city-wide holiday – celebrates the Braderie. Miles of pavement are taken over by professional and amateur traders and stallholders who may sell whatever they like, wherever they like. The pedestrian zone around place Rihour and boulevard de la Liberté are by far the busiest area. The restaurants and cafés traditionally serve mussels and chips, competing with each other to build the highest pile of shells on their doorsteps.

The Giants – Lille's giants, **Phinaert** and **Lydéric**, are paraded through the streets on holidays. According to legend, in about AD 600 a highwayman called Phinaert lived in a château where Lille stands today. One day the highwayman attacked the Prince of Dijon and his wife as they were on their way to England; the prince was killed but his wife was able to escape. Some time later she gave birth to a boy whom she put into hiding, before being caught herself by the highwayman. The baby was taken in by a hermit who baptised him Lydéric and had him suckled by a doe.

Once grown to manhood, Lydéric vowed to avenge the death of his parents; he challenged Phinaert to a fight and slew the highwayman. He then married the sister of King Dagobert and was entrusted with protecting the Flemish forests which had belonged to Phinaert.

A TURBULENT HISTORY

Lille has had a turbulent history having been sometimes Flemish, sometimes French, sometimes under Austrian or Spanish control. The city has faced 11 sieges and has been destroyed several times.

The Counts of Flanders – The name "l'Isle" (pronounced Lille) first appeared in 1066, in the charter of a donation to the collegiate church *(collégiale St-Pierre)* by Baudoin V, Count of Flanders, who owned a château on one of the islands in the Deule River. The town developed around this château and a port which existed on the site of the present avenue du Peuple-Belge.

In 1205 Count Baudoin IX, crowned Emperor of Constantinople during a crusade, died leaving two daughters, Jeanne and Marguerite. The young heiresses were raised by Philip Augustus; Jeanne, the elder daughter, was married to Ferrand of Portugal and the couple was then sent to Lille.

Although a French vassal, Flanders was linked, at least economically, with England and the Holy Roman Empire. Faced with Philip Augustus' claims on the northern regions, a coalition was formed which included the counts of Boulogne, Hainault and Flanders, King John of England and the Holy Roman Emperor Otto IV. The **Battle of Bouvines**, the first great French victory, concluded this war on 27 July 1214. Ferrand was imprisoned in the Louvre, while Jeanne governed Lille.

The Dukes of Burgundy and the Spanish – The marriage of Marguerite of Flanders to Philip the Bold in 1369 made Flanders part of the duchy of Burgundy. The presence of the dukes stimulated trade. **Philip the Good** (1419-67) had Rihour Palace built, where he made the "Pheasant Vow" in 1454 promising to leave for the crusades. His glittering court included the great painter Jan van Eyck.

The marriage of Marie of Burgundy, daughter of Charles the Bold, to Maximilian of Austria in 1477 brought the duchy of Burgundy, including Flanders, under Hapsburg control; the duchy later became Spanish when Charles V of Spain became emperor.

After the Wars of Religion, owing to Spanish domination the situation deteriorated: gangs of peasants in revolt devastated the countryside and sacked the churches. Lille escaped the assault of the "Howlers" *(Hurlus)* thanks only to the inhabitants' energetic defence, led by the inn-keeper **Jeanne Maillotte**.

Lille becomes French – Following his marriage to Maria-Theresa of Spain in 1663, Louis XIV laid claim to the Low Countries, taking advantage of the rights of his wife to a part of Spain's heritage. In 1667 he personally directed the siege of Lille and triumphantly entered the city after only nine days of resistance, after which Lille became capital of the Northern Provinces. The Sun King hastened to have a citadel built by Vauban and enlarged the town, laying down regulations on the height and style of the houses.

Lille under Siege – In September 1792, 35000 Austrians laid siege to Lille which was defended by only a small garrison. Cannon-balls rained down on the town and many buildings were destroyed; nevertheless, the courageous inhabitants held on and the Austrians eventually raised the siege. It is said that a barber who was shaving clients in the street used the fragment of a shell as a shaving dish.

In early October 1914, when six Bavarian regiments tried to breach the fortifications, Lille was very poorly defended. The town was obliged to submit after three days of bloody resistance during which time 900 buildings were destroyed. Prince Ruprecht of Bavaria, receiving the surrender, refused the sword of Captain de Pardieu "in recognition of the heroism of the French troops".

In May 1940 during the Second World War, 40000 French soldiers defending Lille held out for three days against seven German divisions and Rommel's tanks. The French troops finally capitulated on 1 June 1940.

Where to stay and eat

Hôtel Carlton – 3 Rue de Paris, dating from the early 20C, furnished in the Louis XV style.

Hôtel Alliance – 17 Quai de Wault, a former 17C Minim convent.

Hôtel Holiday Inn Express – 75 bis rue Gambetta, a modern hotel near place de la République.

Restaurant À l'Huîtrière – 3 Rue des Chats-Bossus, fish restaurant with original ceramic decoration.

Restaurant Le Lion Bossu – 1 Rue St-Jacques, 17C building with brick ornamentation.

Restaurant La Brasserie André – 71 Rue de Béthune, Flemish-inn atmosphere.

Restaurant L'Alcide – 5 Rue des Débris-St-Étienne, Art-Nouveau decoration.

Restaurant Le Hochepot – 6 Rue du Nouveau-Siècle, local produce, home-made beer.

Tourist information

The tourist office in Lille *(office de tourisme)* provides a town plan indicating 4 tours, each lasting about two hours:
– Old Lille
– Old Jesuit college in Quartier Ste-Catherine
– Quartier St-Sauveur
– 19C Lille.
There are year-round guided tours of Old Lille on foot, on Saturdays at 3pm (2hr); alternatives include an audio-guided tour and taxi tours; inquire at the tourist office.
From mid July to early September, the tourist office proposes a tour of Old Lille by night every Wednesday. The tour ends with a friendly beer-tasting.
To find out what's on in the city (theatres, cinemas, exhibitions, leisure activities etc), obtain a copy of **Sortir**, a free weekly published on Wednesdays, from the tourist office, town hall, cinemas and theatres, cultural centres, the Furet, the FNAC etc. The tourist office has its own data bank and can provide information on cultural events.

Markets

In **Quartier de Wazemmes** the bustling colourful Sunday morning market attracts crowds of people. Antique and bric-a-brac dealers are to be found around Église St-Pierre-St-Paul (**DZ**) while flower sellers congregate in front of the covered market where local produce and seafood is sold. The traditional traders set up their stalls in neighbouring streets.
Beneath the galleries of the **Vieille Bourse** (**EY**), there is a daily flower market as well as a sale of new and second-hand books.
General markets: **place Sébastopol** (**EZ 143**) (Wednesdays and Saturdays) and **place du Concert** (**EY**) (Wednesdays, Fridays and Sundays).

On the town

Evenings out

The brochure "Lille by night", available from the tourist office, contains a list of addresses of bars, discotheques, concert halls, dinner-shows...
Around **rue Masséna** (**DZ**): Club Écossais for an Anglo-Saxon atmosphere or Chez Gino (café and billiards).

Rue Solférino (**DEZ**) – La Boucherie, l'Atomic Club, L'Equateur (very friendly colonial-style pub), L'Irlandais (very convivial atmosphere).

Rue de Paris (**EYZ**) – Le 30 stages jazz concerts every evening from 9pm.

Rue de Béthune (**EYZ**) – A pedestrian precinct to which two grill rooms, Aux Moules and Brasserie André, bring plenty of business day and night alike.

Place Rihour (**EY**) – Cafés filled to overflowing at every hour of the day and night: Le Café de Foy, Le Lobourg, Le Legend Café.

Place de la Gare (**FY 64**) – At the mini-grill room called Les Brasseurs, you can enjoy a cool beer straight from the cellar.

Rue Lepelletier (**EY 102**) – Le Bateau Ivre is an atmospheric café specialising in French songs.

Rue d'Angleterre (**EY**) – The wonderful Anglesaxo is a jazz-café housed in 18C vaulted cellars.

Place Charles-de-Gaulle (**EY 66**) – Start your evening out at Les Messageries, Le Coq hardi, La Houblonnière, Le Président.

Main theatres and shows

Opéra de Lille *(reopening scheduled for the beginning of 2000)* – Place du Théâtre.

Théâtre Sébastopol – Place Sébastopol.

Théâtre du Nord – 4 Place du Général-de-Gaulle.

Lille Grand Palais – Zénith – 1 Boulevard des Cités-Unies.

Nouveau Siècle – 3 Place Mendès-France.

Aéronef – Avenue Willy-Brandt.

"Les folie's de Paris" (cabaret) – 52 Avenue du Peuple-Belge.

Le Petrouchka (theatre-café) – 67 Rue Royale.

ECONOMY

Owing to its location at the centre of a network of major routes and waterways, Lille has always been industrially and commercially important.

Past – During the Middle Ages Lille became famous for its clothmaking; later the high-warp weavers who had been forced out of Arras by Louis XIV came to establish their tapestry workshops here.

Lille devoted itself to cotton and linen milling in the 18C, whereas nearby Roubaix and Tourcoing specialised in wool. Large-scale industry came to Lille at the end of the 18C, creating an urban proletariat with its accompanying miseries: by 1846 the rate of infant mortality in the slums in Saint-Sauveur reached 75% and the cellars where workers laboured achieved a notoriety which Victor Hugo evoked in tragic verse.

Another of Lille's specialities was the milling of linseed, rapeseed and poppyseed to produce oil. Last but not least, it was famous for the production of lace and ceramics.

Present – Lille's urban area is more than ever the economic centre of northern France. Business facilites (conference centre), traditional industries (textiles, mechanics), computer and technology giants, food production companies and research laboratories all co-exist here, side by side with the universities.

The urban area of Lille-Roubaix-Tourcoing is the centre of mail-order selling and also of business, with the Eurabille business centre, the Chamber of Commerce and Industry, and the Stock Exchange.

The metropolis of Lille is at the heart of a highly-developed network of motorways leading to Paris, Brussels, Dunkirk and Antwerp; further, it has the third largest river port in France and an international airport at Lesquin.

Lille is also a retailing centre with shops lining the streets in the pedestrian zone. The city boasts the world's most modern metro, the **VAL**, an entirely automatic system. The rail network, which has a large number of branch lines, uses the new Lille-Europe station built to cater to high-speed trains and the Eurostar service to London and Brussels.

★★OLD LILLE *2hr*

The real renewal of Lille's old district began in 1965, when a few architecture enthusiasts decided to do something to recover the beauty of the 17C and 18C façades, hidden under unsightly rough-rendering. The restorations progressed well and whole blocks of buildings changed completely in appearance. Luxury shops, interior decorators and antique dealers settled in the area which is today an attractive place to explore.

The distinctiveness of the **Lille style** is due to the particular mix of bricks and carved stone. Façades decorated with quarry stones shaped into lozenges (place Louise-de-Bettignies) first appeared in the early 17C; then came the period of the Flemish Renaissance (Vieille Bourse, the Maison de Gilles de la Boé) where the wealth of ornamentation reached its limit. By the end of the 17C the French influence began to be felt in the decoration of the houses and in their arrangement in aligned rows. Ground floors consist of arcades in a close-grained sandstone which prevents humidity reaching the upper floors. The brick above alternates with limestone carved into cherubs, cupids, cornucopias, sheaves of wheat etc.

Leave from place Rihour.

Place Rihour (EY) – The main building on this square is the **Palais Rihour** ⊘ which now houses the tourist office. This Gothic palace was built between 1454 and 1473 by Philip the Good, Duke of Burgundy. Outside, note the beautiful mullioned windows and the graceful octagonal brick turret. The guard-room, with its tall, pointed arches, still exists on the ground floor. The chapel, known as the Conclave Room, is upstairs; the chapel for the Duke's private worship, reached by an elegant stone staircase, has traceried vaults.

A monument to those who died during the two world wars flanks the northeast side of the chapel.

To return to Place du Général-de-Gaulle, take a very busy pedestrian precinct lined with pavement cafés.

On the left, note the 17C houses built in a style that is a combination of Flemish and French. This form of architecture became commonplace in Lille after the town was taken over by Louis XIV.

* **Place du Général-de-Gaulle** (**EY 66**) – The Grand' Place or main square has always been the busy centre of Lille; as early as the Middle Ages it was a market place. The finest building in the square is the Vieille Bourse. *La Voix du Nord*, a daily newspaper, has its offices in the building (1936) with a stepped pediment beside the **Grand' Garde** (**T¹**) (1717), which is surmounted with pediments and once housed the king's guard (this is now the theatre called La Métaphore). **Furet du Nord** (**B**), located in a copy of a 17C house opposite the Vieille Bourse, is said to be the largest bookshop in the world; it has eight floors.

The colonne de la Déesse (1845) rises in the middle of the square, a symbol of the city's heroic resistance during the siege of 1792 *(see above)*.

Lille – Grand'Place

B Kaufmann

** **Vieille Bourse** (**EY**) – The exchange was built in 1652-53 by Julien Destrée, at the request of the tradesmen of Lille who wanted an exchange to rival those of the great cities in the Low Countries. It consists of 24 mansard-roofed houses around a rectangular court which served in the past for commercial deals; today they house second-hand bookshops.

The profusion of decoration on the façade is due to the fact that Destrée was a wood sculptor. The caryatids and telamones on two storeys, the garlands and masks above the outer windows, the fruit and flowers carved on the inner court are all reminiscent of a Flemish chest Bronze busts, and medallions and tablets honouring learned figures and the sciences, can be seen under the arcades.

Place du Théâtre (**EY 150**) – The square is dominated by the imposing Nouvelle Bourse which houses the Chamber of Commerce (**C**) and its neo-Flemish bell-tower. Next to it stands the Louis XVI Opera.

These two buildings date from the beginning of the century and are the work of architect Louis Cordonnier.

Opposite the Nouvelle Bourse stands the **"Rang de Beauregard"** (**EY D**), comprising houses adorned with pilasters surmounted by elegant cartouches. The terrace, built in 1687, is the most characteristic and most interesting example of late-17C architecture in Lille.

Rue de la Bourse – The street is lined with superb 18C housefronts decorated with chubby cherubs and masks on the first floor.

Rue de la Grande-Chaussée (**EY 73**) – The old sandstone houses with their arcades have been renovated and now contain shops selling luxury goods. Some of the wrought-iron balconies and the upper part of the windows are very intricately worked. Note the first house on the right and nos 9, 23 (ship on the keystone of the window) and 29.

Rue des Chats-Bossus (EY 27) – The street acquired its curious name ("Street of the Humpback Cats") from an old tanner's sign.

"L'Huîtrière" (F), a famous seafood restaurant, has a typical Art-Deco front dating from the 1930s.

The VAL

The VAL (literally "véhicule automatique léger") is the most modern driverless metro system in the world and it has been operational in Lille since May 1984. The technology used for the VAL has attracted other cities in France (Bordeaux, Toulouse, Orly) and abroad (Taipei, Jacksonville, Chicago).

A train has two carriages.

There is one train every minute during peak times.

Maximum speed: 80kph/50mph; working speed: 35kph/22mph.

Trains run from 5am to 1am.

Some of the stations are decorated with works of art:

– République: The Muses, a sculpture by Debeve, Spartacus by Foyatier, Autumn and Spring by Carrier-Belleuse, and reproductions of paintings displayed in the Musée des Beaux-Arts.

– Porte de Valenciennes: The Hand by César.

– Wazemmes: The Source of Life, a sculpture made of enamelled lavastone.

– Fives: frescoes by Degand (The Cry and Graffiti).

– Pont de Bois: Bronze sculpture, Paternity, by Mme Leger.

LE MONGY

Inaugurated in 1909, the famous Mongy (named after its inventor) that used to travel along the Grand Boulevard between Lille, Roubaix and Tourcoing, has been replaced by a more modern, elegantly-designed tramway.

The tram is faster than its predecessor, reaching speeds of up to 70kph/44mph.

Place du Lion-d'Or (EY) – At no 15, the Olivier Desforges shop occupies the 18C Maison des Poissonniers.

Place Louise-de-Bettignies (EY 16) – The square bears the name of a First World War heroine. The **demeure de Gilles de la Boé★ (E)**, at no 29 on a corner, was built in about 1636 and is a superb example of Flemish Baroque. The abundant ornamentation includes cornices and prominent pediments. In the past this building stood on the edge of the Basse-Deûle port, in the days when there was a great deal of river traffic.

In 1936 the Basse-Deûle, a bustling harbour until the 18C, was filled in to make way for avenue du Peuple-Belge; the modern tower houses the law courts.

★**Rue de la Monnaie (EY 120)** – The Mint once stood in this street where the restored houses now attract antique dealers and interior decorators. On the left there is a row of 18C houses (note the apothecary's shop sign of a mortar and distilling equipment at no 3). The houses at nos 5 and 9 are decorated with dolphins, wheat-sheaves, palms etc.

At no 10 a statue of Notre-Dame-de-la-Treille adorns the front and at nos 12 and 14 the crow-stepped gable has been rebuilt. Neighbouring houses date from the first third of the 17C and flank the rusticated door (1649) of the Hospice Comtesse.

★**Hospice Comtesse ⊙ (EY)** – The hospital was built in 1237 by Jeanne de Constantinople, Countess of Flanders, to ask for divine intervention on behalf of her husband Ferrand de Portugal, taken prisoner at Bouvines *(see above)*. It was destroyed by fire in 1468 but was rebuilt and enlarged in the 17C and 18C. It became a hospice during the Revolution, then an orphanage. It changed again in 1939 and is today a museum of history and ethnography which also holds concerts and exhibitions.

The monumental 17C main entrance is built from beautiful rusticated sandstone.

Hospital ward – A long, sober building, rebuilt after 1470 on the old 13C foundations, flanks the main courtyard. Inside, the immense proportions of the interior and its panelled timber **vault★★** in the shape of an upturned boat are striking. It contains two beautiful tapestries, woven in Lille in 1704. One represents Baudouin of Flanders with his wife and two daughters; the other portrays Jeanne, the hospital's founder, flanked by her first and second husbands. The **chapel**, which extends the length of the interior, was enlarged and isolated by a rood screen after the fire of 1649. The old 15C window and traces of mural paintings have been revealed on the right wall. The vault is decorated with the heraldic arms of the hospital's benefactors.

Museum – Furniture and artworks evoking the atmosphere of a 17C religious establishment are displayed in the right wing, which was built by the community in the late 15C and heightened in the 17C: the kitchen features blue and white tiles from Holland and Lille; the Baroque overmantel in the dining room frames a 16C Nativity, the sombre Louis XIV panels of the parlour are decorated with a series of 17C votive offerings in the form of portraits of local children. The prayer room is lined with Louis XV wood panelling.

The last two chambers were used as the pharmacy and linen-room.

The former dormitory on the first floor has carved ceiling beams. It contains 17C Flemish and Dutch paintings and a superb 16C wooden Crucifixion from Picardy. The cross-bar and main section of the Cross are decorated with medallions depicting the Evangelists. Two rooms flanking the dormitory are filled with exhibits relating to regional history: architectural features, objets d'art, and paintings by Louis and François Watteau representing Lille in the 18C.

Turn left into rue Au-Pétérinck which still has some 18C houses. The street leads to the delightful little place aux Oignons on which the 17C house fronts have been rebuilt. Continue along rue des Vieux-Murs which follows the line of the town's first walls then turn left into rue des Trois Mollettes. On the left is the impressive **Cathédrale Notre-Dame-de-la-Treille**, a neo-Gothic construction that was never completed. Rue du Cirque leads to rue Basse where parts of the impressive buildings house antique shops (the mansion at no 32 used to belong to the Prince de Soubise). Rue **Esquermoise** is lined with 17C and 18C houses. The Meert cake shop at no 21 has a beautiful 19C interior. At nos 6 and 4 cherubs are shown embracing or turning their backs on each depending on whether or not they belong to the same house. Opposite is a superb restored house that belonged to a furrier (Gailliaerde).

Return to place Rihour via Grand'Place.

★★★PALAIS DES BEAUX-ARTS (FINE ARTS MUSEUM) (EZ)

After a competition, the art gallery was built between 1885 and 1892 to designs by architects Bérard and Delmas. The majestic building stands on Place de la République, opposite the county offices *(préfecture)*. The architects Ibos and Vitard were responsible for the renovation and extension of the gallery (1992-1997).

A narrow building 70m/228ft long and 6m/19.5ft. wide was built to the rear. It contains the café and restaurant on the ground floor, the drawings section and the gallery's offices.

Between the two buildings is the garden. The middle has been given a glass roof which lets light into the temporary exhibition halls below.

The vast entrance hall extending the whole length of the façade is lit by two large coloured-glass chandeliers by Gaetano Pesce. There is free access to the atrium where the bookshop, tearoom and café-cum-restaurant are situated *(garden entrance in rue de Valmy)*.

Basement

Stairs on the left in the atrium.

Archeology – Works from the Mediterranean basin: Egypt, Cyprus, Rome, Greece (three-legged toilet vase known as Exaleiptron, ceramics with black figures);

Middle Ages and Renaissance – The chased-bronze Lille incense-burner (12C Mosan art) is displayed in the centre of the first room. Next to it are a few ivory objets d'art from abbeys of northern France such as the *Old Man of the Apocalypse* (12C from St-Omer).

The vaulted galleries contains rare examples of Romanesque sculpture, including three fragments of a limestone high-relief carving representing the Deposition (c 1170). Gothic art is illustrated by various objects: a reliquary-cross from Wasne-au-Bac said to have contained a piece of the True Cross (1200-1220), *Herod's Feast*, a magnificent low-relief marble sculpture by Donatello, two panels from a triptych by Dirk Bouts *(Paradise* and *Hell)*, the *Virgin and Child from Saint-Sauveur*, in polychrome stone, the large *St George's altarpiece* from southern Tyrol and the *Mysterious Fountain* triptych by J Bellegambe.

Note, in the last room, the famous *Waxhead of a maiden* resting on a terracotta base (18C).

★**Relief maps** – The large hall contains the plans of fifteen towns situated on the northern borders of France at the time of Louis XIV.

Ground floor

Ceramics – *To the left of the atrium.* A superb collection of 18C faience from Lille, Nevers, Strasbourg, Delft and Rouen, as well as German and Walloon sandstone exhibits and 18C porcelain from China and Japan.

Sculpture – *To the right of the atrium.* The collection gives an overview of 19C French sculpture with Frémiet *(The Knight Errant)*, Houdon (bust of *Le Fèvre de Caumartin)*, David d'Angers (original terracotta low-relief sculptures from the Gutenberg memorial on place Kléber in Strasbourg), Camille Claudel *(Giganti, Mme de Massary)*, and Bourdelle *(Penelope*, c 1909).

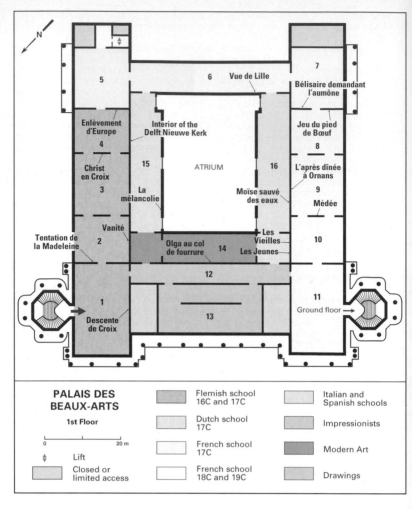

**PALAIS DES
BEAUX-ARTS**

1st Floor

0 ————— 20 m

⇕ Lift

Closed or
limited access

Flemish school
16C and 17C

Dutch school
17C

French school
17C

French school
18C and 19C

Italian and
Spanish schools

Impressionists

Modern Art

Drawings

First floor

The art collections are presented by schools around the atrium.

16C-17C Flemish School – Hermessan's *Vanity* (the museum's latest important acquisition) represents the 16C. Several characteristic canvases by Jordaens are displayed, ranging in themes from the religious *(The Temptation of Mary Magdalene)* to the mythological *(The Abduction of Europa)* or the rustic *(The Huntsman)*; his study of cows was later taken up by Van Gogh. There are important paintings by Rubens and from his workshop: *The Deposition* (1617), a variation of the one in Antwerp, and the original sketch; *The Ecstasy of Mary Magdalene; The Martyrdom of St Catherine; St Francis and the Virgin*. Other paintings include Van Dyck's moving *Christ on the Cross*, David Teniers II's beautifully-coloured *Temptation of St Anthony, The Martyrdom of St Maurice* by Boeckhorst.

17C Dutch School – Dutch masterpieces by de Witte *(Nieuwe Kerk in Delft)* and Ruysdael *(The Wheat Field)* hang with still-life paintings by Van der Ast and Van Beyeren, Van Goyen's *The Skaters* and Pieter Codde's *Melancholy*.

17C French School – Works by Lille artists Wallerand Vaillant *(The Young Draughtsman)* and Monnoyer, Le Sueur, Philippe de Champaigne, La Hyre and Largillière *(Jean-Baptiste Forest)*.

18C and 19C French School – Remarkable works by Boilly (1761-1845), born at La Bassée near Lille, adorn the walls: *Le Jeu du Pied de Bœuf, Marat's Triumph* and numerous portraits, including Jules Boilly as a child and sketches of heads for Isabey's studio. Note Quentin de La Tour's portrait of Madame Pèlerin, the charming paintings by Louis Watteau, who adopted Lille as his permanent home *(Lille Shaving Dish, View of Lille)* and the work by his son François *(Alexander's Battle)*. Other great painters represented include David *(Belisarius Begging for Alms)*, Delacroix, Géricault, Corot and Courbet.

Italian and Spanish Schools – Italy is represented by Liss' *Moses Saved from the Waters*, Tintoretto's *Portrait of a Senator* and a sketch of *Heaven* by Veronese.

The few Spanish paintings are of a rare quality: *Time or The Old Women* and *The Letter or The Young People* two works★ by **Goya**, kind and cruel satirist of his period; and El Greco's *St Francis Praying*.

Impressionists – The end of the 19C is represented by works from the **Masson Bequest**. The pre-Impressionist paintings include canvases by Boudin *(The Port of Camaret)*, Jongkind *(The Skaters)* and Lépine. Impressionism itself is embraced in works by Sisley *(Port Marly, Winter: Snow Effects)*, Renoir *(Young Woman in a Black Hat)* and Monet *(The Disaster, The Houses of Parliament)*. Paintings by Vuillard,

Musée des Beaux-Arts –
Belisarius Begging for Alms by David.

Carrière, Lebourg and several Rodin sculptures complete the collection.

Modern Artists – Figurative and abstract works on show are by Léger *(Women With a Blue Vase)*, Gromaire *(Landscape of the Coalmining Region)*, Poliakoff *(Composition no 2)*, Sonia Delaunay *(Colour Rhythm 1076)* and Picasso *(Portrait of Olga, 1923)*.

Drawings – This is one of the largest collections in France (about 4000 works) especially as regards Italian drawings. The works are displayed on a rotating basis. A few sculptures have also been placed here, in particular the famous *Head of a Young Girl*, a 17C work in wax on a terracotta base attributed to F Duquesnoy, and Georges Lacombe's *Mary Magdalene Kneeling* (1897).

OTHER SIGHTS

★**Église St-Maurice (EFY)** – This vast Gothic edifice was built from the 15C to the 19C. It is a beautiful example of a hall-church, with five aisles of equal height, five roofs and five gables. A 16C Christ of Compassion, often dressed in a long velvet mantle, stands in the chapel of the false left transept; it is venerated as "Jesus Scourged".

South of the church stand two restored houses: the Croix de St-Maurice bakery (1729) and the maison du Renard (1660); opposite *(at no 74 Rue de Paris)* is the maison des Trois Grâces.

Rue Royale (EY) – This was the main route through the elegant district which was built during the 18C between the citadel and the old town. **Église Ste-Catherine**, with its austere 15C tower, stands on the left at the beginning of the street. The handsome private houses bordering Rue Royale show a definite French influence. Note the old *intendance* building at n° 68 **(V)**, built by the Lille architect Lequeux in 1787; it is now the bishop's palace. **Église St-André**, a Carmelite chapel in the 18C, is an example of the Jesuit style. It was topped with a tower in 1890. Charles de Gaulle was baptised here on the day he was born – 22 November 1890.

Maison Natale du Général de Gaulle ⊘ **(EY)** – *9 Rue Princesse.*
Charles de Gaulle was born on 22 November 1890 in this lime-washed brick house in Lille, where his grandfather had a lace works. The old workshop and the house have been turned into a small museum exhibiting photographs and memorabilia. On display are de Gaulle's christening robe and the car in which the General and his wife were travelling on the day of the attempt on their lives in Le Petit-Clamart.

Église Ste-Marie-Madeleine (EY) – The centralised layout of this church and its high dome (50m/164ft) recall Les Invalides in Paris. The building was begun in 1675 and completed at the end of the regin of Louis XIV; the west front was altered in 1884.

LILLE

B «Furet du Nord »
C Chambre de commerce
D «Rang de Beauregard »
E Demeure de Gilles
  de la Boé
F «L'Huîtrière »
H Hôtel de Ville
K Monument aux Fusillés
L Hospice Ganthois
M Musée d'Histoire
  naturelle et de géologie
N Pavillon St-Sauveur
Q Noble Tour
R Chapelle du Réduit
S Hôtel Bidé-de-Granville
T' Grand'Garde
V Ancien hôtel de
  l'Intendance

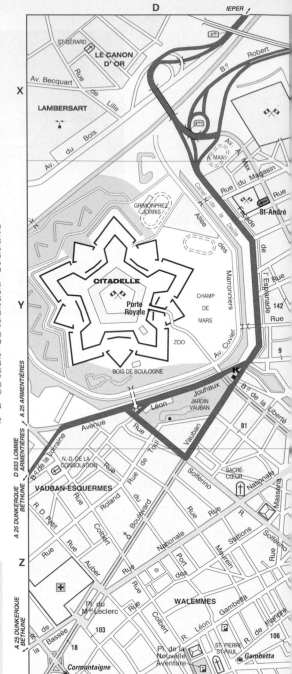

Portes de Gand and de Roubaix (**EFY**) – These massive gates from the 1621 Spanish fortifications are composed of a sandstone base surmounted by a drip-stone and a layer in brick. They were opened in 1875 to allow room for a tramway and their moats have been turned into gardens.

Hôtel Bidé-de-Granville (**FY S**) – The industrialist AD Scrive Labbe estab-lished the first carding machine here in 1821. The building was constructed in 1773 and today houses the offices of the Regional Administration of Cultural Affairs.

Quartier St-Sauveur (**FZ**) – This former working-class district was known for the misery of its slums which inspired Emile Desrousseaux, author of the famous French lullaby Le P'tit Quinquin (statue in rue Nationale on the corner

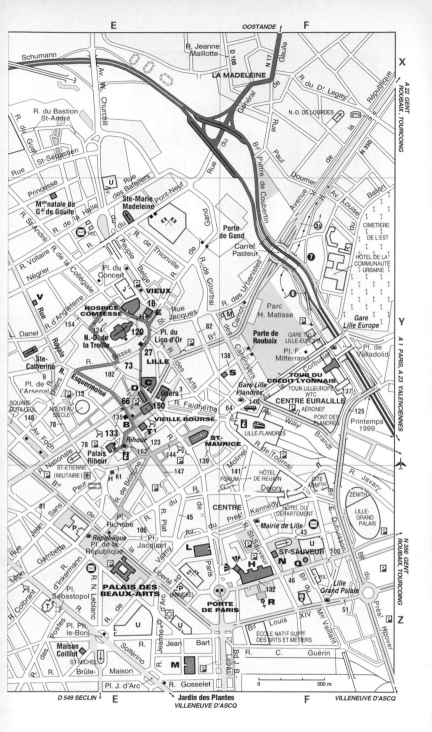

of avenue Foch). The area has today been completely remodelled into a business centre around the town hall. Relics of the past remain dotted among the modern buildings.

Hospice Ganthois (EZ L) – The hospice was founded in 1462 by Jean de la Cambe, known as Ganthois, and is still in use. The original ward has been preserved; its gable, on Rue de Paris, is flanked on either side by 17C buildings. Note the sculpture on the door panels, dated 1664.

★**Porte de Paris** – This gate, built from 1685 to 1692 by Simon Vollant in honour of Louis XIV, is the only example of a town gate which also served as a triumphal arch; it was formerly part of the ramparts. It appears as an arch decorated with the arms of Lille (a lily) and of France (three lilies) on the outward side. Victory stands at the top, honoured by Fames, about to crown Louis XIV represented in a medallion.

Lille – Porte de Paris

H. Gyssels /DIAF

From the inner side the gate has the appearance of a lodge.

Hôtel de Ville ⊘ (**H**) – The town hall was built from 1924 to 1927 by the Lille architect Emile Dubuisson and is overlooked by a tall belfry (104m/341ft). The two Lille giants, Lydéric and Phinaert *(see above)*, are sculpted at its base. The top of the **belfry** *(109 steps then lift)* offers a lovely **view★** over the city and the surrounding area up to 50km/32mi away.

Pavillon St-Sauveur (**N**) – This is the wing of an 18C cloister, preserved when a hospice was demolished in 1959. The brick and stone arches are surmounted by clerestory windows decorated with flowered medallions.

Noble Tour (**Q**) – This keep with its truncated appearance is the only relic of the 15C fortifications; it has become a Resistance memorial. There is a beautiful work by the sculptor Bizette-Lindet.

Chapelle du Réduit (**R**) – This chapel is all that remains of Réduit Fort, built at the same time as the citadel to serve as its counterpart elsewhere in the city. The pretty Louis XIV front is decorated with the arms of France and Navarre. The chapel has been integrated into the engineering regiment's premises.

Maison Coilliot (**EZ**) – *9 Rue de Fleurus.*
Built in 1898 by Hector Guimard for Mr. Coilliot, a local ceramics artist, this house illustrates the Art Nouveau style with its enamelled lavastone façade, curved lines and unusual double roof.

★ Citadelle (Citadel) ⊘ (**DY**) – This citadel is the largest and best preserved in France. It was Louis XIV's first project after the conquest of Lille and is a fine example of Vauban's genius; it is still occupied by the army today. It took three years to build (1667-70) using 2 000 men who first undertook an enormous levelling project then handled 60 million bricks (manufactured in four brickworks created for the purpose) and 3.5 million blocks of concrete. The result was this stone-faced brick construction comprising five bastions and five demilune fortifications, which protect the moats formerly fed by the Deûle River. These defences used to enclose a real town.

The **porte Royale**, which bears a Latin inscription praising Louis XIV, gives onto a vast pentagonal parade ground surrounded by buildings by Simon Vollant: the Classical chapel, the officer's quarters and a superb restored arsenal. These stone and brick buildings are representative of the French-Lille style which developed during this period. The citadel could be completely self-sufficient as it had its own wells, bakery, brewery, tailors, cobblers etc.

During the last two world wars many French patriots were executed by firing squad in the outer moats.

A zoo has been established in the **Bois de Boulogne**, near the Champ de Mars; there is also a tropical house and a playground. The **jardin Vauban** on the Deûle Canal bank is typical of mid-19C country gardens, with its clumps of trees, winding paths, flower beds and ponds. A statue of the Lille poet Albert Samain (1859-1906) stands within it.

Monument aux Fusillés (**DY K**) by Félix Desruelle stands in neighbouring Square Daubenton; it dates from 1915 and commemorates the Lille citizens executed by firing squad. Its most striking feature is the nobility of the victims' bearing.

Musée d'histoire naturelle et de géologie ⊘ (**EZ M**) – The natural history and geology museum was set up in 1822. Its collections were extended at the beginning of the 20C by two local geologists. Facing visitors as they enter the main hall are two impressive whale skeletons, the remains of mammals washed up on the coast.

H. Gyssels /DIAF

New Euralille district

The **zoology** collection on the left includes stuffed mammals and birds, reptiles, batrachia, molluscs, fish, and insects. Dioramas are used to show French fauna in its natural habitat: huge boars, alert deer, beavers etc. The insect houses contain spiders, scorpions and cockroaches. The magnificent ornithological collection boasts more than 5000 birds, including examples of species that are now extinct such as New Zealand huias or great auks.

The section on the right deals with **geology**. Fossils and rocks illustrate the history of Northern Europe from 600 million years BC to the Gallo-Roman period. Numerous plant fossils found in old mine workings are the remains of the dense forest that covered the region 300 million years ago. The work of miners is illustrated by a reconstruction of a coal seam, with its narrow gallery and heavy cart.

Jardin des Plantes ⊘ – *From Boulevard J-B-Lebas* (**FZ**) *take rue de Douai, rue Armand-Carrel and turn right after boulevard des Defenseurs-de-Lille.*
Among the 12ha/27 acres of lawns, trees and rare flowers stands a modern concrete and glass greenhouse containing tropical and equatorial plants.

EXCURSIONS

Marcq-en-Barœul: Fondation Prouvost-Septentrion ⊘ – *9km/5.6mi north. Leave Lille along N 17 then turn right onto D 952 and follow a road on the right which leads to the foundation.* An old farm not far from the Château du Vert-Bois holds temporary exhibitions of paintings, ceramics and objects representative of various civilizations. At the entrance, there is a fine collectin of rare minerals gathered by Anne and Albert Prouvost during their travels.

Euralille

Covering an area of almost 70ha/173 acres beyond Lille city centre is a whole new urban district designed by Dutch town planner Rem Koolhaas. Since May 1993, Lille's railway station, which was renamed **Lille-Flandres**, has catered for most of the high-speed trains from Paris. Linked by a viaduct with four arches, the new station, **Lille-Europe**, easily recognisable for its huge glass frontage, was built as part of the Paris-London and London-Brussels routes using the Channel Tunnel and for the high-speed train services between Lille and Lyon, Bordeaux, Nice, Montpellier etc. Two towers span the new stations, the **Tour Lille-Europe WTC** designed by architect Claude Vasconi and the L-shaped **Tour du Crédit Lyonnais★** designed by Christian de Portzampac.

The **Centre Euralille** was designed by the acclaimed French architect Jean Nouvel. Its spacious walkways and two floors contain more than 130 shops, a hypermarket, restaurants and a cultural centre called l'Espace croisé. It also has a theatre, private apartments, and a business school.

The oval-shaped **Lille Grand-Palais** at the south end stages the city's main events such as conferences, trade fairs, and major shows.

Euralille also includes the 8ha/20 acre Parc Henri-Matisse, and a few developments further to the north at the Portes de Romarin, within the boundaries of La Madeleine.

Château du Vert-Bois

Septentrion also consists of a gallery of contemporary art, a restaurant, a second-hand goods shop, a craft village, shops selling minerals etc.

★**Bondues: Château du Vert-Bois** ⊘ – *11km/7mi north. Leave on N 17 (**FX**) at Bondues turn right onto D 952, then right again to the château. The ticket office is located at the Fondation Prouvost.*
This charming 18C residence, surrounded by water-filled moats, contains splendid 18C furniture, old masters (J Vernet, Van Loo, Lallemant, Bonavia, Linnig), large tapestries and a collection of Persian plates from the 9C to the 13C.

LONGPONT★

Population 298
Michelin map 56 southwest of fold 4 or 237 fold 8

The village lies on the edge of Retz Forest and is overlooked by the ruins of the church and the buildings of the Cistercian abbey founded by St Bernard in the 12C.

Fortified gate – A picturesque 14C **fortified gate**, with four conical turrets, guarding the high street, is all that remains from the original fortifications.

Longpont – The fortified gate of the abbey

★ Abbey ⊘ – The large ensemble formed by the ruined abbey church and the buildings, restored in the 18C, is complemented by internal gardens opening onto a park. The abbey's former size is evoked in a model showing the 14C buildings.

Abbey Church Ruins – The pure Gothic church was consecrated in 1227 in the presence of the young Louis IX and Blanche of Castile. The abbey's possessions, deemed to be national property, were sold during the Revolution. The new owners of the church demolished it little by little, selling its stones until 1831 when it was bought by the Montesquiou family, which still owns it today.

The west front remains but the tracery of the rose-window has disappeared. Inside, the ruined walls and pillars standing among the vegetation give a clear idea of the church's size: 105m/115yd long and 28m/92ft high (Notre-Dame de Paris: 130m/142yd by 35m/115ft high).

Abbey Buildings – The great cloister's south gallery (rebuilt in the 17C) still exists and leads to the unique 13C **calefactory**, preserved intact with its central hooded fireplace. The west building was transformed in the 18C by the commendatory abbots, who had tall windows with large wrought-iron balconies set into the façades, providing a Classical elegance. Inside, the vast entrance hall features a staircase with a beautiful 18C wrought-iron balustrade; the 13C monks' cellars with Gothic vaults have been turned into reception rooms.

Église paroissiale – *Entrance from the square.*
This church takes up four arches of the old undercroft. Two 13C reliquaries have been preserved: the one concerning Jean de Montmirail, councillor to Philippe Auguste, and the head of St Dionysius the Areopagite.

Other Cistercian abbeys in the region include Ourscamp, Valloires and Vaucelles. 1998 marked the 9th centenary of the foundation of the Cistercian Order by Robert de Molesmes. The order later spread throughout Europe under the leadership of St Bernard.

MAINTENON★

Population 4 161
Michelin map 106 fold 26

Access from Paris: *SNCF Rail link from Gare Montparnasse*

This charming town on the banks of the Eure River is renowned for its château, irrevocably linked to the incredible destiny of **Françoise d'Aubigné**; she was born in 1635 to a family with Calvinist views, was orphaned at the age of 12, became the widow of the burlesque poet Paul Scarron at the age of 25, the clandestine governess of Mme de Montespan's children by the age of 34 and, in a secret ceremony, the wife of Louis XIV at the age of 48.

The corridors of power – When her clandestine charge, the duc de Maine, was legitimised, Françoise Scarron made a public appearance at court. Thereafter Louis XIV, who was extremely fond of his son, used to see her every day. Initially, he found her a trifle pedantic but soon revised his opinion of "the Scarron widow" and succumbed to her charm, intelligence and strong temperament. In 1674 Françoise Scarron received the Maintenon estate from the King, who then publicly christened her "Madame de Maintenon".

After the Queen's death, Louis XIV secretly married Mme de Maintenon in the chapel at Versailles during the winter of 1683-84. The morganatic queen acceded to the rank of peer and marquise in 1688 – a privilege bestowed on her directly by the King – and from then on she became an extremely powerful figure in the country's political life. When the King died in 1715, she withdrew to St-Cyr, where she died in 1719.

A Herculean task – Between 1685 and 1688, the area around Maintenon saw one of the century's most ambitious projects: the diverting of the waters of the Eure River to the fountains of Versailles. François Louvois acted as supervisor; he left Sébastien Vauban in charge of the plans and entrusted him with the construction of an 80km/50mi long aqueduct linking Pontgouin *(Michelin map 60 fold 6)* to the Étang de la Tour, which was already linked with the Versailles reservoirs by rivulets from the Trappes plateau.

The Maintenon aqueduct was a colossal enterprise, involving a total length of 4600m/15000ft and three superimposed rows of arches, placed 72m/237ft above the level of the Eure River. In fact, it was only possible to fit in one row of arches. The link with the canals on the plateaux was to be implemented by pressurised pipes acting as a battery of pumps.

The operation was carried out like a military campaign; 20000 soldiers took part in the excavation work, in addition to the 10000 skilled workers summoned from remote villages and the local peasants who helped cart the materials. The Voise and Drouette rivers were canalised and used to convey the freestones and sandstone rubble from the Gallardon and Épernon quarries. The shipments of Newcastle coal needed to work

223

the lime and brick kilns, and the pipes and iron bars despatched from Champagne, Belgium and Pays d'Ouche were carried along the Seine and Eure rivers.

In 1689, the wars triggered off by the Augsburg League interrupted the work. The French troops, in poor physical condition, were sent off to the borders to defend their country. The work was never resumed.

From then on, Mme de Maintenon ceased her visits to the château; she was offered the impressive but unfinished aqueduct to compensate for the damage to her estate.

SIGHTS

★Château ⊘ – The present château occupies the site of a former stronghold circled by the waters of the Eure. The construction work was undertaken by Jean Cottereau, Minister of Finance to Louis XII, François I and Henri II, and completed around 1509 in the Renaissance style.

The estate then came into the hands of the d'Angennes family. In 1674 Louis XIV bought the château from Françoise d'Angennes for 250 000 livres and gave it to the future Marquise de Maintenon. The Marquise left it to her niece, who was married to the Duke of Ayen, son of the first Maréchal de Noailles. The château has remained in this family ever since.

Exterior – The archway, flanked by two protruding turrets and bearing Jean Cottereau's arms (three lizards), leads to the inner court which is the starting-point for tours. The square 12C keep, now crowned with an elegant roof, is all that remains of the original stronghold.

The adjoining wing was built by Mme de Maintenon and the narrow door set in the tower still sports the Marquise's emblem, a griffin's head. A door depicting St Michael and bearing the lizard emblem gives onto a staircase leading to Mme de Maintenon's suite. It consists of an antechamber, a bedroom – where Charles X spent the night on 3 August 1830 when he fled Rambouillet – and a small cabinet. After leaving the main block, visitors are shown round the first floor of the Renaissance pavilion, redesigned to accommodate the apartments of Mme de Montespan and her royal charges.

The tour ends with the reception rooms furnished by the Noailles family in the 19C. The Grand Salon bears portraits of the two royal rivals, Mme de Montespan and Mme de Maintenon. In the Portrait Gallery, a collection of paintings represents the illustrious members of the family. The mortal remains of the Marquise lie in the chapel of St-Cyr Military Academy. A memorial was erected in her honour in 1980.

Parterre – The parterre is flanked by charming canals fed by the waters of the Eure. The bench at the far end offers an extensive view of the Grand Canal and three of the arches of Maintenon aqueduct. Turn round and enjoy the superb **vista★** of the château with its elegant towers and grey and pink stone and brickwork.

Château de Maintenon

★**Aqueduct** – The fifty-odd arches that remain, many of which are crumbling and overgrown with plants and weeds, stretch from Maintenon station to the D 6 road, leading to St-Piat. On the way to Gallardon, the road runs under a curious arch of four ribs of archstones hanging suspended in mid-air.

EXCURSION

St-Piat; L'Arche de la Vallée – *12km/7.5mi southwest, then 1hr on foot there and back. Leave Maintenon by D 6 south towards Chartres via the Eure valley.*

St-Piat – The village has developed around its 16C church and one of the big mills of the area (now disused).

After leaving St-Piat, turn right to climb up to the plateau.

Drive through Chartainvilliers then cross the main Maintenon-Chartres road and follow the signs to Théléville and Berchères-la-Maingot. The line of trees on a hummock to the right indicates a major earth-moving project undertaken to change the course of the River Eure.

The project, called Les Terrasses, was to raise the canal to the upper level of the aqueduct. After leaving Théléville, the road to Berchères descends into a wooded area. At the foot of the incline, park the car at a large crossroads.

L'Arche de la Vallée – *1hr on foot there and back.* In the dip of the valley, take the cart track *(to the right of the Bridge)* which follows the gully of the stream to reach the artificial embankment dividing the valley.

This depression was one of the greatest obstacles lying in the way of the canal (except for the interruption of the river at Maintenon). A stonework aqueduct had initially been planned but, desirous of cutting costs, Vauban installed a closed gallery supported by a ramp, working on the principle of a pump.

Proceed along the foot of the embankment, to the left. This leads to l'Arche de la Vallée, a tunnel supported by intricate brick vaulting, remarkably well-designed for such a small watercourse. *Avoid crossing the river as the ground tends to be muddy.* Go back and turn left into a wide path trodden by horses' hooves leading onto the embankment and to the west funnel, a gallery running to the bottom of the well which was designed to receive the waters from the canal *(bring a torch)*. The passageway used to extend along the upper ridge of the embankment – then much higher – and join up with an east funnel *(private property)*.

Château de MAISONS-LAFFITTE★

Michelin map 101 fold 13 – Michelin plan 18

Access from Paris: *SNCF Rail link from Gare St-Lazare or RER line A 3/A 5*

Président Longueil – The château was built between 1642 and 1651 for René de Longueil, President of the Parlement de Paris, appointed Governor of the royal châteaux at Versailles and St-Germain. The plans were drawn up by the architect **François Mansart**, a difficult man known to be extremely demanding; he would not hesitate to knock down one of his own pavillions and rebuild it if he considered it inadequate. The château was designed to receive royalty as it was one of the official places of residence assigned to French rulers. The palace was inaugurated during a brilliant reception celebrated in honour of Anne of Austria and Louis XIV, then aged 13. The Sun King subsequently took up residence at St-Germain and paid frequent visits to Maisons, as did his successors.

From D'Artois to Lannes – The Comte d'Artois, brother of Louis XVI, acquired the estate in 1777 and gave orders to build the famous racecourse. His extravagant parties were attended by everyone at court. In July 1789 he went into exile, accompanied by a staff of 200, and had to wait 25 years before returning to France. He was crowned King of France in 1824, under the name Charles X, but was exiled a second time in 1830 and died in 1836 at the age of 79.

The estate was sequestered during the Revolution and sold to Marshal Jean Lannes, Duke of Montebello, in 1804. Napoleon I, who enjoyed the Marshal's company, was a regular visitor to the château.

Maisons-Laffitte – In 1818 the famous banker **Jacques Laffitte** (1767-1844) bought the estate, where he entertained the adversaries of the Restoration: General Foy, the Marquis de Lafayette, Casimir Périer, Benjamin Constant etc. Laffitte did much to secure Louis-Philippe d'Orléans' accession to the throne during the revolution of July 1830 which overthrew Charles X. This shrewd financier was made Prime Minister to the new king in 1830 but proved unable to calm the disturbances that had broken out in the capital; mistrusted by both the Orleanists and the moderates, Laffitte was forced to resign in March 1831. Ruined, in debt to the tune of 50 million francs, he dismantled the imposing stables and used the stone to build houses in the Grand Parc.

Château de Maisons-Laffitte

The stables had been two long, beautiful buildings designed by Mansart and erected on the Avenue du Château (now Avenue du Général-Leclerc). They provided a very impressive entrance to the Longueil's estate.

The château frequently changed hands and was bought by the State in 1905.

TOUR ⏱ *1hr*

The château dates from the early part of Louis XIV's reign and has always been considered a model of French architecture. From the main driveway, formerly called the King's entrance – royal visitors generally approached from St-Germain Forest, to the west – there is a splendid view of the high-pitched roofs.

The façade facing the Seine is fronted by a dry moat, a terrace and the main staircase. The stone exterior presents Classical ornamentation: Doric on the ground floor, Ionic on the first floor and Corinthian on the attic storey level with the dormer windows. The alternating fluted columns and engaged pilasters form a pleasing, well-balanced composition.

Interior – Despite minor alterations during the ownership of the Comte d'Artois in the 18C, there are no major discrepancies between the austerity of Mansart's work, completed c 1650 and the cold formality of the neo-Classical features.

Salon des captifs – This drawing room, set in a corner of the château, is decorated with several fine paintings including H Robert's *Landscape with a Waterfall*. The room gets its name from the decoration on the monumental fireplace.

Vestibule d'honneur – Lying in the centre of the château, it constitutes a perfect entrance articulated by eight Doric columns. It was originally enclosed by two imposing wrought-iron gates. They were installed in 1650 and later moved to the Apollo Gallery in the Louvre. A group of mythological figures by Jacques Sarrazin symbolise the four Elements: Jupiter (fire), Juno (air), Neptune (water) and Cybele (Earth).

The eagles are not those associated with the emperor: their "long eye" *(long œil)* is merely a pun on the first proprietor's name.

Grand Escalier – The staircase, one of Mansart's major accomplishments at Maisons, is characteristic of the period: square layout with straight flights of stairs. Groups of children executed by Philippe Buyster symbolise Music and Singing, Science and Art, War and Peace, Love and Marriage.

Appartement du Comte d'Artois – The corner dining room is an excellent example of carved neo-Classical decoration as commissioned by the Comte d'Artois. Two artists with a passionate interest in Antiquity, Bélanger and the sculptor Lhuillier, have left their mark on the room. It has a coffered ceiling, a group of Fames over the door, a fireplace flanked by bacchantes etc.

Appartement du Roi – 1st floor. A suite of rooms built in the Italian style, featuring domed or barrel-vaulted ceilings with no painted decoration. Walk down the Grand Gallery and enter the **Salon d'Hercule** (formerly the king's antechamber), which leads through to the **Chambre du roi.** Admire the domed ceiling, the original parquet floor and the ceremonial bed.

Cabinet des Miroirs – The parquet floor and panelling are masterpieces of marquetry inlaid with wood, bone and pewter.

Chambre Lannes – The passage leading to the bedroom houses a collection of figurines portraying various regiments of Napoleon's Grand Army.
The queen's former bedchamber was redesigned to receive Marshal Jean Lannes. The furniture, chandelier and decoration are all Empire. In the centre stands a magnificent Restoration table inlaid with elm wood. The paintings include a scene which shows Napoleon's ashes being carried past Sartrouville Bridge in 1840.

In the basement, there is a small **racehorse museum**, recalling the major role played by the owners of the château in the history of horse racing.

RACECOURSE AND PARK

The racecourse at Maisons-Laffitte, located on the banks of the River Seine, is well known to Paris racegoers.
The training stables and the tracks, second only to Chantilly in importance, lie to the north of the park, on the edge of the forest.
A walk in the park early in the morning (7am) will reveal the morning training of the various "charges": mounted by stable hands, they will be walking or trotting along the sandy lanes. The most prestigious route, however, for exercising thoroughbreds is a circular ride known as the Cercle de la Gloire (Circle of Glory). The wider tracks used for galloping are not open to the public.

MANTES-LA-JOLIE

Conurbation 189103
Michelin map 106 fold 15

Access from Paris: *SNCF Rail link from Gare St-Lazare or Montparnasse*

This extremely active town has grown considerably with the industrial development of its suburbs.

Henri IV's Conversion – Henri IV, who had taken Mantes from the Catholic League in 1590, returned to the town on account of the ravishing Gabrielle d'Estrées. During one of his stays in May 1593 he decided to renounce Protestantism a second time (he had already done so once to escape the St Bartholomew's Day Massacre).
In view of the ceremony, a number of meetings took place between the king, supported by the Protestants Duplessis-Mornay and Sully, and Cardinal Duperron, the Abbot of St-Denis, as well as various other leading ecclesiastic figures. It was in Mantes, at the end of one of these meetings, that Henri IV replied to Duperron, "I place my soul in your hands. Please take care of it. From where you would have me enter, I shall leave only through death." Tears welled up in his eyes. Taking leave of his Huguenot adviser, he said, "What can I do? If I refused to renounce my faith, that would be the end of France." The famous words, "Paris is well worth a Mass" are said to be a somewhat free interpretation of this sentence. The abjuration ceremony took place in the Basilica of St-Denis on 25 July 1593.

★★COLLÉGIALE NOTRE-DAME ⊙ *30min*

This church – which inspired Corot to paint one of his most beautiful works (now in the Musée des Beaux-Arts, Reims) – would compare favourably with many of France's cathedrals. It was built by the chapter of a collegiate church which owned large estates in the area. The funds for this ambitious project were provided by the municipality, William the Conqueror and several Capetian kings.
The construction of the church, started in 1170, ran into the 13C in the case of the nave and the chancel. The chapels were added in the 14C. The church stood within the fortified bailey that defended the old royal castle *(behind the east end, on the site now occupied by the public gardens).*

Exterior – The west front is the oldest part of the church. The tower on the left and the narrow gallery linking it to the right tower were rebuilt in the 19C.
Three badly-damaged doorways adorn the exterior. The one in the centre is dedicated to the Virgin Mary and was built between 1170 and 1195. Like the north doorway on the left, it features foliated scrolls on the jambs and bases of the colonnettes.
A walk round the right side leads to the protruding 14C Navarre Chapel. Note the unusual east end, with its gabled apses crowned by a gallery and backing onto a high wall circling the ambulatory. This open-work structure admitting large, round bays is supported by hefty buttresses. Above the fortified wall, the upper part of the chancel is supported by a series of sturdy flying buttresses.

Mantes – Musée Luce: The Foundry in Charleroi

Interior – The light, elegant nave (33m/108ft tall) is almost as high as that of Notre-Dame in Paris (35m/114ft). Its elevation of wide arches, brightly-lit galleries and clerestory windows marks the transition from Romanesque to early Gothic. The splendid rose-window (early 13C) in the west front depicts the last Judgement. Walking down the nave, note the arrangement of the sexpartite vaulting. The heavier supporting arches at each end rest on thick pillars, while the lighter ones end in round columns. The deep, well-lit galleries above the aisles – a legacy from Romanesque architecture – open onto the nave by a series of bays with triple arcades. Observe the old-fashioned structure of the galleries in the apse and the north part of the chancel, surmounted by barrel vaulting.

The **Chapelle de Navarre** (Chapel of the Blessed Sacrament), built onto the south side of the chancel, forms a separate ensemble. It resembles a sort of shrine featuring early-14C windows with Radiant Gothic roundels. It is thought the name comes from the kings of Navarre, who belonged to the ruling house of Évreux (the counts of Évreux held the lordship of Mantes from 1328 to 1364).

The entrance to the chapel is graced by four dainty statuettes dating from the 14C. The crowned women carrying a miniature model of the church are probably the founders of Notre-Dame: Jeanne de France, comtesse d'Évreux (1312-49) and Jeanne d'Évreux, Queen of France by her marriage to Charles IV the Fair in 1324. The other two young women are probably Jeanne de France's daughters, Queen Blanche, who married Philip VI of Valois, and Agnès, wife of the famous Gaston Phoebus, comte de Foix.

ADDITIONAL SIGHT

Ancien Hôtel-Dieu – Turned into a museum in 1996, the Hôtel-Dieu stages temporary exhibitions and houses the Musée Luce.

Musée Luce – *Second floor.*

The museum is exclusively devoted to the neo-Impressionist painter **Maximilien Luce** (1858-1941) and contains some 100 of his works (lithographs, etchings, drawings and paintings). A friend of Seurat, Pissarro and of several anarchists, Luce often found his inspiration in the social context of his time: Foundry in Charleroi (1896), Varlin's Execution. He also painted landscapes of the Mantes region, in particular Rolleboise where he spent several months every year.

MARLY-LE-ROI★

Population 16741
Michelin map 101 fold 12 – Michelin plan 18

Although a number of major property developments have spread across the Grandes Terres plateau since 1950, stretching towards Le Pecq, the name of Louis XIV remains firmly attached to this town.

Marly was the Sun King's favourite residence. Unfortunately, its golden age lasted barely twenty years. After the First Empire only the park remained, an impressive display of greenery bordering the old village, which has welcomed many writers and artists: the two Alexandre Dumas, Alfred Sisley, Camille Pissarro, the sculptor Maillol and the tragedienne Mlle Rachel, to name but a few.

The early stages – Marly's construction was due to Louis XIV's desire to retreat from the formal etiquette of Versailles. After the Treaty of Nijmegen in 1678, at the peak of his glory, tired of the continual entertaining at Versailles, the king dreamed of a peaceful country residence, far from the madding crowd. His barony at Marly offered a deep, lush valley which seemed to suit the purpose and he entrusted Jules Hardouin-Mansart with the plans.

Mansart came up with an ingenious idea: instead of designing one huge single pavilion which he knew the king would refuse he conceived a series of 13 separate units. The royal pavilion would stand on the upper terrace, while the other twelve, smaller in size and all identical, would be arranged along a stretch of water. To promote his idea, Mansart explained that the decoration of the king's pavilion could symbolise the sun – Louis XIV's emblem – and that the surrounding buildings could represent the twelve signs of the zodiac. To cut down on costs, it was agreed to replace the carved bas-reliefs by trompe-l'œil frescoes. The King, delighted, gave orders to start building in 1679. It took nine years for the whole project to be completed. After working relentlessly all his life, Mansart died at the château in 1708.

Further embellishments – Right until the end of his reign, Louis XIV applied himself to the improvement of his Marly residence and kept a close watch on the various projects under way. He would even show gardeners how to trim the hedges properly.

Behind the royal pavilion rose the steep, wooded slopes of the hillside. The Sun King gave orders to build the River, also called the Grande Cascade *(illustration above)*, the Wonder of Marly, which was served by the famous "Machine" *(see below)*: starting from the top of the hill, an impressive series of falls poured down a flight of fifty-two steps of pink marble set into the terraced slope. The whole ensemble – adorned with statues, portices and rockeries – was completed in 1699.

The same year, the King decided to clear the main perspective and raze the hillock that stood in the way, an entreprise that occupied 1 600 soldiers for a period of four years.

Archives Nationales, Paris/Revault /PIX

The Grande Cascade at Marly (18C gouache)

Life at Marly – Apart from his close relatives, Louis XIV brought very few guests to Marly; the facilities for accomodation were limited to 24 apartments. It is estimated that 500 lords and 300 ladies altogether were invited to the château over a period of 30 years. The King himself drew up a list of the guests and he personally determined where they should stay; the nearer they were to the royal pavilion, the greater the honour. The "happy few" were not necessarily members of the aristocracy or high dignitaries, but lively, intelligent personalities whose wit and charm would enliven the king's stays.

The formal etiquette of Versailles was dropped at Marly. The king shared his meals with his guests, with whom he conversed in a free, casual manner. Hunts, forest walks, outdoor games, card games, games of chance, balls and concerts were a regular feature of life here. The standard of comfort at the place, however, left something to be desired; in summer the guests caught fever, in winter they shivered with cold or choked with smoke because it was too damp to start a fire. Louis XIV – who personally undertook to tackle the heating problem – introduced new systems every year, in vain. On 9 August 1715, the King suffered a bout of exhaustion after following the hunt in his carriage. He was taken to Versailles, where he died on 1 September, aged 77.

Louis XV and Louis XVI stayed in Marly from time to time. The costly Grande Cascade was abandoned in favour of the present "green carpet". The furniture was sold during the Revolution; in 1800, an industrialist bought the estate and set up a mill there. Having failed in business, he offered Napoleon the opportunity of buying Marly but he was turned down. He then proceeded to demolish the castle and sell the building materials. One year later, Napoleon retrieved the estate which has since been the property of the French state.

★MARLY PARK

Enter Marly Park by the Deux Portes. Take the first right turn through the woods to the car park near the presidential pavilion.

A large esplanade flanked by lime trees in the centre of the park marks the former site of the royal pavilion. A series of slabs defines the layout of the building: the large octagonal drawing room in the centre is surrounded by four corner rooms, separated by vestibules. The decoration in the King's rooms was red, the Dauphin's rooms were green (they were originally intended for the Queen but she never occupied them); the apartments for "Monsieur" (Louis XIV's brother) were yellow and those of "Madame", his second wife Elisabeth of Bavaria, were blue.

This is where the two perspectives of the park meet: across to the drive leading to the Royal Gates, and along the route running from St-Germain and the Seine Valley up to the Grand Mirror fountains and the green "carpet" of lawn.

The plans for one of the guests' pavilions are marked out by the slabs behind the car park.

The present grounds are suggestive of old Marly, with its terraces, fountains and hornbeam arbours. Further information can be obtained from the museum in the new outbuilding near the Grille Royale.

Grille Royale – Louis XIV would use this entrance when he arrived from Versailles. Admire the perspective of the steep road climbing up the hillside and its continuation on the opposite slope, slicing its way through the trees.

Musée-Promenade de Marly-le-Roi-Louveciennes ⊙ – The museum contains precious material on the 13 pavilions and the garden statues which no longer exist; the plans drawn up in 1753 and a miniature model of the whole project give a fair idea of what the king's country residence looked like. Note the interesting 18C approach to ornamental gardening.

The corner of the main pavilion houses the casts of the statues sculpted by Coustou and Lepautre, a painting of the château and its fountains by Martin the Younger (1723) and numerous line drawings of former copses and spinneys.

The room dedicated to Louveciennes displays a number of items concerning Mme du Barry: Pajou's statue of *Loyalty*, a drawing by Moreau the younger portraying a banquet held in the Music Pavilion in honour of Louis XV in 1771. It also features the only religious work by Mme Vigée-Lebrun, as well as her two paintings *Summer* and *Autumn*, which were hung at Marly in 1755. Admire one of Desportes' hunting scenes and a *Lamentation* (1516) from St-Vigor Church.

Before leaving the museum, visit the small chamber presenting the "Marly Machine": it contains drawings and plans, together with a model. The mural painting depicts the waterworks of Versailles.

Return to the car and leave the park by avenue des Combattants. Drive down to the Abreuvoir.

Abreuvoir (Horse-Pond) – After a steep descent – known as Côte du Cœur-Volant – N 386 leads to the horse-pond, once used as a spillway for the waters of Marly park. From here, the water was conveyed back to the Seine by a system of pipes and drains. The terrace flanked by yew trees above the pond used to bear Coysevox' *Winged Horses* and, at a later date, Guillaume Coustou's *Rearing Horses*. Two replicas stand in their place. The original statues once adorned place de la Concorde in Paris and have now been moved to the Louvre. Two reproductions have also been installed on the Parisian square.

EXCURSIONS

Port-Marly

Château de Monte-Cristo ⊙ – *Entrance shared with the Clinique de l'Europe.*
Built in 1846 on a hill overlooking the Seine Valley, this extravagant folly expressed
the eccentricity of **Alexandre Dumas** through a wonderfully eclectic combination of
Gothic, Renaissance and Moorish styles. After holding sumptuous receptions for
the fashionable Paris set when his works *The Count of Monte-Cristo* and *The Three
Musketeers* were enjoying great success, Dumas ran up enormous debts and was
finally forced to sell up. The delightful building has recently been restored. It is
decorated with medallions representing the famous writer and those of his friends
of whom he was particularly fond.

Some of the rooms contain portraits and documents. Visitors can also see the great
man's study and the splendid **Moorish bedroom★** in which the exuberance of the carvings and brilliant stained glass is equalled only by the furniture.

A few yards from the château is the little **Château d'If**, a pseudo-Gothic construction designed by Dumas as a place to which he could retire for peace and quiet.
Note the titles of his works engraved on the freestone walls.

After being abandoned for many years, the **park** has now been exceptionally well
preserved and again provides a charming setting with its grottoes and manmade
features. The many natural springs have been skilfully channelled to form tiny
waterfalls cascading into the basins and ponds. There is also an open-air theatre,
a project planned by Dumas but never completed.

Louveciennes

This small residential town on the edge of Marly Forest still features several large
estates.

The **church** (12C-13C) on the village square retains a Romanesque look, but the
polygonal bell-tower is 19C. The interior boasts an interesting collection of stone
piscinae, resting against the east end.

Walk through the public gardens, along rue de l'Étang and down rue du Pont for
a pleasant view of the 16C **Château du Pont** *(private)*, the groves of trees and the
rippling waters of the moat.

Follow rue du Général-Leclerc to the town hall, opposite which stand arches of the
disused aqueduct that used to convey the waters of the Seine to Versailles thanks
to the "Marly Machine".

From the church, follow rue du Professeur-Tuffier, then rue du Maréchal Joffre as
far as chemin des Gressets to reach **Field Marshal Joffre's Tomb**. The Maréchal's house
can be seen at the corner.

The rotunda-shaped temple seen from the chemin des Gressets was the last resting-
place of the Victor of the Marne and his wife. Joffre, who died in 1931, was
extremely fond of Louveciennes and insisted on being buried here rather than at
Les Invalides in Paris.

The Marly Machine – It was decided to divert the waters of the Seine to supply
the fountains of Marly and, subsequently, those of Versailles.

F. Jalain /EXPLORER

The Moorish bedroom in the Château de Monte-Cristo

Colbert succeeded in finding a Belgian engineer, Arnold Deville, and a master carpenter, Rennequin Sualem, who agreed to take on the daring project of raising the water 150m/493ft above the level of the river. The work started in 1681, took three years and involved a considerable amount of equipment: 13 hydraulic wheels with a diameter of 12m/40ft operated 225 pumps ranged in three ranks, by which the waters were conveyed from the water tower – set at a height of 163m/535ft above the Seine – to the Louveciennes reservoirs via an aqueduct with a capacity of 5000m³/176575cu ft a day. From there they were channelled to Marly or Versailles. Since the 19C, several pumping devices have occupied the site; the last disappeared in 1967.

The site – The road bridge of Ile de la Loge affords a good view of the 18C buildings *(quai Rennequin-Sualem at Bougival)* that contained the Marly Machine, and the pipes lining the hillside. At the top of the rise stands a white lodge by Ledoux: the **"pavillon de musique" de Madame du Barry**. It was inaugurated on 2 September 1771, during a sumptuous banquet attended by Louis XV.

The building was moved to this site and raised a storey in 1934 by the famous perfumer René Coty.

*Bougival

In the 19C Bougival was a centre of art, fêtes and bohemian life. Bizet, Corot, Meissonier and Renoir lived here. The "boaters" – fun-loving, young Parisian men and women – who flocked to the dances at La Grenouillère had their carefree lives evoked by Maupassant in his novels and short stories, and captured on canvas by Impressionists (Renoir, Berthe Morisot, Monet).

Musée Tourgueniev ⊙ – *16 Rue Ivan-Tourgueniev. Access on foot via a small alleyway off N 13 level with the Forest Hill hotel.*

Built on the heights, the house where Turgenev lived in his exile was part of the property owned by his friends Louis Viardot and his wife Pauline, a singer like her sister La Malibran.

On the ground floor are some of the writer's documents, photographs of family and friends, engravings, and his piano. His works are evoked through extracts from novels and essays, among them the *Récits d'un Chasseur* published in 1852, in which he predicted the abolition of serfdom in Russia.

On the first floor, the writer's study and the room where he died on 3 September 1883 have been recreated. His body was taken to St Petersburg on 1 October: a photograph captures Ernest Renan giving a speech at the Gare du Nord in Paris (the "Adieu to Paris"); another shows the funeral procession in St Petersburg.

Forêt de MARLY-LE-ROI

The state forest – once royal hunting grounds, jealously guarded by high walls – covers a rough but picturesque plateau planted with oaks, beeches and chestnut trees. The total area is estimated at 2000ha/5000 acres.

The thicker groves, featuring some beautiful trees, lie west of the road from St-Germain to St-Nom-la-Bretèche, particulary between Etoile des Dames and Etoile de Joyenval.

Consult Michelin map 101 to see which lanes are closed to traffic (barriers). These may however be recommended as cycling paths.

Désert de Retz ⊙ – *Temporarily closed to the public.* The park was created by Monsieur de Monvil, usher to the king's chamber, in the second half of the 18C. It lies on the edge of Marly forest and is adorned with seventeen buildings (Tartars' tent, Greek temple dedicated to Pan, Chinese house, ice-house in the shape of a pyramid etc), an Anglo-Chinese garden, two lakes, an open air theatre etc. Famous figures such as Marie-Antoinette and the King of Sweden visited the Desert.

Domaine du MARQUENTERRE★★

MARQUENTERRE RESERVE

Michelin map 51 fold 11 and 52 fold 6 or 236 fold 11

The Marquenterre area is an alluvial plain reclaimed from the sea; it lies between the Authie and Somme estuaries and its name derives from *mer qui entre en terre* (sea which enters the land).

The stretches of land are made up of briny marshes, salt-pastures and sand dunes secured to the land by vegetation, and are of fairly recent origin. The town of Rue was a seaport in the Middle Ages.

The Marquenterre lands, particularly around the Baie de Somme where vast reaches of sand are uncovered twice a day at low tide, have always been an important stopover for migratory birds and a place of hibernation for many others. It was a paradise for hunters who, from hides, could fire on the hundreds of ducks, geese and sandpipers of all types, to the extent that many species disappeared.

As a result of the decimation, in 1968 the Hunting Commission *(Office de la Chasse)* created a reserve on the maritime land, to ensure the protection of the birds along 5km/3mi of coastline.

The owners of the Marquenterre estate next to the reserve then decided to set up a bird sanctuary within it to allow the general public to watch the extraordinary variety of birdlife in its natural habitat.

The Henson horse breed

This small robust horse is a cross between a French saddle horse and a Norwegian Fjord pony. Its coat varies from light yellow to brown, and its mane is a mixture of black and gold. This breed was developed in 1978 in a small village of the Baie de Somme area, thanks to the determination of Doctor Berquin. Hensons show remarkable endurance: they can remain out in the fields all year round and cover great distances without getting tired. Their docile and affectionate behaviour make them ideal companions for children.and long-distance riders. They also fare very well in team competitions and horse shows generally. A riding centre established next to the bird sanctuary organises excursions for beginners and experienced riders (Centre équestre Henson Marquenterre, Domaine du Marquenterre, 80120 St-Quentin-en-Tourmont, ☎ 03 22 25 03 06)

★★Parc Ornithologique (Bird Sanctuary) ⊘ – *It is advisable to visit on a rising tide when the birds leave the stretches of the Baie de Somme or during the spring and autumn migration periods.*

The Bird Sanctuary was created in 1973 and covers 250ha/627 acres at the edge of the réserve de Marquenterre. Over 300 species of bird have been identified, among them many ducks including the redbeaked sheld-duck, geese, tern, waders such as the avocet with its delicately-curved beak, seagulls, herons, sandpipers, spoonbills etc.

Two different trails are signposted:
– The tour of the lakes and aviaries at the foot of an old coastal dune, offering a close-up view of the birds which live here permanently: ducks, seagulls, geese and herons. Their calls attract wild birds of the same species with their cries.

– The walk *(allow 2hr 30min, binoculars recommended)* follows a path through the dunes to various observation hides, a heronry and a large aviary, from where the habits and movements of numerous species in their natural habitat can be studied.

An additional path (1.5km/1mi) shows the reserve from a completely different angle.

D'après photo by Anthony /JACANA

Avocet

MEAUX★

Canurbation 63 006
Michelin map 106 folds 22, 23 – Local map under Vallée de l'OURCQ

Access from Paris: *SNCF Rail link from Gare de l'Est*

Formerly the property of the house of Champagne, Meaux was an agricultural centre lying between the Petit Morin and Grand Morin rivers, on the edge of the Multien cereal-growing plains and the famous dairy pastures of Brie. It is now an average-sized town, which has been expanding since 1960.

In the summer months, a **son-et-lumière performance** featuring a cast of 2 100 re-enacts Meaux's moments of glory in the charming setting of the Episcopal Precinct *(see Calendar of Events)*.

Jacques Bossuet, Bishop of Meaux – Having completed his tutorial commitments towards the Dauphin, **Bossuet** was made Bishop of Meaux in 1682 at the age of 55. The man later known as the "Eagle of Meaux" exercised his ecclesiastic duties with the utmost assiduity; he kept an attentive eye on catechism, was often seen preaching in his own cathedral and assumed full command of the religious communities in his diocese. For instance, despite his great esteem for Jouarre Abbey, he did not hesitate to have the place besieged when the abbess refused to dismiss two nuns whose presence he considered undesirable.

Bossuet enjoyed working in the huge library of the Episcopal Palace, or in his study at the end of the garden; it was there that he composed five of his most famous funeral orations including those dedicated to Louis XIV's wife Marie-Thérèse and the Great Condé. He also wrote a number of books defending Gallican orthodoxy.

He died in Paris in 1704, aged 77, at the height of his intellectual pursuits. As was his wish, he was buried in his cathedral in Meaux.

★EPISCOPAL PRECINCT *1hr 30min*

★Cathédrale St-Étienne

The construction of the church continued from the late 12C to the 16C, covering the entire gamut of Gothic architecture.

The façade (14-16C) is pure Flamboyant. Only the left tower was completed. The one on the right – a plain bell-tower – is called the Black Tower on account of its dark-coloured shingles. The limestone used for the stonework has crumbled in several places and the exterior decoration is badly damaged. The Wars of Religion brought further destruction.

The south transept façade is an elegant example of Radiant Gothic. The south doorway – in poor condition – is dedicated to St Stephen.

Enter the cathedral through this doorway.

The interior of the cathedral – last restored in the 18C – contrasts sharply with the badly weathered exterior. The lofty, well-lit nave is an impressive sight. The double side aisles are unusually high owing to the suppression of the upper galleries as in Notre-Dame in Paris. These were removed around the middle of the 13C, which had the effect of heightening the aisles.

The two bays of the nave next to the transept date from the early 13C; their austere appearance typifies early Gothic. The west bays were completed in the 14C and the pillars redesigned in the 15C.

The transepts – in particular the south arm – are superb examples of 14C architecture; the elegant, generous proportions characterise the golden age of High Gothic. Below the huge stained-glass window runs an openwork triforium so fine that it allows a full view of the lancets. The chancel – also High Gothic – is a pleasing sight with its double aisles and its five apsidal chapels. Note the pretty 15C Maugarni doorway to the left.

A walk round the ambulatory leads to Bossuet's tomb, marked by a slab of black marble, visible through the parclose enclosing the chancel.

Vieux Chapitre

This is believed to have been the chapter's 13C tithe barn. The external staircase is roofed over and dates from the Renaissance period. The ground floor, linked to the cathedral by a wooden gallery, is used as a sacristy and a chapel annex.

Ancien Évêché ⊘

The old palace houses a **museum** largely dedicated to Bossuet. The building was completed in the 12C and altered in the 17C. The main front overlooks the garden. The two magnificent Gothic rooms facing the park on the ground floor, the lower and the upper chapel are the oldest parts of the palace. The chapterhouse holds temporary exhibitions. The amazing brick ramp was designed by Bishop Briçonnet in the 16C to enable the mules loaded with grain to reach the attics.

Enter the palace through the Salle du Synode which together with the western salons has been made into a Fine Arts Museum (15C to 19C). Among the many artists feature Boullogne, De Troy, Bouchardon, Millet, Courbet and Senelle. The donation made by Annie and Jean Pierre Changeux in 1983 has considerably enriched the collections of 17C and 18C French painting.

Bossuet's apartment, located in the east wing, has retained its original layout but the decoration was renewed in the Louis XV style. Admire Mignard's portrait of the bishop and a splendid Cressent commode (early 18C).

The former library contains an anonymous 17C portrait of Henrietta Maria of England, for whom Bossuet composed his famous funeral oration.

The chapel houses medieval sculptures, a fine reliquary illustrating Christ's Lamentation by Frans Floris.

The history of the town is also presented: 1738 plan by Monvoisin, pictures of the old bridge spanning the Marne with its picturesque mills (sadly disappeared), apothecary's shop of the former hospice, Moisan's electric oven (1892) for studying artificial diamonds.

Gardens

The gardens, shaped like a bishop's mitre, were designed by Le Nôtre in the tradition of French formal gardens.

Anciens remparts

The ramparts are only acessible during the guided tours of the town.

At the top of the steps stands the humble 17C pavilion which Bossuet used as a study. The bishop would retire here to collect his thoughts or to write in the peaceful hours of the night.

The centre of the terrace affords a good **view★** of the gardens, the Episcopal Palace and the cathedral.

EXCURSION

Château de Montceaux ⊙ – *8.5km/5mi east. Leave Meaux by N 3 (east). Beyond Trilport, in Montceaux Forest, turn right onto D 19 (signposted Montceaux-les-Meaux). The lane to the château is on the right.*
Montceaux was known as the Château of the Queens. Catherine de' Medici had it built and Philibert Delorme almost certainly worked on it between 1547 and 1559. Henri IV later gave it to Gabrielle d'Estrées who had work continued by JA du Cerceau (1594-99). On the death of the one who was "almost Queen", the king gave the château to his bride Marie de' Medici who entrusted the works to Salomon de Brosse before he started to build the Luxembourg Palace (1608-22 in Paris). The château fell into disrepair and after 1650 became uninhabitable. Handsome ruins lurk among the trees: from the roofless entrance pavilion, there is an especially good view of a section of wall with gaping windows. The oblong-shaped moat has remained intact.

MEUDON★

Population 45 339
Michelin map 101 folds 23, 24 – Michelin plan 22

Access from Paris: *RER line C 5/C 7 or SNCF Rail link from Gare Montparnasse*

The town is located on the slopes of the plateau covered by the Meudon Forest.
In the mid 18C Mme de Pompadour acquired **Bellevue** estate and gave orders to build the château. Louis XV paid frequent visits to the estate and in 1757 he bought Bellevue from his mistress. He embellished the house, refurbished the grounds and installed a hot water heating system under the flooring. The last occupants were the two unmarried daughters of Louis XV, the aunts of Louis XVI. They added a botanical garden and a charming hamlet. The estate was pillaged during the Revolution and sold as State property. In the 19C it was parcelled out into building plots.
All that remains of the former estate is part of the terrace and its balustrade at the junction of rue Marcel-Allégot and avenue du 11-Novembre. The wonderful panorama of the past has been replaced by a view of modern Paris with, in the foreground, Boulogne-Billancourt and the Ile Seguin.
On 8 May 1842, the small station on the left was the scene of a train crash in which the explorer Admiral Dumont d'Urville died (he had just discovered Adélie Land in the Antarctic), together with 40 other passengers who had been locked in the compartments according to regulations.

CHÂTEAU AND TOWN

The stately Avenue du Château is lined with four rows of lime trees. Half-way down the street, a plaque on the left marks the little house (no 27) where **Richard Wagner** composed the score for the *Flying Dutchman* in 1841.

Château of the House of Guise – A manor house in Meudon dating from the early 15C became the property of the Duchess of Étampes, former mistress to François I, whose generosity graced the estate with two new wings and a park. The domain was subsequently sold to Cardinal de Lorraine, who belonged to the House of Guise. He commissioned the sumptuous grotto (on the site of the Observatory) from Primaticcio, as well as the two superimposed orangeries. For a hundred years Meudon remained in the hands of the Guise. The family later sold the estate to Abel Servien in 1654 owing to financial difficulties.

Meudon at the time of Servien – The wealthy Abel Servien, marquis de Sablé and Minister of Finance, commissioned Le Vau to renovate the château at great expense and gave orders to build the terrace, a large-scale project. Servien led a life of luxury but his fortune soon ran out; when he died in 1659, he was in debt to the tune of 1 600 000 livres. Abel's son sold the estate to Louvois, the lord of Chaville.

Meudon at the time of Louvois – The new owner pursued the efforts of his predecessor, renewing the decoration and embellishing the park. He asked Trivaux to create the perspective and entrusted the plans of the gardens to Le Nôtre, then to Mansart. After Louvois' death, his widow agreed to give Louis XIV her domain in exchange for the Château de Choisy, which belonged to the king's son, the Grand Dauphin.

Meudon at the time of the Grand Dauphin – Of the Sun King's six legitimate children, Monseigneur was the only one who did not die in early childhood. He retained little of the worthy principles his tutor Bossuet imparted to him; it was for the Grand Dauphin that Bossuet had written his *Discours sur l'Histoire Universelle*. The king's son delighted in hunting wolves and stags and his favourite reading matter was the obituary page of the *Gazette de France*. He was however an enthusiastic art lover and made considerable changes in the interior decoration and layout of the Old Château.

In 1706 he dismantled the grotto and replaced it with a new pavilion for his courtiers. This New Château was Mansart's last major accomplishment.

In 1711 Monseigneur died of smallpox and the following year his son the Duke of Burgundy succumbed to the disease. The château came into the hands of a two-year-old boy, who was to become Louis XV. His great-grandfather Louis XIV administered the estate up to 1715.

Meudon abandoned by Royalty – Until the Revolution, Meudon fell into disrepair. In 1793 the chemist Berthollet and Général Choderlos de Laclos – who wrote *Les Liaisons Dangeureuses*, adapted for the cinema by Stephen Frears as *Dangerous Liaisons* and by Milos Forman as *Valmont* – set up an artillery research centre in the Old Château. Unfortunately it was so badly damaged by a fire that the whole building had to be razed in 1804. Only the columns of pink marble still adorn the Luxembourg Palace and the Carrousel Arch, both in Paris.

The flames spared the New Château, which housed a workshop for military balloons. The famous aerostats which contributed to the victory of Fleurus (1789) were manufactured in Meudon. Napoleon I renewed the furniture in the New Château, which was occupied by Marie-Louise and the King of Rome during the Russian campaign.

In 1870 the terrace was turned into a redoubt for a Prussian battery intent on bombarding Paris. When the Germans withdrew the following year, Meudon was burned down along with St-Cloud. Only two small wings still stand. The central section of the building was restored and made into an observatory.

VISIT

★**Terrace** – The terrace (450m/1480ft long and 136m/447ft wide) is planted with handsome trees and sweeping lawns. It lies at an altitude of 153m/502ft and commands an extensive **view**★ of Meudon, the Seine Valley and Paris.

One of the forest's standing stones can be seen to the left of the gates. The pedestal-like pilasters adorning the breast wall of the upper terrace date from the 16C and 17C.

The far end of the esplanade rests on the foundations of the old orangeries of the château. From here, visitors may discover Le Nôtre's beautiful perspective with the modern complex of Meudon-la-Forêt in the far distance.

Observatoire ⊘ – On the right stands the observatory, housing the astrophysics section of the Paris Observatory. A large revolving dome with a diameter of 18.5m/60ft crowns the central block of the New Château. Note the astronomical telescope dating from 1893. Founded in 1876 by the astronomer Janssen, this observatory is considered the most important in France. It is also the leading aerospace research centre in France. A mushroom-shaped tower was added in 1965; its 35m/115ft shaft attracts the rays of the sun, which are then broken down and analysed under a spectroscope.

Musée d'Art et d'Histoire ⊘ – *11 Rue des Pierres, at the foot of the terrace (drive there from the town centre).*

The museum, in the house which Molière's wife Armande Béjart bought in 1676, three years after the writer's death, centres on the history of the town, the celebrities who lived there and the châteaux of Bellevue and Meudon *(information centre)*. It also presents the municipal art collections: Dunoyer de Segonzac, Magnelli, Pape etc. The formal gardens are dotted with contemporary sculptures by Arp, Bourdelle and Stahly.

Musée Rodin, Villa des Brillants ⊘ – *19 Avenue Auguste-Rodin.*

An indispensable complement to the Rodin Museum in Paris. The museum stands next to Villa des Brillants, **Rodin**'s residence and studio from 1895. It contains moulds, drawings and rough sketches by the great sculptor, together with a number of original plaster casts *(The Gates of Hell, Balzac, The Burghers of Calais)*. The façade of the museum was taken from the old château at Issy-les-Moulineaux. Rodin died in 1917 and his grave was laid out in front of the museum. Sitting pensively on the tombstone is his famous statue *The Thinker*.

Use the Index to find more information about a subject mentioned in the guide people, towns, places of interest, isolated sites, historical events or natural features...

MILLY-LA-FORÊT★

Population 4307
Michelin map 106 fold 44

The locality of Milly-la-Forêt developed around the old covered market and it is now an important starting-point for many of the forest lanes crisscrossing the wooded uplands of Les Trois Pignous and Coquibus. Milly has been a long-standing centre for the growing of medicinal plants, including one variety still considered a local speciality: peppermint. Lily of the valley and a wide range of aromatic herbs for cooking purposes are also grown.

Halles – Located on the town square, the market building – made entirely of oak and chestnut wood – dates back to 1479.

Chapelle St-Blaise-des-Simples ⊙ – *On the way out of the village, along the road to Chapelle-la-Reine.*
In the 12C the chapel was part of the St Blaise leper house. More recently, Jean Cocteau decorated the walls in 1959; a huge line-drawing above the altar depicts Christ with a crown of thorns and a mural represents the Resurrection of Christ. The walls of the nave are adorned with illustrations of medicinal herbs or simples (mint, belladonna, valerian, buttercup and aconite).
The chapel houses a bust of Cocteau by the German sculptor Arno Breker, and the poet's grave. The epitaph on the tombstone simply reads: "I remain with you". The garden surrounding the chapel is planted with common medicinal herbs.

EXCURSIONS

Le Cyclop ⊙ – *Leave Milly on the Étampes road (D 837).*
This monumental sculpture was donated to the French government in 1987 by artists Jean Tinguely and Niki de Sainte-Phalle. It represents an enormous head 22.5m/73ft high made with 300 tonnes of steel. The sparkling face conceals a strange world of disorder and utopia. On the top of the piece is a vast water-filled basin dedicated to France's most innovative post-war artist Yves Klein (1928-1962), noted for his use of a rich ultramarine commonly referred to as Yves Klein blue.

MONTFORT-L'AMAURY★

Population 2651
Michelin map 106 north of folds 27, 28

This old town is built on the side of a hill dominated by castle ruins. Before the French Revolution, Montfort was an important county town enjoying far more power than nearby Rambouillet.
The district was founded and fortified in the 11C by the builder Amaury de Montfort. The most famous descendant of this illustrious family was Simon IV, the leader of the Albigensian Crusade, who waged a fierce war against the heretical Cathars of Languedoc. Simon de Montfort was killed by a stone in 1218, while besieging the town of Toulouse.

A Breton outpost in Île-de-France – In 1312 the marriage of the Breton Duke Arthur to one of the Montfort daughters made this citadel a part of Brittany.
Subsequently, when Anne of Brittany, comtesse de Montfort married Charles VIII and then Louis XII, Montfort-l'Amaury became a French fief. The duchy became Crown property after the accession of Henri II, the son of François I and Claude de France – herself the daughter of Louis XII.

SIGHTS

★**Église St-Pierre** – The rebuilding of the church was commissioned by Anne of Brittany in the late 15C. The decoration work continued through the Renaissance and was completed in the early 17C; the nave was uniformly elevated and the bell-tower and the façade were both remodelled.
Walk round the church, surrounded by quaint old houses. Observe the striking gargoyles that adorn the walls of the apse and the high flying buttresses supporting the chancel. The pretty doorway on the south front bears medallions portraying the benefactors whose generosity made it possible to carry out the renovation work in the Renaissance: André de Foix and his wife. The interior features a superb set of Renaissance **stained-glass windows**★ in the ambulatory and around the aisles *(read description in "Montfort-l'Amaury" booklet published by the tourist information centre).* The vaulting above the aisles features many hanging keystones. The historiated bosses in the nave include one bearing the emblem (ermine) of Anne of Brittany.

★**Ancien charnier** – Admire the beautifully carved Flamboyant doorway. This old cemetery is enclosed within an arcaded gallery surmounted by splendid timbered roofing in the shape of an upturned ship. The left gallery is 16C, the other two date from the 17C. In accordance with medieval tradition, these galleries were intended to receive the bones of the dead when there was a lack of space in the graveyard.

Castle Ruins – Take the narrow, twisting road to the top of the hill. Two sections of wall overgrown with ivy are all that remain of the 11C keep. The stone and brick turret belonged to the building commissioned by Anne of Brittany.
The summit offers a good **view★** of the town, the old-fashioned roofs and the edge of the forest.

Musée Maurice-Ravel ⊙ – In 1920 the French composer **Ravel** bought a tiny villa in Montfort-l'Amaury. It was in this house – called Le Belvédère – that he wrote most of his music: *L'Enfant et les Sortilèges*, *Boléro*, *Daphnis et Chloé* etc. The composer developed a brain tumour but stayed on in Montfort, despite doctor's orders to stop working in 1934. He was forced to move back to Paris in 1937, where he died soon afterwards.
The rooms are somewhat cramped and Ravel – who was a short man – had several of them made even smaller. The interior decoration has remained intact; much of the painting was done by Ravel himself and featured dark, sombre tones. The museum exhibits include the composer's piano, his record player and numerous mementoes reflecting his taste for refinement.

EXCURSIONS

Vicq, Musée d'Art naïf de l'Île-de-France ⊙ – *4km/2.5mi north along D 76.*
This museum devoted to the world of fantasy contains the Max-Fourny collection (more than 1 500 works displayed in rotation with temporary exhibitions).

La Queue-les-Yvelines, La Serre aux Papillons ⊙ – *4.5km/3mi northwest. Leave Montfort by D 155 and drive to La Queue-les-Yvelines.*
The butterfly house is part of the Jardinerie Poullain. More than 500 butterflies live in it, in tropical conditions.

Houjarray, Maison Jean-Monnet (Centre d'information sur l'Europe) ⊙ – *4.5km/3mi east. Leave Montfort by D 13 towards Tremblay-sur-Mauldre. Cross N 191 and turn right to Houjarray before Bazoches-sur-Guyonne. The centre is 1 500 m/1mi further on in Houarray.*
Jean Monnet (1888-1979), the political economist and diplomat, bought this country retreat in 1945; it has a thatched roof and a large, gently sloping garden which overlooks the surrounding countryside. Monnet was instrumental in the successful modernisation and strengthening of the tattered French economy after the Second World War, and is also famous for being one of the founders of the European Community (the present European Union).
The text of the declaration regarding the Schuman Plan of 1950 (embodied in a treaty that same year) was conceived and written here; it led to the creation of the European Coal and Steel Community (ECSC).
Monnet would return to this haven of peace after his frequent trips around the world and had many famous figures and heads of state to stay. He retired here in 1975, writing his memoirs until his death. His ashes were transferred to the Panthéon in Paris on 9 November 1988.
Some of the original furnishings remain, together with various possessions: Monnet's *Memoirs*, letters from Schuman, Roosevelt, Adenauer and de Gaulle, various publications with Monnet on the cover, paintings by his wife Sylvia, a bust of Marianne (1945) by the sculptor Paul Belmondo. Display panels recount the important moments of his career.

A taste of castle life

LUXURY

Château du Tremblay – In Tremblay-sur-Mauldre, ☎ 01 34 87 92 92. Enjoy an idyllic stay in this superb 17C castle, in typical Île-de-France style, with its brick and stone façade, and its vast park. Rooms from 600F, menus from 130F.

★Round tour of Rambouillet Forest – *21km/12mi then 30min on foot there and back. See RAMBOUILLET.*

Étang de la Porte Baudet ou des Maurus – *4km/ 2.5mi southwest then 45min on foot there and back. Leave Montfort by D 112 and D 138, towards St-Léger.*

Go past the turning to Gambais *(right)* and turn left into Rue du Vert-Galant. Follow the plateau along the winding route which enters the wood *(the road surface rapidly deteriorates)*. Park the car at the *Zone de Silence de la Mare Ronde*. Certain forests in France have "silent areas" *(zones de silence)* where motor bikes, radios etc are prohibited.

MONT DES CATS

Mont des Cats, or Catsberg (altitude 158m/514ft) is part of the Monts de Flandres range. It lies in pleasant undulating countryside where fields of hops, poplar trees, and red roofs form the "humanised landscape" defined by geographer Brunhes. Gourmets know this area for its wonderful cheeses which are similar to Port-Salut. On top of the hill are the neo-Gothic buildings of a Trappist **monastery** founded in 1826 and restored since that time.

Église paroissiale St-Bernard – In the church to the right of the monastery entrance are some interested stained-glass windows by Michel Gigon (1965) representing Fire and Darkness, Death and Resurrection.

Moulin de Boeschepe ⊙ – The village of **Boeschepe** at the foot of Mont des Cats has a restored windmill next to a delightful bar *(estaminet)*.

EXCURSION

Mont Noir – *7km/5mi east by D 10 and D 318.*
Straddling the border between France and Belgium, Mont Noir (Black Hill), so-called owing to its dark wooded slopes, is part of the Monts de Flandres range. The hill (altitude 131m/429ft) offers views of Ypres, Mont Rouge and Mont des Cats, surmounted by its monastery. Mont Noir is a busy summer resort offering a choice of hotels, bars and recreational facilities (go-carting, camping, playgrounds). Mont Noir has been immortalized in *Archives du Nord (How Many Years)*, the auto-biographical work of writer and French Academy member **Marguerite Yourcenar** (1903-1987) who spent many of her childhood years here.

MONTMORENCY★

This charming town, set on hilly ground, consists of a town centre surrounded by wealthy residences. Its main claim to fame is to have been the home of the celebrated author and social theorist Jean-Jacques Rousseau (1712-78) for a period of his life.

The "First Christian Barons" – The Bouchard family, who held the lordship of Mont-morency, had the reputation of being difficult vassals and it was only after the 12C that they served the French court loyally. Over a period of 500 years, the Montmo-rency family produced six constables, 12 marshals and four admirals. Moreover, their land was made a duchy by Henri II. They had connections with every ruler in Europe and chose to call themselves the "first Christian barons". One of their most celebrated descendants was Constable Anne, companion-in-arms to François I, Henri II and Charles IX and builder of the Château de Chantilly.

The oldest branch of the family died out in 1632 when the constable's grandson Henri II de Montmorency, governor of Languedoc, was beheaded at the age of 37 for having plotted against Cardinal Richelieu. Despite the numerous appeals made to Louis XIII, the King refused to pardon the Duke and ordained that the execution take place. The duchy passed into the hands of Henri de Bourbon-Condé but the title was given to a member of the Montmorency-Boutteville family by Louis XIV.

During the Revolution, the town was called Émile in honour of Rousseau's famous treatise on education. It recovered its former name in 1832.

Jean-Jacques Rousseau's literary retreat – The author lived in Montmorency from 1756 to 1762. Invited by Mme d'Épinay, a society woman who moved in literary circles, Rousseau took up residence in the Hermitage, a small garden pavilion which has since been taken down. He was 44 years old. His short temper and quickness to take offence annoyed the other house guests. He was living with Thérèse Levasseur, a linen maid whom he later married, but fell passionately in love with his hostess's sister-in-law Mme d'Houdetot, who was nearly 20 years his junior.

His romantic involvements caused him to fall out with Mme d'Épinay in 1757, at which point he moved to Montlouis where he completed *The New Eloisa* and published *Emilius and Sophia* and *A Treatise on the Social Compact*. These were his three major works.

The owners of Montlouis – the Maréchal de Luxembourg and his wife – took Rous-seau under their wing. Their admiration for the writer, who would read them his latest chapters, helped them put up with his changing moods. The stately grounds of their estate have survived but the château has been replaced by a modern building.

In 1762 *Emilius and Sophia* was qualified as subversive literature by the Parlement de Paris and a warrant was issued for Rousseau's arrest. Fortunately, the author was forewarned; he fled Montlouis in the marshal's post-chaise and sought refuge in Switzerland. He returned to France in 1767.

Country outings – From the late 18C to the mid-19C, Montmorency and its forest were popular venues for writers, artists, politicians and young Parisian socialites.
Informal picnics and lunches at the Auberge du Cheval Blanc – on the marketplace now called place Roger-Levanneur – were a common feature of life at Montmorency. Visitors were known to sample the local cherries and donkey rides were very much in vogue. Visitors, some of whom were to become leading personalities, engraved their name, together with that of their loved one, on the bark of the chestnut trees or on the mirrors at the inn. Even the crowned heads of France forgot about protocol when they stayed at Montmorency. Queen Hortense, the Duchess of Berry, Napoleon III and the Condé princes would run about the meadows like carefree children, astride their little donkeys.

SIGHTS

★**Collégiale St-Martin** – *Rue de l'Église.* Started in the 16C by Guillaume de Montmorency and completed by his son Constable Anne, St Martin's is characteristic of the Flamboyant Gothic style. It was originally designed to be the mausoleum of the Montmorency family.
Walk round the church to appreciate its **site** which dominates the new town of Montmorency, spread out in the valley. The view extends to the heights of Sannois and the butte d'Orgemont *(tower)*.
The nave features complex ribbed vaulting in keeping with 16C architecture, except for the two ribs in the choir that present ornamental brackets at the point where they meet the pillars.
Certain bosses and bands crowning the columns bear variations on the Greek word *APLANOS (straight ahead)*, which was the Constable's motto.
The chapel was specially designed to receive the remains of the Montmorency family and, in the 18C, the tombs of several members of the Condé family. The tombs were destroyed during the Revolution. Some were salvaged and moved to the Louvre, including those of Constable Anne and his wife Madeleine. The others have disappeared save for the funeral slab of Guillaume de Montmorency and his wife Anne Pot, of the famous Burgundian family; it has been placed at the top of the south aisle.

★ **Stained-glass windows** – *Explanatory plans are attached to the corresponding pillars.* The 14 windows that adorn the apse and the five nearest righthand bays of the chancel provide a fine example of Renaissance decoration, tastefully restored in the 19C. The family connections of the Montmorency are illustrated by the effigies of their ancestors, the brightly-coloured coats of arms and the saints they worshipped. Above the glass cage of the side doorway is a magnificent window representing the famous emblem of this illustrious family: alerions or eagles without beaks or feet painted in blue against a yellow background.
The other windows in the nave – executed in the 19C – harmonise well with the earlier Renaissance windows. They evoke the joys and sorrows of the dynasty up to the execution of Henri II de Montmorency in 1632, which heralded the start of a new era for the Condé.

Montmorency – Detail of stained-glass window in the Collégiale St-Martin

D. Dorval /EXPLORER

The Polish heritage – Behind the west front are a number of busts, recumbent figures and plaques relating to the members of an aristocratic community from Poland who moved to Montmorency in the wake of the failed national insurrection (1831). They were attracted to the town by the fresh, vivifying countryside – reminiscent of their own homeland – and by the literary connections with Rousseau.

In the chancel is a copy of the painting, Our Lady of Czestochowa or the Black Madonna, the patron saint of Poland.

Musée Jean-Jacques-Rousseau ⊘ – *5 Rue Jean-Jacques-Rousseau.*
This is the house where the French writer lived from 1757 to 1762 and where he wrote his major works. The museum evokes the daily life of Thérèse and Jean-Jacques. The old part of the house affords a good view of the valley. The arbour planted with lime trees leads through to the small garden pavilion Rousseau used as a study, which he sardonically called his "keep".
The exhibition hall and audio-visual room in the modern part of the museum present particular aspects of Rousseau's life and work. The 18C house at the edge of the grounds contains a library with numerous studies on Rousseau.

EXCURSIONS

Collégiale St-Martin-de-Groslay – *2km/1.25mi east.*
This 12C and 13C church which was altered and enlarged in the Renaissance features a lovely series of stained glass, among which note the **Tree of Jesse** inspired by the one in Beauvais Cathedral.

Montmorency Forest – *3km/2mi north.*
The area west of Domont and N 309 is the more interesting section of the forest, with deep wooded vales and patches of moist undergrowth. Oaks and chestnut trees are the dominant species, with the occasional birch. The forest boasts several footpaths, a cycle track which cuts through the forest, and the Caesar's Camp recreational area.

Stopover

OUR SELECTION

Au Cœur de la Forêt – Avenue du repos-de-Diane, access via the forest track, ☎ 01 39 64 99 19. Typical Île-de-France pavilion with terrace at the heart of the forest. Fixed-price menu: 190F.

MONTREUIL★

Population 2 450
Michelin map 51 fold 12 or 236 fold 12

Montreuil, which was once "by the sea", occupies a **site★** on the edge of the plateau overlooking the Canche Valley. This peaceful town preserves a certain slightly nostalgic charm in its old streets lined with 17C and 18C houses, and its citadel and shaded ramparts commanding vast horizons.
Montreuil developed around two buildings: the monastery founded in the 7C by St Saulve, Bishop of Amiens, from which the town derived its name; and the fortress built in about 900 by Helgaud, Count of Ponthieu. From the 11C Montreuil became Crown property. In 1537 Charles V of Spain's troops forcibly seized the town, almost completely destroying it in the process. The ramparts were rebuilt by the engineers of François I, Henri IV and Louis XIII; and Montreuil included up to eight churches. In 1804, at the time of the Boulogne Camp, Napoleon stayed in Montreuil and in 1916 Douglas Haig, commander of the British troops, made his headquarters here.
Montreuil's proximity to the coast and particulary to Le Touquet attracts numerous tourists in summer.

A "Storm in the Mind" – Montreuil's setting and surroundings have charmed many writers, among them Laurence Sterne (1713-68), the English writer and author of *A Sentimental Journey through France and Italy*, and also **Victor Hugo**. Hugo visited Montreuil in 1837 and used the town as the setting for one of the main episodes in *Les Misérables*. The novel tells how the convict Jean Valjean, reformed by a life of generosity and sacrifice, becomes mayor of Montreuil; when, however, an innocent man is to be tried in his place, Valjean is subjected to a terrible moral dilemma, immortalised by Hugo under the heading "Storm in the Mind".

CITADEL AND RAMPARTS *1hr*

★**Citadelle** ⊘ – Montreuil citadel was built in the second half of the 16C and was completely remodelled in the 17C by Errard and then by Vauban. Nevertheless, it still incorporates elements of the former castle (11C and 13C).
On the side facing the town, one of Vauban's demilunes protects the entrance. Having crossed this, the tour encompasses:

MONTREUIL

B   Chapelle de l'Hôtel-Dieu

– the two 13C round towers which flank the royal château;
– Tour Berthe (14C), the tower which was the entrance to the town until 1594.
It is part of a 16C bastion and houses the emblems of the lords killed at Azincourt
in 1415. The tower's name evokes Queen Bertha who was repudiated by her
husband Philippe I – who wanted to marry the alluring Bertrade de Montfort – and
shut away in Montreuil château where she lived in such utter poverty that the
people of Montreuil organised collections for her benefit, chanting "Give, give to
your queen".
– the sentry walk, which offers attactive **views**★★ over the Canche valley: the old charterhouse of Notre-Dame-des-Près and the opening of the Course Valley *(right)*, the
wetlands of the Canche, the estuary and Le Touquet marked by its lighthouse *(left)*
– the pillboxes built in 1840 and the 18C chapel.

★**Remparts (Ramparts)** – The red brick and white stone walls with bastions date
largely from the 16C-17C, though some elements of the 13C walls have remained
on the west front.

*Leave the citadel by the bridge which crosses the ditch and turn right into the
small path which runs alongside the walls; continue for 300m/330yd towards the
gate known as Porte de France.*

From the sentry walk there is a lovely perspective of the curtain walls with their
series of 13C towers incorporated into the 16C walls; one side offers a view over
the roofs of Montreuil, the other of the Canche Valley and the plateau of the Montreuil region. For those with time to spare, it is possible to walk right round the
ramparts *(1hr)* along a shaded path offering extensive views over the surrounding
countryside.

ADDITIONAL SIGHTS

Chapelle de L'hôtel-Dieu ⊘ **(B)** – The chapel was rebuilt in 1874 by a follower
of Viollet-le-Duc but retains its Flamboyant 15C doorway. It is adorned inside with
rich 17C **furniture**★, including a unified set of woodwork (carved panels, pulpit,
confessional) and a curious Baroque altar covered with gilding and mirrorwork.

★**Église St-Saulve** – This former Benedictine abbey church dates from the 11C (the
northeasterly face of the belfry-porch in particular) but was altered in the 13C and
again in the 16C following a fire which led to the collapse of the vaults. These
were rebuilt lower than their original height, which accounts for the dim light in
the church.
Inside, the frieze on the capitals to the right of the nave and two large 18C paintings are of particular note: on the main altar, *The Vision of St Dominic* by Jouvenet
and to the left, in the Lady Chapel (the old crossbowmen's chapel), *St Austre-
berthe taking the Veil* by Restout. Note the bases of the Flamboyant Gothic tracery
in the triforium.

Rue du Clape-en-Bas – This charming cobbled street is lined with low, lime-
washed houses with mossy-tiled roofs. They are typical in the Canche Valley.
Craftsmen work here during the season (weavers, potters etc).

Population 4 174
Michelin map 106 fold 46

Access from Paris: *SNCF Rail link from Gare de Lyon*

Moret is a charming riverside town nestling on the banks of the Loing, at a comfortable distance from the busy motorways.

A fortified town and a royal residence – Situated near the Champagne border, Moret and its fortified castle defended the king's territory from the reign of Louis VII up to Philip the Fair's marriage to Jeanne of Navarre, the daughter of the Comte de Champagne (1284), which put an end to the feud between the two families. Its keep and curtain wall – the two gates still stand – lost their strategic value, and Fontainebleau became the official place of residence for French rulers. These fortifications remained until the mid-19C and the part of town traversed by the River Loing kept its quiet, secluded character. The history of Moret was marked by a number of famous women, including Jacqueline de Bueil (1588-1651), one of the last loves of Henri IV, who founded the Notre-Dame-des-Anges hospital and convent. Marie Leszczynska was greeted in Moret by Louis XV on 4 September 1725; a commemorative obelisk marks the place where the betrothed met (at the top of the rise along N 5). The following day they were married in Fontainebeau.

SIGHTS

★**The site** – Branch off the road to St-Mammès and proceed towards le pré de Pin which runs along the east bank of the Loing. Admire the view of the lake, the shaded islets, the fishermen, the church and the ancient keep. It provided inspiration for the Impressionist, Alfred Sisley.

Bridge over the Loing – One of the oldest bridges in Île-de-France, it was probably built around the same time as the town fortifications but was frequently torn down and then widened. On the approach to the Porte de Bourgogne the ramparts and several houses with overhangs – one of which rises out of the Loing waters – come into view.

Église Notre-Dame – The building is reminiscent of many great churches in Île-de-France.
The chancel is believed to have been consecrated in 1166. The original elevation is visible in the apse and on the south side; the main arches resting on round columns are crowned by a gallery opening onto triple arching, surmounted by clerestory windows. The arches and the bays on the north side were walled up to offer greater support to the structurally unsound bell-tower erected in the 15C.
The elevation of the transept with its openwork design, and that of the nave with its tierce-point arches, were undertaken in the 13C and 14C. The Renaissance organ case presents a coffered front with delicate carvings and painted decoration.

Ancien hospice – The corner post at Rue de Grez bears an effigy of St James. A few steps along Rue de Grez a modern cartouche bears the foundation date of the hospital (1638). The place became famous for the Moret barley-sugar sweets made by the nuns. This tradition was continued by the town's confectioners.

Maison de Sisley – Alfred Sisley (1839-99), the Impressionist painter of English parentage, spent the latter part of his life in Moret. His studio was at no 19 Rue Montmartre *(private)*. He turned his back on a life in commerce to paint, and belonged to the Impressionist group but never achieved fame in his lifetime and was continually beset by financial difficulties. A pure landscape painter, Sisley delighted in the scenery of Île-de-France and showed feeling for portraying water, light and air.

Rue Grande – At no 24 a commemorative plaque marks the house where Napoleon spent part of the night on his way back from Elba (19 to 20 March 1815).

Maison de François Ier – *Walk through the town hall porch and into the small courtyard.* Note the extravagant Renaissance decoration of the gallery, and the door crowned by a salamander.

Local products

Sucre d'Orge des Religieuses de Moret – 5 Rue du Puits-du-Four, ☎ 01 60 70 35 63. An exhibition and video-show precede the tasting of this speciality which is still made according to the nuns' techniques passed on to the Rousseau family.

L'échoppe du Bon Saint-Jacques – Place de l'Église. Selection of regional products and souvenirs in the former shop of the Sisters of Charity.

Porte de Samois – Also known as the Paris Gate. A statue of the Virgin Mary adorns the inner façade. Note the old-fashioned royal milestone that once marked out the highway leading from Lyon to Paris (now N 5).

La Grange Batelière ⊘ – *Take rue du Peintre Sisley east and then a private lane which leads off the towpath, on the right, just before the bridge spanning the Loing canal.*
Built in 1926, this was the residence of Michel Clemenceau (1873-1964), who personally supervised the finishing touches. Standing on the banks of the Loing, this charming cottage and its thatched roof was built in imitation of the traditional Vendée cottage. The house of the great statesman has been turned into a museum to his memory and is tended by his daughter-in-law.

BOAT TRIPS ⊘

Embarcation du Vieux Pont. This is the best way to discover the Loing River as you glide along its still waters.

MORIENVAL★

Michelin map 106 fold 11 (inset) or 237 fold 7

The Romanesque church is beautifully set off by the trees and shrubs in the park of the former abbey and the greenery in the surrounding valley.

ÉGLISE NOTRE-DAME

Notre-Dame church depended on a nunnery said to have been founded by King Dagobert in the 7C. It was very well-endowed by Charles the Bald in the 9C but was then destroyed by the Vikings in 885 AD. From the 11C onwards, the church and convent were rebuilt. Abbess Anne II de Foucault commissioned a large number of alterations in the 17C, all of them marked with her cipher (keystones in the nave).
Take the street at the top end of the church close. It runs below the school.

200m/217yd away on the Fossement road, there is a fine view of the church and its east end. Little has changed since the 12C except for the reconstruction of the clerestory in the chancel. The narrow bays visible today date from the last restoration project (1878-1912).

Exterior – The abbey church has a typical silhouette with its three towers, one adjoining the west front and two flanking the chancel; the north tower is marginally shorter and slimmer than the south tower.

The base of the belfry-porch is the earliest part (11C), then the transept, the right bay in the chancel and the two east towers. Originally the belfry-porch stood apart from the Romanesque front and not attached to the extended aisles, an arrangement dating from only the 17C. The church's old porch has been reopened and the restored door reinstated.

Go northwards around the church to the apse; note the ambulatory which was squeezed onto the semi-circle of the chancel at the beginning of the 12C, to give it extra strength as it was threatened by rising damp.

Interior – The extremely narrow ambulatory is the most unusual part of the church. Its arches, dating

Morienval – Notre-Dame Church

H. Veiller /EXPLORER

from about 1125, are some of the oldest in France. Here for the first time ogee arches have been used in the curved part of a building; however, they are an integral part of the areas of vaulting that they support. The transition from groined vaulting to quadripartite vaulting can be seen.

The nave and transept are not so old, having been vaulted in the 17C. The 11C capitals (**a, b, c, d**) – with their spirals, stars, masks and animals, side by side – are the only certain remains of the Romanesque church. A large number of memorial stones stand along the wall of the north aisle; one commemorates the great abbess Anne II Foucault (1596-1635) (**1**). On the wall of the opposite aisle 19C engravings show the church as it was before the last restoration: note the large apsidal windows.

The most notable statues include Our Lady of Morienval (17C) (**2**), the 16C Crucifixion group (**3**) once mounted on a rood beam, and the large 17C terracotta St Christopher (**4**).

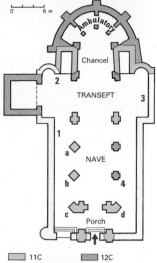

Grottes-refuges de NAOURS★
NAOURS CAVES
Michelin map 52 fold 8 or 236 fold 24 (13km/8mi north of Amiens)

The old village of Naours contains excellent examples of Picardy-style cob houses.
Below the surface of the plateau near Naours there exists the largest number of refuge-caves dug out of limestone; there are many in Picardy and parts of Artois, known as *creuttes*, *boves* or, in Naours, **muches**.
During times of trouble the men of the village would hide *(musser)* there.
The history of the caves of Naours is said to go back to the 9C and the Norman invasions, although they are mentioned in documents only from the 14C. They were much used during the Wars of Religion and the Thirty Years War; in the 18C salt smugglers used them to avoid the collectors of the hated salt tax.
Forgotten for a while, they were rediscovered in 1887 by Abbot Danicourt, the local priest, who explored and cleared them with the help of the villagers. In 1905 treasure was found: 20 gold coins from the 15C, 16C and 17C. In 1942 the caves were occupied by the Germans.

Caves ⊘ – An amusement park stands nearby and it is also possible to climb to the top of the ridge, to the two reconstructed wooden Picardy windmills; there were at one time up to seven windmills in Naours *(bird's-eye view over the town)*. The underground passages form a town which could shelter 3000 people in its 2km/1.25mi of streets and squares, its 300 rooms, three chapels, cattle sheds and stables, bakery with ovens, storerooms etc. Chimneys link the passages to the surface of the plateau, 30m98ft above.
During the tour the different layers of the soil are revealed: chalk, clay in fissures and pockets, flint in parallel bands. The small **Musée du folklore** is housed in a few of the chambers; local crafts are presented in enormous dioramas.

Colline de NOTRE-DAME-DE-LORETTE★
NOTRE-DAME-DE-LORETTE HILL
Michelin map 51 fold 15 or 236 fold 15 (11km/7mi southwest of Lens)

Notre-Dame-de-Lorette is among many places (including Carency, Ablain St-Nazaire, Souchez, Neuville St-Vaast, Vimy and La Targette where **General Pétain** had his command post while the 33rd division pierced the German lines) mentioned in dispatches during the First World War, especially during the first battle of Artois from May to September 1915.
In a dramatically bleak setting, under an often grey sky, the hill at Notre-Dame-de-Lorette (166m/544ft high) is the culminating point of the Artois hill-range. It overlooks the battlefield and was the main target for attack *(bronze viewing table left of the cemetery entrance)*.
The enormous cemetery contains 20000 named French graves; General Barbot's is first left of the main alley. The chapel, in a Romanesque-Byzantine style, is decorated with mosaics and marble.

Colline de NOTRE-DAME-DE-LORETTE

Notre-Dame-de-Lorette

The main ossuary with its lantern tower (52m/170ft high) and the seven other ossuaries house the remains of 20000 unknown soldiers. From the top floor, a vast **panorama★** of the mining basin *(north)*, the Vimy Memorial *(east)*, the ruined church of Ablain St-Nazaire, the towers of Mont-St-Éloi and Arras *(south)*.

Musée vivant 1914-1918 ⊘ – Located 100m/109yd from the basilica, the museum houses many objects (photographs, uniforms, shells, helmets, stereoscopic plates), several reconstructions of underground shelters with laser effects, which recreate the environment of soldiers. Next to the museum, the Champ de bataille extends over an area of 3ha/7.4 acres with its maze of French and German trenches and its mementoes of the First World War (guns, machine-guns, turrets).

Musée de la Targette – *7km southeast along D 937.*
The museum contains over 2000 exhibits, including ancient weapons, but it is mainly devoted to the two World Wars and recreates fighting in the Artois region with the help of reconstructed scenes.

NOYON★

Population 14426
Michelin map 56 fold 3 or 236 fold 36

Noyon is an ancient religious town with a rich history; its buildings are overshadowed by its imposing cathedral.
Originally Gallo-Roman, Noyon was elevated by St Medard to a bishopric linked to Tournai in 581. A century later, St Eligius was one of its bishops. The town has witnessed the splendour of two coronations, Charlemagne's in 768 as King of the Franks and Hugh Capet's in 987 as King of France.
Noyon was one of the first French cities to obtain its own charter, in 1108. It was the homeland of Calvin (1509) and the sculptor Sarazin (1592).
The local industrial activity is varied (smelting, metal furniture, joinery, printing works, food products); agriculture is favoured by the presence of local fertilizer businesses, canning factories and grain storage.

★★CATHEDRAL *30min*

Four buildings preceded the present cathedral, which was begun with the chancel in 1150 and finished in 1290 with the west front; this remarkable example of the early Gothic style has a sober, solid Romanesque appearance combined with the breadth and harmony of the great masterpieces of the golden age of cathedral-building. It was restored after 1918.

Place du Parvis is edged with a semicircle of canons' residences; each entrance is surmounted by a representation of a canon's hat. The square has kept its old charm despite the fact that most of these buildings were rebuilt after 1918.

Exterior – The sparse front is preceded by an early-13C porch with three bays; it was reinforced in the 14C with two flying buttresses decorated with small gables. A gallery with tall, slender colonnettes surmounts the great central bay, framed by two bell-towers with prominent corner buttresses. The more austere south tower is also the older; it was built in 1220. The north tower is one of the loveliest types of bell-towers built in northern France in the 14C; it is discreetly decorated with fine mouldings and twists of foliage on the gallery's arcades, and foliate friezes under the upper shoulders of the buttresses. The crowning of the two towers suggests that the original plan included spires which were never built. The south transept ends in a beautiful semicircle. On the right are the ruins of the episcopal chapel. The east end is surrounded by gardens; the arrangement of the radiating chapels, the ambulatory and the clerestony produces a lovely effect in spite of 18C additions.

To the north stands the old **chapter library** *(private)*, a fine 16C timbered building. It is known for housing the precious Gospel Book from Morienval which dates from the 9C. The north transept arm, surrounded by the canons' residences, is barely visible.

★★ Interior – The proportions of the nave and chancel are extremely pleasing. The nave has five double bays. The elevation rises through four storeys: great arches, large and elegant galleries with double arcading which are particularly striking viewed from the transept crossing, shallow triforium and clerestory.

Among the side chapels, the Lady Chapel (Chapelle de Notre-Dame-du-Bon Secours) in the south aisle contains stellar vaulting with hanging keystones representing sibyls.

The nave's severity is accentuated by the absence of stained-glass windows. The transept arms, like the chancel, are rounded at the end. This feature, found also at Soissons and Tournai cathedrals, is thought to be the result of Rhenish influence.

The chancel vault is as high as the nave's. The eight ribs of the apse radiate from a central keystone and develop into a cluster of small columns. Nine chapels open onto the ambulatory.

Among the furnishings, the Louis XVI high altar shaped liked a temple is of particular interest, as are some largely 18C grilles which enclose the chancel and the chapels in the nave.

Today only a single gallery remains of the **old cloister** *(north aisle)*; the bays with beautiful radiating tracery overlook the garden. The opposite wall is pierced with wide pointed arch windows and a door giving access to the 13C **chapter-house**. The pointed vaults rest on a series of columns.

ADDITIONAL SIGHTS

Musée du Noyonnais ⊙ – This brick and stone Renaissance building (a remnant of the old bishop's palace), with a corner turret and a 17C wing which was rebuilt after the First World War, contains collections on local history. Many objects were discovered during excavations in Noyon and the surrounding area (Cuts, Béhéricourt): 12C chess pieces, a cache of Gallo-Roman money, funeral objects, ceramics. 12C and 13C oak chests from the cathedral are exhibited upstairs.

Hôtel de Ville – Despite several alterations the façade of the Town Hall retains some 16C elements, among them the niches with traceried canopies which used to house statues. The lion-adorned pediment was added in the 17C.

Musée Jean-Calvin ⊙ – The museum is installed in a house built in 1927 partly on the foundations, and following old plans, of the house where Calvin was born which was destroyed at the end of the 16C.

In the ground-floor entrance hall an audio-visual display *(10min)* presents Calvin and his time. The great reformer's room has been recreated and contains authentic portraits and engravings, together with a letter written by Calvin.

On the first floor 16C French Bibles are displayed, including the famous Olivetan Bible and the Lefèvre d'Étaples Bible. There is also a model of a 16C printing works.

Writings by Calvin and his contemporaries are on the second floor, together with models of the round Paradise temple in Lyon (1564) and the galley-ship *La Réale*. The library holds 1 200 books dating from the 16C to the 20C.

To choose a hotel or a restaurant,
to find an auto mechanic,
consult the current edition of the Michelin Red Guide

Château d'OLHAIN*

This medieval **castle** ⊘ is set in a romantic lake at the bottom of a vale. It dates from the 13C-15C and boasts a large bailey from the Middle Ages which has been transformed for agricultural use.

Château d'Olhain

Tour – A drawbridge gives access to the bailey and from there to a watchtower *(staircase with 100 steps)*, a Gothic room known as the Guard-room, cellars with walls 2 to 3m/6.5 to 10ft thick, and a chapel.

Parc départemental de Nature et de loisirs – *1km/0.5mi north on D 57^E.*
In this nest of greenery at the heart of the mining region, numerous facilities have been established: sports grounds, swimming pool, golf, course, tennis, courts, playgrounds, picnic areas, footpaths, etc.

Dolmen de Fresnicourt – *3km/2mi on D 57 and a little road to the right (signposted).*
The "Fairies' Table" is situated at the edge of a small, once-sacred oakwood. It is an impressive sight, even though its capstone has slipped.
The crest of the hill on which the megalith stands, separating Flanders from Artois, provides extensive views.

Vallée de l'OURCQ

OURCQ VALLEY

The River Ourcq rises in Villers-Cotterêts Forest, situated in the Aisne *département*. After La Ferté-Milon, it follows a winding course, which skirts the beds of hard coarse limestone of the Brie subsoil and used to flow into the Marne downstream from Mary-sur-Marne. In 1529 however the magistrates of the City of Paris embarked upon the construction of a canal which diverted the waters to the heart of the capital, where the first shipment of wood and cereals was delivered in 1636.

The Canal de l'Ourcq – In 1802 Bonaparte decided to divert the course of the Ourcq by creating a canal-aqueduct to take the waters to La Villette north of Paris. The canal was inaugurated seven years later and permitted navigation between Paris and Claye-Souilly in 1813. By 1821 it had joined up with the canalised river running from Ourcq to Mareuil-sur-Ourcq. Five locks were built and those which already existed on the canalised watercourse were renewed. From 1920 to 1930 the canal was widened between La Villette and Les Pavillons-sous-Bois and a new lock built at Sevran.
The Canal de l'Ourcq supplies the locks of the St-Denis and St-Martin canals in Paris; it also provides water for factories in Paris. Commercial navigation between La Villette and Meaux ceased in 1960: it has been replaced by pleasure boating.

The navigable section of the Ourcq is 110km/68mi long and may be divided into three parts. The canalised river (10km/6mi – 4 locks) starts upstream from La Ferté-Milon. The canal itself (90km/54mi – 6 locks) links Mareuil-sur-Ourcq to Les Pavillons-sous-Bois: it is 1.5m/5ft deep and 11m/37ft wide. Finally, a wide watercourse (no locks) flows into the "Rond-Point des Canaux" in Paris (La Villette).

Canal cruises along the Ourcq are available in season *(see Practical Information).*

BATTLE OF THE MARNE

The first Battle of the Marne originated with the Battle of the Ourcq, which in fact took place on the heights of the Multien plateau and not in the valley itself. The outcome of this battle did much to secure the success of the general offensive launched between Nanteuil-le-Haudouin, north of Meaux, and Révigny, northwest of Bar-le-Duc.

It is little known that this battle began – on both sides – with the engagement of large reserve units (55th and 56th French Divisions, 4th German Corps). Owing to the hazards of drafting and the movement of retreat, many of the French soldiers were in fact defending their native territory.

The retreat: 24 August to 4 September 1914 – After the invasion of Belgium (4 August) and the defeat at Charleroi (23 August), the Anglo-French armies suffered heavy enemy pressure and were forced to withdraw.

Joffre, who had been appointed commander-in-chief, ordered his men to withdraw in good order. His troops re-formed and he hoped to be able to launch another attack as soon as possible. On 27 August, the 6th Army was created to contain the German advance on the Aisne river; it was led by General Maunoury. It was also to be used as a striking force against the left flank of the enemy pocket. Unfortunately, the retreat continued and by 1 September the Armies had taken up position along a line running west of Beauvais, Verberie, Senlis and Meaux. On the right, it was continued by the 4th British Division led by Sir John French. At this point in the battle, the Germans –

who were marching south west towards Paris – wheeled their right flank southeast. Von Kluck's Army passed Paris.

Gallieni, in charge of the Paris garrison and Maunoury's 6th Army, realised the reason for the manœuvre; Von Kluck wanted to capture the British Army which was withdrawing to Le Grand Morin. After discussing the matter, Gallieni and Joffre decided to attack the enemy's flank and crush the powerful right wing of their invaders. The offensive was scheduled for 6 September.

The check: 4 to 8 September – Gallieni and Maunoury's 6th Army prepared for combat on 4 September. The following day, they endeavoured to reach the position between Lizy-sur-Ourcq and May-en-Multien but ran up against the 4th German Corps. Despite their dominant position, the Germans were afraid of being outflanked and that night evacuated the wooded hills of Monthyon and the village of Penchard. Having suffered badly, the two French Divisions and the Moroccan Brigade – incorporating Lieutenant Juin, who was to rise to the rank of Maréchal – were withdrawn in order that they might re-form. Along the Grand Morin line, Sir John French's Army, exhausted by the retreat, swung slowly towards the north.

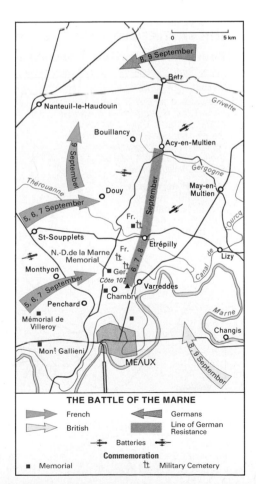

THE BATTLE OF THE MARNE

| French | Germans |
| British | Line of German Resistance |

Batteries

Commemoration

■ Memorial ‡‡ Military Cemetery

On 6 September, from his headquarters in Châtillon-sur-Seine, Joffre launched a moving appeal to all his men: "On the eve of the battle on which the future of our Country depends, it is important to remind all that there must be no looking back".
The French and British Armies advanced a further 200km/120mi; it was the start of a general attack. In the 6th Army sector, the French reached the Chambry-Douy-Bouillancy line.
The day of 7 September was marked by the bloody confrontation with the German front line. The toughest fighting took place in the villages of Étrépilly and Acy-en-Multien, the two bastions of the line, in the valleys of the Thérouanne and the Gergogne. A series of violent bayonet charges were delivered by d'Urbal's light infantry and the Zouaves of Colonel Dubujadoux. French's Army repulsed the German rearguard and took up position along the road from La Ferté-sous-Jouarre to Montmirail.
On 8 September, the war of movement shifted north of Multien to the sector of Nanteuil-le-Haudouin. The previous night the town had received the 7th Division, dispatched by Gallieni and transported by the famous "Marne taxis". It was there that Maunoury and Von Kluck were desperately hoping for a definitive solution, relying on a strategy of encircling movements.

The victory: 9 to 13 September – Wednesday 9 was a turning-point in the Battle of the Marne. On the left, the French troops facing north in the Nanteuil-le-Haudouin sector suffered an assault of such violence that Maunoury began to fear for Paris. The British Army, however, succeeded in crossing the Marne.
In the centre, the French troops entered Étrépilly and Varreddes which had already been evacuated. Von Kluck's Army withdrew. The German commander-in-chief Von Moltke was astonished by the French recovery. An alarming gap separated Von Kluck's 1st Army from Von Bülow's 2nd Army, checked by Foch near the St-Gond marshes, and Von Moltke was afraid that his front line would not hold; he gave orders for a general withdrawal following a line passing north of Soissons, Reims and Verdun.
This war of movement ended on 13 September. In October, the operations became bogged down and the battle developed into trench warfare.
The French offensive failed to fulfil its objective, ie to crush Von Kluck's Army but it halted the invasion at a critical moment. The official telegram sent by Joffre read: "The Battle of the Marne is an undeniable victory for us".

THE BATTLEFIELD AND THE OURCQ VALLEY

Round tour starting from Meaux
96km/58mi – allow 4hr – Local map below

★**Meaux** – See MEAUX.

From Meaux take N 3 (west) towards Paris. After 6.5km/4mi, a memorial paying tribute to Gallieni stands on the left hand side of the road. Turn right onto D 27, towards Iverny, then right again towards Chauconin-Neufmontiers.

Mémorial de Villeroy
– It stands on the site of the early operations of 5 September 1914.

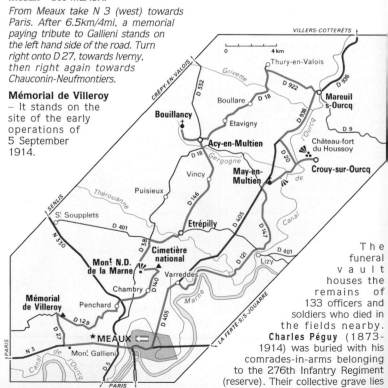

The funeral vault houses the remains of 133 officers and soldiers who died in the fields nearby. **Charles Péguy** (1873-1914) was buried with his comrades-in-arms belonging to the 276th Infantry Regiment (reserve). Their collective grave lies to the right of the vault. The cross celebrating the memory of the writer, philosopher and social reformer has been moved to the intersection of D 27 and D 129. The 19th Company of the 276th Regiment was called in to relieve the Moroccan Brigade who accompanied them and who were dangerously engaged in battle near Penchard. It launched an attack towards Monthyon, under the fire of the enemy, under cover in the valley around the Rutel brook. Péguy was the only surviving officer. He told his men to lie down and was inspecting the German positions when he was struck by a bullet.

At the next crossroads, turn left towards Chauconin-Neufmontiers. Drive through Penchard and follow directions to Chambry. Drive through the village.

The bell-tower of Barcy is visible to the left.

Cimetière National de Chambry — Most of the soldiers buried here died during the fighting that took place on 6, 7 and 8 September when they defended the village of Chambry, which was taken, lost and re-taken several times.

Along the road there is a view of the Chambry-Barcy Plateau covered in war graves that seem to mark out the progression of the Allied troops beneath the fire from the lines of German defence.

Located 500m/500yd east of the crossroads, the German military cemetery marks the place where the main German line — which roughly follows the dirt track — crossed the road to Varreddes.

Turn back, towards Barcy.

Monument Notre-Dame-de-la-Marne — This was erected in response to a vow made by Monseigneur Marbeau, Bishop of Meaux, in 1914 and dominates the whole battlefield. Turn to the north for a good view of the Multien plateau in the far distance.

Proceed towards Puisieux. At the crossroads after the old factory, turn right to Étrépilly. In the centre of the village, 200m/220yd before reaching the church, turn left towards Vincy and Acy-en-Multien.

Étrépilly — The small national cemetery and the memorial evoke the fighting that took place during the night of 7-8 September, reaching a climax near the village graveyard.

Acy-en-Multien — This village nestling in the Gergogne Valley was the scene of intensive warfare on 7 September 1914. The winding alleys, the hillsides planted with small spinneys and the estate walls of the château provided many opportunities for close combat, often ending in tragic death.

Take the left-hand fork out of Acy, to Bas-Bouillancy.

Église de Bouillancy — Located in the lower part of the village. In the quiet valley — rural life is concentrated in the village on the plateau — lies an early Gothic church (12C-13C) of harmonious proportions. Note the bell-tower flanked by buttresses featuring numerous projections.

Turn back to Acy and take D 18 up to the plateau.

Enjoy the **view** of Acy and the elegant village spire. Beyond Étavigny, the road moves away from the battlefield.

Just before Thury-en-Valois take D 922, right.

The road leads to **Mareuil-sur-Ourcq**, marking the start of the canal.

Cross Varinfroy to Crouy-sur-Ourcq.

Crouy-sur-Ourcq — Just after the level crossing, the road skirts the ruins of the **Château Fort de Houssoy**. In order to see the keep, which has remained separate, park the car in the station car park and walk to the courtyard gates. From the top of the tower, there is a fine view of the surrounding area.

Crouy Church features a Gothic interior with two 16C aisles. Admire the beautifully crafted panelling (1670) in the chancel. The colours are particularly harmonious. The patron saints of the church are represented above the altarpiece: St Cyricus, who was martyred at the age of 3, and his mother, St Julitta.

Turn back, and after the bridge turn left towards May.

The twisting, hilly road affords extensive **views** of the surrounding landscape.

May-en-Multien — The village is well situated 100m/330ft above the River Ourcq. It is visible from afar on account of its church tower, one of the highest landmarks in the area.

Drive down to Lizy. Do not cross the canal bridge but go up the hill on the north bank along the road to Congis (D 121).

View of the last loop of the Ourcq, overgrown with greenery.

Cross Congis and Varreddes and join D 405, south.

On the left stands the huge American monument that pays homage to the Marne combatants. The road dips and leads straight down to Meaux.

PARIS★★★

Population 2 152 333 — Conurbation 9 060 257
Michelin map 101 and plan 10 (single sheet) or 11 (atlas with street index)

Paris dominates France's intellectual, artistic, scientific and political life, and has done so since the 12C when the Capetian kings made it their capital. It is today a lively, handsome city with considerable charm, boasting a wealth of attractions. The map and descriptions on the following pages give an outline of the most important sights in Paris, so that the visitor with just a day or two may become acquainted with the capital's landmarks and treasures. Like any city with a rich and varied history, however, Paris needs a little time to get to know; for longer stays in the French capital, consult the **Michelin Green Guide Paris.**

SIGHTSEEING

Civil Architecture

★★★**The Louvre** – The original Louvre was a fortress built in 1200 by Philippe Auguste on the banks of the Seine to protect the weakest point in his new city; it was used as a treasure-house, arsenal and archive. In the 14C the fortress ceased its military functions with the erection of a new perimeter and Charles V converted it into a residence, installing his famous library in one of the towers.

In 1527 François I took up residence in the Louvre. The keep was razed and defences knocked down but it was not until 1546 that a new royal palace was commissioned, on the site of the old keep, which was to become the residence of the kings of France. It was the architect Pierre Lescot who brought the Italian Renaissance style to the banks of the Seine; Jean Goujon added the sculpture. Over the following centuries, almost all the French monarchs added to and altered the evolving Louvre. The Florentine **Catherine de' Medici**, as Regent for Charles IX, ordered Philibert Delorme to build the Tuileries Palace nearby for her while work continued on the Louvre. Charles IX and Henri III both lived in and added to the Louvre, as did Henri IV and Louis XIII who both added pavilions. In 1662 the young King Louis XIV celebrated the birth of the Dauphin with lavish entertainment here.

The monumental, colonnaded façade facing the city was designed by Perrault, aided by Le Brun and Le Vau. It was begun in 1667 but completed only in 1811. Both Napoleon I and Napoleon III continued with additions, alterations and restorations. In 1871 the Communards set the Tuileries Palace and some of the wings of the Louvre ablaze, most of which were subsequently restored or rebuilt. The Tuileries Palace was finally demolished in 1883.

In 1984 President Mitterrand chose the glazed pyramid designed by the American IM Pei as the contemporary entrance to the Louvre Museum.

The **Louvre**★★★ ⊘ is one of the largest and most famous museums in the world. It is divided into seven main sections: Oriental Antiquities, Egyptian Antiquities, Greek, Etruscan and Roman Antiquities, Sculpture, Paintings, Graphic Art and *Objets d'art*. Among its innumerable treasures are Mesopotamian statues; the Frieze of the Archers from Darius' Palace; the jewellery of Rameses II; the Winged Victory of Samothrace and the Venus de Milo; Michelangelo's *Slaves*; Renaissance master paintings by Giotto, Fra Angelico, Leonardo da Vinci *(Mona Lisa)*, through to Veronese, Caravaggio, Van Dyck, Rubens, Rembrandt, Watteau and many more. There are Classical and Romantic works by the great French painters David, Ingres, Delacroix and Géricault.

The *objets d'art* include the Crown Jewels of France; Brussels and Gobelins tapestries; fine furniture, clocks etc.

★★★**Hôtel des Invalides** – Guns captured at Vienna in 1805 line the Esplanade leading to the huge building (designed 1671-76 to house old soldiers invalided out of service) with a front (200m/650ft long) featuring dormer windows in the form of trophies. St Louis' Church within the precinct is the resting-place of some of France's great soldiers; it also contains flags captured from the enemy. Berlioz' *Requiem* was first performed here.

The **Église du Dôme**★★★ ⊘ was designed by Jules-Hardouin Mansart and begun in 1677; it is one of the great works of the Louis XIV style. The façade giving onto Place Vauban has Doric and Corinthian orders, topped with a pediment carved by Coysevox. The soaring, gilded dome stands on a great columned drum supporting a balcony; an elegant lantern rises above.

The church took on its role as military necropolis when Napoleon had Maréchal de Turenne (d 1685) buried here. There is also a memorial to Vauban, the great military architect, and the tomb of Maréchal Foch. In an impressive crypt of green granite stands the unmarked red porphyry mausoleum, which is **Napoleon's Tomb**★★★.

★★★**Arc de Triomphe** ⊘ – The great triumphal arch is one of Paris' main focal points; it stands in Place Charles de Gaulle – known as the Star (l'Étoile) owing to its 12 radiating avenues. The arch was designed in 1806 as one of the landmarks of Napoleon's imperial capital but was finished only in 1836, in the reign of Louis Philippe.

Paris by night – Place de la Concorde and the dome of the Invalides

In 1920 the arch saw the burial of the Unknown Soldier; three years later the flame of remembrance was kindled for the first time. Sculpture on the arch includes Rude's 1836 masterpiece known as *La Marseillaise*, showing the departure of volunteers to fight the invading Prussians (1792).

★★Place de la Concorde – This perfect expression of the Louis XV style was designed by Jacques-Ange Gabriel in 1755 and completed over 20 years. In January 1793 the guillotine was set up here for the execution of Louis XVI and other victims of the Reign of Terror.

The square features colonnaded buildings to the north, massive pedestals, magnificent marble sculptures and the pink granite Luxor Obelisk, 3 300 years old and covered with hieroglyphics, which was brought back from Egypt in 1833.

★★Tour Eiffel ⊘ – The Eiffel tower is Paris' most famous symbol. The first proposal for a tower was made in 1884; construction was completed in 26 months and the tower opened in March 1889.

In spite of its weight (7 000 tonnes) and height (320.75m/1 051ft) and the use of 2.5 million rivets, it is a masterpiece of lightness. The tower actually weighs less than the volume of air surrounding it and the pressure it exerts on the ground is that of a man sitting on a chair.

★Palais de Justice – This, the main seat of civil and judicial authority, has been the residence of Roman governors, Merovinglan kings and the children of Clovis, Dagobert's mint, Duke Eudes' fortress and the royal palace of the rulers of medieval France. The Capetian kings gave it a chapel and a keep and its 1313 Gothic halls were widely admired. Later, Charles V built the Clock Tower *(Tour de l'Horloge)*, the first public clock in Paris.

The **Conciergerie★★** ⊘ served as antechamber to the guillotine during the Reign of Terror; it contains the Prisoners' Gallery, Marie-Antoinette's cell and the Girondins Chapel.

★★Palais-Royal – In 1632 Richelieu commissioned the huge building which became known as the Cardinal's Palace when it was extended in 1639. On his deathbed Richelieu bequeathed it to Louis XIII who renamed it the Palais-Royal. The formal

gardens at the rear and the surrounding arcades were laid out in 1783; the adjoining Théâtre-Français was added four years later. The 260 columns in the outer courtyard were designed in 1986 by Daniel Buren.

★École Militaire – Though lack of funds curtailed the original design, the military academy designed by Jacques-Ange Gabriel is an outstanding example of 18C French architecture.
It was begun in 1752, partly financed by Mme de Pompadour, and completed in 1773; various wings and buildings were added later. True to its original function, it houses the French Army's Staff College. The main front has a projecting central section with Corinthian columns rising through two storeys, crowned with a quadrangular dome and adorned with allegorical figures and military trophies.
The superb **main courtyard★★** is lined by beautiful porticoes with paired columns.

★★Panthéon ⊘ – In 1744 Louis XV made a vow in Metz to replace the half-ruined church of St Genevieve's Abbey: in 1758 Soufflot began building on the highest point of the Left Bank. Despite predictions of collapse, it has stood firm over the years but has undergone extensive alteration. In 1791 it was closed to worshippers and turned into the last resting place of the "great men of the days of French liberty". The building, in the shape of a Greek Cross, is still crowned by Soufflot's dome; the pediment of the Corinthian portico was carved by David d'Angers in 1831. The crypt houses the tombs of the famous.

★★Opéra Garnier ⊘ – This is the National Academy of Music, the magnificent home of French opera. It opened in 1875 and was the work of Charles Garnier. The sumptuous interior is embellished with marble and a ceiling by Chagall.

★★Palais de Chaillot – These elegant inter-war buildings were constructed for the 1937 World Fair. The twin pavilions and wings framing gilded bronze statues house a theatre and four museums: Musée de l'Homme, Musée de la Marine, Musée des Monuments français and Musée du Cinéma. There is a **superb view★★★** over the Seine, the Eiffel Tower and the Champ-de-Mars.

Ecclesiastical Architecture

★★★Cathédrale Notre-Dame – The metropolitan church of Paris is one of the triumphs of French architecture. People have worshipped here for 2 000 years and in many ways Notre-Dame is the cathedral of the nation. Work was begun by Maurice de Sully in 1163 on what turned out to be the last great galleried church and one of the first with flying buttresses.
The chancel was built during the reign of Louis VII and consecrated in 1182 in the reign of Philip Augustus. The double ambulatory and the tracery reinforcing the wide windows set new trends, and the extended spouts of the flying buttresses formed the first gargoyles. By 1210 the first bays of the nave had been built; within 10 years it was completed and the 28 statues of the Kings' Gallery were in place. By 1245 the bulk of the work was complete; St Louis held a ceremony for the knighting of his son and placed the Crown of Thorns here until the Sainte-Chapelle was ready to receive it. In 1250 the twin towers were finished and the nave given side chapels.

In 1430 the young Henry VI of England was crowned King of France in the cathedral; in 1455 a ceremony was conducted to rehabilitate Joan of Arc; in 1558 Mary Stuart was crowned here on becoming Queen of France by her marriage to François II, and in 1572 the Huguenot Henri IV married Marguerite de Valois here; the king converted to the Catholic faith in 1594.

The cathedral square is the point from which distances along the main roads *(routes nationales)* radiating from Paris are measured. Emmanuel, the famous bell weighing 13t, hangs in the south tower; its pure tone is said to be due to the gold and silver jewellery thrown by the ladies of Paris into the molten bronze when the bell was recast in the 17C. The great rose-window above the Kings' Gallery still contains medieval glass.

★★★**Sainte-Chapelle** ⊙ – This masterpiece of High Gothic is strikingly different from Notre-Dame, though built only 80 years later: lighter, with a greater clarity of structure.

The chapel was built for St Louis to house the recently acquired relics of the Passion; it was completed in a record 33 months. Like other royal chapels it is built on two storeys, the upper one for the monarch, the lower one for the palace staff. The upper chapel resembles a shrine with stained-glass walls; 720 of the 1134 different scenes are still of original glass, some created by the masters who had worked on the windows at Chartres.

★★**Église de St-Germain-des-Prés** – With the exception of Clovis, all the Merovingian kings were buried here. The church was subsequently destroyed by the Normans but restored in the 10C and 11C; the west tower has a fortress-like character. Around 1160 the nave was enlarged and the chancel rebuilt in the new Gothic style. From 1631 to 1789 the austere Congregation of St Maur made the church a distinguished centre of learning and spirituality. "Improvements" in the 17C were followed in 1822 by an over-zealous restoration.

★★**Église de St-Séverin** – This Latin Quarter church consists of the portal's lower part and the first three bays of the nave in High Gothic, with the rest largely Flamboyant – note the famous spiral pillar in the ambulatory. In the 18C the pillars in the chancel were clad in wood and marble.

★★**Église St-Eustache** – St Eustache was once the richest church in Paris, with a layout modelled on Notre-Dame when building began in 1532, but it took over a hundred years to finish; tastes changed and the Gothic frame was padded out with Renaissance touches such as Corinthian columns and semicircular arches; the chancel windows and Colbert's tomb, designed by Le Brun with Coysevox and Tuby, are Classical.

★★**Église Val-de-Grâce** – After many childless years, Anne of Austria commissioned François Mansart to design a magnificent church in thanksgiving for the birth of Louis XIV in 1638. The church recalls the Renaissance architecture of Rome; the ornate dome is obviously inspired by St Peter's. Inside, the Baroque spirit prevails: polychrome paving, highly-sculptured vaults, massive crossing pillars and a huge canopy with six twisted columns. The **dome**★★ has a fresco featuring 200 figures.

Urban Design

Since the sweeping away of much of medieval Paris in the 19C, three central districts have come to typify particular stages in the city's evolution.

★★★**Le Marais** – This smart shopping and residential area has Renaissance, Louis XIII and Louis XIV architecture. Charles V's move to the Marais district in the 14C led to the incorporation of a suburban area into Paris; the area soon became fashionable and Rue St-Antoine the city's finest street. It was here that the characteristic French town house, the *hôtel*, took on its definitive form with the collaboration of architects and artists.

The **Hôtel Lamoignon**★ (1584) is a typical example of a mansion in the Henri III style. It was the first time the Colossal Order, with flattened pilasters, Corinthian capitals and a sculpted string-course, was seen in Paris. The Henri IV style appeared in the symmetrical **Place des Vosges**★★★ (completed 1612). The 36 two-storey houses of alternate brick and stone facings have steeply pitched slate roofs pierced with dormer windows.

Louis XIII's reign heralded the Classical style; in 1624 the **Hôtel de Béthune-Sully**★ was built, with a gateway flanked by massive pavilions and a main courtyard with triangular and curved pediments and scrolled dormer windows. The early Louis XIV style is seen in Mansart's fine **Hôtel Guénégaud**★★ (1648) with its simple lines, majestic staircase and small formal garden; in the **Hôtel de Beauvais**★ with its curved balcony on brackets; in the **Hôtel Carnavalet**★★ (now the Museum of Parisian History) built in 1655 by Mansart; and in Cottard's theatrical **Hôtel Amelot de Bisseuil**★ with its cornice and curved pediment decorated with allegorical figures. The Louis XIV style is seen in the **Hôtel de Rohan**★★ with its sculpture of the *Horses of Apollo* and

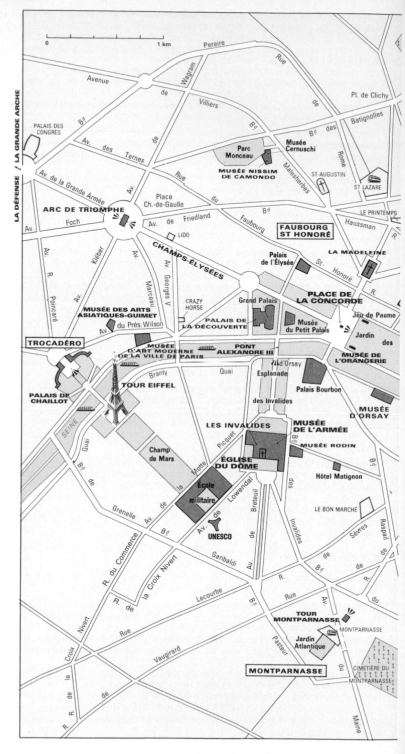

the adjoining **Palais Soubise★★** with its horseshoe-shaped courtyard and double colonnade; both have raised ground floors, massive windows, roof balustrades and sculpture on the projecting central sections.

★★★ **La Voie Triomphale (From the Tuileries to the Arc de Triomphe)** – A great road leading from the courtyard of the Louvre to St Germain had been planned by Colbert but today's "Triumphal Way" was laid out under Louis XVI, Napoleon III and during the years of the Third Republic.

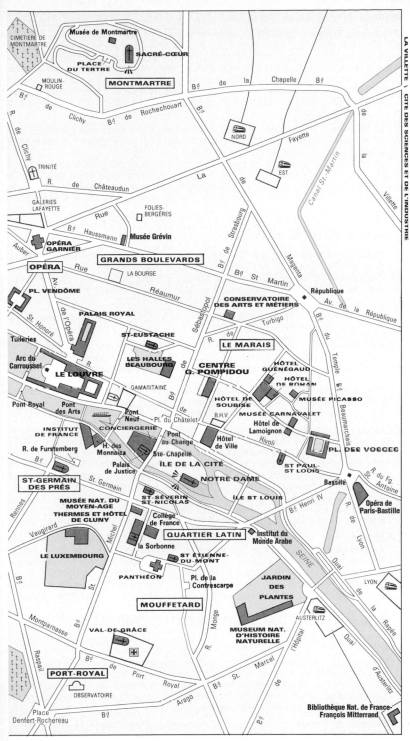

★**Arc du Carrousel** – This pastiche of a Roman arch is decorated with statues of Napoleonic military men. An impressive perspective runs from the Louvre through the arch to the obelisk in Place de la Concorde, then on to the Arc de Triomphe.

★**Jardin des Tuileries** – The gardens were first laid out in the 1560s by Catherine de' Medici in the Italian style. A century later they were remodelled by Le Nôtre who created the archetypal formal French garden.

257

***Place de la Concorde** – See p 253.

Champs-Élysées** – In 1667 Le Nôtre extended the road from the Tuileries to a new focal point, the Rond-Point. The avenue was a service road at the back of smart houses but when refreshment stalls were set up along it crowds began to cluster. In 1724 the Duke of Antin planted rows of elms to extend the "Elysian Fields" up to the Étoile. In 1729 street lanterns lit the evening scene. Finally, in 1836 the **Arc de Triomphe** *(see above)* was completed. The Champs-Élysées became fashionable during the reign of Louis-Napoleon, when high society flocked to its restaurants.

**La Défense – This modern business centre with skyscrapers and pedestrian ter- races descending towards the Seine was planned as an entire project, the individual buildings subordinated to the overall design.
The precincts are overlooked by the enormous cube of the marble-faced Grande Arche (1989) by Danish architect Johan Otto von Spreckelsen, which straddles the view along the Étoile and the Champs-Élysées. The area is also known for its public sculpture: works by Miró, Calder, Takis, Venet, Kowalski etc make it virtually an open-air museum.

THE POLITICAL CAPITAL

Palais de l'Élysée – This has been the Paris residence of the President of France since 1873. It was built in 1718 and was once the property of the Marquise de Pompadour. During the Revolution it housed a public dance-hall, a gaming salon and a picture gallery. In Napoleon's time, Marie-Louise had a boudoir here and the young King of Rome, their son, a set of rooms.

Hôtel Matignon – The attractive town house (1721) has been the residence of the French Prime Minister since 1958.

***Palais Bourbon** – This has been the seat of the Lower House of France's parlia- ment, the Assemblée Nationale, for over 150 years. The Assembly consists of directly elected members; it examines and where necessary amends all draft legis- lation.
The palace was built in 1722; during the Revolution it was the seat of the Council of Five Hundred. The decorative treatment of the façade (1804) which overlooks Place de la Concorde was chosen by Napoleon.

**Palais du Luxembourg – This is the seat of the Senate, the French Upper House. Its 283 members are elected for a period of 9 years but a staggered system ensures that a third of them face reselection every three years.
After the death of her husband the king, the regent Marie de Medici decided to move from the Louvre; in 1615 she commissioned a palace, something to remind her of the Pitti Palace in Florence, from Salomon de Brosse. The result has an exte- rior with ringed columns and rusticated stonework; a courtyard with columns, semicircular windows, curved pediments, balconies and roof balustrades; a south front with a quadrangular dome, a massive pediment and garden terraces.

***Hôtel de Ville** – Central Paris is governed from City Hall. Municipal government was introduced in the 13C under the direction of leading members of the powerful watermen's guild appointed by Louis IX. The place has long been the hub of uprising and revolt: during the Revolution it was held by the Commune, in 1848 it was the seat of the Provisional Government. The Republic was proclaimed from here in 1870 and, in March 1871, the Communards burnt it down. It was rebuilt from 1874.

THE INTELLECTUAL AND ARTISTIC CAPITAL

Intellectual Life

The city as a whole functions as the capital of the country's intellectual life, though there is a particular concentration on the Left Bank, in the Fifth and Sixth *arron- dissements*. The capital's most venerable institutions stand in the area around Mont Ste-Geneviève, in the **Latin Quarter** (so-called because Latin was the language of in- struction right up to the French Revolution).

**Institut de France – The institute originated as the College of Four Nations founded by Mazarin for scholars from the provinces incorporated into France during his ministry (Piedmont, Alsace, Artois and Roussillon). Its building, which dates from 1662, was designed by Le Vau and stands over the river from the Louvre; it is famous for its dome, its semicircular flanking buildings and the tomb of Mazarin in the vestibule. The Institute is made up of five academies:
The **Académie Française**, the most prestigious of all, was founded in 1635 by Riche- lieu; its membership is limited to 40. The members, "Immortals", devote themselves to upholding the quality of the French language and enshrining it in the *Dictionnaire de la langue française*, the country's standard dictionary.

Palais and Jardin du Luxembourg

The **Académie des Beaux-Arts** dates from 1816. It has 50 members who cover painting, sculpture, architecture, engraving and music.
The **Académie des Inscriptions et Belles Lettres** was founded by Colbert in 1663. It deals with literary history and maintains an archive of original documents.
The **Académie des Sciences**, founded by Colbert in 1666, has 66 members working in astronomy, mathematics, medicine and natural sciences.
The **Académie des Sciences morales et politiques** was founded by the Convention in 1795. It has 40 members and is dedicated to philosophy, ethics, law, geography and history.

Collège de France – The college was founded in 1529 by François I under the name of the College of Three Languages (Latin, Greek, Hebrew) in order to combat the narrow scholasticism of the Sorbonne. The present buildings date from the time of Louis XIII, who renamed it the Royal College of France; it underwent major reconstruction in 1778. It was here, in 1948, that Frédéric Joliot-Curie formulated the laws controlling the process of nuclear fission and built a cyclotron to test his theories.

Sorbonne – This is the country's most illustrious university, the successor to the theological college founded in 1253 by Robert de Sorbon for 16 poor scholars. In 1469 France's first printing press was installed here by Louis XI. For many years, the university court constituted the highest ecclesiastical authority beneath the Pope.
The **Sorbonne Church★**, built by Lemercier from 1635, is a fine example of Jesuit architecture. **Richelieu's tomb★** (1694) by Girardon lies inside.

ENTERTAINMENT AND CULTURE

Paris remains a thriving cultural centre, with a large number of different shows, exhibitions and events on at any one time.

Entertainment – There are **about 60 theatres** and over **400 cinemas** in the capital. **Music-hall, variety shows** and **reviews** take place at the Crazy Horse, the Folies Bergères, the Moulin Rouge... There are numerous **concert halls**, some with resident orchestras, as well as the Opera and the Comic Opera. There are also nightclubs, jazzclubs, cabarets, café-theatres, circuses, concerts, recitals in churches etc.

Exhibitions – Paris boasts about 100 museums and 120 art galleries, plus about another 30 places for temporary shows. Museums include the world-famous Louvre, the **Musée d'Orsay★★★** ⊘ (1848-1914 art), the Centre Pompidou *(see below)*, the **Musée de Cluny★★** ⊘ (Museum of the Middle Ages), the **Musée Rodin★★** ⊘ the Military Museum at the Invalides and the fascinating **Cité des Sciences et de l'Industrie★★★** ⊘ at La Villette.

Tourist Paris – Certain parts of the city have come to be identified in the visitor's mind with the very essence of Paris itself.

★★★**Montmartre** – The "Martyrs' Mound" became the haunt of artists and Bohemians in the late 19C; its steep and narrow lanes and precipitous stairways still evoke the picturesque village it once was. The mound rises abruptly above the city's roofs and at its centre is **Place du Tertre★★** with its "art market".

The exotic outline of the **Sacré-Cœur Basilica**★★ a place of perpetual pilgrimage, rises nearby. The basilica offers an incomparable **panorama**★★★ over the whole city.

★★★**Champs-Élysées** – *See above.* ★★★Notre-**Dame** – *See above.*

★★★**Tour Eiffel** – *See above.* ★★★Le **Marais** – *See above.*

★★★**Louvre** – *See above.* ★★★**Centre Georges-Pompidou** ⓥ – The old Beaubourg district has been transformed by the construction of this cultural centre with its library, exhibitions and **Musée National d'Art Moderne** ⓥ.

★★**La Défense** – *See above.* ★★Palais **de Chaillot** – *See above.*

PÉRONNE

Population 8 497
Michelin map 53 fold 13 or 236 fold 26

At the confluence of the River Cologne and the Somme stands the old fortified town of Péronne-en-Vermandois, stretching between fish-filled lakes and "**hardines**", marshland vegetable gardens similar to the *hortillonages* of Amiens. This is an eel centre, which is reflected in the local gastronomy: eel pâté, smoked eels.
The commercial port, on the north canal, is flanked by a marina.

The Meeting in Péronne – In 1468, a meeting was attended by **Charles the Bold** and **Louis XI**, who both wanted Picardy as part of their territory. Louis was a sly, wily man who had supported the uprising of the town of Liège against Charles; as a result he had been shut away in Péronne by his rival. Before he could recover his freedom, the King of France was forced to sign a humiliating treaty that went against the grain and his interests since it obliged him to take up arms against the people of Liège. He was to remember the insult in future years and tradition has it that his bitterness was kept alive by a parrot which kept repeating, "Péronne! Péronne!".

Miseries of War – In 1536 the town suffered a violent assault by the troops of Charles V of Spain; one heroic woman, however, saved the day: **Marie Fouré** managed to galvanise a resistance and the assailants were forced to lift their siege. Each July a procession through the town and a fête commemorate the occasion.
In 1870 Péronne was besieged by the Prussians who bombarded the town for 13 days. During the Battle of the Somme in 1916 Péronne was occupied by the Germans. That year and the next saw the destruction of virtually the entire town.

SIGHTS

★**Historial de la Grande Guerre** ⓥ – The unusual and innovative Museum of the Great War is housed in a modern building standing on piles behind the 13C castle, on the banks of the Étang du Cam. Access to the museum is through an opening carved into the wall of the castle. Louis XI was held prisoner by Charles the Bold in one of the towers here.
The museum presents an insight into European society on the eve of the First World War and throughout hostilities.

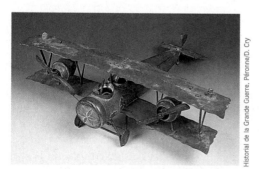

Historial de la Grande Guerre, Péronne/D. Cry

Miniature aeroplane made from shrapnel and bullets

Maps, some of them illuminated, illustrate at regular intervals the development of various fronts. A large collection of objects, works of art, documents, letters and postcards reveal the thoughts and the pattern of daily life for those caught up in the conflict.
In shallow white marble excavations representing the trenches are uniforms, arms and personal effects.
Clips from archive films are shown on videos dotted around the museum; a film by a British soldier shows the Battle of the Somme.

A signposted itinerary leads from Péronne to Albert and indicates the main battlefields and memorials erected in memory of the soldiers who fought there.

Hôtel de Ville – *Place du Cdt-Daudré.*
The Town Hall has a Renaissance façade flanked by turrets towards the square, and a Louis XVI front towards rue St-Sauveur.
Inside, the **Musée Danicourt** ⓥ contains a precious collection of ancient coins and Greco-Roman and Merovingian jewellery.

Porte de Bretagne — *Off rue St-Sauveur.*
This gateway dates from 1602 and was one of two entrances giving access through the town walls, which were destroyed before the First World War. It is now a free-standing brick pavilion with a slate roof, and is adorned with the emblem of Péronne. The wooden gates have been retained.
Beyond the moat, walk through the gate of the demilune and follow the old brick **ramparts** with stone courses (16C-17C) for an attractive view over the lakes and the "hardines".

EXCURSION

Athies — *10 km/6mi south along D 44, then D 937 towards Ham.*
Emperor Clovis' son, Clothar I, King of the Franks, had a palace here in which his future wife, Radegonde, was brought up. She later retired to Poitiers where she founded a convent and was canonised.
The church has a beautiful 13C portal with carved tympanum representing the Nativity and the Flight into Egypt.

Château de PIERREFONDS★★

Michelin map 106 fold 11 (inset) or 237 fold 8 — Local map see Forêt de COMPIÈGNE

This famous castle rises above a pretty town which, in its heyday, was a fashionable spa resort. A small lake adds to the romantic image.
A **tourist train** ⊙ offers various rides across the town.

Louis of Orléans' Castle — A castle has stood on this site since the 12C. The Valois earldom — which was elevated to a duchy when Charles VI gave it to his brother, Louis of Orléans — consisted of the castellany of Pierrefonds together with Béthisy, Crépy and La Ferté-Milon.
Louis of Orléans assumed the regency during the king's madness but was assassinated in 1407 by his cousin John the Fearless, Duke of Burgundy. Before his death he constructed a chain of fortresses on his Valois lands, of which Pierrefonds was the linchpin; to the south, barely 7mi apart, stand the castles of Verberie, Béthisy, Crépy, Vez, Villers-Cotterêts and La Ferté-Milon forming a barrier from the River Oise to the Ourcq.
The Prince also had the medieval castle completely rebuilt by the King's architect, Jean le Noir, and Pierrefonds triumphantly withstood sieges by the English, the Burgundians and the royal troops. In the 16C the castle passed to Antoine d'Estrées, Marquess

Château de Pierrefonds

of Cœuvres and father of the beautiful Gabrielle. On the death of Henri IV the Marquess took sides with the Prince of Condé against the young Louis XIII; besieged once again by the royal forces, the castle was finally seized and dismantled.

Viollet-le-Duc's Castle – In 1813 Napoleon I bought the castle ruins for a little under 3 000 francs. Napoleon III, an enthusiastic archeologist and since his days in the army passionate about the art of siege warfare, entrusted its restoration in 1857 to **Viollet-le-Duc**. It was only a matter of returning parts of it (the keep and annexes) to an inhabitable condition, leaving the curtain walls and towers as "picturesque ruins". At the end of 1861, however, the programme of works took on an altogether different, larger dimension; Pierrefonds was to be transformed into an Imperial residence. Work lasted until 1884 and cost 5 million francs, 4 million of which was deducted from the Emperor's civil list.

Fascinated by medieval life and Gothic architecture in particular, Viollet-le-Duc set about a complete reconstruction of the castle, following the basic shapes that were already outlined by the numerous walls and fragments remaining at the time. Aiming at all times to "adapt the medieval architecture to modern needs" the architect nevertheless did not hesitate to invent parts of the building – encountering severe criticism from specialists in military architecture and purists when he did – and to give free rein to his ideas for the painted and carved decoration.

TOUR ⊙

Leave the car in Place de l'Hôtel-de-Ville and approach the main entrance to the castle at the foot of the Arthus Tower.

Exterior – The quadrangular castle (103m/337ft long, 88m/288ft wide) has a large defensive tower at each corner and in the middle of the walls. On three sides it overlooks the village, almost vertically; to the south a deep moat separates the castle from the plateau.

The walls have two sentry walks, one above the other: the covered lower one is dressed with machicolations; the upper one only has merlons. The towers (38m/124ft high with walls 5 to 6m/16 to 20ft thick) are crowned with two storeys of defences; from the cart track *(route charretière)* they are a formidable sight. Eight statues of named military heroes *(preux)* adorn them, indicating the building's political significance: Arthus, Alexander, Godefroy, Joshua, Hector, Judas Maccabaeus, Charlemagne and Caesar.

On the chapel roof stands a copper statue of St Michael.

Having walked along the esplanade, cross the first moat to the forecourt known as Les Grandes Lices. A double drawbridge (**1**) (one lane for pedestrians, the other for vehicles) leads to the castle doorway which opens into the main courtyard.

Interior – A permanent exhibition in the barracks celebrates Viollet-le-Duc and his work (engravings, paintings, photographs of the ruins, history of the castle etc). Another exhibition illustrates the Middle Ages by using strip cartoons.

The main front appears with its basket-handled arcading forming a covered shelter, surmounted by a gallery. Neither of these existed in the original castle, but were created by Viollet-le-Duc, freely inspired by the courtyard at the Château de Blois. The equestrian statue of Louis of Orléans (**2**) by Frémiet (1868) stands before the monumental stairway. The inside of the chapel, heightened by Viollet-le-Duc, presents a bold elevation with a vaulted gallery above the apse, which was another of the architect's inventions.

The doorway pier incorporates a figure of St James the Great with Viollet-le-Duc's features.

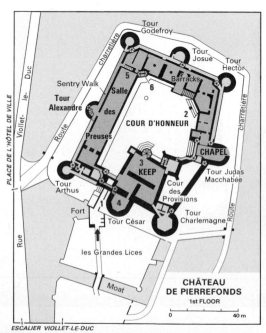

CHÂTEAU
DE PIERREFONDS
1st FLOOR

0   40 m

ESCALIER VIOLLET-LE-DUC

The keep, where the lord had his living quarters, stands between the chapel and the entrance. Viollet-le-Duc accentuated its residential function by giving it an elegant open stairway. It is flanked by three towers. The two on the outside are round; the one on the inside is square.

The provisions courtyard between the keep and the chapel communicates with the main courtyard by means of a postern gate and with the outside world by another postern, 10m/30ft above the foot of the castle walls. To introduce food and other supplies into the fortress, a steeply inclined wooden ramp was lowered; provisions were then dragged up.

Keep (Logis au donjon) – Reaching the first floor of the keep, the tour leads through the Imperial couple's rooms: the Grande salle (**3**) with woodwork and a few, rare pieces of furniture designed by Viollet-le-Duc. Among the symbolic decorative motifs, notice the Napoleonic eagle, the thistle (Empress Eugénie's emblem) and on the chimneypiece the heraldic arms of Louis of Orléans (the "broken" arms of France) and another family emblem, a knotted staff. Beyond the Chambre de l'Empereur (**4**) (view down over the fortified entrance) the tour leads to the salle des Preuses, leaving the keep.

Salle des "Preuses" – This timber-ceilinged hall (52m by 9m/170ft by 29ft) was created by Viollet-le-Duc. The roof is shaped like an upturned ship. The mantelpiece of the double fireplace (**5**) is decorated with statues of nine women, heroines from tales of chivalry. The central figure of Semiramis, Queen of Assyria and legendarily of captivating beauty, has the features of the Empress whilst the others are portraits of ladies of the court.

Tour d'Alexandre et chemin de ronde Nord (Sentry walk) – The original walls on this side of the ruins still stand 22m/72ft high; note the different colour of the stones. Along the sentry walk Viollet-le-Duc highlighted the last step forward in defence systems before the arrival of the cannon: level walkways without steps or narrow doorways, which allowed the defenders (housed in nearby barracks) to muster quickly at critical points without blundering into obstacles. The view extends over Pierrefonds Valley.

Salle des gardes ou des mercenaires – A double spiral staircase (**6**) leads down to this guard-room which now houses beautiful lapidary fragments; remains of the original 15C statues of the heroic figures on each tower. The tour ends at the model of the castle.

Return to the town by the direct staircase (towards the car park).

POISSY

Population 36745
Michelin map 101 folds 11, 12

Access from Paris: *RER line A 5 or SNCF Rail link from Gare St-Lazare.*

The town of Poissy, situated on the banks of the Seine, was a royal residence as early as the 5C. St Louis was christened here in 1214; the king's private correspondence was even signed Louis de Poissy. The castle used to stand on place Meissonnier but it was demolished by Charles V.

An Augustinian convent founded in the 11C was given to the Dominican order by Philip the Fair. From 9 September to 13 October 1561 the abbey refectory hosted the Poissy Symposium; Catholics and Protestants were invited to discuss their differences at the instigation of Chancellor Michel de l'Hôpital. The debate was attended by the papal legate, 16 cardinals, 40 bishops and the generalof the Jesuit order on the one side, and by an important group of theologians led by Theodore Beza on the other. The symposium lasted seventeen days, but these high-level talks proved vain for the divide between the two parties was even greater after the conference.

Up to the middle of the last century, Poissy was the main Paris cattle market. Today, it is the site of a large automobile plant (Peugeot).

★**Collégiale Notre-Dame** – The greater part of the collegiate church is Romanesque, dating from the 11C and 12C. Several chapels were added in the 15C and the whole church was restored by Viollet-le-Duc. The front tower, built in the Romanesque style, once served as a belfry-porch. The square base of the tower develops to an octagonal section on the highest level, ending in a stone spire. The central tower, also Romanesque, is eight-sided through two floors, and ends in a timberwork spire.

Interior – The vaulting of the nave now features ribbing. The capitals of the south columns in the first two bays were recarved in the 17C. The other capitals feature interlacing, monsters and foliage motifs. Some of them are thought to be older than this building and were probably taken from another church. The nave is very well lit owing to the installation of a triforium by Viollet-le-Duc in the three bays nearest to the chancel, which is circled by an ambulatory with groined vaulting. The side chapels – added in the 15C – pay homage to the various trade guilds: butchers, fishermen, etc.

The first chapel to the right of the doorway contains fragments of the font used for St Louis' christening. For many centuries, the faithful would scrape the stone sides, dissolve the dust in a glass of water and drink the potion as a remedy for high fever. This explains why the font is in such bad condition.

The central Lady Chapel is the work of Viollet-le-Duc. The statue of the Virgin and Child is attributed to the Duchess of Uzès (c 1890).

The most impressive furnishings are in the first chapel on the right: majestic 15C statues of John the Baptist and St Barbara, and a superb 16C Entombment *(see below)* portraying Mary, John, Mary Magdalene, the Holy Women, Nicodemus and Joseph of Arimathea.

16C Entombment, Collégiale Notre-Dame

Musée du Jouet ⊘ – The toy museum is housed in the building flanked by two towers that used to mark the fortified entrance to the abbey. This was once a **Priory** dedicated to **St Louis** and it was here that a famous meeting was held in 1561.

The toys and games exhibited in the museum date back to the days before the introduction of television. There is a large number of dolls showing the changes in production from porcelain and biscuit (Jumeau, 19C) to the celluloid used by French and German manufacturers in the 1930s.

On the first floor, there is a display case full of clockwork toys, another filled with teddy bears and yet another with lead and paper soldiers dating from the 19C.

On the top floor are collections of cars and trains, some clockwork, others powered by steam. An electric train track dating from the 1930's operates automatically as visitors approach.

The winding street in the old enclosure leads to **Parc Meissonnier** (10ha/25 acres), laid out like English gardens.

Musée d'Art et d'Histoire ⊘ – *12 Rue St-Louis.*
The history of Poissy from Merovingian times (sarcophagi) up to the present day (automobile industry) is presented in a simple, pleasing manner. One of the glass cabinets displays numerous seals, some of which date back to the 12C, other exhibits include a painting by Meissonnier depicting summer bathing in the Seine, a splendid 16C painted wooden statue taken from the Church of Our Lady etc.

★**Villa Savoye** ⊘ – *82 Rue de Villiers.*
This masterpiece of modern architecture was designed in 1929 by **Le Corbusier** and Pierre Jeanneret for the industrialist Savoye. The use of cylindrical piles made it possible to do away with load-bearing walls and introduce huge glass surfaces. The main rooms are located on the first floor, at a height of 3.5m/12ft. They are arranged around a large terrace which opens onto the countryside, as does the solarium occupying the top level of the house. The Villa Savoye features a ramp leading to the upper levels and a spiral staircase with vertical lines deliberately brought in to counter the horizontal configuration of the villa.

Centre de production Peugeot ⊘ – This ultra-modern car plant has a large number of industrial robots. It produces more than 1 200 cars every day.

Musée Caapy ⊘ – The museum contains some forty-five veteran and vintage cars.

Waterside stopover

OUR SELECTION

Le Bon Vivant – 30 Avenue Émile-Zola in Poissy, ☎ 01 39 65 02 14. This restaurant is located on an attractively decorated barge. Menu: 200F.

Les Romanciers – Quai de Seine in Médan, ☎ 01 39 75 82 22, fax 01 39 75 44 88. This restaurant-hotel, facing Platais Island (Villennes beach) and close to Zola's house, offers a peaceful shaded setting on the south bank of the River Seine. Menu: 149F, double room: 390F.

LUXURY

Le Moulin d'Orgeval – Rue de l'Abbaye in Orgeval, ☎ 01 39 75 85 74, fax 01 39 75 48 52. Closed from 20 to 30 December and Sunday evening from November to March. Peaceful and refined establishment in the middle of a park with a pond. Menus from 210F, double room: 800F.

Abbaye de PORT-ROYAL-DES-CHAMPS★

Michelin map 101 fold 21 or 106 fold 29

Little remains of this famous abbey, which was the scene of a serious religious dispute for more than one hundred years of French history.

An abbess aged eleven – In 1204 a Cistercian convent was founded in Porrois, a town later known as Port-Royal. Although this order was supposed to be strict, the rules grew extremely lax over a period of five centuries and by the turn of the 17C, the 10 nuns and 6 novices who resided at the abbey were leading a most unsaintly life; the cloister had become a promenade, fasting was a bygone practice and the vows of poverty were hardly compatible with the entertaining carried out at the abbey, including Carnival celebrations. In 1602 **Angélique Arnauld**, the 11-year-old daughter of an influential family of lawyers was passed off as 17 and appointed Abbess of Port-Royal.

A reformer without mercy – Recovering from a bout of ill health, Mother Angélique realised where her duty lay and set about reforming her nunnery. She re-instated the enclosure and would not receive her mother, nor her father, except in the parlour, despite their repeated supplications and threats (1609). She introduced the perpetual adoration of the Blessed Sacrament, and imposed observance of the Cistercian rule, meditation and manual labour. The abbey was transformed and greeted an increasing number of novices.

Mother Angélique chose Jean Duvergier de Hauranne, better known as the Abbot of St-Cyran, and Antoine Singlin to be the directors of Port-Royal-des-Champs. Like Angélique's parents and close relatives, many of whom were Calvinists, these austere confessors aspired to draw man away from earthly pleasures, make him see how corrupt he was and persuade him that divine grace alone could save him.

In 1618, the Cistercian order sent Mother Angélique to Maubuisson where she was to reform the abbey. While she was absent, one of her younger sisters, Mother Agnès, headed the Port-Royal community.

By 1625 when Mother Angélique returned to her abbey it became necessary to find new premises; the conventual buildings were too cramped and the surrounding marshes were ruining the nuns' health. The community moved to the capital, where it occupied new buildings and was renamed Port-Royal-de-Paris (now a maternity clinic).

Angélique Arnauld by Philippe de Champaigne
(Musée de Versailles)

The "Messieurs" of Port-Royal – One of Angélique's brothers was a theologian with great influence over his friends and relations, all of whom shared the pessimistic views propounded by the Abbot of St-Cyran. These men – known as the *Solitaires* or the *Messieurs de Port-Royal* – decided to withdraw from society in order to take up prayer and meditation. In 1637 they left Port-Royal-de-Paris and moved to Port-Royal-des-Champs, which had remained empty. There they applied themselves to the renovation of the abbey: they drained the land, raised the ground and enlarged the buildings. The following year, the Abbot of St-Cyran was incarcerated on the orders of Cardinal Richelieu, whom he had refused to serve. He died in 1643. Mother Angélique returned to Port-Royal-des-Champs in 1648 and from then on she and her flourishing community spent their time between this abbey and the one in Paris. The *Solitaires* were lodged in Les Granges perched on top of a hill overlooking the old town of Porrois.

Influenced by Saint-Cyran and haunted by the importance of early education, they set up the "Petites Ecoles" in the hope of achieving salvation. Here they provided an education that was widely acclaimed for its excellence and effectiveness. The "gentlemen of Port-Royal" included some of the greatest minds of the day, among them the Great Arnauld, Arnauld d'Andilly, their relatives the Lemaistres (including Lemaistre de Sacy who translated the Bible), Lancelot the Greek scholar, Nicole the philosopher and Hamon.

The Jansenist Movement – The growing influence that Port-Royal exerted over people at court and in Parliament, as well as over the younger generation, was resented by the Jesuits. They were especially indignant because Port-Royal published the works of Cornelius Jansen, the former Bishop of Ypres, who had been entrusted by Louvain University with the task of refuting the doctrine advocated by the Jesuit Luis de Molina. Molina maintained that man could attain self-improvement through his own will-power, overcome all the problems in this world if he genuinely wished to do so and expect God to come to his assistance in any circumstances, simply on account of his merits; quite the opposite of the *Solitaires'* belief.

Cornelius Jansen died in 1638, soon after he completed his treatise *Augustinus*, unaware of the dramatic developments that were to follow its publication.

Problems of conscience – The theologians connected to Port-Royal approved of *Augustinus* because it confirmed their views, many of which were close to the Calvinist theory. They circulated it in France. The Jesuits retaliated by accusing the Jansenists of holding heretical views and produced a text of heretical "quotes" by Jansen. The Church eventually took action with the result that, from 1653, nuns and priests were required to sign a document condemning these quotations taken out of context; the nuns at Port-Royal agreed that they could not sign the document without making a few reservations since the incriminated quote did not appear in the same form in Jansen's work. They nevertheless agreed that the actual quotes were heretical.

The theological war raged on. In 1656 the celebrated mathematician and religious philosopher **Blaise Pascal**, who was in retreat near Port-Royal-des-Champs, published a series of pamphlets – the **Provinciales** – which attacked Jesuit theory and staunchly defended the cause at Port-Royal.

From 1661 Jansenists were again persecuted (the Pope's death in 1655 had produced a brief lull) and in that year Mother Angélique died after a long illness during which each week brought new torment. For some ten years from 1669 onwards, with new publications and religious studies, the Jansenist question seemed to fade into oblivion.

In 1679 Louis XIV decided to settle the whole affair once and for all: the noviciate was forbidden, the *Solitaires* were dispersed and some went into exile. The nuns at Port-Royal-de-Paris disowned their counterparts at Port-Royal-des-Champs, who were the object of continual persecution. By 1705 they numbered only 25, the youngest being 60 years old. On 20 October 1709 the remaining nuns were expelled by 300 musketeers. The mortal remains of Jean Racine, who had been buried in the northern cemetery, were moved to St-Étienne-du-Mont, in Paris, and he now rests beside Blaise Pascal.

In 1710 the monastery buildings were razed to the ground. The graveyard was desecrated and the bones of the nuns thrown into a communal grave in the cemetery of St-Lambert. The religious objects and furnishings went to a number of neighbouring parishes. The tombstone slabs which once paved the church at Magny-les-Hameaux have now been re-assembled.

The Jansenist doctrine continued to arouse controversy during Louis XV's reign. The Parlement de Paris refused to ratify royal edicts and ordinances, and priests refused to distribute the Blessed Sacraments. Clandestine publications began to circulate. Jansenism became a religious sect and it was only after the Revolution that its influence over French society started to decline.

RUINS AND MUSEUMS *2hr*

The tour of Port-Royal estate comprises two parts. The pilgrimage to the abbey ruins is enhanced by a visit to the park (Porte de Longueville, canal, view of the ruins). The Little Schools building is situated on a plateau, surrounded by pleasant, shaded grounds. It now houses a national museum, containing a wide range of documents on the former teaching colleges. The farmhouse where the *Solitaires* used to stay is a farming concern closed to the public.

Ruins and Abbey Museum ⊘ – The shaded path leading to the abbey branches off the Dampierre-Versailles road. *Park in the car park.*

The guided tour begins in a square area defined by avenues of lime trees, which was the site of the former cloister. The graveyard where the Cistercian nuns were buried after 1204 has been planted with grass. The church adjoined the cloister. Because the *Solitaires* had raised the floor level in an attempt to ward off the dampness, the building was razed down to the paving. When the original level was restored, the work uncovered the base of the pillars and the walls of the first building.

An oratory built in 1891 stands on the site of the chancel.

Next to the dovecote, a 17C barn houses a collection of paintings, engravings and memorabilia which illustrate and enliven the tour of the estate.

Les Granges, where the *Solitaires* lodged, lies above the valley on the north side screened by trees. Ascending and descending the steep slope daily to attend Mass in the abbey must have required great effort; it is said that the Hundred Steps were designed by the *Messieurs* themselves. The Hundred Steps are no longer open to the public.

Musée National des Granges de Port-Royal ⊘ – The building was specially designed for the Little Schools (established by the *Messieurs* to provide religious education) in 1651-52 and presents a suitably austere front. In the 19C a Louis XIII-style wing was added.

Most of the rooms have been restored to their former condition and contain books, engravings and drawings on the history of the abbey and the Jansenist movement, the *Solitaires* and the Little Schools. Other exhibits include a series of portraits by Philippe de Champaigne depicting the principal Jansenist leaders. Note the touchingly naïve collection of 15 gouache paintings portraying the life of the Cistercian nuns.

Jean Racine lived at Port-Royal between the ages of 16 and 19, with a break at college in Paris. He was taught Greek and Latin and French versification, and was lectured on diction and rhetoric. The French poet learned much from his tutors and he soon became an outstanding reader. Louis XIV was spellbound by his beautiful voice and Racine's advice was sought by many an actor. The good Dr. Hamon, of whom he was very fond, often used to take Racine with him when he went to treat poor patients, knitting clothes for them as he trotted along on an old donkey. Although the Jansenists were sceptical about the Arts, they accepted paintings inspired by authentic religious feelings. The exhibition hall dedicated to Philippe de Champaigne reminds visitors of the strong ties that linked this painter to the abbey: every day the nuns could admire his two works *Ecce Homo* and *Mater Dolorosa*. The museum building overlooking the farmyard once accommodated another celebrity who came here on a retreat. It was Blaise Pascal who wrote his *Mystery of Jesus* here in 1655. Tradition has it that his knowledge of mathematics came in use during his stay at the abbey when he produced the calculations for a new winch for the well: this enabled the nuns to draw a huge bucket as big as nine ordinary buckets from a depth of 60m/197ft with no extra effort.

ADDITIONAL SIGHT

Église St-Lambert – This small picturesque country church is perched above the village. A granite pyramid erected in the church cemetery in the early 20C marks the communal grave that received the remains of the Cistercian nuns and the *Solitaires*.

To the right of the drive stands a cross bearing the words "To the human race" *(A la personne humaine)*. It was set up in 1944 and celebrates the memory of those who suffered most during the Second World War, in particular in concentration camps, irrespective of race, nationality or creed.

PROVINS★★

Population 11 608
Michelin map 61 fold 4 or 237 fold 33

Access from Paris: *SNCF Rail link from Gare de l'Est*

Whether approaching Provins from the Brie plateau to the west or from Champagne and the Voulzie Valley, this medieval town presents the eye-catching and distinctive outlines of the Tour César and of the dome of St-Quiriace Church.

The lower town, a lively shopping centre, sits at the foot of the promontory and extends along the Voulzie and Durteint rivers. The town is of monastic origin, developing from the 11C around a Benedictine priory.

The Provins fairs – In the 10C Provins became one of the economic capitals of the Champagne region, thanks to its two annual fairs which, with those of Troyes, were among the largest in the region. Traders from the north and from the Mediterranean came here for business.

Common Rose of Provins

Linens, silks, spices from the Orient and wine were traded, attracting people from many walks of life: money agents and merchants among whom mingled the hard-working *bourgeoisie* of the region. These fairs were prosperous until the early 14C, when the political and economical weight shifted to Paris, eclipsing the Champagne region.

Roses – According to tradition it was Thibaud IV the Troubadour who brought roses back from Syria and grew them successfully here in Provins. Edmund Lancaster (1245-96), brother of the King of England, married Blanche of Artois and was for a while suzerain of Provins, at which time he introduced the red rose into his coat of arms.

June is the best month to visit the rosebeds at the **Pépinières et Roseraies Vizier** ⊘, Rue des Prés.

★★UPPER TOWN *1hr 30min*

It is advisable to park in the car park near Porte St-Jean. This is the location of the Tourist Office and the departure point for the small tourist train which tours the Upper Town and then returns to the Lower Town.

Maison du visiteur – The visitors' centre near the car parks houses the tourist office and provides a full range of information about local sightseeing and special events. It also provides "day passes" and guided tours of the town, and includes a model of the medieval town as well as an audio-visual presentation of its history.

Porte St-Jean (**DYZ**) – St John's Gateway was built in the 13C. This stocky construction is flanked by two projecting towers which are partially hidden by the buttresses which were added in the 14C to support the drawbridge.

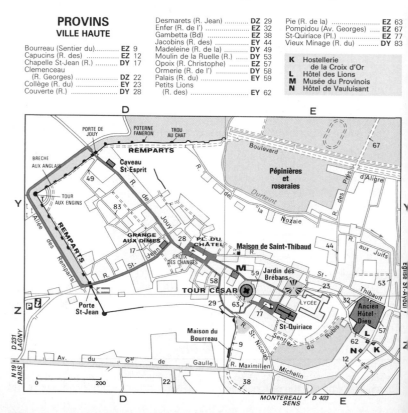

PROVINS' FESTIVE MOOD

Medieval feast	2nd weekend in June
Son et lumière	2nd and 3rd weekend in June
Jousting	Sundays at 4pm in June, July and August
Les Aigles de Provins	free-flying birds of prey, April to October
A l'Assaut des remparts	medieval war machines storming the ramparts, April to October
Harvest feast	August
Second-hand market	3rd Sunday of every month

Inquire at the tourist office, ☎ 01 64 60 26 26.

Follow allée des Remparts which overlooks the old moat.

★★Remparts – The town walls were built in the 12C and 13C along an existing line of defence, then altered on several occasions. They constitute a very fine example of medieval military architecture. The most interesting part runs between Porte St-Jean and Porte de Jouy. The Tour aux Engins, on the corner, links the two curtain walls; it derives its name from a barn nearby in which engines of war were housed. In summer, on a space behind this tower, within the ramparts, the falconners of the "Aigles de Provins" company put on a **show** ⊙ of birds of prey; other birds of prey are displayed in shelters.

Beyond the 12C Porte de Jouy take rue de Jouy, which is lined by picturesque low houses with long tiled roofs or an overhanging upper storey. **Caveau St-Esprit** *(open during special events)* was once the store of an old hospital which was destroyed by fire in the 17C.

★Grange aux Dîmes ⊙ (**DY**) – *Rue St-Jean.*
This massive 13C building belonged to the canons of St-Quiriace, who hired out the space to merchants during the major fairs. When the fairs went into decline the barn became a store for the tithes *(dîmes)* levied on the harvests of the peasants.

Provins – Tour César

Stopover

BUDGET

Le Petit Écu – 9 Place du Châtel, ☎ 01 60 67 62 22. This charming timber-framed house with terrace houses a small bistro-like restaurant. Menus from 65F, medieval buffet: 100F at weekends.

OUR SELECTION

Aux Vieux Remparts – 3 Rue Couverte, ☎ 01 64 08 94 00, fax 01 60 67 77 22. Located at the heart of the upper town, this interesting house combines style and comfort. Double room from 440F, menu: 350F.

The atmosphere of the town's famous fairs is realistically recreated in a permanent exhibition entitled, "**Provins au temps des foires de Champagne**".

Place du Châtel (**DY**) –– This vast, peaceful square, rectangular in shape, is bordered by attractive old houses: the 15C Maison des Quatre Pignons (southwestern corner), the 13C Maison des Petits-Plaids (northwest corner), the Hôtel de la Coquille to the north. The remains of Église St-Thibault (12C) stand on the northeastern corner.

In the centre, next to an old well with a wrought-iron cage, stands the Croix des Changes, where the edicts of the Counts of Champagne were posted.

Musée du Provinois ⊘ (**M EY**) – This local museum is housed in one of the oldest buildings in the town, "The Romanesque House".
On the ground floor are displayed **the sculpture and ceramic collections★**, valuable works of local medieval and Renaissance art.
Exploiting the underground clay quarries enabled potters to produce pieces now noted for their remarkable variety and timelessness.

Église St-Quiriace (**EZ**) – The church was begun in the 11C. The transept and nave date from the 13C, the dome from the 17C. On the square in front of the church stands a cross on the site of the old bell-tower which collapsed in 1689.

★★**Tour César** ⊘ (**EYZ**) – This superb 12C keep, 44m/144ft high and flanked by four turrets, is the emblem of the town. It was once part of the walls of the upper town. The pyramidal roof was built in the 16C.
The revetment wall which encloses the base of the keep was added by the English during the Hundred Years War, in order to house the artillery.
The guard-room on the first floor is octagonal and 11m/36ft high; it is topped by vaulting formed of four arcades of pointed arches ending in a dome and pierced by an orifice through which the soldiers on the floor above were passed supplies.
The gallery encircling the Keep at the height of the turrets was originally roofed over. One **view★** extends over the town and the surrounding countryside.
A very narrow stairway leads to the upper level. Under the fine 16C wooden roof are the bells of St-Quiriace, which have hung here since the church lost its bell-tower.

ADDITIONAL SIGHTS

Église St-Ayoul – In 1048 Thibaud I, count of Troyes and Meaux (and also count of Blois under the name Thibaud III), grand protector of the abbeys, installed the monks from Montier-la-Celle in the St-Ayoul district in the Lower Town.
The three doorways project far beyond the line of the gable on the west front. Missing parts of the central doorway were replaced with new pieces by the sculptor Georges Jeanclos, who was responsible for the bronze **statues★** with antique patina which now harmonise well with the medieval reliefs.
Inside, in the north aisle, stand 16C **statues★★**: a graceful if rather affected Virgin Mary and two **angel musicians** with wonderfully draped clothes.

Souterrains à graffiti ⊘ (**EZ**) – *Entrance in rue St-Thibault, left of the doorway to the Ancien Hôtel-Dieu* (**EZ**). There is a substantial network of underground passages around Provins, some marked with ancient graffiti. The section which is open to the public runs through a layer of a tufa which lies parallel to the base of the spur on which the Upper Town stands. The entrance is through a low-roofed chamber with ribbed vaulting in the old hospice.

Maison du Bourreau (**EZ**) – The last executioner to live here was Charles-Henri Sanson who executed Louis XVI.

Admission times and charges for the sights described are listed at the end of the guide. Every sight for which there are times and charges is identified by the symbol ⊘ in the Sights section of the guide.

Le QUESNOY★

Population 4 890
Michelin map 53 fold 5 or 236 fold 18

This quiet town of low, white-washed houses lying in a lush, lake-filled setting close to Mormal Forest is a fine example of French military architecture.

★FORTIFICATIONS *1hr*

The perfectly preserved fortifications still show clearly the unique qualities of the old stronghold. Built of coarse stone, flint and lime mortar covered with bricks, they form a polygon of defensive curtain walls with projecting bastions; despite apparently being in the style of Vauban these defences in fact date in part from the time of the Emperor Charles V (16C), for example the bastions with projecting towers. Various all-season paths offer pleasant walks, enabling enthusiasts of military architecture to study the layout of the defences *(information panels)*.

Leave from place du Général-Leclerc and head for the postern gate by avenue d'Honneur des Néo-Zélandais.

The gateway gives access to the moat, to the spot where the men of the New Zealand Rifle Brigade scaled the walls in November 1918. The Monument des Néo-Zélandais commemorates their exploits.

Walk in the moat around the south front of the ramparts.

From **Étang du Pont Rouge** continue to **Lac Vauban** which lies at the foot of the ramparts to each side of the Porte Fauroeulx.
The bridge provides a lovely view of the red-brick curtain walls and bastions and their reflection in the calm waters.

Étang du Fer à Cheval – Lying northwest of the town, the lake was dug to a design by Vauban during Louis XIV's reign.
The calm and verdant setting is extremely peaceful.

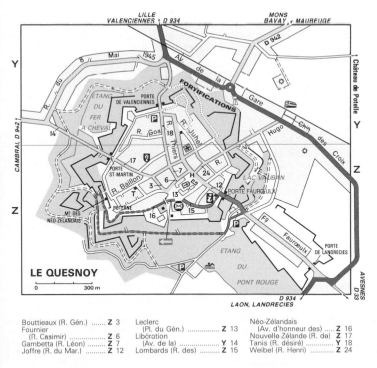

Boutieaux (R. Gén.) .... **Z** 3	Leclerc (Pl. du Gén.) .... **Z** 13	Néo-Zélandais (Av. d'honneur des) ..... **Z** 16
Fournier (R. Casimir) .... **Z** 6	Libération (Av. de la) .... **Y** 14	Nouvelle Zélande (R. de) **Z** 17
Gambetta (R. Léon) .... **Z** 7	Lombards (R. des) .... **Z** 15	Tanis (R. désiré) .... **Y** 18
Joffre (R. du Mar.) .... **Z** 12		Weibel (R. Henri) .... **Z** 24

EXCURSION

Château de Potelle – *2km/1mi east; take the road to Bavay and turn right beyond the railway.* In the 15C, this small medieval castle and chapel *(private)* were the property of Jean Carondelet, Chancellor to the Dukes of Burgundy.

Going fishing? Remember to check the national regulations on minimum size. Pike under 40cm and trout under 23cm should be returned to the water.

RAMBOUILLET★

Population 24 343
Michelin map 106 fold 28

Access from Paris: *SNCF Rail link from Gare Montparnasse*

The combination of attractive château, park and forest makes Rambouillet one of the main sights in Île-de-France. Since 1897 it has been the official summer residence of the President of the French Republic.

HISTORICAL NOTES

The death of François I – At the age of 52, François I fell ill and his health started to decline. He became restless and left his St-Germain residence in February 1547. He went to stay with his major-domo at Villepreux, paid a visit to his treasurer's widow in Dampierre, spent Shrove Tuesday in Limours with his mistress the Duchess of Étampes and indulged in a three-day hunt in Rochefort-en-Yvelines. On the way back, he dropped in to see the captain of his bodyguard Jacques d'Angennes at the Château de Rambouillet. The château was built in 1375 by Jean Bernier – a prominent court figure under Charles V – and had remained the property of the d'Angennes family since 1384. During his stay at Rambouillet François I's condition grew worse. Feeling that his end was drawing near, the King summoned his son Monseigneur le Dauphin and placed his servants and the French people in his hands. He died on 30 March 1547.

18C – In 1706 Louis XIV bought Rambouillet for the Comte de Toulouse, one of Mme de Montespan's legitimated sons. The Comte trebled the private apartments and added two perpendicular wings onto the main building.
Under Louis XVI the estate came into the hands of the Comte de Toulouse's son the **duc de Penthièvre**. Like his father, he was a dedicated governor who applied himself to the improvement of his domain. He refurbished the grounds for his daughter-in-law the Princesse de Lamballe. A close friend of Marie-Antoinette, the princess was butchered in the old La Force prison in Paris on 3 September 1792.
Louis XVI was an enthusiastic hunter who enjoyed staying at Rambouillet and he purchased the estate, and the opportunities it offered for hunting, in 1783. The Queen was bored by life at the château, which she referred to as a "Gothic toad hole". In an attempt to amuse her, the King gave orders to build the Dairy, a small pavilion reminiscent of the Trianon at Versailles. A landscape garden was started by Penthièvre and completed in accordance with plans by Hubert Robert.

A sense of destiny – In 1814 Marie-Louise met up with her father François II in Rambouillet; she decided to leave Napoleon and accompany the King of Rome to Vienna. A year later, on 29 June 1815, Napoleon made an unexpected stop here on his way from Malmaison to St Helena, to spend a night of melancholy reflection on his time here with Marie-Louise after he had divorced Joséphine.
On 31 July 1830 at about 6pm Charles X arrived at Rambouillet, fleeing the insurrection at St-Cloud. For three days the ageing ruler debated what course of action to choose. The troops under his command disbanded and an army of citizens was approaching from Paris. He eventually abdicated and set sail for England.
It was in Rambouillet – where he stayed from 23 to 25 August 1944 – that General de Gaulle gave orders for the Leclerc Division to march on Paris.

CHÂTEAU ○ *1hr*

Leave from Place de la Libération, the site of the Town Hall *(if the car park is full, leave the car in the park – parking is tolerated in certain spots).*
The château presents a triangular shape owing to the fact that Napoleon dismantled the left wing. The large François I tower belonged to the 14C fortress. It is difficult to distinguish because of the numerous additions made by the Comte de Toulouse.

Mezzanine – The reception rooms commissioned by the Comte de Toulouse are embellished with superb rococo **wainscoting★**. Note the charming boudoir designed for the Comte's wife.
The corridor adjoining the François I tower leads through to the Imperial bathroom suite, adorned with Pompeian frescoes. This opens onto the Emperor's Bedchamber, where he spent the night on 29 June, and the study. It was in the dining room – the former ballroom – that Charles X signed the abdication document. The view of the park is stunning.

Ground Floor – The Renaissance-style Marble Hall, dating from the time of Henri II, is entirely lined with marble tiles.

★PARK ○

Parterre – The château is set in a pleasant formal garden. On the right stands a quincunx, around several copses. The perspective ends with the Rondeau Basin and a sweeping avenue of swamp cypresses planted in 1805.

Rambouillet – Napoleon's bathroom

Jardins d'eau – These water gardens were remodelled by the duc de Penthièvre. The central canal is continued by a green carpet of lawn. The other canals with their geometric lines enclose islets of greenery: Île des festins, Île des Roches etc.

★**Laiterie de la Reine** – Louis XVI had the dairy built to amuse his wife Marie-Antoinette. The small sandstone pavilion resembling a neo-Classical temple consists of two rooms. The first – which houses the actual dairy – features marble paving and a marble table dating from the First Empire. The Sèvres porcelain bowls and jugs used for tasting have disappeared.

The room at the back was designed as an artificial grotto adorned with luxuriant vegetation. It includes a marble composition by Pierre Julien depicting a nymph and the she-goat Amalthea (1787).

★**Chaumière des Coquillages** – The landscape garden in the park features a charming cottage built by Penthièvre for the Princesse de Lamballe. The walls of the rooms are encrusted with a variety of sea shells, chips of marble and mother-of-pearl. A small boudoir with painted panelling adjoins the main room.

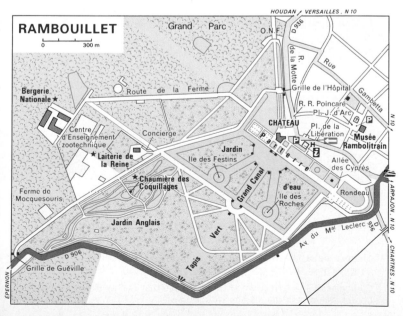

ADDITIONAL SIGHTS

★Bergerie Nationale ⊘ – In 1786 Louis XVI decided to add to his experimental farm with the production of fine wool and so he purchased a flock of merinos from Spain. The sheep farm buildings were completed during the First Empire. Today it houses around 800 animals, including 120 merino sheep.

Local products

La Boutique Gourmande – This shop facing the Bergerie nationale has a choice of regional gourmet specialities together with products made from the sheep's wool.

Musée Rambolitrain ⊘ – An astounding collection of more than 4000 toy trains and models explains the history of the railway from its early beginnings to the present day. A large O-shaped circuit occupies the whole of the second floor.

★RAMBOUILLET FOREST

This vast forest has some delightful footpaths for those who enjoy walking. Some twenty or more lakes with picturesque banks, including the **Étangs de Hollande** ⊘, and a number of villages with old houses that are now holiday homes give it a very special charm.

Geographical Notes – This is part of the ancient Yveline Forest which stretched in Gallo-Roman times as far as the outskirts of Nogent-le-Roi, Houdan, Cernay-la-Ville and Etampes.

Of the total 20000ha/50000 acres, 14000/35000 are State-owned. They cover a clay plateau with an altitude of between 110m/358ft and 180m/585ft, crisscrossed by sandy valleys. In the Middle Ages, wide-scale deforestation took place and the vast clearances now divide it into three main areas of woodland: St-Léger and Rambouillet itself, the most popular areas with tourists situated north of Rambouillet, and Yvelines to the south which is rather more divided up into private estates.

At present the policy is to create copses. There is a predominance of oak (60%) followed by pine (30%) and other varieties (10%) such as birch and beech. The forest round Rambouillet is damper and has more rivers, lakes and ponds than the one at Fontainebleau. From time immemorial it has been particularly well-stocked with game such as deer, roe-deer and wild boar – and it remains so today.

Sights

Espace Rambouillet ⊘ – *Car park and visitors centre 500m – 540yd to the south-west of the Rambouillet-Clairefontaine road (D 27).*
This 250ha/625 acres wildlife park has been divided into three areas:

Forêt des Aigles, with more than 100 birds of prey in aviaries. Free flight shows.

Forêt des Cerfs, where observation hides provide a view of deer, stags, and wild oxen.

Forêt Sauvage, a 180ha/450 acres site in which the animals roam free.
Binoculars are recommended.

Étangs de Pourras et de St-Hubert – *30min on foot there and back. Leave from the large star-shaped St-Hubert crossroads. Follow the continuation of N 191, a rough track flanked by houses which leads to the road running between the two ponds.*
The ponds were part of one of Vauban's projects to create reservoirs for Versailles' water requirements. A series of six ponds separated by paths was laid out near the Étang de Hollande. Only the two end basins are filled with water. The two central ponds – known as Bourgneuf and Corbet – are now nothing more than by a rivulet overgrown with aquatic plants.

Cycle tracks – *See Michelin map 106.*

Round tour starting from Montfort-L'Amaury
21km/12mi and 30min on foot there and back

Château de la Mormaire – Built of stone and brick under Henri IV, this castle is reminiscent of the houses on place des Vosges in Paris.

Gambaiseuil – A former woodcutter's village that is now almost deserted. A few houses still exist in the old church quarter.

Étang Neuf – Situated in a remote corner of the forest, this pond is a popular fishing haunt. It lies in pleasant surroundings planted with beech trees.

Carrefour du Grand Baliveau – The road to the right of the sign "Route Forestière du Parc d'en Haut" offers a charming walk through a lovely green glade. One of the clearings affords a good **view**★ of a secluded valley.

Round tour starting from Rambouillet

41km/25mi – about 1hr then 1hr 30min on foot there and back

Leave Rambouillet by the Maintenon road. At Gazeran (5km/3mi) turn left onto D 62; after 6.5km/4mi leave the car in the parking area down in the Drouette Valley.

Réserve Zoologique de Sauvage ⊙ – This 40ha/100 acre park is surrounded by oak woods and dotted with boulders. It contains free-roaming antelopes, deer and kangaroos, and many aquatic birds including rare swans and ducks together with a colony of flamingoes.

The Tropical Aviary in which the temperature and humidity are kept at a constant level features many tropical bird species: toucans, eclectus parrots, gouras, hornbills etc.

Return to Gazeran and continue north.

Roches d'Angennes – *Leave from the parking area of the "Zone de Silence des Rabières".* Walk 100yd through the village up the steeper slope of the valley to find the right path leading to the summit. Go past an arena-shaped shelf circled by boulders to reach the crest: **view** of Guesle Valley and Angennes lake, bordered by bulrushes, reeds and other aquatic plants.

Carrefour du Haut Planet – *Leave your vehicle on the car park at La Croix Pater and walk back to this crossroads (shelter).* The ledge of the Haut-Planet plateau – planted with birches and conifers – commands a sweeping **view**★ northwards over the hills of St-Léger.

★ **Balcon du Haut Planet** – Bear right and take the straight path leading to Haut Planet, which crosses rough, hilly ground. After passing a spring fenced by wire netting on the right, the lane reaches a shaded terrace on the edge of the plateau *(shelter for ramblers)*.

The path – offering beautiful vistas all the way – eventually leads to a rocky promontory. *Return to the car.*

Château fort de RAMBURES★

Michelin map 52 fold 6 or 236 fold 22 (6km/4mi northeast of Blangy-sur-Bresle)

The **castle** ⊙ is an interesting example of 15C military architecture; during the Hundred Years War it played an important role as a French enclave in the middle of the English-occupied territories, and it came to be called "the key to the Vimeu". The castle has remained in the same family since the 15C.

From the outside the castle retains the look of a powerful fortress, with its enormous machicolated round towers and its rounded curtain walls (so that there were no level surfaces for the enemy to fire against), its deep moat and its tall watchtower. It was designed to resist the artillery of the time and its brick walls are 3m/10ft thick. In the 18C the castle was converted into a country residence and the courtyard façade was pierced with huge windows.

Inside, for many of the rooms the only source of daylight is still through loopholes, though the alterations begun in the 18C did provide reception rooms decorated with woodwork and marble chimneypieces *(first floor)*.

After a glance over the 15C watch-path, the tour continues on the second floor, to the library-billiards room hung with a collection of portraits.

The kitchen is located in the old guard room above the dungeons; the cellars were used to shelter the villagers during invasions.

The informal park is planted with ancient trees.

Help us in our constant task of keeping up-to-date.
Send us your comments and suggestions to
Michelin Travel Publications
38 Clarendon Road – WATFORD Herts WD1 1SX
☎ *(01923) 415000/ANG*
Web site: www.michelin-travel.com

La ROCHE-GUYON★

Population 561
Michelin map 106 fold 2

This village lies between the River Seine and the Vexin plateau. It developed at the foot of an old stronghold; its crumbling keep still dominates the steep, rocky ledge. Life at La Roche-Guyon has resumed its peaceful character since the bombings of July 1944 and the Battle of Normandy, when Marshal Rommel established his headquarters in the castle. In the 13C, a residential château was erected at the foot of the cliff not far from the fortress; it was linked to the keep by a flight of steps carved in the rock. François I and his numerous retinue took up residence here in 1546. Their stay was marred by an unfortunate incident; the young comte d'Enghien – whose glowing accomplishments in Ceresole two years earlier had earned him public recognition – died of a fractured skull when a chest fell out of a window. La Roche-Guyon was made a duchy-peerage in 1621. Thirty-eight years later the title came into the hands of **François de La Rochefoucauld**, who wrote many of his famous *Maximes* at the château.

In 1816 Louis-François Auguste, **Duc de Rohan-Chabot**, acquired the estate. He lost his wife in 1819 and took holy orders at the age of 31. On his return, he continued to entertain at the château, combining acts of charity with the fashionable manners of pre-Revolutionary France. Among the guests were fellow students at St-Sulpice Seminary and the young Romantic authors Victor Hugo, Alphonse de Lamartine, Hugues Lamennais, Henri Lacordaire and Father Dupanloup.

They delighted in the grand but respectful services celebrated in the underground chapel to the strains of a superb Italian organ. In 1829 the duke was appointed Archbishop of Besançon, and then Cardinal, and sold the château and its grounds to François de la Rochefoucauld-Liancourt. La Roche-Guyon has remained in this family ever since.

★**The banks of the Seine** – The quayside promenade commands a good **view**★ of the sleepy countryside and the meandering river. Behind, the two castles stand side by side. The abutment pier of the former suspension bridge (dismantled in the 19C) provides a good observation point.

A de Vairoger /MICHELIN

La Roche-Guyon – The castle and the keep

★ **Château** ⊘ – The superb wrought-iron gates bearing the La Rochefoucauld crest open onto the courtyard and 18C stables which now house the reception desk and temporary exhibitions. The house still has some 13C features such as the towers flanking the main apartments. Built in the 16C, they stand on a terrace supported by arcaded foundations. The rooms are empty of furniture. The parapet walkway and "southeast" tower provide some wonderful panoramic views of the Seine Valley. A newly-restored corridor leads to the three chapels. The main one is dedicated to Our Lady of the Snows. During the German occupation, numerous pillboxes were built into the cliffs. They now house a retrospective look at Rommel's visit to the château. The remainder of the buildings in the cliffs, including the orangery, are now used as the backcloth for a sound and light show about regional art, entitled "**Parcours de lumière en Vallée de Seine**".

★**Route des Crêtes** – *und tour of 4km/2.5mi.*
Take the road to Gasny which passes the entrance to the famous troglodyte caves or stables called **boves**, carved in the chalk. On reaching the pass, turn right into

D 100, also known as "Route des Crêtes". When the estates no longer conceal the view of the river, park the car on a belvedere near a spinney of pine trees.

View★★ of the meander of the Seine carpeted with the trees of the Forêt de Moisson and, further along the promontory, of the spurs of the Haute-Isle cliffs. In the foreground, down below, the truncated **keep** ⊘ of the Château de La Roche-Guyon.

Continue along D 100. At the first junction, turn right into Charrière des Bois, which leads back to the starting point. The road follows a steep downward slope and passes under the 18C aqueduct that supplies water to the village and the château.

Arboretum de La Roche – *On D 37 towards Amenucourt.*
The arboretum, which spreads over 12ha/29 acres, has been planted to reproduce the geography of the Île-de-France area. Each *département* is distinguished by a different species: oak for Seine-et-Marne, maple for Essonne, hornbeam for Val-de-Marne, ash for Val-d'Oise, cherry for Seine-Saint-Denis, lime for Les Hauts-de-Seine, and beech for Yvelines. The plane-trees in the middle represent Paris. They are all young trees, apart from the twenty year-old Lebanese cedar at the central roundabout. Among the plantations, snaking stretches of lawn evoke the valleys.

Abbaye de ROYAUMONT★★

Royaumont Abbey is an impressive symbol of the wealth that often accrued to the great French abbeys of the Middle Ages. A tour of this sanctuary is strongly recommended.

The abbey, founded in 1228 and completed in 1235, was occupied by members of the Cistercian Order. It was richly endowed by the king and his successors, which explains the size and beauty of the buildings. Six of St Louis' relatives – three children, a brother and two grandsons – were buried in the abbey. Their remains have since been moved to St-Denis.

In 1791 Royaumont was sold as State property and the church dismantled. Since 1923 the abbot's palace and the grounds forming the estate have been separated from the abbey itself.

In 1964 the last owners Isabel and Henri Gouïn (1900-77) created the Royaumont Foundation for the Advancement of Human Science, to which they donated the estate.

Abbaye de Royaumont

A cultural calling – In 1978 the abbey was assigned a new cultural mission. The *Centre Culturel de rencontre* set up on its premises ensures the preservation of the abbey; it also organises concerts, lectures, training seminars and exhibitions in its regional vocal arts centre, literary centre and ethnology centre.

TOUR ⊘

Church ruins – *See plan.* Royaumont Church was consecrated in 1235. The fragments of columns that remain mark the foundations of this unusually large building (101m/330ft long).

The chancel and its radiating chapels break with Cistercian tradition in that they

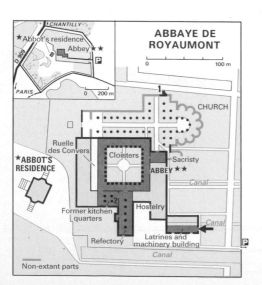

do not feature a flat east end (eg Fontenay in Burgundy). A corner turret (**1**) belonging to the former north transept gives a fair idea of its elevation (the keystone was 28m/91ft above ground).

Abbey buildings – The cloisters surround a delightful garden. The west gallery (opposite the entry) is paralleled, at the back, by a narrow, uncovered passageway known as the "ruelle des Convers". It was built for the lay brothers in order that they might have access to their wing and to the church without passing through the cloisters, habitually reserved for the monks.

278

Refectory – This spacious dining hall – which consists of two aisles – is a masterpiece of Gothic architecture. It could accommodate 60 monks without difficulty (note the monolithic shafts of the columns).

St Louis would take his turn at serving the monks at table while they sat in silence listening to the reader who stood erect in a pulpit carved out of the thick stone wall.

Former kitchen quarters – The kitchens house a statue of the Virgin of Royaumont (**2**), carved in the 14C.

The strange building resting on 31 semicircular arches astride the canal is the **latrines and machinery building**. In former times, the water reached a higher level and activated the machinery in the workshops. One of the water wheels has remained intact.

★ Abbot's Residence (Palais Abbatial) – Built on the eve of the Revolution for the last commendatory abbot of Royaumont, this white cubic construction is reminiscent of an Italian villa. In neo-Classical style, it is the work of Louis Le Masson. The façade facing the road to Chantilly is reflected in the waters of a charming pond.

RUEIL-MALMAISON★★

Population 66 401
Michelin map 101 folds 13, 14 – Michelin plan 18

Access from Paris: *RER line A 1*

The town of Rueil is famed for Malmaison, the delightful estate that remains firmly attached to the name of Napoleon Bonaparte.

Malmaison during the Consulate – Marie-Joseph-Rose Tascher de la Pagerie, born in Martinique in 1763, the widow of Général de Beauharnais, married General **Bonaparte** in 1796. Three years later, while Napoleon was away on campaign, she bought Malmaison and the 260ha/640 acres surrounding the château.

When Napoleon was First Consul he lived at the Tuileries, which he found "grand and boring". He decided to spend the end of each ten-day "week" at Malmaison. These were the happiest moments of his married life. Elegant, lively **Josephine** – she had 600 dresses and would change five or six times a day – was the spirit of the party at Malmaison. Life was carefree and formal protocol was dropped.

Malmaison in Imperial times – Crowned Emperor in 1804, **Napoleon** had no alternative but to stay at St-Cloud, Fontainebleau and the Tuileries, which were the official places of residence. Visits to Malmaison were too rare for the Empress' liking; she began to miss her splendid botanical and rose gardens, unparalleled in France. Josephine was a generous person with expensive tastes who spent money like water. When she ran into debt, her husband would complain bitterly but he invariably gave in, grumbling that this would be "the last time".

Malmaison after the divorce – Josephine returned here after her divorce in 1809. Napoleon had given her Malmaison, the Élysée and a château near Évreux. She fled the estate in 1814 but the Allied powers persuaded her to return. She behaved a little rashly by entertaining the Russian Tsar and the King of Prussia at Malmaison. She caught cold while staying with her daughter Hortense at the Château de St Leu and died on 29 May 1814, at the age of 51. The debts she left behind were estimated at 3 million francs.

The farewell to Malmaison – Ten months after Josephine's death, Napoleon escaped from Elba and revisited Malmaison.

At the end of the Hundred Days he returned to the estate and stayed with Hortense, who had married Napoleon's brother, Louis, and was to give birth to Napoleon III. On 29 June 1815 the Emperor paid a last visit to the château and his family before leaving for Rochefort and St Helena.

The dining-room at Malmaison

F. Jalain /EXPLORER

★★MUSEUM ⊙

After Josephine's death, the Château de Malmaison and its 726ha/1 800 acres of land passed to her son Prince Eugène, who died in 1824. The château was sold in 1828 and changed hands several times until it was bought by Napoleon III for the sum of one million francs. The Emperor undertook to restore the architecture and interior decoration to its former glory.

By 1877 the château was in a sorry state and the grounds reduced to a mere 60ha/148 acres. Malmaison was sold as State property and saw yet another succession of owners. The last proprietor, a Mr Osiris, acquired the estate – by now reduced to 6ha/15 acres – in 1896, restored the château and gave it to the State in 1904.

The site of the Mausoleum of the Imperial Prince was bequeathed to Malmaison by Prince Victor-Napoleon. Mr and Mrs Edward Tuck, an American couple who owned Bois-Préau Château, also gave their residence and its 19ha/47 acre park, formerly part of Josephine's private gardens.

The entrance gate still sports its old-fashioned lanterns. The **château** was built around 1622 and when Josephine bought it in 1799 it featured only the central block; the square, jutting pavilions were added soon after and the conservatory in 1801-02. The museum was founded in 1906. It houses many exhibits which were purchased, donated or taken from either Malmaison, St-Cloud and the Tuileries, or from other national palaces connected with the Imperial family.

Ground Floor

1) Vestibule built in the Antique style: busts of Napoleon's family.

2) Billiards Room: furniture belonging to the former gallery.

3) Drawing room: beautiful furniture, including Marie-Louise's weaving loom. Note the splendid fireplace, flanked by two paintings by Gérard and Girodet (based on the poems by Ossian).

4) Music Room: elegant furniture by the Jacob brothers, the Empress's harp, piano belonging to Queen Hortense.

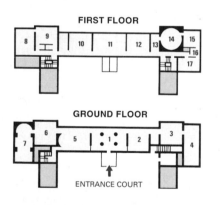

FIRST FLOOR

GROUND FLOOR

ENTRANCE COURT

5) Dining Room: walls adorned with paintings over stuccowork.

6) Council Chamber: tent-shaped decor, embellished with military trophies. The armchairs were taken from the former château at St Cloud.

7) Library: original decoration by Percier and Fontaine (note how mirrored panels cleverly conceal heating vents), furniture by the Jacob brothers. The books, furniture and military maps come from Malmaison and the Tuileries.

First Floor

The first rooms were occupied by the Emperor when he spent his last days in Paris (June 1815), between the Battle of Waterloo and his departure for St Helena.

8) Imperial Salon: several large portraits of the Imperial family, painted by Gérard.

9) Emperor's Bedroom: Prince Eugène's bed and a private collection of furniture, both taken from the Tuileries. The Victory standing on a pedestal table is the same one the Emperor was holding at the top of the Grand Army column on Place Vendôme in Paris (it was torn down by the Commune in 1871). The walls are decorated with white hangings.

10) Marengo Room: paintings by David and Gros, ceremonial sabre and sword belonging to the First Consul.

11) Josephine's Room: portrait of the Empress, various personal items, porcelain dinner services manufactured in Sèvres and Paris, picture representing the Emperor surrounded by the marshals who took part in the Battle of Austerlitz.

12) Exhibition Gallery: frieze taken from the Paris mansion where the Imperial couple lived, located in rue Chanteraine, later renamed rue de la Victoire. Josephine's dressing table, bust of the Empress by Chinard.

13 to 17) Josephine's Suite (antechamber, State bedchamber, ordinary bedroom, bathroom, boudoir): portraits of the Empress by Gérard and Prud'hon.

Second Floor – One of the rooms contains glass-fronted cupboards containing a few of the Empress' clothes. In the next room is a display of ceremonial robes. Other rooms contain furniture and personal mementoes belonging to Queen Hortense as well as objects connected with Prince Eugène and others who frequented Malmaison.

The last room houses an exhibition relating to the history of the château and the estate.

Pavilions – The **Pavillon Osiris** contains all the collections that have been donated over the years: the works of art and Antique pieces belonging to Mr Osiris, a remarkable selection of snuff boxes, glass objects and caskets relating to the Napoleonic legend. The central area is dominated by Gérard's full-length portrait of Czar Alexander I. The **Pavillon des Voitures** displays several Imperial carriages, including the landau that Blücher captured at Waterloo in June 1815.

Park – In the park (now limited to 6ha/15 acres) note the Marengo cedar tree planted soon after the victorious battle of 14 June 1800, the rose garden and a number of rare tree species. At the end of an avenue of stately lime trees stands the **Pavillon de Travail d'Été** that Napoleon used in conjunction with the library.
Leave the estate on foot and turn right to skirt the park along avenue Marmontel (gates). On the left lies the Mausoleum of the Imperial Prince, the son of Napoleon III, who was killed by members of the Zulu tribe in 1879. The statue of the prince playing with his dog Nero is a replica of Jean-Baptiste Carpeaux' work; the original is in the Louvre.

★**Château de Bois-Préau** ⊘ – This château, bought by Josephine in 1810 and rebuilt in 1855, and its park were bequeathed by Mr and Mrs Edward Tuck. The Malmaison museum housed in this château contains memorabilia of Napoleon's exile on St Helena and reminders of the return of his ashes. There is also an extensive display concerning the Napoleonic legend.

Église St-Pierre-St-Paul – Built in the late 16C and completed under Richelieu, this church was restored thanks to the generosity of Napoleon III.
The interior is Renaissance. The **organ case**★, made in Florence in the late 15C, is among the most beautiful in France and was a present from Napoleon III.
To the right of the chancel lies the white marble tomb of the Empress Josephine. She is portrayed kneeling in formal attire, just as she was in David's painting of the coronation ceremony. Nearby stands a small mausoleum in memory of her uncle, governor of Martinique. The funeral monument to Queen Hortense – who died in 1837 – lies to the left of the chancel. The high altar features a beautiful 17C bronze low-relief sculpture representing the Embalming of Christ. It used to adorn the chapel in the Château de Malmaison.
Leave the church and bear left along D 39. Turn right onto rue Masséna to reach rue Charles-Floquet, which becomes chemin de Versailles. Enter the forest and continue to Etang de St Cucufa. Park nearby.

Forêt de Malmaison – This 200ha/500 acre forest is planted with oaks and chestnut trees; it is believed that a chapel was once built in the forest in honour of St Cucufa, who martyred in 304 during the rule of Diocletian.
In a small, wooded vale lies **Etang de St Cucufa**★, a small lake which is covered with water-lilies during the summer months. Josephine gave orders to build a dairy at the water's edge and it supplied the château with milk, butter and cheese. It has since disappeared. The wooden cottages lining the shores of the lake were built by Empress Eugénie.
Return to the car. On leaving the forest, take the first turning on the right.

Avenue de la Châtaigneraie and rue du Colonel-de-Rochebrune (D 180) cross the **Buzenval** district, where the heroes of the Paris Commune fought bravely in January 1871. A memorial has been erected on the top of the mound, which commands an extensive view of the northern lowlands.

ST-AMAND-LES-EAUX

Population 16776
Michelin map 51 fold 17, 236 fold 17 or 111 fold 36

The town is set on the west bank of the River Scarpe, which separates it from a vast forest; its name derives partly from St Amand, who was Bishop of Tongres in the 7C and founder of a Benedictine monastery here which became one of the most important abbeys in the north of France, and partly from its hot springs, used for the treatment of rheumatism and respiratory disorders. The four mineral springs produce water bottled by the Société des Eaux Minérales de St-Amand, the fifth largest producer in France.

Abbey – The last reconstruction of these monastic buildings was undertaken c 1625 by Abbot Nicolas du Bois, with their solemn inauguration in 1673.
After the Revolution, only the impressive abbey tower and the magistrates' buildings remained.

★**Abbey Tower - Museum** ⊘ – This is a colossal building (82m/269ft high) in a traditional Baroque style and was the narthex of a church with a nave (non-extant) which occupied much of what is now the public garden.
The façade is divided into five levels, each using a Classical order: from the bottom to the top the orders run through Tuscan, Doric, Ionic, Corinthian and Composite.

The columns and mouldings set the rhythm for the design which is unusual for the plethora of carvings. The damaged statues show God the Father, St Amand, St Benedict, St Martin and others. At the centre of the first level, a *trompe-l'œil* depiction of a church sheltered a now-faint scene of Christ expelling the money-lenders from the Temple.

The tower above the balustrade is crowned with a vast dome surmounted by a generously carved lantern turret and lantern; inside hangs the 17C Great Bell, weighing 4560kg/nearly five tons.

Interior – The superb ground-floor chamber has carved stone vaulting around a central void to allow for the passage of the bells. Masks and scrolls, niches and stoups are reminiscent of the Antwerp mannerist style. Temporary exhibitions are held here.

The first floor, with its lovely ribbed vault, houses a collection of 18C faiences from the two local potteries, Desmoutiers-Dorez and Fauquez; the collection includes over 300 pieces.

Climbing the tower *(362 steps)* gives a good **view** of the 17C timberwork. The workings of the 17C clock can be seen before reaching the bells themselves (48 of them), electrically operated each day between 12 noon and 1230.

An outside gallery offers a wide **panorama** over the Scarpe Valley and Raismes Forest as far as Valenciennes.

Échevinage ⊙ – The priory was designed by Nicolas du Bois as an entrance pavilion to the abbey, and was also used by the "magistracy" comprising the mayor and his aldermen.

The façade, flanked by towers with domes and a lantern, has a sandstone base and

D'après photo Bottin

St-Amand-les-Eaux – Échevinage

is in typically Flemish Baroque style; stone surrounds with vermiculated rustication, ringed columns, sculpted cartouches. The door is surmounted by a proclamations balcony or bartizan and the belfry houses the original "proclamations bell".

Inside, on the first floor, the Salle de Justice de Paix still has its original decor.

On the second floor, two symmetrical rooms beneath the domes are covered by beautiful domed vaulting with radiating ribs. The Salle des Échevins reserved for the local council, has been entirely redecorated; the **Salon Watteau**, so-named because in 1782 Louis Watteau of Lille, great-nephew of the great painter, adorned it with religious and allegorical paintings, has kept its atmosphere.

Maison du Parc – *357 Rue Notre-Dame d'Amour.*
The visitors centre gives an insight into the beauty spots and natural environments contained within the regional park covering the Scarpe and Escaut Plains.

Établissement thermal – *4km/2.5mi east by D 954 and D 151.*
Fontaine-Bouillon was known to the Romans for the curative powers of the spring water and was also a place of worship. When the exploitation of the waters began again in the 17C, under Vauban's direction, several ex-voto wooden statues left by those who had taken the waters in the past were found at the bottom of the basin. The waters and mud, bubbling up at a temperature of 26°C/82°F, are among the most radioactive in France; they are used mainly for the treatment of rheumatism and for physiotherapy.

The **établissement thermal**, which was rebuilt after the Second World War, also houses a hotel and a casino; its park (8ha/20 acres) extends into the forest along Drève du Prince which was marked out on the orders of Louis Bonaparte, who took the waters here in 1805. A tall beech grove stretches nearby to the south.

In March 1793 the Château de Fontaine-Bouillon (since demolished) served as the headquarters for **Dumouriez** after he was evacuated from Belgium. It was here that the victor of the battles of Valmy and Jemmapes received the commissioners of the Convention who had come to arrest him; Dumouriez instead delivered them to the Austrian general Clairfayt. He then went over to the enemy with his staff, which included General Égalité, ex-duke of Chartres and future King Louis-Philippe.

Forêt de Raismes-St-Amand-Wallers – This forest (4600ha/11370 acres), an important section of a larger, 10000ha/24710 acre Regional Nature Park (parc naturel régional), is however only a sliver of the great mantle which covered the

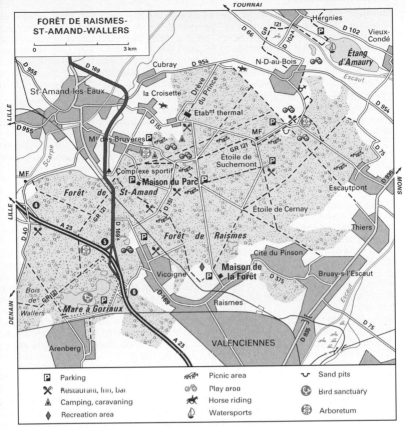

FORÊT DE RAISMES-
ST-AMAND-WALLERS

	Parking		Picnic area		Sand pits
	Restaurant, inn, bar		Play area		Bird sanctuary
	Camping, caravaning		Horse riding		Arboretum
	Recreation area		Watersports		

Hainault region in the Middle Ages. The flat sand and clay soil, combined with the quarries of former mining works, has resulted in marshes and small lakes throughout the forest, which is made up of oak, beech, birch and poplar groves. Amenities include trails, bridleways, picnic areas, a recreation area *(base de loisirs)*, a watersports centre at the 100ha/247 acre **Amaury Lake** *(étang d'Amaury)* and the **Goriaux Pool** *(Mare à Goriaux)* bird sanctuary *(réserve ornithologique)* where numerous bird species such as the crested grebe, the common coot and the little ringed plover live. A marked itinerary in the area leads to several local dovecotes including that at **Bouvignies** ⊙ where documents and objects related to the breeding and training of pigeons are displayed.

ST-CLOUD★★

Population 28 597
Michelin map 101 folds 14, 24 – Michelin plan 22

Access from Paris: *Metro line 10 (station: Boulogne-Pont de St-Cloud)*

St-Cloud is situated on the west bank of the River Seine and belongs to the residential suburbs of the French capital. It is known mostly for its park, which once surrounded a splendid château.

Clodoald – Unlike his unfortunate brothers, Clodoald, the grandson of Clovis and Clotilda, escaped murder and became a disciple of the hermit Severin. He founded a monastery, where he died in 560; his tomb soon became a place of pilgrimage and the town of Nogent, which surrounded it, was subsequently renamed St-Cloud. The saint bequeathed his seignorial rights to the Bishops of Paris who, until 1839, held the title of Dukes of St-Cloud and Peers of France.

The assassination of Henri III – In 1589 Henri III laid seige to Paris, which had fallen into the hands of the **Catholic League**: this religious alliance between members of the French nobility (led by the Guise and Montmorency families) and Spain had been formed in order to gain military and political power during a time of weak monarchy in France. Following the King's alliance with his cousin, the Protestant Henri of Navarre, a vengeful young Jacobin friar called Jacques Clément gained admission to the King's presence and stabbed him in the abdomen. Henri III died two days later.

Monsieur's Castle – In 1658 the episcopal building became the property of Louis XIV's brother, known to all as "Monsieur". His first wife Henrietta of England died there in 1670. The Sun King's brother later married Charlotte-Elisabeth of Bavaria. He extended the grounds to 590ha/1 460 acres and asked Jules Hardouin-Mansart to draw up the plans for a series of beautiful buildings. The park and its impressive cascade were designed by **Le Nôtre**. Marie-Antoinette bought the estate in 1785 but it became State property during the Revolution.

The 18 Brumaire – When General Bonaparte returned from his campaign in Egypt, the army troops and the French people saw him as the leader who would restore peace and order. On 18 Brumaire of the year VIII in the new French calendar (9 November 1799), the seat of the Consulate was moved to St-Cloud.
The following day, the Five Hundred held a meeting at the Orangery, presided over by Napoleon's brother Lucien Bonaparte. The General was greatly disconcerted by the hostile reception he got and was saved only by the swift intervention of his brother. Lucien summoned Joachim Murat, who cleared the assembly room instantly. The Directoire was abolished.

St-Cloud during the Empire – In 1802 Bonaparte was appointed consul for life and St-Cloud became his favourite official residence. He celebrated his civil wedding with Marie-Louise on the estate and followed it with a religious ceremony in the Square Salon of the Louvre (1810).
Later, in 1814, the Prussian Marshal Gebhard Blücher took up residence at the château. In an act of vengeance, he cut the silk hangings to ribbons, and wrecked both the bedroom and the library.
It was at St-Cloud that Charles X signed the Ordinances of July 1830, which abolished the Charter and precipitated his down fall. It was also from St-Cloud that he went into exile.
On 1 December 1852 the Prince-President Louis-Napoleon was made Emperor. A meeting was held at the Château de St-Cloud on 15 July 1870, during which it was decided to declare war on Prussia. The building was badly damaged in a fire three months later; it was finally razed to the ground in 1891.

★★PARK ⊘

The 450ha/1 110 acre park which spreads from the slopes of the Seine Valley to the Garches plateau has retained most of the original layout designed by Le Nôtre. In the former Guards' Pavilion, a **Musée Historique** ⊘ tells the story of the estate and its château destroyed by fire in October 1870.

★**Grande Cascade** – Designed in the 17C by Lepautre, these impressive falls were later enlarged by Jules Hardouin-Mansart. Dominated by allegorical statues of the rivers Seine and Marne, the waters of the cascade flow into a series of basins and troughs before reaching the lower falls, from where they are channelled down to the edge of the park. The whole works are about 90m/296ft long. The **Grandes Eaux**★★ ⊘ fountain display is quite remarkable.

Grand Jet – Nestling in greenery near the Great Cascade, it is the most powerful fountain in the park and rises to a height of 42m/138ft.

Terrace – A cluster of yew trees and a marble layout mark the former site of the château, which was also the start of the lawns and their continuation, the Allée de Marnes. The private gardens used to spread on either side of this avenue.

★**Jardin du Trocadéro** – These gardens were laid out on the site of the former château; they date from the Restoration period. This beautiful landscape garden features a charming pond and an aviary.
The far end of the terrace commands a view of Paris. In the foreground, note the Pavillon d'Artois, part of which was built in the 17C. It now houses the École Normale Supérieure (the prestigious teachers' training college).

Tapis vert – Running from the Grande Gerbe to Rond-Point des 24 Jets, these lawns command a lovely view of the flowerbeds and the city of Paris.

Rond-Point de la Balustrade – On this site Napoleon erected a monument surmounted by a lantern which was lit when the Emperor was staying at the château. It was based on a model from ancient Greece, which is why the Parisians called it Demosthene's lantern. It was blown up by the Prussians in 1870. The terrace offers a superb **panorama**★★ of Paris, stretching from the Bois de Boulogne to the woods at Clamart and Meudon.

Pavillon de Breteuil – This 18C pavilion – St-Cloud's former Trianon – houses the Bureau International des Poids et Mesures, the world centre for scientific measurement. The Bureau still has the old standard metre.

La Fayette Memorial – *West of the park, along Boulevard Raymond-Poincaré (N 307)*. The memorial was erected by an American foundation. It pays homage to the 209 pilots from the United States who volunteered to take part in the La Fayette

Squadron during the First World War. The monument consists of an arch and a colonnade reflected in a small pond. The crypt beneath the terrace contains the mortal remains of the 67 pilots who perished, including the ace fighter Lufbery.

★**Institut Pasteur – Musée des Applications de la Recherche** ⊙ – *3 Boulevard Raymond-Poincaré*. In 1884 when **Louis Pasteur**, who had already done considerable research work, lacked space in Paris to pursue his studies on rabies, a decree ruled that he could move to the now State-owned Villeneuve-l'Étang estate; in 1885 he successfully invented the first vaccine for human use, crowning a lifelong career.

The museum is housed in the Hundred Guards' Pavilion, occupied by Napoleon III's soldiers in the 19C. It presents the history of the struggle against infectious diseases through the accomplishments of Pasteur and his disciples: Pierre Roux, Yersin, Gaston Ramon, Albert Calmette, Nicolle and Laveran, and concentrates on three major fields of research: serum therapy, vaccination and

Louis Pasteur

chemotherapy. The techniques used to overcome diseases such as diphtheria, tetanus, typhus, cholera, tuberculosis and polio are explained, together with the progress of modern research into hepatitis B, AIDS, immunology and artificial vaccines. The room where Pasteur died in 1895 remains intact and features the family measuring rod bearing inscriptions made by Mme Pasteur. The study of Gaston Ramon, who discovered toxoids, has been reconstructed. The former drawing room houses a collection of 19C instruments from medical laboratories: Elie Metchnikoff's microscope, Chamberland's sterilizer and Doctor Roux' optical bench.

TOWN

Overlooked by the spire of the Eglise St-Clodoald (1865), the steep, narrow streets of the old town wind their way up the hillsides of the Seine Valley.

★**Eglise Stella-Matutina** – *Place Henri-Chrétien along Avenue du Maréchal-Foch.* The church was consecrated in 1965; it is shaped like a huge circular tent made of wood, metal and glass. It is fixed to a concrete base by nine pivots and fronted by a porch roof in the shape of a helm. The converging lines of the copper roofing and the pine timbering create an impression of loftiness and soaring height which is further emphasised by the concentric rows of fews round the altar.

Pont de St-Cloud – In the 8C a bridge was built across the River Seine. According to tradition, no king was to set foot on it, or he would die a sudden death. Until the middle of the 16C, French rulers would cross the river in a boat.

However when François I died in Rambouillet, it was decided that the funeral procession would cross the famous bridge; no ill omens were feared as the King was already deceased. This put an end to the long-standing tradition. François' son Henri II replaced the old wooden bridge with a magnificent stone construction featuring 14 arches. The local people were astonished by such a massive display of stonework, which they claimed was the Devil's work, and the bridge had to be exorcised.

ST-DENIS★★★

Population 89 988
Michelin map 101 fold 16 – Michelin plan 20

Access from Paris: *Metro line 13 (station: St-Denis-Basilique). By RER, line B, La Plaine-Voyageurs or line D, gare SNCF de Saint-Denis.*

Saint-Denis is an industrial and cultural town dating far back in history. For centuries, its destiny was directly linked to that of the abbey, then of the cathedral. Its economic development began with the setting up of dyeing and printing works. Its proximity to Paris, however, brought it into the forefront of wars and epidemics. This may go some way towards explaining its active role in the French Revolution in 1789. It was then renamed Franciade, a name which it kept until 1800. During the second half of the 19C, the town attracted heavy industries. The **Stade de France**, inaugurated in January

1998, has given the town a boost, and stimulated the economy. The means of transport and the accommodation infrastructure were expanded for the France 98 Football World Cup. This opportunity is already leading to a wide range of projects such as a Cité du Sport, an international football museum etc.

Effigies of Marie-Antoinette and Louis XVI

"Monsieur Saint-Denis" – St Denis was a preacher, and the first Bishop of Lutetia. Legend has it that, after being beheaded in Montmartre, he·picked up his head and walked away with it. He finally died in the country and was buried by a pious woman. An abbey was built over the grave of the man popularly known as "Monsieur (or Monsignor) Saint-Denis" and soon attracted large crowds of pilgrims. That, at least, is the legend. In fact, a Roman town stood on the site of Saint-Denis. It was called Catolacus and it had stood on the site since the 1C AD as it was possible to keep watch over the Paris-Beauvais road and the river from this spot. It was in a field outside this town that St Denis was said to have been buried in a secret ceremony, after his martyrdom.

In 475, the first large church was built. Dagobert I had it rebuilt in 630 and set up a Benedictine community there with orders to take charge of the pilgrimage. The abbey was the wealthiest and most illustrious in France. The church was again rebuilt c 750 by Pepin the Short who included a "martyrium" under the chancel, a crypt in which people could pray at saints' tombs. The building we see today, however, dates mainly from the days of Suger in the 12C and Pierre de Montreuil in the 13C.

Abbot Suger – Suger is *the* outstanding figure in the history of St-Denis. He came from a poor family and was "given" to the abbey at the age of 10. His exceptional gifts gave him immense power over his fellow pupil, the son of Louis VI the Fat, who became a close friend of the young monk, summoned him to the royal court and consulted him on every possible subject. Suger was elected Abbot of St-Denis in 1122 and drew the plans of the present minster himself. As a minister during the reign of Louis VII, he was appointed Regent while the king was away fighting in the Second Crusade. His wisdom and his care for the public good were so great that, on his return, Louis VII called him the "Father of the Country".

The Lendit Fair – The fair was instigated by the abbey in 1109 and was held in the plain at St-Denis. For six hundred years, it enjoyed fame throughout Europe. Twelve hundred wooden stalls were set up for the merchants. Every year, the University of Paris attended the fair in order to buy the parchment in the various faculties.

★★★ BASILICA CHURCH ⊘

The burial ground of kings – For twelve hundred years from Dagobert to Louis XVIII, almost all the Kings of France were buried here. In 1793, Barrère asked the Convention for permission to destroy the tombs. The bodies were thrown into communal graves. Alexandre Lenoir saved the most precious tombs by taking them to Paris, storing them in the Petits-Augustins which was to become the Musée des Monuments Français. In 1816, Louis XVIII returned the tombs to the basilica.

Construction – The structure is of prime importance in the history of architecture. It had the first large chancel and was a prototype, providing inspiration for the architects of countless late-12C cathedrals such as the ones in Chartres, Senlis and Meaux. Suger had the west front and first two bays built between 1136 and 1140, followed by the chancel and crypt from 1140 to 1144. The Carolingian nave was retained as a temporary measure but was refaced (1145-1147). The amazing speed with which the building was erected can be explained by Suger's skill and knowledge, and by the assistance provided by the congregation. They pulled the carts loaded with building stone quarried in Pontoise.
Early in the 13C the left tower was topped with a magnificent stone spire. Then work began again on the chancel. The transept and the nave were totally rebuilt. St Louis commissioned Pierre de Montreuil to do the work. He was employed here from 1247 until his death in 1267.

Decline and Fall – In later years, the basilica was poorly maintained and the French Revolution brought with it further damage. In his work *Genius of Christianity*, Chateaubriand described the desolate atmosphere, "Saint-Denis is deserted. Birds fly through it and grass grows on the broken altars..." Napoleon had the most urgent repairs carried out and returned the basilica to the Church in 1806.

Restoration – The architect Debret took charge of the church in 1813 but he knew little or nothing about medieval architecture and his work raised public indignation. He began to work on the magnificent spire but used materials that were too heavy and the delicate balance was destroyed. In 1846, the spire threatened collapse and had to be removed.

Viollet-le-Duc, who replaced Debret in 1847, gathered up documents that enabled him to restore the building to its original condition. From 1858 until his death in 1879, he undertook a considerable amount of work and the church we see today is due to his efforts.
Digs carried out in the crypt have revealed stretches of wall from the Carolingian martyrium and a Merovingian burial ground including the late 6C tomb of Princess Arégonde, Clothar I's wife, some magnificent sarcophagi, and several admirable pieces of jewellery. Foundations of earlier churches have also been uncovered.

TOUR *1hr*

Exterior – The absence of the north tower mars the harmony of the west front. In the Middle Ages the building was fortified and some crenellations are still visible at the base of the towers. The tympanum on the central doorway represents the Last Judgment, that on the right doorway (it has been recarved) depicts the Last Communion of St Denis and on the left the Death of St Denis and his companions Rusticus and Eleutherus (also recarved). The door jambs feature the Wise and Foolish Virgins *(centre)*, the labours of the months *(right)* and the signs of the Zodiac *(left)*.
On the north side of the cathedral, the nave is supported by double flying buttresses. The transept, which presents a wonderful rose-window, was initially to have had two towers but work stopped after the first floor. If the original plans had been carried out, the church would have had six towers altogether.

The basilica has been floodlit every night since June 1998; the lighting by Yann Kersalé which illuminates the west front recreates the warm colours of stained glass.

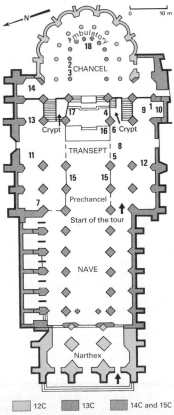

Interior – The cathedral is 108m/354ft long, 39m/128ft wide in the transept and 29m/95ft high, making it slightly smaller than Notre-Dame in Paris.

The narthex is formed by the two bays beneath the towers. Part of its pointed vaulting, which rests on a series of sturdy pillars, was designed by Suger. The elegant nave is attributed to Pierre de Montreuil. The bays in the triforium open onto the exterior (one of the first examples of such arrangements). The stained-glass windows in the nave are modern.

★★★**The tombs** – St-Denis houses the tombs of kings, queens and royal children, as well as those of leading personalities who served the French court, such as Bertrand du Guesclin (**1**). The mausoleum may be seen as a museum of French funeral art through the Middle Ages and during the Renaissance period (79 recumbent figures). The tombs have been empty since the Revolution.

After the 14C it was customary to remove the heart and viscera from the bodies of French kings before embalming them. The inner organs, the heart and the body were all buried in different places. The bodies were taken to St-Denis.

Up to the Renaissance, the only sculpture adorning tombs were **recumbent figures**. Note the tombs of Clovis (**2**) and Fredegunde (**3**), featuring a copper cloisonné mosaic made in the 12C for St-Germain-des-Prés Church.

Around 1260 St Louis commissioned a series of effigies of all the rulers who had preceded him since the 7C. The figures were purely symbolic but they provide a telling example of how royalty was portrayed towards the mid 13C. They include the imposing tomb of Dagobert (**4**), with its lively, spirited scenes, the recumbent statues of Charles Martel (**5**) and Pepin the Short (**6**), and a female effigy carved in Tournai marble (**7**).

The statue of Philippe III the Bold (**8**), who died in 1285, shows an early concern for accurate portraiture and bears a strong resemblance to the living character.

Towards the middle of the 14C well-known people had their tomb built when they were still alive. The effigies of Charles V by Beauneveu (**9**), Charles VI and Isabella of Bavaria (**10**) are therefore extremely lifelike.

During the Renaissance, these **mausoleums** took on monumental proportions and were lavishly decorated. They were laid out on two levels, contrasting sharply with one another. The upper level featured the king and his wife, kneeling in full regalia. On the lower level, the deceased were pictured lying down as naked cadavers. Admire the twin monument built for Louis XII and Anne of Brittany (**11**), and that of François I and Claude de France (**12**), sculpted by Philibert Delorme and Pierre Bontemps.

Catherine de' Medici, who survived her husband Henri II by 30 years, gave orders to build the royal tomb. When she saw how she had been portrayed according to tradition, she fainted in horror and ordered a new effigy which substituted sleep for death. Both works are on display in the cathedral. Their making was supervised by Primaticcio (**13**), and Germain Pilon (**14**), respectively.

Chancel – The beautiful pre-Renaissance stalls (**15**), in the forward part of the chancel, were taken from the Norman Castle in Gaillon. On the right stands a splendid 12C Romanesque **Virgin Mary**★ in painted wood (**16**), brought from St-Martin-des-Champs. The bishop's throne opposite (**17**) is a replica of Dagobert's royal throne (the original is in the Medals and Antiquities Gallery at the Bibliothèque Nationale in Paris).

At the end, the modern reliquary of the Saints Denis, Rusticus and Eleutherius (**18**) flanks Suger's **ambulatory**★, characterised by wide arches and slim columns.

The radiating chapels are decorated with several altarpieces and fragments of stained glass dating from the Gothic period.

★★**Crypt** – The lower ambulatory was built in the Romanesque style by Suger (12C) and restored by Viollet-le-Duc (capitals with plant motifs). In the centre stands a vaulted chapel known as Hilduin's Chapel (after the abbot who had it built in the 9C).

Beneath the pavement lies the burial vault of the Bourbon family, which houses the remains of Louis XVI, Marie-Antoinette and Louis XVIII, among others. The communal grave in the north transept received in 1817 the bones of around 800 kings and queens, royal highnesses, princes of the blood, Merovingians, Capetians and members of the Orléans and Valois dynasties.

ADDITIONAL SIGHTS

Former Abbey ⓥ – It adjoins the cathedral that was once the abbey church. The present conventual buildings date from the 18C and are the work of Robert de Cotte. In 1809 Napoleon I made the abbey the seat of a college for the daughters of holders of the French order of merit, the **Légion d'Honneur**.

Musée d'Art et d'Histoire ⓥ – *22 bis Rue Gabriel-Péri.*

The museum is set up in the former Carmelite convent, part of which has been restored. The convent was founded by Cardinal de Bérulle in 1625 and occupied by Louis XV's daughter Madame Louise de France between 1770 and 1787. The refectory and the kitchen contain archeological exhibits discovered in St-Denis (fragments of medieval pottery). Many of the items on display come from the old hospital, including a superb reconstruction of an apothecary's shop that is of particular interest to ceramics enthusiasts (17C and 18C jars) apothecary's collection of ceramic phials and jars (17C and 18C).

The cells on the first floor contain many works of art, mementoes and paintings, including several by Guillot, evoking the daily life of the Carmelite nuns. Mystical adages have been inscribed on the walls.

On the second floor, once reserved for the king when he visited his daughter, there are numerous drawings, paintings and documents relating to the Paris Commune of 1871. One of the rooms contains works by the Impressionist painter Albert André.

The former Louis XV pavilion, now renovated, houses an exhibition of the works of Paul Eluard, with a collection of personal memorabilia.

The **former Carmelite chapel** has a splendid Louis XVI dome. It was here that the prioress Louise de France died in 1787.

Musée Bouilhet-Christofle ⓥ – *112 Rue Ambroise-Croizat.*
The famous gold and silverware manufacturing company – the first to apply the principle of electroplating – set up premises here in 1875. They became official supplier to Napoleon III and their silver pieces still adorn the tables of many heads of State and rulers throughout the world. The museum presents a number of rare exhibits and some beautiful reproductions crafted in the St-Denis workshops in the late 19C. The history of the silverware industry covers Antiquity, the Gallo-Roman period (Hildesheim treasure), the Renaissance (Henri II's ceremonial armour), the 18C (Vinsac ewer), the Second Empire and the present century up to 1960 (objects by Gio Ponti Sabattini, Wirkkala etc). There is an annexe of this museum in Paris (9 rue Royale, 75008); it is also possible to visit the workshops on request.

The French football team, winner of the 1998 World Cup

Stade de France – The France 98 Football World Cup was the force that generated it, and now it is the biggest multi-function Olympic-sized stadium in the world. The elliptic structure is 270m/295yd long, 230m/240yd wide, 35m/115ft high and covers an area of 17ha/42 acres. Thanks to its variable capacity, it can host all kinds of sporting and entertainment events. The circle of stands (25 000 seats) nearest the track can be reconfigured to accommodate athletics competitions. The middle stand has a capacity of 30 000 and the upper stand 25 000. When the field is used for concert fans, the total capacity reaches 105 000.

Parc de la Courneuve – *2.5km/1.5mi east along rue de Strasbourg and N 301 (on the right).*
This 440ha/1 090 acre stretch of greenery features a cycling track, bridlepath, a ski jump, a little train, sports facilities, and playgrounds for children. Rowing boats and pedaloes may be hired to explore the 12ha/30 acre lake *(bathing prohibited).*

ST-GERMAIN-EN-LAYE★★

Population 39926
Michelin map 101 fold 12 – Michelin plan 18

Access from Paris: *RER line A 1*

St-Germain is both a residential district and a popular resort with many tourists, attracted by its château, its huge terrace and its forest.

HISTORICAL NOTES

The Old Castle – In the 12C Louis VI, the Fat, eager to exploit the strategic position of the St-Germain hillside, built a fortified stronghold on the site of the present château. In 1230 St Louis added a charming little chapel which still stands today. The fortress was destroyed during the Hundred Years War and restored by Charles V around 1368.

In 1514 Louis XII married his daughter Claude de France to the duc d'Angoulême, who became François I the following year. The young ruler was acquainted with Italian culture and the ancient citadel was hardly suited to his taste for palatial comfort and luxury. In 1539 he had the whole building razed with the exception of Charles V's keep and the chapel built by St Louis. The reconstruction was entrusted to Pierre Chambiges, who produced the present château.

New Château – Even the new building presented itself as a fortified structure equipped with machicolations and defended by a garrison numbering 3000. Henri II, who wanted a real country house, commissioned Philibert Delorme to draw up plans for a New Château on the edge of the plateau. The construction work was completed under Henri IV. The château became famous on account of its fantastic location and the terraces built along the slopes overlooking the River Seine.

The area beneath the foundation arches has been arranged into artificial grottoes where hydraulically-propelled automatons re-enact mythological scenes: Orpheus playing the viola and attracting animals who come to listen, Neptune's chariot in full motion etc. Henri IV was a mischievous man; he installed a system whereby fountains of water would spring out from all directions at the end of the show, drenching the King's guests. This wonderful mechanism was the work of the Francine, a family of Italian engineers, to whom Louis XIV later entrusted the water-works of Versailles.

Chronology of court events – The court occupied both the New Château and the Old Castle which were used as a palatial residence, or a safe retreat when riots broke out in Paris.

Henri II, Charles IX and Louis XIV were all born at St-Germain. Louis XIII died here. Mary Queen of Scots lived here between the ages of 6 and 16. In 1558 she married the Dauphin François, aged only 15, and was crowned Queen of France the following year.

Her husband died after a year, however, and she was forced to return to Scotland, where her tragic destiny led her to die on the scaffold.

Mansart's improvements – Louis XIV – who was born, christened and brought up at St-Germain – grew fond of the château. As king, he paid frequent visits to the estate. The apartments of the Old Castle had become too cramped for Louis' liking and he commissioned **Jules Hardouin-Mansart** to build five large pavilions as a replacement for the five corner turrets adjoining the outer walls. Le Nôtre drew up the plans for the park, the terrace and the forest; in 1665 the grounds were replanted with five and a half million trees. In 1682 the court moved from St Germain to Versailles. In 1689 the deposed King of England James II came to stay at the Old Castle, where he died, in great financial straits in 1701, a well-loved figure (funeral monument in St Germain Church, facing the château).

Maréchal Louis de Noailles (1713-93) subsequently became the important figure at St Germain as governor of the château and its estate, which was divided up and acquired the reputation of being the most fashionable residential area in town.

Final developments – In 1776 the badly dilapidated New Château was ceded to the comte d'Artois by his brother Louis XVI. The future king Charles X had the building demolished, except for the Henri IV pavilion on the terrace and the Sully Pavilion, in Le Pecq. He originally intended to reconstruct the building according to new plans but he dropped the work at St Germain when he purchased the château at Maisons-Laffitte. The remains, together with the park, were sold during the Revolution.

The Old Castle was stripped of its furniture. Under Napoleon I it was the seat of a cavalry college, under Louis-Philippe it housed a military penitentiary but Napoleon III ordered its closure in 1855. It was then entirely restored under the guidance of the architect Millet, succeeded by Daumet.

The five pavilions added by Mansart were demolished and the building regained the appearance it had during the reign of François I.

In 1867 Napoleon III inaugurated the National Museum of French Antiquities which he had set up on the premises. The signing of the 1919 peace treaty with Austria took place in the château at St Germain.

THE CHÂTEAU AND ITS NEIGHBOURHOOD *3 hr 30min*

The most striking approach to the château is from the north, along the road from Les Loges. The tour starts from the square beside the château, Place Charles-de-Gaulle. The express RER line (which runs underground at St-Germain and has an exit giving onto the square) has replaced the famous railway track between Paris and St-Germain; its inauguration between Le Pecq and the French capital on 26 August 1837 was an unprecedented landmark in the history of French railway services.

★Château – The château is the shape of an imperfect pentagon; its moats were originally filled with water. The feudal foundations are distinguishable together with the covered watch-path and a series of machicolations restored by Daumet. The roof, laid out as a terrace edged with vases and a balustrade and dominated by tall chimneys, was an innovative idea.

At the northern end of the façade overlooking place Charles-de-Gaulle stands the quadrilateral keep built by Charles V, to which a bell-tower was added under François I.

Senior officers were housed on the ground floor while the mezzanine apartments were occupied by princes of the blood, ladies-in-waiting, mistresses and ministers, among them Mazarin, Colbert and Louvois.

The royal suites were on the first floor; the king and the dauphin lived in the wing facing the parterres, the queen's suite looked towards Paris and the children's rooms were in the wing which now faces rue Thiers. Under Henri IV twelve of the fourteen royal infants, born to five different mothers, romped noisily in these quarters.

The château now houses the Museum of Antiquities.

★Ste-Chapelle – Built by St Louis from 1230 to 1238, this chapel precedes the Ste-Chapelle in Paris by some ten years. It was probably designed by the same architect, Pierre de Montreuil, but its tall windows do not have the stained glass that gives such dazzling splendour to its counterpart in Paris. The fine rose-window in the west front was blocked off by other buildings.

Within the thickness of the keystones are carvings of figures thought to represent St Louis, his mother Blanche of Castille, his wife, and other people close to him. If this is true, it would make these precious images the oldest pictures of royal families in existence.

★★Musée des Antiquités Nationales ⓥ – The museum contains many rare archeological exhibits relating to France's early history, ranging from the first signs of man's existence (Paleolithic Age) to the Middle Ages.

Prehistory and protohistory (Mezzanine) – The Paleolithic or early Stone Age goes back one million years before our era.

The glass cabinets on the right provide general information on materials such as stone (flint), quartz, bone and antlers, and displays tool-making techniques of that period. Note the traces of man's existence in prehistoric times: photographs of the handprints at Gargas, mould of the footprints found in a cave at Aldène. The left-hand cabinets displaying the results of the excavations are in chronological order.

Château de St-Germain-en-Laye, main courtyard

The major works of art dating from the Paleolithic Age are surprisingly small: the **Lady of Brassempouy** (height: 3.6cm/1.44in), the oldest human face found to date (c 20000 BC), a bison licking itself (Magdalenian – c 16000 BC), the Bruniquel baton in the shape of a jumping horse (c 13000 BC), the Mas-d'Azil head of a neighing horse (c 10000 BC) etc.

During the Neolithic Age, man developed farming and cattle rearing, community life in huts and the use of ceramics. He produced arms and tools by polishing very hard stones (jadeite).

The discovery of an alloy combining copper and tin led to the early stages of metallurgy (Bronze Age). Gold too was widely used and the museum displays several objects and pieces of jewellery made of solid gold or gold leaf. Note the numerous weapons (daggers, axes with curved blades) and the metal necklaces and other decorative objects (open bracelets) which give these particular collections the sparkle that characterised some of the so-called "primitive" civilisations of the modern world.

The large iron sword is typical of the items from princely burial sites dating from the early Iron Age (the period known as Hallstatt). It was found together with clasps, ceramics, pieces of furniture (Magny-Lambert cist), horses' tack and even four-wheel funeral carriages.

The La Tène period that followed benefited from the contributions made by foreign civilisations and especially the increasingly important trade relations with the Mediterranean world. Most of the objects exhibited here come from excavation sites in Champagne and Burgundy (jewellery, vases). Gallic tribes still buried funeral chariots in their tombs, worked gold (jewellery) and minted coins. The fall of Alésia (52 BC) put an end to their own culture.

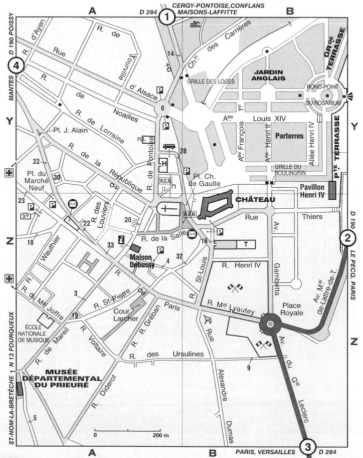

Gallo-Roman and Merovingian Antiquities (First floor) – The lengthy period of Roman peace *(Pax Romana)*, the indulgence of the victors and the deeply-rooted religious feeling for indigenous gods gave rise to a flourishing industry of mythological and funeral sculpture (until then the Celts had shown little interest in statuary art). Note the large collection of gravestones.

Ceramic pieces played an important role in domestic life; one of the cabinets offers a fairly comprehensive presentation of "sigillate" ceramics, decorated with stamped motifs, made in workshops at Lezoux, La Graufesenque, Banassac etc (1C-4C AD).

Little is known about the following period (3C-8C AD), though its heritage consists mostly of Merovingian burial places rich in arms – swords with damascene blades – and items of finery: heavy flat buckles for belts, S-shaped clasps etc.

Lady of Brassempouy, Musée des Antiquités Nationales

The large ballroom in the château – also called the Salle de Mars – is a beautiful vaulted room with ornate stone ribbing and a fireplace bearing François I's emblem, the salamander. It is dedicated to comparative archeology; a superb selection of objects from all five continents makes it possible to draw parallels between techniques and life-styles belonging to geographically distant civilisations, from very different historical periods.

The displays are carefully arranged according to two thematic approaches; the transition from one continent to another is evident if the visit runs from one end of the room to the other, while the chronological evolution of technology is clear when visiting one side and the other in succesion.

Observe the splendid Egyptian collections dating from pre-Dynastic times, a set of bronze sculptures from Kodan and Armenian Talysh (Asia), **Mérida's Chariot** (6C BC), a masterpiece of Iberian workmanship. The impressive ethnographical exhibits from Oceania feature a magnificent wooden statue depicting the god Rao (Gambier Islands).

EXTERIOR

Parterres (BY)   Enter the gardens through the gate on place Charles-de-Gaulle and skirt the château. Built into the façade is the loggia opening onto the inner main staircase. The moat contains restored megalithic monuments and replicas of Roman statues.

The east esplanade – now the site of a pillbox – was the scene of the last judicial duel during which the will of God was invoked. The duel opposed Jarnac and La Châtaigneraie and was attended by Henri II, accompanied by his retinue of courtiers. La Châtaigneraie, one of the finest swordsmen in Europe, was confident about the outcome of the battle. Jarnac, however, had learnt a new tactic: he severed the left hamstring of his adversary, who collapsed and slowly died.

Pavillon Henri-IV (BY) – The brick pavilion was built on the very edge of the escarpment; it is crowned by a dome, and, together with the **Sully Pavillon** set lower down on the hillside at Le Pecq, is all that remains of the New Château. It contains the Louis XIII oratory where Louis XIV was baptised on 5 September 1638, the day he was born.

The hotel which opened in this historic building in 1836 became an important meeting-place for 19C writers, artists and politicians. Alexandre Dumas wrote *The Three Musketeers* and *The Count of Monte Cristo* while he was staying here, Offenbach composed *The Drum Major's Daughter* and Léo Delibes produced the ballet *Sylvia*. The statesman and president Thiers died here in 1877.

★★**Terrace (BY)** – The Small Terrace starts beside the hotel and extends to the Rosarium roundabout. There, a worn Touring Club of France viewing table is a reminder of past views towards the western suburbs of Paris.

The Grand Terrace extends beyond the roundabout. It is one of Le Nôtre's finest accomplishments and was completed in 1673 after four years of large-scale construction work. Lined with stately lime trees, it is 2400m/8000ft long and is one of the most famous promenades around Paris.

The vista from the terrace being the same all the way along, visitors pressed for time may return to their car through the lovely **landscape garden**★.

ADDITIONAL SIGHTS

★**Musée départemental du Prieuré** ⊙ **(AZ)** – The Priory was founded in 1678 by Mme de Montespan and was originally designed as a royal hospital. In 1915 it became the property of the painter **Maurice Denis** (1870-1943), who moved there with his large family and frequently entertained his friends of the Nabis movement. The rooms are former dorters and attics joined by double spiral staircases featuring surbased groined vaulting.

The museum explains the origins of the **Nabis** group – founded by Paul Sérusier in 1888 – and illustrates their passion for various forms of pictorial and decorative expression: painting, posters, stained glass etc. The works assembled in the priory testify to the considerable influence the symbolic movement – the "search for the invisible" – had on the art world at large: literature, decorative arts, sculpture, painting and music. The Pont-Aven School is represented by Gauguin, Émile Bernard, Filiger, Moret, Slewinsky, Seguin etc.; the Nabi group by Sérusier, Ranson, Bonnard, Vuillard, Maurice Denis, Cazalis, Lacombe, Rousseli, Valloton and Verkade. The museum also displays works by Toulouse-Lautrec, Anquetin, Mondrian, Lalique etc.

Chapelle – The chapel was entirely decorated by Maurice Denis between 1915 and 1928: stained glass, frescoes, liturgical furnishings...

Atelier – Maurice Denis had this studio built by his friend Auguste Perret in 1912 when he was working on the decoration for the ceiling of the Théâtre des Champs-Élysées, an undertaking which required a vast amount of space.

Park – A series of terraced flower beds are pleasantly dotted with statues by Antoine Bourdelle. The park offers a charming vista of the priory façade and its elegant severity.

Maison Debussy ⊙ **(AZ)** – *38 rue au Pain*. This house was the birthplace of the composer Claude Debussy on 22 August 1862. The restored building contains the Tourist Office on the ground floor and mementoes of the composer on the first floor.

Forêt de St-Germain

Circled by one of the Seine's loops, the forest was once part of the Forest of Laye. It is planted with oaks, beeches and hornbeams, with conifers on the poorer soil of the northern massif. 120km/74mi of footpaths and 60km/37mi of bridleways skirt hunting lodges, wayside crosses, old gates and clearings.

Forêt de ST-GOBAIN★★
ST-GOBAIN FOREST
Michelin map 56 fold 4 or 236 fold 37

This beautiful forest (6000ha/14000 acres) between the Oise and the Ailette rivers covers a plateau pitted with quarries and furrowed with vales which are dotted with lakes. Tree species include oak and beech, with ash on the clay, birch over the sand and poplar in the valleys.

The region is rich in deer and used to be the home of wolves and wild boar. Deer-hunting, a tradition here since the time of Louis XV, still continues today; the Rallye Nomade Hunt and Kennels are based at **Folembray** *(see p 156)*.

Signposted trails penetrate the forest; in season, the area provides a rich crop of mushrooms and lily of the valley.

ROUND TOUR FROM ST-GOBAIN
23km/14mi – about 2hr 45min.

St-Gobain – The town was established as a consequence of pilgrims visiting the Irish hermit Gobain, and rises on the edge of a band of fossil-rich limestone which reaches a height of 200m/656ft in parts.

St-Gobain is best known for its **Mirror Factory** *(manufacture de glaces)* founded by Louis XIV at Colbert's request, and established in 1692 in the ruins of the castle

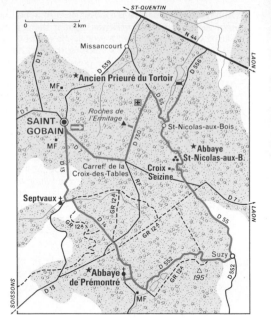

that had belonged to the Lords of Coucy. It was the first to use a method of casting which allowed the production of very large mirrors. The factory's entrance has a monumental 18C gateway.

Take D 7 (Laon road) east for 3km/2mi; at the crossroads (La Croix-des-Tables) turn left onto D 730.

The **Roches de l'Ermitage** *(15min on foot there and back)* are very picturesque.

D 730 joins D 55.

Turn right onto D 55 and first left onto D 556.

★**Le Tortoir** – The walls of Le Tortoir, a 14C fortified priory which was a daughter-house of the abbey of St-Nicolas-aux-Bois, appear in a clearing surrounded by lakes where teal and moorhen are to be found.

Around the courtyard of the priory (now a farm) stand the guest house (28m/91ft long) and the prior's residence with its elegant mullioned windows; the chapel dates from the early 14C.

Return to D 55 and continue south.

Soon after the village of St-Nicolas-aux-Bois, the ruins of the abbey become visible *(right)*.

★**Abbaye St-Nicolas-aux-Bois** The Benedictine abbey, the remains of which have been incorporated into a private property, occupied a delightful setting here on the floor of a valley. The road first skirts the moat which protected the abbey walls and then two ponds encircled by greenery, beyond which the 15C abbey buildings appear.

Croix Seizine – *400m/440yd from D 55.* This expiatory monument was erected by Enguerrand IV, Lord of Coucy, who was condemned in 1256 by St Louis for having executed four students from St-Nicolas-aux-Bois who were caught hunting on his land.

Continue along D 55.

At the picturesque village of **Suzy** turn right onto D 552.

Former Priory of Le Tortoir

295

★Abbaye de Prémontré ⊘ – This former abbey nestling in a wooded valley was founded by **St Norbert**, who was born at the end of the 11C near the Rhine in the Duchy of Cleves. He lived a wordly life until one stormy day he was thrown from his horse like St Paul and a voice reproached him for his dissolute living. Touched by grace, Norbert sold all his possessions and retreated to Prémontré where he founded the abbey and the order which took its name.

The **Premonstratensian order**, which adopted St Augustin's rule, was recognised by the pope from 1126 and prospered – numbering 1 500 houses for men and women. The fathers wore the biretta (cap) and white habits.

The abbey was rebuilt in the 18C, converted to a glassworks in 1802 and is now a psychiatric hospital. Three buildings stand around the flowerbeds; they feature remarkable "colossal Ionic" pilasters which set the rhythm for the façade. The main body has a round outer porch with an unusual curved triangular pediment, with a cardinal's shield above. Note the wrought-iron balcony with the cardinal's arms and the finely carved keystones of the windows.

The wings are simpler; their porches are topped with a shell framed by monumental urns. The left-hand building contains a stairway of advanced design, entirely supported by the walls of the oval well.

The abbey church was not built; an adjacent building housed the canons' chapel.

Follow D 14 to Septvaux.

Septvaux – The Romanesque church with its two belfries was served by the Premonstratensians before the Revolution; it stands on a mound overlooking the lovely 12C wash-house *(on the road to Coucy).*

D 13 returns to St-Gobain.

ST-LEU-D'ESSERENT★

Population 4 288
Michelin map 106 north of folds 7 and 8 – northwest of Chantilly

The Archbishop of Sens, St Leu, who died in 623, gave his name to several French localities. St-Leu-d'Esserent, located on the banks of the River Oise, boasts a magnificent church which the philosopher and historian Ernest Renan once compared to a Greek temple on account of its pure, harmonious lines.

★CHURCH *30min*

Leave Chantilly and proceed towards St-Leu along D 44. The bridge over the Oise affords the best **general view** of the church from a distance. Nearby quarries produced the lovely stone which was used for the construction of many other churches and cathedrals as well as the palace at Versailles.

The Germans converted these quarries into workshops for their V-1 missiles. As a result, the town was repeatedly bombed and the church wrecked in 1944.

Exterior – The façade has been significantly restored since the 19C – in particular the sculpted decoration – and is separate from the nave. It forms a Romanesque block (first half of the 12C) presenting a porch and, on the upper level, a gallery, each consisting of three bays. The bell-tower and its stone spire were to be counter-balanced by a north tower; note the two lines of toothings on the left. Four centuries later, the west front gable above the nave, set back slightly, was given a Flamboyant Gothic rose-window.

Skirt the right side of the church, walking past the entrance to the former priory.

The chancel is dominated by two square towers with saddle-back roofs. It is surrounded by the ambulatory and its five radiating chapels which date back to the second half of the 12C. The flying buttresses were added to consolidate the buttresses which supported the transept crossing.

★Interior – The nave offers a superb perspective. It is filled with a golden light filtering through modern stained glass (1960). The chancel and the first two bays of the nave are Romanesque (12C) while the rest of the nave is 13C.

Originally the chancel was to include galleries, as is usual with Romanesque buildings. In the 13C, however, when the flying buttresses were added to support the east end, the architects realised that the counter-thrust provided by galleries was no longer necessary and so replaced them with a single triforium. They decided to apply this principle to the whole building.

Before returning to the car, stroll to the nearby cemetery.

View of the upper part of the church.

ST-OMER★★

Conurbation 53 062
Michelin map 51 fold 3 or 236 fold 4

St-Omer is an aristocratic, wealthy and religious town which has largely retained its ancient appearance. It is characterised by quiet streets lined with 17C and 18C pilastered mansions and houses with sculpted bays. This refined atmosphere is in contrast to the simpler nature of the northern suburbs, where low Flemish houses line the quays of the River Aa.

Clerics Take Action – In the 7C Benedictines from Luxeuil evangelised the Morini region, a marshy land with Thérouanne as its capital. They were led by the future **St Omer**, joined by Bertin and Mommolin who founded a monastery on the island of Sithieu in the Aa marshes; it was named St Bertin's. Omer, for his part, had been named Bishop of Thérouanne and in 662 had a chapel built on the hill overlooking Sithieu island; a small market-town quickly formed around it.

St-Omer developed from the joining of the monastery and the chapel, by-then collegiate; the link between the two religious establishments is reflected in the town's layout.

★★CATHEDRAL DISTRICT *3hr*

★★**Cathédrale Notre-Dame** – The cathedral is the most beautiful religious building in the region and is surprisingly large and majestic. It stands at the heart of a peaceful area which was formerly the canons' "Notre-Dame cloister". The chancel dates from 1200, the transept from the 13C, the nave from the 14C and 15C; the powerful west front tower (50m/164ft) with its network of vertical, English-style blind arcades is crowned by 15C watch-turrets. The pier of the large south door is ornamented with a 14C Virgin Mary and the tympanum bears a Last Judgement in which the chosen are very few. In a corner of the chancel stands an octagonal Romanesque tower.

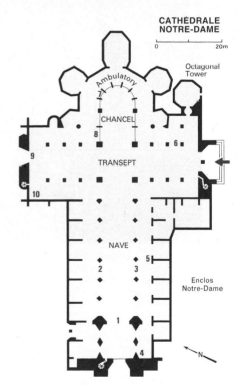

CATHÉDRALE NOTRE-DAME

0   20m

The complex arrangement of the vast interior (100m/110yd long, 30m/33yd wide, 23m/75ft high) consists of a three-storey nave (arcades, a tall, blind triforium and clerestory) flanked by side aisles, a transept with aisles, and a chancel with ambulatory and radiating chapels. The chapels off the side aisle, formerly reserved for the canons, are screened by richly traceried and painted marble.

★★**Works of Art** – Among the numerous interesting pieces, note in particular:

– the 1717 organ case (**1**) surmounted by statues of King David and St Cecilia;

– the 13C cenotaph (**2**) of St-Omer *(left of the nave)*;

– the 16C mausoleum (**3**) of Eustache de Croy, Provost of the St-Omer Chapter and Bishop of Arras. This striking work by the Mons artist Jacques Du Broeucq presents the deceased kneeling in his episcopal robes and also lying nude in the Antique manner *(right of the nave)*.

– 15C engraved gravestones and a *Descent from the Cross* by Rubens *(first bay of the south aisle)* (**4**);

– 15C funerary monuments and 16C and 17C carved alabasters (**5**) with a charming Madonna with Cat *(south aisle)*;

– the 13C statue of Notre-Dame-des-Miracles (**6**), a highly venerated object of pilgrimage *(south transept)*;

– a 13C low-relief Nativity (**7**) with a Syrian inscription; the 8C tomb of St Erkembode (**8**), Abbot of St Bertin's *(ambulatory)*;

– the Astronomical Clock (**9**) with a mechanism dating from 1558 *(north transept)*:
– the "Great God of Thérouanne" (**10**), a famous 13C carved group which stood at a height of 20m/65ft, over the portal of Thérouanne Cathedral which was destroyed by Charles V of Spain. The shapes, which seem deformed, were foreshortened by the artist to take into account the distorting effect of perspective *(north transept)*.

Take rue des Tribunaux.

The street runs behind the east end of Notre-Dame and in front of the **palais épiscopal** (**J**), which dates from the 17C and is today the law courts, leading to place Victor-Hugo. The square is the busy centre of St-Omer and features a fountain placed there to celebrate the birth of the Count of Artois, the future Charles X.

Rue Carnot leads to Hôtel Sandelin.

★**Hôtel Sandelin** ⊙ – The house was built in 1777 for the Viscountess of Fruges. It is set between a courtyard and a garden, with access through a monumental portal with an elegant Louis XV gate.

Ground Floor – The drawing rooms overlooking the gardens form a charmingly old-fashioned suite of rooms with light-coloured, finely carved wainscoting and 18C fireplaces that form a beautiful setting for the Louis XV furniture and the paintings

G. Guittot /DIAF

Base of the Saint Bertin Cross, Hôtel Sandelin

from the bequest of Mme du Teil-Chaix d'Est-Ange. Among the paintings are Lépicié's *Rising of Fanchon* in the style of Chardin, the portrait of *Mme de Pompadour as Diana the Huntress* by Nattier, the more conventional *Portrait of a Man* by Greuze and four lively works by Boilly *(The Visit, The Improvised Concert, The Quenching of the Flame of Love, The Jealous Lover)*. There is also a *grisaille* work from the same period entitled *Ah ça ira*.

The woodcarving room (religious sculptures and medieval tapestries) and the Salle Henri Dupuis containing ebony cabinets made in Antwerp lead to the **Salle du Trésor** where exhibits include the famous **base of the St Bertin Cross★** (12C), a masterpiece of Mosan art made of gilt and enamel. It is decorated with the Evangelists and enamelled scenes from the

Old Testament and comes from the abbey of St Bertin, as does the beautiful ivory representing one of the old men of the Apocalypse. Note, too, the **Cross-reliquary** with its double crossbar (1210-1220) from the abbey in Claimarais. The rear has fine filigree work and is encrusted with gemstones.

The small wall cabinets in the chapel corridor (so-called because of the impressive altar made of ebony, tortoiseshell and gilded bronze) contain various pieces of gold and silverware and ivories.

The rooms overlooking the courtyard have an interesting collection of works by Flemish Primitives: *St Crispin and St Crispinian* altarpiece (c 1415), *The Holy Family and an Angel* by Gérard David's school, a triptych of *The Adoration of the Magi* by the Master of the Adoration, Khanenko, *The Flemish Feast* by Hell Brueghel, and several works by lesser-known 17C Flemish and Dutch masters including *The Smoker* by Abraham Diapram, *Lizard and Shells* by Balthasar Van der Ast, *Portrait of a Woman* by Cornelis de Vos, and *The Bawdy Woman* by Jan Steen.

First and Second Floors – Collection of ceramics including some produced in Saint-Omer. Also an outstanding series of **Delft** (750 items).

Continue along rue Carnot and take the second turning right, onto rue St-Denis.

Église St-Denis ⊙ – This church, restored in the 18C, still has its proud 13C tower and the 15C chancel hidden by 18C wainscot (rich canopy with a gilded coffered ceiling). A chapel left of the chancel houses an alabaster Christ attributed to Du Broeucq.

From rue St-Bertin turn onto the street which runs beside the Jesuit chapel.

★ **Ancienne chapelle des Jésuites** – This chapel, now the chapel of a secondary school *(lycée)*, is an example of early Jesuit style. Gothic influences can be seen in the shape of the bays and the layout with ambulatory. The chapel was designed by Du Blocq, a Jesuit from Mons, and completed in 1629. Its height is striking, as are the alignment of the scrolling in the nave and the narrow square towers enclosing the chancel in the Tournai tradition. The most beautiful part of the building, however, is the monumental brick-and-white-stone façade, five storeys high and adorned with sculptures.

Turn left onto rue Gambetta.

Bibliothèque ⊘ – The library contains 350 000 volumes including over 1 600 manuscripts (11C Life of St Omer) and nearly 200 early printed books or "incunabula" (famous Gutenberg Bible). They are presented in bookcases from St Bertin's Abbey.

Turn round and return up rue Gambetta.

Rue Gambetta, which is lined with affluent homes, leads to **place Sithieu**. The square has kept its provincial charm which was described by Germaine Acremant in her novel *Ces Dames aux Chapeaux verts*.

Returning to the cathedral square, the "Canon's Door" in the south corner opens into rue de l'Échelle which runs down to the ramparts in a flight of steps.

ADDITIONAL SIGHTS

Ruines de St-Bertin – All that remains of the abbey are a few arches and the lower part of the tower (1460). The square in which the ruins lie contains a marble statue of Suger, who was a benefactor to the abbey. Rue St Bertin provides a lovely view of the ruins surrounded by great trees.

★ **Jardin public** – This vast park (20ha/48 acres) is located on part of the old 17C ramparts. The moat has been turned into a formal French garden; the slope bears an English garden with winding paths shaded by beautiful trees. There are lovely views of the bastion, the roofs and the cathedral tower. The large moat south of the garden now contains a swimming pool.

Ancien Collège des Jésuites – The school was built in 1593 and became a military hospital. Altered in 1726, it features a beautiful front decorated with garlands and pilasters surmounted by composite capitals.

Musée Henri-Dupuis ⊘ – The museum is housed in an 18C mansion with a beautiful period Flemish kitchen. The ground floor houses a large collection of birds from the Arctic to Indonesia in their natural habitat (dioramas, information panels). On the first floor, an impressive collection of **shells**★ is on display, reminding visitors of an 18C natural history room.

Place du Maréchal-Foch – The Town Hall was built between 1834 and 1841 using stones from the former abbey church dedicated to St Bertin. A veritable theatre was set in the centre of the building. At 42 bis, the **Hôtel du Baillage** (now the Caisse d'Epargne or savings bank) was originally the royal courthouse which opposed the authority of the town's aldermen. It is an elegant Louis XVI building decorated with pilasters, Doric capitals, wrought ironwork, and garlands of flowers. The four statues on the balustrade represent Virtues.

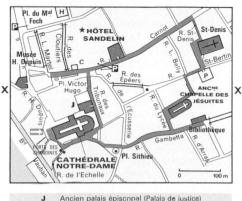

J   Ancien palais épiscopal (Palais de justice)

Église Saint-Sépulchre – This hall-church (the three aisles are of the same width and height) was consecrated in 1387 and used to be the seat of the largest parish in the town. It has a spire 52m/169ft high. The name of the church is uncommon; there are only seven churches named after the Holy Sepulchre in France. It comes from the involvement of three local lords in the Crusades. The church inherited a doorway from the abbey dedicated to St Bertin, a masterpiece of joinery. It also has two Baroque statues of St John the Evangelist and St John the Baptist. The chancel contains fine 19C stained-glass windows connected with the Holy Sepulchre.

L'AUDOMAROIS

This region gets its name from the Latin word *Audomarus* meaning "Omer" and it covers the area around St-Omer. It also corresponds to one of the sectors in the regional country park. The area known as the Marais audomarois, or Omer Marshes, is one of the most unusual parts of the park.

La **Grange-Nature** ⊘ in Clairmarais is the visitor centre for the St-Omer section of the **Parc naturel régional**; it contains exhibitions and audio-visual presentations on nature and wildlife. The centre is also the starting-point for footpaths, some within the Romelaere nature reserve (observation and study trails).

Marais audomarois – *4km/2 .5mi northeast on D 209.*
The marshes sit in a vast depression (3 400ha/8 401 acres) stretching from Watten in the north to Arques just south of St-Omer, and from Clairmarais Forest (north-east) to the Tilques watercress beds (northwest). They are the result of painstaking efforts begun in the 9C by St Bertin's monks to transform the area.
Today the marshes encompass a series of small plots of land linked by **waterways** *(watergangs)*, which are used by large flat-bottomed boats known as *bacôves*. A large number of the plots are devoted to market gardening; their most famous vegetable is the St-Omer cauliflower. The marshes also provide good fishing: pike, eel, sauger, perch, roach... and bird-watching as they are a stopover for migratory birds (heronry). From D 209 beside Neuffossé canal the circulation and drainage canals can be seen here and there, crossed by culverts and lift bridges; but for a proper **tour of the marshes** ⊘ it is necessary to hire a boat or join one of the tours in a *bâcove* or other vessel.

EXCURSIONS

Forêt de Rihoult-Clairmarais – *4.5km/2.5mi northeast on D 209.*
When he stayed at St-Omer, Charlemagne hunted here in the oak groves; in the 12C it was the property of Cistercian monks.
The forest (1 167ha/2 884 acres) is now managed with tourists in mind *(picnic tables)*, especially around **Étang d'Harchelles**, the last of seven ponds dug by the Cistercians for peat or for fish. It is circled by a path *(30min on foot).*

Arques – *4km/2.5mi southeast. Leave St-Omer by N 42.*
Arques, which is an industrial town known chiefly for its crystal glassware, is also an important port at the junction of the canalised Aa and the Neuffossé Canal, linking the River Aa to the River Lys. Le Grand Vannage houses the Maison du parc de l'Audomarois, a white-stone and pink-brick building spanning the Aa. The sluice gate room where the river level is regulated can be visited.

Verrerie Cristallerie d'Arques ⊘ – Founded in 1825, this undertaking is now a world leader in fine tableware production. Every day, six million items in glass, opal and crystal are manufactured. A tour of the premises provides a close look at the magical materials used to make so many lovely things.

In Arques, take N 42 east towards Hazebrouck; about 1km/0.5mi beyond the bridge over the Aa, turn right onto a small road marked "Ascenseur des Fontinettes" which ends near a factory.

★ **Ascenseur à bateaux des Fontinettes** (Fontinettes Barge Lift, Arques) ⊘ – The barge lift, which was in use from 1888 to 1967, is an interesting remnant of 19C technology. It was built on the Neuffossé Canal to replace the five locks needed to negotiate the 13.13m/43ft drop in the canal. The principle is simple: the barges took their place in one of two water-filled basins, attached to two enormous pistons which were a kind of hydraulic balance; one went up while the other simultaneously went down.
A visit to the engine room and a working model help to understand how it functioned. The lift was replaced by an impressive **giant lock**, 500m/550yd upriver. This can contain six barges and requires 20 minutes to operate.

★ **Blockhaus d'Eperlecques** ⊘ – *15km/9mi northwest. Leave St-Omer by D 928 and turn left at Watten.*
This 22m/72ft concrete mountain rising out of the forest is the largest concrete bunker ever built; V2 bombs loaded with explosives with which to bombard London were to be launched from here. Its construction – in fact only a third of its planned size – involved over 35 000 French, Belgian, Dutch, Polish, Russian and other prisoners during 1943 and 1944. On 27 August 1943, 187 British "flying fortresses" bombed the bunker, disabling it at the cost of numerous lives of detainees working there. After this episode the bunker was enlarged to become a factory making liquid oxygen; a film inside evokes these tragic events.

Abbaye St-Paul-de-Wisques – *7km/4mi west. Leave St-Omer by N 42.*
Benedictine monks occupy the château which consists of both old buildings (15C tower, 18C house and portal) and modern buildings (chapel, cloister, refectory and bell-tower). The bell-tower houses Bertine, the bell from St Bertin's abbey church, which dates from 1470 and weighs 2 600kg/over 2.5t.
The road *(D 212)* continues past the Petit Château (1770) and climbs to a summit where the abbaye Notre-Dame, the Benedictine monastery, stands.

Return to St-Omer by D 208.

The route offers pretty **views** over the town, dominated by the basilica church (Notre-Dame) and the Jesuit chapel.

Esquerdes – *8km/5mi southwest.* This village lies in the Aa Valley and has been famous for papermaking since 1473. It still has several paper mills.
The **Maison du papier** ⊙ was built on the ruins of the old Confosse mill. The exhibition explains papermaking techniques from the earliest used in China to the most modern. Visitors can try making their own sheet of paper in the workshop, an unusual souvenir to take home.

Marché aux Puces de ST-OUEN

Michelin plan 11 fold 7: A 13, A 14
Metro line 4: Porte-de-Clignancourt station

The flea market takes place from Saturday to Monday in St-Ouen, on the outskirts of the capital. In the past, rag and bone men used to offer their finds to onlookers passing the time eating chips and dancing the polka. Around 1920, a few masterpieces, discovered among the mediocre objects on offer, made the market fashionable overnight. Today there are numerous antique and second-hand furniture dealers who attract a cosmopolitan clientele on the lookout for unusual and picturesque objects. The old fashioned stands tend to be replaced by boutiques; however it is still possible to stumble on an interesting object or piece of furniture.

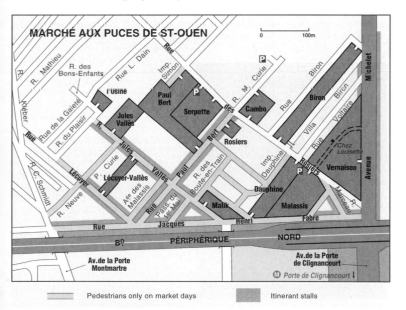

The market is divided into specialised areas:
Vernaison: period furniture, trinkets.
Biron: antiques, valuable objects.
Cambo: furniture, paintings.
Rosiers: furniture, trinkets, paintings.
Serpette: antique and rustic furniture, trinkets.
Paul-Bert: bric-à-brac, bronze objects.
Jules Vallès: rustic furniture.
Malik: second-hand clothes, glasses, records.
Dauphine: antique furniture, contemporary art.
Malassis: antiques.

Stands are also set up in neighbouring streets.

ST-QUENTIN

Conurbation 69 188

Michelin map 53 fold 14 or 236 fold 27

St-Quentin is perched on a limestone hill riddled with caves and underground passages, and overlooks the canalised Somme River which crosses the Isle marshlands. St-Quentin's waterways and railways link it to the north European capitals and the Ruhr, making it a transportation centre between Paris, the English Channel, the countries north of France and the Champagne region. It suffered terribly during the First World War but has since strengthened its industrial position; its heritage of textile works (mills, machine weaving, fine articles) has now been overtaken by chemicals, machinery and food products.

St-Quentin Canal – Before the Canal du Nord was built, this was the busiest canal in France. It links the Somme and Oise river basins to the Escaut (Scheldt) River, flowing for about 100km/62mi between Chauny and Cambrai. Napoleon considered it one of the period's greatest achievements.

It is made up of two sections: the Crozat Canal, running between the Oise and Somme rivers, which was named after the financier who had it constructed, and the St-Quentin Canal proper, which crosses the plateau between the Somme and Escaut rivers partly through tunnels at Tronquoy (1km/0.5mi long) and Riqueval. It is the St-Quentin Canal which is used for regular shipments of sand, gravel and especially grain to the Paris region. The enlargement of the canal, which is part of a long-term project, will improve the town's links with Dunkirk.

The Battle of St-Quentin – St-Quentin was the prize in a bloody battle in 1557: the army led by Constable de Montmorency, which had come to the rescue of the beleaguered citizens of St-Quentin, was defeated by Spanish troops on St Lawrence's Day. A vow made by **Philip II** at this victory resulted in the building of the Escurial near Madrid.

SIGHTS

Musée Antoine-Lécuyer ⊙ – The pride of the museum is the splendid **portrait collection★★** by the pastel artist **Quentin de La Tour** (1704-88), who was born and died in St-Quentin. La Tour, who painted all the important 18C society figures, is representative of an age marked by the importance of individuality. His works, both sensitive and honest, are "incomparable illustrations of moral anatomy": each smile has its own personality, whether spontaneous, ironic, mischievous, benevolent, embittered etc.

Self-portrait by Quentin de la Tour,
Musée Antoine-Lécuyer

The main room is devoted to the 17C and 18C French schools. The next three rooms are set aside for La Tour and contain 78 remarkable portraits: princes and princesses, great lords, financiers, clerics, men of letters (Jean-Jacques Rousseau) and artists. The greatest are perhaps of Father Huber reading; of Marie Fel, a friend of the artist; and a self-portrait, which is an exceptional study, both introspective and penetrating.

A bust of the artist by JB Lemoyne stands in the second room. Downstairs is an exhibition of 18C faience.

A room upstairs displays 19C painting, illustrating various artistic movements: works by Lebourg, Corot, Fantin-Latour and Renoir (pastel portrait of Mlle Dieterle). Another room presents 20C painting with works by Gromaire, Ozenfant and Lebasque.

There are also interesting collections of ivories and enamels; among the 18C furniture, note the 1750 harpsichord.

★Basilica ⊙ – The Basilica of St Quentin is a mainly Gothic building which could rival many of the great cathedrals. It began as a collegiate church dedicated to St Quentin, who worked as a missionary in the region and was martyred at the end of the 3C; it became a basilica in 1876.

After the famous 1557 siege, a fire in 1669 and bombing in 1917, the basilica came close to total destruction in October 1918.

Exterior – The west front incorporates a massive belfry-porch; its lower part dates from the late 12C while the upper storeys were rebuilt in the 17C and the top after 1918. Left of the church, Square Winston Churchill (wrought-iron well) offers a good **view★** over the large and small transepts and the east end; note the soaring, triple flying buttresses.

A walk around the church continues to offer interesting views of this remarkable building. At the south arm of the small transept stands the St Fursy Chapel, which was tacked on in the late 15C. The pretty, Flamboyant Lamoureux porch can be seen on the left.

The spire dates from 1976 and reaches the height of the original one (82m/269ft).

Interior – The impressively large 13C **chancel** consists of a double transept, double aisles, an ambulatory and radiating chapels. The vaulting of the chapels right of the ambulatory rests on two columns, following the elegant arrangement of the Champagne region. The Lady Chapel contains old stained-glass windows depicting the Life of the Virgin Mary; a 13C statue of St Michael stands left of the chapel entrance.

The Art Deco Trail

St-Quentin suffered extensive damage during the First World War and was partially rebuilt during the 1920s to designs by the architect Guindez. A walk through the town's streets reveals numerous housefronts decorated with bow windows, projecting balconies, floral or geometric motifs, coloured mosaics, wrought-ironwork etc.

Among the most outstanding buildings are the post office in rue de Lyon, the council chamber in the Hôtel de Ville (town hall), the Carillon (cinema in rue des Toiles), the music school at 47 rue d'Isle, the buffet in the railway station, the bridge flanked by lantern towers next to the station, and the war memorial.

The chancel screen, reworked in the 19C, portrays scenes from the life of St Quentin; on the left sits the stone chest *(sacrarium)* (1409) in which church plate was kept. Note the great hieratic figures of the stained glass adorning the clerestory in the centre, and the 16C glass in the north arm of the small transept, portraying the Martyrdom of St Catherine and that of St Barbara.

The bold, 15C nave (34m/111ft high) has a long maze (260m/284yd) traced on its floor, which the faithful followed on their knees. The superb organ case (1690 1703) was designed by Bérain; the instrument itself, by Clicquot, was destroyed in 1917; it was replaced by a modern organ with 74 stops.

The sculpted Tree of Jesse, at the start of the south aisle, dates from the early 16C; the second chapel bears 16C mural paintings.

During the summer, a tour of the upper section provides a view of the pinnacles, piers and surrounding countryside as far as Laon.

J.-P. Demolin /CAMPAGNE CAMPAGNE

St-Quentin – Hôtel de Ville

Champs-Élysées – The site of the original fortification was turned during the Restoration into a pleasant park (10ha/24 acres): playgrounds, sports field, flower garden.

★**Hôtel de Ville** ⊘ – This is a gem of late Gothic architecture (early 16C). The vigorous design of the façade includes ogival arches topped with pinnacles, mullioned windows and a traceried gallery beneath three gables. It is decorated with picturesque carvings in the Flamboyant Gothic style. The campanile was rebuilt in the 18C. It houses a peal of 37 bells.

Interior – The gables on the façade correspond to the vaulting of three aisles in the shape of an upturned ship. The **Salle des Mariages** still has its old rafter and a huge Renaissance fireplace. Note the carvings representing the town's main celebrities: the treasurer, the executioner etc. The **Salle du Conseil** has an Art Deco interior (lamps made of wrought-iron and glass paste, Brazilian rosewood wainscoting with medallions representing various trades).

Espace St-Jacques – *14 Rue de la Sellerie.*
This neo-Gothic building was built on the site of Église St-Jacques and was formerly the seat of the Chamber of Commerce. Today it houses temporary exhibitions on the ground floor, with an entomological museum on the first floor.

Musée des Papillons ⊘ – This collection of butterflies and other insects is the largest in Europe. It includes about 600 000 specimens, of which about a fifth are exhibited at any given time.

There are many different forms and colours in the butterflies, especially the ones from tropical countries. They include the metallic blue Morpho, the Thysania from Guyana (the world's largest butterfly), leaf miners, and a yellow and black species found locally.

Rue des Canonniers – The 18C **Hôtel Joly de Bammeville** has a fine staircase with wrought-iron banisters. It houses the town library (a major venue during the *Festival de la Nouvelle*). The entrance to the old **Hôtel des Canonniers** *(no 21)* has military trophies carved in low relief.

The **Festival de la Nouvelle** was created in 1985. It includes exhibitions, markets, readings, and meetings with the best-known short story writers and with new talent. The literary prize known as the Prix Goncourt de la Nouvelle is awarded during the festival. Other prizes are also awarded such as the St-Quentin Prize for an unpublished short story.

Béguinages – Beguine convents were founded in the Middle Ages for pious women who did not take their final vows. In St-Quentin, the tradition dates back to the 13C. The population explosion that occurred in the 19C led to a need for accommodation for single or elderly people and the name *béguinage* was extended to cover such housing. Only six large enclosures have survived, grouping some forty houses around a communal garden. There are also six small enclosures. The most interesting ones are to be seen in rue Quentin-Barré (crowstepped gables), rue de Bellevue and rue du Moulin.

Marais d'Isle – This zone covering over 100ha/247 acres has been provided with fishing and watersports facilities, and it also includes a **nature reserve** ⊘ which lies along the route taken by migratory birds from Northern and Eastern Europe.
The flora of wetlands is very varied and includes rare species like water hemlock (also known as dropwort or cowbane) or strange ones like bladderwort, a carnivorous plant. Among the numerous birds here there are nest-building species (crested grebes) and overwintering species (ducks).

The **Maison de la nature**, a small visitors centre in Rouvray presents an audio-visual show and documents relating to the ecosystem of the lake. A path around the reserve allows a view of some of the birds.

Chemin de fer touristique du Vermandois ⊘ – A steam train or old rail-car runs from St-Quentin to Origny-Ste-Benoîte, following the Oise Valley after Mézières-sur-Oise over a total distance of 22km/14mi.

EXCURSION

North of St-Quentin *Round trip of 30km/18mi*
Take N 44 north for 15km/9mi.

Mémorial américain de Bellicourt – The memorial stands north of the village over the Riqueval tunnels. It consists of a white stone cenotaph which commemorates the 1918 attack by the US Army's 2nd Division against Hindenburg's line. From the surrounding area there is a **panoramic view** of the plateau bearing traces of the German trenches (American cemetery at Bony).
Continue on N 44 and turn first right to Mont St Martin.

Mont St-Martin – The ruins of an old Premonstratensian abbey may be seen here. North of the village, a path gives access to the **source of the Escaut (Scheldt) River** which is hidden in a quiet and mysterious spot, once a place of pilgrimage. The clear water flows between rows of aspens and ash trees which form a leafy vault in summer: this is the beginning of the river's 400km/250mi course through France, Belgium and Holland.

Drive north along D 71 to Gouy and turn right (D 28) to Beaurevoir.

Beaurevoir – This village has preserved a tower of the château where Joan of Arc was a prisoner from August to November of 1430. She was held by the Count of Luxembourg, who handed her over to the English.

ST-RIQUIER★

Population 1 166
Michelin map 52 fold 7 or 236 folds 22, 23 (9km/5.5mi northeast of Abbeville)

The little town of St-Riquier grew around an ancient Benedictine abbey which boasts an imposing Gothic church to rival many cathedrals.

A Hermit and a Son-in-Law – The town was called Centule when, in 645, the hermit **Riquier** died in Crécy Forest, near what is now the village of Forest-Moutiers. This ceno-bite monk who came from a noble family had previously evangelised the Ponthieu region; after his death his body was transported to Centule where it became the object of an important pilgrimage.

A Benedictine monastery was founded as a result and prospered so much that in 790 Charlemagne gave it to his son-in-law, the poet **Angilbert**, the "Homer of the Palatine Academy". Angilbert, to whom the Emperor paid several visits, gave a new lease of life to the abbey and had the buildings rebuilt in the most precious materials: Italian porphyry, marble and jasper. At that time the monastery also included a main church, which housed the tomb of Riquier, and two secondary churches (St Benedict and St Mary) with a triangular cloister in the middle.

★CHURCH ⊘ 45min

Despite having been destroyed and rebuilt several times, the present, largely Flam-boyant (15C-16C) church has nevertheless retained some 13C architectural elements (lower parts of the transept and chancel).
The ensemble was restored by Abbot Charles d'Aligre (17C) who also had the fur-niture renewed; it is the same in use today.

Exterior – The west front is essentially made up of a large square tower (50m/164ft high) flanked by stairtowers and covered in abundant, finely carved orna-mentation. Above the central doorway, the gable bears a Holy Trinity surrounded by two abbots and the Apostles, as at St Wulfram's Church in Abbeville. Higher still stands a Crowning of the Virgin Mary. Finally, between the two windows of the belfry, a statue of St Michael can be seen. Above the vaulting of the right doorway a St Genevieve holds a candle which, according to legend, the devil used to blow out and an angel used to relight.

★★Interior – The beauty, size and simplicity of the architecture are worth admiring. The two storeys of the large central nave (13m/42ft wide, 24m/78ft high, 96m/314ft long) are separated by a frieze as in Amiens Cathedral and by a balustrade. The chancel still has its 17C decoration and furniture: wrought-iron **grilles★** lectern and monks' stalls, marble screen surmounted by a large wooden Crucifix by Girardon.
The south transept is unusual: its end is cut off by the sacristy and the treasury above it which occupy three bays of the cloister gallery. The wall of the treasury is decorated with fine sculptures and statues.
In the first of the ambulatory's radiating chapels, on the right after the staircase, note the painting by Jouvenet *Louis XIV Touching Those Afflicted with the King's Evil*. The lady chapel contains stellar vaulting with ribs running down to historiated corbels (Life of the Virgin Mary); at the entrance, *The Apparition of the Virgin to St Philo-mena* (1847) is by Ducornet, an artist who painted with his feet as he had no arms. In St Angilbert's chapel the five coloured statues of saints are typical of 16C Picardy sculpture: they show *(left to right)* Veronica, Helen, Benedict, Vigor and Riquier.
The north transept contains a Renaissance font, its base carved with low reliefs showing the Life of the Virgin Mary and the Baptism of Christ.

Treasury ⊘ – This was the abbot's private chapel. The walls of the beautiful early 16C vaulted chamber are decorated with murals from the same period; the best of them depicts the Meeting of the Three Dead and the Three Living, which sym-bolises Life's brevity.
The treasury contains a 12C Byzantine Crucifix 13C reliquaries, a 15C alabaster altarpiece and a curious 16C hand-warmer.

Abbey buildings – Rebuilt in the 17C during the d'Aligre abbacy, they now house the **Centre culturel départemental de l'abbaye de St-Riquier** that includes a **museum** ⊙ of rural life and crafts and a conference centre with seminar rooms and accommodation.

The rooms used for temporary exhibitions also host concerts and conferences.

ADDITIONAL SIGHTS

Belfry – Turrets with lookout posts above crown this 16C tower. Its mighty outline is a reflection of the importance of the town that used to have fortifications.

Hôtel-Dieu ⊙ – The hospital dates from the early 18C. It stands to the left behind the belfry. The chapel has some attractive wrought-iron grilles. The altarpiece is decorated with a painting by Joseph-François Parrocel. The two angels and the statues of St Nicholas and St Augustin are by Pfaffenhoffen who lived in St-Riquier for many years.

Maison Petit – *On the Abbeville road. Turn left after the church.*
This house was built for one of Napoleon's soldiers. Its gable resembles Napoleon's hat.

ST-VALERY-SUR-SOMME★

Population 2 942
Michelin map 52 fold 6 or 236 folds 21, 22

St-Valery (pronounced Val'ry), the capital of the Vimeu region, occupies a lush setting overlooking the peaceful countryside of the Somme Bay. It consists of an upper town with a lower town beside the port.

The port, which is used by coasters, handles numerous yachts and fishing boats known as *sauterelliers* (a *sauterelle* is a grey shrimp).

St-Valery began as an abbey founded by a monk called Valery from Luxeuil in Lorraine. In 1066 William the Conqueror stopped here before invading England; Joan of Arc passed through the town in 1430 as prisoner of the English, on the way from Le Crotoy.

The Somme Bay – Like all bays, the Somme suffers from the flow of water and silt which settles and tends to widen the sandbanks; these become covered with grass, creating the **mollières** or salt-pastures where lambs now graze.

The silting-up combined with a gradual increase in the size of boats in general has considerably affected the formerly active traffic here; the development of the Somme canal from 1786 to 1835 and the creation of a sheltered port at Le Hourdel merely slowed its decline. It is worth noting, however, that during the First World War the bay served as a British base: in 1919, traffic reached an exceptional 125 000 tonnes.

Hunting and fishing – The bay's three fishing ports (St-Valery, Le Crotoy and Le Hourdel) specialise in shellfish and squid fishing.

When the tide is out fish are also caught in the channels, pools and ruts on the shore: cockles, mullet, eels and flatfish, either speared or just picked up by hand. Wildfowl hunters lie in wait either in special boats or in hides formed in grassy mounds pierced with firing holes, using domestic or artificial ducks as decoys. The Marquenterre reserve and bird sanctuary, northwest of the Somme Bay, nevertheless serve as a stopping-off place for migratory birds; 315 of the 452 species found in Europe have been identified in the area (the Camargue region is host to 360 species).

SIGHTS

Ville basse – The lower town extends for almost 2km/1.25mi, to the mouth of the River Somme where the port is located.

★**Promenade** – The promenade, which is shaded in summer by plane and lime trees, leads to a sheltered beach and offers lovely views over the Somme Bay to Le Crotoy and the headland at Le Hourde. Pleasant villas set in gardens stand inland; beyond the Relais de Normandie are the ramparts of the upper town, overlooked by St Martin's church.

Calvaire des Marins – Access from Rue Violette and Sentier du Calvaire, through the sailors' district which is full of charming painted cottages. **View** over the lower town and the estuary.

★**Écomusée Picarvie** – This appealing little museum faithfully recreates regional life before the industrial age. Reconstructions of workshops and stalls show the work of basket weavers, cobblers, locksmiths, coopers, blacksmiths, joiners, etc and there is also a village with a school, café and barbershop. An entire period farm has been recreated on the first floor, with the bedroom, kitchen, cowshed, stable, cider-press and the barn where flax, grown in the surrounding villages, was beaten to make linen.

Ville haute – Part of the fortifications have been preserved.

Porte de Nevers – The name of this 14C gate, which was heightened in the 16C, harks back to the dukes of Nevers who owned St-Valery in the 17C.

Église St-Martin – The exterior of this Gothic building bordering the ramparts is of flint and sandstone laid in a chequered pattern. In the month aisle, a Renaissance triptych portrays the Crucifixion, the Baptism of Christ and the Martyrdom of John the Baptist.

Porte Guillaume – The 12C gate stands between two majestic towers; extensive view over the Somme Bay.

Chapelle des Marins – Take rue de l'Abbaye beyond the Porte Guillaume: **St Valery's Abbey** used to lie in the vale to the left. The abbey's brick and stone château survives, with a carved 18C pediment.

From place de l'Ermitage take the path to the chapel *(30min there and back)*. The chequered sandstone and flint chapel houses the tomb of St Valery. Overlooking the Somme Bay, the chapel offers an extensive **view★** of the salt meadows and the estuary as far as the Marquenterre reserve in the distance.

FROM ST-VALERY TO CAYEUX-SUR-MER
14km/81.5mi – about 2hr

Leave St-Valery by D 3 (west) and follow signs to Maison de l'Oiseau.

★**Maison de l'Oiseau** ⓥ – A superb collection of stuffed birds assembled by an inhabitant of Cayeux was the basis for the Bird House, which is fittingly located in the ornithologically-rich Somme Bay area. A building round a courtyard was especially constructed, following the layout of traditional farms.

Inside, displays highlight local birds in their natural habitat: cliffs, sand and mudflats, dunes and gravel pits... In a room dedicated to ducks, a reconstructed hide looks out over a pond behind the house where wild duck, geese, waders etc live. Films, exhibitions and information for fledgling birdwatchers complete the presentation.

Return to D 3, turn left then right into D 102 to Le Hourdel.

Le Hourdel

Le Hourdel – The typical Picardy houses of this small fishing harbour and yachting marina stand at the tip of an offshore bar which begins at Onival. The bar consists of pebbles which are crushed to make emery powders and filtering materials. Views over the bay.

It is possible, with a good pair of binoculars, to observe seals sprawled on the sand lining the estuary, ready to flee at the first sign of danger. A surveillance system has been set up by Picardie Nature to keep human interference to a minimum so that females can give birth without being disturbed; at the moment, two baby seals are born every year.

D 102 skirts the shingle beach and the dunes.

Phare de Brighton ⊘ – The top of the lighthouse provides lovely views over the sea and Cayeux-sur-Mer.

Cayeux-sur-Mer – This resort is bordered by a promenade and an 1 800m/over 1mi long wooden path lined with more than 400 cabins. The long beach of hard sand extends from the Hâble d'Ault to the pointe de Hourdel; footpaths crisscross the woods of Brighton-les-Pins.
The **Chemin de fer de la baie de Somme** ⊘ offers steam train excursions in the region *(see Le CROTOY)*.

SCEAUX★★

Population 18 052
Michelin map 101 fold 25 – Michelin plan 22

Access from Paris: *RER line B 2*

In 1670 Louis XIV's superintendant of buildings **Colbert** commissioned Claude Perrault Le Brun, Girardon and Coysevox to build a superb residence in Sceaux. The two groups of sculptures flanking the entrance pavilion were created by Coysevox: the dog and the unicorn, representing loyalty and honesty, were Colbert's emblems. The grounds were laid out by Le Nôtre, who succeeded admirably in spite of the rough, uneven terrain. The canal, basins and fountains were supplied by the waters diverted from the hillsides of Le Plessis-Robinson. The château was inaugurated in 1677 at a lavish reception attended by the Sun King in person; one of the many attractions that night was the performance of Jean Racine's famous tragedy *Phaedra*.
In 1685 Colbert's son Seignelay entertained Louis XIV and Mme de Maintenon at the château, an occasion for which Racine and Lulli composed their *Ode to Sceaux*.

Sceaux in the hands of the duc du Maine – In 1700 the estate became the property of the duc du Maine, the legitimated son of Louis XIV and Mme de Montespan. The King often came to stay with his favourite son.
The duchesse du Maine, the Great Condé's grand-daughter, surrounded herself with a large court of brillant personalities. She entertained on a grand scale, providing opera, ballet, comedy and tragedy for her many guests. The dazzling "Nights of Sceaux", enhanced by superb displays of fireworks and twinkling lights, were the talk of all Paris and Versailles.
On the eve of the Revolution, the estate of Sceaux belonged to the duc de Penthièvre the duc du Maine's nephew, for whom the fabulist Florian acted as librarian. The domain was confiscated and subsequently sold to a tradesman who had the château razed to the ground and the park turned into arable land.

Sceaux today – In 1856 the duc de Trévise, who inherited the estate through his wife's family, built the château that stands today. The grounds gradually slipped into a state of neglect; Alain-Fournier found inspiration there for his novel *Le Grand Meaulnes*. In 1923 the château was bought by the Seine *département*, which undertook to restore both the building and its park. The Île-de-France Museum was installed in 1936. The estate now belongs to the Hauts-de-Seine département.

The famous physicists **Pierre** (1859-1906) and **Marie** (1867-1934) **Curie** and their daughter **Irène Joliot-Curie** (1897-1956) lived in Sceaux. Their remains were transferred to the Panthéon in Paris in 1995.

★★PARK ⊘

Main Entrance – Designed for Colbert, the two entrance pavilions with sculpted pediments are flanked by two small lodges surmounted by Coysevox's groups of statues.

Orangery ⊘ – This conservatory (60m/196ft long) was designed by Jules Hardouin-Mansart in 1685. It is decorated with a series of carved pediments. In summer it was used as the ballroom – note the interior decoration – and in winter it sheltered the 300 orange trees of Sceaux Park.
Today the Orangery is a venue for conferences, exhibitions and concerts *(see Calendar of Events)*.

★**Musée de l'Île-de-France** ⊘ – The museum is housed in the château that once belonged to the Duc de Trévise. It was refurbished in 1994 and is laid out on the basis of four themes: Sceaux, the estate and its owners; ceramics from the Paris Basin; royal and princely residences; and scenery in the Paris Basin from the 18C to 20C.
The estate in Sceaux has a long history which is illustrated in the small drawing room where the main architectural feature is the superb marquetry floor. The reception rooms contain numerous portraits of successive owners, among them Colbert (French School, 17C) and the Duc de Penthièvre painted by JB Charpentier.

The oval room is given over to Sceaux faience and boasts the largest existing collection of this local production. The "japanned faience" *(see Introduction, Faience and porcelain)* by J Chapelle make renewed use of the Rococo style. Two other rooms are part of this section of the museum. The library has 18C porcelain (Vincennes, Sèvres, St-Cloud etc) and the Millet room on the first floor includes fine 19C faience recognisable for its unusual background colouring and decoration (ropework for Montereau, flowers for Creil).

The luxurious residences built in the vicinity, some of which have since been demolished, are illustrated at length. There are etchings by Rigaud, oils including the *Château de St-Cloud* by C Troyon, furniture such as the elegant bureau made by Riesenburg (Château de St-Hubert) and Caroline Murat's bed produced by the Jacob brothers (Château de Neuilly).

The variety of landscapes in the Paris Basin has provided much inspiration for artists such as AH Dunoy, G Michel, Lebourg, Utrillo, Luce etc. The museum has a large collection of works by Paul Huet, André Dunoyer de Ségonzac and Jean Fautrier.

Painted wainscoting from the folly built by the famous 18C dancer "La Guimard" in Pantin decorates a small drawing room.

The **Centre de Documentation** ⊙ houses several million written documents about and illustrations of the Île-de-France area.

★**Grandes Cascades** ⊙ – The waters are approached from allée de la Duchesse; they spring out of carved masks by Rodin and tumble down a series of ten terraces before flowing into the Octagonal Basin. The sight of these various fountains and cascades is particularly spectacular when all the fountains are playing during the **Grandes Eaux**★. This perspective is continued by a green lawn.

L'Octogone – The basin has kept its original design by Le Nôtre. Of ample proportions, circled by a row of plane trees, it exudes a majestic, peaceful atmosphere. The jets of water reach a height of 10m/32ft.

Pavillon de Hanovre – The pavilion was built by the architect Chevotet in 1760 and moved from the Boulevard des Italiens in Paris to Sceaux in 1930.

★**Grand Canal** – It is as long as the Petit Canal at Versailles (1 030m/3 380ft) and flanked by a double row of Lombardy poplars.

Terrasse des Pintades – From the canal, two ramps lead up to a terrace which is the starting-point for the park's two sweeping perspectives: one extends towards the château while the other follows the line of the Grand Canal.

Petit Château – An elegant early-17C building which was incorporated into the estate by Colbert. The children of the duchesse du Maine were brought up here.

The Grandes Cascades at Sceaux

Pavillon de l'Aurore – This charming pavilion crowned by a dome is attributed to Claude Perrault. It is approached by a series of staircases featuring dainty, neatly-arranged balusters. The interior decoration forms a harmonious ensemble: wainscot, flooring, ceilings and a superb dome by Le Brun, reproducing the delicate tints of sunrise.

It was here that Colbert received the French Academy in 1677. For this momentous occasion the poet Quinault composed a poem of 900 lines on the subject of Le Brun's fresco. He read it out to the members of that prestigious assembly, who spent most of the evening craning their necks towards the ceiling to follow Quinault's detailed explanations.

Intendance – This is a splendid Louis XVI building, and was formerly the residence of the intendant of Sceaux.

Anciennes Écuries – The stables were built under Colbert, after studies made by Le Pautre. Facing the stables stands a horse-pond *(visible from the esplanade)*.

TOWN

Jardin des Félibres – Florian, the celebrated fabulist from the Cévennes, died in 1794 and was buried at Sceaux. Since the 19C this garden has been a place of pilgrimage for Provençal poets and writers – known locally as *Félibres* – who come and pay their respects once a year (on a Sunday in June). The garden contains several busts of Provençal poets, including one of Frédéric Mistral.

Église St-Jean-Baptiste – The church was rebuilt in the 16C and was given a façade and a spire under Louis-Philippe. The 17C *Baptism of Christ* by Tuby behind the high altar was taken from the chapel of the former château. The altar in the north aisle is adorned with a medallion of the Virgin Mary by Coysevox (18C).

Jardin de la Ménagerie – This menagerie used to belong to the duchesse du Maine and to the burial place of her canaries (beneath the columns) and her favourite cat (in a funeral urn). It was used to host popular dances during the Revolution; the famous *Bal de Sceaux*, attended by the *Muscadins* and the *Merveilleuses*, was very much in vogue at the time and gave its name to one of Honoré de Balzac's novels. Subsequently it went out of fashion and was replaced by dancing at Robinson.

Ancienne manufacture de céramique – The old works were founded by the duchesse du Maine and lie at the corner of rue des Imbergères. The ceramics production is on display at the Île-de-France Museum.

SENLIS★★

Population 14 432
Michelin map 56 fold 11

Access from Paris: *SNCF Rail link from Gare du Nord to Chantilly; bus link to Senlis.*

Senlis derives its romantic charm from its picturesque old streets, its connections with Frankish rulers, enterprising bishops and abbots, the rich cornfields of Valois and the wooded horizons.

The election of Hugh Capet – The conquerors of Senlis built a massive strong-hold over the first Gallo-Roman ramparts of the town. The kings of the first two Frankish dynasties would often take up residence here, lured by the game in the nearby forests. The Carolingian line died out when Louis V suffered a fatal hunting accident. In 987 the Archbishop of Reims called a meeting at Senlis Castle in which he and the local lords decided that Hugh Capet – the Duc des Francs – would be the next king.

Senlis went out of fashion as a royal place of residence and was gradually replaced by Compiègne and Fontainebleau. The last French ruler to have stayed at the castle was Henri IV.

OLD TOWN *1hr*

Jardin du Roy ⊘ – These gardens occupy the former moat of the Gallo-Roman ramparts which, at their widest point, measured 312m/1 024ft across and at their narrowest 242m/794ft. Twenty-eight towers (7m/23ft high and 4m/14ft thick) defended the city walls; 16 remain today, some still intact, others badly damaged. There is a lovely **view★** of the ramparts and the towers, the cathedral and the scattered buildings that once formed the castle.

Return to rue de Villevert and proceed towards place du Parvis.

★**Place du Parvis** – A charming little square beside the cathedral.

★★**Cathédrale Notre-Dame** – Its construction was started in 1153 – 16 years after St-Denis and 10 years before Notre-Dame in Paris – but progressed at a slow pace owing to insufficient funds. The cathedral was consecrated in 1191. In about 1240 a transept which had not originally been planned and a spire were added. The building was struck by lightning in June 1504; as a result, the clerestory and the transept walls needed to be rebuilt. A set of new side aisles was also added, giving the cathedral its present appearance. Initially, the two towers were identical. It was only towards the mid 13C that the right tower was crowned with the magnificent **spire**★★ which was to have such a strong influence over religious architecture in the Valois area *(see below)*. The spire reaches a height of 78m/256ft.

The **main doorway**★★ – dedicated to the Virgin Mary and celebrating her Assumption - is strongly reminiscent of the doorways at Chartres, Notre-Dame in Paris, Amiens and Reims. The lintel features two famous low-relief carvings representing the Dormition of the Virgin Mary and the Assumption. The realism and freedom of expression of the sculpture were unusual for the 12C; note the touching swiftness with which the angels raise Mary off the ground and remove her to the celestial skies.

The embrasures are adorned with eight figures from the Old Testament, depicted in a lively manner. The heads were smashed during the Revolution and remodelled in the 19C. On the left, Abraham is about to sacrifice his son Isaac, while an angel holds the sword in an attempt to stop him. The statues rest on square bases presenting a series of light-hearted panels sculpted into the labours of the months. The calendar starts with January, on the right-hand side near the door.

South front – Constructed by Pierre Chambiges in the 16C, the **transept crossing**★★ contrasts sharply with the west front. It is interesting to follow the evolution of Gothic architecture from the austere 12C to the 16C, when late Flamboyant already showed signs of Renaissance influence, introduced after the Italian wars. The clerestory and its huge Flamboyant windows were also completed in the 16C.

Senlis Cathedral – South Front

A de Valroger /MICHELIN

The lower part (12C) of the east end and the radiating chapels are intact. The axial chapel was replaced by a larger structure in the 19C. The galleries – dating from Romanesque times – support the nave and chancel with the help of Gothic flying buttresses.

Interior – Enter through the south doorway. The church interior is 70m/230ft long, 9.2m/30ft wide and measures 24m/79ft to the keystone. Above the organ, the 12C vaulting which escaped the ravages of the fire in 1504 marks the original height of the church: 17m/56ft. The nave and the chancel, comparatively narrow in spite of their height, are graced with an airy lightness. The triforium galleries above the aisles are among the finest in France.

The first chapel to the right of the south doorway features superb vaulting with pendant keystones, a 14C stone Virgin and a lovely set of stained-glass windows. These are the only original panes to have remained intact. A statue of St Louis from the 14C is placed in the south aisle of the ambulatory. The north transept chapel houses a 16C Christ made of larch.

Leave through the north door.

The left-hand aisle features an elegant statue of St Barbara dating back to the 16C.

North doorway – The north side is similar to the southern façade but less ornate. The gable surmounting the doorway bears François I's salamander and the capital F as a reminder of the 16C reconstruction campaign, financed by the generous contributions of the French King.

North side – The cathedral's setting on this side is much less solemn; it features several patches of greenery and is extremely picturesque. Skirt the little garden that follows the east façade of what was once the bishop's palace. The building rests on the ruins of the old Gallo-Roman ramparts; the base of one tower remains. Lovely view of the cathedral's east end.

Église St-Pierre ⊘ – The church was started in the 12C and underwent extensive alteration in the 17C. The small left tower and its stone spire are both Romanesque, while the heavier tower on the right dates from Renaissance times (1596). The badly damaged but very elaborate façade is characteristic of Flamboyant Gothic.

The church was abandoned during the Revolution. It is now used as a venue for a variety of cultural activities.

★**Musée d'Art et d'Archéologie** ⊘ (**M¹**) – The Art and Archeology Museum is housed in the old bishop's palace, which is made up of a series of buildings dating from the 13C to the 18C.

The Gallo-Roman collections are exhibited on the ground floor: glass, merovingian jewellery, small bronze statues, strange votive offerings carved in stone from a small sanctuary in Halatte Forest *(see below)*, a **bronze base**★ dating from AD 48 and engraved with a dedication to Emperor Claudius.

In the crypt there are traces of a house built on this site in the early 2C; the foundations of the Gallo-Roman wall (3C) are also visible, made up of fragments of columns, pilasters and carved stonework from buildings of the earlier town which stood here.

SENLIS

D   Hôtel des Trois-Pots
F   Hôtel de la Chancellerie
H   Hôtel de ville
M¹ Musée d'Art et
        d'Archéologie
M² Musée des Spahis
M³ Musée de l'Hôtel de
        Vermandois

In the Gothic Room (late 14C) there are striking medieval sculptures including the **Head of a Bearded Man**★ (early 13C) and a majestic marble **Virgin and Child** (late 14C). Note also the entertaining series of small figures of painted and gilded wood which came originally from a depiction of the Passion on a late-15C altarpiece made in Antwerp.

At the bottom of the stairs the mid-12C stained-glass windows recount the creation of Eve and the Temptation of Adam and Eve.

Paintings dating from the 17C to 20C are on display in the four rooms on the first floor: Philippe de Champaigne, Luca Giordano, Francesco Solimena, Corot, Boudin, Sérusier, Thomas Couture (1815-79) who was born in Senlis. Centring on works by Séraphine Louis, nicknamed Séraphine de Senlis, is a collection of works by 20C naive artists.

Return to place du Parvis and, before entering the castle courtyard, start to walk up rue du Châtel to see the original fortified entrance to the stronghold now walled up. Adjoining the old doorway, the 16C Hôtel des Trois Pots (**D**) proudly sports its old-fashioned sign.

Musée des Spahis ⏱ (**M²**) – *By the entrance to the old Royal Castle.*
This museum retraces 150 years of history of the North African cavalry, which held a special place in the French Army from 1880 to 1814 and from 1830 to 1964. It largely concentrates on the old Spahis (native Algerian horsemen), Goumiers (indigenous horsemen and foot soldiers), Meharists (dromedary riders) and Saharans (cameleers).

Ancien Château royal ⏱ – This fortified site was occupied at least as early as the reign of the Emperor Claudius (AD 41-54). Throughout its history, up to the time of Henri II, it has featured a charming collection of ruins.

The sturdy square "praetorium" tower is the most striking piece of architecture that still stands today; the 4.5m/15ft thick walls are further supported by a set of hefty buttresses. Athough apparently dating from the Middle Ages, its history is not entirely clear.

Musée de la Vénerie (Hunting Museum) ⏱ – In the 13C St Louis founded St-Maurice priory next to the royal castle. The relics of St Maurice of Agaune were kept here by the monks until the Revolution. A new building was built in the early 18C which now houses the Hunting Museum.

The works presented here were chosen from among the many illustrations of stag hunts which have enriched French culture. Desportes (1661-1743) and Oudry (1688-1755) represent the *Ancien Régime*, while later animal painters include Carle Vernet, Rosa Bonheur, Charles Hallo (the founder of the museum) etc. The walls are hung with numerous trophies and stags' heads.

The display of historical hunting gear renders the exhibition particularly interesting. The hunting costume of the Condé – fawn and amaranth-purple – can be seen on a figure representing a Chantilly forest warden, and in the painting depicting the young duc d'Enghien (1787). Note the famous collection of hunting "buttons", which were the most highly prized trappings of a hunting outfit, chased hunting knives, horns (including a beautiful silver hunting horn made in 1817) etc.

★**Old Streets** – *Follow the route indicated on map above.*
Rue du Châtel used to be the main street through Senlis for those travelling from Paris to Flanders. This is why its southern continuation is named "rue Vieille de Paris". In 1753 it was succeeded by rue Neuve de Paris, now called rue de la République.

Take the charming **rue de la Treille** and walk to the "Fausse Porte", which was the postern of the former Gallo-Roman ramparts. On the left stands the Chancellerie (**F**), flanked by two towers.

The **Town Hall** (Hôtel de Ville – **H**) on place Henri-IV was rebuilt in 1495. The front bears a bust of Henri IV and an inscription conveying his affection for the town of Senlis. These date back to a visit by Charles X on his way back from his coronation in Reims Cathedral (1825).

Senlis intra-muros

BUDGET

Vieille Auberge – 8 Rue Long Filet, ☎ 03 44 60 95 50. Closed Sunday evenings. Traditional restaurant with a pleasant summer terrace. Menu: 109F.

OUR SELECTION

Le Bourgeois Gentilhomme – 3 Place de la Halle, ☎ 03 44 53 13 22. Closed Sunday evenings and Mondays. This restaurant overlooking the large market square offers a cosy atmosphere and a vaulted basement for drinks before dinner. Menu: 145F.

Travellers' addresses

Chapelle Royale St-Frambourg ⓥ – Hugh Capet's wife the pious Queen Adelaide founded this chapel before 990 to house the relics of a recluse from the Bas-Maine, known as St Frambourg or St Fraimbault. The chapel was rebuilt by Louis VII after 1177 but abandoned during the Revolution.

The chapel was restored as the Franz Liszt Auditorium in 1977, through the efforts of the pianist Georges Cziffra. The Cziffra Foundation organises concerts and exhibitions for lovers of classical music.

The **church** and its single Gothic nave have been restored to their former grandeur. Descend to the archeological **crypt**. Excavations have revealed the floor of a sanctuary dating from about AD 1000 featuring fragments of columns. Two fragments of pilasters belonging to the flat east end of this church still bear the mural paintings of bishops. At the east end the crypt comes to rest on a sturdy round tower of fine brickwork and on the inner ramparts of the town, which follow the old Gallo-Roman wall.

ADDITIONAL SIGHTS

Ancienne Abbaye St-Vincent ⓥ – *Southwest of the town, via rue l'Apport-au-Pain and rue de Meaux.*
St Vincent's Abbey was founded in 1060 by Henri I's wife Anne of Kiev, following the birth of their son Philippe, heir to the throne, possibly owing to a vow. The child's christening marked the introduction into France of the Byzantine name Philippe.

A 12C open-work belltower – one of the finest and the most delicate in Ile-de-France – dominates the church, the silhouette of which has been marred by successive building and reconstruction campaigns.

The former abbey buildings, rebuilt in the 17C, house a cloister with classical features: colonnettes with Doric capitals and stone vaulting with coffering.

Rempart Bellevue – *Start from St Vincent's. Turn right (east) onto rue de Meaux, a staircase in a recess to the left leads up to the ramparts. Turn right and follow the walls.*
View of the countryside around St Vincent's, and the Nonette river.

Musée de l'Hôtel de Vermandois ⓥ (**M³**) – This small museum installed in a 12C mansion – a lovely example of Romanesque vernacular architecture – illustrates the history of the town and its cathedral through an audio-visual presentation. Sculpture plays a large part: a 12C head of an angel from one of the doorways of Notre-Dame; carved capitals and consoles from the cathedral and from the priory chapel. One of the brackets is decorated with a carving of "The Wrestlers" (1260). The original spire of the cathedral has been placed in one of the two rooms.

EXCURSIONS

★**Forêt d'Halatte** – This large forest north of Senlis includes beech groves, cherished by the Capetians, and oaks, hornbeams, pine trees etc to the south.

Aumont-en-Halatte – This charming village houses a museum on the activist author Henri Barbusse (1873-1935), best known for his wartime novel *Under Fire* (1917) recounting life as a French soldier in the trenches.

★**Butte d'Aumont** – *30min on foot there and back from Aumont church: towards Apremont take the first public lane on the left (chain), a sandy track flanked by wire fences.* The hillock offers a superb **panorama★** over the wooded horizon and the towns.

Mont Pagnotte – *Northeast of the forest.* One of the heights of the Paris region, Mont Pagnotte reaches an altitude of 221m/727ft (television transmitter). A footpath runs along the edge of the plateau at its summit.

Pont-Ste-Maxence – *11km/7mi north by N 17.* Because of its old bridge spanning the River Oise, the town has always been an important staging post. It owes the second part of its name to an Irish saint who was martyred here in the 5C. East of the town stands **Abbaye du Moncel** ⓥ which Philip the Fair had built next to a royal castle, two towers of which still remain. The abbey, dedicated to the Order of St Clare, found favour with Philippe VI, the first ruler of the Valois dynasty (1328-50); in 1347 the abbey received the mortal remains of his wife Jeanne of Burgundy, and after Philippe's death, his second wife Blanche of Navarre retired there.

The main façade still looks medieval and offers two imposing chimneys. The **courtyard★** is surrounded by three wings crowned with tall roofs of brown tiles (restored). Other elements of note include one of the galleries from the 16C cloister, the storeroom and its pointed vaulting, the Gothic chapter-house and the amazing 14C **timberwork★** above the nuns' dorter, made with oak from Halatte Forest.

Château de Raray – *13km/8mi northeast by D 932ᴬ. At Villeneuve-sous-Verberie, turn right.*
Standing on the edge of a charming hamlet, the château (now part of a golf club) is famous for the striking decoration of its main courtyard, used in Jean Cocteau's film *Beauty and the Beast*. Its game pens consist of an alternating series of arcades, recesses and niches housing busts of the gods of Antiquity and 17C historical figures. These are crowned by two lively hunting scenes carved in stone, a stag hunt and a boar hunt.

St-Vaast-de-Longmont – *16km/10mi northeast by D 932ᴬ.*
Seen from the village cemetery, the Romanesque bell-tower and its stone spire appear to be extremely ornate: cornices with billet moulding, arcades resting on colonnettes decorated variously with spiralling, zig-zag or torus motifs.
At **Rhuis** nearby *(west on D 123)*, the 11C Romanesque church has an elegant bell-tower with a double row of twinned windows. The tower is believed to be one of the oldest in Île-de-France. The interior features four bays and an apsidal chapel with no vaulting.

The Belltowers of the Valois area – *Tour of 48km/29mi. Allow 2hr 30min.* This tour leads across the arable plains which lie near the forest and through a string of small villages with charming 19C farmhouses. The route is dotted with bell-towers, the slender spires of which feature crockets.
Leave Senlis to the southeast, past the abbaye St-Vincent – the first bell-tower of the tour – and then the Ponte de Meaux. Turn left soon afterwards and right onto D 330, towards Mont-l'Évêque. After passing over the motorway, take a right turning.
Villemétrie – The bridge spanning the Nonette river offers a pleasant vista of the old mill, an ancient stone cross and the shady grounds of a park.
Turn round and proceed along D 330ᴬ.
Baron – Note the **church** ⊘ and its crocketed steeple (45m/148ft). The nave was rebuilt in the 16C and features many ornate embellishments on the exterior: stone buttresses round the roof, and rounded, pot-bellied piers at the east end. The 14C stone Virgin and the 18C **panelling★** inside were taken from the abbaye de Chaalis.
Versigny – Presents a bell-tower typical of the Senlis style. Observe the strange **château** ⊘ on the opposite side of the road. This long, low, U-shaped building of Italian inspiration was first started in the 17C and subsequently remodelled under Louis-Philippe: the balustrades, curved pediments, steps and columns date from the Restoration period.
Proceed towards Nantouil-le-Haudouin but on reaching the edge of the château grounds take a right turning at the next junction and follow directions to Montagny-Ste-Félicité. Drive up to the isolated church.
Montagny-Ste-Félicité – Superb open-work **bell-tower★**, rising 65m/213ft above the ground.
Turn round. At the crossroads north of Montagny, turn left to Baron and take the road to Senlis. Do not follow the direct route. Instead, at the Fontaine-Chaalis Junction, turn right towards Montépilloy.
Fourcheret – A former **barn** ⊘ belonging to the Abbaye de Chaalis still stands, supported by 18 pillars. Built in the 13C, this monastic structure (65m/213ft long and 18m/60ft wide) features an impressive display of timberwork.
Montépilloy – The ruins of the old stronghold – presently occupied by a farmhouse - are perched on top of the plateau that rises between the shallow valleys of the rivers Nonette and Aunette. On 15 August 1429 Joan of Arc spent the night at Montépilloy, having fought the English troops of Bedford who occupied Senlis. A commemorative plaque has been affixed onto the church exterior. The 13C entrance gatehouse – itself a small castle – offers a view of the farmhouse and, in the background, the ruins of the 14C keep which stand 40m/130ft high.

Use the Index to find more information about a subject mentioned in the guide people, towns, places of interest, isolated sites, historical events or natural features...

SÈVRES★★

Population 21 990
Michelin map 101 fold 24 – Michelin plan 22

Access from Paris: *Metro line 9 (station: Pont de Sèvres)*

The **Manufacture Nationale de Porcelaine** (National Porcelain Factory) established here in the 18C has made the name of Sèvres famous throughout the world. The present buildings date back to 1876.

★★MUSÉE NATIONAL DE LA CÉRAMIQUE ⊘

Founded in 1824 by Brongniart, the museum has an outstanding collection of pottery, faience, and porcelain classified by origin and by historical period. *(See Introduction, Faience and porcelain).*

On the **ground floor** are the collections of Islamic ceramics, some very old and very rare pottery (8C-18C) and a superb collection of Renaissance faience. Opposite is an exhibition and sale room presenting a range of pieces made in the pottery, some of them traditional models and others contemporary creations.

The collections on the **first floor** show changes in clay and decorative techniques in Sèvres, Europe and worldwide. In the central room, note the Chinese porcelain *(famille verte* and *famille rose)* and the decoration on the pieces of Meissen from Saxony (Kakiemon and Imari styles).

Sèvres pot-pourri vases (18C)

The rooms on the right focus on soft paste porcelain (18C-20C). French works are particularly well represented through Chantilly, St-Cloud, Vincennes and Sèvres. In the raised display cabinets, note the various background colours (green, purple, blue). The 19C collection includes the industrial arts service painted by Devely from 1823 onwards. It is representative of the Sèvres porcelain which, unlike others, must include gold.

The rooms on the left have some splendid pieces of high-fired ceramics from French and European works. The decoration can be in a range of blues, like the porcelain from Rouen or Marseille (late 17C) but much of the high-fired porcelain has multicoloured decoration. This is shown in the magnificent pieces of regional porcelain dating from the 18C. The last rooms are given over to Nevers and Delft.

ADDITIONAL SIGHT

Maison des Jardies (Maison de Léon Gambetta) ⊘ – *14 Avenue Gambetta.*
This modest gardener's lodge was once part of the Jardies estate, where Honoré de Balzac lived and attempted the cultivation of pineapples, unsuccessfully. Corot stayed here and Gambetta died here on 31 December 1882. Several of the politician's mementoes have been kept and are on show to the public. At the crossroads near the villa stands a memorial to Gambetta, by Bartholdi.

The length of time given in this guide
- for touring allows time to enjoy the views and the scenery;
- for sightseeing is the average time required for a visit.

SOISSONS★

Population 29 829
Michelin map 56 fold 4 or 236 fold 37

Soissons rises in the midst of rich agricultural land which is overlooked by the tall spires of the town's abbey visible from far around. Although the town was largely rebuilt after the First World War, it retains many old monuments.

The Frankish Capital – The town played an important role at the time of the Frankish monarchy; it was at this town's gates that Clovis defeated the Romans, ruining them for his own benefit. The famous story of the **Soissons Vase** took place after this battle: Clovis demanded that his booty include a vase which had been stolen from a church in Reims. A soldier angrily opposed him, broke the vase and cried "You will have nothing, O King, but that which Destiny gives you!" The following year, while Clovis was reviewing his troops he stopped before the same soldier, raised his sword and split the soldier's skull saying, "Thus you did with the Soissons vase". This episode is illustrated in a low-relief carving on the war memorial.

Clotaire I, son of Clovis, made Soissons his capital as did Chilpéric, King of Neustria and husband of the notorious Frédégonde; the latter was famous for her rivalry with Brunhilda, whose sister she had had assassinated.

The election of Pepin the Short in the 8C, naming him successor to the fallen Merovingians, also took place in Soissons and in 923, following a battle outside the town walls, Charles the Simple gave up his throne in favour of the house of France.

★★ANCIENNE ABBAYE DE ST-JEAN-DES-VIGNES ⊙ *1hr*

The old Abbey of St John of the Vines, which was founded in 1076, was one of the richest monasteries of the Middle Ages. The generosity of the kings of France, bishops, great lords and burghers allowed the monks to build a great abbey church and large monastic buildings in the 13C and 14C. In 1805, however, an imperial decree approved by the Bishop of Soissons ordered the demolition of the church, so that its materials could be used to repair the cathedral; the resulting outcry led to the preservation of the west front.

West front – The cusped portals are delicately cut and surmounted with late 13C gables; the rest of the front dates from the 14C except for the bell-towers which were built in the 15C. An elegant openwork gallery separates the central portal from the great rose-window, which has lost its tracery. Statues of the Virgin Mary and the saints are placed in pairs beside the piers on the towers.

The two Flamboyant bell-towers are extremely graceful. The **north tower** is the larger, taller and more ornate. the platform of the buttresses is finely worked; the spires of the openwork turrets bear prominent groins and crockets; on the western side, against the mullion of the upper window, a Christ on the Cross stands with statues of the Virgin Mary and St John at his feet.

The back of the façade is much plainer, the north tower having been gutted from this side. The south portal contains a 13C door which linked the church and cloister.

★Réfectoire – The **refectory** was built into the extension of the west front, at the back of the great cloister. The 13C construction has two naves with pointed vaulting. The transverse arches and ribs rest on seven slender columns with foliate capitals. Eight great lobed rose-windows pierce the east and south walls. The reader's pulpit still exists.

Cellier – This magnificent **undercroft**, located under the refectory and of the same shape, has pointed vaulting resting on solid octagonal pillars.

The building opposite was rebuilt in the 16C to serve as the abbot's residence.

Cloîtres – All that remains of the **great cloister★** are two 14C galleries. The pointed arches separated by elaborate buttresses had a graceful blind arcade, remains of which can be seen in the south bays. The delicately worked capitals represent flora and fauna.

The **small cloister** nearby has two Renaissance bays.

Maison franque – The reconstruction of this 6C house was based on findings from excavations at Juvincourt, a village in the Aisne region.

★★CATHÉDRALE ST-GERVAIS-ET-ST-PROTAIS *1hr*

The pure lines and simple arrangement of St Gervase and St Protase Cathedral make it possibly one of the most beautiful examples of Gothic art.

Construction of the cathedral began in the 12C with the south transept; the chancel, nave and side aisles rose during the 13C; the north transept and the upper part of the façade were not completed until the early 14C. The Hundred Years War brought work to a halt before the north bell-tower was built; it was never to be finished.

After the First World War only the chancel and the transept remained intact.

Exterior – The asymmetrical front gives no hint of the beauty of the interior; some unfortunate 18C alterations, partly corrected in 1930, have disfigured the portals and today only their deep arching remains. The rose-window, surmounted by a graceful gallery, is set within a pointed arch. Rue de l'Evêché offers a good view over the south transept which ends in a semicircle; place Marquigny overlooks the solid and austere east end.

A portal with a soaring gable supported by two buttresses stands east of the north transept; the more ornate decorative art of the 14C may be seen here. The transept's façade is decorated with radiating blind arcades, also 14C, and is pierced by a great rose-window set within a pointed arch, topped by a gable flanked by two pinnacles.

** **Interior** – Excluding the transept arms, the cathedral (116m/380ft long, 25.6m/83ft wide and 30.33m/99ft high) is perfectly symmetrical; no superfluous detail breaks the perfect harmony of the vast nave. Cylindrical columns separate the bays of the nave and chancel. Their sparsely decorated capitals bear the weight of the great pointed arches. They also serve to support five shafts sustaining the vaulting, which are extended down to the base by an engaged column. The arcades are surmounted by a triforium and twinned clerestory windows.

The **south transept**** presents an extremely graceful arrangement, due largely to the ambulatory and the gallery above it. A two-storey chapel opens onto the ambulatory. A beautiful keystone adorns the intersection of the vaulting's ribs, which rest on fine columns framing the windows and on two huge columns at the entrance. The upper chapel, similar to the lower one, leads to the transept gallery.

The **chancel** is one of the earliest examples of the decorated Gothic style. The five lancet windows are embellished with beautiful 13C and 14C stained glass. The high altar is framed by two white marble statues representing the Annunciation. The pointed vaulting of the five radiating chapels links up with that of the ambulatory; the eight ribs of the vaulting intersect at the same keystone.

The **north transept** has the same arrangement as the nave; the rose-window containing old glass was a 14C addition. The *Adoration of the Shepherds* on the left was painted by Rubens for the Franciscans, to thank them for their care at Soissons.

ADDITIONAL SIGHTS

Musée municipal de l'ancienne abbaye de St-Léger ⊘ – St Leger's Abbey was founded in 1152 but devastated in 1567 by Protestants who also demolished the nave of the church.

Église – The 13C chancel and transept are lit by high and low windows. The chancel has a cant-walled east end. The west front and the nave with its double side aisles were rebuilt in the 17C. Note the tympanum and capitals from the old abbey at Braine.

Crypte – The crypt contains two galleries and two bays from the late 11C. The groined vaults are supported by pillars which are flanked by columns with square foliate capitals. The nave leads into the 13C polygonal apse with pointed vaulting.

Salle capitulaire – The 13C chapter-house gives onto the cloister of the same date. The six quadripartite vaults rest on two columns.

Museum – The museum's various collections are housed in the old monastery buildings.

The prehistoric, Gallic and Gallo-Roman exhibits are on display on the ground floor. The first floor is devoted to 16C-19C painting: Northern school (Francken), Italian school (Pellegrini) and French school (Largillière, Courbet, Boudin and Daumier). The other room has maps, documents, paintings and models tracing the history of the town.

Avenue du Mail offers a view of both the east end of the church and the town hall which was the Intendancy under the *Ancien Régime*.

Abbaye de St-Médard ⊘ – This abbey was very well known during the Frankish period; today only the 9C pre-Romanesque crypt remains. It used to contain the tombs of St Médard and the founding Merovingian kings, Clotaire and Sigebert.

EXCURSION

Courmelles – *4km/2.5mi south; take D 1 for about 2km/1.5mi then take the small road on the right.*

The 12C **church** with its squat bell-tower has preserved its rounded Romanesque east end. Four buttresses of slender columns with finely carved capitals separate the rounded-arch windows, which are decorated with stars and surmounted by blind arcades of pointed arches. The projecting central window was formerly a recess for the altar.

Vallée de la SOMME★

SOMME VALLEY

Michelin map **52** folds 6 to 10 or **236** folds 22 to 26

The slow-moving waters of the River Somme, "which made Picardy as the Nile made Egypt" (Mabille de Poncheville), often burst their banks to spill into silvery ponds or dark peat bogs and have formed a wide, lush valley in Picardy's chalky plateau.

As the Somme is a natural barrier and has long been a regional frontier, it has been the site of numerous encounters; it has given its name to two battles, one in 1916, the other in 1940.

The source of the river is upstream of St-Quentin, at an altitude of 97m/318ft; from there it flows 245km/152mi westwards. The gentleness of this descent, together with the absorbent quality of the peat through which the river meanders, largely explains the lazy pace of the waters.

The regular flow of the river is, however, assured by the uninterrupted seeping from the chalk plateau, which produces numerous springs along the sides of the valley. This moisture is the reason for the fresh, green countryside.

Along the river bed, edged with willows and poplars, the waters are separated in places by small islands.

During their journey, the waters wind past peat bogs hidden under tall grasses, and meadows where laundry used to be spread out to bleach in the sun; past farmed fields and slopes pitted with quarries; past woods revealing shaded springs... In places, the bogs have been drained and turned into vegetable plots *(hortillonnages)*.

The deep-looking, rectangular ponds were formerly peat bogs. In the past the dense, black **peat** *(la tourbe)* was used as a household fuel in modest Picardy homes. It formed in the swamps when vegetation decomposed, producing 60% carbon. The peat was cut out in bars with special shovels *(louchets)* and cut up into blocks; these were then dried in the meadows or in small barns *(hallettes)*. Navigation on the river has always been limited owing to the fords and the shallowness of the water, but the Somme River nevertheless once carried **gribannes** between Amiens and St-Valery. these heavy skiffs transported wheat from Santerre and wool from Ponthieu downstream; salt and wine were brought upstream. In the 19C a few steamboats joined this traffic.

The **Somme Canal** which was finally completed in the 19C links St-Quentin and St-Valery. Sometimes it follows the course of the river, at other times it runs alongside it or takes shortcuts across the meanders. The canal was hardly used, however, as there was never a true maritime port at the end.

Hunting and Fishing – Hunting chiefly consists of lying in wait for wildfowl, in either a boat or the shelter of a hide *(see St-Valery)*. A great quantity of duck and snipe provide the game here; hunting wild swans, however, has not been allowed since the early 18C. The river, ditches and ponds teem with fish, although the salmon and sturgeon which were so numerous in the 18C are rarely seen. Excellent pâté is made from the abundant swarms of eels which share the waters with pike, carp, perch, tench etc.

AMIENS TO ABBEVILLE

58km/36mi – about 3hr

★★★ **Amiens** – See AMIENS

Leave Amiens on N 235 (west) towards Picquigny; follow the road parallel to the Paris-Calais railway line.

Ailly-sur-Somme – The market town is overlooked by the sober lines of the modern church: its unusual design comprises a great slanting roof like the sail of a boat, which on one side rests on a stone wall and on the other, the ground.

Cross to the north bank of the Somme and turn left towards La Chaussée Tirancourt.

★ **Parc Samara** ⊙ – This park (25ha/62 acres) lies at the foot of a Celtic settlement overlooking the Somme River (known as the Samara in the days of the Gauls). Footpaths lead to an **arboretum** (110 species), a botanical garden with quite a few rare plants, the marshes at the bottom of the valley and reconstructions of dwellings from the Neolithic, Bronze and Iron Ages. The working of flint, wood and pottery is brought to life by demons-

Reconstructed Prehistoric dwellings

Meissonnier /CAMPAGNE CAMPAGNE

trations of prehistoric techniques. Various ecosystems are cultivated and explained in this educational park, including the peat bog, where peat is extracted using techniques which were once common and have almost completely gone out of use.

Daily life in Piracy from the Paleolithic era to the Gallo-Roman period is evoked in the **exhibition pavilion**: a reindeer hunter's house, a bronzesmith's and an Iron Age ironsmith's workshop, a Gallic village street, Gallo-Roman kitchen etc. Visitors can have a look at the whole park from a tethered hot air balloon, which carries 30 passengers at a time, aloft at 150m/500ft.

Picquigny – In 1475 Trève Island in the middle of the Somme was the setting for the Peace Treaty of Picquigny signed by **Louis XI** and **Edward IV** of England.

The town itself defends a passage across the Somme and is crowned by the ruins of a **castle** ⊘: its 14C fortifications include a massive keep with walls 4m/13ft thick. A beautiful Renaissance kitchen, a great chamber, underground passages and prisons may all be seen. The château is early 17C. The church contains a 13C nave with 15C apse and tower.

Take D 3 (northwest) out of Picquigny.

Abbaye du Gard – This abbey was founded in 1137 by the Cistercians; in the 17C Mazarin was its commendatory abbot. After the Revolution the buildings were used by the Trappists, the Fathers of the Order of the Holy Spirit and Carthusian reclusive nuns; they were then abandoned and fell into ruin.

In 1967 the Abbey was bought by the monks of St-Riquier *(see ST-RIQUIER)* who restored the beautiful 18C main building and gave the abbey back its role as a place of prayer and meeting.

Continue on D 3 to Hangest.

Hangest-sur-Somme – The village specialises in growing watercress. The 12C-16C **church** ⊘ contains 18C furniture from the abbaye du Gard.

After Hangest, the road climbs a hill offering extensive views of the valley.

In 1940 the German 7th Tank Division commanded by **Rommel** crossed the Somme River between Hangest and Condé-Folie using the only railway bridge that had not been blown up; large French military cemetery at **Condé-Folie**.

Longpré-les-Corps-Saints – The town derives its name from the relics which the church founder, Aléaume de Fontaine, sent from Constantinople during the Crusades. The **church** ⊘ features a portal with a tympanun depicting the Death and Resurrection of the Virgin Mary. The reliquaries are on display at the end of the chancel.

1km/0.5mi beyond Longpré, turn right at Le Catelet onto D 32 towards Long.

The road crosses the floor of the valley, here dotted with ponds, offering a lovely view of the Château de Long.

Long – The great church in this pretty hillside village was rebuilt in the 19C, in the Gothic style, but retained its 16C spire; Cavaillé-Coll organ.

The elegant Louis XV **château** ⊘ has a slate mansard roof and red brick and white stone. Note the unusual, rounded wings and the graceful openings surmounted by keystones carved with masks and other ornamentation. It resembles the Château de Bagatelle *(see ABBEVILLE).*

Cross the Somme again and return to D 3.

Liercourt – The charming Flamboyant **church** with its gable tower stands just before the village. The fine basket-handled doorway is surmounted by the arms of France and a recess containing a statue of St Riquier.

Turn right onto D 901, crossing the Paris-Calais railway line.

Château de Pont-Remy – This château was built on an island near Pont-Remy in the 15C but was rebuilt in 1837 in the "Gothic Troubadour" style.

Return to D 3.

The road runs along the bottom of the hillside, skirting ponds and meadows, and approaches the Monts de Caubert; at their base, turn right to Abbeville.

Abbeville – *See ABBEVILLE.*

La THIÉRACHE★

Michelin map 53 folds 15 and 16 or 236 folds 28, 29, 39

The Thiérache region forms a green patch in the bare, chalky plains of Picardy and Champagne. The high altitude (250m/820ft in the east) provides greater rainfall which, combined with the terrain's lack of porousness, creates a well-watered area, devoted to forestry and especially grazing. The main lines of communication follow the deep valleys of the Oise and Serre Rivers and their tributaries.

The woodland is interspersed with meadows, cider-apple orchards and a scattering of farms. For eight months of the year black and white Friesian cows graze in the pastures. Their milk is dispatched throughout the region and to Paris; some of it is used to make butter, milk powder or the French Maroilles and Edam cheeses; the whey is kept for the pigs. Basket-making is a speciality around **Origny**, which is not suprising, in light of the many graceful basket willows growing there.

★FORTIFIED CHURCHES

Until the reign of Louis XIV the Thiérache region was a frontier and so repeatedly invaded – by 14C mercenaries led by Du Guesclin, by German foot soldiers and by Republicans – particularly during the Hundred Years War, the Wars of Religion and the conflicts between France and Spain under Louis XIII and Louis XIV. From the late 16C and during the 17C, local inhabitants, lacking fortresses and ramparts, fortified their churches. This accounts for the watch-turrets, round towers and square keeps pierced with arrow slits found on most of the 12C and 13C buildings, resulting in an uncomfortable architectural mix of brick and stone. Other fortress-churches, such as that at Plomion, date entirely from the turn of the 17C. The interiors of these churches were adapted to receive soldiers and shelter villagers: the naves have low ceilings owing to an extra room being included upstairs; fireplaces, a bread oven and a well allowed those taking refuge within to survive for some time. About sixty of these curious churches still exist in the Thiérache region and the Oise Valley.

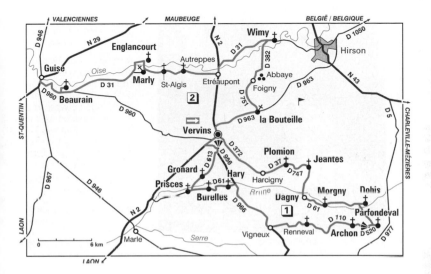

1 Round Trip starting from Vervins
65km/40mi – about 3hr

Vervins – The charm of the town, which is the region's capital, lies in its ramparts, its cobbled and winding streets and its squares bordered by houses with steeply pitched slate roofs and brick chimneys. The **church** features a 13C chancel, 16C nave and imposing brick tower (34m/111ft tall) with stone string courses (note the double buttresses on the corners).
Inside, 16C mural paintings adorn the piers and a huge, brightly coloured composition by Jouvenet (1699) portrays *Supper in the House of Simon*; 18C organ case and pulpit.
Leave Vervins by D 372 (southeast); at Harcigny take D 37 east.

Plomion – The 16C church features a fine west front flanked by two towers; note the square keep with its great hall leading up to the garret.
A large covered market in front of the church testifies to Plomion's commercial activities.
Take D 747 east towards Bancigny and Jeantes.

Jeantes – The façade of the **church** is flanked by two towers. Expressionist frescoes on the walls of the interior, representing scenes from the Life of Christ, are the work of painter Charles Van Eyck (1962). Note the 12C font.

Dagny – This old village has preserved its cob houses and half-timbered houses with brick courses.

Morgny-en-Thiérache – The chancel and nave of the church date from the 13C. Fortification mainly affected the chancel, which was raised by a storey to create an extra room for those seeking a safe refuge.

Dohis – There are many half-timbered and cob houses here. The church (12C nave) is particularly interesting because of its porch-keep, added in the 17C.
Turn around from the church and take the first road on the left (south); fork left to Parfondeval.

Plomion – The church

Morcime /CAMPAGNE CAMPAGNE

Parfondeval – This lovely village stands perched on a hill, its warm-toned brick houses clustering around a broad green. The 16C **church** rises at the end of the square, an indisputable fortress behind a fortification of neighbouring houses. The white stone portal is in the Renaissance style. On the walls, glazed bricks form a crisscross design.

Back at the entrance to the village take D 520 (west) to Archon.

The road offers a good view over Archon and the undulating countryside dotted with copses.

Archon – Cob-walled and brick houses encircle the church, which is guarded by two great towers; a footbridge between the towers also served as a lookout point. Follow D 110 west through **Renneval** (stone church with fortified chancel) to Vigneux.

At Vigneux take D 966 northwest to Hary.

Hary – A 16C brick keep rises above the chancel and nave of this 12C, white stone, Romanesque church.

Burelles – The 16C and 17C village **church** has a number of defences: arrow slits; a reinforced keep with watch-turrets; barbicans and watch-turrets above the months transept; the chancel flanked by a turret. The upper floor of the transept has been turned into a vast fortified room.
The brick bonding adds some attractive variation in colour.

Prisces – The 12C chancel and nave of the **church** ⊘ were given an enormous, square brick keep (25m/82ft tall) with two turrets on diagonally-opposing corners. The four floors inside allowed about a hundred soldiers to take shelter with their arms and provisions.
Cross the Brune River and follow D 613 to Gronard.

Gronard – The façade of the church is almost hidden behind lime trees.
The keep is flanked by two round towers.
Return to Vervins along D 613 and D 966.
The route offers a picturesque view of Vervins and its surrounding area.

② **From Vervins to Guise**
51km/32mi – about 2hr

This tour largely follows the Oise Valley which also features many fortified churches.

Vervins – *See above.*
From Vervins take D 963 to La Bouteille.

La Bouteille – The church has thick walls (over 1m/3ft) and is flanked by four turrets. It was built by Cistercians from the nearby Abbaye de Foigny, now in ruins.
D 751 and D 382 lead to Foigny. Cross D 38 and take the little road which runs beside the abbey ruins, to Wimy.

Wimy – The enormous keep of the fortified church is flanked by two large, cylindrical towers. Two fireplaces, a well and a bread oven were added inside. The first floor has a vast room for those seeking refuge.

D 31 crosses Etréaupont and continues through **Autreppes**, a village of brick buildings. The road runs in front of the fortified church and continues past the village of **St Algis** which is overlooked by its church keep.

Marly – The 13C and 14C sandstone church has a beautiful, pointed arch portal to which two great watch-turrets were added. The large arrow slits near the base allowed crossbows to be used.

Take D 774 north to Englancourt.

Englancourt – The fortified **church**, in a pretty location overlooking the Oise River, has a west front flanked by watch-turrets, a square keep in brick and a chancel with a flat east end reinforced by two round towers.

Return to D 31 via D 26.

Beaurain – The **church** stands isolated on a hill which rises from lush surroundings. The beautiful fortress dates entirely from the same period. The great square keep is flanked by towers, as is the chancel. A Romanesque font stands by the entrance.

Follow D 960 to Guise.

Guise – *See GUISE.*

THOIRY★★

Population 835
Michelin map 106 folds 15, 16

Access from Paris: *By car, take A 13. Leave the motorway at the Bois d'Arcy exit to Dreux and rejoin N 12. In Pontchartrain, turn into D 11 to Thoiry.*

Thoiry is a vast estate comprising a large Renaissance château and 250 ha/625 acres of gardens and park. The family who has owned it for the past four hundred years or more has undertaken a considerable amount of work to turn it into a magical spot where history and nature merge.

Château ⊘ – Raoul Moreau, Treasurer to Henri II, was passionately interested in alchemy and esoterics. It was he who had this "solar house" built on a magnetic fault, to designs using the Golden Section. This outstanding position on a hilltop enables the château to act as a solar instrument, with spectacular sights such as the sunrise or sunset in line with the façade at the solstices.
The house is also a "time machine" which has come down to us through the centuries and now gives an insight into an eventful history. The ancestors conversing from their picture frames in the portrait gallery (no, you are not dreaming!) and the spicy tales uncovered in the 50 trunks full of family archives are all rather unconventional means of taking a look at history.

Zoological and botanical park ⊘ – The area of park adjacent to the château has been laid out as a zoo, with numerous special events. The most impressive section is the tiger enclosure which visitors cross on a concrete footbridge among the trees. It is also possible to see the animals from the glass tunnel in which only the

X L'Hospice-Château de Thoiry

African wildlife park – Lions

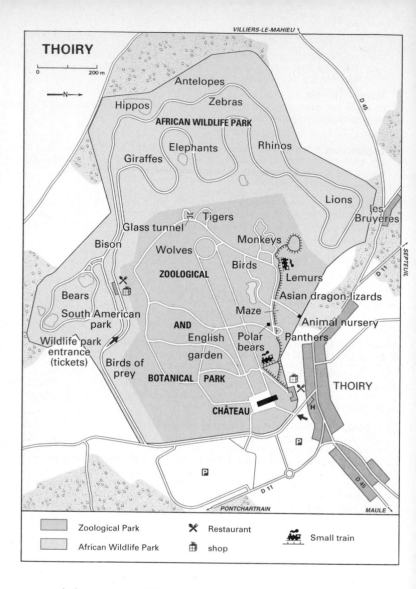

THOIRY

VILLIERS-LE-MAHIEU

0   200 m

—N→

Antelopes

Hippos   Zebras

AFRICAN WILDLIFE PARK

Elephants   Rhinos

Giraffes

Lions

les
Bruyères

Tigers

Glass tunnel   Monkeys

Bison   Wolves   Birds

ZOOLOGICAL   Lemurs

Bears   Asian dragon-lizards

South American   Maze
park   Animal nursery

Wildlife park   **AND**   Panthers
entrance   English   Polar
(tickets)   Birds of   garden   bears
                   prey

BOTANICAL   PARK   THOIRY

CHÂTEAU   H

P

P

D 11

PONTCHARTRAIN   MAULE

	Zoological Park	✕	Restaurant		Small train
	African Wildlife Park	🎁	shop		

armoured glass separates visitors from the claws and teeth of these wild beasts. Various trails pass the elegant but fearsome black panthers, the emus and cassowaries, the mandrill island, and a tribe of lemurs running free. There are demonstrations of birds of prey in flight. The trees, too, speak to visitors about the natural environment. Do not miss the impressive Asian dragons (5m/16ft long) and become familiar with the ecosystem of European rivers (otters).
The park is also appreciated for its varied vegetation: an audio-guided trail makes it easy to discover its diversity.

African wildlife park ⊙ – The park is visited by car since the animals roam free. For your own safety, please comply with the rules.
The park is so vast that many different species of African wildlife can live together quite happily. The road covers a distance of 10km/6mi and visitors can see antelopes with strangely shaped horns, bison, giraffes, zebras, elephants, rhinos, and hippos. A drive through two high-security enclosures provides a close-up view of lions and bears.

The most important sights in this guide can be found on the Principal Sights map, and are described in the text. Use the map and plans, the Calendar of events, the index, and read the Introduction to get the most out of this guide.

Le TOUQUET ☆☆☆

Population 5 596

Michelin map 51 fold 11 or 236 fold 11

Named "Paris Beach" (Paris-Plage) when it was inaugurated in the 19C, the resort was almost immediately adopted by the English and took the name Le Touquet Paris-Plage in 1912. Since then it has developed into an all-year European resort with a substantial hotel trade, year-round sporting activities and a thalassotherapy centre.

The Town – Le Touquet lies between the sea and the forest, its parallel streets intersected by access roads to the beach. The liveliest area of the town – which boasts sporting facilities and a pony club – is around **rue St-Jean** and **rue de Paris**. Rue Jean-Monnet continues through the arch of the **covered market** (**AZ K**), a monumental, half-moon-shaped ensemble, to the town hall and church facing each other.

Église Ste-Jeanne-d'Arc (**AZ**) – Joan of Arc's Church was built in 1912 and restored in 1955; it is decorated with clear figurative glass and with decorative ironwork by Lambert Rucki.

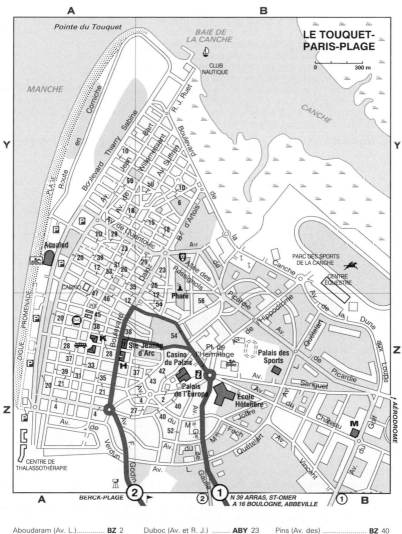

Aboudaram (Av. L.) .... **BZ** 2	Duboc (Av. et R. J.) .... **ABY** 23	Pins (Av. des) .... **BZ** 40
Atlantique (Av. de l') .... **ABZ** 4	Garet (Av. et R. L.) .... **ABY** 26	Recoussine (Av. F.) .... **BZ** 42
Bardol (R. E.) .... **BY** 6	Genets (Av. des) .... **ABZ** 27	Reine May (Av. de la) ...... **ABZ** 43
Bourdonnais	Grande Rue .... **AZ** 28	St-Amand (R.) .... **AZ** 45
(Av. de la) .... **ABY** 10	Hubert (Av. L.) .... **ABY** 29	St-Jean (R.) .... **AZ** 46
Bruxelles (R. de) .... **AYZ** 12	Londres (R. de) .... **AYZ** 31	St-Louis (R.) .... **AZ** 47
Calais (R. de) .... **BY** 15	Metz (R. de) .... **AYZ** 33	Tourville
Desvres (R. de) .... **ABY** 18	Moscou (R. de) .... **AYZ** 35	(Av. de l'Amiral) .... **ABY** 50
Dr J. Pouget	Oyats (Av. et R. des) ...... **ABZ** 37	Troènes (Av. des) .... **BZ** 52
(Bd. du) .... **AYZ** 20	Paix (Av. et R. de la) ...... **ABZ** 38	Verger (Av. du) .... **BZ** 54
Dorothée (R.) .... **AZ** 21	Paris (R. de) .... **AYZ** 39	Whitley (Av. J.) .... **BZ** 56

H Hôtel de ville	**K** Marché couvert	**M** Musée

Hôtel de Ville (**AZ H**) – The town hall was built from local stone in 1931 in Anglo-Norman style and is flanked by a belfry (38m/125ft tall).
Along the sea front, the **promenade** is edged by numerous gardens and car parks.

The Beach and Port – The gently sloping beach of fine, hard sand, which is uncovered for 1km/0.5mi at low tide and stretches as far as the mouth of the River Authie (12km/7.5mi), attracts many sand yachts. The **coast road** which follows the line of the dunes leads to the marina, well sheltered by the headland known as Pointe du Touquet.

Aqualud ⊘ (**AY**) – This lively aquatic leisure complex consists of an indoor section under a glass pyramid with a wave pool, a giant flume, an infant's pool, a sauna etc, and outdoor swimming pools and slides for warmer days.

Lighthouse (**BY**) – The lighthouse (53m/173ft) which was rebuilt after 1945 stands inland between the town and the forest. Its hexagonal red-brick column is crowned with two white balconies.

Forêt – The forest (800ha/1900 acres) was planted in 1855; its maritime pine, birch, alder, poplar and acacia trees protect about 2000 luxury villas – either Anglo-Norman in style or resolutely modern – from the wind.
Near the attractive shopping galleries of the Hermitage district are the **Sports Centre** (Palais des Sports) (**BZ**) with its heated pool, horse show arenas and 38 tennis courts, the select **Casino du Palais** (**BZ**), the **Palais de l'Europe** (**BZ**) where conferences and cultural exchanges take place and the **École hôtelière** (**BZ**), the catering college which presents a curious external arrangement of reversed stars.
Three golf courses extend south of the forest.
Along the River Canche are the racecourse, the equestrian centre and the **airport** from which there are regular flights to Lydd in England; from the observation terrace there is a good **view** over the bay, spanned by the road and rail bridges of Étaples, a small port where the railway station is located.

Museum ⊘ (**BZ M**) – The museum's original collection consists of works by the Étaples School (1880-1914). It also includes paintings by Le Sidaner and a section devoted to modern art.

EXCURSIONS

Stella-Plage – *8km/5mi. Leave Le Touquet by S on the map (south) and after 5km/3mi, turn right into D 144.*
Behind the dunes which extend along the beach are villas dotted across the woods forming a continuation of the woods in Le Touquet.

St-Josse – *10km/6mi southeast by* ① *on N 39, D 143 and D 144* (views of Étaples).
St-Josse, which stands on a hill, was once the home of an abbey founded by Charlemagne in memory of St Josse, a 7C pilgrim and hermit whose reliquary is venerated in the church's early 16C chancel.
About 500m/550yd east, in the middle of a wooded close, stand St Josse's chapel, which is a place of pilgrimage, and St Josse's fountain.

★**Parc d'attraction de Bagatelle** ⊘ – *13km/8mi south. Leave Le Touquet by* ② *and continue on D 940.* Located between Berck and Le Touquet some 5km/3mi from the sea, this amusement park occupies a sprawling 26ha/62 acre replete with rides, games, shows and a zoo.

VALENCIENNES

Conurbation 33 6481
Michelin map 51 fold 17 or 236 folds 17, 18

This busy commercial town, located on the River Escaut (Scheldt), is surrounded by boulevards which replaced the former ramparts. Only the 15C Tour de la Dedenne has survived.
The architectural variety in Valenciennes is a result of the damage inflicted on the town during sieges and wars over the centuries; the bombings of 1940 and 1944 completely destroyed the old, wood-built centre.
Valenciennes was once the capital of the steel industry and metallurgy in the north, while the coal basin nearby was fully active. Today these industries have decreased markedly but have been replaced by others: rolling stock, car manufacturing, paints, pharmaceutical laboratories, mechanical engineering, electronics etc. The presence of a science faculty has contributed to his growth.
Among the culinary specialities of Valenciennes is *langue Lucullus*, smoked ox tongue cut into slices and covered in foie gras.
Toyota is building a car-manufacturing plant in Onnaing, near Valenciennes.

Athens of the North – Valenciennes earned this nickname because of the town's long-standing interest in the arts and the many artists who were born here.

Native sculptors include André Beauneveu (14C) – the "image-maker" of Charles V – who was also a painter; Antoine Pater (1670-1747); Saly (1717-76) who went to work for the court of Denmark; Philippe Dumont (18C), creator of the beautiful bust of his fellow citizen, actress Rosalie Levasseur, and in particular **Carpeaux** (1827-75), who brought new life to French sculpture.

Famous local painters are also numerous: notably Simon Marmion, who died in Valenciennes in 1489; in the 18C, the great **Antoine Watteau** (1684-1721) and Jean-Baptiste Pater (1695-1736) who both specialised in genre painting in the *fête galante* style; Eisen (1720-78), painter, draughtsman and engraver; Dumont "the Roman"; Louis and François Watteau, grand-nephew and great-nephew of Antoine; and in the 19C, the landscape painter Henri Harpignies (1819-1916) and the portrait painter Abel de Pujol (1785-1861).

In the 18C the citizens of Valenciennes, wishing to encourage the arts, founded an Academy, a Salon and a School of Fine Art. The granting of scholarships was also established with the same aim.

There are many treasures in the town's museum.

Jean-Baptiste Carpeaux

Jean-Baptiste Carpeaux (Valenciennes 1827-Courbevoie 1875) was a sculptor, painter and draughtsman. He won the Grand Prix de Rome in 1854.

Having become an official sculptor, he produced a large number of elegant busts of celebrities during the Second Empire and was also involved in the decoration of public buildings:
– *Triumph of Flora*, a low relief for the pediment of the Louvre's Flora pavilion in Paris;
– *Dance*, a group sculpture for the front of the Paris opera house, now in the Musée d'Orsay;
– *The Four Quarters of the Globe* for the fountain at the Observatoire in Paris;
– A statue of Watteau in Valenciennes.

A commemorative statue by Félix Desruelles was erected in memory of the great man in Avenue du Sénateur-Girard in Valenciennes.

Other works, plaster casts or earthenware models can be seen in the Musée d'Orsay and the Musée du Petit Palais in Paris, the Musée Roybet-Fould in Courbevoie and the Musée des Beaux-Arts in Valenciennes.

Traditions – Each year, on the second Sunday in September, the **Tour du St-Cordon** takes place, a procession of the statue of the Virgin Mary kept in the neo-Gothic Basilica of Notre-Dame-du-St-Cordon. This tradition dates back to the 11C when Valenciennes was threatened by the plague; the Virgin Mary is said to have appeared uncoiling a long scarlet cord around the town to protect it.

In the 17C and 18C fine Valenciennes **lace** was particularly famous; lacemaking is once more taught today.

SIGHTS

★**Musée des Beaux-Arts** ⊙ – This vast museum, which was built at the beginning of the century, has a particularly large collection of works from the 15C-17C Flemish school (Rubens), 18C French works and 19C sculptures (Carpeaux). It has been renovated throughout and now has a bookshop and gift shop, café, lecture hall etc.

15C-17C Flemish school – The first room contains a double panel by Hieronymus Bosch, *St James and Hermogenes the Magician*, next to Van Leyden's triptych of *The Last Judgement* and Marinus Van Reymerswaele's *Tax Collector*.

The next three rooms cover the 17C with major works from the Dutch, French, Italian and, more particularly, Flemish schools.

In the Rubens room, works by the great artist from Antwerp include the triptych depicting the *Martyrdom of St Stephen* that used to hang in the abbey in St-Amand, and two large paintings entitled *Elija and the Angel* and *The Triumph of the Eucharist*. The vast gallery deals with Flemish religious painting from Mannerism until the Baroque period. It contains *The Adoration of the Magi* and the *Holy Family* by Martin de Vos, *Calvary* by Janssens, *St Augustin's Ecstasy* by Crayer, *St Paul* and *St Matthew*, two heads by Van Dyck. The other two rooms show changes in genres such as portraits (*Elisabeth of France* by Pourbus), still-life painting (Snyders' *Store Cupboard*, Beuckelaer's *Vegetable Carrier*), genre painting (*The Young Chatter like the Old Sing* by Jordaens), landscapes (*Kidnapping of Proserpine* and *Ceres and Cyane* by Soens, *Landscape with Rainbow* by Rubens).

18C French school – The French school is divided between two rooms. The first one contains two works by Watteau, a portrait of the sculptor Antoine Pater and a work painted in his youth, *Real Jollity*. Note, too, the *Portrait of Jean de Jullienne*, a friend and patron of the artist by François de Troy; the *Rustic Concert* and the *Joys of Country Life* by JB Pater who worked with Watteau. In the second room is a view of the Capitol in Rome by Hubert Robert and a set of works by Louis and François Watteau, the latter being better known as Watteau of Lille (*The Battle of the Pyramids, The Four Hours of the Day* – a series of four paintings). These works are characteristic of the taste of these lesser-known artists for genre painting.

Carpeaux – In the centre of the museum, in a vast hall filled with light, is a set of sculptures that reveal the changes in Carpeaux' artistry. There are huge works such as *Ugolin and his Children*, the *Triumph of Flora*, and the Watteau fountain, nu-

merous busts (Charles Garnier, the architect of the Paris opera house, composer Charles Gounod), and sketches of women and children showing the artist's fascinating ability to suggest movement and life. A few paintings illustrate the artist's social life *(Masked Ball in the Tuileries)* and his skills as a portraitist (series of self-portraits) or as a visionary artist *(Scene of Madness)*. Next to his works are others by contemporary artists such as Lemaire *(Young Girl frightened by a Snake)*, Crauk *(Morning)*, and Desruelles *(Job)*.

19C-20C French school- The huge size of the canvases show the popularity of historical paintings at this time. They include *The Death of Maréchal Lannes* by Guérin, *The Youth of Peter the Great* by Steuben, *The Execution of Mary Queen of Scots* by Abel de Pujol, or *The Sword of Damocles* by Félix Auvray. Landscapes are well re-

Detail of a statue by Carpeaux

presented with Charlet, Boudin, Rousseau, Lépine, Zicau and Harpignies.
The small 20C section illustrates the search for line and colour by artists such as Herbin or Félix Delmarle *(The Harbour)*.

Archeological crypt – From the centre of the museum, steps lead down to the regional archeological collections. There are murals from Famars, bronzes and a silver platter from the Gallo-Roman period, cloisonné enamel jewellery, funerary paintings (Abbaye de Beaumont) and medieval tombs (Jean d'Avesnes, 14C).

Maison espagnole – This 16C half-timbered, corbelled house was built during the Spanish occupation. It has been restored and is today the home of the tourist office.

Église St-Géry ⊘ – This old Recollect church was built in the 13C and altered in the 19C. Restoration has reinstated the original Gothic purity to the nave and chancel.
The fountain in nearby **Square Watteau** is overlooked by a statue by Carpeaux of Antoine Watteau, who was born at 39 rue de Paris.

Bibliothèque municipale – The library is housed in the buildings of the old **Jesuit school**. It was founded in the early 17C. The pleasing brick and stone façade has Louis XVI garlands and bull's-eye windows on the ground floor.
On the first floor is the **Bibliothèque des Jésuites** ⊘ with painted decoration dating from the 18C. This library contains more than 100 000 works. They include the manuscript of St Eulalie's famous *Cantilene*, the oldest known poem in French written in the language of northern France c 880 AD, very old books (incunabula), rare or valuable printed books dating from the 17C to 20C etc.

The **Église St-Nicolas**, once the Jesuit chapel, has a delightful 18C west front. It is no longer consecrated and has been turned into the Auditorium St-Nicolas.

Maison du Prévôt Notre-Dame – At the corner of rue Notre-Dame is one of the oldest buildings (15C) in the town, constructed in brick and stone. The mullioned windows, crowstepped gable, and turret with bellcote give it a certain elegance.

EXCURSIONS

St-Saulve – *2km/1.25mi northeast. Leave Valenciennes by avenue de Liège, N 30.*
Chapelle du Carmel – *1 Rue Barbusse.* This Carmelite chapel, which was completed in 1966, was inspired by a model created by the sculptor Szekely and then built to plans prepared by the architect Guislain who favoured effects of mass and the use of simple materials. The chapel stands back from the road and is flanked by an asymmetrical bell-tower. The interior is bathed in a gentle light which filters in above the altar through stained-glass windows featuring geometric designs.

Sebourg – *9km/5.5mi east. Leave Valenciennes by D 934 towards Maubeuge, turn left at Saultain on D 59; beyond Estreux turn right onto D 350.*
This little market town attracts people from Valenciennes owing to its still-rural aspect: it stretches over the verdant slopes of the Aunelle Valley.
The 12C-16C **church** ⊘ is the destination for pilgrimages to St Druon; the 12C shepherd-hermit is invoked to cure hernias. In the south aisle lie 14C recumbent effigies of Henri of Hainault, Lord of Sebourg, and his wife.

Bruay-sur-l'Escaut – *5km/3mi north by D 935.*
The **church** ⊘ contains the **cenotaph** of St Pharaïlde, the sister of St Gudule; the 13C block of white stone depicts a graceful woman's form.

Denain – *10km/6mi southwest by N 30.*
Denain is famous for Maréchal de Villars' defeat of the army led by Prince Eugène on 24 July 1712.
After the discovery of coal in 1828, this rural village became a major industrial centre. The town had up to fifteen mine shafts at one time (the last one, the Puits du Renard, was closed in 1948 but its slag heap still dominates the town). It was in this town and in the countryside nearby that Zola came to seek inspiration for his work *Germinal*. Traces of the town's heyday are still visible. One large building (1852) remains of the mining community in avenue Villars; it is now the academy of music. It was here that the poet-miner Jules Mousseron (1868-1943) lived.
The **Cité Ernestine** *(park your car and take the alleyway between 138 and 140 Rue Ludovic-Trarieux)* has retained its working-class atmosphere. It consists of twenty or more semi-detached miners' houses (known locally as *corons*). The **Cité Bellevue** to the north consists of a fine group of foremen's houses, some of them built to each side of the bread oven.

Abbaye de VALLOIRES★

Michelin map 51 fold 12 or 236 fold 12

The old Cistercian abbey is located on a solitary site in the Authie Valley, surrounded by woods and orchards; it is a rare and beautiful example of 18C architecture.

War and Peace – The abbey was founded in the 12C by a Count of Ponthieu and became a burial place for his family. In 1346 the bodies of knights killed at Crécy were transported here.
In the 17C the abbey was ravaged by several fires, but the monks were wealthy and in 1730 the abbot ordered that huge amounts of wood be cut in order to begin rebuilding. Reconstruction, following plans by Coignard, took place from 1741 to 1756. The decoration is the work of Baron **Pfaff de Pfaffenhoffen** (1715-84) from Vienna who was forced to leave his city after a duel; he settled in St-Riquier in 1750.
From 1817 to 1880 the **Basiliens**, members of a lay congregation founded in Mons in 1800, lived in Valloires. All members of the community exercised their profession, scrupulously fulfilled their religious duties and wore an all-blue outfit: a cotton cap, loose shirt and leggings. The monastery is today a child-care centre.

ABBEY ⊘

A 16C dovecote stands in front of the long building which is extended to the left and rear by the east front of the **abbey lodgings**; these in turn are surrounded by smaller buildings. The chapter-house is no longer near the church as in the Middle Ages, but is in the main building itself; Pfaffenhoffen's elegant decoration has given it the look of a drawing room.
The simple cloister gallery has groined vaulting. The refectory is located on the ground floor of the east wing; the abbot's rooms and the monk's cells are upstairs. The vestry is decorated with wood panels by Pfaffenhoffen and paintings by Parrocel.

Stopover

Abbaye – The abbey has six guest rooms overlooking the gardens; elegant 18C decor. Room for two persons, including breakfast: 440F; information, ☎ 03 22 29 62 33.

★ **Church** – "It would delight Mme de Pompadour yet St Bernard would see nothing to take exception to". This comment by an English traveller illustrates the balance between the building's architectural restraint and the elegant ornamentation of its decor.

Inside, the **organ** (**1**) is supported by a gallery carved by Pfaffenhoffen with musical instruments; the statues at each side symbolise religion. The balustrade and small organ case are decorated with *putti* and cherub musicians. Caryatids support the great organ case, which is crowned by a statue of King David accompanied by angel musicians.

The beautiful **grilles**★ (**2**) are of a graceful and light design: the central part is surmounted by the Valloires arms and Moses' brazen serpent (prefiguration of the Crucifixion), framed by baskets of flowers. The creator of the grilles, Jean Veyren, was also responsible for those in the cathedral in Amiens.

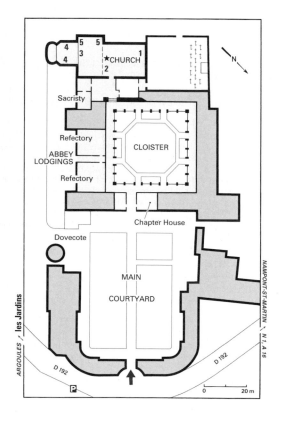

Two adoring angels in gilded lead by Pfaffenhoffen are located around the high altar (**3**), dominated by a curious and rare eucharistic monstrance in the form of an abbot's crook, another masterpiece of ironwork by Jean Veyren. Two white *papier mâché* angels seem to be flying over the altar.

Carved religious emblems adorn the stalls (**4**); those reserved for the abbot and the prior stand on either side of the entrance to the apsidal chapel, which is decorated with wood panels by Pfaff.

The south transept houses recumbent effigies of a Count and Countess of Ponthieu (**5**). In the north transept is the window through which sick monks could follow services.

GARDENS ⊘

This 7ha/17 acre landscaped park at the foot of the abbey contains 4000 species of plants and trees. Part of it is laid out in the formal French style with a magnificent rose-garden containing a hundred varieties, including the Valloires rose created in 1992. The roses grow among aromatic plants and medicinal herbs, such as would have been found in the monks' garden.

The English-style park is laid out on high ground and includes an Island Garden whose colours change with the seasons.

The Garden of the Five Senses contains a selection of plants and trees connected with the different senses: strawberries and apples (taste), thorny plants (touch), aspens with leaves that rustle with the slightest breeze (hearing), colourful petunias (sight), jasmine, lily and mint (smell).

Lower down lies the wilder Marsh Garden with its artificial canal reminiscent of the arm of the River Authie which used to flow across the estate.

Château de VAUX-LE-VICOMTE★★★

Michelin map 106 folds 45, 46 – 6km/4mi northeast of Melun

This château, built by Fouquet, remains one of the greatest masterpieces of the 17C.

The rise of Nicolas Fouquet – Born to a family of magistrates, Fouquet became a member of the Parlement de Paris by the age of twenty. He was made Procureur Général of this respectable assembly and was appointed Superintendent of Finances under Mazarin. Owing to the customs of the time and the example of Cardinal Mazarin, he acquired the dangerous habit of confusing the credit of the State with his own. He was forever surrounded by a large retinue of senior personalities whose services cost vast sums of money. Intoxicated with success Fouquet chose a squirrel as his emblem – in Anjou patois *fouquet* means a squirrel – and decreed his motto would be *Quo non ascendam* (How high shall I not climb?).

In 1656 Fouquet decided to grace his own seignory of Vaux with a château worthy of his social standing. He showed excellent taste when it came to choosing his future "collaborators": the architect **Louis Le Vau**, the decorator **Charles Le Brun** and the landscape gardener **André Le Nôtre**. He was equally discerning in other matters; the famous chef Vatel was hired as his major-domo and La Fontaine as close adviser.

The builders were given carte blanche. A total of 18 000 workers took part in the project, which involved the demolition of three villages.

Le Brun created a tapestry works at Maincy to fulfil his commission. After Fouquet's fall it was moved to Paris, where it became the Manufacture Royale des Gobelins. The whole operation took five years to complete and the result was a masterpiece that Louis XIV wished to surpass with the construction of Versailles.

An invitation to royal vexation – On 17 August 1661 Fouquet organised a fête for the King and his court, who were staying at Fontainebleau. The reception was one of dazzling splendour. The King's table featured a service in solid gold; this detail annoyed him intensely as his own tableware had been sent back to the smelting works to meet the expenses incurred by the Thirty Years War.

After a banquet at which Vatel had surpassed himself, the guests could feast their eyes on the garden entertainments, enhanced by 1 200 fountains and cascades. The programme included country ballets, concerts, aquatic tournaments and lottery games in which all the tickets won prizes. It also included the premiere of *Les Fâcheux*, a comedy-ballet by Molière, performed by the author and his troupe against a delightful backdrop of greenery.

The King was vexed by such an extravagant display of pomp and luxury, unparalleled at his own royal court. His first impulse was to have Fouquet arrested immediately but Anne of Austria managed to dissuade him.

The fall of Nicolas Fouquet – Nineteen days later, the Superintendent of Finances was sent to jail and all his belongings sequestrated. The artists who had designed and built Vaux entered the King's service and were later to produce the Palace of Versailles. At the end of a three-year trial, Fouquet was banished from court but this sentence was altered by the King to perpetual imprisonment. Only a few close friends remained loyal to the fallen minister: Mme de Sévigné and La Fontaine, who composed *Elegy to the Nymphs of Vaux*.

On account of her dowry, Fouquet's wife was entitled to recover the ownership of the château. After the death of her son, the estate was bought by the Maréchal de Villars in 1705, when it was made a duchy-peerage. It was sold in 1764 by one of Louis XV's ministers the duc de Choiseul-Praslin, and survived the Revolution without suffering too much damage.

In 1875 Vaux was bought by a wealthy industrialist Mr Sommier, who applied himself to restoring and refurnishing the château, as well as refurbishing its grounds. This task has been continued by his heirs.

TOUR

★★Château ⊘ – The château stands on a terrace surrounded by a moat. The impressive approach leads towards the château's imposing northern front, with its tall windows indicating the *piano nobile* on a raised ground floor. The building is characteristic of the first period of Louis XIV architecture.

The glass doors in the entrance hall – presently covered up by tapestries – opened onto the Grand Salon and the perspective of the formal gardens. This vestibule leads up to the first floor, occupied by the suites of M and Mme Fouquet.

Visitors are shown the superintendent's antechamber (large ebony desk inlaid with gilt copper), his study and his bedroom (superb ceiling decorated by Le Brun), followed by Mme Fouquet's boudoir (portrait of Fouquet by Le Brun), the Louis XV study and bedroom embellished with contemporary furniture (large tester bed attributed to F Leroy) and the Louis XVI bedchamber.

Back on the ground floor, enter the Grande chambre carrée, a square chamber that has the only Louis XIII interior in the château, with a French-style ceiling.

Six reception rooms giving onto the gardens are laid out on either side of the Grand Salon. The ceilings were decorated by Le Brun, who conferred a sense of unity to the ensemble. Admire his rendering of *The Nine Muses* in the Salon des

Vaux-le-Vicomte – Dresser

Musés *Hercules Entering Mount Olympus* in the Salon d'Hercule. The latter houses an equestrian statue of Louis XIV by François Girardon. It is a miniature bronze of the monument set up on Place Vendôme in 1699 and destroyed during the Revolution.

★**Grand Salon** – This room, crowned by the central dome, was left unfinished after Fouquet's arrest and suffers from the absence of decoration (the various studies made by Le Brun are on display). The sixteen caryatids supporting the dome symbolise the twelve months and the four seasons of the year. The only remains of the original furnishings are two marble tables, as well as six statues and six paintings discovered by M Sommier when he moved in.

★★**Chambre du Roi** – The King's bedchamber communicates with the former ante-chamber (now a library beautifully furnished in the Regency style).

Its decoration is characteristic of the Louis XIV style that was to leave its mark on the State Apartments at Versailles. The ceiling features stuccowork by Girardon and Legendre, and a central painting by Le Brun representing *Time Taking Away Truth from the Skies.* Below the cornice is a frieze of palmette motifs alternating with tiny squirrels.

The Salle des Buffets probably served as a dining room in Fouquet's time. It gives onto a wood-panelled passageway hung with paintings, where a long row of dressers would receive the bowls of fruit and other dishes brought from the distant kitchens.

A tour of the basement shows a number of rooms (Salle des Plans, Salle des Archives) and the kitchen quarters, which were used up to 1956. Note the servant's dining hall, complete with a fully laid table.

★★★**Gardens** ⊘ – M Sommier carefully restored Le Nôtre's masterpiece, of which the most striking feature is its sweeping perspective. The grounds offer several "optical illusions", including the discovery of basins which are not visible from the château. Walk to the far end of the upper terrace to get a good view of the southern façade. The central dome and its surmounting lantern turret, the corner pavilions, heavier than on the north side, and the decoration of the forepart, crowned by statues form an impressive, if somewhat heavy, composition.

Starting from the château, walk past the *boulingrin* or former bowling green, two areas of garden laid out like a piece of lacework.

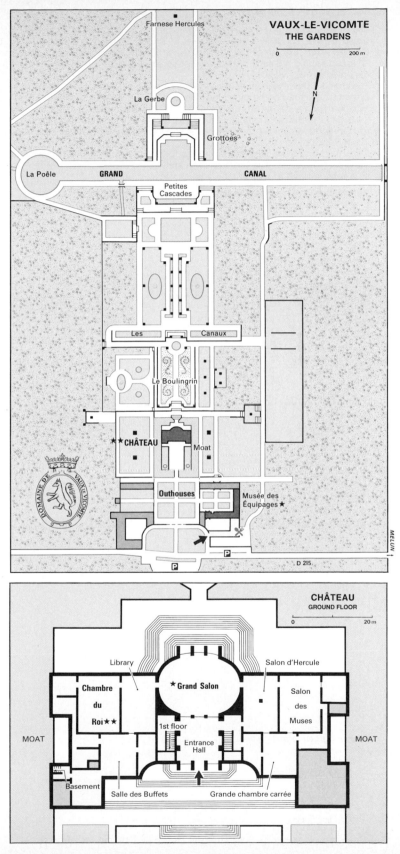

VAUX-LE-VICOMTE
THE GARDENS

0   200 m

N

Farnese Hercules

La Gerbe

Grottoes

La Poêle   GRAND   CANAL

Petites
Cascades

Les   Canaux

Le Boulingrin

★ ★ CHÂTEAU   Moat

Outhouses   Musée des
Équipages ★

DOMAINE DE VAUX LE VICOMTE

P   P   D 215

MELUN

CHÂTEAU
GROUND FLOOR

0   20 m

Library   Salon d'Hercule

Chambre   ★ Grand Salon   Salon

du   des

Roi ★ ★   Muses

1st floor

MOAT   Entrance   MOAT
            Hall

Basement

Salle des Buffets   Grande chambre carrée

The three main water perspectives – the moat, the two rectangular canals and the Grand Canal – suddenly come into view in a most impressive manner. Owing to the prevailing customs of that period, the artificial grottoes appear to have been arranged around the edge of the very last square basin, as the Grand Canal is optically hidden from view.

The Grand Canal – known as the *"poêle"* (frying pan) on account of its rounded extremity – is approached by a steep flight of steps level with the Petites Cascades located opposite the grottoes. The niches at each end house two statues of river gods, some of the most important examples of 17C sculpture at Vaux; these Mlle de Scudéry fondly imagined to be the Tiber and the Anqueuil (local name given to the Almont stream).

Skirt the Grand Canal and walk up to the foot of the Farnese Hercules which ends the great perspective. The very last basin aptly called the spray – *La Gerbe* – affords an extensive **view★** of the château and its stately grounds.

Outbuildings – The **Musée des Équipages★** ⊘ lies in the western outbuildings, next to the visitors' entrance. It presents harnessing and saddlery, an old-fashioned smithy and fully equipped carriages.

Michelin green tourist guides
Landscapes
Monuments
Scenic routes, touring programmes
Geography
History, Art
Places to stay
Town and site plans
Practical information
A collection of guides for your travels in France and around the world.

Access from Paris: *see p 365*

Versailles was created during the golden age of French royalty and, except under the Regency, it remained the seat of government and the political centre of France from 1682 to 1789. It owes its reputation to the outstanding royal residence consisting of the palace, its grounds and the Trianons.

The town was built as an annexe with a view to housing the numerous titled and untitled people who served the French court: dukes, ministers, craftsmen, civil servants etc. Owing to its former duties, the town has retained a certain austere charm. Versailles will delight all those interested in the Bourbons' penchant for splendour and the insurrectionary beginnings of the French Revolution.

The prestigious domain is now protected as one of UNESCO's World Heritage sites.

P. Viard /PIX

Louis XIII's Château – In the 17C the locality of Versailles was the seat of a medieval castle perched on a hillock. At the foot lay the village, surrounded by marshes and woodland abounding in game. Louis XIII used to come hunting here fairly often and in 1624 he bought part of the land and gave orders to build a small country residence. In 1631 the Archbishop of Paris Monseigneur Gondi granted him the lordship of Versailles, and he commissioned Philibert Le Roy to replace the manor with a small château built of brick, stone and slate.

The glorious task of taming nature – 1661 marked the year of Louis XIV's accession to the throne. The King hired the various artists, builders, designers and landscape architects who had produced Vaux-le-Vicomte and entrusted them with an even more challenging task. Louis was wary of settling in Paris following the Fronde uprisings and so searched for a site in the outskirts of the capital. He chose Versailles as he had spent many happy days there as a boy and, moreover, he was fond of hunting. It was by no means an ideal site; the mound was too narrow to allow Louis XIII's château to be enlarged. Although the surrounding land was swampy, and therefore unsuitable for growing ornamental plants, it did not yield enough water to supply the many fountains and canals that were an essential part of 17C gardens. The King ruled that nature be tamed and gave orders to divert the waters of nearby rivers, drain the land and bring in heavy loads of earth to consolidate the site.

In the early stages, **Louis Le Vau** built a stone construction around the small château in 1668; it was reminiscent of Italian architecture and was aptly named the "Envelope". André Le Nôtre designed the new gardens and created his celebrated perspectives. The first receptions were held at the new château in 1664.

A massive operation – In 1678 **Jules Hardouin-Mansart**, aged only 31, was appointed head architect, a position he kept until he died in 1708. From 1661 to 1683 **Charles Le Brun** supervised a team of accomplished painters, sculptors, carvers and interior decorators. **Le Nôtre** applied himself to the embellishment of the grounds. When designing the waterworks, he joined forces with the Francines, a family of Italian engineers. Louis XIV kept a close watch on the various works under way, except when he marched to war. He was a critical overseer who made numerous comments aimed at altering, rectifying and improving the plans of his new residence.

In 1684, two years after the King and his elegant courtiers had moved to Versailles, the *Journal de Dangeau* reported that a total of 22 000 labourers and 6 000 horses were at work on the different sites. It was necessary to build a hill to accommodate the entire length of the château (680m/2230ft). Whole forests were transplanted and the King's gardeners produced 150 000 new flowering plants every year. The orangery housed around 3 000 shrubs: orange and pomegranate trees, oleanders...

The problem of water supply was of great concern to Colbert, and later Louvois. The waters of Clagny Pond – located near the present Rive Droite railway station – proved insufficient and the builders were forced to divert the course of the Bièvre and drain the Saclay plateau. The Marly Machine conveyed the waters pumped from the river Seine but the diversion of the Eure *(see Maintenon)* was a fiasco.

It took fifty years to complete the structural work on the palace at Versailles, allowing for the interruptions and slack periods attributed to contemporary wars. It was only in 1710 that the last chapel was finished. By that time, Louis XIV had reached the age of 72.

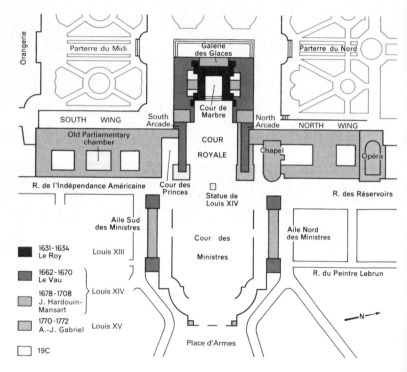

Life at Court – When the King and his entourage moved to Versailles, the palace and the adjacent outbuildings were required to lodge at least 3 000 people.

The Fronde movement had been a humiliating experience for the King, who had witnessed many intrigues involving men in high places. Consequently, his main concern was to keep the aristocracy with him at court, in an attempt to stifle opposition that might threaten the stability of the throne. The lavish entertainments suited his extravagant tastes and served to keep the nobility under his thumb. For the first time in French history, the royal suites in the palace were given fixed, permanent furnishings. Thanks to Colbert's efforts to encourage the production of luxury goods (tapestries, furniture, lace etc) on a national scale, the palace – which remained open to the public – offered a standing exhibition of arts and crafts in France.

Strict etiquette governed the visits that the French people would pay Versailles. The famous chronicler Saint-Simon described a day at court as a "clock-work ceremony" consisting of a series of banquets, audiences and entertainments. After 1684, the pious Mme de Maintenon put an end to these large-scale festivities; the court had to find other ways to overcome its boredom.

When Louis XIV died in 1715 his successor was still a young boy. The Regent Philippe d'Orléans administered the king's affairs from the Palais-Royal, his Paris residence. During this time, the court left Versailles and moved to the Tuileries.

In 1722 Louis XV, aged twelve, decided to settle at Versailles. In order that royal etiquette might not interfere with his private life, he gave orders to convert several of the private apartments. He dreamed of having the front of the palace remodelled, a task he entrusted to Jacques-Anges Gabriel. Unfortunately, no major alterations could be carried out owing to insufficient funds, but the Petit Trianon was built.

Louis XVI and Marie-Antoinette commissioned no further works. The Queen was perfectly happy to stay in the Petit Trianon; it was for her that the hamlet and the present grounds were designed in 1774. On 6 October 1789, the national insurrection forced the royal family to return to Paris. After that date, Versailles ceased to be a place of residence for the kings of France.

To the glory of France – After the storming of the Tuileries and the fall of the monarchy on 10 August 1792, most of the furniture was removed and auctioned. The major works of art – paintings, carpets, tapestries and a few items of furniture – were kept for the art museum which opened in the Louvre in August 1793. After the renovation work undertaken by Napoleon and Louis XVIII, Versailles was threatened once more; it was spared demolition by Louis-Philippe, who contributed a large part of his personal fortune to turn it into a museum of French history in 1837.

More recently, Versailles was restored following the First World War, thanks to the generosity of the Academy of Fine Arts and the handsome contributions made by a number of wealthy patrons, including the American JD Rockefeller.

Restoration – A major restoration campaign was launched in the early 1950s, permitting the renovation of the Royal Opera, the installation of central heating and electric lighting, and the completion of various refurnishing and maintenance projects. In 1980 the King's Bedroom and the Hall of Mirrors were both restored to their 18C splendour.

Phases of construction and other historical events

1631	Completion of Louis XIII's château.
1643	Death of Louis XIII. Five-year-old **Louis XIV accedes to the throne.** France is ruled by the Regent Anne of Austria and Cardinal Jules Mazarin.
1661	Louis XIV comes of age. After Mazarin's death, he decides to reign without the assistance of a Prime Minister.
1664	The first sumptuous receptions are held.
1666	The Versailles fountains play for the first time.
1668	Louis Le Vau starts work on the château.
1671	Charles Le Brun and his team of artists begin the interior decoration.
1674	Louis XIV's first major stay at Versailles.
1682	The court and government officials take up residence at the palace.
1683	Death of Marie-Thérèse of Austria. Louis XIV is secretly married to Mme de Maintenon.
1684	The Hall of Mirrors is completed.
1687	The Porcelain Trianon is replaced by the Marble Trianon.
1710	Birth of Louis XV, great-grandson of the Sun King.
1715	Death of Louis XIV. Five-year-old **Louis XV accedes to the throne.** France is ruled by the Regent Philippe d'Orléans. The court leaves Versailles.
1722	The court returns to Versailles.
1729	Birth of the Dauphin, later father to Louis XVI, Louis XVIII and Charles X.
1745	Mme de Pompadour becomes Louis XV's mistress. Her "reign" was to last fifteen years.
1754	Birth of Louis XVI.
1770	Marriage of Louis XVI to the Austrian Archduchess Marie-Antoinette.
1774	Death of Louis XV. **Louis XVI accedes to the throne.**
1783	The Treaty of Versailles is signed, granting independence to 13 American States.
1789	The States-General meet in the town. The royal family leaves Versailles.

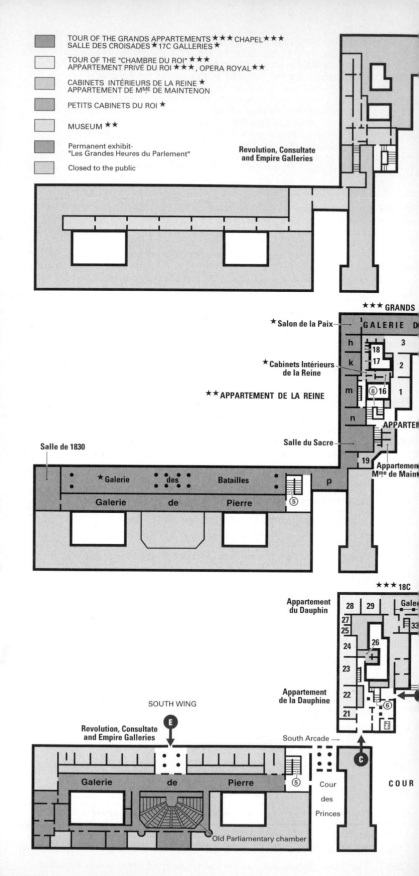

TOUR OF THE GRANDS APPARTEMENTS ★★★ CHAPEL ★★★
SALLE DES CROISADES ★ 17C GALLERIES ★

TOUR OF THE "CHAMBRE DU ROI" ★★★
APPARTEMENT PRIVÉ DU ROI ★★★, OPERA ROYAL ★★

CABINETS INTÉRIEURS DE LA REINE ★
APPARTEMENT DE Mme DE MAINTENON

PETITS CABINETS DU ROI ★

MUSEUM ★★

Permanent exhibit-
"Les Grandes Heures du Parlement"

Closed to the public

Revolution, Consultate
and Empire Galleries

★★★ GRANDS

★ Salon de la Paix

GALERIE D

h   18   3
k   17   2

★ Cabinets Intérieurs
de la Reine

m   ⑥ 16   1

★★ APPARTEMENT DE LA REINE

n   APPARTEM

Salle de 1830   Salle du Sacre

19   Appartemen
Mme de Main

★ Galerie   des   Batailles   p

Galerie   de   Pierre   ⑤

★★★ 18C

Appartement
du Dauphin   28   29   Gale

27
25   33
24   26
23

Appartement
de la Dauphine   22   ⑥
21   T

SOUTH WING   ⑦

Revolution, Consultate   E
and Empire Galleries

South Arcade →

Galerie   de   Pierre   ⑤   Cour   COUR

C

des

Princes

Old Parliamentary chamber

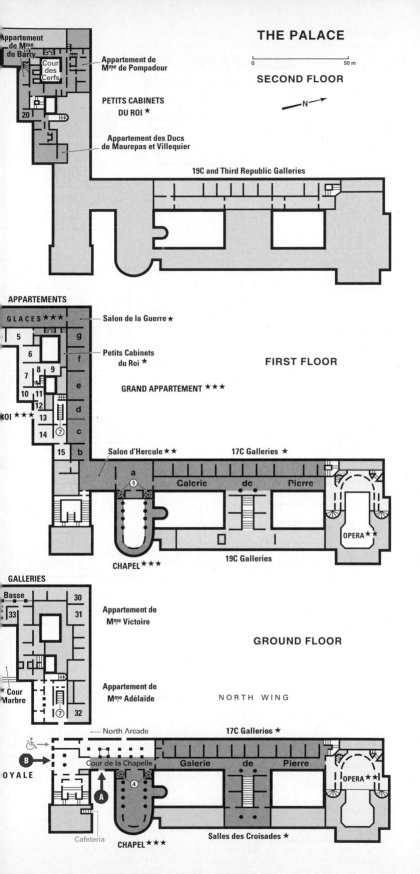

THE PALACE

0 ——————————— 50 m

SECOND FLOOR

→N→

Appartement de Mme du Barry

Appartement de Mme de Pompadour

Cour des Cerfs

20

PETITS CABINETS DU ROI ★

Appartement des Ducs de Maurepas et Villequier

19C and Third Republic Galleries

APPARTEMENTS

GLACES ★★★

Salon de la Guerre ★

5

g

6

f

Petits Cabinets du Roi ★

7   8 9

e

10   11

12

d

ROI ★★★   13   ⑦

c

14

15   b

GRAND APPARTEMENT ★★★

FIRST FLOOR

Salon d'Hercule ★★

a

①

17C Galleries ★

Galerie   de   Pierre

OPERA ★★

CHAPEL ★★★

19C Galleries

GALLERIES

Basse

30

33

31

Cour Marbre

⑦

32

Appartement de Mme Victoire

Appartement de Mme Adélaïde

GROUND FLOOR

NORTH WING

North Arcade

17C Galleries ★

B

OYALE

Cour de la Chapelle

④

A

Galerie   de   Pierre

OPERA ★★

Cafeteria

CHAPEL ★★★

Salles des Croisades ★

339

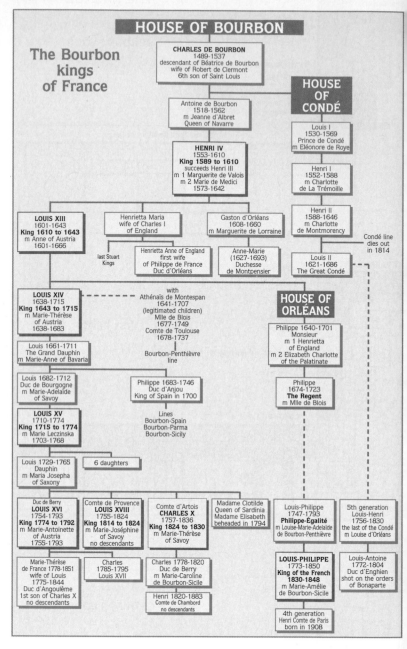

VERSAILLES-PALACE AND ITS SURROUNDINGS

★★Place d'Armes

This huge square was the junction of the three wide avenues leading to Paris, St-Cloud and Sceaux, separated by the **Écuries Royales**★, the stables built by Jules Hardouin-Mansart. Identical in size, the Grande and the Petite Écuries were so named for reasons of convenience: the former houses the **Musée des Carrosses** ⊙ where various carriages can be seen, while the latter was used for carriagehorses. Its ring was often the scene of impressive equestrian entertainments.

★★★Courtyards

The wrought-iron railings date from the reign of Louis XVIII. Beyond them stretches a series of three courtyards.
The forecourt or **Cour des Ministres** is flanked by two long wings linking the four pavilions in which the king's ministers were accommodated.

An equestrian statue of Louis XIV, commissioned by Louis-Philippe, stands in the middle of the drive. The **Cour royale** was separated from the outer courtyard by railings through which only persons of high rank (peers, princes of the blood, noblemen etc) might pass in carriages. The two wings lining this court were originally separate from the palace and used as outbuildings. They were joined to the main building and fronted by a set of colonnades under Louis XV and Louis XVIII. Beyond the North Arcade – leading through to the park – and the South Arcade stand three gilded gates marking the entrance to the State Apartments. On the left rises the Queen's Staircase. The original entrance lay to the right but it was blocked up after the Ambassadors' Staircase was destroyed in 1752.

The **Cour de Marbre**★★ (Marble Court) – paved with slabs of black and white marble – has been raised to its original level. It is surrounded by Louis XIII's old château, the façades of which were altered and greatly improved by Louis Le Vau and Jules Hardouin-Mansart: balustrades, busts, statues, vases etc. On the first floor of the central pavilion, the three arched windows belonging to the king's bedroom are fronted by a gilded balcony resting upon eight marble columns.

★★★Garden Façade

Walk under the North Arcade, skirt the main part of the palace and step back to get a good view.

The huge building occupies a total length of 680m/2230ft and yet its general appearance is not monotonous; the central body stands proud from the wings, and the length of the façade is articulated with intermittent rows of sculpted columns and pillars to break the rigidity of the horizontal lines. The flat roof, built in the Italian style, is concealed by a balustrade bearing ornamental trophies and vases. The statues of Apollo and Diana, surrounded by the Months of the Year, surmount the central body which housed the Royal Suite. Certain members of the royal family, including several of the King's children, stayed in the South Wing.

The terrace extending in front of the château commands an extensive view of the park and its many perspectives. It bears two **giant vases**★, one at each end; the one to the north was executed by Coysevox and symbolises War, while the south vase, attributed to Tuby, is a representation of Peace. They are appropriately placed outside the bay windows of the Salon de la Guerre and the Salon de la Paix respectively.

At the foot of the main building lies a row of four sculptures, the very first to be cast by the Keller brothers who drew inspiration from a classical model: Bacchus, Apollo, Antinoüs and Silenus.

The terrace offers a general view of the grounds and their distinctive features *(description below)*: in the foreground the Water Gardens *(Parterres d'Eau)*, with a sweeping perspective as far as the Grand Canal: on the left the South Parterre *(Parterre du Midi)*; on the right the North Parterre *(Parterre du Nord)* and groves *(Bosquets du Nord)*, cut across by another canal leading to the Neptune Basin.

Return to the cour de Marbre through the South Arcade in the south wing.

TOUR OF THE GRANDS APPARTEMENTS

The visitors' entrance Entrance (**A**) leads through to a vestibule which houses the ticket office. From there, go to the Salles des Croisades.

★Salles des Croisades

The five rooms, decorated in a neo-Gothic style, illustrate events which took place during the crusades and contain a collection of paintings commissioned by Louis-Philippe, including a copy of *The Crusaders Enter Constantinople* by Delacroix (the original is in the Louvre), *The Defence of Rhodes* by the Belgian painter G Wappers and the colourful *Capitulation of Ptolemais* by MJ Blondel. the emblems of the families who took part in the crusades decorate the pillars, coffered ceilings and part of the walls.

17C Galleries

These small rooms – occupying the greater part of the north wing – feature a charming selection of paintings and portraits, also busts and console tables.

Ground Floor – The vestibule by the chapel leads to this suite of eleven rooms. The first six were once occupied by the duc de Maine, the son of Louis XIV and Mme de Montespan, while the last four housed the apartments of the Princes of Bourbon-Conti.

The series of portraits includes Henri IV, who enjoyed visiting the site of Versailles, and Louis XIII, the founder of the original château. Works by Vouet, Philippe de Champaigne, Deruet and Le Brun tell of the men and the events that marked French history between Louis XIII's reign and the early days of Louis XIV's. The room dedi-

Versailles, garden façade

cated to Port-Royal features several portraits by Philippe de Champaigne and gouaches attributed to Magdeleine de Boullongne. The rare collection of paintings in the Versailles room illustrates the various stages of construction of the palace.

First Floor – Portraits of the royal family, Mme de Maintenon, Louis XIV's legitimised children and the celebrated figures of the King's reign, painted by Le Brun, Mignard Van der Meulen, Coypel, Rigaud Largillière etc, bring these rooms to life. Note the set of portraits of famous men (Colbert, Racine, Molière, La Fontaine, Le Nôtre and Couperin) and the vast battle scenes by Van der Meulen, characterised by attention to detail and a true love of nature.

The galleries offer a lovely view of the gardens.

★★★Chapel

Dedicated to St Louis (Louis IX), the chapel at Versailles is an elegant display of stonework decorated in white and gold tones. This masterpiece is the work of Mansart and was completed by his brother-in-law Robert de Cotte in 1710. The pillars and arches bear exquisite bas-reliefs by amongst others Van Clève, Le Lorrain, Coustou.

As the usual place for an organ is occupied by the royal gallery it stands instead at the east end in the gallery, a splendid piece of craftsmanship by Clicquot, enhanced by fine carvings based on studies by Robert de Cotte.

The marble altar is attributed to Van Clève. The altar front features a low relief in gilded bronze representing the *Pietà*; it is the work of Vassé.

The painting in the apse is by La Fosse and depicts the Resurrection.

While the members of the royal family were seated in the gallery, the courtiers stood in the nave.

★★Salon d'Hercule

This drawing room stands on the site formerly occupied by the fourth and penultimate chapel of the original château. Construction of the room was started in 1712, the year in which the St Louis Chapel was inaugurated; the decoration was completed by Robert de Cotte in 1736, during the reign of Louis XV.

The room boasts two splendid compositions by Veronese. **Christ at the House of Simon the Pharisee**★ was a present to Louis XIV from the Venetian Republic. The room was in fact designed to house this huge painting, which has been returned to its precious gilt frame. The second work *Eliezer and Rebecca* hangs above the marble mantelpiece which is richly adorned with gilded bronze.

The ceiling – representing Hercules entering the Kingdom of the Gods – was painted by François Lemoyne, who spent three years on the 315m²/3 390sq ft fresco. His work met with widespread acclaim, but the following year the artist suffered a nervous breakdown and committed suicide (1737).

★★★Le Grand Appartement

In former times, the apartment was approached from the Royal Court by means of the Ambassadors' Staircase (destroyed in 1752).

It provides a splendid example of early Louis XIV decoration. Note the use of noble materials such as multicoloured marble, bronze and copper, chased and gilded in the Italian Baroque style. Impressive rock crystal chandeliers hang from the ceiling and candelabra adorn the pedestal tables.

The suite of six salons was sparsely furnished with a few stools, folding chairs pedestal and console tables. The Grand Appartement – running from the Salon d'Hercule, dedicated to a man endowed with divine powers, to the Salon d'Apollon, built in honour of the son of Jupiter and Latona – symbolised the solar myth to which Louis XIV claimed to belong. The six rooms were all built by Le Vau in 1668 and decorated by Le Brun. The rooms are named after the subjects painted on the ceiling frescoes.

Three times a week, between 6 and 10pm on Mondays, Wednesdays and Thursdays, the king held court in the Grand Appartement. The ceremony was enhanced by dancing and gaming.

Salon de l'Abondance (b) – At the time of Louis XIV, on the days when the king held court, this reception room contained three buffets: one for hot drinks, two for cold drinks such as wine, eaux-de-vie, sorbets and fruit juice. The walls are hung with the winter furnishings, made of embossed velvet in deep emerald tones. Admire the four portraits of the royal family, painted by Rigaud and Van Loo: the Grand Dauphin, Philippe V, the Duke of Burgundy and Louis XV.

The next two rooms were originally vestibules leading to the Ambassadors' Staircase. The magnificent walls lined with marble are in keeping with the ornate decoration of the former main staircase.

Grands Appartements (State Apartments) ⊘

These consist of the various reception rooms – the Salon d'Hercule and a suite of six rooms known as the Grand Appartement – together with the famous Hall of Mirrors *(Galerie des Glaces)* and the living quarters where the king and queen would appear in public.

While visiting the palace, it is helpful to remember a few facts concerning the layout of great châteaux of Classical and Baroque inspiration.

Generally speaking, French rulers would spend their day between the ornate reception rooms of the State Apartments – their official, semi-public quarters – and the private apartments which afforded a certain amount of privacy. In the 18C, Louis XV and later Louis XVI enjoyed a greater degree of intimacy in the Petits Appartements.

A standard example of State Apartments – The two suites belonging to the king and the queen are placed symmetrically on either side of the central pavilion. Each suite consisted of at least one guard room, several antechambers, the bedroom, the grand cabinet and a number of private drawing rooms (it was through these that the two royal suites communicated).

At Versailles, this symmetrical disposition was applied only between 1673 and 1682. When Marie-Thérèse died in 1683, there was no question of Mme de Maintenon occupying the apartments of the former queen. Louis XIV moved into new quarters giving onto the Marble Court. His former suite had just been transformed, at great cost, into a series of reception rooms.

Summer and winter furnishings – In the living quarters of the palace, the hangings were changed twice a year, at the beginning of summer and before the onset of winter. Thus the summer furnishings (silk) would alternate with the winter furnishings (velvet).

The fabric-dressed walls were then hung with paintings inspired by religious themes, by artists of the Italian School: Poussin, Veronese, Titian etc.

Salon de Vénus (c) – As in the following, the ceiling reception rooms, the ceiling was painted by Houasse. It features decorated panels framed by heavy gilt stucco.

Salon de Diane (d) – This used to be the billiard room under Louis XIV. Observe the **bust of Louis XIV** by Bernini (1665), a remarkable piece of Baroque workmanship. The room displays several paintings by De Lafosse and Blanchard.

Salon de Mars (e) – The lavish decoration (wall hangings) is a reminder that this room once belonged to the royal suite (guard room). Louis XIV subsequently used it for dances, games and concerts. The two galleries which housed the musicians were placed on either side of the fireplace. They were dismantled in 1750. The 18C paintings include *Darius' Tent* by Le Brun and *The Pilgrims on the Road to Emmaüs* after Veronese.

The side walls bear Rigaud's portrait of Louis XV and a painting of Marie Leczinska by Van Loo. The martial scenes on the ceiling are attributed to Audran, Jouvenet and Houasse. One of the Sun King's favourite paintings hangs above the fireplace: Domenichino's *King David*, in which he is portrayed playing the harp. It was originally displayed in the king's bedchamber.

Salon de Mercure (f) – A fire was lit in this former antechamber on the evenings when the king held court. It was here that Louis XIV lay in state for one week after his death in 1715. Seventy-two ecclesiastics took turns to watch over him, ensuring that four Masses could be said at the same time between 5am and midday. The ceiling was decorated by JB de Champaigne.

Salon d'Apollon (Throne room) (g) – The former throne room. The throne was placed on a central platform covered by a large canopy. The three hooks to which the canopy was attached still remain.

Louis XIV received ambassadors in this chamber. When he held court, it was used for dances and concerts. The ceiling sports a fresco by De Lafosse: *Apollo in a Sun Chariot*.

This room marks the end of the Grand Appartement. Set at a perpendicular angle, the Hall of Mirrors and the adjacent rooms dedicated to war and peace occupy the entire length of the main front giving onto the palace gardens.

*Salon de la Guerre (War Salon)

This is a corner room joining the Hall of Mirrors and the Grand Appartement; it features a huge oval low relief sculpture by Coysevox, representing the king defeating his enemies.

VISITING TIPS

Versailles is one of the most popular tourist attractions in France. This means that a minimum amount of organisation is required in order to see it comfortably. See the chapter *Admission times and charges* for details of opening times and entrance fees.

Visiting programmes

For visitors with little time to spare, it is advisable to follow one of the following programmes:

One-day visit: In the **morning**, visit the exterior and the Appartements du Roi et du Dauphin.
In the **afternoon**, have a stroll in the gardens, visit the Petit and Grand Trianons and then tour the Grands Appartements (they are quieter in the afternoon).

Two-day visit: Round off the first day's tour with the exhibition "Les Grandes Heures du Parlement". Ensure that you miss nothing out in the Trianon by taking an additional guided tour *(ask for information on the day of your visit, Entrance D)* or take a stroll in the park. Details of the tourist train and other activities (boat or cycle hire) are given in the *Admission times and charges* chapter.

Access for visitors

The entrances, which are marked on the plan, vary according to the areas you wish to visit:
Entrance A: **Grands appartements** ⊘ (individual visitors)
Entrance B: Grands appartements (parties)
Entrance C: **Appartements du Roi et du Dauphin** ⊘ (individual visitors with audio-guiding facilities)
Entrance D: **Guided tours** ⊘ (individual visitors, book on day of visit)
Handicapped visitors enter beside Entrance B.
Entrance to the permanent exhibition entitled **"Les Grandes Heures du Parlement"** ⊘ is via the left wing of the château *(Entrance E)*.

***Galerie des Glaces (Hall of Mirrors)

The Hall of Mirrors was completed by Mansart in 1687. It covered a short-lived terrace (1668-78) that Le Vau had built along the side overlooking the gardens. Together with the Salon de la Guerre and Salon de la Paix, it is the most brilliant achievement by Le Brun and his team of artists. The hall is 75m/246ft long, 10m/33ft wide and 12m/40ft high. The 17 large windows are echoed by 17 mirrors on the wall opposite. These are made up of 578 pieces of the largest size possible at the time. This hall was designed to catch the golden rays of sunset. The ceiling fresco – painted by Le Brun in amber, flame-coloured tones – pays tribute to the early reign of Louis XIV (from 1661 to 1678, up to the Treaty of Nijmegen).
The capitals of the pilasters bear an unusual ornamental feature; made of gilded bronze, they represent the "French order", which combines antique motifs with fleurs-de-lis and stylised cocks (the emblem of French patriotism).
In 1980 the Hall of Mirrors was restored to its former glory. With its crystal chandeliers and new set of candelabra – cast after the six surviving originals – it presents the same dazzling appearance as in 1770 when Marie-Antoinette was married to the Dauphin, the future King Louis XVI.
The Hall of Mirrors was used for court receptions, formal ceremonies and diplomatic encounters. On these occasions, the throne was placed under the arch leading into the Salon de la Paix. It is easier to picture the hall during court festivities, when it was thronged with elegant visitors in formal attire, brightly lit by the thousands of flickering candles reflected in the mirrors. The tubs bearing the orange trees, as well as the chandeliers and other furnishings, were made of solid silver under Louis XIV. For a period of ten years, part of the country's monetary reserves was thus shaped into works of art.
It was here that the German Empire was proclaimed on 18 January 1871, and that the Treaty of Versailles was signed on 28 June 1919.
The central windows offer a splendid **view***** of the Grand Perspective.

★Salon de la paix (Peace Salon)

Placed at the southern end of the Hall of Mirrors, this chamber counterbalances the Salon de la Guerre. Originally designed as an extension of the great gallery, it was made into an annexe of the Queen's Suite towards the end of Louis XIV's reign; it communicated with the Hall of Mirrors by means of a movable partition. Above the mantelpiece hangs *Louis XV Bringing Peace to Europe*, a painting by François Lemoyne.

★★Appartement de la Reine (Queen's Suite)

This suite was created for Louis XIV's wife Marie-Thérèse, who died here in 1683.

Chambre de la reine (h) – In 1975, after a restoration programme lasting 30 years, this room regained its summer furnishings of 1787. Originally designed for Maria-Theresa, the bedchamber was later occupied by the wife of the Grand Dauphin, Louis XIV's son; by the duchesse de Bourgogne, wife of the Sun King's grandson, who gave birth to Louis XV here; by Marie Leszczynska, wife of Louis XV (for 43 years); and by Louis XVI's wife Marie-Antoinette. Nineteen children belonging to French royalty – among them Louis XV and Philippe V of Spain – were born in this bedroom.

A long-standing tradition ruled that the delivery of royal infants should be made public. Even the proud Marie-Antoinette had to comply with the French custom, surrounded by a crowd of curious onlookers.

The ornamental motifs on the wainscot and the ceiling were designed and made for Marie Leszczynska by the Gabriels, while the fireplace, imposing jewel chest, sphinx-shaped andirons, fire screen and bedspread were designed for Marie-Antoinette.

Note the magnificent silk hangings and furnishings decorated with flowers, ribbons and peacock's tails, which were rewoven to the original pattern in Lyon.

Salon des Nobles de la Reine (k) – The official presentations to the Queen took place in this former antechamber. It was also here that the queens and *dauphines* of France used to lie in state prior to the burial ceremony. The original fresco on the ceiling, attributed to Michel Corneille, has been preserved. The rest of the decoration was considered staid and old-fashioned by Marie-Antoinette, who had it

Marie-Antoinette and her Children by Vigée-Lebrun

entirely refurbished by the architect Richard Mique (1785). Furnished with commodes and corner cupboards by Riesener and embellished with magnificent green silk hangings, the salon looks very much as it would have done on the eve of the French Revolution in 1789.

Antichambre du Grand Couvert (**m**) – This chamber was used as a guard room under Marie-Theresa. It was here that Louis XV and Marie Leszczynska – and later Louis XVI and Marie-Antoinette – would dine in full view of the public.
A family portrait of Marie-Antoinette and her children (1787) by Mme Vigée-Lebrun shows, from left to right, Mme Royale, the Duke of Normandy – who became Louis XVII – and the Dauphin, who died in 1789. He is portrayed pointing to an empty cradle which symbolises the premature death of his sister "Mme Sophie".

Salle des Gardes de la Reine (**n**) – The decoration was the work of Le Brun and N Coypel. It was moved from its original setting – the Salon de Jupiter – when the Hall of Mirrors was completed in 1687; the Salon de Jupiter was subsequently renamed the Salon de la Guerre. On 6 October 1789, several of the queen's guards were stabbed to death by a group of dedicated revolutionaries. The Louis XIV decor – featuring sumptuous marble-lined walls – has been beautifully preserved.

Salle du sacre (Coronation Room)

This room was initially used as a chapel between 1676 and 1682. The Parlement de Paris used to hold its sessions in this former guard room. It was altered by Louis-Philippe in order to accommodate several huge paintings depicting the Emperor's coronation. David's second *Coronation of Napoleon* – painted between 1808 and 1822 – lies to the left of the entrance. The original is exhibited in the Louvre Museum (Salle Mollien). On the opposite wall hang David's *Distribution of Eagles on the Champ de Mars* and a painting by Gros representing *Murat at the Battle of Aboukir* (1806).

Salle de 1792 (**p**)   This large, unfurnished room lies at the junction of the south wing and the main central pavilion. The walls are hung with portraits of soldiers, paintings of famous battles and war scenes. Cogniet's work *The Paris National Guard* shows Louis-Philippe proudly sporting his Lieutenant-General's uniform.

*Galerie des batailles

Created in 1836 on the site of the princes' suite in the south wing, the Galerie des Batailles caused quite a stir because of its huge dimensions: 120m/394ft by 13m/43ft. It was designed to house the 33 paintings of France's major victories under the *Ancien Régime*, the Empire and the Republic, from Tolbiac *(first on the left when entering)* to Wagram *(first on the right)* by Horace Vernet, Louis-Philippe's favourite painter (who also painted Iéna, Fontenoy, Bouvines and Friedland), and including works by Eugène Delacroix (Taillebourg) and Baron Gérard (Austerlitz).

Salle de 1830

Commissioned by Louis-Philippe, this room is devoted to the last king of France who was known as the "citizen-king".
Take the Princes' Staircase ⑤ down to the Cour des Princes.

***TOUR OF THE "CHAMBRE DU ROI"
Audio-guided tour, Entrance C.

***Appartement du roi ⊘ (suite of Louis XIV)

The king's quarters are arranged around the Cour de Marbre. They were designed by Jules Hardouin-Mansart and set up in Louis XIII's château between 1682 and 1701. The style shows a marked change in the Louis XIV period. The ceilings are no longer coffered but painted white, the marble tiling has been replaced by white and gold panelling, and large mirrors adorn the stately fireplaces.

Escalier de la Reine (**6**) – Towards the end of the *Ancien Régime*, the Queen's Staircase was the official entrance to the royal apartments. The decoration of the staircase is extremely ornate; from the top landing, admire the elegant display of multi-coloured marble designed by Le Brun. The huge *trompe l'œil* painting is jointly attributed to Meusnier, Poerson and Belin de Fontenay.
The guard room (**1**) and a first antechamber (**2**) lead to the Salon de l'Œil-de-Bœuf.

Salon de l'Œil-de-Bœuf (second antechamber) (**3**) – The Bulls'-Eye Chamber was originally two rooms: the king's bedchamber between 1684 and 1701 – the part nearest to the two windows giving onto the Cour de Marbre – and a small study.

Versailles – Louis XIV's bedroom

The two were united under the supervision of Mansart and Robert de Cotte. Lightness and elegance are the principal characteristics of this charming drawing room, which contrasts sharply with the earlier achievements of Louis' reign. Level with the famous bull's-eye – echoed by a mirror on the opposite wall – runs a frieze depicting children at play. Note Coysevox' bust of Louis XIV.

The paintings by Veronese and Bassano have been replaced by a number of royal portraits, including an allegorical rendering of Louis XIV's family by Nocret.

It was in this antechamber that the courtiers assembled before witnessing the rising and retiring ceremonies of the king.

Chambre du Roi (4) – This became Louis XIV's state bedroom in 1701.

At the centre of the palace, this bedroom, which gave onto the Cour de Marbre, looks out in the direction of the rising sun. Louis XIV, suffering from a gangrenous knee, died here on 1 September 1715.

The ritual rising and retiring ceremonies took place in this room from 1701 to 1789. Daytime visitors were requested to make a small bow when passing in front of the bed, which symbolised the divine right of the monarchy.

The King's bedroom is hung with its summer furnishings of 1723 – Louis XV's second year at the palace – and its decor has been scrupulously reconstructed. Beyond the beautifully-restored gilded balustrade lies a raised four-poster bed, complete with canopy and curtains. The gold and silver embroidered brocade used for the bed and wall hangings, upholstery and door coverings has been entirely rewoven. Six religious works – including Valentin de Boulogne's *Four Evangelists* – lie level with the attica. Above the doors hang *St Madeleine* by Domenichino, *John the Baptist* by Caracciolo and several portraits by Van Dyck.

Grand Cabinet du Roi (5) – Like the Salon de l'Œil-de-Bœuf, it originally consisted of two rooms: the Cabinet des Termes and the Cabinet du Conseil. The decoration of the present room – created under Louis XV – was entrusted to Gabriel. The mirrors dating from Louis XIV's reign were replaced with wainscoting by Rousseau, who produced a splendid Rococo interior.

Over a period of one hundred years, many grave decisions affecting the destiny of France were taken in this council chamber, including that of France's involvement in the American War of Independence in 1775.

As you go by, admire the decoration of Louis XV's bedroom (open door on the right) before walking across the Hall of Mirrors and back to the Salon de l'Œil-de-Bœuf.

Appartement du Dauphin ⊘

Go down a small staircase leading to the Dauphin's apartments.

The entrance was through the Salle des Gardes (on the right), which is now decorated with splendid Gobelins tapestries

The **Dauphin's Bedchamber (29)**, occupied by Louis XVI's son, has retained its original 1747 décor: wardrobe with lacquered panels (Bernard Van Rysenburgh – BVRB), commode by Boudin and an 18C embroidered canopied bed. The fireplace is among the finest in the palace.

The **Grand Corner Cabinet** (**28**) houses portraits of Mesdames Adélaïde, Louise, Sophie and Victoire by Nattier, as well as some beautiful pieces of furniture by Jacob, taken from Louis XVI's gaming room at St-Cloud.

The **library** (**27**) boasts magnificent wooden panelling in deep amber tones, enhanced by turquoise relief work. Admire Vernet's delicate seascapes above the doors. This room leads to the Dauphine's apartments which are visited backwards.

Appartement de la Dauphine

The **Cabinet Intérieur** (**25**) features 1748 Vernis Martin wainscoting as in the Dauphin's library. Note Gaudreaux' commode and a writing desk by BVRB. The rooms (**26**) in the Dauphine's apartments that are included in the tour of the Queen's apartments were refurbished under Louis XVIII for the Duchesse d'Angoulême, the daughter of Louis XVI: couch formerly belonging to the Comtesse de Provence, antechamber, study-library and servant's quarters.

The **Dauphine's Bedroom** (**24**) contains a Polish-style bed and a magnificent set of six armchairs by Heurtaut. Note Nattier's two portraits of Mme Adélaïde and Mme Henriette, portrayed respectively as Flora and Diana.

The **Dauphine's Grand Cabinet** (**23**) evokes the marriage of Marie Leszczynska to Louis XV. It also presents Lemaire's sculpted barometer, offered on the occasion of Marie-Antoinette's marriage to the Dauphin, and several corner cupboards by Bernard Van Risenburgh (BVRB).

The fireplace in the **Second Antechamber** (**22**), adorned with a bust of the Regent, was taken from the Queen's Bedroom at the time of Marie Leszczynska. Savonnerie tapestry.

The **First Antechamber** (**21**) houses a number of pictures representing the rulers who succeeded the Sun King: portrait of the five-year-old Louis XV by Alexis Belle (1723), *Cavalcade of the King (Louis XV) After His Coronation on 22 October 1722* by Pierre-Denis Martin.

★★★APPARTEMENT PRIVÉ DU ROI (Suite of Louis XV) *guided tour*

Appartement intérieur du Roi

This suite of rooms, with its superb wainscoting by Gabriel, provides a delightful feast for the eyes. The fine Rococo carvings are the work of Verberckt.

Chambre à coucher (**6**) – The absence of furniture makes it difficult to picture this room in its original state. Owing to the constraints of court etiquette, Louis XV (after 1738) and then Louis XVI (up to the end of the *Ancien Régime*) daily had to leave this room and slip away to the State bedroom, where they "performed" the rising and retiring ceremonies.
It was here that Louis XV died of smallpox on 10 May 1774.
The original paintings above the doors were taken down and replaced by portraits of the three daughters of Louis XV.

Cabinet de la Pendule (**7**) – This room was named after the famous **astronomical clock**★★★ by Passemant and Dauthiau, with bronze embellishments by Caffiéri, which was brought to the palace in January 1754; a copper line running across the floor indicates the Versailles meridian.
In the centre of the room stands the equestrian statue of Louis XV by Vassé. It is a replica of Bouchardon's sculpture which initially adorned the Place Louis XV – now called Place de la Concorde – in Paris and which was destroyed in 1792.

Antichambre des Chiens (**8**) – A charming passageway off the king's private staircase (known as *degré du Roi*). The decoration features Louis XIV panelling, in sharp contrast with the adjoining rooms.

Salle à manger dite des Retours de chasse (**9**) – Between 1750 and 1769 hunts were organised every other day in the forests surrounding Versailles. Louis XV and a few privileged fellow hunters would come here to sup after their exertions.

Cabinet intérieur du Roi (**10**) – This masterpiece of 18C French ornamental art was commissioned by Louis XV. Gabriel and the accomplished cabinet-maker Verberckt were responsible for the stunning Rococo decor.
The celebrated **roll-top desk**★★★ by Oeben and Riesener (1769) was among the few prestigious works of art to be spared in 1792.
The medal cabinet attributed to the cabinet-maker Gaudreaux (1739) is heavily decorated with gilded bronze: it bears the 1785 candelabra commemorating the role played by France in the American War of Independence, flanked by two Sèvres

The King's desk

vases (bronzes by Thomire). Two corner cupboards made by Joubert in 1755 to house Louis XV's ever-increasing collections, were added subsequently, as was a set of chairs attributed to Foliot (1774).

The room was originally private but under Louis XVI it took on a semi-official character. In 1785 it was the scene of a formal encounter attended by Marie-Antoinette, at which the King informed Cardinal de Rohan that he would shortly be arrested for his involvement in the Diamond Necklace Affair.

The Corner Room leads through to the study (**11**) where Louis XV and Louis XVI kept all confidential documents relating to state affairs, and where they granted private audiences.

Cabinet de Madame Adélaïde (**12**) – This was one of the first "new rooms" laid out at the instigation of Louis XV. It overlooks the Royal Court and was designed by Louis XV for his favourite daughter Madame Adélaïde (1752). The ornate decoration features delightful Rococo wainscoting and gilded panelling embellished with musical instruments, as well as fishing and floral motifs: the room was used as a music room by the king's daughter. It is believed that the young Mozart performed on the harpsichord before the royal family in this very room, during the winter of 1763-64. Louis XVI later made the room his "jewel cabinet". Note the extraordinary medal cabinet attributed to Bennemann; each drawer is decorated with melted wax, delicately blended with feathers and butterfly wings and carefully poured onto thin glass plates.

Bibliothèque de Louis XVI (**13**) – Designed by the ageing Gabriel and executed by the wood carver Antoine Rousseau, this extremely refined library is a perfect example of the Louis XVI style (1774). The austere appearance of the bookcases, in which the door panels are concealed by a set of false decorative backs, is countered by the gay Chinese motifs on the upholstery and the curtains. Next to Riesener's flat-top desk stands the vast mahogany table where the King spent many enjoyable hours correcting geographical maps.

Salon des Porcelaines (**14**) – This room was used as the Hunters' Dining Hall under Louis XV, and from 1769 to 1789 under Louis XVI. It houses numerous exhibits of Sèvres porcelain, painted after drawings by Oudry. The whole collection was commissioned by Louis XVI.

Salon des Jeux de Louis XVI (**15**) – From the doorway admire the full effect of this perfect vignette of 18C furniture and ornamental art: corner cupboards by Riesener (1774), set of chairs by Boulard, curtains and upholstery in a rich crimson and gold brocade.

Walk down the Louis-Philippe staircase ⑦ and leave by the North Arcade (a public passageway leading through to the park). The room on the ground floor houses a miniature replica of the Ambassador's Staircase (Escalier des Ambassadeurs). Ask to view the model.

★★Opéra Royal

Gabriel started work on the opera house in 1768 and completed it in time for the wedding ceremony of Marie-Antoinette and the future King Louis XVI in 1770.

It was the first oval-shaped opera house in France and although it was built during the reign of Louis XV, its decoration was later to be termed Louis XVI. Pajou's work, inspired by the classical models of Antiquity, remains surprisingly modern-looking. The court engineer Arnoult designed the sophisticated machinery required for the new opera house. For banquets and formal receptions, the floor of the stalls and of the circle could be raised level with the stage. This auditorium – its interior decoration made entirely of wood – enjoys excellent acoustics and can seat 700. The seating capacity could virtually be doubled by means of additional galleries set up on the stage.

In the middle of the circle lies the royal box, fronted by a mobile grid and surmounted by an elegant alcove. A number of other boxes, also enclosed by grilles, may be seen up above in the flies.

The low-reliefs adorning the boxes were executed by Pajou. They represent the Gods of Mount Olympus (dress circle), groups of children and the signs of the Zodiac (upper circle).

Although initially reserved for members of the court, the opera house at Versailles was later used for lavish receptions organised on the occasion of official visits. A number of foreign rulers were received at the palace, including the King of Sweden (1784), Marie-Antoinette's brother the Emperor Joseph II (1777 and 1781) and Queen Victoria (1855). The sessions of the National Assembly were held in the Royal Opera between 1871 and 1875. It was here that the Wallon Amendment was voted on 30 January 1875, laying the foundation stone of the Third Republic. The latest restoration ended in 1957 and was marked by an official reception in honour of Queen Elizabeth II and Prince Philip.

LES GRANDES HEURES DU PARLEMENT

Self-guided tour, Entrance E

Versailles is a magnificent reminder of life during the days of the monarchy; it has also been the cradle of French democracy since 1789. Even now, the semicircular chamber in the south wing accommodates members of parliament when changes are made to the Constitution. A permanent exhibition illustrates the history of French democracy and the parliamentary systems in various countries throughout the world. An audio-visual show (20min) sums up the main debates which marked France's national and international politics.

★CABINETS INTÉRIEURS DE LA REINE (Queen's Private Suite)

These somewhat cramped apartments giving onto two inner courtyards were used as a daytime retreat by the queens of France. Unlike the king, the queen was not allowed to live anywhere but in her State Apartment. The 18C decoration and layout were designed by Marie-Antoinette, who gave the suite a delicate, feminine touch.

Cabinet doré (16) – The panelling by the Rousseau brothers marks the revival of Antique motifs: frieze with rosettes, sphinx, trivets, small censers... A lovely chandelier features among the magnificent bronze works. The commode was made by Riesener. Naderman's harp reminds visitors that the Queen was an enthusiastic musician in her spare time; she would often play with Grétry, Gluck or even his rival Piccinni. It was in this cabinet that Mme Vigée-Lebrun worked on her portrait of Marie-Antoinette.

Bibliothèque (17) – Note the drawer handles in the shape of a two-headed eagle, the emblem of the House of Hapsburg.

Méridienne (18) – This little octagonal boudoir was used for resting by Marie-Antoinette. It was designed in 1781 by the Queen's architect Mique in honour of the birth of the first Dauphin. The decoration evokes romance and the period leading up to the Dauphin's birth: lilies, hearts pierced with arrows and the famous dolphin.

The boudoir – embellished with blue silk hangings – is furnished with two armchairs by Georges Jacob and the original day couch.

Two of the many prestigious works of art given to the Queen are exhibited here: a clock presented by the City of Paris and a table on which the top is made of petrified wood (a present from one of Marie-Antoinette's sisters).

The second floor houses Marie-Antoinette's Apartment (open by prior arrangement).

APPARTEMENT DE Madame de MAINTENON
(Open only for temporary exhibitions)

This suite was located away from the throngs of courtiers but next to the King's apartments, reflecting a situation enforced by the king during the last 32 years of his reign, with a view to establishing an atmosphere of tact and mutual respect. The Grand Cabinet (**19**) was a private drawing room decorated with red hangings where Mme de Maintenon entertained members of the royal family – her favourite was the Duchess of Burgundy – and where Racine recited his famous plays *Esther* and *Athalie*.

★PETITS CABINETS DU ROI (King's Private Apartments)

A tour of these apartments is recommended to visitors who are already acquainted with Versailles and who have a particular interest in 18C decorative art.
Louis XV did not share the taste for publicity which had been such a dominant trait of the Sun King's personality. Consequently he created a suite of private apartments to which he could retire and receive his mistresses, close friends and relatives. Some of the rooms overlooked the inner courts, others were located in the attics. They were approached by a series of narrow passages and staircases. In the privacy of these rooms the King would read, study, carve ivory and wooden pieces or eat on the tiny roof-top terrace, surrounded by tubs of flowers and several delightful aviaries. The decoration of these apartments was renewed at regular intervals – as were their occupants. Four of the rooms housed Mme de Pompadour's first suite from 1745 to 1750. Louis XVI used the rooms giving onto the Cour des Cerfs when he wished to study or indulge in one of his favourite pastimes.

Appartement de Madame de Pompadour – *2nd floor. (Closed).* This was the first suite occupied by Louis XV's mistress between 1745 and 1750. The Grand Cabinet features splendid carved woodwork by Verberckt.

Appartement de Madame du Barry – *2nd floor.* The wooden panelling has been meticulously restored to its original colours. The suite looks out onto the Cour des cerfs and the Cour de Marbre. It consists of a bathroom, a bedroom, a library and a corner drawing room (**20**) which was one of Louis XV's favourite haunts; he would enjoy sitting here and gazing out at the town of Versailles nestling among wooded slopes.

Appartements des ducs de Maurepas et Villequier – *2nd floor.* These apartments were occupied by two ministers of Louis XVI. The decoration appears rather austere when compared to that of the royal suites. Most of the furniture was donated by the Duke and Duchess of Windsor.

★★MUSEUM

The museum houses several thousand paintings and sculptures which present French history from the 17C to the 19C.

17C Galleries *see the Tour of the Grands Appartements*

★★★18C Galleries

Appartements du Dauphin et de la Dauphine – *See the Tour de la Chambre du Roi.*

Galerie basse – Divided into apartements under Louis XVI and partly restored under Louis-Philippe, the gallery now stands as it did under Louis XIV. From 1782 to 1789 the rooms in this gallery were used by Marie-Antoinette and her children.

Appartement de Madame Victoire – The Sun King's former bathroom and its two marble piscinae underwent several alterations before being used as the antechamber to this suite, occupied by the fourth daughter of Louis XV.
The **Grand Cabinet** (**30**) is an exquisite corner room with a delightful carved cornice and panelling by Verberckt. It has retained its original fireplace.
Mme Victoire's former bedroom (**31**) has been furnished with some outstanding pieces, set off by the newly-restored summer hangings.

Appartement de Madame Adélaïde – These rooms housed the second suite of Mme de Pompadour, who died here in 1764. Five years later, Mme Adélaïde moved into the suite, which consisted of a private cabinet, a bedroom and a grand cabinet. The **Salle des Hocquetons** (**32**) was an annexe adjoining the former Ambassadors' Staircase, destroyed in 1752. The stately proportions of this room, its *trompe l'œil* fresco and its splendid marble paving give an idea of how magnificent the flight of stairs once looked. Note the huge **clock**★ by Claude Siméon Passement with bronze ornamentation by Caffiéri; it dates from 1754 and illustrates the creation of the world. The last rooms, overlooking the Cour de Marbre, housed the apartments of the Captain of the Guard.

Salle des Hocquetons

The ground-floor suite of Marie-Antoinette, which she occupied during her last days at Versailles, has been partly recreated but of the furniture in the bedroom and the bathroom (**33**) only the console table and the recently re-embroidered bed-spread date from her period.

Revolution, Consulate and Empire
South attic (By appointment only)

A detailed exhibition of documents, drawings, engravings, watercolours and paintings, surrounded by wall-hangings of corresponding periods, brings to life the historic encounters, anecdotes, battles, ceremonies and the great figures of the Napoleonic period and the Bonaparte family who changed the course of French history.

19C Galleries
2nd Floor – North attic (by appointment only)

Galleries dedicated to the Restoration, the July Monarchy, the Second Empire and the Third Republic – Numerous painting illustrate the major events which marked this period of French history: the *Entente Cordiale*, cemented with the official visits of Louis-Philippe and Queen Victoria, the conquest of Algeria, the Revolutions of 1830 and 1848, the Franco-Prussion War of 1870 and the Paris Commune, the signing of the Treaty of Versailles. Note the portraits of Louis XVIII, Charles X, Louis-Philippe and his family, Napoleon III and Eugénie.

★★★VERSAILLES – PARK ⊘

Facts and figures ⊘ – The **gardens** cover an approximate area of 100ha/250 acres and the distance between the palace and their perimeter (the Apollo Basin) is about 950m/1 040yd.

Beyond the actual gardens of Versailles, the Versailles estate used to incorporate the **Petit Parc,** which already included the Grand Canal and the Trianon. Under the Second Empire its area gradually shrank from 1 700ha to 600ha/4 200 to 2 000 acres; a large part of this land was used as a terrain for military training. The royal gates at the exit of the Petit Parc marked the entrance to the **Grand Parc,** a 6 000ha/15 000 acres hunting reserve surrounded by 43km/27mi of walls punctuated by a series of 25 "royal" gates. The Grand Parc was entirely divided up during the Revolution.

The palace was built on top of a small hillock consolidated by vast loads of earth. The terrace rises above the Latona Basin by a height of 10.5m/35ft, the Apollo Basin by 30m/100ft, the Grand Canal by 32m/105ft and the Orangery by 17m/56ft.

The flower beds – To ensure that all the beds would be in full bloom during the month of August, the gardeners had to supply 150 000 plants, including 32 000 for the North Parterre, 35 000 for the South Parterre and 35 000 for the Latona beds. During the reign of Louis XIV, the plants which were all in pots would be changed up to fifteen times a year.

★★★Gardens

Quick tour: allow 3hr

A typical formal garden – Versailles is a superb example of a genre perfected by André Le Nôtre: the formal garden.

The terrace and parterres provide a perfect balance to the monumental front of the palace which screens the town of Versailles. Lower down, the lawns and the Grand Canal cut across the middle of the grounds, creating a sweeping perspective that extends into the far distance.

Numerous groves and straight paths are laid out on either side of this central axis. Their asymmetrical designs, basins and sculptures add a touch of variety to Le Nôtre's formal layout. The two hundred sculptures which adorn the park make it one of the biggest open-air museums of classical sculpture.

The view towards the south extends to the heights of Satory.

The gardens in former times – Today the branches of the trees lining the paths join so as to form a roof of foliage. In Le Nôtre's time, visitors to Versailles could look up and see the sky. The trees were not planted along the edge of the avenues but set back very slightly; their shadows would not even fall on the statues. The garden paths were flanked with a variety of colourful trellises, and arbours averaging 7.5m/25ft in height. These were fronted by tubs of orange and pomegranate trees, box trees and clipped yew trees.

Louis XV and Louis XVI did not alter the layout of the gardens but under Louis XVI replanting became necessary in 1776. This operation was renewed in 1860 and 1987.

★★★**Grandes Eaux** – *When the fountains are in operation (see Calendar of Events), the gardens may be entered only by the North Parterre (Parterre du Nord), the South Parterre (Parterre du Midi) the Great Staircase of 100 Steps (Escalier des Cents marches), the two gates at the end of the Grand Canal and the Dragon Gate (at the end of rue de la Paroisse).*

This magnificent display of fountains and groves presents a modified version of the splendour of the 18C. *Brochures of the tour may be obtained at the reception desk.* Start the tour from the top of the steps overlooking the Latona Basin. Start walking as soon as the fountains begin to play and carry on at a brisk pace, paying special attention to the groves, which are open only on these particular days especially the Salle de Bal and the Bosquet d'Apollon which is not visible from the garden paths. The grand finale *(at 5.20pm for 10min)* takes place at the Neptune and Dragon Basins. It involves 99 fountains. The one in the Bassin du Dragon rises to a height of 42m/138ft.

★★★**Illuminations** – *Every year the dates are fixed in advance for the whole season (see Calendar of Events).*

The night illuminations are organised four times a year during summer at the Bassin de Neptune and end with a fireworks display.

Grande Perspective

★★**Parterres d'eau** – The two huge basins that front the stately palace constitute a sort of aquatic esplanade where the three main perspectives meet: the central view, and the line along the North and South Parterres. The extremities of the basins bear allegorical statues of French rivers (portrayed as men) and their tributaries (portrayed as women). Lengthways are arranged groups of children at play, alternating with reclining water nymphs. These outstanding bronze sculptures were made by the Keller brothers.

Degré de Latone (Latona Staircase) – An imposing flight of steps and a double ramp flanked with yew trees and replicas of antique statues lead from the parterres d'eau down to the Bassin de Latone. From the top of the steps admire the wonderful view★★★ of the gardens and the Grande Perspective.

The two fountains – These stand to the left and the right of the steps. They were originally called the *Cabinets d'animaux* on account of the bronze works depicting dogs fighting wild beasts. They were named after the most striking statue of the three standing on the edge of the basins.

Fontaine au Point du Jour (**1**) – Dawn – whose head is crowned by a star – is the work of Gaspard Marsy. The other two figures are Water and Spring.

★**Fontaine de Diane** (**2**) – Le Hongre's statue Air is the one looking in the direction of Dawn. At its side stands the hunting goddess Diana, by Desjardins. The third statue was carved by Marsy and represents Venus, the goddess of love. These sculptures are among the finest works in the gardens.

All these statues were part of the massive ensemble commissioned by Colbert in 1674: a total of thirty marble sculptures, including 24 statues divided into six themes. The four Elements, the four Times of Day, the four Poems, the four Seasons, the four Continents and the four Temperaments were to be installed on the terrace fronting the château.

The initial plan was however never carried out; the court architects thought it a pity to break the classical lines of the esplanade with a row of great pale figures. Finally it was decided to adopt a more original approach: most of the bronze statues were cast as reclining figures and arranged around the basins while the others were set out in appropriate spots among the flowerbeds.

★**Bassin de Latone (Latona Basin)** – This vast composition by Marsy was the very first marble sculpture to grace the gardens of Versailles (1670). It tells the story of Latona (the statue is a mould of the original), the mother of Apollo and Diana, who was showered with insults by the peasants of Lycea and prevented from quenching her thirst. She appealed to Jupiter, the father of her children, who promptly avenged the offence by turning the culprits into aquatic animals. The Bassins des Lézards on the side picture the early stages of the metamorphosis... Originally the statue of Latona looked towards the palace, a clear indication of how the King viewed the public or private insults concerning his love life.

At the foot of the steps, to the right, lies the charming **Nymph with a Shell** (**3**), a modern replica of Coysevox' statue. The original work – inspired by the statues of Antiquity – has been moved to the Louvre.

★★**Tapis Vert** – The "Green Carpet" has been entirely replanted according to Le Nôtre's plans. From the foot of the Esplanade de Latone, admire the Grande Perspective leading up to the palace and extending beyond the Tapis Vert (Green Carpet), towards the Grand Canal.

This long stretch of lawn is lined with a superb collection of ornamental vases and statues, among them Cyparissus and his pet stag by Flamen and Poulletier's Dido. A stroll along the Allée du Midi leads to the **Richelieu Venus** (**4**), sculpted by Le Gros after an Antique bust that featured among the Cardinal's private collections.

Leave the Tapis Vert and enter the Bosquet du Midi.

Bosquets du Midi (South Groves)

★**Bosquet de la Salle de Bal** (**5**) – This elegant grove, also known as Bosquet des Rocailles, was part of Le Nôtre's original plans. Shaped as a circular stage, it is surrounded by gentle slopes, grassy banks and tiered rockeries where small cascades tumbled down. This outdoor theatre was used for performances given by members of the court or a corps de ballet.

Bassin de Bacchus (or Bassin de l'Automne) (**6**) – Attributed to Gaspard Marsy. The basins of the Four Seasons are laid out to plans by Le Brun in the form of a quadrangle flanked by the main paths. These groups of lead figures were recently re-gilded and decorated in "natural tones".

Bosquet de la Reine (**7**) – This grove lies on the site of a former maze and was created in 1775, at the time of the great replanting campaign.

In its centre stand a number of busts and bronze statues cast after Antique models: Aphrodite, a Fighting Gladiator etc. The maple groves are a magnificent sight in autumn.

Bassin du Miroir d'Eau (**8**) – Of the two basins circling the Royal Isle, the larger one began to silt up and Louis XVIII replaced it by a landscape garden, known as the Royal Garden. The only one to survive is the Bassin du Miroir d'Eau (Vertugadin), handsomely adorned with statues.

★**Jardin du Roi** – A dazzling sight in summer, when all the flowers are in full bloom, this garden is a welcome change from the formal groves of Versailles. The wonderful central lawn is flanked by a charming selection of rare species of tree.

Bassin de Saturne (or Bassin de l'Hiver) (**9**) – This basin was designed by François Girardon.

★★**Colonnade** – *This grove is usually closed but can be seen quite clearly through the railings.*

Jules Hardouin-Mansart built this circular colonnade in 1685 with the help of fifteen fellow sculptors. One of its most pleasing features is the elegant display of multi-coloured marble: blue, red, lilac and white. Observe the carved masks on the keystones and, on the spandrels, the delightful groups of children playing musical instruments.

★Bassin d'Apollon (Apollo Basin)

The whole composition was made by Tuby. Apollo the Sun God is portrayed seated in his chariot, surrounded by marine monsters, rising from the ocean waters to bring Light to the Earth. This basin is continued by an esplanade leading to the Grand Canal. It is bordered by statues, parts of which are genuine antiquities (note the cracks where the different fragments join).

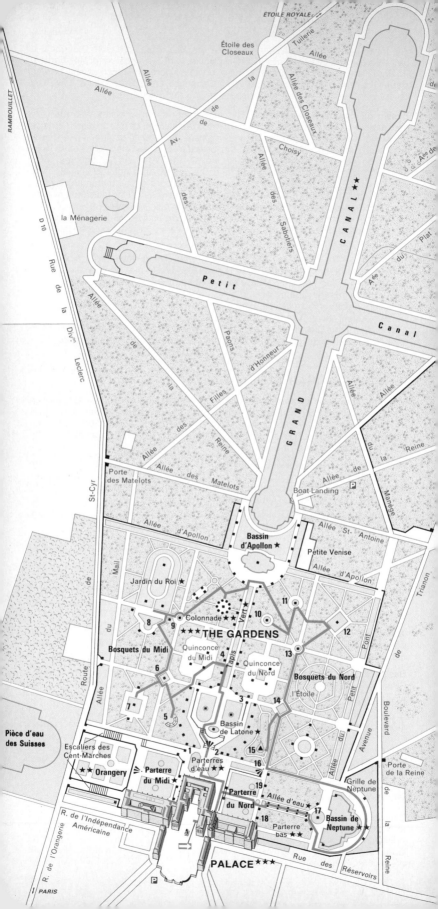

ÉTOILE ROYALE

RAMBOUILLET

Étoile des
Closeaux

Tuilerie

Allée

Allée

de

Av.

de

des

la

Choisy

Allée

des

Allée des Closeaux

CANAL ★★

Aée

du

Plat

des

Sabotiers

D 10

la Ménagerie

Rue de la Div^on Leclerc

Allée

de

la

des

Reine

Allée

des Matelots

Allée

des

Matelots

St-Cyr

Porte
des Matelots

Petit

Canal

Paons

Filles

d'Honneur

des

GRAND

Canal

Allée

de

la

Reine

Manège

Allée St-Antoine

Boat Landing P

Allée   d'Apollon

Bassin
d'Apollon ★

Petite Venise

Allée   d'Apollon

Mail

du

Route

Allée

Jardin du Roi ★

Colonnade ★★

★★★ THE GARDENS

Bosquets du Midi

Quinconce
du Midi

tapis

Vert

Quinconce
du Nord

Bosquets du Nord

l'Étoile

Trianon

Pont

de

Boulevard

Porte
de la Reine

8

9

10

11

12

13

14

6

4

7

5

3

Bassin
de Latone ★

15 ▲

16

Pièce d'eau
des Suisses

Escaliers des
Cent-Marches

★★ Orangery

★ Parterre
du Midi

Parterres
d'eau ★★

2

19

Parterre
du Nord

Allée d'eau

17

Bassin de
Neptune ★★

Grille de
Neptune

Avenue

Allée

du

18

Parterre
bas ★★

R. de l'Indépendance
Américaine

R. de l'Orangerie

PARIS

PALACE ★★★

Rue

des

Réservoirs

la

Reine

de

P

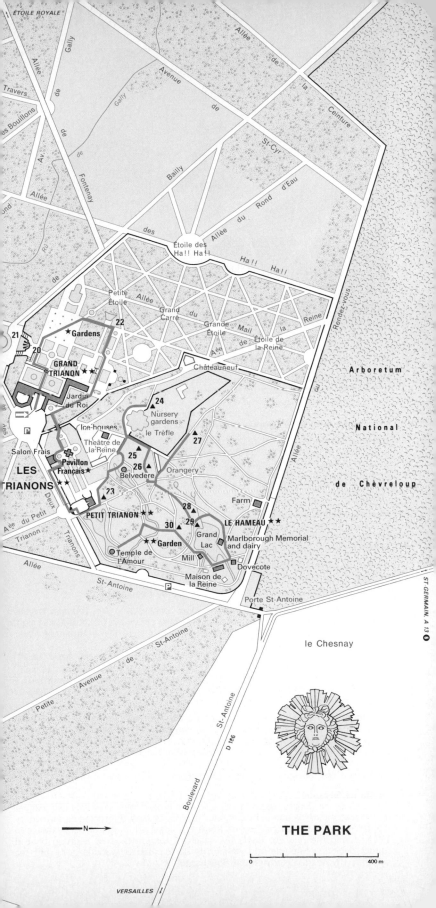

THE PARK

The Apollo Basin at Versailles

Bosquets du Nord (North Groves)

Bosquet des Dômes (**10**) – The grove was named after two pavilions crowned by domes which were designed by Mansart. They were demolished in 1820.
A series of low reliefs adorns the edge of the basin, representing the weapons used in different countries. It has the unmistakably elegant touch of Girardon. Among the fine statues feature two works by Tuby, Acis and Galatea.

★**Bassin d'Encelade** (**11**) – The stark realism of this recently restored Baroque composition by Marsy contrasts sharply with the other groups dotted around the gardens. A head and two arms is all that is visible of the Titan Enceladus, slowly being dragged down towards the bowels of the earth by the very rocks of Mount Olympus by which the Titan had hoped to reach the sky (a clear warning to Fouquet).

Bassin de l'Obélisque (**12**) – Designed by Mansart, this raised basin is surrounded by a flight of stone steps and several lawns. When the fountains are in operation, the central sculpture lets out a gigantic spray of water which resembles a liquid obelisk.

Bassin de Flore (or Bassin du Printemps) (**13**) – Another of the four seasons series by Tuby.

Bassin de Cérès (or Bassin de l'Été) (**14**) – Made by Regnaudin.

★**Bosquet des Bains d'Apollon** (**15**) – *Open only during the fountain display (Grandes Eaux).* Designed by Hubert Robert in the early days of Louis XVI's reign, this grove heralded the Anglo-Chinese Garden which Marie-Antoinette later adopted for the Trianon park.
On the edge of a small lake, a charming artificial grotto houses the **Apollo Group**★. Its lush, verdant setting is a far cry from the austere 17C Versailles. The Sun God, tired by the day's exertions, is portrayed resting, waited upon by a group of nymphs (Girardon and Regnaudin). The horses at his side are being groomed by tritons (Marsy and Guérin).

Carrefour des Philosophes (**16**) – Flanked by impressive statues. The "philosophers" crossroads offer an interesting sideways **view**★★ of the palace (northwest corner). The sweeping perspective on the right is lined with a double row of yew trees and a set of bronze statues, including Girardon's Winter.

Bassins de Neptune, du Dragon

★★**Bassin de Neptune** – *Stand in line with the basin, near the statue of Fame.*
This is by far the largest basin in Versailles. Its proportions are wildly extravagant by classical standards and it extends northwards beyond the rectangle formed by the gardens. It was designed by Le Nôtre but acquired its present appearance in 1741, during the reign of Louis XV, when it was enriched by a group of lead statues depicting Neptune and Amphitrite surrounded by various gods and sea monsters (by Adam, Lemoyne and Bouchardon).

Bassin du Dragon (17) – This allegorical sculpture evoking the victory over deep-sea monsters is a direct allusion to the crushing of the Fronde Revolt, symbolised by a wounded dragon. Though the dragon's body is the original, the remaining pieces were recast in 1889.

★ **Allée d'Eau** – A double row of 22 small white marble basins bears delightful bronze groups of three children, each holding pink marble vessels.

The Parterres and Orangery

Parterre du Nord (North Parterre) – The very first royal suite looked out onto this "terrace of greenery".

Bassin des Nymphes de Diane (18) – The pond is surrounded by fine low-relief carvings by Girardon which inspired 18C and 19C painters such as Renoir.

★★ **Parterre Bas** – Close to the groves, along its northern and western boundaries, the terrace is flanked by bronze statues representing the four Continents, four Poems, four Seasons and four Temperaments. The lead **Pyramid Fountain★ (19)**, made by Girardon from a study by Le Brun, combines grace with originality: dolphins, crayfish and tritons.

At the top of the steps leading to the Parterres d'Eau note the **Knifegrinder**, a bronze replica of a classical statue. Coysevox' **Venus on a Tortoise** – called Venus as a Paragon of Modesty under Louis XIV – is a bronze cast, also inspired by Antique sculpture. The original is exhibited in the Louvre and is among the artist's finest works.

★ **Parterre du Midi (South Parterre)** – These flower beds were laid out in front of the queen's apartments. With their vivid blossoms and their pretty boxwood patterns, they are a hymn to Nature. The terrace running along the Orangery offers a good **view★** of the 700m/2275ft long Pièce d'Eau des Suisses and, in the far distance, the wooded heights of Satory.

★★ **Orangery** – One of Mansart's creations, the Orangery forms the foundations of the South Parterre. It extends south by means of two corner pavilions set at right angles which support the colossal **Escalier des Cent-Marches**, a flight of 100 steps. At the time of Louis XIV, the Orangery housed 3000 shrubs in tubs; 2000 of these were orange trees. Today it contains 1200 bushes, some of which date back to before the French Revolution. The Orangery looks splendid during the summer season, when the orange trees and palm trees (a recent introduction) are brought outside and arranged around the flower beds.

★★Le Grand Canal

The Grand Canal, which was completed in 1670, is shaped like a large cross: the long canal is 1670m/5480ft long by 62m/204ft wide; the shorter one measures 1070m/3500ft long by 80m/263ft wide.

The nearby buildings make up Petite Venise which housed the Venetian gondoliers in charge of the king's fleet (gondolas, models of battleships and merchant ships). Boat trips and tourist train starting point nearby.

★★Grand Trianon *2hr*

Access on foot – *Avenue de Trianon (1km/0.5mi) starts at the Neptune Gate and leads directly to the Trianons. The avenue starting from the eastern extremity of the Grand Canal also leads there.*

Access by car – *See map above.*

A pavilion known as the Trianon de Porcelaine, faced with blue and white Delft tiling, used to be a quiet, secluded meeting-place for Louis XIV and his favourite Mme de Montespan. It stood for eighteen years, from 1670 to 1687. When Mme de Montespan fell from favour, the pavilion deteriorated and was eventually taken down. In just six months, Jules Hardouin-Mansart completed the Trianon de Marbre, a retreat built in honour of Mme de Maintenon.

It was stripped of its furniture during the Revolution. Napoleon I commissioned major renovation work and refurnished the building on the occasion of his marriage to Marie-Louise. The Marble Trianon was restored under Louis-Philippe.

The latest renovation programme took place in 1962 at the instigation of General de Gaulle, who wished to use the Trianon for official receptions.

★★ **Château** – Walk past the low railings and enter the semicircular courtyard to discover two buildings with a flat terrace roof, joined by an elegant peristyle. Note the delicate colours in the marble with pink overtones. Another wing called Trianon-sous-Bois *(private)* stands at a right angle to the righthand gallery, but it is not visible from the court.

The peristyle overlooks both the court and the gardens. It was designed by Robert de Cotte and adopted by Louis XIV despite Mansart's scepticism. It was used for banquets and formal receptions.

Apartments – The austere interior decoration has changed very little since the days of Louis XIV. The apartments were occupied by Napoleon and Louis-Philippe and their respective families. The furniture is either Empire, Restoration or Louis-Philippe and the paintings were by 17C French artists.

The Salon des Glaces in the left pavilion was used as a council chamber. Admire the splendid Empire furniture and the lavish silk hangings, rewoven according to the original pattern ordered by Marie-Antoinette (the four Continents of the World). The bedroom contains the bed Napoleon commissioned for his apartments at the Tuileries: it was later altered for Louis-Philippe's use. The wall put in by Bonaparte level with the columns has been dismantled and the room has been restored to its original size. The reception rooms in the right wing were remodelled by Louis-Philippe, who gave them a more personal touch. These salons are enhanced by a collection of paintings by famous 17C French artists, dedicated to mythological subjects.

In Louis XIV's former Music Room, the musicians' loggias are enclosed by a series of shutters.

Louis-Philippe created a family drawing room, in which the two tables feature numbered drawers reserved for the princesses' needlework.

The Salon des Malachites was first the Sun King's Grand Cabinet and then the bedroom of the Duchess of Burgundy. It owes its name to the various objects encrusted with malachite given to Napoleon by Tsar Alexander I following their talks in Tilsit (1807): basins, candelabra, bookcase etc. Malachite is a green semi-precious stone found in Siberia, and is easy to polish.

The north-facing drawing room houses four paintings representing the early days of Versailles, following the plans drawn up by Mansart (display of documents showing the palace and the grounds). The two filing cabinets (1810) and the console table (1806) were made by Jacob Desmalter from a drawing by Charles Percier.

The Salon des Sources – where Napoleon kept his various maps and plans – leads to the Imperial Suite *(open on request)*.

Placed at a right angle, the **Gallery★** houses an extremely precious collection of 24 paintings by Cotelle. They conjure up a vivid picture of the palace and its stately grounds at the time of Louis XIV. The lovely Empire chandeliers were manufactured in the Montcenis glassworks in the Burgundian town of Le Creusot. At the end of the Gallery, the luminous Salon des Jardins features a fine set of chairs from the Château de Meudon.

★**Gardens** – They derive their simple charm from the impressive displays of flower beds and the absence of allegorical meanings.

The terrace of the Lower Gardens *(Jardins Bas)* (**20**) commands a good view of the Lower Basin *(Bassin Bas)* (**21**), which is reached via a horse-shoe staircase, and of the Grand Canal beyond, seen from the side.

Beyond the parterres lies a charming wood featuring fine avenues, rows of stately trees and several small ponds *(best seen when the Trianon fountains are playing)*. The only sculpture with a mythological theme in the Trianon gardens is Mansart's Buffet d'Eau (**22**), completed in 1703. It pictures the Sea God Neptune and Amphitrite, surrounded by a cluster of smaller statues.

Skirt Trianon-sous-Bois and walk through what was once the king's private garden. It is flanked by two square pavilions which housed the apartments of Mme de Maintenon and Louis XIV towards the end of the Sun King's reign.

To reach the Petit Trianon, cross the bridge erected by Napoleon I, known as Pont de Réunion.

★★Petit Trianon *1hr 30min*

It was Louis XV's love of gardening and farming that prompted the construction of the Petit Trianon. The King gave orders to build a menagerie (experimental farm) and commissioned his "botanical expert" Claude Richard to design the greenhouses and botanical gardens. A College of Botanical Science was founded and entrusted to the famous botanist Bernard de Jussieu.

Gabriel finished the Petit Trianon in 1768, shortly before Louis XV's reign ended. Mme de Pompadour, the woman behind the initial project, never saw the château. Louis XVI gave the Petit Trianon to his wife Marie-Antoinette. The Queen would often come here with her children and her sister-in-law Mme Elisabeth, relieved to get away from court intrigues and the formal etiquette that was expected from a woman of her rank. She insisted on a number of changes: the grounds were redesigned, a theatre was built and Jussieu's botanical gardens, complete with their experimental hothouses, were destroyed. On 5 October 1789 the Queen was resting in a grotto near the Belvedere when a messenger informed her that the mob was marching on Versailles. She left Trianon in great haste and was never to return.

Later, Empress Eugénie, who felt great sympathy for Marie-Antoinette, formed a collection of her personal mementoes and had the château refurnished in 1867.

★Pavillon français – This pavillon was built by Gabriel for Louis XV and Mme de Pompadour in 1750. It is surrounded by an enchanting formal garden. The cornice features a sculpted frieze representing the farm animals that were raised on the estate. Visitors can get a glimpse of the highly-refined interior decoration through the large French windows.

The cool **Summerhouse** at the southern end of the gardens was rebuilt in 1982.

★★Château – The façade facing the courtyard is austere in the extreme. It overlooks the formal gardens and is a perfect example of Gabriel's talent; the four regulary-spaced columns are crowned by a balustrade and two fine flights of steps lead from the terrace down to the gardens.

Enter the château and walk up the imposing flight of stone stairs lit by an old-fashioned lantern. The wrought-iron banisters are stamped with a decorative monogram, believed to be that of Marie-Antoinette.

First Floor Apartments – Guibert's craftsmanship is evident in the superb **panelling★★** in the dining room and the drawing room. The decoration of the dining-room presents fruit, flower and foliage motifs, set off against a pale green background, a welcome change from the "Trianon grey" prevalent throughout the 19C. The drawing room – partly refurnished by the Empress Eugénie in the 19C (chairs, 1790 pianoforte) – houses one of Riesener's greatest acheivements: the famous astronomical writing desk (1771).

The furniture in Marie-Antoinette's bedroom was designed by Jacob and adorned with ears of corn. Jacob also designed several pieces for the comtesse de Balbi; they have been placed in a recently-restored boudoir with unusual movable mirrors.

★★Gardens – This charming Anglo-Chinese garden including a brook, several ornamental ponds, some fine trees and an interesting collection of manmade features was designed by an amateur, the comte de Caraman, and built by the Queen's architect Mique who received advice from Hubert Robert.

Several of the trees are 150 to 200 years old and some were probably planted by Bernard de Jussieu in his botanical gardens. The oldest of all is a damaged pagoda tree (**23**) planted during the reign of Louis XV, which stands near the northeast corner of the château.

Belvedere – This delightful pavilion designed by Mique was also called the Music Room. It overlooks the Petit Lac and the interior decoration offers painted arabesques of the utmost refinement.

Off the winding paths of the landscape garden lies the Jardin Charpentier, planted with remarkable trees. Go on to the grounds of the Grand Trianon to have a look at the superb Lebanese cedar tree (**24**) near the Bassin au Trèfle, as well as the two entirely-restored 17C ice-houses standing in the background. Return to the Jardin Charpentier and note the two huge Wellingtonias (**25**) and single fastigiate oak (**26**). Bear left after the Orangery to an ancient Siberian elm (**27**) with unusually deep striations. Start walking towards the Hamlet. Before the lake is a tulip tree from Virginia (**28**) and two spinneys of stately swamp cypresses (**29**).

★★Le Hameau (Hamlet) – The grounds around the lake (Grand Lac) are dotted with a dozen pretty cottages featuring cob walls and thatched or tiled roofs, inspired by the hamlet at Chantilly. Contrary to popular belief, the Queen was far too steeped in formal protocol to indulge in any farming activities.

Le Petit Trianon

The Memorial to Marlborough is a reminder of the popular nursery rhyme, "Chanson de Marlborough", introduced to Louis XVI's court by the Dauphin's nanny. On the way to the Temple de l'Amour, notice a remarkable plane tree (**30**) with thick spread-eagled roots.

Temple de l'Amour – One of Mique's creations (1778), the Temple of Love stands on a tiny islet. In the centre, Bouchardon's statue shows Cupid making his Bow from the Club of Hercules (original in the Louvre). The sculpture is fronted by a row of Corinthian columns resting on a circular flight of six steps.

★★VERSAILLES – TOWN

In 1671 Louis XIV decided that plots of land would be granted to those citizens who put in a request, in exchange for a levy of five sous for each arpent (3 194m²/3 833sq yd). The new buildings had to conform to the rules laid down by the Service des Bâtiments du Roi, a building commission answerable to the court. The purpose of these measures was to achieve architectural unity. Moreover, in order that the palace might continue to dominate the area, the roofs of the village houses were not to exceed the height of the Cour de Marbre. Today very little remains of these 17C buildings. Most of the old town was completed in the 18C, enlarged and renovated in the 19C.

The Notre-Dame district features the oldest church in Versailles and a few houses built under Louis XIV, situated near the Notre-Dame market-place.

The St-Louis district south of Avenue de Sceaux contains the official buildings of the former ministries, the Real Tennis Court or **Jeu de Paume** ⊙ where the National Assembly took their famous oath on 20 June 1789, "old Versailles" built around the former village square and an 18C estate on the former Parc aux Cerfs, located close to Satory heights.

★**Musée Lambinet** ⊙ – This museum is housed in the woodpanelled drawing rooms of the charming Hôtel Lambinet built in 1750 for Joseph-Barnabé Porchon, building contractor to the King, whose initials can be seen in the wrought iron-work on the balcony in the middle of the pleasing façade.

The atmosphere of an 18C townhouse is recreated by the period furniture, paintings and sculptures (Pajou, Houdon). At the same time, the museum illustrates the history of Versailles through numerous objects and documents.

Room 2 is given over to a ceramics collection with a large number of pieces of Parisian porcelain from the last quarter of the 18C described as "Vieux Paris". It is famous for the whiteness of its paste which made it a worthy rival of Sèvres.

Room 4 is an incursion into the 19C with the reconstruction of actress Julie Bartet's "green drawing room". She was a member of the Comédie Française and was well-known for her roles in Racine's works. Her skill in interpreting Victor Hugo's heroines placed her on a par with Sarah Bernhardt.

Room 5 contains several works by an artist from Versailles named H Collin de Vermont (story of Cyrus) and ceramics from Rouen, Strasbourg, Eastern France and China.

Rare 18C engraved copper plates are exhibited in Room 6. They were used to print the calico known as *toile de Jouy*.

The first floor houses an extensive collection of items related to Revolutionary events and figures: the arrest of **Charlotte de Corday** (Room 9), events in Versailles during 1789 with, in particular, the Declaration of Human Rights (Room 13), Général Hoche, one of Versailles' most famous sons (Room 14), and **Marat** (Room 16). On the landing are 12 commemorative plates made in 1889 to mark the centenary of the Revolution. Note the beautiful "golden drawing room" with its ornate woodwork and marquetry furniture.

On the second floor in the room devoted to **religious art★** (Room 23) there are two magnificent **abbesses' crooks** with rock crystal scrolls. They come from Maubuisson and Le Lys.

Rooms 26, 27 and 28 deal with Versailles in the 17C and 18C. Room 27 houses a large collection of high-fired ceramic apothecary's jars, most of which come from the works in St-Cloud. Note the display case in Room 28 containing miniatures on ivory representing the palace and park.

The final room (29) contains weaponry made by the famous manufacturer Boutet, the managing director of the little-known **Manufacture d'armes de Versailles**. The factory enjoyed an excellent reputation during the days of the Empire for the quality of the workmanship. This is evident in the collection of ceremonial arms (sabres, rifles) and the very fine boxed pistols with accessories said to have belonged to Général Scherer.

Back on the ground floor, the last rooms display 19C and 20C works of art: Boilly, Isabey, Carrière, Le Sidaner and Dunoyer de Segonzac.

ON THE TOWN: VERSAILLES

Transport

Access – It is particularly easy to travel from this royal town to Paris by RER from Versailles Rive-Droite (SNCF to La Défense, St-Lazare), Versailles Rive-Gauche (RER line "C" to Invalides) and Versailles Chantiers (RER line "C" and rail service to Montparnasse).

Public transport – The easiest means of transport is the bus. The main bus stations are on Avenue de l'Europe and opposite Versailles Rive-Gauche station.

Where to stay

BUDGET

Home St-Louis – 28 Rue St-Louis, ☎ 01 39 50 23 55, fax 01 30 21 62 45. Situated in the quiet St-Louis district, this small two-star renovated hotel offers good value for money within a stone's throw of the castle. Double room: 320F.

OUR SELECTION

Résidence du Berry – 14 Rue d'Anjou, ☎ 01 39 49 07 07, fax 01 39 50 59 40. Well-appointed, comfortable and charming 18C building (three stars) close to the Potager du Roi. Double room from 450F.

Versailles – 7 Rue Ste-Anne, ☎ 01 39 50 64 65, fax 01 39 02 37 85. Comfort and closeness to the castle are the main assets of this convivial hotel. Double room from 460F.

Where to eat

BUDGET

Le Fahler – 22 Rue de Satory, ☎ 01 39 50 57 43. Convivial restaurant in a lively pedestrianised street, close to the castle. Menus from 128F.

La Flotille – Parc du château, at the beginning of the Grand Canal, ☎ 01 39 51 41 58. Decorated like a country bistro, this restaurant offers its clients a fine terrace within the beautiful Versailles Park. Rather go there for lunch as it closes early in the evening. Menus from 132F.

OUR SELECTION

Le Chevalet – 6 Rue Philippe-de-Dangeau, ☎ 01 39 02 03 13. Closed from 10 to 25 August, February holidays, Monday evenings and Sundays. Decorated with paintings by the chef, this small restaurant offers a pleasant setting and imaginative cuisine. It is advisable to book in advance as the dining room is small. Menus from 145F.

Brasserie La Fontaine – 1 Boulevard de la Reine, ☎ 01 30 84 38 47. Closed in August. Located in the annexe of the Trianon Palace. Menus: 165F.

Le Potager du Roy – 1 Rue du Maréchal-Joffre, ☎ 01 39 50 35 34. Closed Sunday evenings and Mondays. Situated near the famous garden of the same name, this restaurant serves fresh garden or market produce. Menu: 169F.

FOR GOURMETS

Les Trois Marches – 1 Boulevard de la Reine, ☎ 01 39 50 13 21. Closed in August. This legendary restaurant enjoys the luxury setting of the Trianon Palace alongside the park of the Château. Menu: 610F.

Out and about

Shops – The main shopping streets are Rue de la Paroisse with Place du Marché, Les Manèges (opposite Versailles Rive-Gauche station), Rue Royale and Rue du Général-Leclerc. Passage de la Geôle near Place du Marché contains a large number of antique shops. Large stores such as FNAC, Printemps, BHV etc. are all in the Parly II shopping precinct on the Versailles-St Germain road.

Theatre – The Montansier, Rue des Réservoirs, is directed by Francis Perrin. It has recently been renovated and it stages a wide range of classical plays and variety performances.

Music – The Centre de Musique Baroque de Versailles organises concerts in the chapel or the opera house within the palace *(see Calendar of Events)*. Programmes are available from the tourist office.

Having a drink – Le Molière, a piano bar in Les Manèges, provides a friendly, relaxing atmosphere. There are many bars, grill rooms and pubs in the avenues around Place du Marché. The piano-bar and grillroom called Trianon Palace, 1 Boulevard de la Reine is outstanding for its interior decoration.

Église Notre-Dame – The church built in the Rue Dauphine – renamed Rue Hoche – by Jules Hardouin-Mansart in 1686 was the parish church attached to the king and his court. The king would attend Solemn Masses such as Corpus Christi here. The requirements of the Service des Bâtiments du Roi explain why the church presents a flattened front flanked by truncated towers.

A large open-work dome graces the church interior, characterised by Doric embellishments. The nave *(explanatory notices)* is surrounded by 12 carved medaillions representing Apostles and figures from the New Testament; these were the works presented by the new entrants to the Académie Royale de Sculpture et de Peinture between 1657 and 1689. The axial chapel – the chapel of the Blessed Sacrament – houses the *Assumption*, a 16C painting by Michel Corneille.

Rue de l'Independance-Américaine – In the 18C this street housed many buildings occupied by ministries and public services, in particular the Grand Commun – now the Military Hospital – which lodged a total of 1 500 officials, cooks etc.

At no 5 stands the former **Ministry of the Navy and Foreign Affairs**, fronted by a magnificent gate crowned by statues of Peace and War. It was here that an alliance was signed (1762) between France and the American "insurrectionaries", acting as a prelude to the 1783 treaties granting the independence of the United States. The mansion has been made into a public library **(bibliothèque municipale ⊙)**.

★**Cathédrale St-Louis** – St Louis' Cathedral was built in 1754 to serve the "old Versailles" and the Parc aux Cerfs, and lies close to the King's Vegetable Garden *(Potager du Roi)*. The west front with its two towers, and the dome above the transept crossing are reminiscent of the great classical churches.

Several official celebrations were held at the cathedral: the inauguration ceremony of the States General on 4 May 1789, attended by the deputies who had formed a procession starting from Notre-Dame in Paris; the session of 22 June which authorised the reunion of Clergy and Nobility; the Mass of the Holy Ghost which opened the 1875 sitting of the National Assembly at which the members voted on the constitutional law that founded the Third Republic.

The noble, austere nave still contains its organ and collection of 18C paintings, but the most interesting furnishings are the religious works dating from the 19C.

Carrés St-Louis – Louis XV gave orders to create a "shopping area" near St Louis Church, along the streets presently named rue Royale and rue d'Anjou (1755). The shops – featuring mansard roofs – were arranged around four small squares known as *carrés*: Carré au Puits, Carré à l'Avoine, Carré à la Fontaine, Carré à la Terre. Some of these houses still exist and have been converted into antique shops.

★**Potager du Roi** – 6 Rue Hardy, École nationale supérieure du paysage. This "kitchen garden" was commissioned by Louis XIV from **JB Quintinie** (1624-1688) to supply the king's table with a variety of fruit and vegetables. The result amounted to 29 separate gardens surrounding a large central square and protected by walls and terraces.

Parc Balbi – 12 Rue du Maréchal-Joffre. This small Anglo-Chinese garden was commissioned for the countess of Balbi. Gradually restored, the park has regained the refined charm of a romantic garden so much appreciated in the 18C.

EXCURSION

Arboretum National de Chèvreloup ⊙ – *Leave by D 186 north and turn left before entering Rocquencourt. Opposite the Parly II shopping centre.*

In 1927 a plot of land formerly belonging to the Grand Parc *(see description of the Park of Versailles above)* was offered to the Natural History Museum of Paris so that the Botanical Gardens *(Jardin des Plantes)* could enrich their collection of tree species. The first steps were to set up a Tree Centre.

Visitors may tour only the southeast part of the park, planted with clusters and rows of conifers. Several types of horticultural species which do not grow locally are cultivated here: a row of Lawson cypresses, of unusual shapes and sizes; large groups of thujas next to yew trees and weeping conifers. The broad-leaved trees include birches and willow trees at the height of their development. The oldest species of all is one of the pagoda trees planted at the time of Louis XV and restored to life thanks to modern tree surgery.

Through-roads and access roads are shown in red or yellow on town plans.

VÉTHEUIL

Population 732
Michelin map 106 fold 3

This former wine-growing village has a lovely riverside setting: it lies on the steep banks of one of the Seine's meanders, not far from La Roche-Guyon. The village houses – built with a fine pale yellow stone – are characteristic of the French Vexin region. The small town was made famous by the Impressionists, in particular Claude Monet who lived here for three years and whose wife Camille died in Vétheuil in 1879.

Church ⊙ – Perched right above the village the church makes a picturesque sight, but the Impressionist painters were more interested in the area around Lavacourt, on the south bank of the Seine.

From the main village crossroads take rue de l'Église which leads straight to the entrance steps.

Although the chancel was first started in the late 12C the church was only completed under Henri II, when the last chapels were consecrated in 1580. The building is presently undergoing restoration.

Exterior – The west front dates from the mid-16C; the three levels of Renaissance galleries are flanked by two square turrets. The pier features a 16C statue depicting Charity.

The south façade presents a doorway fronted by a Renaissance porch – note the 16C panels. Walk past the 16C nave to the late-12C chancel, which shows the transition from Romanesque to Gothic. A broad view of the elevation of the church reveals small round windows (oculi) on the first floor and a series of stepped buttresses around the east end. The bell-tower was built in the 13C: it was the subject of many Impressionist paintings.

Interior – The church houses a number of **statues★** (14C-16C), a few 16C and 17C painting and several interesting carvings. The first chapel on the left – formerly dedicated to one of the brotherhoods of charity – is enclosed by a Renaissance parclose. In the third chapel stands a lively statue of St James (Burgundian School – 15C) and the north aisle bears a 16C *Ecce Homo.* Note the 14C Virgin and Child in the south transept crossing (Notre-Dame-de-Grâce de Vétheuil) and, in the adjacent chapel, St Veronica, a colourful stone statue dating from the 14C.

Domaine de VILLARCEAUX★

Michelin map 106 fold 3
8km/4.5mi northeast of La Roche Guyon

Access – From Chaussy, follow D 71 towards Magny-en-Vexin. Drive past the Louis XV-style castle and take the first road to the right (signposted "La Comté"). A little further on the right, a new access road leads to a vast parking area.

J Cabanou /DIAF

Villarceaux – Ninon's pavilion

Domaine de VILLARCEAUX

Villarceaux estate is set in rolling surroundings at the heart of the French Vexin. It is graced by a magnificent setting and two châteaux: a 15C-16C manor house which belonged to the celebrated beauty Ninon de Lenclos, and a Louis XV château.

Approaching the estate from the south, the road from Villers-en-Arthies offers a glimpse of the little 19C Château du Couvent surrounded by a golf course.

Ninon de Lenclos – When Ninon (1620-1705) died at the age of 85, she had witnessed Louis XIII's reign and the absolute monarchy of Louis XIV. She was acquainted with all the leading personalities of her time and virtually became a legendary figure of the 17C because of her charm and her wisdom; few of her contemporaries could claim to possess such an impressive collection of memories. It was at Villarceaux that she received the young Françoise d'Aubigné, the future Mme Scarron and Mme de Maintenon, who 32 years later was to marry Louis XIV. It was also here that she had a love affair with Louis de Mornay, the Marquis de Villarceaux. The youthful Voltaire was officially presented to her shortly before her death.

Restoration work may lead to modifications in the tour of the estate.

Manoir de Ninon – Prolonged by vast outbuildings forming a courtyard, the manor replaced in the 16C a former fortified house now reduced to the Tour St-Nicolas. Ninon's pavilion ends with Ninon's tower which houses a charming Italian closet and an intriguing hideout dimly lit by a loophole.

★ Gardens ⓥ – They illustrate the evolution of gardens through the centuries. The former Renaissance terraces on the left of the entrance are overlooked by the unusual St-Nicolas tower, known as the "tower of the condemned" because witches were hanged there. The tour of the large pond leads past Ninon's pool, supplied by an Italian waterfall, and reveals a view of the south front of the Louis XV castle. The other façade of the 18C castle overlooks the open Vexin countryside.

Discover the suggested Touring Programmes at the beginning of the guide Plan a trip with the help of the Map of Principal Sights.

VILLENEUVE-D'ASCQ
Population 65 320
Michelin map 51 fold 16 or 236 fold 16 – 8km/5mi east of Lille

In 1970 the *communes* of **Annappes, Flers and Ascq** were grouped together to form Villeneuve-d'Ascq, one of nine new towns in France. The three centres of the old towns have remained hubs of activity.

From the 1960s universities had established themselves in the Annappes area. The Triolo, Cousinerie, Brigode and Pont de Bois residential and commercial districts developed around the science park (cité scientifique). Industries and research centres followed. Today most of the region's universities are located in Villeneuve-d'Ascq; over 30 000 students are enrolled here.

A stroll through the town reveals new concepts in urban living: overhead pedestrian walkways straddle the main roads; residential areas merge into commercial centres; there are numerous large civic amenities: a 35 000 seater stadium, a cultural centre, museums etc.

The town is linked to the remainder of the Lille conurbation by a network of motorways and an automatic *métro* system: the Val.

The town's name, Ascq, is a reminder of the tragic massacre of 86 patriots on 2 April 1944, which is commemorated by a monument and a museum (**M¹**).

Routhier
Motherhood by Modigliani
(Musée d'Art Moderne)

★★ MUSÉE D'ART MODERNE ⓥ

Leave N 227 at "Château de Flers" exit.

Lying by a lawn above Lac du Héron, the huge building by architect Rolland Simounet suggests a set of brick and glass cubes. The foyer leads to the permanent and temporary exhibitions *(right)*, and to the reception and other services *(left)*: library, cafeteria, classrooms used for courses in the plastic arts.

The collection – Roger Dutilleul's collection, which contains over 230 works mainly from the first half of the 20C, was presented to the museum by Geneviève and Jean Masurel, Dutilleul's nephew. Dutilleul made his first acquisitions in 1907 and from the beginning recognised the talent of artists who were not then understood: one of the first paintings he bought was Braque's *Houses and Tree* which had just been refused at the Salon d'Automne.

The collection contains many Fauvist, Cubist, primitive and abstract works. The Fauvists include Rouault, Derain and Van Dongen *(Pouting Woman* – 1909). Cubism is represented in paintings by Braque *(Houses and Tree, The Factories of Rio Tinto)* and Picasso *(Seated Nude, Bock, Spanish Still-Life)*; this section also contains collages: Picasso's *Head of a Man* and Braque's *The Little Scout*. Several works by **Fernand Léger** follow his development from a 1914 landscape to his sketch for a mural (1938), encompassing works such as *The Mechanic* (1918) and *Still-Life with Fruit Dish* and his studies of volume and mass. One room is devoted to **Modigliani**, seven of whose paintings are included in the collection, together with five drawings. His beguiling portraits reveal subtle plays of line and colour, especially in *Motherhood* (1919), *Seated Nude with a Shirt* (1917) and *The Red-Headed Boy* (1919). Works of abstract art featured are by Kandinsky, Miró, Klee and Nicolas de Staël. De Staël knew Roger Dutilleul through the painter Lanskoy, who was the collector's protégé, and many examples of the latter's work are also on show.

Outside, a pleasant stroll through the public gardens (Parc du Héron) beside the lake leads to the mills and the adjacent museum.

B	Forum des Sciences – Centre François Mitterrand	**F⁴**	Ferme D'en haut
F¹	Ferme Dupire	**F⁵**	Ferme Descamps
F²	Ferme St-Sauveur	**F⁶**	Ferme Petitprez
F³	Ferme Verbecque-Courouble	**M¹**	Monument et musée du Souvenir
		M²	Moulins et musée

TRADITIONAL ACTIVITIES

Mills ⓥ (**M²**) – Next to the traditional **flour mill** (1776) stands the **oil mill** (1743) which was used for processing linseed. In the 19C there were 200 of these oil presses around Lille; this is the last to have survived.

After visiting the mills, it is interesting to tour the **museum** ⓥ managed by a regionally based association Les Amis des Moulins. Exhibits describe the various mechanisms used in the mills, and include the tools used by carpenters, millers, woodcutters etc in the 18C and 19C. There are countless millstones, ranging from a hand-operated prehistoric stone to stones worked by an electric motor.

In June 1915, **Neuville-St-Vaast** further south was captured from the German troops by the 5th Infantry Division led by Général Mangin, after eight days of bloody fighting.

The national mill fair takes place every year on the 3rd Sunday in June.

Musée du Terroir ⊙ – Delporte Farm in the old centre of Annappes is a typical local *cense*, built of Lezennes stone and brick; it now houses the folk museum. In the courtyard and buildings a collection of agricultural tools are displayed, along with traditional workshops: foundry, locksmith's, joinery, saddlery, dairy etc.

ADDITIONAL SIGHTS

Forum des Sciences-Centre François-Mitterrand ⊙ (**B**) – Inaugurated in 1996, this centre is devoted to new technology and stages temporary exhibitions on scientific themes; there is a workshop for youngsters, early-learning area for children aged 3 to 6 and an information centre. The hemispheric planetarium (14m/46ft in diameter) offers an introduction to a study of the sky, the comets, the planets, time...

Château de Flers ⊙ – This Flemish castle, built in 1661 is surrounded by a moat once spanned by a drawbridge. The brick buildings with stone ties, surmounted by stepped gables, house the tourist office and an archeological museum (temporary exhibitions) in the basement.

Parc archéologique ⊙ – This 6ha/15 acre park contains reconstructions of regional dwellings from the Neolithic Era to the end of the Middle Ages: houses, barns, workshops.

VILLERS-COTTERÊTS

Population 8 402

Michelin map 56 north of fold 13 or 237 fold 8

Villers-Cotterêts is a peaceful little town, almost entirely surrounded by Retz Forest; it was the homeland of the Orléans family until the Revolution and developed owing to the royal passion for hunting. It was the birthplace of Alexandre Dumas senior in 1802.

Birth of the State – In 1535 François I replaced the first 12C royal castle with a Renaissance building and added to the outbuildings which dealt with the management of the royal hunts.

It was here that the King announced the famous Statute of Villers-Cotterêts in 1539 prescribing the substitution of French for Latin in public registers and legal documents. Among its 192 articles it stated that parish priests should keep registers of the parishioners' dates of birth and death; here then, are the foundations of the modern registry system. Previously, except in noble families where records were kept, ordinary people had to rely on the memory of witnesses to prove identity. It was another 250 years (1792) before the keeping of State registers was entrusted to the local authorities.

A Child of the Islands – The first of the three generations – grandfather, father and son – of the famous Dumas family was the son of a Dominican settler, Marquess Davy de la Pailleterie, and Marie-Cessette Dumas, a coloured girl. Thomas-Alexandre assumed his mother's surname and pursued a career in the army where he later rose to become General, but his Republican opinions led to his being disgraced by Napoleon Bonaparte. He retired to Villers-Cotterêts which was his wife's homeland and lived a quiet life until his death, four years after the birth of his son Alexandre, the future novelist.

Alexandre Dumas' Youth – Many hard years passed for the widow and her son; Alexandre entered the study of one of the town's notaries and copied deeds there until he was 20. One day his mother told him that only 253 francs remained; Dumas took 53 francs as his share, left the rest for his mother and headed for Paris. He played billiards, gambling the cost of his fare to the capital, and won which allowed him to arrive in the capital with his nest egg intact. His beautiful handwriting landed him a job in the secretary's office of the Duc d'Orléans, future King Louis-Philippe. His prodigious literary career was about to begin.

Château François I ⊙ – In 1806 Napoleon turned the empty château into a workhouse for the *département* of Seine; today it is a retirement home.

Within the courtyard, the east and west sides are bordered by buildings which retain Renaissance features: high attic windows in brick flanked by pillars crowned with urns. At the end stands the main front, with a shallow recessed loggia on the first floor.

The **main staircase★** alone is worth a visit; it is a Renaissance masterpiece, a double flight of stairs dating from the period of François I. The carvings on the coffered ceiling – crowned Fs, salamanders, fleurs-de-lis – are from the school of Jean Goujon. The same motifs are used in greater abundance in the State Room, which was originally the chapel. The vaulting is concealed by a false ceiling. The stonework of the Renaissance altarpiece remains. At the end of the gallery *(display on local history)* the **King's staircase**, contemporary with the main staircase, has its original decoration of carved scenes from The Dream of Polyphyle.

Parc – All that remains of Le Nôtre's work are the outlines of the parterre and the perspective of the Allée Royale ending at a telecommunications tower.

Musée Alexandre-Dumas ⊙ – Three small rooms are dedicated to the famous "Three Dumas": Thomas-Alexandre the General; Alexandre senior, author of *The Three Musketeers*, *The Count of Monte Cristo* and *The Black Tulip*; and Alexandre junior, author of *La Dame aux Camélias*.
Alexandre senior was born in the house at no 46 rue Alexandre Dumas.

EXCURSION

Montgobert – *10km/6mi northeast by N 2 and D 2 (left). Turn onto a small road towards Montgobert.*

Musée du Bois et de l'Outil (Wood and Tool Museum) ⊙ – The museum is housed in the **Château de Montgobert**, on the edge of Retz Forest. The 18C building was originally the property of Pauline Bonaparte and her husband, General Leclerc, who is buried in the park.
On the ground floor traditional woodworking tools used by cartwrights, sawyers, coopers, carpenters, joiners etc are displayed.
The first floor is dedicated to the life and management of the forest; exhibition on the role of the French Forestry Commission *(Office National des Forêts)*.
The second floor focuses on occupations related to wood within the forest (charcoal burning, woodcutting) together with reconstructions of workshops (joinery, spinning mill, dairy etc).

Mémorial canadien de VIMY★

Michelin map 51 fold 15 or 236 fold 15

Vimy Ridge, which overlooks the mining region, was captured in April 1917 by the four divisions of the Canadian Expeditionary Corps, which was part of the British Third Army under General Allenby. Despite this success, the German lines held.
The Ridge was the strongest defensive position in northwestern France and of enormous importance: this 61m/200ft barrier on the plain safeguarded mines and factories which were in production for Germany, and covered the junction of the main Hindenburg Line and the defences stretching

north to the coast. Despite the Canadians' great success, however, the German front was not penetrated.
The impressive white stone **memorial** ⊙, which was the result of a design competition won by a Toronto sculptor who said the idea came to him in a dream, is made of "trau" stone from the Dalmatian coast; its construction began in 1925 and lasted 11 years. The two great shafts symbolise the Canadian and French forces; various figures represent Canada, Peace, Justice, Truth, Knowledge... An inscription at the base of the memorial commemorates the Canadian soldiers (over 66 000 of them) who died during the War, and the ramparts bear the names of a further 11 000 men missing, presumed dead.
The foot of the memorial offers views over the old mining basin; the ossuary on Notre-Dame de Lorette Hill can be seen to the west.
To the south, on the slope of the hill, a network of Canadian and German trenches, dug-outs and **tunnels** have been restored. The tunnel Grange was originally 750m/2 430ft long. The area is still littered with shell holes and mine craters.

The Canadian memorial at Vimy

The chapter on Practical Information at the end of the guide lists:
local or national organisations providing additional information,
recreational and spectator sports,
thematic tours,
suggested reading,
events of interest to the tourist,
admission times and charges.

Rolleboise – the Seine meanders through Île-de-France

Practical
information

Planning your trip

When to go

While the beaches of the Opal Coast are spectacular, stretching out for 1km/0.5mi at low tide, the relatively cool weather and the chilly waters of the Channel are generally more appealing for shell-seekers, horse riders, landsailers and kite-flyers than for swimmers. In the winter months, the coast is often buffeted by strong winds. Statistically, June is the sunniest month on the coast, August the warmest. It rains most in November, and least in April (for a total of 170 days per year). Peak summer temperatures usually hover around 25°C/75°F.

Inland, the winters are chilly and darkness falls early in the northern latitudes. As spring turns to summer, the days grow deliciously long and warm; in June the sun lingers until past 10pm.

For information, brochures, maps and assistance in planning a trip to France travellers should apply to the official French Tourist Office in their own country:

Australia – New Zealand

Sydney – BNP Building, 12 Castlereagh Street
Sydney, New South Wales 2000
☎ (61) 2 231 52 44 – Fax: (61) 2 221 86 82.

Canada

Montreal – College Suite 490
Montreal PQ H3A 2W9
☎ (514) 288-4264 – Fax: (514) 845 48 68.

Eire

Dublin – 38 Lower Abbey St, Dublin 1
☎ (1) 703 40 46 – Fax: (1) 874 73 24.

United Kingdom

London – 179 Piccadilly, London WI
☎ (0891) 244 123 – Fax: (0171) 493 6594.

United States

East Coast: New York – 444 Madison Avenue, NY 10022
☎ 212-838-7800 – Fax: (212) 838 7855.

Mid west: Chicago – 676 North Michigan Avenue, Suite 3360
Chicago, IL 60611
☎ (312) 751 7800 – Fax: (312) 337 6339.

West Coast: Los Angeles – 9454 Wilshire Boulevard, Suite 715
Beverly Hills, CA 90212.
☎ (310) 271 2693 – Fax: (310) 276 2835.

Cyberspace

www.info.france-usa.org
The French Embassy's Web site provides basic information (geography, demographics, history), a news digest and business-related information. It offers special pages for children, and pages devoted to culture, language study and travel, and you can reach other selected French sites (regions, cities, ministries) with a hypertext link.

www.fr-holidaystore.co.uk
The new Travel Centre in London has gone on-line with this service, providing information on all of the regions of France, including updated special travel offers and details on available accommodation.

www.visiteurope.com
The European Travel Commission provides useful information on travelling to and around 27 European countries, and includes links to some commercial booking services (ie, vehicle hire), rail schedules, weather reports and more.

LOCAL TOURIST OFFICES

In addition to the French tourist offices abroad listed above, visitors may wish to contact local offices for more precise information, to receive brochures and maps. Below, the addresses are given for each local tourist office by *Région* and *département*. The index lists the *département* after each town; the *Introduction* at the beginning of this guide also gives information on the administrative divisions of France.

For **regional** information, address inquires to the *Comité régional de tourisme (CRT)*:

Nord-Pas-de-Calais, 6 Place Mendès-France, 59800 Lille, France. ☎ 03 20 14 57 57.

Picardie, 11 Mail Albert 1ᵉʳ BP 2616, 80026 Amiens Cedex, France. ☎ 03 22 91 10 15.

Île-de-France, 26 Avenue de l'Opéra, 75001 Paris. ☎ 01 42 60 28 62.

For information on each **département**, contact the *comités départementaux de tourisme (CDT)*:

Nord: 15-17 Rue du Nouveau-Siècle, BP 135, 59027 Lille Cedex. ☎ 03 20 57 00 61.

Pas-de-Calais: 24 Rue Desille, 62204 Boulogne-sur-Mer Cedex. ☎ 03 21 83 32 59.

Aisne: 1 Rue Saint-Martin, BP 116, 02006 Laon Cedex. ☎ 03 23 26 70 00.

Oise: 19 Rue Pierre-Jacoby, BP 822, 60008 Beauvais. ☎ 03 44 45 82 12.

Somme: 21 Rue Ernest-Cauvin, 80000 Amiens, France. ☎ 03 22 92 26 39.

Eure-et-Loir: 10 Rue du Docteur Maunoury, BP 67, 28002 Chartres Cedex. ☎ 02 37 36 36 39.

Essonne: 2 Cours Monseigneur Roméro, 91025 Evry Cedex. ☎ 01 64 97 35 13.

Hauts-de-Seine: Change of address underway. ☎ 01 46 42 17 95.

Seine-et-Marne: Hôtel d'Albe, 9 et 11 Rue Royale, 77300 Fontainebleau. ☎ 01 60 39 60 39.

Seine-St-Denis: 1 Ruede la République, 93000 St-Denis. ☎ 01 42 43 33 55.

Val-d'Oise: Château de la Motte, 95270 Luzarches. ☎ 01 34 71 90 00.

Yvelines: 2 Place André-Mignot, 78012 Versailles. ☎ 01 39 02 78 78.

Maison de province – The **Maison du Nord-Pas-de-Calais**, 25 Rue Bleu, 75009 Paris ☎ 01 48 00 59 62 provides documents on the region, sells books and regional products and organises special events.

Offices de tourisme – In the *Admission times and charges* section of this guide, the address and phone number of the tourist offices for the main towns are listed next to town.

Travellers with special needs – The sights described in this guide which are easily accessible to people of reduced mobility are indicated in the *Admission times and charges* by the symbol &.

Useful information on transportation, holidaymaking and sports associations for the disabled is available from the *Comité National Français de Liaison pour la Réadaptation des Handicapés* (CNRH), 236 bis, rue de Tolbiac, 75013 Paris. Call their international information number ☎ 01 53 80 66 44, or write to request a catalogue of publications. Web-surfers can find information for slow walkers, mature travellers and others with special needs at www.access-able.com. If you are a member of a sports club and would like to practice your sport in France, or meet others who do, ask the CNRH for information on clubs in the *Fedération Française du Sport Adapté* (FFSA – Paris, ☎ 01 48 72 80 72). For information on museum access for the disabled contact La Direction, *Les Musées de France, Service Accueil des Publics Spécifiques*, 6, rue des Pyramides, 75041 Paris Cedex 1, ☎ 01 40 15 35 88.

The **Michelin Red Guide France** and the **Michelin Camping Caravaning France** indicate hotels and camp sites with facilities suitable for physically handicapped people.

FORMALITIES

Passport – Visitors entering France must be in possession of a valid national passport. In case of loss or theft report to the embassy or consulate and the local police.

Visa – No entry visa is required for Canadian and US citizens staying less than three months; it is required of Australian citizens in accordance with French security measures. If you need a visa, apply to the French Consulate (visa issued the same day; longer if submitted by mail).

US citizens should obtain the booklet *Safe Trip Abroad* ($1.25) which provides useful information on obtaining a passport, visa requirements, customs regulations, medical care etc for international travellers. It is published by the Government Printing Office and may be ordered by phone (1-202-512-1800), consulted or ordered via Internet (www.access.gpo.gov). General passport information is available by phone toll-free from the Federal Information Center (item 5 on the automated menu) ☎ 800-688 9889. US passport application forms can be downloaded from http://travel.state.gov.

Customs – Apply to the Customs Office (UK) for a leaflet on customs regulations and the full range of duty-free allowances. The US Customs Service offers a publication *Know Before You Go* for US citizens. For the office nearest you, look in the Federal Government section of your phone book, under US Department of the Treasury (or consult www.customs.ustreas.gov). There are no customs formalities for holidaymakers bringing their caravans into France for a stay of less than six months. No customs document is necessary for pleasure boats and outboard motors for a stay of less than six months but the registration certificate should be kept on board.

Americans can bring home, tax-free, up to US$400 worth of goods; Canadians up to CND$300; Australians up to AUS$400 and New Zealanders up to NZ$700. Persons living in a Member State of the European Union are not restricted in regard to purchasing goods for private use, but the recommended allowances for alcoholic beverages and tobacco are as follows:

Spirits (whisky, gin, vodka etc)	10l	Cigarettes	800
Fortified wines (vermouth, ports etc)	20l	Cigarillos	400
Wine (not more than 60 sparkling)	90l	Cigars	200
Beer	110l	Smoking tobacco	1kg

EMBASSIES AND CONSULATES

Australia Embassy 4 Avenue Jean-Rey, 75015 Paris
☎ 01 40 59 33 00 – fax: 01 40 59 33 10.

Canada Embassy 35 Avenue Montaigne, 75008 Paris
☎ 01 44 43 29 00 – fax: 01 44 43 29 99.

Eire Embassy 4 Rue Rude, 75016 Paris
☎ 01 44 17 67 00 – fax: 01 45 00 84 17.

New Zealand Embassy 7 ter Rue Léonard-de-Vinci, 75016 Paris
☎ 01 45 00 24 11 – fax: 01 45 26 39.

UK Embassy 35 Rue du Faubourg St-Honoré, 75008 Paris
☎ 01 42 66 91 42 – fax: 01 42 66 95 90.

Consulate 16 Rue d'Anjou, 75008 Paris ☎ 01 42 66 06 68 (visas).

USA Embassy 2 Avenue Gabriel, 75008 Paris
☎ 01 43 12 22 22 – fax: 01 42 66 97 83.

Consulate 2 Aue St-Florentin, 75001 Paris
☎ 01 42 96 14 88.

Consulate 15 Avenue d'Alsace, 67082 Strasbourg
☎ 03 88 35 31 04.

PUBLIC HOLIDAYS

Museums and other monuments may be closed or may vary their hours of admission on the following public holidays:

1	January	New Year's Day (Jour de l'An)
		Easter Day and Easter Monday (Pâques)
1	May	May Day
8	May	VE Day
		Whit Sunday and Monday (Pentecôte)
		Ascension Day (Ascension)
14	July	France's National Day (Bastille Day)
15	August	Assumption (Assomption)
1	November	All Saint's Day (Toussaint)
11	November	Armistice Day
25	December	Christmas Day (Noël)

National museums and art galleries are closed on Tuesdays; municipal museums are generally closed on Mondays. In addition to the usual school holidays at Christmas and in the spring and summer, there are long mid-term breaks (10 days to a fortnight) in February and early November.

Getting there

By air – Most major airlines operate flights to Paris (Charles-de-Gaulle/Roissy located 27km/14mi north of Paris or Orly located 16km/10mi south). There are also direct flights from London to Lille-Lesquin airport, located fifteen minutes from the centre of Lille in northern France. Contact airlines and travel agents for information on package-tour flights with rail or coach link-ups or fly-drive schemes.

The major French carriers – Air Inter Europe, Air France, Air Liberté – offer frequent domestic flights between major French cities.

By rail – French Railways (SNCF) and British companies operate a daily service via the Channel Tunnel on Eurostar (3hr) between London (Waterloo International Station, ☎ 0345 881 881) and Paris (Gare du Nord).

Rail passes offering unlimited travel, and group travel tickets offering savings for parties are available under certain conditions. **Eurailpass, Flexipass** and **Saver Pass** are options available in the US for travel in Europe and must be purchased in the US – ☎ 1 800 4 EURAIL or www.raileurope.com.us; Eurporail provides timetables and information on special fares via internet www.eurail.on.ca (☎ 1-888-667-9731, fax 1-519-645-0682); or consult your travel agent.

In the UK, information and bookings can be obtained from French Railways, 179 Piccadilly, London W1V 0BA, ☎ 0891 515 477, in mainline stations, or from travel agencies.

The SNCF operates a telephone information, reservation and pre-payment service in English, from 7am to 10pm (French time). In France, ☎ 08 36 35 35 39. From abroad, ☎ 00 33 8 36 35 35 39. Internet: www.sncf.fr. Ask about discount rates if you are over 60, a student, or travelling with your family.

A rail ticket used within France must be validated *(composter)* by using the orange automatic date-stamping machines at the platform entrance.

Baggage trolleys (10F coin required – refundable) are available at mainline stations.

By coach (bus) – Regular coach services are operated from London to Paris. For further information, contact **Eurolines**:

London: 52 Grosvenor Gardens, Victoria, London SW1W 0AU. ☎ 0171 730 8235.

Paris: 28, avenue du Général de Gaulle, 93541 Bagnolet. ☎ 01 49 72 51 51.

By sea – There are numerous **cross-Channel services** (passenger and car ferries, hovercraft, SeaCat) from the United Kingdom and Eire. For details contact travel agencies or:

P&O Stena Lines, Channel House, Channel View Road, Dover CT17 9TJ. Reservations: ☎ 0990 980 980.

Portsmouth Commercial Port, George Byng Way, Portsmouth, Hampshire PO2 8SP. ☎ 01705 297 391.

Hoverspeed, International Hoverport, Marine Parade, Dover, Kent CT17 9TG. ☎ 01304 240 241.

Brittany Ferries, Millbay Docks, Plymouth, Devon PLI 3ᴱW. ☎ 0990 360 360. The Brittany Centre, Wharf Road, Portsmouth, Hampshire PO2 8RU. ☎ 01705 827 701.

Sally Direct, Ferry Terminal, Ramsgate, Kent CT11 8RP ☎ 0845 600 2626, fax 01843 853 536.

To choose the most suitable route between your point of arrival and your destination, use the **Michelin Motoring Atlas France** or Michelin maps from the 1:200 000 series with yellow covers.

Motoring in France

Planning your route – The area covered in this guide is easily reached by main motorways and national routes. **Michelin map 911** indicates the main itineraries as well as alternate routes for avoiding heavy traffic during busy holiday periods, and gives estimated travel times. **Michelin map 914** is a detailed atlas of French motorways, indicating tolls, rest areas and services along the route; it includes a table for calculating distances and times. In France, use the Minitel service **3615 MICHELIN** to plan an itinerary. The newest Michelin route-planning service is available on Internet, **www.michelin-travel.com**. Travellers can calculate a precise route using such options as shortest route, route avoiding toll roads, Michelin-recommended route, and gain access to tourist information (hotels, restaurants, attractions). The service is available on a pay-per-route basis or by subscription.

Documents – Travellers from other European Union countries and North America can drive in France with a valid national or home-state **driving licence**. An **international driving licence** is useful because the information on it appears in nine languages (keep in mind that traffic officers are empowered to fine motorists). A permit is available (US$10) from the National Auto Club, Touring Department, 188 The Embarcardero, Suite 300 San Francisco CA 94105; or contact your local branch of the American Automobile Association. For the vehicle it is necessary to have the registration papers (logbook) and a nationality plate of the approved size.

Insurance – Certain motoring organisations (AAA, AA, RAC) offer accident insurance and breakdown service schemes for members. Check with your current insurance company in regard to coverage while abroad. If you plan to hire a car using your credit card, check with the company, which may provide liability insurance automatically (and thus save you having to pay the optional fee for optimum coverage).

Highway Code – The minimum driving age is 18. Traffic drives on the right. It is compulsory for the front-seat passengers to wear **seat belts** and it is also compulsory for the back-seat passengers when the car is fitted with them. Children under the age of 10 must travel on the back seat of the vehicle. Full or dipped headlights must be switched on in poor visibility and at night; use side-lights only when the vehicle is stationary.

In the case of a **breakdown** a red warning triangle or hazard warning lights are obligatory. In the absence of stop signs at intersections, cars must **yield to the right**. Traffic on main roads outside built-up areas (priority indicated by a yellow diamond sign) and on roundabouts has right of way. Vehicles must stop when the lights turn red at road junctions and may filter to the right only when indicated by an amber arrow.

The regulations on **drinking and driving** (limited to 0.50 g/litre) and **speeding** are strictly enforced – usually by an on-the-spot fine and/or confiscation of the vehicle.

Speed limits – Although liable to modification, these are as follows:
- toll motorways *(péage)* 130kph-80mph (110kph-68mph when raining);
- dual carriageways and motorways without tolls 110kph-68mph (100kph-62mph when raining);
- other roads 90kph-56mph (80kph-50mph when raining) and in towns 50kph-31mph;
- outside lane on motorways during daylight, on level ground and with good visibility – minimum speed limit of 80kph (50mph).

Parking Regulations – In town there are zones where parking is either restricted or subject to a fee; tickets should be obtained from the ticket machines (*horodateurs* – small change necessary) and displayed inside the windscreen on the driver's

side; failure to display may result in a fine, or towing and impoundment. In some towns you may find blue parking zones *(zone bleue)* marked by a blue line on the pavement or road and a blue signpost with a P and a small square underneath. In this case you have to display a cardboard disc with various times indicated on it. This will enable you to stay for 1hr 30min (2hr 30min over lunch time) free. Discs are available in supermarkets or petrol stations (ask for a *disque de stationnement*); they are sometimes given away free.

Tolls – In France, most motorway sections are subject to a toll *(péage)*. You can pay in cash or with a credit card (Visa, Mastercard).

Car Rental – There are car rental agencies at airports, railway stations and in all large towns throughout France. European cars have manual transmission; automatic cars are available in larger cities only if an advance reservation is made. Drivers must be over 21; between ages 21-25, drivers are required to pay an extra daily fee of 50-100F; some companies allow drivers under 23 only if the reservation has been made through a travel agent. It is relatively expensive to hire a car in France; Americans in particular will notice the difference and should make arrangements before leaving, take advantage of fly-drive offers, or seek advice from a travel agent, specifying requirements.

Central Reservation in France:
Avis: 01 46 10 60 60   **Europcar**: 01 30 43 82 82
Budget: 01 46 86 65 65   **Hertz**: 01 47 88 51 51
Baron's Limousine and Driver: 01 45 30 21 21

Global Motorhome rents fully-equipped recreational vehicles in a range of sizes; Paris pick-up. The toll-free US number is 800-468-3876 (order a video "Europe by RV" ☎ 800-406-3348).

Petrol (US: gas) – French service stations dispense: *sans plomb 98* (super unleaded 98), *sans plomb 95* (super unleaded 95) and *diesel/gazole* (diesel). Petrol is considerably more expensive in France than in the USA, and also more expensive than in the UK.

Accommodation

HOTELS

The **Places to Stay** map in the Introduction indicates recommended places for overnight stops, weekend breaks, shorts holidays, as well as rating seaside resorts according to the range of activities they offer. Use the map in conjunction with the **Michelin Red Guide France** which lists a selection of hotels and restaurants.

Loisirs-Accueil is a booking service which has offices in most French *départements*. For information contact Réservation Loisirs Accueil, 280 Boulevard St-Germain, 75007 Paris; ☎ 01 44 11 10 44.

Accueil de France tourist offices which are open all year make hotel bookings for a small fee, for personal (non-business) callers only. The head office is in Paris (127 Avenue des Champs-Élysées, ☎ 01 49 52 53 54 for information only) and there are offices in many large towns and resorts.

Logis et Auberges de France publishes a brochure (a selection of inns) which is available from the French Government Tourist Office.

Relais et Châteaux, 9 Avenue Marceau, 75016 Paris, ☎ 01 47 42 20 92, lists hotel accommodation in châteaux and manor houses around France.

FARM STAYS AND HOLIDAY RENTALS

Maison des Gîtes de France has a list of self-catering (often rural) accommodation where you can stay in this region (and all over France). Generally, the service lists cottages or apartments decorated in the local style where you will be able to make yourself at home. Gîtes de France have offices in Paris: 59 Rue St-Lazare 75009 Paris, ☎ 01 49 70 75 75.
You must purchase the list (a small guide book with details and ratings) for the area that interests you and make reservations directly through the proprietor.

The **Fédération française des Stations Vertes de Vacances** publishes an annual list of **rural localities**, selected for their tranquillity, and the outdoor activities available. Information from the Federation, 16 Rue Nodot, 21000 Dijon, ☎ 03 80 43 49 47. Among the localities in this region are **Bergues** in Nord, **Montreuil-sur-Mer** in Pas-de-Calais and **Poix-de-Picardie** in Somme.

The guide **Bienvenue à la ferme** (Editions Solar) includes the addresses of farmers providing guest facilities who have signed a charter drawn up by the Chambers of Agriculture. *Bienvenue à la ferme* farms, vetted for quality and meeting official standards, can be identified by the yellow flower which serves as their logo. Address inquiries to:

– *Bienvenue à la ferme dans l'Aisne*, Agriculture and tourisme 02, Maison de l'Agriculture, 38 Boulevard de Lyon, 02007 Laon Cedex, ☎ 03 23 22 50 94.
– *Bienvenue dans les fermes du Pas-de-Calais*, Relais départemental agriculture et tourisme, 56 Avenue Roger-Salengro, BP39, 62051 St-Laurent Blangy Cedex, ☎ 03 21 24 07 07.
– *Bienvenue dans les fermes de l'Oise*, Chambre d'Agriculture, Service tourisme, Rue Frère-Gagne, 60021 Beauvais Cedex, ☎ 03 44 11 44 50.
The guide-book entitled *Vacances et week-ends à la ferme* published by Editions Balland also gives a list of addresses.

Ramblers can consult the guide entitled *Gîtes et refuges France et Frontières* by A and S Mouraret (Editions La Cadole, 74 Rue Albert-Perdreaux, 78140 Vélizy, ☎ 01 34 65 10 40).
The guide has been written mainly for those who enjoy rambling, riding and cycling holidays.

BED AND BREAKFAST

Gîtes de France *(see above)* publishes a booklet on bed and breakfast accommodation *(chambres d'hôte)* which include a room and breakfast at a reasonable price.
You can also contact **Bed & Breakfast (UK and France)**, 94-96 Bell St, Henley-on-Thames, Oxon RG9 1XS, ☎ 01491 578 803, Fax: 01491 410 806; e-mail: bookings@bed-break.demon.co.uk.

YOUTH HOSTELS

There are two main youth hostel associations *(auberges de jeunesse)* in France: **Ligue Française pour les Auberges de Jeunesse**, 38 Boulevard Raspail, 75007 Paris, ☎ 01 45 48 69 84, fax: 01 45 44 57 47 and **Fédération Unie des Auberges de Jeunesse (FUAJ)** 27 Rue Pajol, 75018 Paris, ☎ 01 44 89 87 27, fax: 01 44 89 87 10.

The **International Youth Hostel Federation** (www.iyhf.org) is establishing a computerised booking network (IBN), which allows hostellers to view bed availability and to reserve as much as six months in advance. The annual guide *Hostelling International Europe* is on sale in book shops and can be ordered from your national association. US: American Hostels Inc, 733 15th Street NW, Suite 840, Washington DC 20005. UK: Youth Hostels Association, Trevelyan House, 8 St Stephen's Hill, St Albans, Hertfordshire AL1 2DY.

FUAJ publishes booklets in French and English for hostellers and adventurers. Order from the address listed above or via the Internet (www.fuaj.org).

CAMPING

There are numerous officially graded sites with varying standards of facilities along the coast and elsewhere. The **Michelin Guide Camping Caravaning France** lists a selection of camp sites. An International Camping Carnet for caravans is useful but not compulsory; it may be obtained from motoring organisations or from the Camping and Caravaning Club (Greenfields House, Westwook Way, Coventry CV4 8JH, ☎ 01203 694 995).

Eating out

Guide Rouge Michelin France – This guide-book provides a very wide selection of restaurants serving the finest specialities in Flanders, Picardy, Paris and the Île-de-France region. When the word *repas* ("meal") is printed in red, it refers to a high-quality but reasonably-priced meal. This is a gourmet guide you can trust.

Armengaud/Association des Amis de Felleries et des Bois-jolis, Felleries

Traditional Avesnois butter moulds

Fermes-auberges (Farm-inns) – Farm-inns may or may not offer accommodation. They serve farm produce and local speciality dishes. They are open at weekends but advanced booking is required. Contact the Association des fermiers aubergistes de France, **Ferm'Auberge**, Les Perriaux, 89350 Champignelles. ☎ 03 85 45 13 22.

Brasseries in northern France – The best place to discover the friendliness of people in the north of France is one of the many *brasseries* (the name derives from the French for "brewery"; hot and cold dishes are usually available all day long) often located on the main square, beside the belfry. This is also the best place to taste the traditional dish of mussels and French-fried potatoes, or a sugar tart washed down with a glass of beer. The ambience is lively well into the night.

In the Nord-Pas-de-Calais area, there are still several **traditional breweries** which produce beer in the old-fashioned way, even where ultra-modern equipment has been introduced. Some of them are open to the public:

– **Brasserie d'Annœullin**, 4 Grand'Place, 59112 Annœullin. ☎ 03 20 86 83 60.
– **Brasserie Castelain**, 13 Rue Pasteur, 62410 Bénifontaine. ☎ 03 21 40 38 38 (1hr guided tour by appointment).
– **Brasserie Castelain**, 13 Rue Pasteur, 62410 Bénifontaine. ☎ 03 21 08 68 61.
– **Brasserie Bécu**, 10 Rue Verlaine, 62118 Fampoux. ☎ 03 21 55 97 57
– **Heineken**, Rue du Houblon, ZI de la Pilaterie, 59370 Mons-en-Barœul. ☎ 03 20 33 67 56.
– **Brasserie Thiriez**, 22 Rue de Wormhout, 59470 Esquelbecq. ☎ 03 28 62 88 44.

Possibilité de restauration:
– **Les Trois Brasseurs**, 22 Place de la Gare, 59800 Lille. ☎ 03 20 06 46 25.
– **Taverne de l'Écu**, 9 Rue Esquermoise, 59800 Lille. ☎ 03 20 57 55 66.
– **Beck**, Eckelstraete, 59270 Bailleul. ☎ 03 28 49 03 90.
– **Au Baron**, Place du Fond-des-Rocs, 59570 Gussignies. ☎ 03 27 66 88 61.
– **Brasserie St-Poloise**, 2 Rue de la Calandre, 62130 St-Pol-sur-Ternoise. ☎ 03 21 41 91 00.

To make one litre of beer, it takes:
– 200g (1 cup) of grain (mainly barley)
– 2g (1/2 teaspoon) of hops
– 1cl (0.33oz) of yeast
– pure water

Estaminets – Food and drink are also served in the cafés known locally as *estaminets* (originally, a café where smoking was permitted). The warm, unpretentious atmosphere is typical of the region, as is the good beer served there.
– **De Vierpot**, 125 Rue du Moulin, 59299 Boeschepe.
– **Het Blauwershof**, 9 Rue d'Eecke, 59270 Godewaersvelde.
– **L'Estaminet flamand**, 6 Rue des fusilliers-marins, 59140 Dunkerque.
– **Le St-Georges**, 5 Rue de Caëstre, 59114 Ecke.
– **L'Haezepoel**, 3451 Chemin de l'Haezepoel, 59122 Hondschoote.
– **'T Kasteelhof**, next to the milll, 59670 Cassel. Sharing premises with the *estaminet*, la **Maison du Pays** offers crafts and speciality foods from Flanders, Hainaut and Artois *(open from 10am to 7pm Wed-Sun; every day in June, July and August, ☎ 03 28 40 59 29)*.

The coast – Those who enjoy fish will remember that Boulogne is France's leading fresh fish port. In addition to the gourmet restaurants serving fish soup, turbot with cream sauce, *sole meunière*, or a fish platter known as *la gainée* consisting of three different types of fish with a shrimp sauce, there are also fishmongers' stalls selling cod, herring and fresh eels.

Picardie – Soup has pride of place in this region and one of the best-known is the *soupe des hortillons*, made with fresh vegetables. Water fowl is used in many different ways, for example duck or snipe paté. The *ficelle picarde* is a ham pancake rolled up and filled with mushrooms then smothered in bechamel sauce and baked in the oven until the top is crisp and golden. Leek quiche also forms part of a simple but delicious meal.

You can obtain a copy of the *Guide des produits et de la gastronomie* for the Nord-Pas-de-Calais area and for Picardy by contacting:
– Chambre régionale d'agriculture Nord-Pas-de-Calais, 56 Avenue Roger-Salengro, BP 39, 62051, St-Laurent-Blangy Cedex, ☎ 03 21 60 57 86.
– Terroirs de Picardie, comité de promotion, BP 2626, 80026 Amiens Cedex, ☎ 03 22 97 39 49.

Gourmet guide – The Picardy region boasts some spots which appeal to the gourmet tourist interested in discovering local specialities. Among the places which have been awarded the *Site remarquable du goût* (for "remarkable taste sensations") distinction are Houille, Loos and Wanbrechies, on the outskirts of Lille, known for *genièvre* (a juniper-flavoured eau-de-vie similar to gin); the port of Boulogne famous for its fish; the market gardens of the Marais audomarois in St-Omer; and the *Hortillonnages* marshland in Amiens, for fruits and vegetables (traditional floating market on the 3rd Sunday in June, canal festival in September).

Michelin Maps are updated constantly.
Always travel with the latest edition.

General information

Medical treatment – First aid, medical advice and chemists' night service rota are available from chemists/drugstores *(pharmacie)* identified by the green cross sign.
It is advisable to take out comprehensive insurance cover as the recipient of medical treatment in French hospitals or clinics must pay the bill. Nationals of non-EU countries should check with their insurance companies about policy limitations. Reimbursement can then be negotiated with the insurance company according to the policy held.
All prescription drugs should be clearly labelled; it is recommended that you carry a copy of the prescription. American Express offers its members a service, "Global Assist", for any medical, legal or personal emergency – call collect from anywhere in France ☎ 01 47 16 25 29.

British and Irish citizens should apply to the Department of Health and Social Security for Form E 111, which entitles the holder to urgent treatment for accident or unexpected illness in EU countries. A refund of part of the costs of treatment can be obtained on application in person or by post to the local Social Security Offices *(Caisse Primaire d'Assurance Maladie)*.

The American Hospital of Paris is open 24hr for emergencies as well as consultations, with English-speaking staff, at 63 Boulevard Victor-Hugo, 92200 Neuilly-sur-Seine, ☎ 01 46 41 25 25. Accredited by major insurance companies.

The British Hospital is just outside Paris in Levallois-Perret, 3 Rue Barbès, ☎ 01 46 39 22 22.

Time – France is 1hr ahead of Greenwich Mean Time (GMT).
When it is **noon in France**, it is

3	am	in Los Angeles
6	am	in New York
11	am	in Dublin
11	am	in London
7	pm	in Perth
9	pm	in Sydney
11	pm	in Auckland

R. Corbel

In France "am" and "pm" are not used but the 24-hour clock is widely applied.

Electricity – The electric current is 220 volts. Circular two-pin plugs are the rule. Adapters should be bought before your leave home; they are on sale in most airports.

CURRENCY

There are no restrictions on the amount of currency visitors can take into France. Visitors carrying a lot of cash are advised to complete a currency declaration form on arrival, because there are restrictions on currency export.

Notes and coins – *See illustration following*. The unit of currency in France is the French Franc subdivided into 100 centimes. European currency units known as **Euros** are being printed, and as of January 1999 the banking and finance industries began making the changeover. Banknotes are scheduled to go into circulation in January 2002, with national instruments phased out by July of that year. In the meantime, both euro and franc values (1 euro is about 6 francs 50 centimes) are given in more and more instances (store and restaurant receipts, bank documents etc).

Banks – Banks are open from 9am to noon and 2pm to 4pm and branches are closed either on Monday or Saturday. Banks close early on the day before a bank holiday. A passport is necessary as identification when cashing travellers or ordinary cheques in banks. Commission charges vary and hotels usually charge more than banks for cashing cheques for non-residents. Most banks and many larger post offices have **cash dispensers** (ATM) which accept international credit cards (have your PIN number handy). These machines *(distributeurs)* are located outside many different banks, and easily identified by the luminous sign showing a hand holding a card. Visa and Mastercard are accepted almost everywhere; American Express cards can only be used in dispensers in Paris at 11, rue Scribe (Amex office), and inside the Gare de Lyon and the Gare Montparnasse train stations.

Credit Cards – Visa, Mastercard-Eurocard, American Express and Diners Club are widely accepted in shops, hotels and restaurants and petrol stations. If your card is lost or stolen, call the following 24-hour hotlines:

American Express	01 47 77 72 00	Visa	01 42 77 11 90
Mastercard/Eurocard	01 45 67 84 84	Diners Club	01 47 62 75 00

You must report any loss or theft of credit cards or travellers' cheques to the local police who will issue you with a certificate (useful proof to show the issuing company).

Tipping – Since a service charge is automatically included in the price of meals and accommodation in France, it is not necessary to tip in restaurants and hotels. However taxi drivers, bellboys, doormen, petrol station attendants or anybody who has been of assistance are usually tipped at the customer's discretion. Most French people give an extra tip in restaurants and cafés (at least 50 centimes for a drink and several francs for a meal).

POST AND TELEPHONE

Main post offices open Monday to Friday 8am to 7pm, Saturday 8am to noon. Smaller branch post offices generally close at lunch time between noon and 2pm and at 4pm.

Postage via air mail:

> UK: letter (20g) 3.00 F
>
> North America: letter (20g) 4.40 F
>
> Australia and NZ: letter (20g) 5.20F

Stamps are also available from newsagents and *bureaux de tabac*. Stamp collectors should ask for *timbres de collection* in any post office.

Public Telephones – Most public phones in France use pre-paid phone cards *(télécartes)*, rather than coins. Some telephone booths accept credit cards (Visa, Mastercard/Eurocard: minimum monthly charge 20F). *Télécartes* (50 or 120 units) can be bought in post offices, branches of France Télécom, *bureaux de tabac* (cafés that sell cigarettes) and newsagents and can be used to make calls in France and abroad. Calls can be received at phone boxes

where the blue bell sign is shown; the phone will not ring, so keep your eye on the little message screen.

National calls – French telephone numbers have 10 digits. Paris and Paris region numbers begin with 01; 02 in northwest France; 03 in northeast France; 04 in southeast France and Corsica; 05 in southwest France.

International calls – To call France from abroad, dial the country code (33) + 9-digit number (omit the initial 0). When calling abroad from France dial 00, then dial the country code followed by the area code and number of your correspondent.

International dialling codes (00 + code):

Australia	61	New Zealand	64
Canada	1	United Kingdom	44
Eire	353	United States	1

To use your **personal calling card** dial:

AT&T....................	0-800 99 00 11	Sprint....................	0-800 99 00 87
MCI	0-800 99 00 19	Canada Direct........	0-800 99 00 16

International Information, US/Canada: 00 33 12 11

International operator: 00 33 12 + country code

Local directory assistance: 12

Toll-free numbers in France begin with 0 800.

Emergency numbers:

Police:	17	**"SAMU"** (Paramedics):	15
Fire *(Pompiers)*:	18		

Minitel – France Télécom operates a system offering directory enquiries (free of charge up to 3min), travel and entertainment reservations, and other services (cost varies between 0.37F – 5.57F/min). These small computer-like terminals can be found in some post offices, hotels and France Télécom agencies and in many French homes. 3614 PAGES E is the code for **Directory assistance in English** (turn on the unit, dial 3614, hit the "connexion" button when you get the tone, type in "PAGES E", and follow the instructions on the screen). For route planning, use Michelin services **3615 MICHELIN** (tourist and route information) and **3617 MICHELIN** (information sent by fax).

Cellular phones in France have numbers which begin with 06. Two-watt (lighter, shorter reach) and eight-watt models are on the market, using the Itinéris (France Télécom) or SFR network. "Mobicartes" are pre-paid phone cards that fit into mobile units. Cell phone rentals (delivery or airport pickup provided):

Ellinas Phone Rental	01 47 20 70 00
Euro Exaphone	01 44 09 77 78
Rent a Cell Express	01 53 93 78 00

Conversion tables

Weights and measures

1 kilogram (kg)	2.2 pounds (lb)	2.2 pounds
1 metric ton (tn)	1.1 tons	1.1 tons

to convert kilograms to pounds, multiply by 2.2

1 litre (l)	2.1 pints (pt)	1.8 pints
1 litre	0.3 gallon (gal)	0.2 gallon

to convert litres to gallons, multiply by 0.26 (US) or 0.22 (UK)

1 hectare (ha)	2.5 acres	2.5 acres
1 square kilometre (km²)	0.4 square miles (sq mi)	0.4 square miles

to convert hectares to acres, multiply by 2.4

1 centimetre (cm)	0.4 inches (in)	0.4 inches
1 metre (m)	3.3 feet (ft) - 39.4 inches - 1.1 yards (yd)	
1 kilometre (km)	0.6 miles (mi)	0.6 miles

to convert metres to feet, multiply by 3.28. kilometres to miles, multiply by 0.6

Clothing

Women	EU	US	UK
	35	4	2½
	36	5	3½
	37	6	4½
Shoes	38	7	5½
	39	8	6½
	40	9	7½
	41	10	8½
	36	4	8
	38	6	10
Dresses & Suits	40	8	12
	42	12	14
	44	14	16
	46	16	18
	36	08	30
	38	10	32
Blouses & sweaters	40	12	14
	42	14	36
	44	16	38
	46	18	40

EU	US	UK	Men
40	7½	7	
41	8½	8	
42	9½	9	
43	10½	10	Shoes
44	11½	11	
45	12½	12	
46	13½	13	
46	36	36	
48	38	38	
50	40	40	Suits
52	42	42	
54	44	44	
56	46	48	
37	14½	14,5	
38	15	15	
39	15½	15½	Shirts
40	15¾	15¾	
41	16	16	
42	16½	16½	

Sizes often vary depending on the designer. These equivalents are given for guidance only.

Speed

kph	10	30	50	70	80	90	100	110	120	130
mph	6	19	31	43	50	56	62	68	75	81

Temperature

Celsius (°C)	0°	5°	10°	15°	20°	25°	30°	40°	60°	80°	100°
Fahrenheit (°F)	32°	41°	50°	59°	68°	77°	86°	104°	140°	176°	212°

To convert Celsius into Fahrenheit, multiply °C by 9, divide by 5, and add 32.
To convert Fahrenheit into Celsius, subtract 32 from °F, multiply by 5, and divide by 9.

Notes and coins

500 Francs featuring
scientists
Pierre and Marie Curie
(1858-1906). (1867-1934)

200 Francs featuring
engineer Gustave Eiffel
(1832-1923)

100 Francs featuring
Post-Impressionist painter
Paul Cézanne
(1839-1906)

50 Francs featuring
pilot and writer
Antoine de Saint-Exupéry
(1900-1944)

20 Francs

10 Francs

5 Francs

2 Francs

1 Franc

50 Centimes

20 Centimes

10 Centimes

5 Centimes

Sports and recreation

WATER SPORTS

Fishing – This is an area crossed by a myriad of rivers, waterways and lakes, a paradise for anglers, especially along the rivers Somme, Course, Lyse, Aisne, Oise, Aa and in the seven-valley region (Canche, Authie, Ternoise etc.).

The map-brochure with commentary entitled *Pêche en France* can be obtained from the *Conseil Supérieur de la pêche*, 134 Avenue de Malakoff, 75116 Paris, (☎ 01 45 02 20 20) or from the *Fédération de pêche* (angling union) in each *département*.

Obligatory fishing permits *(cartes de pêche)* are often for sale on site in cafés or sports shops located near popular spots.

Boat trips for anglers are organised in Berck (Les Sternes: ☎ 03 21 84 43 48), Boulogne (Les Arsouins: ☎ 03 21 87 55 99) and Etaples (May to September: contact the Tourist Office: ☎ 03 21 09 56 94 or the Pavillon de la mer, ☎ 03 21 94 17 51). Boat trips for non-anglers can also be arranged.

Sailing and windsurfing – There are sailing schools all along the coast from Bray-Dunes to Auly-Onival. Some of the inland lakes are also ideal for these sports, for example the Val-Joly recreation area in the Avesnois region *(see map under L'AVESNOIS)*, the Etangs de la Sensée and Escaut, and the Lac de Monampteuil near Soissons. For information, contact the *Fédération française de voile*, 55 Avenue Kléber, 75784 Paris Cedex 16. ☎ 01 45 53 68 00.

Cruising the waterways – The rivers and canals once plied by well-laden barges constitute over a thousand miles of navigable waterways providing holidaymakers with an opportunity to enjoy a cruise or hire their own boat, both excellent ways of visiting the region.

Voies Navigables de France, 175 Rue Ludovic-Boutleux, 62408 Béthune Cedex ☎ 03 21 63 24 24, can provide information on travelling the waterways. They also have offices in Calais, Douai, Dunkerque, Lille, Margny-lès-Compiègne, St-Quentin and Valenciennes.

Crown Blue Lines rents self-skippered boats accommodating two to eight passengers in 10 regions of France. Weekly rates range from $1 320 for a two-person boat to $4 620 for an eight-person vessel. Rates are lowest in April and Ocotber, then May and September; the high season is July and August. Bike rental and car parking cost extra. Headquarters in Britain: 1603 630513. Toll-free US number: 800-355-9394. Internet: www.crown-holidays.co.uk.

Marne Loisirs – Quai Jacques-Prévert Prolongé, 77100 Meaux, ☎ 01 64 34 97 97. House boats (no permit required) for 2 to 12 people.

Nogent-sur-Marne Marina – ☎ 01 48 71 41 65. Peddle boats and small motor boats for rent.

Le Comité régional de tourisme d'Île-de-France has joined with the Paris Port Authority and *Voies Navigables de France* to publish a brochure on boating opportunities in Île-de-France: *Prenez le large en Île-de-France*; they can also provide *Tourisme fluvial – Guide pratique*, which gives addresses of rental agencies and marina facilities.

Visit the canals of northern France aboard a barge

Boat tours:
– in the Audomarois region *(see St-Omer)*.
– around the market garden district of Amiens *(see Amiens)*.
– **Paris Canal** – Bassin de La Villette, 19-21 Quai de la Loire, 75019 Paris, ☏ 01 42 40 96 97. On the canals of Paris and along the meanders of the Marne (Paris-Chennevières-Paris).
– **Un canal deux canaux** – 15 Allée du Canal, 77440 Lizy-sur-Ourcq, ☏ 01 60 01 13 65.

THE NATURAL ENVIRONMENT

Regional nature parks have brought a breath of fresh air to the landscapes of the Paris-Ile-de-France region and northern France. They are promoted as protected areas, not only in regard to the natural environment but also for traditional lifestyles, crafts and trades. Information can be obtained from the *Maison du Parc* associated with each one.

In the Paris region, the Château de Dampierre et de Breteuil and the Abbaye de Port-Royal-des-Champs (see description in the Sights section) are within the **Parc naturel régional de la Haute Vallée de Chevreuse**, created in 1985 (Maison du Parc, ☏ 01 30 52 09 09). Woods and farmlands alternate on the plateau along with lush valleys. The park offers over 200km/125mi of blazed hiking trails.

In the northern area covered in this guide, the **Parc naturel régional Nord-Pas-de-Calais** is divided into several sectors (Audomarois, Boulonnais, Plaine de la Scarpe et de l'Escaut, Avesnois, Monts de Flandre, Littoral Nord), managed by the *Espace naturel régional*, 17 Rue Jean-Roisin, 59800 Lille. ☏ 03 20 12 89 12. Discover dunes, forests, bays and wetlands by following itineraries on foot, horseback or bike. The park also offers cultural and thematic programmes.

Conservation district – To protect coastal areas, the **Conservatoire du Littoral** (Corderie Royale, BP 137, 17300 Rochefort ☏ 05 46 84 72 50) was set up in 1975 to safeguard and maintain ecological balance. There are now 339 protected sites, including the dunes at Garennes-de-Lornel in Pas-de-Calais, the first to be covered by preservation measures.

Wildlife reserves – These areas are protected by virtue of the rare or remarkable flora and fauna found there, exceptional geological characteristics, or their role as a way-station for migratory species. Some reserves are vast while others are quite modest. Waymarked footpaths allow visitors to observe the natural habitat. These include:

– **le Platier d'Oye**, Pas-de-Calais. Information at the Espace naturel régional;
– **la Dune Marchand**, part of the Conservatoire du littoral, guided tour, ☏ 03 28 26 50 20.
– **la Baie de Canche**, observation points along the trails. Information at the Clos St-Victor musuel in Étaples.
– **l'Étang de St-Ladre**, la Somme. Information from the Association de gestion de l'Étang de St-Ladre, 22 Rue Victor-Hugo, à Boves.
– **le Marais d'Isle**, in the Aisne, *see St-Quentin*.
– **la Baie de Somme** (the largest reserve in the region). Information at the Parc du Marquenterre.

WALKING, CYCLING, RIDING

Rambling – There is an extensive network of well-marked footpaths in France which make rambling *(la randonnée)* a breeze. Several **Grande Randonnée (GR)** trails, recognisable for the red and white horizontal marks on trees, rocks and in town on walls, signposts etc, go through the region. Along with the GR exist the **Petite Randonnée (PR)** paths, which are usually blazed with blue (2hr walk), yellow (2hr 15min-3hr 45min) or green (4-6hr) marks. Of course, with appropriate maps, you can combine walks to suit your desires.

To use these trails, obtain the **Topo-Guide** for the area published by the *Fédération Française de la Randonnée Pédestre*, 9 Rue Geoffroy-Marie, 75009 Paris, ☏ 01 48 01 80 80. Some English-language editions are available. An annual guide **(Rando Guide)** which includes ideas for overnight itineraries and places to stay as well as information on the difficulty and accessibility of trails, is published by the *Comité national des sentiers de Grande Randonnée*, 64 Rue de Gergovie, 75014 Paris, ☏ 01 45 45 31 02. Another source of maps and guides for excursions on foot is the *Institut National Géographique (IGN)*, which has a boutique in Paris at 107 Rue de la Boétie (off the Champs-Elysées); to order from abroad, contact IGN-Sologne, Administration des Ventes, 41200 Romorantin-Lanthenay, ☏ (33) 2 54 96 54 42, fax (33) 2 54 88 14 66, or visit the Web site (www.ign.fr) for addresses of wholesalers in your country. Among their publications, France 903 is a map showing all of the GR and PR in France (29F); the "Série Bleue" and "Top 25" maps, at a scale of 1:25 000 (1cm=250m), show all paths, whether waymarked or not, as well as refuges, camp sites, beaches etc (46-58F) for a precise area.

The *Conseil général du Nord* publishes, jointly with the *Association départementale de la randonnée*, itineraries covering various distances, with maps and information. Contact the *Comité départemental de tourisme du Nord (address under Tourist Information above)*.

An association publishes a *Guide des Sentiers de Promenade dans le Massif Forestier de Fontainebleau*, in the famous forest southeast of Paris, a popular spot for ramblers, climbers, mushroom hunters and cyclists on day trips, and provides guided tours that are open to all. For a programme, please send an international reply coupon to **Association des Amis de la Forêt de Fontainebleau**, 26 Rue de la Cloche, BP 14, 77301 Fontainebleau, or call ☏ 01 64 23 48 45 (answering machine). To join up with fellow ramblers, try the **Randonneurs d'Ile-de-France** club, which organises walks in the region (small membership fee): 67 Rue du Moulin-Vert, 75014 Paris. ☏ 01 45 42 24 72.

Cycling – The network of country roads is ideal for cycling. Lists of cycle hire businesses are available from local tourist offices.

Bikes are carried free of charge on many regional trains and on the Paris-Amiens-Boulogne line. The presence of cycle hire firms near or in train stations located in proximity to the main forests makes it easy to organise a cycle tour.

The **Fédération française de Cyclotourisme, Ligue Île-de-France** (8 Rue Jean-Marie-Jégo, 75013 Paris, ☏ 01 44 16 88 88) supplies itineraries covering most of France, outlining mileage, the level of difficulty of routes and sights to see.

The **Office National des Forêts** edits publications for mountain bike enthusiasts, Guides VTT Evasion (nos 1 to 8). They include itineraries covering between 15 and 30km/9 to 18mi. In Ile-de-France ☏ 01 40 19 58 82.

Moutain biking, or off-road cycling has become very popular in France. There are many courses laid out in the region, suitable for both new and experienced riders. For the Somme, a topo-guide pulished by the *Comité départemental du tourisme* in Amiens maps out a dozen itineraries of different lengths and levels of difficulty. Maps for other routes (baie de Somme, vallée de la Somme, vallée du Scardon, forêt de Crécy) area available from the *Syndicat intercommunal de développement économique et d'aménagement du Ponthieu-Marquenterre* (3 Rue de l'École-des-Filles, 80135 St-Riquier).

Riding – The Nord-Pas-de-Calais and Ile-de-France regions have hundreds of miles of bridlepaths running through forests or along the coast.

The *Délégation Nationale au Tourisme Équestre* (30 Avenue d'Iéna, 75116 Paris ☏ 01 53 67 44 44) publishes an annual review called *Tourisme et loisirs équestres en France*. It lists all the possibilities for riding by region and *département*.

Addresses of riding stables and information on bridlepaths are available from:

– **Association régionale de tourisme équestre Nord-Pas-de-Calais**, Le Paddock, 62223 St-Laurent-Blangy. ☏ 03 21 55 40 81.

– **Association régionale de tourisme équestre Picardie**, 8 Rue Fournier-Salovèze, B.P. 354, 60203 Compiègne Cedex. ☏ 01 44 40 19 54.

– **Association régionale de Tourisme Équestre d'Île-de-France (ARTEIF)** – 30 Avenue d'Iéna, 75116 Paris, ☏ 01 40 93 01 77. The brochure *Chevauchée en Île-de-France* lists the main clubs in the region.

Racing – The Paris region has the largest number of race tracks anywhere in France, hosting all types of horse races. **France Galop** specialises in improving breeds of horses in France and manages the flat racing tracks in the Paris area: 46 Place Abel-Gance, 92655 Boulogne Cedex. ☏ 01 49 10 20 30.

Track	Trotting	Flat course	Steeplechase	Main races
Chantilly		●		Prix Diane-Hermès (June) Prix du Jockey-Club (June)
Enghien	●	–	●	Prix de l'Atlantique (April) Prix d'Europe (July) Grand Steeple-Chase (October)
Longchamp		●		Grand Prix de Paris (June) Arc de Triomphe (October)
Maisons-Lafitte		●	Cross-country	Prix Robert Papin (July)
Saint-Cloud		●		Grand prix de St-Cloud (July) Critérium de St-Cloud (October)

The region also includes the Parisian race tracks in Auteuil (steeplechases) and Vincennes (trotting races).

AND MORE...

Landsailing – Landsailers are a strange combination of three-wheeled go-kart and sailboat. Powered solely by the wind, they may exceed 100kph/62mph on the vast stretches of fine, hard sand along the coasts of northern France at low tide. In addition to landsailers, there are also speedsail boards which resemble windsurfing boards on wheels. For information, contact the **Fédération française de char à voile**, zone industrielle de la Vigogne, BP 165, 62605 Berck-sur-Mer. ☏ 03 21 84 27 69.

J. Guillard /SCOPE

Landsailing at Hardelot-Plage

Sky High – **Tourist flights** are provided by **Vue de ciel** from Toussus-le-Noble (near Versailles): Paris, Forêt de Rambouillet, Vallée de Chevreuse, Versailles etc. ☎ 01 49 52 53 42.

Flights in small planes from the Aérodrome de Cerny, 91590 Cerny. ☎ 01 64 57 55 85.

Hot-air ballooning from Maintenon, daily, April to October. For information, contact Loisirs-Accueil, 10 Rue du Docteur Maunoury, BP 67, 28002 Chartres Cedex. ☎ 02 37 84 01 00.

Ultra-light flights from Dreux or Houville-la-Branche (east of Chartres) daily, April to October. For information, contact Loisirs-Accueil d'Eure-et-Loir (address and phone number above).

Golf – Golfers can enjoy their favourite sport and take part in competitions in the region. Courses abound in the Nord-Pas-de-Calais region, in pleasantly rustic settings taking players up hill and over dale, on the edge of forests, or overlooking the sea. Contact the Comité régional de tourisme *(address under Tourist Information above)* to obtain the brochure entitled *Golfs Nord-Pas-de-Calais*. Picardy has golf courses in Fort-Mahon, Quend-Plage, Grand-Laviers, Nampont-Saint-Martin, Salouel (3km/2mi from Amiens) and Querrien (7km/4mi from Amiens).

Something different...

DANCE HALLS

After the golden age of Impressionism in the late 19C, dance halls located along canals in the countryside around Paris, known as *guingettes*, gradually disappeared from Ile-de-France. These dance halls, serving drinks and meals, with music provided by a band, were reintroduced as part of regional policy and as a result of the enthusiasm of the *Culture Guingette* association. They are now springing up again on the banks of the Marne and Seine, bringing back to life the picturesque atmosphere of the turn-of-the-century.

You may prefer to be a casual spectator, enjoying simple fare at a riverside table. But if you have your dancing shoes on, dress with flair as the regulars do (men may need a tie to enter the ballroom). Brush up on your passo doble, tango and cha-cha-cha, and they'll be sure to take you for a native.

Association Culture Guinguette – 13 Rue Jean-Guy-Labarbe, 94130 Nogent-sur-Marne, ☎ 01 48 73 44 11. This assocation for the promotion of these traditional gathering places can inform tourists of special events, and the dance styles – ranging from athletic rock to energetic polka by way of the classic waltz – practiced in the member clubs:

– **Domaine Ste-Catherine**, 22-24 Allée Centrale, Pont de Créteil, Île de Brise Pain, 94000 Créteil, ☎ 01 42 07 19 18.
– **L'Île du Martin-Pêcheur**, 41 Quai Victor-Hugo, 94500 Champigny-sur-Marne, ☎ 01 49 83 03 02.
– **Le Moulin Vert**, 103 Chemin du Contre-Halage, 94500 Champigny-sur-Marne, ☎ 01 47 06 00 91.
– **Quai 38**, 38 Quai du Viaduc, 94500 Champigny-sur-Marne, ☎ 01 47 06 24 69.
– **La Goulue**, 17 Quai Gabriel-Péri, 94340 Joinville-le-Pont, ☎ 01 48 83 21 77.
– **Le Petit Robinson**, 164 Quai de Polangis, 94340 Joinville-le-Pont, ☎ 01 48 89 04 39.
– **Chez Gégène**, 162 Quai de Polangis, 94340 Joinville-le-Pont, ☎ 01 48 83 29 43.
– **La Grenouillère**, 68 Avenue du 11-Novembre, 94210 La Varenne-St-Hilaire, ☎ 01 48 89 23 32.
– **Le Canotier**, 2 Rue du Bac, 77410, Précy-sur-Marne, ☎ 01 60 01 62 12.
– **L'Auberge Charmante**, 20 Quai de la Rive-Charmante, 93160 Noisy-le-Grand, ☎ 01 45 92 94 31.

TOURIST ROUTES

These are itineraries based on architectural heritage presented in its historical context. There are several historical routes in the area covered in this guide:
– Route du **Camp du Drap d'Or**, the "Cloth of Gold" route from Calais to Arras.
– Route du **Roman au Gothique**, Romanesque and Gothic architecture, through the royal forests in Oise.
– Route des **Valois**, the Valois dynasty.
– Route des **Abbayes Renaissantes**, abbeys.
– Route du **Lys de France et de la Rose de Picardie**, "Lily of France and Rose of Picardy".

Baie de la Somme – All aboard!

– Route de la **Vallée de l'Oise**, the Oise Valley from Conflans-Ste-Honorine to Chimay (Belgium).

– Route des **Hauts Dignitaires**, from Breteuil to Fontainebleau.

– Route des **Parcs et Jardins d'Île-de-France**, parks and gardens in Ile-de-France.

– Route des **Peintres Impressionnistes**, Impressionists in the Val d'Oise.

– Route du **Roy Soleil**, the Sun King Louis XIV.

These and other special itineraries are the subject of brochures which can be found in most local tourist offices.

Route des villes fortifiées – This itinerary was set up by an association for the promotion of the **walled towns** in the Nord-Pas-de-Calais region. It includes 13 of the area's main citadels: Arras, Avesnes-sur-Helpe, Bergues, Boulogne-sur-Mer, Calais, Cambrai, Condé-sur-l'Escaut, Gravelines, Lille, Maubeuge, Montreuil-sur-Mer, Le Quesnoy, and St-Omer. The itinerary is 500km/310mi in length but is subdivided into shorter distances that provide many possibilities for excursions and tours. Each of the towns has a *Route des villes fortifiées* signpost at its entrance, accompanied by a logo. A map and brochure recounting the history of each town are available from the local tourist offices and from the Comité régional de tourisme du Nord-Pas-de-Calais *(address under Tourist Information above)*.

TOURIST TRAINS

Le p'tit train de la Haute-Somme – South of Albert, 3km/2mi from Bray-sur-Somme, there is a narrow-gauge railway running from Froissy to Dompierre via the Cappy Tunnel (300m/325yd). The round trip covers a distance of 14km/9mi and takes about 1hr 30min. A visit to the railway museum rounds off the trip.

The train runs from May to September on Sundays and public holidays from 2.15pm to 6pm. Additional trips 15 July to 5 September, Wednesdays and Saturdays at 2.30pm and 4pm; also Thursdays in August, 2.30pm and 4pm. Adults 40F, children 28F.

For information and bookings, contact APPEVA, BP 106, 80001 Amiens Cedex 1. ☎ 03 22 44 55 40.

Le chemin de fer de la baie de Somme – A train with old carriages with platforms runs through fields and salt marshes between Le Crotoy, Noyelles, St-Valery-sur-Mer and Cayeux-sur-Mer *(see Admission times and charges: Le CROTOY)*.

Chemin touristique du Vermandois – From St-Quentin to Origny Ste-Benoîte (44km/27mi round trip) a steam train or an old-fashioned rail motor car runs down into the Oise Valley from Mézières-sur-Oise.

For information, contact the Office du tourisme de St-Quentin, ☎ 03 23 67 05 00 or C.F.T.V., BP 152, 02104 St-Quentin Cedex. For bookings, ☎ 03 23 07 88 02.

The train runs from early June to the end of September on Sundays and public holidays.

WINDMILLS

Once a common sight in the region, surviving examples of windmills have been taken under the wing of a local association which has begun to restore and develop them. The **Centre régional de molinogie** (59650 Villeneuve-d'Ascq, ☎ 03 20 05 49 34), can provide brochures, maps and books on the subject. Most of the windmills cited in this guide are open to visitors. In addition, tourists are welcome at the Moulin de la Tourelle in Achicourt, south of Arras *(Friday from 5pm to 7pm and Sunday from 3pm to 6pm, ☎ 03 21 71 68 68); the oil mill at St-Vaast-en-Cambrésis (open to visitors May to September, Sunday from 2pm to 7pm, call M. Bisiaux ☎ 03 27 37 10 97 or M. Leclercq ☎ 03 27 37 21 39)*.

On the plains of the Beauce and the Brie, a few sails still catch the wind. Listed below are a few operating windmills whose owners allow visitors, at least for a look around the outside of the mill.

In the Beauce (Michelin map 60, folds 18, 19; off the A 10 "Allainville" exit or, from Orléans, "Allaines-Chartres"):

– **Ouarville** (☎ 02 37 22 13 87): visits from 2pm to 6pm, Sundays, Easter to 11 November, 10F;

– **Levesville-la-Chenard** (☎ 02 37 22 18 60): Sunday afternoons, June to August, or by appointment.

In the Brie region (Michelin map 106, fold 36, 8km/5mi north of Nangis):

– The **Moulin Choix** in Gastins (☎ 01 64 08 08 11) is open by appointment.

The following windmills are described in the Sights section of this guide.

– Moulin de St-Maxent *(see ABBEVILLE)*.

– Moulin Den Leew à Pitgam *(see BERGUES)*.

– Moulin de CASSEL, Steenmeulen (at Terdeghem), Drievemeulen, Noordmeulen near Steenvoorde, Moulin de la Briarde at Wormhout *(see CASSEL)*.

– Noord-Meulen *(see HONDSCHOOTE)*.

– Moulin de Boeschepe *(see MONT DES CATS)*.

– VILLENEUVE D'ASCQ (windmill and museum)

The association's annual windmill festival is held around the region in June.

CARILLONS

Chiming bells are part of everyday life in many towns in northern France and particularly in Flanders. A carillon consists of several bells hung in a bell-tower or belfry. The bells ring out different refrains to indicate the hour, the quarter and the half hour. The word comes from a medieval term "quadrillon", a peal of four bells ringing in harmony. In the Middle Ages, clocks were mechanical; they included small bells which the bell-ringer struck using a mallet or hammer. After a gradual increase in the number of bells, the mallet was replaced by a keyboard. The automatic system with cylinder used in some places is tending to be replaced by an electrical system which is easier to maintain.

The main carillons in area are as follows:

Tourcoing – Eglise St-Christophe: 61 bells

Douai – Town Hall: 62 bells

Bergues – Belfry: 50 bells

Avesnes-sur-Helpe – Collégiale St-Nicolas: 48 bells

Capelle-la-Grande – Belfry: 48 bells

Dunkirk – Tour St-Eloi: 48 bells

Le Quesnoy – Town Hall: 48 bells

St-Amand-les-Eaux – Tower on the abbey church: 48 bells

Seclin – Collégiale St-Piat: 42 bells

Carillon concerts are held regularly in certain towns (for information, contact the Tourist Office).

KID STUFF...

Below is a selection of some of the numerous theme parks and recreational areas in the regions covered in this guide.

Northern France

Aqualud, 62520 Le Touquet, ☎ 03 21 05 63 59 *(see le TOUQUET)*.

Bagatelle, 62155 Merlimont, ☎ 03 21 94 60 33 *(see le TOUQUET: Excursions)*.

Bal Parc, 207 Rue du Vieux-Château, 62890 Tournehem, ☎ 03 21 35 61 00.

Le Fleury, 5 Rue de Bouchain, 59111 Wavrechain-sous-Faulx, ☎ 03 27 35 71 16.

Moulin de la Tour, 62560 Dennebrœucq, ☎ 03 21 95 11 39.

Olhain, 62150 Houdain, ☎ 03 21 27 91 79 *(see Château d'OLHAIN)*.

Prés du Hem, 7 Avenue Marc-Sangnier, 59280 Armentières, ☎ 03 20 44 04 60.

Saint-Paul, 60650 St-Paul, ☎ 03 44 82 20 16.

Val Joly, 59132 Eppe-Sauvage, ☎ 03 27 61 84 16.

Loisinord, 62290 Nœux-les-Mines: water sports, ☎ 03 21 26 89 89, and downhill skiing on an artificial slope (slag heap), ☎ 03 21 26 84 84.

Île-de-France

Parc Astérix, 60128 Plailly ☎ 08 36 68 30 10 *(see Parc ASTÉRIX)*.

Disneyland Paris, 77777 Marne-la-Vallée ☎ 01 64 74 30 00; advance booking, schedules and prices at www.disneylandparis.com *(see DISNEYLAND PARIS)*.

Mer de Sable, 60950 Ermenonville ☎ 01 44 54 00 96 *(see Abbaye de CHAALIS)*.

France Miniature, 78990 Elancourt ☎ 08 36 68 53 35 *(see FRANCE MINIATURE)*.

Thoiry, 78770 Thoiry ☎ 01 34 87 40 67 *(see THOIRY)*.

Further reading

TOURISM, ILLUSTRATED BOOKS

Cruising the French Waterways, Hugh McKnight *(London: A&C Black, 1991)*

The Fair Face of Flanders, Patricia Carson, *(Tielt: Lannoo, 1991)*

Gothic Art, Andrew Martindale *(New York: Praeger, 1967)*

Impressions of the Seine, Carey More and Julian More *(New York: Rizzoli, 1991)*

Royal Palaces of France, Ian Dunlop *(London: Hamish Hamilton, 1985)*

HISTORY, COMMENTARY

Another World, Anthony Eden *(London: A Lane, 1976)*

Fatal Avenue: A Traveller's History of the Battlefields of Northern France and Flanders, 1346-1945, Richard Holmes *(London: Pimlico)*

Great Battles: Agincourt 1415, Christopher Hibbert *(Windrush Press)*

The Invention of Truth, Marta Morazzoni *(New York: AA Knopf, 1993)*

Our Fathers Have Told Us: The Bible of Amiens, John Ruskin *(London: George Allen, 1907)*

The Sands of Dunkirk, Richard Collier *(London: Collins, 1961)*

FICTION, LITERATURE

Complete Letters of Van Gogh, *(Boston: Bullfinch Press, 1991)*

Confessions, Jean-Jacques Rousseau

Germinal, Emile Zola

Letters of a Traveller, George Sand

The Middle Parts of Fortune: Somme and Ancre, 1916, Frederic Manning *(New York, St. Martin's Press, 1977)*

The Snow Goose, Paul Gallico *(New York: AA Knopf, 1942)*

Ursule Mirouët, Honoré de Balzac

A FEW WEB SITES

www.pas-de-calais.com is the regional tourist office site, with a complete English version. On it, you will find maps, useful addresses, scheduled events, information for booking *Gîtes* and other furnished accommodation, bed and breakfast establishments. There is a space for E-mailing your specific questions for reply.

www.chateauversailles.fr is a site as sumptuous as the palace, offering 360° views of the Hall of Mirrors and other highlights. The English version includes schedules of concerts and other special events.

www.francetourism.com is the official Web site for the French Government Tourist Office in the United States. It offers a very wide range of topics for perusal: history and culture, family activities, special interest events, news and general information.

www.franceway.com is an on-line magazine with a focus on culture and heritage. For each region, there are also suggestions for activities and practical information on where to stay and how to get there.

Calendar of events

FESTIVALS, FÊTES AND FAIRS

Saturday
Chartres................................... "Les samedis musicaux de Chartres" (classical music, jazz, folk music). Information at the l'Office de tourisme, place de la Cathédrale (☎ 02 37 27 18 52).

2nd half of February
Chambly .... "Bois-Hourdy" folk festival.

March
Senlis...................................... Music Festival (☎ 03 44 53 19 96).
Beauvais................................. "Cinémalia" film festival.

Saturday from March to July
Versailles................................ Baroque music concert series (☎ 01 39 20 78 00).

April
Abbeville et baie de Somme .... Ornithology Film Festival, ☎ 03 22 24 02 02 (screenings, exhibits, nature walks, lectures).
Valenciennes........................... Action and Adventure film festival.

Palm Sunday weekend (Friday to Monday)
Coulommiers............................ Cheese and wine fair (☎ 01 64 03 88 09).

One weekend in April
St-Jean-de-Beauregard............. Perennial plant festival (☎ 01 60 12 00 01).

3rd Sunday in May
Rambouillet .... Lily-of-the-Valley festival (☎ 01 34 83 21 21).

3rd weekend in May and in October
Courson .... Plant day (☎ 01 64 58 90 12).

May, June
Auvers-sur-Oise........................ Music Festival (☎ 01 30 36 77 77).

3rd Sunday after Pentecost
Lille .... "Fêtes de Lille": various events around the city.

June
Boulogne-sur-Mer..................... Music & Remparts.

1st weekend in June
Bièvres .... Photo fair (☎ 01 69 41 30 32).

Mid June (odd-numbered year)
Aérodrome du Bourget............. International Air and Space Show (☎ 01 47 20 61 09).

2nd weekend in June
Provins .... Medieval festival (☎ 01 64 60 26 26).

3rd Sunday of June
Gerberoy.................................. "Fête des roses".
Windmills around the region ... National Windmill Day. Information: ARAM ☎ 03 20 05 49 34.

23 June
Long.. "Feux de la Saint-Jean" mid-summer festival.

Late June to mid August
St-Germain-en-Laye.................. "Fête des Loges" fun fair (☎ 01 30 87 21 70).

Saturday or Sunday, from June to September
Royaumont .... Concert series at the abbey (☎ 01 30 35 59 83).

July
Côte d'Opale............................ Music Festival, ☎ 03 21 30 40 33.
St-Riquier .... Classical music festival.

1st Sunday in July
Noyon...................................... Red fruits market.

Around 14 July

Bray-Dunes .... World Folklife Festival.

Loison-sur-Créquoise .... Groseille (red current) festival.

July and August

Gravelines .... "Les Estivales" (outdoor theatre festival – night-time).

Hardelot .... Music Festival.

3rd Sunday in July

Buire-le-Sec .... Crafts and Trades Fair.

Tuesday, Thursday and Saturday at 9.15pm in July and August

Chartres .... "Soirées Estivales" (summer nights festival).

From July to October

Sceaux .... "Saison musicale d'été" (summer music festival) (☎ 01 46 60 07 79).

August

Le Touquet .... International music festival.

September

In Picardie .... "Festival des cathédrales", ☎ 03 22 97 37 49.

1st Sunday in September

Arleux .... Garlic Fair.

Aire-sur-la-Lys .... Andouille (sausage) festival.

1st weekend in September

Lille .... "Grande braderie" flea market and sale.

Lille – "Grande Braderie", place du Lion d'Or

F. Balloy /DIAPHOR

2nd Sunday in September

Armentières .... "Fête des Nieulles".

3rd weekend in September

Arpajon .... Bean fair (☎ 01 64 90 08 39).

Les nieulles

The name of these little biscuits (pronounced *nee-uls*) comes from the Spanish *niola*, which means "crumb". In 1510, a banquet was held in the reception rooms of the hôtel de ville, presided by the Count of Luxembourg, Lord of Armentières. When the guests had finished feasting, the Count stepped out on the balcony. A crowd of children gathered below, holding their hands out for alms. The Count flung the crumbs from the cake at them, as if they were so many hungry birds.

Last weekend in September (odd-numbered years)

Senlis... "Rendez-vous de Septembre": city without cars, music festival in the streets (☎ 03 44 53 06 40).

Late September, early October

Chatou....................................... "Grande foire nationale à la brocante et aux jambons" (flea market and ham fair) (☎ 01 47 70 88 78).

1st Sunday in October

Steenvoorde............................. Hops festival.

Suresnes................................... "Rues de Rêve" street theatre festival (☎ 01 41 18 18 76).

October

Barbizon................................... Painting awards.

3rd Sunday in October

Sains-du-Nord.......................... Cider festival.

Early November

St-Jean-de-Beauregard............. Fair: "Fruits and vegetables from the past and present" (☎ 01 60 12 00 01).

3rd weekend in December

Licques..................................... Turkey festival.

PAGEANTS, "SON ET LUMIÈRE", FOUNTAINS

Daily from Easter to 1 November

Provins..................................... Falconry show.

2nd and last Saturday of the month, April to October

Vaux-le-Vicomte........................ Fountains in the garden.

Provins – Jousting tournament

J.-F. Bénard /Office de Tourisme de Provins

3rd Sunday of the month, May to September

Parc de Marly-le-Roi................ Grand fountain (☎ 01 30 61 61 35).

Sunday from May to September (3.30pm to 5pm)

Versailles................................. Fountains and music in the palace garden (☎ 01 39 50 36 22).

Saturday and certain holidays from May to mid October between 8.30pm and 11pm

Vaux-le-Vicomte........................ Candlelight visit of château and gardens (☎ 01 64 14 41 90).

Friday and Saturday from mid June to mid July and early September

Meaux....................................... "Son et lumière" ("The Song of the Stones") (☎ 01 64 33 95 15).

2nd and 3rd weekends in June
Évry-Courcouronnes................ "Son et lumière" on the lake, with fountains (☎ 01 64 97 89 07).

3rd weekend in June
Chantilly .... "Nuits de Feu" international fireworks competition (☎ 03 44 45 82 12).

Saturday evening from June to September
Moret-sur-Loing...................... "Son et lumière" ("Reflections of History") (☎ 01 60 70 41 66).

Certain Saturdays from June to September
Versailles .... "Grandes Fêtes de Nuit au bassin de Neptune", fireworks, fountains and music in the palace garden (☎ 01 39 50 36 22).

Sunday in June
St-Cloud .... Fountains (☎ 01 41 12 02 90).

Sunday at 4pm in July and August
Provins .... Jousting tournament (☎ 01 64 60 26 26).

SPORTS EVENTS

Mid February
Le Touquet............................. "Enduro des sables" endurance race.

End March to end November
Fontainebleau .... La Solle racetrack open (☎ 01 64 22 29 37).

In April
Berck.. International kite festival.

2nd Sunday in April
Roubaix .... "Paris-Roubaix" cycling race.

Last Sunday in April
Villes fortifiées
du Nord-Pas-de-Calais.............. Regional "fortified towns" festival, ☎ 03 27 49 50 05.

May
Dunkerque .... Cycling race.

Weekend of Pentecost
St-Quentin .... "Fêtes du Bouffon".

Weekend of Pentecost
Aérodrome de Cerny............... Vintage aircraft show (☎ 01 64 57 55 85).

1st Sunday in June
Chantilly .... "Prix du Jockey-Club" race.

2nd Sunday in June
Chantilly .... "Prix de Diane-Hermès" race.

June
La Courneuve.......................... international Pétanque festival.

End July
St-Omer .... Procession of floats on the canal.

Mid August to mid September
Fontainebleau .... "Grande semaine du cheval", Sporting horse breeders' week. (☎ 01 64 23 42 07).

3rd weekend in September
Chantilly .... "Trophée de Polo", French championship.

October
Berck-sur-Mer .... Land sailing competition.

October
Fontainebleau
(hippodrome du Grand Parquet) "Grande semaine du cheval" (French championship: jumping and dressage).

CARNIVALS AND GIANTS IN THE NORTH

Sunday before Mardi Gras and Mardi Gras Tuesday

Dunkerque................................. Carnival.

Bailleul..................................... Carnival with giant Gargantua.

Sunday after mardi gras

Malo-les-Bains.......................... Carnival.

Sunday mid-Lent

Hazebrouck.............................. Grand parade in traditional costumes, giants on parade. Carnival the following Sunday.

Easter Monday

Cassel...................................... Giants on parade: Reuze-Papa and Reuze-Maman.

Denain..................................... Carnival.

May

Amiens.................................... Carnival.

Carnival Giants

In the dialect of Picardie, they are *gayants*; in the Flemish vernacular, *reuzes*; the French call them *géants*. The numerous (about 200) larger-than-life characters come out to play at carnival time and for other local festivities; in Hazebrouck they are displayed in the museum year-round.

The first carnival giants appeared in Portugal in the 13C, and in the northern part of France in the 16C: 1530 in Douai, 1556 in Maubeuge, 1559 in Cambrai. Since the early 20C, the family has grown.

In recent years, they have held international family reunions, *Rondes de Géants* (1992 in Barcelona, 1993 in Steenvoorde, 1994 in Maastricht and Folkestone). The association **La ronde des géants**, 7 Rue St-Bernard, 59000 Lille, ☎ 03 20 93 94 67, serves to promote and protect this age-old tradition.

One Sunday in June

Bourbourg map 51, fold 3 ...... Giants on parade: Gédéon, Arthurine et Florentine.

July

Hazebrouck .... Summer Carnival featuring giants Roland, Tisje, Tasje, Toria et Babe Tisje.

Sunday following 5 July

Douai....................................... Grand parade featuring the Gayant (giant) family.

15 August

Cambrai................................... Giants on parade: Martin et Martine.

2nd weekend of September

Valenciennes............................ "Les Folies de Binbin".

2nd Sunday in October

Comines................................... "Fête des Louches" featuring giants Grande Gueuloutte et P'tite Chorchine.

24 December

Boulogne-sur-Mer.................... "Fête des Guénels" (a *guénel* is sort of like a jack o'latern, carved out of a beet!).

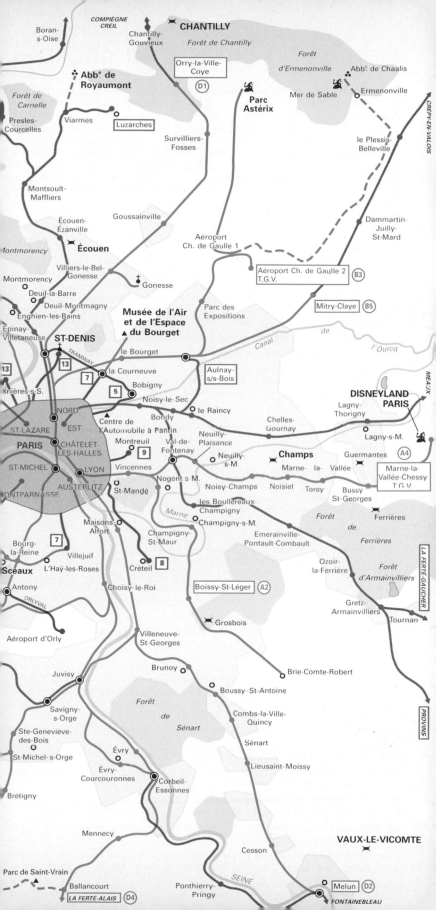

Admission times and charges

The following pages contain useful visiting information for each sight identified with the ⊙ in the main section of this guide. Sights are generally listed under the name of the city or town in which they are located.

Opening hours and admission charges are liable to alteration without prior notice. Due to fluctuations in the cost of living and the constant change in opening times, the information below is given only as a general indication. Dates given are inclusive.

The information applies to individual adults and, whenever possible, children. For groups, however, special conditions regarding times and charges are common and arrangements should be made in advance. Ticket offices often close 30-45 minutes before the actual closing time.

Churches and other places of worship *are usually closed from noon to 2pm. Tourists should refrain from visits when services are being held. Times are indicated if the interior is of special interest and the church, chapel etc. has unusual opening times. Visitors to chapels are sometimes accompanied by the person who keeps the key. A donation is welcome.*

Guided tours *– When these are indicated, the departure time of the last tour of the morning or afternoon will be up to an hour before the actual closing time. Most tours are conducted by French-speaking guides but in some cases the term "guided tours" may cover group-visits with recorded commentaries. Some of the larger and more frequented sights may offer guided tours in other languages. Enquire at the ticket office or book stall. Other aids for the foreign tourist are notes, pamphlets and audio-guides.*

Ensure no valuables are left in unattended vehicles in car parks or isolated sites.

The symbol **🄱** *appears before the address of the local* **Tourist Information Office** *(Office de tourisme).*

The **&** *symbol indicates that the sight has facilities designed for* **handicapped people**.

A

ABBEVILLE
🄱 1, place Amiral-Courbet – 80100 ☎ 03 03 22 24 27 92

Musée Boucher de Perthes – Open year round, daily (except Tues), 2-6pm. Closed 1 Jan, 1 May, 14 Jul, 1 and 25 Nov. No charge. ☎ 03 22 24 08 49.

Château de Bagatelle – Guided tours (45min) July and Aug, daily (except Tues), 2-6pm. Closed the rest of the year. 40F. ☎ 03 22 24 02 69.

AMBLETEUSE

Fort d'Ambleteuse – Open July and Aug, Sat-Mon, 3-7pm; Apr to June, Sept and Oct, Sun, 3-7pm. Last entry 30min before closing. Closed Nov to Mar. 15F. ☎ 03 20 54 61 54.

Musée historique de la Deuxième Guerre mondiale – & Open Apr to mid-Oct, daily, 9.30am-7pm; mid-Oct to Mar, Sat, Sun and public holidays, 10am-7pm. Closed Dec and Jan. 30F. ☎ 03 21 87 33 01.

AMIENS
🄱 6 bis, rue Dusevel – 80000 ☎ 03 22 71 60 50

Guided tours of the town 🄰 – Apply to the tourist office.

Cathedral – Guided tours July and Aug, Mon-Fri, Sun at 3pm, Sat at 10.30am; Sept to June, Sun and public holidays at 3pm. Closed 25 Decand 1 Jan. ☎ 03 22 71 60 50.

Towers- Open June-Sept daily except Tues 1.30-6pm; April, May, Oct on Wed 1.15-5.15pm; Nov-March weekends, holidays and school holidays 2pm-4.15pm. Closed 1 Jan, 24-25 and 31 Dec. 15F. 03 22 80 03 41.

Stalles - April-Oct daily except Sat, 3-4pm; Nov-Easter, weekends, holidays and school holidays, 3-4pm. Closed 1 Jan. No charge.

Trésor – Currently closed. Apply to the tourist office.

Musée de Picardie – & Open year round, Tues-Sun, 10am-12.30pm, 2-6pm. Closed 1 Jan, 1 May, 14 July, 11 Nov and 25 Dec. 20F. ☎ 03 22 97 14 00.

Musée d'Art local et d'Histoire régionale – Open year round, Thur-Sun, 2-6pm. Closed 1 Jan, 1 May, 14 July, 11 Nov and 25 Dec. 10F. ☎ 03 22 97 14 00.

Hortillonnages – Boat trips (1hr) Apr to Oct, daily from 2pm. Apply to the Maison des hortillonnages, 54 boulevard Beauvillé. 30F (adult), 15F (child). ☎ 03 22 92 12 18.

Centre de documentation Jules Verne – Guided tours (1hr) year round, Mon-Fri, 9am-noon, 2-6pm; Sat, 2-6pm. Closed Sun and public holidays. 15F. ☎ 03 22 45 37 84.

Galerie du Vitrail – Guided tours (1hr) year round, Mon-Sat 3pm. Closed public holidays. 10F. ☏ 03 22 91 81 18.

Maison de la Culture – Open early Sept to mid-July, Tues-Fri, noon-7pm, Sat and Sun, 2-7pm. Closed public holidays and mid-July to early Sept. ☏ 03 22 97 79 77.

Parc Zoologique – Currently closed for work. Planned to reopen in spring 1999. ☏ 03 22 69 61 00.

ARQUES

Ascenseur à bateaux des Fontinettes – Open mid-June to mid-Sept, daily, 3-6.30pm; Apr to mid-June and mid-Sept to Oct, Sat, Sun and public holidays, 3-6.30pm. Last departure at 5.30pm. Closed Nov-Mars. 25 F.☏ 03 21 12 62 30.

ARRAS

🅱 Hôtel de ville, place des Héros – 62000 ☏ 03 21 51 26 95

Guided tours of the town 🄰 – Apply to the tourist office.

Hôtel de ville – Guided tours. Apply to the tourist office.

Belfry – Free access during opening times of the underground passages.

Tour of the underground passages – Guided tours (45min) May-Sept, 9am-6.30pm, Sun and holidays 10am-1pm and 2.30-6.30pm; Oct-April.; 9am-noon, 2-6pm, Sun and holidays 10am-12.30pm and 3-6.30pm. 22F. ☏ 03 21 51 26 95.

Musée des Beaux-Arts – Open Oct to Mar, Mon, Wed, Fri and Sat, 10am-noon, 2-6pm, Thur, 10am-6pm, Sun, 10am-noon, 3-6pm; Apr to Sept, Mon, Wed, Fri, 10am-noon, 2-5pm, Thu, 10am-5pm, Sat, 10am-noon, 2-6pm, Sun, 10am-noon, 3-6pm. Closed 1 Jan, 1, 8 May, 14 July, 1, 11 Nov and 25 Dec. 20F (no charge first Wed and first Sun of each month). ☏ 03 21 71 26 43.

Cathedral – Open year round, afternoons.

Citadelle – Guided tours (1hr) May to Sept, Sun at 3pm and 4pm. Closed Oct to Apr. 15F. Bring proof of identity. ☏ 03 21 51 26 95.

Église St-Nicolas-en-Cité – Open Thurs afternoons.

Parc ASTÉRIX

Open Apr, daily, 10am-6pm; July and Aug, daily, 9.30am-7pm; May and June, Mon-Fri (except the occasional Mon or Fri), 10am-6pm, Sat and Sun, 9.30am-7pm; Sep, Wed, 10am-6pm, Sat and Sun, 9.30-7pm; first two weeks in Oct, Wed, Sat and Sun, 10am-6pm. Closed mid-Oct to Mar. Enquire before visiting as dates and times may vary. 160F (adult), 110F (child 3-11), no charge (under 3s). ☏ 08 36 68 30 10 or Minitel 3615 ASTERIX.

AUVERS-SUR-OISE

Maison de Van Gogh – Open year round, Tues-Sun, 10am-6pm. Closed 1 Jan and 25 Dec. 30F, family ticket 60F. ☏ 01 30 36 60 60.

Musée de l'Absinthe – Open June to Sept, Wed-Sun, 11am-6pm; Oct to May, Sat and Sun only, 11am-6pm. 25F. ☏ 01 30 36 83 26.

Château d'Auvers (Journey Back to the Days of the Impressionists) – Self-guided tours (1hr 30min) Apr to Sept, Tues-Sun, 10am-7.30pm; Oct to Mar, Tues-Sun, 10.30am-6pm. Ticket office closes 1hr 30min earlier. 60F. b 01 34 48 48 48. Intenet www.chateau-auvers.fr.

AZINCOURT

Musée des Traditions populaires et d'Histoire locale – 🚻 Open Apr to Oct, daily, 9am-6pm; Nov to Mar, daily,10am-5pm. Closed 1 Jan and 25 Dec. 10F. ☏ 03 21 04 41 12.

B

Parc d'attraction de BAGATELLE

Open Apr to Sept, daily, 10am-7pm. 98F (adult), 78F (child 3-7), no charge (under 3s). ☏ 03 21 89 09 99.

BARBIZON

🅱 55, Grande rue – 77630 ☏ 01 60 66 41 87

Auberge du Père Ganne – Open year round, Mon, Wed-Fri, 10am-12.30pm, 2-6pm, Sat, Sun and public holidays, 10am-6pm (Oct to Mar, 5pm). 25F. ☏ 01 60 66 22 27.

BARON

Church – Guided tours year round, Mon-Fri. Apply to the vicarage (presbytère), 3, rue du Cimetière, 60300 Baron. ☎ 03 44 54 25 48.

BAVAY

Musée archéologique – Open July and Aug, Mon, Wed-Sat, 10am-noon, 2-6pm, Sun, 9.30am-noon, 2-7pm; Sept to 24 Decand Jan to June, Mon, Wed-Sat, 9am-noon, 2-5pm, Sun, 9.30am-noon, 2-5pm (Sept, 7pm). Closed 25 Dec to early Jan, 1 May, 1, 11 Nov. 20F. ☎ 03 27 63 13 95.

BEAUVAIS
🛈 1, rue Beauregard – 60000 ☎ 03 44 45 08 18

Guided tours of the town 🄰 – Apply to the tourist office.

Cathédrale St-Pierre: Astronomic clock – Son et lumière display (25min) with individual ear phones, June to Aug, daily at 10.40am, 11.40am, 12.40pm, 2.40pm, 3.40pm and 4.40pm; Sept to May, daily, 10.40am, 11.40am, 2.40pm, 3.40pm and 4.40pm. Closed 1 Jan. 22F. ☎ 03 44 48 11 60.

Musée départemental de l'Oise – Open year round, daily (except Tues), 10am-noon, 2-6pm. Closed 1 Jan, Easter Mon, Whitsun, 1 May, 1 Nov and 25 Dec. 16F (no charge on Wed). ☎ 03 44 11 43 83.

Galerie nationale de la Tapisserie – Open, Apr to Sept, Tues-Sun, 9.30am-noon, 2-6.30pm; Oct to Mar, Tues-Sun, 10am-noon, 2.30-5pm. Closed 1 Jan, 1 May and 25 Dec. 25 F. ☎ 03 44 05 14 28.

Église de Marissel - July-Aug, guided tours available on request. ☎ 03 44 05 46 43.

BELLIGNIES

Musée du marbre – Open mid-Feb to mid-Dec, daily, 2-6pm. Closed the rest of the year. 12F. ☎ 03 27 66 89 90.

BERGUES
🛈 place de la République – 59380. ☎ 03 28 68 60 44

Belfry – Open in season, daily, 9.30am-12.30pm, 2-6pm; the rest of the year, Mon-Fri, 9.30am-noon, 2-6pm, Sat, Sun and public holidays, 10am-noon, 2-5.30pm. 10F. ☎ 03 28 68 71 06.

Carillon concerts – Year round, Mon at 11am, the eve of public holidays at 5pm.

Musée municipal – Open Feb to Dec, daily (except Tues), 10am-noon, 2-5pm. Closed Jan. 15F. ☎ 03 28 68 13 30.

BIÈVRES

Musée Français de la Photographie – Open year round, daily (except Tues), 10am-noon, 2-6pm. Closed public holidays. 20F. ☎ 01 69 35 16 50.

BLÉRANCOURT

Musée national de la coopération franco-américaine – ♿ Open year round, daily (except Tues), 10am-12.30pm, 2-5.30pm. Closed 1 Jan, 1 May, 25 Dec. 16F. ☎ 03 23 39 60 16.

BOESCHEPE

Moulin de Boeschepe – Open July and Aug, daily, 2-6pm; Apr to June and Sept, Sun and public holidays, 3-6.30pm. Closed Oct to Mar. 10F. ☎ 03 28 42 50 24.

BOUGIVAL

Musée Tourgueniev – Open end of Mar to mid-Dec, Sun and public holidays, 10am-6pm. Closed the rest of the year. 25F. ☎ 01 45 77 87 12.

BOULOGNE-SUR-MER
🛈 quai de la Poste – 62200. ☎ 03 21 80 56 78

Guided tours of the town 🄰 – Apply to the tourist office.

Nausicaa – ♿ Open July and Aug, daily, 9.30am-8pm; Sept to June, daily, 9.30am-6.30pm. Closed first three weeks in Jan and 25 Dec. 65F (adult), 45F (child 3-12). ☎ 03 21 30 98 98.

Belfry – Open year round, Mon-Fri, 8am-6pm, Sat, 8am-noon. Closed public holidays. No charge. ☎ 03 21 87 80 80.

Basilique Notre-Dame – Open May to Oct, Mon-Sat, 9am-noon, 2-7pm, Sun and public holidays, 2.30-7pm; Nov to Apr, Mon-Sat, 9am-noon, 2-5pm, Sun and public holidays, 2.30-5pm. Crypt and Treasury, 2.30-5pm only. 10F. ☎ 03 21 99 75 98.

Château-musée – Open year round, Mon, Wed-Sat, 10am-12.30pm, 2-5pm, Sun, 10am-12.30pm, 2.30-5.30pm. Closed 1 Jan, 1 May and 25 Dec. 20F. ☎ 03 21 10 02 20.

Musée d'Histoire naturelle – Open year round, Mon-Fri, 10am-11.45am, 2-5.45pm, Sat and Sun by appointment only, 2-5.45pm. Closed 1 Jan and 25 Dec. No charge. ☎ 03 21 80 09 80.

Casa San Martin – Guided tours (30min) daily except Wed and Thurs, 10am-noon, 2pm-6pm, Closed Jan and public holidays. No charge.☎ 03 21 31 54 65.

Colonne de la Grande Armée – Open year round, Thur-Mon, 9-11.30am, 2-7pm (Oct to Mar, 4pm). Closed 1 Jan, 1 May, 1, 11 Nov and 25 Dec. No charge. ☎ 03 21 80 43 69.

Musée de l'air et de l'espace du BOURGET

Museum – Open year round, Tues-Sun, 10am-6pm (Nov to Apr, 5pm). Closed 1 Jan and 25 Dec. 30F (adult), 22F (child). ☎ 01 49 92 71 99.

BOURRON-MARLOTTE

Château – Grounds open mid-Apr to Oct, Sat, Sun and public holidays, 2-6pm. 10F. Castle open Mar to Oct, by appointment, for groups only. ☎ 01 64 78 39 39.

BOUVIGNIES

Dovecote – Open Apr to Sept by appointment with the town hall 15 days in advance. ☎ 03 27 91 20 13, except Wed afternoon.

Château de BRETEUIL

Guided tours (45min) year round, Mon-Sat, 2.30-5.30pm (Sat, 6pm), Sun, public holidays and Paris school holidays, 11am-6.30pm. Historical tours May to mid-Oct. Grounds open year round from 10am. 57F (adult), 47F (child). Park only 38F. ☎ 01 30 52 05 02.

BRUAY-SUR-L'ESCAUT

Church – Apply to the vicarage *(presbytère)*. ☎ 03 27 47 60 89.

BY-THOMERY

Atelier Rosa-Bonheur – Guided tours (30min) year round, Wed and Sat, 2-5pm. 15F. ☎ 01 60 70 04 49.

C

CALAIS 🛈 12, boulevard Clemenceau – 62100 ☎ 03 21 96 62 40

Guided tours of the town – Private groups only.

Musée des Beaux-Arts et de la Dentelle – Open year round, Mon, Wed-Sat, 10am-noon, 2-5.30pm (Sat, 6.30pm), Sun, 2-6.30pm. Closed public holidays. 15F (no charge on Wed). ☎ 03 21 46 48 40.

Musée de la Guerre – Open Apr to Sept, daily, 10am-6pm; Feb-Mar and Oct-Nov, daily (except Tues), 11am-5pm. Closed Dec and Jan. 20F. ☎ 03 21 34 21 57.

CAMBRAI 🛈 48, rue de Noyon – 59400 ☎ 03 27 78 36 15

Guided tours of the town 🅰 – Apply to the tourist office.

Chapelle du Grand Séminaire – Apply to the tourist office.

Église St-Géry – Open year round daily except Sun afternoons outside of school holidays. ☎ 03 27 81 30 47 (tourist office).

Musée municipal – Open year round, Wed-Sun, 10am-noon, 2-6pm. Closed 1 Jan, 1 May, 15 Aug and 25 Dec. 20F. ☎ 03 27 82 27 90.

Château de Selles – Not open to the public. For further information, apply to the tourist office.

CAP BLANC-NEZ

Musée National du Transmanche – Open July and Aug, daily, 10am-6pm; Apr to June and Sept, Tues-Sun, 10am-6pm. Closed Oct to Mar. 20F. ☎ 03 21 85 57 42.

CAP GRIS-NEZ

Musée du mur de l'Atlantique – Open May to Sept, daily, 9am-7pm; Feb to Apr, Oct and Nov, daily, 9am-noon, 2-6pm. Closed Dec and Jan. 30F. ☎ 03 21 32 97 33.

CASSEL

🛈 Grand-Place – 59670 ☎ 03 28 40 52 55

Windmill – Guided tours (30min), June to Sept, 10am-noon, 2-6pm; Oct to May, during school holidays only, 10am-noon, 2-5pm. 15F. ☎ 03 28 40 52 55.

Museum – Currently being restored. Closed until 2001.

Abbaye de CHAALIS

Château-Musée – Guided tours (1hr 15min) Mar to 11 Nov, Mon-Fri 10.30am-12.30pm, 2-6pm. Non-guided tours, Mar to 11 Nov, Sat, Sun and public holidays, 10.30am-12.30pm, 2-6.30pm. Park open 10am-6.30pm. Closed the rest of the year. 35F (park only 15F). ☎ 03 44 54 04 02.

CHAMBOURCY

Désert de Retz – Currently closed to visitors.

Château de CHAMPS

Park – Open July and Aug, daily (except Tues), 9.30am-8pm; Sept to June, daily (except Tues), 9am until dusk. No charge. ☎ 01 60 05 24 43.

Château – Open year round, Mon, Wed-Fri, 10am-noon, 1.30-4.30pm, Sat, Sun and public holidays, 10am-noon, 1.30-6pm (Mar, 5.15pm, Oct, 5.30pm, Nov to Feb, 4.45pm). Closed 1 Jan, 1 May, 1, 11 Nov and 25 Dec. 32F. ☎ 01 60 05 24 43.

Château de CHANTILLY

Museum – Open Mar to Oct, daily (except Tues), 10am-6pm; Nov to Fev, Mon-Fri, 10.30am-12.45pm, 2-5pm, Sat, Sun and public holidays, 10.30am-5pm. Museum and grounds 39F (84F including balloon flight). ☎ 03 44 62 62 62.

The three Graces by Raphael, Château de Chantilly

Appartements des Princes – Same admission times and charges as the museum.

Petits Appartements – Guided tours Mar to Oct, daily at 11.15am, 2.15pm, 3.45pm and 4.45pm; Nov to Feb, daily at 11.15am, 2.30pm and 3.15pm. Phone the day before visiting to check opening times. 50F. ☎ 03 44 62 62 62.

Park – Same admission times and charges as the château. 17F. ☎ 03 44 62 62 62.

Aérophile et Hydrophiles – Balloon flights (15min) or boat trips (30min) Mar to 11 Nov, daily, 10am-7pm. Flights depend on weather. 45F (adult), 25F (child). ☎ 03 44 57 35 35.

Musée Vivant du Cheval et du Poney – Open Apr to Oct, daily (except Tues), 10.30am-5.30pm (Sat, Sun and public holidays, 6pm); Nov to Mar, Mon, Wed-Fri, 2-5pm, Sat, Sun and public holidays, 10.30am-5.30pm. Closed 1 Jan and 25 Dec. 50F. ☎ 03 44 57 13 13.

CHARTRES

🛈 place de la Cathédrale – 28000 ☎ 02 37 21 50 00

Guided tours of the town – Apply to the tourist office.

Cathedral

Access to New Bell-tower – Open May to Aug, daily (except Sun mornings), 9am-6.30pm; Mar, Apr, Sept and Oct, daily (except Sun mornings), 9.30-11.30am, 2-5.30pm; Nov to Feb, daily (except Sun mornings), 10-11.30am, 2-4.30pm. Closed 1 Jan, 1 May, 1, 11 Nov and 25 Dec. 25F. ☎ 02 37 21 22 07.

Treasury – Open year round, Tues-Sun (except Sun mornings), 10am-noon, 2-6pm (Nov to Mar, 4.30pm). Closed most public holidays. ☎ 02 37 21 56 33.

Crypt – Guided tours (30min) Apr to Oct, daily at 11am, 2.15pm, 3.30pm and 4.30pm (June to mid-Sept, additional tour at 5.15pm); Nov to Mar, Mon-Sat at 11am and 4.15pm, Sun and public holidays at 4.15pm. Closed 1 Jan, 21 June and 25 Dec. 11F. Apply to the Maison de la Crypte, near the south doorway. ☎ 02 37 21 56 33.

Tourist Train – Tours (40min) with commentary mid-Mar to Oct, daily, 10am-7pm. Departure from the cathedral. 30F (adult), 18F (child). ☎ 01 42 62 24 00.

Centre international du Vitrail – & Open year round, Mon-Fri, 9.30am-12.30pm, 1.30-6pm, Sat, Sun and public holidays, 10am-12.30pm, 2.30-6pm. Closed 1 Jan, 25 Dec and a few days in Apr, Oct and Nov. 20F. ☎ 02 37 21 65 72.

Musée des Beaux-Arts – Open year round, daily (except Sun mornings and Tues), 10am-noon, 2-6pm (Nov to Apr, 5pm). Closed 1 Jan, 1, 8 May, 1, 11 Nov and 25 Dec. 10F. ☎ 02 37 36 41 39.

Le COMPA – Open year round, Tues-Fri, 9am-12.30pm, 1.30-6pm, Sat, Sun and certain public holidays, 10am-12.30pm and 1.30-7pm. Closed 1 Jan, 1 May, 1 Nov and 25 Dec. 25F. ☎ 02 37 36 11 30.

Musée de l'Ecole – Open year round, Mon-Fri, 10am-noon, 2-6pm. Closed public holidays. 15F (adult), 10F (child). ☎ 02 37 30 07 69.

Maison Picassiette – Open Apr to Oct, daily (except Sun mornings and Tues), 10am-noon, 2-6pm. Closed Nov to Mar, 1, 8 May and 25 Dec. 10F. ☎ 02 37 36 41 39/34 10 78.

Le CHEMIN DES DAMES

Museé du Caverne du Dragon – Apply to ☎ 03 23 25 92 93.

Arboretum de CHEVRELOUP

Open Apr to mid-Nov, Mon, Sat and Sun, 10am-5pm. Closed mid-Nov to Mar. 15F. ☎ 01 39 55 53 80.

COMPIÈGNE
🛈 place de l'Hôtel-de-Ville – 60200 ☎ 03 44 40 01 00

Guided tours of the town 🅰 – Apply to the tourist office.

Palais

Appartements Historiques – Guided tours (1hr) Mar to Oct, daily (except Tues), 10am-6pm; Nov to Feb, daily (except Tues), 10am-4.30pm. Last entry 45min before closing. Closed 1 Jan, 1 May, 1 Nov and 25 Dec. 35F (23F on Sun). ☎ 03 44 38 47 00 / 02.

Musée du Second Empire – Same admission times and charges as the Appartements historiques. Guided tours available. ☎ 03 44 38 47 02.

Musée de la voiture – Guided tours (1hr) year round. Same admission times as the Appartements historiques. 25F (17F on Sun). ☎ 03 44 38 47 02.

Musée de la Figurine historique – Open Mar to Oct, Tues-Sat, 9am-noon, 2-6pm, Sun and public holidays, 2-6pm; Nov to Feb, Tues-Sat, 9am-noon, 2-5pm, Sun and public holidays, 2-5pm. Closed 1 Jan, 1 May, 14 July, 1 Nov and 25 Dec. 12F. ☎ 03 44 40 72 55.

Musée Vivenel – Open Mar to Oct, Tues-Sat, 9am-noon, 2-6pm, Sun, 2-6pm; Nov to Feb, Tues-Sat, 9am-noon, 2-5pm, Sun, 2-5pm. Closed 1 Jan, 1 May, 14 July, 1 Nov and 25 Dec. 12F. ☎ 03 44 20 26 04.

Forêt de COMPIÈGNE

Wagon du Maréchal Foch – Open Apr to mid-Oct, daily (except Tues), 9am-12.15pm, 2-6.15pm; mid-Oct to Mar, daily (except Tues), 9-11.45am, 2-5.15pm. Closed 1 Jan and 25 Dec. 10F. ☎ 03 44 85 14 18.

CONTY

Église St-Antoine – Apply to the vicarage *(presbytère)*, 4, rue Guy-de-Segonzac.

CORBIE

Église St-Pierre – Open Apr to Sept, Tues-Fri and Sun afternoons; Oct to Mar, Tues-Fri. ☎ 03 22 96 95 76 (tourist office).

Museum - Open daily except Mon, 3-7.30pm; Sun and holidays on request. No charge. ☎ 03 22 96 43 37.

CÔTE D'OPALE

Site des deux caps – Guided tours July and Aug around various natural beauty spots (Platier d'Oye, Cap Blanc-Nez, Cap Gris-Nez, dunes and Slack Estuary, Canche Bay, Authie Dunes). For information apply to Eden, 3, square Bernard-Shaw, 62930 Wimereux. ☎ 03 21 32 13 74.

COUCY-LE-CHÂTEAU-AUFFRIQUE

Château – Open May to Aug, Mon-Fri, 10am-noon, 2-6pm, Sat, 10am-noon, 2-6.30pm, Sun, 10am-6.30pm; Mar, Apr, Sept and Oct, Mon-Fri, 10am-noon, 2-5.30pm, Sat, 10am-noon, 2-6pm, Sun, 10am-6pm; Nov to Feb, Mon-Fri, 10am-noon, 2-4pm, Sat, 10am-noon, 2-4.30pm, Sun, 10am-4.30pm. Closed 1 Jan, 1 May, 1, 11 Nov and 25 Dec. 25F. ☎ 03 23 52 71 28.

COUCY-LE-CHÂTEAU-AUFFRIQUE

Musée historique – Open Mar to Sept, Mon-Sat, 10.30am-12.30pm, 2-6pm, Sun and public holidays, 2-6.30pm; Oct to Feb, Mon-Fri, 2-5pm, Sat, Sun and public holidays, 2-5.30pm. Closed 25 Dec to 1 Jan. No charge. ☎ 03 23 52 44 55.

Église St-Sauveur – Guided tours. Apply to the tourist office. ☎ 03 23 52 44 55.

Château de COURANCES

Guided tours (30min) Apr to Oct, Sat, Sun and public holidays, 2-6.30pm (Oct, 5.30pm). Closed Nov to Mar. 38F (grounds only 25F). ☎ 01 40 62 07 62.

CRÉPY-EN-VALOIS

Abbaye de St-Arnoul – Open Apr to Oct, Sun, 2-7pm. Closed Nov to Mar. Apply to the Association St-Arnoul. ☎ 03 44 59 17 76.

Musée de l'Archerie et du Valois – Open 3rd weekend in March to 11 Nov, Mon and Wed-Sat, 10am-noon, 2-6pm; Sun and public holidays, 10am-noon, 3-7pm. Closed the rest of the year. 20F. ☎ 03 44 59 21 97.

Le CROTOY

Chemin de fer de la Baie de la Somme – Departures from Le Crotoy July and Aug, Tues-Fri at 3.30pm, Sat, Sun and public holidays at noon and 3.30pm; Apr to June and Sept, Wed, Sat, Sun and public holidays at 3.30pm.
Departures from St-Valery July and Aug, Tues-Fri at 3.30pm, Sat, Sun and public holidays at 10.45am and 3.30pm; Apr to June and Sept, Wed, Sat, Sun and public holidays at 3.30pm.
Departure from Cayeux July and Aug, Sat, Sun and public holidays at 3.30pm.
Return ticket 35F to 66F depending on age and length of trip. No charge for bicycles. ☎ 03 22 26 96 96.

D

Château de DAMPIERRE
Guided tours (45min) Apr to mid-Oct, Mon-Fri, 2-6.30pm, Sun and public holidays, 11am-noon, 2-6.30pm. Grounds open daily, 11am-6.30pm. Closed mid-Oct to Mar. 50F (grounds only 32F). ☎ 01 30 52 53 24.

Bois de DELVILLE

Mémorial Sud-Africain et musée commémoratif – &. Open Apr to mid-Oct, Tues-Sun, 10am-5.45pm; mid-Oct to Nov, Feb and Mar, Tues-Sun, 10am-3.45pm. Closed Dec, Jan and public holidays. No charge. ☎ 03 22 85 02 17.

DISNEYLAND PARIS

Open in high season, Mon-Fri, 10am-6pm, Sat, Sun and public holidays 9am-8pm; mid-July to Aug, daily, 9am-11pm; in low season, Mon-Fri, 10am-6pm, Sat, 9am-8pm. For further information apply to ☎ 01 60 30 60 30. For guided tours apply to the City Hall on Town Square, off Main Street, USA. 50F (adult), 35F (child). Parking: 40F (car), 25F (motorcycle).
Disneyland one-day pass: high season, 200F (adult), 155F (child 3-11). Two-day pass: 385F (adult), 300F (child). Three-day pass: 545F (adult), 420F (child).
The two- or three-day passes do not have to be used on consecutive days. Further information also on Minitel 3615 DISNEYLAND or Internet www-disneylandparis.com
Visitors wishing to leave the park for a short time should have their hand rubber-stamped. Please make sure you have your pass and parking ticket with you.

DOUAI   🛈 70, place d'Armes – 59500 ☎ 03 27 88 26 79

Guided tours of the town 🄰 – Apply to the tourist office.

Belfry – Guided tours (1hr) July and Aug, daily at 10am, 11am, 2pm, 3pm, 4pm and 5pm; Sept to June, Mon-Sat at 2pm, 3pm, 4pm and 5pm, Sun and public holidays at 10am, 11am, 3pm, 4pm and 5pm. Closed 1 Jan and 25 Dec. 11F. ☎ 03 27 88 26 79.

Carillon concerts – Year round Sat, 10.45-11.45am, public holidays at 11.30am. July and Aug summer season concerts at 9pm.

Musée de la Chartreuse – Open year round, Mon, Wed-Sat, 10am-noon, 2-5pm, Sun, 10am-noon, 3-6pm. Closed public holidays. 12F (no charge on first Sat of each month). ☎ 03 27 71 38 80.

Église St-Pierre – Open year round, Tues-Sun.

Palais de Justice – Tours possible May to Oct, one Sun in each month. The schedule is set up by the tourist office, 70, place d'Armes. ☎ 03 27 88 26 79.
Visits of the cells July and Aug, Thur-Sun, 2-8pm. No charge.

Boat trips – Cruises (30min) July and Aug, Thur-Sun, 2-8pm. Departure from quay beside the Law Courts. 20F (adult), 10F (child).

Église Notre-Dame – Open year round, Tues-Sun.

DUNKERQUE ◻ Beffroi, rue de l'Amiral-Ronarc'h – 59240 ☎ 03 28 66 79 21

Boat trips round the harbour – Departures (from Place du Minck, Bassin du Commerce), depending on reservations, July-early Sept, daily at 10.30am, 3pm, 4.30pm, and Sun and holidays at 11am, 3pm, 4.30pm, 5.30pm; May-June, Sun and holidays at 3pm, 4.30pm. 40F. ☎ 03 28 63 47 14.

Musée portuaire – Open Sept to June, daily (except Tues), 10am-12.45pm, 1.30-6pm; July and Aug, daily (except Tues), 10am-6pm. Closed 1 Jan, Mon before Lent, 1 May and 25 Dec. 25F. ☎ 03 28 63 33 39.

Musée d'Art contemporain – Not open to the public. ☎ 03 28 59 21 65.

Beffroi – Guided tours (30min) July and August, Mon-Sat at 9.30am, 10.30am, 11.30am, 2.30pm, 3.30pm, 4.30pm and 5.30pm. Closed public holidays. 12F. ☎ 03 28 66 79 21.

Église St-Eloi – Open year round, daily (except Sun afternoons).

Musée des Beaux-Arts – Open year round, daily (except Tues), 10am-noon, 2-6pm. Closed on certain public holidays. 20F (no charge on Sun). ☎ 03 28 26 25 60.

E

ÉCOUEN

Musée national de la Renaissance – ♿ Open year round, daily (except Tues), 9.45am-12.30pm, 2-5.15pm. Closed 1 Jan, 1 May and 25 Dec. 25F (17F on Sun). ☎ 01 34 38 38 50.

ÉPERLECQUES

Blockhaus d'Éperlecques – Open July and Aug, daily, 10am-7pm; June and Sept, Mon-Sat, 10am-noon, 2.15-7pm, Sun, 10am-7pm; Apr, Oct and Nov, daily, 2.15-6pm; May, Mon-Sat, 2.15-6pm, Sun, 10am-7pm; Mar, Sun, 2.15-6pm. Last entry 1hr before closing. Closed Dec to Feb. 39F. ☎ 03 21 88 44 22.

ERMENONVILLE

Parc J-J Rousseau – Open daily, except Tues year round, 2-6.15pm, Sun and public holidays, 2-7pm (Oct to Mar, 6.15pm). 12F (adult), 6F (child). ☎ 03 44 54 01 58 (tourist office).

Mer de Sable – Open daily June to Aug, Mon-Sat, 10.30am-6.30pm, Sun and public holidays, 10.30am-7pm; Apr, May and Sept, apply for opening times. Closed Oct to Mar. 82F. ☎ 03 44 54 00 96.

ESQUERDES

Maison du papier – ♿ Open mid-Feb to mid-Nov, Mon-Fri, 9am-12.30pm, 2-6.30pm, Sun and public holidays, 2-6.30pm. 25F. ☎ 03 21 95 45 25.

F

FELLERIES

Musée des Bois-Jolis – ♿ Open Apr to Oct, daily, 2.30-6.30pm. 15F. ☎ 03 27 59 03 46.

Château de FERRIÈRES

Château – Guided tours (30min) May to Sept, Wed-Sun, 2-6pm; Oct to Apr, Wed, Sat and Sun, 2-5pm. Closed 1 Jan and 25 Dec. 32F (includes access to park). ☎ 01 64 66 31 25.

Musée de l'Imaginaire – Open May to Sept, Thur and Fri (except from 15 July to 20 Aug), 2-6pm, Sat, 3-6pm, Sun, 2-7pm; Oct to Apr, Sat, 3-5pm, Sun, 2-5pm. 16F. ☎ 01 64 66 31 25.

Park – Same admission times as the château. 16F. ☎ 01 64 66 31 25.

FOLLEVILLE

Church – Open Apr to mid-Oct, Wed-Sat, 10am-noon, 2-7pm, Sun, 2-7pm; mid-Oct to mid-Dec, Feb and Mar, Wed-Sat, 10am-noon, 2-5pm, Sun, 2-5pm. Closed mid-Dec to Jan. 15F (20F guided tour). ☎ 03 22 41 42 52.

FONTAINEBLEAU

🛈 4, rue Royale – 77300 ☎ 01 60 74 99 99

Palace

Cour Ovale – Apply to the Administration du Domaine. ☎ 01 60 71 50 70.

Grands Appartements – ♿ Open May to Oct, daily (except Tues), 9.30am-5pm (July and Aug, 6pm); Nov to Apr, daily (except Tues), 9.30am-12.30pm, 2-5pm; Closed 1 Jan, 1 May and 25 Dec. 35F (adult), no charge (under 18s). ☎ 01 60 71 50 60.

Appartement intérieur de l'Empereur – See Grands Appartements.

Musée chinois – See Grands Appartements. Phone in the morning to check opening times. ☎ 01 60 71 50 60.

Petits Appartements et Galerie des Cerfs – Guided tours (45min) year round, daily (except Tues), 2-5pm. Last entry 1hr before closing. Phone on the day to check opening times. Closed 1 Jan, 1 May and 25 Dec. 16F. ☎ 01 60 71 50 60.

Musée Napoléon I – Guided tours (45min) year round, daily (except Tues), 9.30am-12.30pm. Last entry at 11am. Phone in the morning to check opening times. 16F. ☎ 01 60 71 50 60.

Musée napoléonien d'Art et d'Histoire militaires – Open year round, Tues-Sat, 2-5pm. Closed public holidays. 10F. ☎ 01 60 74 64 89.

FOURCHERET

Barn – Apply to ☎ 03 44 54 20 66.

FOURMIES

Musée du Textile et de la Vie sociale – ♿ Guided tours (1hr 30min) July and Aug, Mon-Fri, 9am-6pm, Sat, Sun and public holidays, 2.30-6.30pm; Sept to Dec and Feb to June, Mon-Fri, 9am-noon, 2-6pm, Sat, Sun and public holidays, 2.30-6.30pm. Closed Jan and 25 Dec. 30F. ☎ 03 27 - 60 66 11.

Fourmies – Musée du Textile et de la Vie sociale housed in a reconverted spinning mill

FRANCE MINIATURE

♿ Open mid-Mar to mid-Nov, daily, 10am-7pm. Last entry 1hr before closing. Closed the rest of the year. 75F (adult), 50F (child). ☎ 08 36 - 68 53 35.

FRIVILLE-ESCARBOTIN

Musée des Industries du Vimeu – Guided tours (1hr) Easter Day to Oct, Mon-Fri, 2.30-5.30pm, Sun and public holidays, 2.30-6.30pm. 15F. ☎ 03 22 26 42 37.

G – H

GRAVELINES

Musée du Dessin et de l'Estampe originale – Open year round, Mon, Wed-Fri, 2-5pm, Sat and Sun, 10am-noon, 3-6pm (Oct to Apr, 3-6pm only). Closed 1 Jan, 1, 8 May, 14 July and 25 Dec. 10F. ☎ 03 28 23 15 89.

GUÎNES

Musée municipal E-Villez – Open May to Sept, daily, 3-6pm by appointment only. No charge. ☎ 03 21 35 73 73.

GUISE

Château fort des ducs de Guise – Guided tours (1hr) year round, daily, 10am-noon, 2-6pm (in winter, 5.30pm). Closed mid-Dec to early Jan. 30F. ☎ 03 23 61 11 76.

Familistère Godin – Guided tours (1hr 30min), Apr to Oct, Tues-Sun at 2.30pm and 4.30pm, Jan to Mar, Nov and Dec, Sat at 2.30pm. Closed late Dec to mid-Jan. 20F. ☎ 03 23 61 35 36.

HANGEST-SUR-SOMME

Church – Apply to the town hall, open Mon, Tues, Thur and Fri, 3-6pm, Sat, 9am-noon. ☎ 03 22 51 12 37.

L'HAŸ-LES-ROSES

Roseraie – ⅘ Open mid-May to mid-Sept, daily, 10am-8pm. Closed the rest of the year. 10F. ☎ 01 43 99 82 80.

HONDSCHOOTE

Moulin Spinnewyn – Open year round, daily. It is recommended to phone first. 6F. ☎ 03 28 62 54 20.

Hôtel de ville – Open year round, Mon-Fri, 9am-noon, 2-5pm. Closed public holidays. 6F. ☎ 03 28 62 53 00.

Noord-meulen – Apply to the tourist office. 6F. ☎ 03 28 62 53 00.

HOUJARRAY

Maison Jean-Monnet: Centre d'Information sur l'Europe – Open year round, Mon-Fri, 10am 5pm, Sat, 1-6pm, Sun and public holidays, 9am-6pm. Audio-visual presentation: 12min. No charge. ☎ 01 34 86 12 43.

HUPPY

Church – Open year round, daily, 2-5pm.

HYDREQUENT

Masion du Marbre et de la Géologie – ⅘ Open July and Aug, daily, 10am-12.30pm, 2-6.30pm; Sept to June, Mon-Fri, 9am-12.20pm, 1.30pm-6pm, Sat and Sun, 2-6pm. Closed mid-Dec to mid-Jan. 25F. ☎ 03 21 83 19 10.

I – J

L'ISLE-ADAM

Église St-Martin – Open year round, Mon-Fri, 8.30am-noon, 2-5pm. ☎ 01 34 69 01 88.

Abbaye de JOUARRE

Tower – Open year round, daily (except Tues), 10am-noon, 2-6pm (Nov to Mar, 5pm). Closed 1 Jan, 1 May, 1, 11 Nov and 25 Dec. 15F (joint ticket with the crypt 30F). ☎ 01 60 22 64 54.

Crypt – Guided tours (30min). Same admission times as the tower. 20F.

Musée Briard – Guided tours (30min). Same admission times as the tower. 12F. ☎ 01 60 22 64 54.

JOUY-EN-JOSAS

Musée de la toile de Jouy – Open daily, except Mon, 2-6pm; Nov to Feb, 2-5pm. Closed 25 Dec. 25F.☎ 01 39 56 48 64.

Musée Léon-Blum – Open May, June, Sept and Oct, Sun, 2-5pm. Closed the rest of the year. 20F. ☎ 01 39 20 11 11 (town hall).

L

LAON
🅱 place du Parvis-de-la-Cathédrale – 02000 ☎ 03 23 20 28 62

Guided tours of the town  – Apply to the tourist office.

Maison des Arts – Open year round, Tues-Sat, noon-7pm, Sun, 3-7pm. Closed public holidays and during Christmas holidays. No charge. ☎ 03 23 26 30 30.

Museum – Open year round, daily (except Tues), 10am-noon, 2-6pm (Oct to Mar, 5pm). Closed 1 Jan, 1 May, 14 July and 25 Dec. 16F (no charge on Sun from Oct to Mar). ☎ 03 23 20 19 87.

Chapelle des Templiers – Open year round, daily (except Tues), 10am-6pm (Oct to Mar, 5pm). Closed 1 Jan, 1 May, 14 July and 25 Dec. No charge. ☎ 03 23 20 19 87.

Église St-Martin – Open July and Aug, daily, in the afternoon; Sept to Mar by appointment only. ☎ 03 23 20 28 62 (tourist office).

Centre historique minier de LEWARDE

Guided tours of the mine (1hr 30min) and non-guided tour of the exhibits July and Aug, Mon-Thur, Sat and Sun, 9am-5.30pm, Fri, 9am-8pm; Mar to June, Sept and Oct, 9am-5.30pm; Nov to Feb, Mon-Sat, 1-5pm, Sun and public holidays, 10am-5pm. Closed 1, 15-31 Jan, 1 May, 1 Nov and 25 Dec. High season 64F (adult), 32F (child); low season 56F (adult), 28F (child). ☎ 03 27 95 82 82.

LILLE
🅱 Palais Rihour – 59000 ☎ 03 20 21 94 21

Guided tours of the town  – Apply to the tourist office.

Palais Rihour – Open year round, Mon-Sat, 9.30am-6.30pm, Sun and public holidays, 10am-noon, 2-5pm. Closed 1 Jan, 1 May and 25 Dec. ☎ 03 20 21 94 21.

Hospice Comtesse – Open year round, daily (except Tues), 10am-12.30pm, 2-6pm. Closed 1 Jan, 1 May, 14 July, first weekend in Sept, 1 Nov and 25 Dec. 15F. ☎ 03 20 49 50 90.

Musée des Beaux-Arts – ♿ Open year round, Mon, 2-6pm, Wed, Thur Sat and Sun, 10am-6pm, Fri, 10am-7pm. Closed 1 Jan, 1 May, 14 July, first weekend in Sept, 1 Nov and 25 Dec. 30F. ☎ 03 20 06 78 00.

Citadelle – Guided tours (2hr) June to Aug, Sun, 3-5pm. Closed Sept to May. 45F. ☎ 03 20 21 94 21.

Hôtel de ville: belfry – Currently being restored.

Maison natale du Général de Gaulle – Open year round, Wed-Sun, 10am-noon, 2-5pm. Closed public holidays. 15F. ☎ 03 28 38 12 05.

Musée d'Histoire naturelle – Open early June to end of Jan, Mon, Wed-Fri, 9am-noon, 2-5pm, Sun, 10am-5pm; Feb to early June (exhibits), Mon, Wed-Fri, 9am-noon, 2-5pm, Sun, 10am-1pm, 2-6pm. Closed 1 Jan, 1 May, 14 June and 25 Dec. No charge on weekdays from June to Dec. ☎ 03 28 55 30 80.

Flea market at the Place du Lion-d'Or, Lille

Jardin des Plantes – Open May to Sept, daily, 7.30am-9pm; Oct to Mar, daily, 8.30am-6pm, Apr, daily, 7.30am-6pm. Greenhouse: 7.30-11.30am (8.30-11.30am in winter), 1-4pm. No charge.

LONG

Château – Guided tours (30min) mid-Aug to Sept, daily, 10am-noon, 2-5pm. 30F. ☎ 03 22 31 84 99.

LONGPONT

Abbey – &. Guided tours (30min) mid-Mar to Oct, Sat, 2.30-6.30pm, Sun and public holidays at 11am and 2.30-6.30pm. 28F. ☎ 03 23 96 01 53.

LONGPRÉ-LES-CORPS-SAINTS

Church – Apply to the tourist office several days in advance. ☎ 03 22 31 72 02.

M

MAINTENON

Château – Open Apr to Oct, Mon, Wed-Sat, 2-6pm, Sun, 10am-noon, 2-6pm; Nov to Mar, Sat, Sun and public holidays, 2-5pm. Closed mid-Dec to mid-Jan. 38F. ☎ 02 37 23 00 09.

Château de MAISONS-LAFFITTE

Open year round, daily (except Tues), 10am-noon, 1.30-6pm (mid-Oct to Mar, 5pm). Closed 1 Jan, 1 May, 1, 11 Nov and 25 Dec. 32F. ☎ 01 39 62 01 49.

MANTES-LA-JOLIE 🗉 place Jean XXIII – 78200 – ☎ 01 34 77 10 30

Collégiale Notre-Dame – For guided tours, apply to ☎ 01 34 77 10 30.

MALO-LES-BAINS

Musée aquariophile – Open year round, daily (except Tues), 10am-noon, 2-6pm. Closed 1 Jan, 1 May and 25 Dec. 12F (no charge on Sun). ☎ 03 28 59 19 18.

MARLY-LE-ROI

Musée-Promenade – &. Open year round, Wed-Sun, 2-6pm. Closed public holidays. 15F. ☎ 01 39 69 06 26.

Château de Monte-Cristo – Open Apr to Oct, Tues-Fri, 10am-12.30pm, 2-6pm, Sat, Sun and public holidays, 10am-6pm; Nov to Mar, Sun, 2-5pm. Last entry 1hr before closing. 30F. Guided tours (45min) Sun afternoons. 40F. ☎ 01 30 61 61 35.

MARQUENTERRE

Parc Ornithologique – Open April to Sept, daily, 9.30am-7pm; Oct to mid-Nov, daily, 10am-5pm; mid-Nov to Mar, Sat, Sun, public holidays and school holidays, daily, 10am-5pm. Last entry 1hr 30min before closing. Closed 25 Dec. 49F (adult), 39F (child). ☎ 08 36 68 80 21.

MEAUX 🗉 2, rue St-Rémy – 77100 ☎ 01 64 33 02 26

Guided tours of the town Ⓐ – Apply to the tourist office.

Ancien Évêché – &. Open Apr to Sept, daily (except Tues), 10am-12.15pm, 2-6pm; Oct to Mar, Wed-Sat, 10am-noon, 2-5pm, Sun, 2-5pm. Closed 1 Jan, 1 May, 14 July and 25 Dec. 15F (no charge on Wed). ☎ 01 64 34 84 45.

MEUDON

Observatoire – Temporarily closed to the public. ☎ 01 45 07 75 30.

Musée d'Art et d'Histoire – Open Jan to July and Sept to Dec, Wed-Sun, 2-6pm. Closed Aug and public holidays. 15F. ☎ 01 46 23 87 13.

Musée Rodin: Villa des Brillants – Open May to Oct, Fri-Sun, 1-6pm. Last entry 45min before closing. Closed Nov to Apr. 10F. ☎ 01 41 14 35 00.

MILLY-LA-FORÊT

Chapelle St-Blaise-des-Simples – &. Open Easter Day to 1 Nov, daily (except Tues), 10am-noon, 2.30-6pm; the rest of the year, Sat, Sun and public holidays, 10.15am-noon, 2.30-5pm. Closed last two weekends in Nov and the three weekends following 15 Jan. 10F. ☎ 01 64 98 84 94.

Le Cyclop – Guided tours (30min) May to Oct, Fri, 10.15am-4.15pm by appointment with the tourist office, Sat, 11am-5pm (Oct, 4.15pm), Sun, 11am-5.45pm (Oct, 5pm). Closed Nov to Apr. No children under 10. 35F. ☎ 01 64 98 83 17.

MIMOYECQUES

Forteresse de Mimoyecques – ♿ Open July and Aug, daily, 10am-7pm; Apr to June and Sept to mid-Nov, Mon-Sat, 2-6pm, Sun and public holidays, 10am-6pm. Closed mid-Nov to Mar. 30F. ☎ 03 21 87 10 34.

Abbaye de MONCEL

Guided tours (1hr) year round, daily (except Wed), 10am-noon, 2-6pm. 35F. ☎ 03 44 72 33 98.

MONTCEAUX-LES-MEAUX

Château – Park open year round, daily, 9am-6pm. 8F. ☎ 01 64 35 92 43.

MONTFORT-L'AMAURY

Musée Maurice-Ravel – Guided tours (1hr) year round, Wed-Fri, by appointment, only, Sat, Sun and public holidays at 10am, 11am, 2.30pm, 3.30pm and 4.30pm (Apr to Sept, also at 5.30pm). Closed 25 Decto 1 Jan. Maximum 7 people. 30F. ☎ 01 34 86 00 89.

Excursions

Vicq: Musée d'art naïf de l'Île-de-France – Open year round, daily, 9am-noon, 2-6pm. 36F. ☎ 01 34 86 12 18.

MONTGOBERT

Musée du Bois et de l'Outil – Open July and Aug, daily (except Tues), 2-6pm; Apr to June, Sept and Oct, Sat, Sun and public holidays, 2-6pm. Closed Nov to Mar. 20F. ☎ 03 23 96 36 69.

MONTMORENCY

Musée Jean-Jacques-Rousseau – Guided tours (30min) year round, Tues-Sun, 2-6pm. Closed 1 Jan, 1 May, 24, 25 and 31 Dec. 25F. ☎ 01 39 64 80 13.

MONTREUIL
🛈 place Darnétal – 62170 ☎ 03 21 06 04 27

Citadelle – Open Apr to Oct, daily (except Tues), 9am-noon, 2-6pm; Nov to Mar, daily (except Tues), 10am-noon, 2-5pm. Closed during Christmas and Feb school holidays. 15F. ☎ 03 21 06 10 83.

Chapelle de l'Hôtel-Dieu – Open for major liturgical festivals and some Sat and Sun in the year.

MORET-SUR-LOING
🛈 place Samois – 77250 ☎ 01 60 70 41 66

Guided tours of the town – Apply to the tourist office.

La Grange Batelière – Guided tours (1hr 30min) Easter Day to Aug, Sun at 3pm; Sept and Oct, Sun at 2.30pm; the rest of the year by appointment only. 50F. ☎ 01 60 70 51 21 / 41 66 (tourist office).

Boat trips – Trips along the Seine, the Yonne, and Loing Canal. Departure from St-Mammès, opposite Bourse de l'affrètement, May to 1 Nov, Sun and certain public holidays at 3pm. Duration depends on destination. For further information apply to Larguez-les-Amarres, 55, rue Gambette, 77670 St-Mammès. ☎ 01 64 23 16 24.

MORIENVAL

Église Notre-Dame – Apply to 4 Place de l'Eglise.

N

NAOURS

Caves – Guided tours (1hr) Feb to mid-Nov, daily, 9am-noon, 2-6pm. 47F (adult), 37F (child). ☎ 03 22 93 71 78.

Colline de NOTRE-DAME DE LORETTE

Musée vivant 1914-1918 – ♿ Open year round, daily, 9am-8pm. Closed 25 Dec. Museum 20F, battle field 5F. ☎ 03 21 45 15 80.

NOYON

🏠 place de l'Hôtel-de-Ville – 60400 – ☎ 03 44 44 21 88

Guided tours of the town
🅰 – Apply to the tourist office.

Musée du Noyonnais – Open year round, daily (except Tues), 10am-noon, 2-6pm (Nov to Mar, 5pm). Closed 1 Jan, 11 Nov and 25 Dec. 15F (joint ticket with the Musée Jean-Calvin). ☎ 03 44 09 43 41.

Musée Jean-Calvin – Open year round, daily (except Tues), 10am-noon, 2-6pm (Nov to Mar, 5pm). Closed 1 Jan, 11 Nov and 25 Dec. 15F (joint ticket with the Musée du Noyonnais). ☎ 03 44 44 03 59.

13C oak chest in the Musée du Noyonnais

O – P

Château d'OLHAIN

Open Apr to 1 Nov, Sun and public holidays, 3-6.30pm; summer school holidays, Sat, 3-6.30pm. 25F. ☎ 03 21 27 94 76.

PARIS

🏠 127, avenue des Champs-Elysées – 75008 – ☎ 01 49 52 53 54

Musée du Louvre – ♿ Open year round, daily (except Tues and certain public holidays), 9am-6pm (Mon, 9.45pm for parts of the museum, Wed, 9.45pm for the entire museum). Rooms begin to close 30min before closing. The medieval sections and rooms dealing with the history of the Louvre are open 9am-9.45pm; bookshops, restaurants and cafés in the Carrousel du Louvre 9.30am-9.45pm. Temporary exhibitions beneath the pyramid 10am-9.45pm; permanent exhibitions before 3pm 45F, after 3pm and Sun 26F. No charge on first Sun of each month and for visitors under 18 years. Tickets are valid for a full day (visitors may leave and return to the museum). Ticket office closes at 5.15pm or 9.15pm. The "Carte Musée et Monuments" pass giving admission for 1, 3 or 5 days to 65 museums and historic buildings can be purchased from the ticket offices at the Carrousel du Louvre. The "Carte Louvre jeunes" for visitors under 26 years is valid for 1 year and can be purchased beneath the pyramid. It gives free admission to the museum and temporary exhibitions but not reserved cultural events. The pass does not give reductions on lectures or guided tours. The "Carte des Amis du Louvre" (valid for 1 year) can be purchased from the Amis du Louvre ticket office next to the Engravings section between the pyramid and the reverse pyramid. It gives free admission to the museum and temporary exhibitions and reductions on other exhibitions with admission charges elsewhere in Paris. Recorded information in 5 languages. ☎ 01 40 20 51 51. Reception ☎ 01 40 20 53 17. Internet: www.louvre.fr.

Hôtel des Invalides

Église du Dôme – Open June to Aug, daily, 10am-7pm; Sept and Apr to June, daily, 10am-5.30pm, Oct to Mar, daily, 10am-4.30pm. Closed 1 Jan, 1 May, 1 Nov and 25 Dec. 37F. ☎ 01 44 42 38 42.

Arc de Triomphe – Open April to Aug, daily, 9.30am-11pm (Sun and Mon, 6.30pm); Oct to Mar, daily, 10am-10.30pm (Sun and Mon, 6pm). 35F. ☎ 01 43 80 31 31.

Eiffel Tower – Open (all 3 floors) 15 June to Aug, daily, 9.30am-midnight; the rest of the year, daily, 9.30am-11pm. Charges for lift: 20F to first floor (children 10F), 42F to 2nd floor (children 21F), 57F to 3rd floor (children 28F). ☎ 01 44 11 23 23.

La Conciergerie – Open Apr to Sept, 9.30am-6.30pm; Oct to Mar, daily, 10am-5pm. Closed 1 Jan, 1 May, 1, 11 Nov and 25 Dec. 32F. ☎ 01 43 54 30 06.

Panthéon – Open Apr to Sept, daily, 9.30am-6.30pm; Oct to Mar, daily, 10am-5.30pm. Closed 1 Jan, 1 May, 11 Nov and 25 Dec. 32F. ☎ 01 43 54 34 51.

Opéra Garnier – Open year round, daily (except during matinees and certain events), 10am-4.30pm. Guided tours (1hr 30min) through foyers and museum, daily (except Mon), 1pm. Meet 15min before in the entrance foyer in front of the statue of Rameau. Entrance charge 30F (no charge for children under 10), guided tour 60F (25F children under 10). Closed 1 Jan and 1 May. ☎ 01 40 01 22 63.

PARIS

Sainte-Chapelle – Open Apr to Sept, daily, 9.30am-6.30pm; Oct to Mar, daily, 10am-5pm. Closed 1 Jan, 1 May, 1, 11 Nov and 25 Dec. 32F. ☎ 01 43 54 30 09.

La Grande Arche – &. Open Apr to Sept, daily, 10am-6pm; Oct to Mar, Mon, Wed-Fri, 11am-5pm, Sat and Sun, 10am-5pm. 40F. ☎ 01 49 07 27 57.

Musée d'Orsay – Open 20 June to 20 Sept, Tues-Sun, 9am–5.30pm (Thur, 9.15pm); the rest of the year, Tues-Sun, 10am-5.30pm. Closed 1 Jan, 1 May and 25 Dec. 39F (27F for youth aged 18-25). Recorded information ☎ 01 45 49 11 11.

Musée de Cluny – Open year round, daily (except Tues), 9.15am-5.45pm. Closed 1 Jan, 1 Nov and 25 Dec. 30F. ☎ 01 53 73 78 16. Musuem book and card shop.

Musée Rodin – Open year round, Tues-Sun, 9.30am-5.15pm (Oct to Mar, 4.15pm). Closed 1 Jan, 1 Nov and 25 Dec. 28F. ☎ 01 44 18 61 10.

Cité des Sciences et de l'Industrie – &. Open year round, Tues-Sun, 10am-6pm (Media library, noon-8pm, no charge). Closed 1 May and 25 Dec. 45F; joint Cité-Pass ticket including visit to "L'Argonaute" submarine, Cité des Enfants, 25F; joint ticket Cité and Géode 92F. Triple-ticket Cité-Géode-Cinaxe 121F. Reservations (recommended for the films) ☎ 01 40 05 12 12. ☎ 01 36 68 29 30 (recorded information) or ☎ 01 40 05 70 00. Internet: www.cite-science.fr.

Centre Georges-Pompidou – Open year round, Mon, Wed-Fri, noon-10pm, Sat and Sun 10am-10pm. Closed 1 May.

Musée national d'art moderne 38F. One-day pass including Musée national d'art moderne, all exhibitions and special events 70F. ☎ 01 44 78 12 33.The museum will be closed for restoration until Dec 1999.

PÉRONNE

🛈 1, rue Louis XI – 80200 – ☎ 03 22 84 42 38

Historial de la Grande Guerre – &. Open May to Sept, daily, 10am-6pm; Oct to Apr, Tues-Sun, 10am-6pm. Closed mid-Dec to mid-Jan. 39F. ☎ 03 22 83 14 18.

Musée Danicourt – Open Tues, Thur and Fri, 2-6pm, Wed, 8am-noon, 2-6pm, Sat, 8am-noon, 2-5pm by appointment only. Apply to the town hall. ☎ 03 22 73 31 00.

PICQUIGNY

Castle – Guided tours (1hr 15min) July and Aug, daily (except Tues) at 10am, 11.30am, 2pm, 3.30pm and 5pm. Easter Day to June and Sept, Sat, Sun and public holidays at 2pm, 3.30pm and 5pm. 20F. ☎ 03 22 51 46 85.

Collégiale St-Martin – Same admission times and charges as the castle.

Château de PIERREFONDS

Tourist train – 4km/2.5mi ride (30min) mid-July to mid-Sept, daily at 2pm; Mar to mid-July and mid-Sept to Oct, Sat and Sun at 2pm. Closed the rest of the year. 30F (adult), 15F (child). Departure from the car park at the town hall. ☎ 03 44 86 49 35.

Château – Open May to Aug, daily, 10am-6pm; Mar, Apr, Sept and Oct, Mon-Sat, 10am-12.30pm, 2-6pm, Sun, 10am-6pm; Nov to Feb, Mon-Sat, 10am-12.30pm, 2-5pm, Sun, 10am-5.30pm. Closed 1 Jan, 1 May, 1, 11 Nov and 25 Dec. 32F. ☎ 03 44 42 72 72.

PITGAM

Den Leeuw – Guided tours (30min), Apr to Sept, third Sun of each month, 3-7pm. 10F. ☎ 03 28 62 10 90.

POISSY

Musée du Jouet – Open year round, Tues-Sun, 9.30am-noon, 2-5.30pm. Last entry 45min before closing. Closed public holidays. 15F (adult), 10F (child). ☎ 01 39 65 06 06.

Musée d'Art et d'Histoire – Open year round, Wed-Sun, 9.30am-noon, 2-5.30pm. Closed public holidays. No charge. ☎ 01 39 65 06 06.

Villa Savoye – Open year round, daily (except Tues), 9.30am-12.30pm, 1.30-6pm (Nov to Mar, 4.30pm). Closed 1 Jan, 1 May, 1, 11 Nov and 25 Dec. 25F. ☎ 01 39 65 01 06.

Centre de production Peugeot – Guided tours (3hr) Apr to Oct, Mon-Thur. Plant closed Aug and end Dec. Visitors must be at least 15 years of age. Apply 2 to 3 months in advance to Peugeot-Poissy, Relations Extérieures, Visites d'usine, 45, rue J.-P. Timbaud, 78300 Poissy Cedex. ☎ 01 39 19 30 50.

Musée Caapy – &. Guided tours (1hr 15min) Sept to July, Mon-Sat, 10am-noon, 2-5pm. Closed Aug and public holidays. 15F. ☎ 01 30 19 41 15.

Abbaye de PORT-ROYAL-DES-CHAMPS

Ruins and Abbey Museum – Guided (1hr) or non-guided tours 21 June to mid-Oct, Mon, Wed-Fri, 2-6pm, Sat, Sun and public holidays, 11am-noon, 2-6pm; the rest of the year, Mon, Wed-Fri, 2-5pm, Sat, Sun and public holidays, 11am-noon, 2-5pm. Closed 1 Jan and 25 Dec. 20F. ☎ 01 30 43 74 93.

Musée national des Granges de Port-Royal – Open year round, daily (except Tues), 10am-noon, 2-6pm (mid-Oct to Feb, 5.30pm). Closed 1 Jan and 25 Dec. 16F. ☎ 01 30 43 73 05.

Abbaye de PRÉMONTRÉ

Apply to the gatekeeper at the hospital 8 days in advance. ☎ 03 23 23 66 66.

PRISCES

Church – Currently being restored. ☎ 03 23 98 11 98.

PROVINS
🅱 chemin de Villecran BP 44 – 77160 ☎ 01 64 60 26 26

Guided tours of the town 🄰 – Apply to the tourist office.

Pépinières et Roseraies Vizier – ♿ Open year round, daily without a break. Closed late Dec to early Jan. ☎ 01 64 00 02 42.

Grange aux Dîmes – Open Apr to Aug, daily, 10am-6pm; Sept and Oct, Mon-Fri, 2-6pm; Nov to Mar, Sat, Sun, public holidays and daily during school holidays, 2-5pm. Closed 25 Dec. 22F.

Musée du Provinois – Open Apr to 1 Nov, daily, 2-6pm; the rest of the year, Sat, Sun, public holidays and daily during school holidays, 2-5pm. Closed 25 Dec. 22F. ☎ 01 64 60 26 26.

Tour César – Currently being restored. Apply to the tourist office.

Souterrains à graffiti – Guided tours (45min) Apr to 1 Nov, Mon-Fri at 3pm and 4pm, Sat, Sun and public holidays, 11am-6pm; the rest of the year, Sat, Sun, public holidays and daily during school holidays at 3pm and 4pm. Closed 25 Dec. 22F.

Q

QUAËDYPRE

Church – Apply to the town hall, Mon-Fri, 8.30-11.30am, 1.30-5pm, Sat, 9-11.30am. ☎ 03 28 68 66 03.

La QUEUE-LES-YVELINES

Serre aux Papillons – ♿ Open Apr to mid-Nov, daily, 9.30am-12.15pm, 2.30-6pm. Closed mid-Nov to Mar. 35F. ☎ 01 34 86 42 99.

R

RAMBOUILLET
🅱 Hôtel de Ville – 78120 ☎ 03 34 83 21 21

Guided tours of the town – Apply to the tourist office.

Château – Guided tours (30min) year round, daily (except Tues), 10-11.30am, 2-5.30pm (Oct to Mar, 4.30pm). Closed 1 Jan, 1 May, 1, 11 Nov, 25 Dec and when the French President is in residence. 32F. ☎ 01 34 83 00 25.

Park – Open May to Aug, daily, 6.30am-7.30pm; Feb to Apr, Sept and Oct, daily, 7am-6pm; Nov to Jan, daily, 8am-5pm. Closed when the French President is in residence. No charge. ☎ 01 34 94 28 79.

Laiterie de la Reine et Chaumière des Coquillages – Guided tours (45min), year round, daily (except Tues), 10-11.30am, 2-5.30pm (Oct to Mar, 3.30pm). Closed 1 Jan, 1 May, 1, 11 Nov and 25 Dec. 15F. ☎ 01 34 83 29 09.

Bergerie Nationale – ♿ Open year round, Wed-Sun and public holidays, 2-5pm. Guided tours (1hr) available Sat and Sun. Closed during the Christmas holidays. 25F (adult), 15F (child). ☎ 01 34 83 68 00.

Musée Rambolitrain – Open year round, Wed-Sun, 10am-noon, 2-5.30pm. Closed 1 Jan and 25 Dec. 22F. ☎ 01 34 83 15 93.

Forêt de RAMBOUILLET

Etangs de Pourras et de St-Hubert – To find out about regulations regarding fishing in the Etang St-Hubert, apply to the Fédération des Yvelines pour la Pêche et la Protection du Milieu Aquatique, 19, rue du Docteur Roux, 78520 Limay. ☎ 01 34 77 58 90.

Forêt de RAMBOUILLET

Espace Rambouillet – Open Apr to Oct, daily, 9am-6pm; Nov to Mar, Tue-Sun, 10am-5pm. Mar to Nov, display of birds of prey in flight. Closed 1 Jan and 24, 25 and 31 Dec. 45F (adult), 35F (child). ☎ 01 34 83 05 00 or MINITEL 3614 ESPACE RAMB.

Château-fort de RAMBURES

Guided tours (1hr) Mar to Oct, daily (except Wed), 10am-noon, 2-6pm; Nov to Feb, by appointment only. Closed 1 Jan and 25 Dec. 30F. ☎ 03 22 25 10 93.

RAMOUSIES

Church – Open in summer, daily; in winter, Sun. ☎ 03 27 59 06 04.

RÉTY

Church – Open year round, Sun during Mass or apply to 5, rue de l'Église.

La ROCHE-GUYON

Château – Open second weekend in Mar to second weekend in Nov, Mon-Fri, 10am-6pm, Sat, Sun and public holidays, 10am-7pm; the rest of the year, Sat, Sun and public holidays, 2-6pm. Candlelit tour by appointment in season. 40F (adult), 20F (child). ☎ 01 34 79 74 42.

Abbaye de ROYAUMONT

Open year round, daily, 10am-6pm (Nov to Feb, 5.30pm). Guided tours available Sat, Sun and public holidays in the afternoon. 25F. ☎ 01 30 35 88 90.

RUEIL-MALMAISON

Museum – Open year round, Mon, Wed-Fri, 10am-noon, 1.30-5pm (Oct to Mar, 4.30pm), Sat, Sun and public holidays (guided tours, 1hr), 10am-5.30pm (Oct to Mar, 5pm). Closed 1 Jan and 25 Dec. 30F (20F on Sun). ☎ 01 41 29 05 55.

Château de Bois-Préau – Currently being restored. ☎ 01 41 29 05 55.

S

SAINS-DU-NORD

Maison du Bocage – Open Apr to Oct, Mon-Fri, 2-6pm, Sat, Sun and public holidays, 2.30-6.30pm. 20F. ☎ 03 27 59 82 24.

ST-AMAND-LES-EAUX

Abbey Tower – Museum – Open Apr to Sept, Mon, Wed-Fri, 10am-12.30pm, 2-5pm, Sat, Sun and public holidays, 10am-12.30pm, 3-6pm; Oct to Mar, daily (except Tues), 10am-12.30pm, 2-5pm. Closed 1 Jan, 14 July, 1, 11 Nov, and 25 Dec. 10F. ☎ 03 27 22 24 55.

Échevinage – Guided tours year round, Mon, Wed, Thur and Sat, 10am-noon, 3-6pm, Fri, 3-6pm, Sun, 10am-noon. Closed public holidays. 1F. ☎ 03 27 22 24 55.

ST-CLOUD

Park – Open May to Aug, daily, 7.30am-10pm; Mar, Apr, Sept and Oct, 7.30am-9pm, Nov to Feb, 7.30am-8pm. Cars 20F, no charge for pedestrians. ☎ 01 41 12 02 90.

Musée Historique – Open year round, Wed, Sat, Sun and public holidays, 2-6pm. ☎ 01 44 61 21 70.

Grandes Eaux (Fountain display) – *See Calendar of events.*

Institut Pasteur – Musée des Applications de la Recherche – ♿ Open Sept to July, Mon-Fri, 2-5.30pm. Closed Aug and public holidays. 20F. ☎ 01 47 01 15 97.

ST-DENIS

🛈 1, rue de la République – 93200 ☎ 01 55 87 08 70

Guided tours of the town 🄰 – Apply to the tourist office.

Basilica: Tombs and Crypt – Open Apr to Sept, daily, 10am-6.30pm; Oct to Mar, daily, 10am-4.30pm. Closed 1 Jan, 1 May, 1, 11 Nov and 25 Dec. 32F. ☎ 01 48 09 83 54.

Former Abbey – Guided tours organised by the tourist office. ☎ 01 55 87 08 70.

Musée d'Art et d'Histoire – Open 5 June to 12 July, daily (except Tues), 10am-7pm, the rest of the year, Mon-Sat, 10am-5.30pm, Sun, 2-6.30pm. Closed public holidays. 35F. ☎ 01 42 43 05 10.

Musée Christofle – Guided tours (1hr) year round, Mon-Fri, 2-5.30pm by appointment with the Musée, 112, rue Ambroise-Croizat, 93206 St-Denis. Closed public holidays. ☎ 01 49 22 41 15.

ST-GERMAIN-EN-LAYE

🖪 38, rue de Pain – 78100 ☎ 01 34 51 05 12

Guided tours of the town 🅰 – Apply to the tourist office.

Musée des Antiquités Nationales – ♿ Open year round, daily (except Tues), 9am-5.15pm. Closed 1 Jan and 25 Dec. 25F (adult), no charge (under 18s). ☎ 01 39 10 13 21.

Musée Départemental du Prieuré – Open year round, Wed-Fri, 10am-5.30pm, Sat and Sun, 10am-6.30pm. Closed 31 Jan, 1 May and 25 Dec. 25F. ☎ 01 39 73 77 87.

Maison Debussy – Open year round, Tues-Sat, 2-6pm. Closed public holidays. No charge. ☎ 01 34 51 05 12.

ST-OMER

🖪 boulevard Pierre-Guillain – 62500 ☎ 03 21 98 08 51

Hôtel Sandelin et Musée – Currently being restored. For information apply to ☎ 03 21 38 00 94.

Église Saint-Denis – Open for religious services.

Bibliothèque (Library) – ♿ Open year round, Tues-Sat, 9am-noon, 1-6pm. Closed Easter Sat, Sat before Whitsun and public holidays. ☎ 03 21 38 35 08.

Musée Henri-Dupuis – Open year round, Wed-Sun, 10am-noon, 2-6pm (Fri, 5pm). Closed public holidays. 15F. ☎ 03 21 38 24 13.

L'Audomarois

Tour of the marshes – Boat trips with commentary (1hour 45min) through the marshes on the Emeraude, July and Aug, daily in the afternoon; Apr to June and Sept, depending on availability of the boat. Departure from St-Omer, in Faubourg de Lysel, 2km/1mi from the railway station, beside the bridge over the Canal de Neuffossé on D 209 between Clairmarais and St-Omer. Phone in advance. ☎ 03 21 98 66 74.

La Grange-Nature – Open Easter and summer school holidays, daily, 9.30am-12.30pm, 2.30-6.30pm; Apr to June and Sept, Sat, 2.30-6.30pm, Sun, 9.30am-12.30pm, 2.30-6.30pm; Oct, Sat and Sun, 2.30-5.30pm; Mar and first two weeks in Nov, Sat and Sun, 2.30-5.30pm. Closed the rest of the year. Rue du Romelaere, 62500 Clairmarais. ☎ 03 21 38 52 95.

Excursions

Arques: Cristallerie d'Arques – Guided tours (1hr 30min), Mon-Sat, every 20min, 9-10.30am, 2-4pm. 35F. ☎ 03 21 12 74 74.

ST-QUENTIN

🖪 14, rue de la Sellerie – 02100 ☎ 03 23 67 05 00

Guided tours of the town 🅰 – Apply to the tourist office.

Musée Antoine-Lécuyer – Open year round, Mon, Wed-Fri, 10am-noon, 2-5pm, Sat, 10am-noon, 2-6pm, Sun, 2-6pm. Closed 1 Jan, 1 May, 1 Nov and 25 Dec. 15F (no charge on Wed). ☎ 03 23 64 06 66.

Basilica – Guided tours (2hr, basilica and town hall) July and Aug, daily (except Sat) at 3pm; June, Sun at 3pm. 30F. Visit of upper sections 2-30 Aug, Sat at 9pm. ☎ 03 23 67 05 00.

Hôtel de ville – Guided tours (2hr, town hall and basilica) July and Aug, daily (except Sat) at 3pm; June, Sun at 3pm. 30F. ☎ 03 23 67 05 00.

Musée entomologique – Open year round, Mon, Wed-Sat, 2-6pm, Sun and public holidays, 3-6pm. Closed 1 Jan, 1 May, Whitsun, 14 July, 1 Nov and 25 Dec. 15F. ☎ 03 23 06 30 92.

Marais d'Isle – Open year round, Mon-Fri, 10am-noon, 2-5.30pm, Sat and Sun, 10am-noon, 2-6pm. Park open Apr to Sept, daily, 8am-8pm; Oct to Mar, daily, 9am-6pm. Closed 1 Jan, 1 May, 1 Nov and 25 Dec. No charge. ☎ 03 23 05 06 50.

Chemin de fer touristique du Vermandois – Apply to the tourist office in St-Quentin, 27, rue Victor-Basch, ☎ 03 23 67 05 00 or to CFTV, BP 152, 02104 St-Quentin Cedex, ☎ 03 23 64 88 38.

ST-RIQUIER

Church and Treasury – Guided tours (1hr) Apr to Oct, daily (except Wed afternoon and Sun morning) at 9.30am, 10.30am, 11.30am, 2pm, 3pm, 4pm and 5pm; Nov to Mar, daily (except Wed afternoon and Sun morning) at 11am, 2pm and 3pm. Closed last two weeks in July. 10F. ☎ 03 22 28 20 20.

Centre culturel départemental: Museum – Open July and Aug, daily, 10am-6pm; May to June and Sept, daily, 10am-noon, 2-6pm; mid-Feb to Apr, Oct and Nov, Mon-Fri, 2-6pm, Sat, Sun and public holidays, 10am-noon, 2-6pm. Closed Dec to mid-Feb. No charge. ☎ 03 22 68 20 20.

Hôtel-Dieu – ♿ Guided tours (15min) year round, Mon-Sat, 9-11.30am, 2-4.30pm. Closed public holidays. No charge. ☎ 03 22 28 92 52.

ST-VALERY-SUR-SOMME

Musée Picarvie – Open mid-Mar to mid-Nov, daily (except Tues), 2-7pm. Closed the rest of the year. 25F. ☎ 03 22 26 94 90.

Maison de l'Oiseau – &. Open mid-Feb to mid-Nov, daily, 10am-6pm (July and Aug, 7pm). Closed mid- Nov to mid-Feb. 34F (adult), 27F (child). ☎ 03 22 26 93 93.

Phare de Brighton – Closed to the public.

Chemin de fer de la Baie de Somme – *See Le CROTOY.*

Parc SAMARA

Open July and Aug, daily, 10am-7.30pm; Sept to mid-Nov and mid-Mar to June, Mon-Fri, 9.30am-5.30pm, Sat, Sun and public holidays, 9.30am-6.30pm. Closed mid-Nov to mid-Mar. 59F (adult), 45F (child). ☎ 03 22 51 82 83.

SARS-POTERIES

Musée du Verre – Open year round, Mon-Fri, 2-6pm, Sat, Sun and public holidays, 2-7pm. Closed 1 Jan and 25 Dec. 16F. ☎ 03 27 61 61 44.

Watermill – Open July and Aug, daily (except Tues) from 3pm; Apr to June, Sept and Oct, Sun and public holidays, 3-6pm. Closed Nov to Mar. 15F. ☎ 03 27 61 60 01.

SAUVAGE

Réserve zoologique – Open year round, daily, 9am-7pm (in winter, 6pm). 40F (adult), 25F (child). ☎ 01 34 94 00 94.

SCEAUX

Park – Open year round, daily, sunrise to sunset. ☎ 01 46 61 44 85.

Orangery: chamber music concerts – For a programme, apply to "Saison Musicale d'été de Sceaux", BP 52, 92333 Sceaux Cedex. ☎ 01 46 60 07 79.

Musée de l'Ile-de-France – &. Open year round, daily (except Tues), 10am-6pm (Oct to Mar, 5pm). Closed most public holidays. 22F. ☎ 01 41 13 70 41.

Centre de Documentation – Open year round by appointment. ☎ 01 46 61 06 71.

Grandes Cascades – Operates year round, Wed, Sat, Sun and public holidays, 11am-9pm (in winter, 5pm). ☎ 01 46 61 44 85.

SEBOURG

Church – Guided tours by appointment. ☎ 03 27 26 51 87 (Mr Heuclin) or 03 27 26 54 09.

SENLIS
🖪 place du Parvis Notre-Dame – 60300 ☎ 03 44 53 06 40

Guided tours of the town 🅰 – Apply to the tourist office.

Jardin du Roy – Public garden. Open year round, daily. No charge.

Église St-Pierre – Guided tours by appointment with the tourist office. ☎ 03 44 53 06 40.

Musée d'Art et d'Archéologie – Open year round, daily (except Wed morning and Tues), 10am-noon, 2-6pm (Nov to Feb, 5pm). Closed 1 Jan, 1 May and 25 Dec. 15F (joint ticket with the Musée de Vermandois). ☎ 03 44 53 00 80 ext 1247.

Musée des Spahis – Open year round, daily (except Wed morning and Tues), 10am-noon, 2-6pm (Nov to Feb, 5pm). Closed 1 Jan, 1 may and 25 Dec. 15F (joint ticket with the Musée de la Vénerie). ☎ 03 44 53 00 80 ext 1315.

Ancien Château royal – Same admission times and charges as the Musée des Spahis.

Musée de la Vénerie – Same admission times and charges as the Musée des Spahis.

Chapelle royale St-Frambourg – Open May to Oct, Sat, Sun and public holidays, 3-6.30pm; Nov to Apr, Sun, 3-5pm. 20F. ☎ 03 44 53 39 99.

Ancienne Abbaye St-Vincent – Open year round, Sun, 9am-5pm.

Musée de l'Hôtel de Vermandois – Same opening times and charges as the Musée d'Art et d'Archéologie.

SÈVRES

Musée national de la céramique – &. Open year round, daily (except Tues), 10am-5pm. Closed most public holidays. 22F. ☎ 01 41 14 04 20.

Maison des Jardies – Guided tours (1hr) year round, Mon and Fri, 2.30-3.45pm. Closed 1 May, 1 Nov and 25 Dec. 25F. ☎ 01 45 34 61 22.

SOISSONS

🏛 cour St-Jean-des-Vignes – 02200 ☎ 03 23 53 17 37

Guided tours of the town 🅰 – Apply to the tourist office.

Ancienne abbaye de St-Jean-des-Vignes – Open year round, Mon-Fri, 9am-12.30pm, 1.30-6pm, Sat, 9am-12.30pm, 1.30-7pm, Sun, 10am-12.30pm, 1.30-7pm. Closed 1 Jan, 1 May and 25 Dec. No charge. ☎ 03 23 59 15 90.

Musée municipal de l'ancienne abbaye de St-Léger – Open mid-June to Aug, daily (except Tues), 10am-6pm; Sept to mid-June, daily (except Tues), 10am-noon, 2-5pm. Closed 1 Jan, 1 May and 25 Dec. No charge. ☎ 03 23 59 15 90.

Abbaye de St-Médard: Crypt – Open by appointment with the tourist office. ☎ 03 23 53 17 37.

STEENVOORDE

Steenmeulen – Open Apr to Sept, last Sun of each month, 2-6pm. 10F. ☎ 00 32 69 35 29 80.

Drievenmeulen – Open in season. Apply to the town hall. ☎ 03 28 49 77 77.

Noordmeulen – Guided tours (30min) Easter Day to Oct, by appointment with the town hall, ☎ 03 28 49 77 77. Visit possible with the presence of a miller. 5F.

T – V

THOIRY

Château – ♿ Guided tours (30min). Enquire before your visit as closed on certain days. 38F (adult), 30F (child). ☎ 01 34 87 40 67 or MINITEL 3614 THOIRY.

Zoological park – Same admission times as the African wildlife park. 79F (adult), 65F (child).

African wildlife park – Open Easter Day to 1 Nov, Mon-Sat, 10am-6pm, Sun and public holidays, 10am-6.30pm; the rest of the year daily, 10am-5pm. 100F (adult), 79F (child), joint ticket with the Zoological park. ☎ 01 34 87 40 67.

Le TOUQUET

Aqualud – July-early Sept: 10am-7pm; Feb school holidays, some weekends in Mar and Apr, Wed-Sun in May-June, weekends Sept-Oct and November school holidays: 10am-6pm. 72F (55F for 3hr, 6F for every additional hour). ☎ 03 21 05 63 59.

Museum – Open July and Aug, daily (except Tues), 10am-noon, 3-7pm, Sept to June, Mon, Wed-Sat, 10am-noon, 2-6pm, Sun and public holidays, 10am-noon, 2.30-6pm. Closed 1 Jan, 11 Nov and 25 Dec. 20F. ☎ 03 21 05 62 62.

TRÉLON

Atelier-musée du verre – ♿ Open Apr to Oct, Mon-Fri, 2-6pm, Sat, Sun and public holidays, 2.30-6.30pm. 30F. ☎ 03 27 59 71 02.

VALENCIENNES

🏛 1, rue Askièvre – 59300 ☎ 03 27 46 22 99

Musée des Beaux-Arts – ♿ Open year round, daily (except Tues), 10am-6pm (Thur, 8pm). Closed 1 Jan, 1 May, Mon following second Sun in Sept and 25 Dec. 20F (no charge on first Sun of each month). ☎ 03 27 22 57 20.

Église St-Géry – Guided tours. Apply to the vicarage (presbytère). ☎ 03 27 46 22 04.

Bibliothèque des Jésuites – Open during library opening hours, Tues and Thur, 2-6.30pm, Wed and Sat, 10am-noon, 2-6.30pm, Fri, 10am-8pm. Guided tours available Sat at 11am and by appointment. ☎ 03 27 22 57 00.

Abbaye de VALLOIRES

Guided tours (45min) April to 11 Nov, daily, 10am-noon, 2-6pm (Oct to 11 Nov, 5pm). 28F. Closed the rest of the year. ☎ 03 22 29 62 33.

Gardens – Open mid-May to mid-Sept, daily, 10am-7.30pm; mid-Sept to mid-Nov and mid-Mar to mid-May, daily, 10am-6pm. Last entry 1hr before closing. Closed mid Nov to mid-Mar. 36F. ☎ 03 22 23 53 55.

Abbaye de VAUCLAIR

Abbey ruins and park – ♿ Open year round, daily, 8am-8pm. ☎ 03 23 22 40 87.

VAUX-DE-CERNAY

Abbey ruins and grounds – Open year round, Sat, Sun and public holidays, 2-6pm (Apr to Oct, 7pm). 25F. ☎ 01 34 85 23 00.

Château de VAUX-LE-VICOMTE

Château – Open Mar to 11 Nov, Mon-Sat, 10am-1pm, 2-6pm, Sun, 10am-6pm; the rest of the year enquire. Candlelit tour, May to mid-Oct, Sat and public holidays, 8.30-11pm. 56F (castle, grounds and carriage museum), 75F (candlelit tour). ☎ 01 64 14 41 90.

Gardens – ♿ Same admission times as the château. 30F (joint ticket with the Musée des Equipages), 45F (candlelit tour). Electric cars available (45min: 80F, deposit 600F) near the château. ☎ 01 64 14 41 90.

Musée des équipages – ♿ Same opening times as the gardens. 30F (45F candlelit tour). ☎ 01 64 14 41 90.

VERSAILLES

🏠 7, rue des Réservoirs – 78000 ☎ 01 39 50 36 22

Access to the courtyards and gardens of Versailles Palace and Trianon, and to the park (23F for cars) is free every day from sunrise to sunset. However, there is a charge to visit the gardens during the Grandes Eaux Musicales, June to Aug, Sat, 1-5pm; Apr to Oct, Sun, 1-5pm.

Palace

Guided tours – Tues-Sun. Book in advance on day of visit. Entrance D. 1hr: 25F; 1hr 30min: 37F; 2hr: 50F (this is in addition to the entry charge of 45F). ☎ 01 30 83 77 88.

Musée des Carrosses – ♿ Open year round, Sat and Sun, 2-6.30pm (Oct to Apr, 5.30pm). 12F (no charge for under 18s). ☎ 01 30 83 77 88.

Chapel and Grands Appartements – As well as the traditional visit of the Grands Appartements, the new tour usually includes the Crusade Rooms, the 17C rooms, the Galerie des Batailles and the 1830 Room. Open May to Sept, Tues-Sun, 9am-6.30pm; Oct to Apr, Tues-Sun, 9am-5.30pm. Last entry 30min before closing. 45F (reduced rate 35F, Tues-Sun from 3.30pm). ☎ 01 30 83 76 20.

Appartements du Roi – Audio-guided visit (1hr) in 6 languages. Entrance C. 25F (plus a variable charge according to age which gives access to the Grands Appartements). ☎ 01 30 83 76 20.

"Les Grandes Heures du Parlement" – Audio-guided visit (1hr 30min) year round, Tues-Sat, 9am-5.30pm (May to Sept, 6.30pm). Last entry 1hr before closing. 20F (no charge for under 18s). ☎ 01 39 67 07 73.

Park

Small train – Round trip (40min) with a stop at Trianon. Departures May to Aug, daily (except on occasions and Mon from mid-Nov to mid-Feb), 10am-6.15pm; Sept, daily, 10.30am-6.15pm; Mar, Apr and Oct, daily, 10.30am-5pm; Nov, daily, 11am-4.30pm; the rest of the year , enquire. Departure from the Palace terrace (north arcade). 33F (adult), 21F (child). ☎ 01 39 54 22 00.

Cycle Hire – There are two cycle hire points in the park:

Near the Grand Canal, Feb to Mar, daily (except when raining), 10am-6.30pm. 32F for 1hr.

At the entrance to the park, by the Grille de la Reine, July and Aug, Mon-Fri, 1-6.30pm, Sat, Sun and public holidays, 10am-6.30pm; Feb to June, Sept and Oct, Wed, 1-6.30pm, Sat, Sun and public holidays, 10.30am-6.30pm. 27F for 1hr. ☎ 01 39 66 97 66.

Boat Hire – Boating on the 24ha-Grand Canal. Landing-stage open July and Aug, daily, 10.30am-7pm; Apr to June, Mon-Fri, 11.30am-6pm, Sat, Sun and public holidays, 10.30am-7pm; Mar, Tues-Thur, 1-5.30pm, Sat, Sun and public holidays, 11am-5.30pm; Sept and Oct, Mon-Fri, 1-5.30pm, Sat, Sun and public holidays, 11am-5.30pm. Times and duration depend on weather. Boat for 4 people 73F for 1hr, 51F for 30min. ☎ 01 39 54 22 00.

Grand Trianon at Versailles

Grand Trianon – Petit Trianon
Open May to Sept, Tues-Sun, 10am-6.30pm; Oct to Apr, Tues-Fri, 10am-12.30pm, 2-5.30pm, Sat and Sun, 10am-5.30pm. Last entry 30min before closing. Grand Trianon 25F (reduced rate 15F), joint ticket with Petit Trianon 30F (reduced rate 20F). ☎ 01 30 83 76 20.

Town of Versailles
Guided tour – Apply to the tourist office.

Jeu de Paume – Open year round, Sat and Sun, 2-5pm. No charge. ☎ 01 30 83 77 88.

Musée Lambinet – Open year round, Tues and Fri, 2-5pm, Wed and Thur, 1-6pm, Sat and Sun, 2-6pm. Closed public holidays. 25F. ☎ 01 39 50 30 32.

Bibliothèque municipale – Occasional guided tours of the reception rooms. Apply to the tourist office.

Château de VERT-BOIS

Château – Guided tours (1hr) July and Aug, Wed-Sun, 2-6pm. Closed the rest of the year. 40F. ☎ 03 20 46 26 37.

Fondation Septentrion – Open July and Aug, Wed-Fri, 9am-noon, 2-6pm, Sat, Sun and public holidays, 2-6pm; Sept to June, Mon-Fri (except Mon and Tues during temporary exhibitions), 9am-noon, 2-6pm, Sat, Sun and public holidays, 2-6pm. Closed 1 Jan and 25 Dec. 20F. ☎ 03 20 46 26 37.

VERSIGNY

Château – Grounds open July and Sept, daily, 2-6.30pm. ☎ 01 44 88 04 35.

VÉTHEUIL

Church – Open Easter Day to 1 Nov, Sun, 3-6pm; otherwise apply to the Association Notre-Dame de Vétheuil. ☎ 01 34 78 12 17.

Domaine de VILLARCEAUX

Gardens and tower – Open May to Oct, Sat, Sun and public holidays, 2-6pm. No charge. ☎ 01 34 67 74 33.

VILLENEUVE-D'ASCQ

Musée d'Art moderne – &. Open year round, daily (except Tues), 10am-6pm. Closed 1 Jan, 1 May and 25 Dec. 43F. ☎ 03 20 19 68 69.

Mills and museum – Guided tours (45min to 2hr) year round, Mon-Fri, 2-5pm, Sun, 3-6pm. Closed mid-Dec to mid-Jan and public holidays. 30F. ☎ 03 20 05 49 34.

Musée du Terroir – Open June to Sept, Tues-Sat, 2.30-6pm, Sun, 9.30am-1pm, 2.30-6pm; mid-Mar to May, Oct and Nov, Tues-Thur and public holidays, 2-5.30pm, Sun, 9.30am-1pm (second and fourth Sun of each month, 2.30-5.30pm); Dec to mid-Mar, Sun, 9.30am-1pm. 15F. ☎ 03 20 91 87 57.

Forum des Sciences – Centre Francois-Mitterrand – &. Open school holidays, Tues-Fri, 8.45am-7pm, Sat, Sun and public holidays, 2-7pm; outside of school holidays, Tues-Fri, 8.45am-5.30pm, Sat, Sun and public holidays, 2-7pm. Closed first three weeks in Sept, 1 Jan, 1 May and 25 Dec. 50F. ☎ 03 20 19 36 36.

Château de Flers – &. Open year round, Tues-Fri, 2-5.30pm; Sat and the first Sun of the month, 9am-noon. No charge. ☎ 03 20 43 55 70 / 82.

Parc archéologique – Open May to Oct, Sun, 3-6.30pm. No charge. ☎ 03 20 43 55 70.

VILLERS-COTTERÊTS

Château François I – Guided tours (45min) year round, daily (except Tues) at 10.30am, 2.30pm and 4pm. Closed 1 Jan and 25 Dec. 20F. ☎ 03 23 96 55 10.

Musée Alexandre-Dumas – &. Open year round, daily (except Tues and last Sun of each month), 2.30-5pm. Closed public holidays. 20F. ☎ 03 23 96 23 30.

Mémorial canadien de VIMY

The historical centre, the memorial and the trenches are open year round, daily. Guided tours of the tunnel (30min) Apr to Nov, daily, 10am-5.30pm. No charge. ☎ 03 21 48 72 29.

VULAINES

Musée départemental Stéphane-Mallarmé – Open year round, Tues-Sun, 10am-noon, 2-6pm. Closed 1 Jan and 25 Dec. 15F. ☎ 01 64 23 73 27.

W

Le WAST

Church – To visit, apply to Colembert vicarage, ☎ 03 21 33 30 96 or to Mme Bourdon, 8, rue de la Vallée, ☎ 03 21 33 32 05 (mornings).

Manoir du Huisbois – Open Apr to Sept, Mon-Fri, 8.30am-noon, 1.30-6pm, Sun, 3-7pm; Oct to Mar, Mon-Fri, 8.30am-noon, 1.30-6pm. No charge. ☎ 03 21 83 38 79.

WEST-CAPPEL

Église St-Sylvestre – Guided tours. Apply to the town hall. ☎ 03 28 68 66 03.

WIGNEHIES

Observation Trails – Signposted trails starting from the church square. Leaflets available at the Ecomusée. ☎ 03 27 60 66 11.

WISSANT

Musée du Moulin – Open year round, daily, 2-6pm. 14F. ☎ 03 21 35 91 87.

WORMHOUT

Moulin Deschodt – Open June to Aug, first two Sun of each month, 3-6pm. Closed Sept to May. 11F. ☎ 03 28 62 81 23.

Musée Jeanne-Devos – Open year round, daily (except Wed), 9.30am-noon, 2-5pm (first and second Sun of each month, 3-6pm). Closed public holidays. 11F. ☎ 03 28 62 81 23.

Excursions

Friville-Escarbotin: Musée des Industries du Vimeu - Easter to end October, guided tour (1hr) daily except Sat 2.30-5.30pm; Sun and holidays 2.30-6.30pm. 15F. ☎ 03 22 26 42 37.

Useful French words and phrases

ARCHITECTURAL TERMS

See the ABC of Architecture in the Introduction

SIGHTS

abbey	abbaye	house	maison
belfry	beffroi	market	marché
cemetery	cimetière	monastery	monastère
cloisters	cloître	windmill	moulin
courtyard	cour	museum	musée
convent	couvent	square	place
lock (canal)	écluse	bridge	pont
church	église	port/harbour	port
covered market	halle	quay	quai
garden	jardin	tower	tour
town hall	mairie		

NATURAL SITES

dam	barrage	lake	lac
viewpoint	belvédère	beach	plage
waterfall	cascade	river	rivière
ledge	corniche	stream	ruisseau
coast, hillside	côte	beacon	signal
forest	forêt	spring	source
cave	grotte	valley	vallée

ON THE ROAD

car park	parking	petrol/gas station	station essence
driving licence	permis de conduire	right	droite
east	Est	south	Sud
garage (for repairs)	garage	toll	péage
left	gauche	traffic lights	feu tricolore
motorway/highway	autoroute	tyre	pneu
north	Nord	west	Ouest
parking meter	horodateur	wheel clamp	sabot
petrol/gas	essence	zebra crossing	passage clouté

TIME

today	aujourd'hui	Monday	lundi
tomorrow	demain	Tuesday	mardi
yesterday	hier	Wednesday	mercredi
winter	hiver	Thursday	jeudi
spring	printemps	Friday	vendredi
summer	été	Saturday	samedi
autumn/fall	automne	Sunday	dimanche
week	semaine		

NUMBERS

0	zéro	10	dix	20	vingt
1	un	11	onze	30	trente
2	deux	12	douze	40	quarante
3	trois	13	treize	50	cinquante
4	quatre	14	quatorze	60	soixante
5	cinq	15	quinze	70	soixante-dix
6	six	16	seize	80	quatre-vingts
7	sept	17	dix-sept	90	quatre-vingt-dix
8	huit	18	dix-huit	100	cent
9	neuf	19	dix-neuf	1000	mille

SHOPPING

bank	banque	grocery	épicerie
bakery	boulangerie	newsagent, bookshop	librairie
big	grand	open	ouvert
butcher shop	boucherie	post office	poste
chemist's/drugstore	pharmacie	push	pousser
closed	fermé	pull	tirer
cough mixture	sirop pour la toux	shop	magasin
entrance	entrée	small	petit
exit	sortie	stamps	timbres
fishmonger's	poissonnerie		

FOOD AND DRINK

beef	bœuf	knife	couteau
beer	bière	lamb	agneau
butter	beurre	lunch	déjeuner
bread	pain	green salad	salade
breakfast	petit-déjeuner	meat	viande
cheese	fromage	mineral water	eau minérale
chicken	poulet	mixed salad	salade composée
dessert	dessert	orange juice	jus d'orange
dinner	dîner	plate	assiette
fish	poisson	pork	porc
fork	fourchette	salt	sel
fruit	fruits	spoon	cuillère
sugar	sucre	vegetables	légumes
glass	verre	water	de l'eau
ice cream	glace	white wine	vin blanc
ice cubes	glaçons	yoghurt	yaourt
ham	jambon		

PERSONAL DOCUMENTS AND TRAVEL

airport	aéroport	shuttle	navette
credit card	carte de crédit	suitcase	valise
customs	douane	train/plane ticket	billet de train/d'avion
platform	voie	wallet	portefeuille
railway station	gare		

CLOTHING

coat	manteau	socks	chaussettes
jumper	pull	stockings	bas
raincoat	imperméable	suit	costume/tailleur
shirt	chemise	tights	collant
shoes	chaussures	trousers	pantalon

USEFUL PHRASES

goodbye	au revoir	thank you	merci
hello/good morning	bonjour	yes/no	oui/non
excuse me	excusez-moi, pardon	please	s'il vous plaît

Do you speak English?	Parlez-vous anglais?
I don't understand	Je ne comprends pas
Talk slowly	Parlez lentement
Where's...?	Où est...?
When does the ... leave?	A quelle heure part...?
When does the ... arrive?	A quelle heure arrive...?
When does the museum open?	A quelle heure ouvre le musée?
When is breakfast served?	A quelle heure sert-on le petit-déjeuner?
What does it cost?	Combien cela coûte?
Where is the nearest petrol/gas station?	Où se trouve la station essence la plus proche?
Where can I change traveller's cheques?	Où puis-je échanger des traveller's cheques?
Where are the toilets?	Où sont les toilettes?
Do you accept credit cards?	Acceptez-vous les cartes de crédit?
I need a receipt.	Je voudrais un reçu.

Index

A

B

F

H

G

I

J

K – L

M

T – V

W – Y – Z

Manufacture Française des Pneumatiques Michelin
Société en commandite par actions au capital de 2 000 000 000 de francs
Place des Carmes-Déchaux – 63 Clermont-Ferrand (France)
R.C.S. Clermont-Fd B 855 200 507

© *Michelin et Cie, Propriétaires-éditeurs, 1999*
Dépôt légal juin 1999 – ISBN 2-06-134403-8 – ISSN 0763-1383

Compogravure : NORD COMPO, Villeneuve d'Ascq
Impression – brochage : I.F.C.–ASKREA, St-Germain-du-Puy

Cover illustration by Didier WIBROTTE/Pascal VITRY